Thomas Waters is a lect[...] specialist in the modern h[...] of witchcraft and magic.

Further praise for *Cursed Britain*:

'A timely account of the ebb and flow of belief in the black arts in modern times. It's fascinating, well researched, and utterly compelling.' Michelle Paver, author of *Wakenhyrst*

'Authoritative and engaging, Waters' book explores and explains why we should seek to understand the magical beliefs of our recent ancestors, and also requires us to reflect on the continued belief in malign forces.' Owen Davies, author of *A Supernatural War*

'An important and timely investigation into how malevolent magic and counter magic have survived, adapted, declined, and revived in the modern age. This is also a very human history of fear, power, influence, and imagination. Fascinating.' Karl Bell, author of *The Magical Imagination*

THOMAS WATERS

CURSED BRITAIN

A History of
Witchcraft
and
Black Magic
in Modern Times

YALE UNIVERSITY PRESS
NEW HAVEN AND LONDON

For information about this and other Yale University Press publications, please contact:
U.S. Office: sales.press@yale.edu   yalebooks.com
Europe Office: sales@yaleup.co.uk   yalebooks.co.uk

Set in Minion Pro Regular by IDSUK (DataConnection) Ltd
Printed and bound in Great Britain by Clays Ltd, Elcograf S.p.A.

Library of Congress Control Number: 2019939094

ISBN 978-0-300-22140-4 (hbk)
ISBN 978-0-300-25477-8 (pbk)

A catalogue record for this book is available from the British Library.

10 9 8 7 6 5 4 3 2

CONTENTS

Preface to the paperback edition   *vii*

One   **Black magic in modern times**   1

Two   **Blood the witch, swim the wizard: 1800–30**   9
         1804: William Ettrick's evil year—Wizardry at Wickham
         Skeith—Magic in Monmouthshire—Brutal beliefs—Milder
         means—Evil traditions—Indulgent magistrates—Shy
         demonologists—Critics muster

Three **Tough superstitions: 1830–60**   38
         Outrage in Oxfordshire: the case of the 'Little Tew ghost'—
         Cursing, Irish and otherwise—The drive against 'popular
         superstition'—A resilient creed—Progress for the few,
         witchcraft for the many—Conjurors and constables,
         magistrates and magic—Spellbound or mesmerised?

Four   **Secret beliefs: 1860–1900**   73
         Investigating witchcraft with the folklorists—Witch hares in
         the Western Isles—Regional witchcraft—Witch villages and
         cursing wells—Who were the witches?—Women and
         witchcraft

Five   **Healing black magic: The unwitchers of late**   106
         Victorian Britain
         An Aberdeenshire Warlock—Cunning-folk—From cards to
         curses: fortune-telling—Roma go 'dukkerin'—Unwitching as
         mental health care—Why unwitching worked

Six   **Occultists study dark arts: 1850s–1900**   139

From crisis of faith to occult revival—Spiritualism and evil magnetism—Theosophy and Indian witches—Black magic and the Golden Dawn—Christian Science: a new witchcraft—Baphomet and paganism—Strident Christians revive demonology

Seven   **Gone native: Witchcraft in the British Empire and beyond** 156

Baptist meets witch—Superstition and imperialism—The occult in the outback—Māoris and makutu: witchcraft in New Zealand—Slavery and sorcery: obeah in the Caribbean—Beyond colonial power: witchcraft and witch-hunting in India—The curse of a continent? Witchcraft in Africa—Bringing magic back

Eight   **Witchcraft's decline: 1900–60s**   187

Under psychic attack: How Violet Firth became Dion Fortune—Witchcraft's decline: 1900–1930s—A twentieth-century white witch: the late career of Mother Herne—The war against quackery—The last conjurors in Wales—Witchcraft's collapse: 1940s–1960s—Why did witchcraft decline?—Roma doing less dukkerin, but still cursing—Pagan witch cults and a magic murder—Wicca

Nine   **Multicultural magic: 1970–2015**   221

The evolution of enchantment: John Lundy's curse—Old stories and alternative lifestyles: witchcraft in the countryside—Voodoo London: magic in the urban environment—Out of Africa? Witchcraft and child abuse—The deliverance ministry: a new demonology—The occult online

Ten   **Conclusion: Witchcraft's decline and return**   261

Endnotes   266
Select bibliography   326
List of maps and illustrations   334
Acknowledgements   336
Index   337

PREFACE TO THE PAPERBACK EDITION

Curses, sorcery, and harmful types of witchcraft are the focus of this book. It explains how, in comparatively rich parts of the world, during relatively recent times, those eerie ideas have continued to shape, shake, mark, and haunt people's lives. Its characters are strained individuals and careworn families, overawed by growing problems, desperately seeking solutions. Friends who, witnessing this, suggest that dark forces might be at play. Charismatic magicians and (latterly) pastors, who respond by diagnosing witchcraft and promising deliverance, for a price. Innocent women, men, and (recently) children who are wrongly accused of being in league with evil powers, and on that account defamed, abused, attacked, and in a few dreadful instances killed. And embittered people, who really do attempt to settle scores magically.

I should like to very briefly describe my method for excavating these occult experiences and esoteric ways of thinking. What follows is intended to be a carefully researched, empathetic, and evocatively written social history, which is enriched with healthy doses of folklore, anthropology, antiquarianism, sociology, cultural studies, and reportage of various kinds. I've tried to explore this grimly fascinating topic by combining brisk, big-picture approaches with personal and biographical studies. This, I hope, will help readers to appreciate how wider patterns of belief and practice seeped into people's lives, why witchcraft changed over time, and above all how individuals who had once been resolutely sceptical of the notion of magic came eventually to believe that weird powers really were at work in daily life. Geographically, the action takes place largely in the regions and nations of Britain, and to a lesser extent the (now dismantled) British Empire. Chronologically, it occurs during what historians class as the modern period – that is, since roughly 1800.

People often react strongly to witchcraft, though they do so in different ways. Bringing up in conversation the 'deed without a name', as the three witches called it in *Macbeth*, can inspire curious responses. Wide-eyed fascination, intakes of breath, and words to the effect of 'tell me more'. Stifled laughs, blushes, and giggles. Grumpy debunking and dismissive disdain. Or most curiously of all, a twitchy nervousness, which in some cases is combined with a stark unwillingness to discuss the matter further. Historically, witchcraft inspired similarly mixed reactions, reflected in its racy yet evasive epithets such as 'the damned art', 'the dark art', and (as Daniel Defoe preferred in his 1727 history) 'the black art'. Whatever term or euphemism we use, we're clearly dealing with some of humanity's strangest, most unsettling, but also most compelling fears, anxieties, and terrors. For all their strangeness, they are in certain core ways remarkably persistent throughout human history, and strikingly prevalent across human societies. Yet too often these fears, anxieties, and terrors have been ignored, sidelined, laughed away, or pushed out of view when they surface close to home.

The distancing of harmful, antisocial, and maleficent (to use a previously obscure Latin word that literally means doing or making bad, and which is now rather better known thanks to a 2014 Disney movie) witchcraft usually happens in one of two ways. Either witchcraft is historicised as belonging to the mental baggage of the pre-modern past, the stifling debris of the ancient systems of thought that so befuddled and bewildered our ancestors. Or it is exoticised as belonging to cultures in distant parts of the world, usually in economically underdeveloped and exploited places.

Casting magic's dark shadow over our forebears and onto foreigners in this way certainly results in a comforting tale for contemporary Westerners to tell themselves: a reassuring fable about rich nations being such advanced, orderly, and sophisticated places that their citizens and policymakers needn't concern themselves with the currency of radical beliefs about sinister occult powers. Yet this self-aggrandising myth, of a largely secularised and securely disenchanted West, is not only empirically wrong but actively harmful too. As well as being implicitly chauvinistic, it obscures a litany of experiences, suffering, attitudes, problems, traditions, and beliefs that really do deserve our attention.

Although we might like to think otherwise, the notion of harmful witch-craft, or 'mystic interpersonal harm' as I more broadly define it in the text, resonates in numerous different forms in the modern West. It haunted the imaginations of considerable numbers of Britons during the nineteenth century, affected rather fewer during the twentieth, and yet it still resonates today, partly because it has undergone a modest revival since the 1970s. What this reminds us is that witchcraft evolves when the zeitgeist alters. It adapts as the conditions of life and the nature of governance change. It finds niches. As a result, it continues to have serious consequences for people's health, wealth, reputations, and safety.

I want to make my particular focus on malevolent magic clear at the outset because, today, witchcraft denotes very many things indeed. I don't just mean figuratively, metaphorically, and imaginatively. Literally and concretely, witchcraft now stands for a huge range of practices, rites, identities, religions, styles, and spiritualities. This proliferation began primarily in mid-twentieth-century England, with the creation of the modern pagan religion of Wicca. A female-centric, nature-focused, countercultural creed, Wicca powerfully rejected the historical image of witches as wicked magicians – as supernatural death-dealers who enjoyed nothing more than blighting their neighbours with vicious spells.

In time, Wicca's reinterpretation of witchcraft spread to fertile grounds in the Americas, Australasia, and continental Europe. Smaller numbers of adherents coalesced in Russia, South Africa, Japan, and elsewhere. While this was happening, Wicca subdivided into numerous different styles and traditions, eventually inspiring other types of modern witchcraft that neither identified themselves as Wiccan nor pagan. Since the millennium, this diversification has accelerated, resulting in a remarkably creative outpouring of witchcraft-related spirituality, learning, ritual, writing, commerce, and fashion. Today, hundreds of thousands – if not millions – of people worldwide are experimenting with, studying, adapting, and creating different iterations of modern witchcraft. As a result, we now have not only Wicca but also Hedge Witchcraft, Urban Witchcraft, Fairy Witchcraft, Queer Witchcraft, Art Witchcraft, Traditional Witchcraft, Backwoods Witchcraft, Mountain Witchcraft, and (from the deltas of the United States) Swamp Witchcraft. And this is to name just a few.

At this point, I feel I should acknowledge the importance of interfaith dialogue by underlining a truth that will be obvious to some, but is by no means universally recognised. I would like to reassure readers who may be new to the contemporary history of witchcraft and who might also feel uneasy about the growth of these new and highly spiritual forms of magic, perhaps from having heard hostile material like that voiced in some (though not all) evangelical and Pentecostal churches, which portrays all witchcraft as profoundly evil. Sincerely, it is not. I have been fortunate to meet, teach (in my capacity as an academic historian), and befriend quite a few modern witches. In my admittedly partial experience, they are overwhelmingly decent people: thoughtful, artistic, caring, peaceful, ecologically conscious, and politically engaged. The modern witches I know are dedicated to exploring spirituality, folklore, landscapes, aesthetics, and the rich history and anthropology of magic. They are certainly not trying to harness occult powers in order to smite others. It is true that, in the late 2010s United States, some politically progressive modern witches, and some magical novices too, devised a 'Magical Resistance' against President Donald Trump, designed not to physically injure him but to cast mass 'binding spells' to stop him from doing harm to others. This controversial blend of magic and politics is not supported by all modern witches, however.

Yet today, some people undoubtedly do throw curses, enact wicked spells, and cast hexes. Or at least, they try. They are not necessarily people who are learned in the magical arts, with long-developed spiritual interests and well-established esoteric identities, although some are. Amateurs, novices, and individuals who have probably never thought about harmful witchcraft before might find their minds turning in dark directions, in malicious or vengeful moments. I am reminded of this when I look up my writings on the history of witchcraft and cursing online. When I do this lamentably self-regarding thing, Google punishes me by suggesting a list of what it thinks are related searches. This includes charming questions such as 'how to put the evil eye on someone', 'how to curse a business', and 'how to hex'. Reddit, Yahoo Answers, and other internet forums have similarly anti-social threads, begun by people asking the internet for help to do this sort of thing.

During the course of researching this book, several people told me that they had thrown curses. One, surely, was a fantasist. A successful entrepreneur (this part was true, I was able to confirm), he volunteered a lavish tale of how he had gone about cursing business rivals and those who didn't pay up when they had promised to. Something about his brash, loud account didn't ring true. It was the way he extravagantly revelled in the details of the formulas he'd spoken, the signs and symbols he'd used, and the effects his curses apparently had. I doubt whether anyone who seriously believed in these horrible powers would have spoken about them in such an unguarded, boastful sort of way, though it is hard to say for sure. His manner was totally unlike that of other cursers who whispered about their actions. With them, it was only after knowing me for some time, and after hearing me speak at length about the intricate history of maleficent magic, that, in small voices, they told me that they had done it too. In every case I've been told about, magical revenge was taken after someone was bullied, harassed, assaulted, or mistreated. In one instance, it had taken the form of an improvised chant, said while holding hands with a boyfriend and a sibling. A single event, which had occurred decades earlier. Yet the memory was painfully fresh. The little details that coloured the story chastened the atmosphere in the room. Everyone present held their breath, leaned in, and listened. Experiences like these leave lasting marks.

Historically, too, there were people who looked to maleficent magic either for revenge, or to achieve a sort of satisfaction rooted in sadism and jealousy. But as this book shows, harmful witchcraft is something that over-whelmingly begins in the minds of its victims – in the heads of people who come to believe that they have been bewitched, cursed, hexed, or in some way attacked by occult forces. To say this is not to dismiss, denigrate, or minimise the experiences of people who sincerely believe that they have been cursed. One of the wider themes of this book is the incredible power of belief, though I don't mean belief as an ordinary unit of thought, an intention, or a notion, as in 'I believe I'll have eggs for breakfast'. I mean believing in the sense of a willed, cultivated, tempting, and passionate state of mind; one that seems to make an 'electrical connection with your nature', as the late-nineteenth-century American philosopher and psychologist William James put it. The determined act of believing shapes key areas of human life, particularly politics, religion, and morality. It is also central to the art of magic, past and present. It can inspire powerful, energised, and determined states, making people learn and do things they never thought possible, including immersing themselves in rich traditions of witchcraft and counter-witchcraft. To what end? Some people, suffering terrible problems, reinter-pret them as the result of harmful witchcraft, embrace magic to rid themselves of these apparent powers, and do finally say they feel better as a result. But beliefs like these can also lend themselves to fraud, persecution, abuse, ostracism, violence, and even death. It's not all bad, but it's certainly not all good either.

A major lesson from the history of witchcraft is that belief-based justice can be terribly wrong. Somewhere in the region of 50,000 people were executed in Europe during the witch trials of the early modern period, between approximately the late fifteenth and early eighteenth centuries. Today, across the globe, large numbers of people continue to be harmed after being identified as witches. Reporting on this secretive and taboo topic is distinctly patchy, but instances noted recently in the British press show that these problems are found to some degree in the West too. In 2018, for example, a woman from Leicester wrote to her local paper to warn readers about an unscrupulous faith healer operating in the city, who was fracturing families by claiming that his clients' misfortunes were caused by evil spells cast by their own relatives. In London in 2019, a mother and her adult son were convicted of harassing a neighbour, whom they blamed for making them ill with witchcraft. They had spent months retaliating with curses and evil prayers, chanting 'death by fire' through the walls during the small hours, begging God to kill the 'witch', and even telling the poor woman's 7-year-old daughter that her mother was evil. Far worse was the dreadful case of Michael Oluronbi, a self-styled prophet and pastor from Birmingham, convicted of rape and child abuse in 2020 after telling children and young women in his congregation they would become witches if they refused his advances. Just three anecdotes, but figures collated by the Office for National Statistics point to more widespread problems. Between April 2016 and March 2019, it found evidence of 4,990 cases of child abuse linked to faith and belief, many of which seem to have involved accusations of diabolical possession and witchcraft, with violent or traumatic exorcisms providing the purported cure. These social problems need solving. But to do so, we need to better understand the nature of witchcraft beliefs, along with the experiences and lifestyles that underlie them.

The British Isles
with key places of
witchcraft and magic
mentioned in
the text.

Shetland

Orkney

Atlantic
Ocean

North Sea

SCOTLAND

Meikle Wartle
Aberdeenshire

Isle of Gigha

Edinburgh

NORTHERN
IRELAND

Durham

Stokesley,
North Yorkshire

Irish Sea

IRELAND

Liverpool

Leeds

ENGLAND

St. Elian's
cursing wells

Leicester

Wickham
Skeith,
Suffolk

WALES

Long Compton,
Warwickshire

Llanfoist,
Abergavenny

Little Tew,
Oxfordshire

London

Boscastle,
Cornwall

Charlton Horethorne,
Somerset

Turners Puddle,
Dorset

Lamerton,
Devon

English Channel

N

W   E

S

FRANCE

0   kilometres   100

0   miles   100

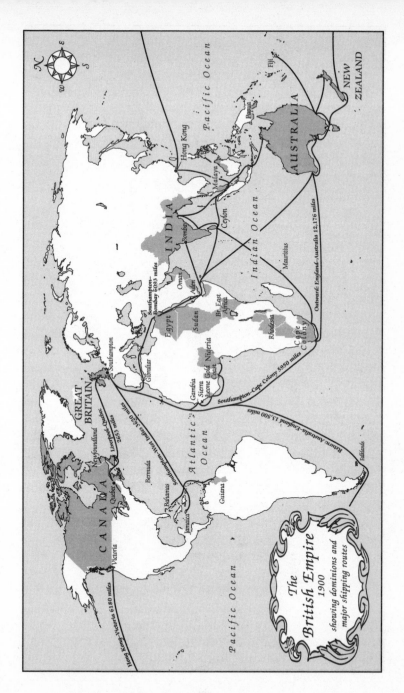

The
British Empire
1900
showing dominions and
major shipping routes

GREAT BRITAIN

CANADA

INDIA

AUSTRALIA

NEW ZEALAND

Pacific Ocean

Atlantic Ocean

Indian Ocean

Pacific Ocean

Egypt

Sudan

Br. East Africa

Rhodesia

Cape Colony

Gambia

Sierra Leone

Gold Coast

Nigeria

Oman

Aden

Ceylon

Mauritius

Hong Kong

Malaya

Borneo

Fiji

Newfoundland

Quebec

Victoria

Bermuda

Bahamas

Jamaica

Guiana

Falklands

Gibraltar

Bombay

Southampton

Hong Kong–Victoria 6180 miles

Liverpool–Quebec 2653 miles

Southampton–West Indies 3620 miles

Southampton–Cape Colony 5950 miles

Southampton–Bombay 6093 miles

Outward: England–Australia 12,176 miles

Return: Australia–England 13,500 miles

XV

ONE

BLACK MAGIC IN MODERN TIMES

Imagine: troubles mounting swiftly, quietly. Just bad luck you said, at the start. Jobs lost, businesses bankrupt, investments collapsing. Insomnia and, if sleep comes, nightmares. Sick children, enduring illnesses the doctors don't understand. Pets dead, work animals dying. And stranger happenings, at home. Thuds at night, scratches on the roof, doors banging inexplicably. Accidents, oversights, mishaps, missteps. Fraying family ties. Finally, a lover gone, perhaps somewhere else, maybe to someone else.

Individually, these misfortunes would be bad. But imagine they've occurred simultaneously, relentlessly, in a cluster. You could lose your mind, watching your disasters swell. Emotionally, it's overwhelming.

Except, as the crisis peaks, a friend makes a strange comment. Perhaps someone has a grudge against you. Maybe you're cursed.

Cursed, hexed, bewitched, jinxed, ill-wished, overlooked. Utter nonsense, you once thought. Idiocy epitomised. Now though, you begin to wonder. Could apparently unrelated misfortunes share a common origin, a single mysterious cause? Is someone close to you not just enjoying your problems, but also conjuring them? Are they, out of envy and spite, destroying you with black magic? And if they are, what should you do about it?

*   *   *

1

This book is about witchcraft. Not witchcraft as in Wicca, the peaceful nature religion also known as Modern Pagan Witchcraft, though it features in later chapters. Not witchcraft in the sense of childish tales about the Wizard of Oz and Harry Potter, either. Instead, this book is concerned with black witchcraft, curses, hexes, jinxes, damaging esoteric influences and harmful spells. The sort of evil mysticism that takes hold when terrible things happen, disasters mount, and families face desperate stresses and strains. The sort of magic that really matters.

It's a violent, disturbing, yet strangely empowering way of thinking. Witchcraft in the sense of mystic interpersonal harm is a deeply ingrained idea, found to a greater or lesser extent in most cultures and during every era of recorded history. From ancient Egypt in the twelfth century BC to Britain in the 2010s, people have thought it's possible to hurt enemies with black magic, whether by mumbling maledictions, jabbing pins into dolls, casting elaborate spells, commanding spirit familiars, or even just an evil stare.[1] The basic notion of witchcraft is so widespread that it's tempting to wonder whether our brains evolved to recognise it, perhaps because thinking in this way conferred some sort of competitive advantage in the prehistoric environment.

Everyone knows that, in Europe and North America, witchcraft was a powerful concept between roughly the 1400s and 1700s, in the era of the 'witch craze'. Many people also know that, today, witchcraft is a dangerous idea across much of the world, particularly in Africa, Melanesia and rural South Asia.[2] Few of us, however, are aware of the fact that black magic haunts the modern West too, albeit more secretively and subtly. Long after witchcraft was decriminalised and declared impossible by courts and parliaments, black magic continued to trouble vast numbers of Europeans and North Americans. Witchcraft still exists, or is thought to by sophisticated folks with university degrees and access to scientific medicine, state welfare and advanced technology. If anything, in recent decades evil magic has become more common across much of the West.

This sinister topic is the focus of a growing body of academic research.[3] But there's so much left to say. What exactly is black magic and how has it changed over time? What role did witchcraft play in our ancestors' lives and what is its status today? What are the harms and are there any benefits? Above all, what should we do about the recent resurgence in dark mysticism?

This book is designed to help answer those questions. I've dedicated well over a decade to researching the modern history of black magic. I expect to the bafflement of my family and friends, I've spent the best part of my adult life rummaging through musty manuscripts, trawling bleary-eyed through historical newspapers, scouring old barns for ritual markings, interviewing exorcists and magicians, as well experiencing modern magic for myself. The result, I hope, is both intriguing and important. There is an unknown story of black magic in modern Britain, stretching from the rural world of Thomas Hardy to the multicultural present day. Here, the strange tale is told in full for the first time.

* * *

The history of black magic in modern times is a cosmopolitan drama. Human movement rapidly accelerated from the nineteenth century. People, goods, technologies and ideas began crossing the earth at a dizzying rate. Travellers took their magical beliefs abroad and encountered new mysticisms when they got there. Empires regulated their colonial subjects in all sorts of ways, including how they dealt with witches. Witchcraft became more international, though at the same time it remained fundamentally rooted in local circumstances. This means that, to understand modern witchcraft, we need to combine a global orientation with a local focus. An excellent place for that local focus is a large island, lying on the eastern edge of the North Atlantic Ocean: Britain.

Britain is an ideal place to study the dark arts. Partly because it has many sources for this secretive subject, including personal papers, social investigations, folklore reports, legal and government records, archaeology and above all a vast newspaper archive. Britain is also a dynamic, diverse, globally connected place. As a result, it exhibits many different styles and types of modern witchcraft.

Britain changed profoundly during the era covered by this book. In 1800 it was home to 10 million mostly churchgoing country dwellers. A century later, in the early 1900s, approaching 40 million mostly urbanites lived on the mainland, while abroad the British Empire had become the largest in history, ruling around a quarter of the globe. The empire was long gone by the early 2000s, by which time over 60 million people representing many creeds and backgrounds lived in Britain, largely in towns, cities and suburbs. Throughout this period, Britain was a land of great variety, between its multicultural cities and its regions, like the folklore-rich West Country, the isolated mountains of North Wales, the Highlands of Scotland, the lonely Shropshire hills, the fenlands of East Anglia and the almost 200 inhabited islands surrounding the mainland. It was known both for its traditions and for its modernity, with a long-established welfare state, a highly financialised economy and, as of the late 2010s, among the highest smartphone ownership and internet access in the world. British culture mingled new and old, archaic and advanced, homespun and exotic. This mix made witchcraft in Britain eclectic, shifting and adaptable.

The history of modern British witchcraft is full of surprises. Spells for good and evil. Magic markings and esoteric objects. Sincere supernatural healers and cynical hoodwinkers. Innocent victims, falsely accused of being witches, and people who really did claim they possessed evil powers. Witchcraft makes the nineteenth and twentieth centuries, those well-known and well-studied epochs, look weird and odd.

The tale begins in the largely rural world of the early 1800s, the era of George III and George IV. The Industrial Revolution was under way. The seeds of modernity were germinating. The Enlightenment, an intellectual movement for reason and liberty, had come and gone. Witchcraft hadn't been a crime for at least two generations, since the 1730s. And yet, as Chapter 2 shows, in early 1800s Britain witchcraft was widely believed in. Magical traditions, traceable to the period of the witch trials and before, were strong. Villagers and townsfolk ducked, mobbed, attacked and bullied witches. Privately, many sophisticated and wealthy people sympathised. Not with victims of superstitious violence, but with the perpetrators.

Things were changing, as Chapter 3 shows. But they were changing slowly and not really because of reason or enlightenment. Between about the 1830s and 1860s, campaigners against superstition strove to convince their compatriots that witchcraft was risible nonsense. These campaigners failed because ridding people of their occult beliefs is far harder than many non-believers imagine. It wasn't social activism but the growth of professional policing that stopped mobs from attacking eccentric, vulnerable and usually innocent people. Alleged witches were somewhat safer, but knowledge of the occult's finer details remained rife.

4

During the later 1800s, the subject of Chapter 4, better policing stemmed one-on-one violence against witches. Vicious individual attacks on spell-casters waned and many commentators concluded that belief in witchcraft had disappeared. Finally, the dismal superstition was dead. But it was not so. Hidden beneath the veneer of late Victorian civilisation, dark forces were at work, or were believed to be. Hundreds, if not thousands, of people continued to be harassed, defamed, spat at and carefully roughed up, in the name of punishing witchcraft. Across Britain's regions, there remained tons of local magical traditions – stories about the dark arts, dialect words for magic, cursing wells, rumours about places where witches met, and special spells. As had been the case for centuries, black magic continued to be strongly linked with women.

Throughout the Victorian era, thousands of magicians made money from the dark arts. These urban fortune-tellers, itinerant Roma women, and powerful characters known as 'cunning-folk' are the focus of Chapter 5. Their weird work could be misleading, downright fraudulent and outrageously expensive. At the same time, the techniques Victorian magicians used to cure witchcraft did some good for their clients. Unwitching, the practice of removing harmful spells, functioned as a form of cryptic mental health care, which helped despairing people cope with terrible problems. It was all about creating a strong, ardent belief in the reality of mystic powers. This was difficult. Yet it was often better than the paralysing alternative – the awful idea that life's most precious things can be destroyed by mere bad luck.

Witchcraft didn't beguile only rustic simpletons, during the Victorian era. In cities and suburbs, behind expensive curtains and in bay-windowed houses, avant-garde types experimented with new forms of occultism. Spiritualism, theosophy, Christian Science and extremely complex ritual magic – these types of mysticism are often seen as positive, therapeutic and emancipating. In many ways they were, but as we shall see in Chapter 6, the late Victorian occult revival had dark sides too. Many occultists were intrigued by evil powers and some were absolutely obsessed with them. These characters, with their strange theories and esoteric investigations, helped to refresh the idea of witchcraft, rendering it in terms that befitted the modern age.

From Victorian Britain, Chapter 7 moves out to the immense territories of the British Empire. From Africa to India to New Zealand, the empire was run by white Britons who often tried to stop indigenes from attacking witches. It was part of Britannia's 'civilising mission' to the 'primitive' peoples of the world. Yet, after years abroad in foreign climes, something strange happened to many colonists. Secretly, unintentionally, they found themselves wondering. Were the locals partly right about the existence of evildoers with supernatural powers? Perhaps there was 'something in it' after all. Witchcraft was a contagious idea. A good education and a strong sense of personal superiority were small protection against it.

Back in Britain, Chapter 8 explores witchcraft's major decline. It occurred much later than many people realise: during the first half of the twentieth century. Britons were living healthier, more comfortable lives. Their 'stiff upper lip' mentality was hardly consistent with making themselves believe in the reality of terrible magic. They no longer entertained themselves with tales of local witches: radio, cinema and television were more fun. But the main reason Britons stopped blaming their misfortunes on evil spells lay elsewhere. The state was growing, its tentacles reaching into previously ignored areas. Health care was becoming more regulated and professional magicians began to suffer. Cunning-folk, fortune-tellers and itinerant Roma women had skirted around hostile laws, designed to stop them from making money with magic. No longer. Professionals who cured witchcraft almost entirely disappeared. Without them, only a tiny fraction of the public continued to seriously ponder the dark arts.

This situation of very low levels of witchcraft didn't last. From the 1970s the mood, the atmosphere and the state, changed. Liberalism was triumphant. Alternative cultures and alternative medicine flourished. Multiculturalism was ascendant. Minority religions and spiritualities were protected. In this environment, new and diverse types of witchcraft emerged. Some were brought by migrants from South Asia, Africa and the Caribbean, before catching on among the wider population. Other varieties of witchcraft were created in Britain or imported by the churches. *Obeah* men, African spiritual healers, white witches, hedge witches, traditional witches, deliverance ministers, Islamic *hakims*, *jinn* removers, and Hindu *vaids*. By the close of the twentieth century, a huge range of healers and religious figures were providing curse removal services. Doubtless there were benefits in terms of individual freedom, spiritual fulfilment, and maybe even emotional consolation. At the same time, the revival of witchcraft had damaging consequences. Financial frauds involving black magic became more common. Violence against alleged witches or possessed people returned. Worst of all, it was now also directed at children.

*   *   *

Investigating black magic is difficult because witchcraft is a secretive, conspiratorial subject. People dislike talking candidly about it, often going to extraordinary lengths to avoid doing so. This means we have to interpret utterances about witches carefully, in a way that is mindful of the eerie idea that discussing dreadful things makes them more likely to happen. 'Speak of the devil', as the phrase goes, 'and he shall appear.' Another problem is that one can be misled by eccentric theories or, worse, become enraptured by wild imaginings. We should not be complacent about this, assuming that because we're reasonably sensible people we're immune from extreme fantasies. Remember the panic about satanic ritual abuse, a modern witch-hunt that swept the western world during the 1980s and 1990s. That almost entirely baseless delusion led to hundreds, if not thousands, of fake testimonies, along with a good number of wrongful convictions.[4]

There's an easier way to misapprehend the shadowy realm of witchcraft. You can overlook important features of this topic by viewing it primarily from the witches' perspective. We naturally sympathise with innocent people, unfairly accused of controlling occult powers. We're also fascinated by the few individuals who genuinely strive to injure their enemies with magic, whether or not they succeed, whether or not their purported supernatural powers really exist. Witches are tragic, beguiling, sometimes empowering figures. But when it comes to witchcraft, they are not the most important characters. Purveyors of supernatural evil, whether they're called witches or something else, are antagonists, vital but secondary actors in the drama. So are the professionals offering to cure curses and banish bewitchments, the 'service magicians' as they have been usefully termed.[5] These witch doctors, mediums, white witches and cunning-folk, as they were usually known in Britain before the 1950s, are also secondary characters.

In the world of witchcraft, the principal characters, the protagonists, are the victims. The supposedly cursed, hexed, bewitched, overlooked or otherwise bedevilled people. That's why this book focuses primarily on them.

7

Witches and witch doctors figure throughout, but not in every case considered here. Bewitched people didn't always identify the witches who were responsible for their ills. Other cursed individuals couldn't quite bring themselves to believe in service magicians, in mystics who offered to solve terrible problems with magic. Cursing, witchcraft and evil magic begin with a victim, with someone who concludes their diverse sufferings are in some sense uncanny. Often, it goes no further than that. Victims of black magic are the only constant, so focusing on them is the best way to unlock this mysterious belief system.

Beyond homing in on people who think they're cursed, a second key theme of this book is 'belief'. This may sound dated or old-fashioned to some experts in the field, who are more used to terms like 'discourse'. But I do not use belief vaguely, as just another synonym for 'idea'. Here, 'belief' conveys something specific and vital about magic. For it to work, you must quash your doubts.

Cunning-folk, professional magicians who removed witchcraft, insisted on one thing. Their clients had to believe. They needed faith that the prescriptions worked, the potions cured, the charms protected, and the witch-bottles really did send the evil back to the person it came from.[6] It was hard to believe something like that, and that was the point. People seeking the help of spell-breakers deliberately suppressed their cynicism, repressed their unease, and silenced their nagging doubts. Today, professional curse removers do something similar, by asking their customers to believe wholeheartedly in their treatments.

Witchcraft is more like a religious faith than a scientific or common-sense theory of how the world works. It is an imaginative, uncanny and wishful way of thinking. This explains why people can go from being sardonic cynics one moment to ardent believers the next. If we want to understand witchcraft, to appreciate why it's so difficult to dislodge and often impossible to eradicate altogether, we need to grasp this above all. Witchcraft is a willed belief, driven by desperation and not by cool calculation.

TWO

BLOOD THE WITCH,
SWIM THE WIZARD
1800–30

'Legendary nonsense, unworthy even of being ranked with those pretty stories which divert the nursery.'[1] At the dawn of the nineteenth century, 'witchcraft' was a byword for odious causes and idiotic doctrines.

Objections to free trade were as deluded as believing in witchcraft.[2] Political corruption was as lamentable as the old witchcraft laws.[3] Lord Castlereagh's enemies thought it was easier to have faith in magic than in the Minister for War.[4] Napoleon's hold over France seemed to owe something to the dark arts.[5] Abolitionists highlighted slavery's link with witchcraft (some slaves, according to the tribal leaders who sold them to European traders, were guilty of sorcery).[6] 'Witchcraft', in the usage of the great and the good, meant inanity at best and insanity at worst. It was preposterous, outrageous and ridiculous. Witchcraft, a genteel antiquary wrote in 1821, was 'an absurdity too great to be endured even by children'.[7]

Was it really? Britain's courts certainly no longer prosecuted witches. Between the fifteenth and early eighteenth centuries, around 500 people had been convicted and executed for practising sorcery in England, and perhaps as many as 2,500 in Scotland, though its population was below a third of the size.[8] Mercifully, between the 1690s and 1720s the witch trials ended, mostly because judges came to doubt whether any evidence could be sufficiently conclusive to prove that someone had dallied with the devil. After the trials subsided, and to surprisingly little comment, the crime of witchcraft was abolished in 1736 and replaced with a new offence of 'pretences' to sorcery, designed to stop anyone from making money by selling purported magic.[9]

The law had changed, yet old anxieties persisted. How far was much debated. Some critics thought witchcraft possessed 'a strong hold upon the minds of the few illiterate vulgar'.[10] Others warned that fears concerning spells and curses were 'general among the lower classes'.[11] A few even claimed that 'popular errors' about magic were 'not confined to the very lower orders of society'.[12] They were, on the contrary, entertained by 'many persons of the middle class'.[13]

In my view, the observers who stressed witchcraft's wide currency were right: observers like James Paterson, a clergyman from Midmar in Aberdeenshire. Paterson's regular contact with 'men of the ordinary ranks of life' showed him 'how generally a belief in Witchcraft prevails among them, and the strong conviction they feel of its truth'.[14] Witchery, he discovered, extended well beyond the working classes. A sign of this was that, in north-eastern Scotland, it was hard to discuss it, even with educated people. Witchcraft was too unsettling, too scary. The Reverend couldn't raise the horrid topic with his parishioners 'without observing the rooted conviction of its existence in their minds'.[15]

Some readers may find it hard to believe that, in the era of Jane Austen and the Napoleonic Wars, good numbers of respectable Britons credited witchcraft. Scepticism about supernatural superstitions, it's often said, became widespread among affluent and sophisticated people during the eighteenth-century Enlightenment, before gradually percolating down to the masses over the course of the nineteenth century.[16] Any remaining convictions about witchcraft were passive and insignificant background prejudices.

In reality, witchcraft troubled many well-to-do folk during the early 1800s. This chapter explores a remarkable area of common ground between the masses, the upper classes and those in the middle. More often than we might expect, they agreed with each other: sorcery was real, and witches deserved to be punished.

1804: WILLIAM ETTRICK'S EVIL YEAR

Great wealth, an expensive education and high rank didn't stop people from crediting witchcraft. Witness William Ettrick (1757–1847), scholar at Blake's

Grammar School in York, graduate of Lincoln College and fellow of University College, Oxford, ordained minister of the Church of England, descendant of the Earl of Dumbarton, and heir to the Ettrick family's estates at High Barnes, Sunderland.[17] No idiot. And not, perhaps, the type of man we'd expect to be troubled by witches. Yet in 1804 the Rev. Ettrick experienced what he called his '*annus malignus*', his evil year. Beset by travails, fearing for his family's survival, this upstanding member of the gentry found his thoughts turning in occult directions.

By 1804, when the events unfolded, William Ettrick was in his late forties and serving as vicar of Turners Puddle, Dorset. He'd lived in that village, near England's south coast, for about a decade and a half with his wife Elizabeth and their growing brood of children. The area became notorious during the 1830s when some local labourers were prosecuted for forming a trade union. Unlike those poverty-stricken workers, we might imagine that the Rev. Ettrick enjoyed an idyllic existence, the charmed life of a genteel country parson. Yet even wealthy men like him found rural life cold, dirty, difficult and dangerous. In his diaries, the main sources for this study, William recorded a cornucopia of folk cures and recipes, showing the lack of effective medicines and the difficulties of household management.[18] For bowel complaints: beef suet, mixed with water and wheat, taken three times a day. For 'the bile': boiled carrots. Instructions for making ink, polish, fish sauce, essence of peppermint, for curing outbuildings of rats, and more. Survival depended on resourcefulness and self-sufficiency.

Country life was always hard. But it was perilous when animals died, people sickened, crops failed and food spoiled. Troubles mounted for the Rev. William Ettrick in February 1804, when his new horse fell ill. The expensive animal, needed for work and transport, got worse when William hired a local farrier, who bled it and prescribed an ointment that blistered the horse's throat. In September the poor beast died and at the same time some pigs ailed. Worse, William and Elizabeth's infant son became seriously unwell. Unlike the horse he was not bled, though copious opiates were administered to help him sleep.

The Ettricks had recently employed Susan Woodford, a local woman, to help farm the gardens, nurse the children and run the house. One day in November 1804 they spoke with her about their desperately ill child, who, despite the drugs, wouldn't settle at night. Rather than commiserate, Susan

11

mocked the family's misfortunes, or so it appeared to the sleep-deprived parents. All she would say were strange fatalisms and riddles. These mystic-sounding remarks, William later recalled, were 'the thing that first excited our suspicions'.

William and Elizabeth Ettrick knew Susan Woodford had an evil reputation. In Turners Puddle and the surrounding villages she was known as a witch, someone with special powers who blighted her neighbours with spells and other malignant abilities, for no other reason than spite and envy. The villagers shared their suspicions with the parson. Some even said they'd harmed the witch with counter-magic. Initially though, the Rev. Ettrick ignored these rumours. Susan Woodford was insolent. But she was a good worker too, quick with the hoe, knowledgeable about plants and crops. William gladly employed her, yet when his multiple misfortunes unfolded, in what seemed like an escalating pattern, he began thinking differently. Searching for a culprit, he remembered that, as well as talking in a witchy way, Susan once asked for a hair from his horse's tail. No doubt she was undertaking the common folk cure for warts, which involved tying them with a horse's hair.[19] Suspicious and disorientated, Ettrick imagined she wanted it for a malicious spell.

In his diary, William reviewed Susan's work. A pattern emerged. The crops she planted didn't sprout. The potatoes she dug up rotted, though every care was taken to store them properly. The beehives she tended died off, or failed to swarm. The raspberries she watered went bad. Everything the old witch touched turned to dust, shrivelling and dying as it came into contact with her malefic power. William and Elizabeth's baby became uncomfortable in Susan's presence, as if it could sense her malignity. Desperately, the parson put his immense learning to magical uses, writing out a biblical verse in Hebrew, attaching it to a piece of string and hanging it around the child's neck. Soon after, the babe fell into a deep healing sleep, barely leaving time for opiates to be administered. There were other signs witchcraft really was at work. One night, amidst his troubles, William dreamt he saw a black bird flying round his hall, pecking him until at last he grabbed it, and broke its neck. Even the starving cat refused to touch the beast on the floor.

'I was once incredulous about the powers of witchcraft, but have no doubts remaining.' So William Ettrick wrote, on 14 November 1804. He'd revised his once sceptical views and now took seriously the village tales about Susan Woodford's witchcraft. But the parson was more disposed to believe than he was willing to acknowledge, even in the privacy of his diary. William was independent to the point of eccentricity, and not a man to be cowed into accepting the fashionable, sneering doctrines of his atheistically minded contemporaries. (As an illustration of his independence, Ettrick was one of the few people in British history to marry himself – that is, conduct his own wedding ceremony, to save money.) William also had a prophetic, occult cast of mind. He wrote several obscure works of Christian prophecy, predicting the Apocalypse's imminent onset.[20] Perhaps it seemed plausible, at the dawn of the nineteenth century, as Napoleon crowned himself Emperor of France (1804) and amassed troops just across the English Channel, ready to invade.[21] A strong supporter of Church and state, William Ettrick despised free-thinkers, deists, secularists like Thomas Paine and Joseph Priestley, and the French *philosophes* of the Enlightenment. This distressed, conspiratorial, reactionary Dorset parson was just the type of educated man who'd be prepared to credit the existence of immanent supernatural forces.

Although he tried magical remedies, the Rev. Ettrick ultimately dealt with his bewitchment by distancing himself from Susan, the witch. In January 1805, eleven months after his misfortunes began, William sacked her. The poor, hardworking and skilful woman wanted an explanation and made several attempts to bring herself back within the fold. William was unmoved and, though he never accused Susan directly, he revealed his suspicions to other locals. With Susan gone, Ettrick's problems gradually eased, or he thought they did. Yet for the Ettrick family, life couldn't just return to normal. In 1806, after almost two decades at Turners Puddle, William made it known that he intended to resign his living and depart the parish. In 1808, following the death of his father, he finally left, relocating to the family estate in High Barnes, Sunderland, about 350 miles north and four days' travel away by coach.

Even as master of a great estate, William didn't fully escape the witchcraft he dreaded. An experience like his was impossible to forget, and he never quite felt safe again. In May 1825, two decades after his *annus malignus*, Ettrick made a foreboding note in his diary: 'Another Old Sue!'[22] Once again, his horses and cattle had fallen ill. Once again, he dreamt evil was upon him. In the nightmare he was walking in his garden when he noticed something in the soil, which on inspection turned out to be 'scorpions, pointing their venomous crab like stings in my direction'. William knew what it meant. He had another witch in his employ, a servant named Ann. As before, he resolved the problem by sacking the no doubt blameless woman.

As a clergyman, landowner and person of rank, Ettrick had considerable influence over his neighbours. Gentry like him set the tone of local society, funded church building, provided employment, arranged charity and administered the law as Justices of the Peace (JPs, Justices). These responsibilities determined how the Rev. Ettrick dealt with his witches. Shy and secretive with his suspicions, there was no question of someone like William directly confronting the women he blamed for his troubles. As for attacking his witches – that was unthinkable.

But what would happen if someone like the Rev. William Ettrick, in his capacity as Justice of the Peace, was called upon to settle conflicts between villagers and witches? Where would the magistrate's sympathies lie? Might he permit intimidation, even violence? We can begin to form answers to these questions by examining the humiliations of a notorious wizard from eastern England, called Isaac Stebbings.

WIZARDRY AT WICKHAM SKEITH

Isaac Stebbings was a thin little man, aged about 67, from the Suffolk village of Wickham Skeith.[23] A hawker of sorts, Stebbings earned his living by going door to door, selling cheap wares. By the mid-1820s he was badly off. Unable to exploit the markets of distant towns and villages, as he would have in his youth, with the passing years old Isaac's patch must have shrunk to the point where he relied entirely upon his neighbours for sales. Any income he had, he owed to them. If they refused to buy, he went without. It was more like begging than hawking.

Imagine how Isaac's neighbours felt when he called. Annoyed and obligated, probably. Angry and resentful too. Above all guilty, if they sent him away penniless. Painful encounters, similar to some of the confrontations that generated witchcraft accusations during the period of the witch trials.[24] Does someone wish you ill? Anyone pondering that ominous question could easily fix their suspicions on a character like Isaac Stebbings, with whom they had frequent but fraught dealings.

By 1825, Isaac was blamed for a spate of mishaps. He'd caused a thatcher's wife to become 'afflicted in mind', it was said, and an old farmer too. The

14

local shoemaker even accused him of magically spoiling his wax. Dubbed 'a wizard beyond all doubt', Isaac's neighbours tormented and threatened. It became so bad that Isaac proposed he be tried by ordeal. He should be 'swam for a wizard' in the village pond. His tormentors would be silenced. His innocence would be proven.

Except it wasn't. The practice of 'ducking' or 'swimming' witches, trial by water or the water test as it was more formally known, dated from the early 1600s, when it was imported to Britain from France.[25] The rite may well have become more popular during the eighteenth century, as it filled the gap left by the official courts refusing to prosecute witches. The basic theory was that innocent people sank while the guilty floated, because their very malevolence caused the waters to reject them. This was what Isaac Stebbings proposed to test.

At two o' clock on a Saturday afternoon, early in July 1825, he was brought to a large pond, known locally as the 'Grimmer', by Wickham Skeith village green. Four men chaperoned him into the water. From the banks, a crowd looked on.[26] The theatrical, open and formal arrangement conferred a sense of legitimacy on the affair. So did the presence of the parish constable, who, far from putting an end to Stebbings' ordeal, was there to ensure it proceeded in an orderly fashion.[27]

Wearing breeches and a shirt, Isaac was led into the water until it reached his waist. The four guards then lifted him up and laid him on his back. There the old man bobbed for ten minutes. One can only guess how he felt, as the waters seemed to pronounce their guilty verdict. 'Give him another,' was the cry from the shore. The rite was repeated, with the same result. 'Try him again, and dip him under the water,' someone called. This was done, so that Isaac's head was submerged, while his heels came out of the water. 'In a word,' a journalist from the *Suffolk Chronicle* reported, 'he was like a piece of cork in the water.' Held in the cold depths for three-quarters of an hour, when the old man finally came ashore he was described as being 'more dead than alive'. Some spectators still weren't satisfied. Another man, they said, of the same size and weight ought to be swum with Stebbings, to confirm the test's accuracy. Amazingly, Isaac agreed. Next Saturday, there'd be a retrial. Isaac, it was said, 'was determined to get rid of the imputation, or die'.

When the retrial day arrived, hundreds came to watch, from Wickham Skeith and the surrounding villages. Apparently, when Stebbings underwent his first immersion, the farmer he bewitched became agitated, crying, 'I can see the imps all about me.' Surely, this was another sign of Isaac's guilt. Luckily, there was never a chance to find out. At last the parson and church-wardens used their influence to keep the swimmers away from the pool. Yet it was not quite the end of Isaac's tribulations. A farmer from the neighbour-hood took up the issue with a 'cunning-man' – a professional provider of occult services, from fortune-telling to counter-witchcraft therapies. This conjuror confirmed that Stebbings was indeed a wizard. For the substantial sum of £3, he agreed to focus his powers on the old man so that he would be 'killed by inches' (a cliché witchcraft phrase, meaning slowly and painfully). It didn't work. Seventeen years later, at the time of the 1841 Census, Isaac was still living in Wickham Skeith, having reached the grand age of 80.

How could an old man suffer like this, in George IV's England, in the year that the world's first passenger railway opened and horse-drawn omni-buses took to London's streets? Essentially, because witchcraft was widely believed in, and people who credited it were given a good deal of leeway by those in authority. This is confirmed by a third and final case: the mobbing of Mary Nicholas.

MAGIC IN MONMOUTHSHIRE

Llanfoist, a village near the Welsh town of Abergavenny.[28] In 1827 William Watkins, a prosperous farmer, was suffering unusual losses in his herd. Eventually, he concluded that a local woman, 90-year-old Mary Nicholas, was the cause. Surely, she was the witch. To put things right Mr Watkins recruited the parish constable and a couple of servants, sought Mary out and dragged her to his fold-yard. 'There is some of your work,' he said, gesturing at beasts lying dead in his fields.

Meanwhile, a crowd of perhaps one hundred gathered. Mr Watkins made Mary kneel behind a colt, take hold of the animal's tail, and pray for the Almighty to bless the cattle. As Mary made her recitations, he pulled a briar rose from a nearby hedge. The farmer walked to where the old woman knelt and drew the thorns across her arm, with the idea that spilling the old witch's blood would diffuse her magic. Then the ordeal took a more abusive turn.

Was there physical evidence of witchcraft? Watkins and his helpers stripped Mary and began looking for 'the mark of where the devils sucked', a reference to familiars, the witch's evil servants. Finding nothing on her body, they came across something plausible on her head, which they cut off along with her remaining hair. Someone suggested ducking Mary – apparently to test her witchcraft. This was too much for a least one member of the crowd whose warnings, along with the desperate entreaties of Mary's daughter, persuaded Mr Watkins to release his now delirious prisoner. 'Oh, my dear child, they have killed me,' Mary cried, falling into her daughter's arms.

Thankfully, they hadn't. A tough and hearty old woman, Mary Nicholas lived to see her tormentors stand trial for instigating a riot. Unfortunately, they evaded this very serious charge and were found guilty only of committing assault. To some minds, even this seemed severe. William Watkins was a 'respectable farmer' and a man of means. He commissioned his attorney to draw up a petition requesting the sentences be commuted.[29] The ninety-three signatures adorning this obsequious document give a sense of where the local community's sympathies lay. A few were written in uncertain, shaky hands. Most were confident and elegant. The witch-mobbers' supporters were absolutely not illiterate peasants. Among the signatories were three surgeons, three lawyers, a magistrate and a general.

Not quite everyone condoned commuting Watkins' sentence. The Rev. William Powell, Vicar of Abergavenny and the magistrate who orchestrated the prosecution, was appalled enough to write a four-page letter to the Home Secretary, imploring him to ignore the petition.[30] Powell admitted the signatories were 'both many and I must say, respectable as to ranks in life'. Still, he did his best to discredit the extraordinary levels of local sympathy for the witch-mobbers. The petition's signatories, he suggested, had been misled by contagious example, were ignorant of the case's details, and acted according to their 'constitutional good nature'. 'The most numerous portion of the agricultural population,' the Rev. Powell warned, 'almost universally believe in sorcery, conjuring, [and] witchcraft.' A reprieve would make things worse, by giving the impression 'that even in more enlightened minds, some learning may exist in favour of this ridiculous but mischievous superstition'.[31]

BRUTAL BELIEFS

Witch-scratchers and witch-abusers carried out their crimes publicly. They expected, and received, sympathy.

Not just in remote villages and far-flung hamlets, either: in towns like Sheffield (1802), Bridport (1824), Manchester (1826) and Leeds (1828), witches were attacked in full view of their neighbours and passers-by.[32] Such was the fate of Anne Burgess – a 68-year-old woman from Wiveliscombe (Somerset). In 1822 she was mobbed by the women of the Bryant family.[33] The Bryants thought Anne had bewitched Lizzie (22) for at least a year, but they only became violent when Anne confronted them about their suspicions. Following some abuse ('yes, you have you damned old witch') Lizzie pinned Anne down while her mother and sister set about cutting the witch's arm with a knife and a nail. In the middle of the street, while Anne cried out 'murder', a crowd gathered. For ten minutes they watched. Finally, a Good Samaritan dragged Anne away from the women's fury.

Witches were assaulted in places like Leeds, Sheffield and Manchester because suspicions about the black art thrived in Georgian Britain's towns and cities. In the heyday of the first Industrial Revolution, urban centres were rapidly and haphazardly expanding, with thousands of mostly young rural workers arriving annually in search of higher-paying jobs. The number of people living in Carlisle, a town in north-western England, tripled between the 1780s and 1840s.[34] In just one decade, the 1820s, Bradford's population grew by 66 per cent, Sheffield's by 41 per cent, Manchester's by 46 per cent and Bristol's by 70 per cent.[35] When they arrived in town, newcomers didn't just forget the fears they'd acquired during their country childhoods.[36] Why would they?

Chaotic growth meant cities teemed with misfortunes that were plausibly blameable on witchcraft. Before the sanitary reforms of the mid-Victorian period, contagious diseases like typhoid abounded, thanks to filth, overcrowding, pigs and cows living in backyards, and contaminated water supplies. In the industrial towns of Lancashire and the West Midlands, average life expectancy barely reached 30, and around a fifth of newborns died before their first birthday.[37] Survivors grew up stunted: central Londoners were on average two-thirds of an inch shorter than country-folk.[38] Beyond want and disease, there were other reasons for thinking about sorcery in town. Most neighbourhoods were dense, close-knit places, riven with the sort of personal animosities that could easily be associated with witchcraft. Cities were scary in other ways too. At eventide, alleyways and courtyards filled with strange sounds, exhorting preachers, rowdy drinkers, crying babies and pealing bells. When darkness fell and you had to find your way home, few if any flickering gas lamps lit the way.[39]

In this environment, black magic was deeply serious. It could inspire extreme violence, disturb communities and fracture families. For Henry and Mary Ibbortson, a poor and bewitched couple from Sheffield, it did all three. The Ibbortsons blamed their niece Elizabeth for their sufferings, and planned to draw her blood to 'break the charm that afflicted them'.[40] One Saturday evening, late in July 1802, they carried out their scheme in just about the most public place imaginable – Sheffield Market. Mary grabbed Elizabeth and bit her 'inhumanly' on the arm. Simultaneously, her husband stabbed the poor girl several times. 'A stout athletic young man' from Manchester was just as brutal when, in 1826, he burst into an elderly couple's house, attacked them, then dragged the old woman into the street by her hair.[41] Robert and Mary Northover were worse still, when they assaulted Elizabeth Parsons in the Dorset town of Bridport. Insensible with rage, swearing about the damned 'bitch who murdered six of my horses and a pig', they broke down the terrified woman's door and began thrashing her. Beaten, bleeding, and promised death, Elizabeth's ordeal ended when she was thrown almost naked into the street.[42]

Witch-scratchings were frantically and sometimes hysterically barbaric, but they were also magical acts. Drawing blood – 'scoring' or 'sloving' the witch, Lowland Scots called it – was supposed to be uniquely effective at nullifying evil powers.[43] Especially so if the cut was made 'above the breath', meaning on the witch's head. The gory rite had been practised in Britain for generations, since at least the period of the witch trials.[44] '*Blood will I draw on thee*, thou art a Witch', Shakespeare made Talbot say in *Henry VI*, his play of 1591. Witch-scratching's deeper origin, however, was uncertain. Perhaps the symbolic assault took inspiration from the Old Testament story of David humiliating his enemy Saul, by sparing his life but secretly cutting off a portion of his robe.[45] This motif may have mingled with deeper feelings about the magical potency of blood and the power of blood-letting to release evil spirits, which can be traced back to ancient times and found across the world.[46] To take one of many examples, nineteenth-century Icelandic folktales suggested that a troll's enchantment could be broken by drawing its victim's blood.[47]

Witchcraft vigilantes were furious because they were desperate. Sorcery, they supposed, acted like a slow but lethal poison. It began by injuring. Left unchecked, it could kill.[48] Betty Townsend, a beggar from the Somerset town of Taunton, exploited this idea in 1810 and 1811, to extort money from a labourer's daughter. She'd 'die by inches' if she didn't pay, Betty said. Fearing a long, painful demise, the girl borrowed what added up to a tidy sum from a local shopkeeper and gave it to Betty.[49] Eventually, her parents found out. Betty said she'd make them 'die by inches' too, if they told anyone. Mrs Poole, the girl's mother, knew what to do. Taking a pin from her clothes, she scratched Betty in three places. Unfortunately, even this potent antidote didn't free her daughter from the wicked woman's power. The girl was terrified, to the point of sickness. Like people from historical Europe to modern Australasia and Africa, she was so disturbed by the thought she'd been bewitched, so convinced she was going to die, that she stopped eating.[50] Witchery may not have been literally magical. Yet it had genuine psychosomatic powers, inspiring fears that manifested themselves in real physical and mental suffering. 'Few English people,' it's been said, 'were excessively preoccupied with witchcraft after 1700.'[51] The experiences recounted here suggest otherwise. Witchcraft was no longer a capital crime, but for those who thought they were under its spell, it was a matter of life and death.

Witchcraft could kill, but the ills laid at its door were almost innumerable. Sick animals were good candidates (occasionally, investigations revealed that apparently bewitched animals had in fact been poisoned).[52] Fits, madness, distraction and melancholy in people were credited to evil magic.[53] 'Dr' John Bird, a cunning-man from Leeds, convinced a couple that their son's consumption was actually a result of him 'labouring under the effects of witchcraft'.[54] On the relatively trivial end, others blamed witchcraft for destroying clothes, tainting food, souring beer, and even stopping smoke from going up the chimney.[55] Stranger, uncanny happenings were also attributed to sorcery, ranging from sleep paralysis (often called 'hag riding') to unexplained fires and intense internal burning sensations.[56] Witchcraft wasn't invoked to explain single, one-off disasters, unless the trouble was really unusual. Nobody concluded magic was at play without first trying conventional explanations and remedies. But if an illness lingered, baffling a succession of doctors – that might be a sign that witchery was at work.[57] Alternatively, witchcraft functioned as the ultimate cause for the onset of a spate of misfortunes, far vaster and more disastrous than you'd expect in the ordinary run of things. From the trivial to the deadly, from the mundane to the mysterious, witchcraft poisoned an individual's entire life, including their relatives and possessions. The witch, as one journalist deftly surmised, was 'the cause of every misfortune by which the family were afflicted'.[58]

Witches weren't just bullied by adults. Adolescents could be worse, because their intimidation was hard to prosecute. It was still scary for people like the old woman from Truro, Britain's most southerly city, who late in the spring of 1821 was 'hunted' through the town's streets by a gang of children, threatening to tear her gown and draw her blood so 'she might have no power over them'.[59] In Tysoe (Warwickshire), the village lads put crossed pieces of wood in the path of a reputed witch as she trudged up the high street, while yelling 'Old Mother Alcock's a witch. Stick a pin in the witch.'[60] Parents and communities tacitly condoned this sort of harassment. If they'd wanted to, they could have stopped it. But in their minds, witches were appalling evil-doers who deserved mistreatment and more.

MILDER MEANS

Cursed people scratched or mobbed their witches as a last resort. Typically, they used ritualistic violence after they'd tried to stem the evil with less confrontational forms of counter-magic.

We can see this in the behaviour of an ill shoemaker from the Welsh town of Narberth. In 1829 he drew his witch's blood, but only once he'd first failed to nullify her magic by getting her to pronounce thirteen times the benediction: 'God bless him and his family.'[61] Making witches cast blessings or renounce their spells had been very popular during the period of the witch trials, and may well have been the normal response to witchcraft.[62] The method persisted into the nineteenth century, though it appears infrequently in the newspaper sources. Perhaps a witch's blessing wasn't considered newsworthy. More likely, it didn't happen as much as it used to, because witchcraft was no longer illegal. Without the deadly threat of a formal prosecution, it was harder to make innocent people renounce curses that they'd never actually laid.

With the witch's blessing less available, other forms of apotropaic (evil-averting) magic filled the gap. A horseshoe nailed above a door, found on 'many a house' from Somerset to Scotland, was the most obvious way to guard a home or a barn against malign influences.[63] Branches of rowan and alder trees were used for similar reasons, especially in northern Britain.[64] A downside of these methods was that they marked the inhabitants out as rather nervous believers in occult powers. There were solutions for this difficulty. As in the era of the witch trials, during the early nineteenth century people who were scared of sorcery defended themselves with special ritual markings and various witchcraft-repelling objects, which they secretly concealed around their households.[65] These items included crossed knives, opened scissors, spoons, shoes placed within roof cavities and 'witch-bottles' – gruesome concoctions designed to direct magic back to its sender, that were buried or occasionally hidden up chimneys. However, these charms also had an insurmountable problem. Like horseshoes, they didn't protect you when you went outside.

What if you met your witch while walking along the village street or in town? How to shield yourself from his or her wicked wishes and evil eye? There were answers, in the capitalistic world of early nineteenth-century Britain, but they generally came at a price. Professional magicians sold protective objects for carrying around, including amulets made of biblical writings, or more unusual evil-averting items like feathers filled with quicksilver.[66] In Scotland, there was an attractive and relatively new alternative. It involved special ornaments known variously as 'luckenbooth brooches', 'heart brooches', 'fairy brooches' and 'witch brooches'.[67] First produced sometime around 1700, by jewellers in Edinburgh's Luckenbooth workshops (hence the name), luckenbooth brooches were made from silver (notoriously anti-magical and not too expensive) or gold (for the rich), shaped like a heart with a pin through the middle, perhaps embellished with some mother-of-pearl, and sometimes bearing a crown on the top.[68] Their anti-witchcraft qualities may have been suggested by the design, which was reminiscent of the powerful anti-witchcraft technique of sticking pins into an animal's heart.[69] Apart from the obvious fact that they repelled malign influences, several trends made luckenbooth brooches attractive during the 1700s and early 1800s. The dainty ornaments had a characteristic Scottish look, and there were stories of them being worn by romantic national heroes like Mary Queen of Scots and Bonnie Prince Charlie.[70] This made luckenbooth brooches perfect purchases in an era of growing consumerism and cultural nationalism. But if you wanted your brooch to repel evil powers it had to be fastened in a special way. Like so much to do with witchcraft, this meant secretly and silently. A Scottish folklorist recalled how he experienced this, as a lad growing up in early nineteenth-century Aberdeenshire. While his half-sceptical mother looked the other way, his Highland grandmother scooped him up, then quietly fastened a witch-brooch onto his undergarments.[71]

'Reform' was abroad, 'improvement' was under way, and the 'intellect' was marching.[72] Influential Britons, usually rich and powerful men, celebrated the progress that was transforming the country, from the growth of towns to the building of canals and factories, the growing efficiency of the government (the first census was conducted in 1801) and the private campaigns designed to civilise the rebellious masses. One of these campaigns made a powerful counter-witchcraft technique hard to practise. The urban middle classes, particularly, were becoming concerned about the welfare of animals, founding in 1824 the Society for the Prevention of Cruelty to Animals.[73] As well as objecting to fighting dogs, baited bears and flogged horses, proponents of animal welfare also targeted the ritualistic burning of farm stock – an expensive but apparently effective method for removing witchcraft from herds and flocks. Initially, they used shame. Newspapers denounced farmers who sacrificed cows, ducks, pigs or sheep to the flames, as in Kent in 1809 and south Lanarkshire in 1812.[74] Particularly notable was the case of a Cumbrian farmer who was widely vilified when he ordered his workers to incinerate a calf in 1810.[75] Legislation followed in 1822, prohibiting the ill-treatment of horses and cattle. Neither moral pressure nor the new laws were sufficient to entirely stop the brutish rite of animal burning, as a case from Perth in 1826 illustrates.[76] But it certainly became more difficult.

With powerful anti-witchcraft techniques frustrated, opportunities grew for cunning-folk. They were professional magicians who told fortunes, found stolen goods, enacted love magic, and healed bewitched people when disasters struck. The cunning-craft had existed for centuries, certainly since the time of the witch trials and perhaps since as long ago as the Anglo-Saxon era.[77] A sense of its primordial origins can be inferred from the fact that there were also cunning-folk working on the European continent: in Denmark they were called 'kloge folk'.[78] Back in Britain, these controversial characters went under many intelligent-sounding names: wise-folk, clever-folk, canny-folk, wizards, warlocks, white witches, conjurors and so on.[79] Technically, their work contravened the terms of the 1736 Witchcraft Act, which proscribed all 'pretenses' to witchery and magic. However, the legislation was cumbersome and heavy handed, requiring an expensive trial before a judge at the Quarter Sessions. Occasionally, it was invoked: cunning-folk were prosecuted at Ipswich in 1801, Cardiff in 1807, Leeds and Hull in 1808, Lancaster in 1809, Beverley in 1813, and Norwich and Leeds in 1819 (note the craft's urban profile).[80] To increase the rate of prosecution, new legislation was enacted in 1824 that allowed local magistrates to prosecute professional magicians.[81]

It took more than one new law to stop Britain's cunning-folk. They were sly and imposing characters who adapted to changing circumstances and were good at spotting new opportunities. A colourful illustration of this comes from Stokesley, a market town on the edge of the North Yorkshire moors, and home to a part-time shoemaker and cunning-man (a typical combination of occupations) named John Wrightson (c. 1780–1846). To critics, he was a person of 'ill fame and dishonest persuasion', a 'charlatan and impostor' who prospered from deceit and was unwilling 'to get his livelihood by honest labour'.[82] Mr Wrightson's customers, the desperate and needy folk of North Yorkshire, disagreed. Their cunning-man, 'famed all the country round', was so respected that local people regularly asked him to be godfather to their children.[83]

Why was the conjuror so esteemed? Largely, because John Wrightson acted like an impressive figure. He went to church dressed like a true Regency gentleman, in crimson knee britches, a scarlet coat and a frilly shirt. Describing himself as the seventh son of a seventh daughter, he attended his customers in a room filled with exotic objects, from dried herbs to a globe and a human skull. When his clients arrived, he already seemed to know why they'd come (critics speculated that he must have used informants). He could write a little Latin and even some Hebrew, which he used to embellish the evil-averting written charms he sold to local farmers. (What his clients didn't know was that John's knowledge of Hebrew didn't go beyond some rather impressive-looking letters.) Wrightson's witchcraft cures were similar to those prescribed by cunning-folk around Britain. Invariably, they involved sympathetic magic, animal hearts stuck with pins, biblical readings, and incantations uttered at midnight. The absolute prerequisite was to 'keep all very secret and have a Strong faith', as John insisted in some written instructions.[84] He may not have genuinely rid his clients of witchcraft. But if the cunning-man inspired strong faith or powerful belief, he probably helped his customers in another way, by activating powerful placebo effects and enhancing their bodies' self-healing processes. That, at any rate, is the conclusion we could draw from a growing body of research into what has been described as 'medicine's last great frontier': the healing power of faith.[85]

Much of John Wrightson's magic was traditional, but he was also a savvy businessman who turned it to new uses. When, during the 1790s, men from around Stokesley were balloted to serve in the army, to fight in Europe against French forces, Mr Wrightson espied an opportunity. He began telling fortunes to predict whose name would be drawn. Presumably some of his predictions were wrong because, in 1797, an aggrieved customer prosecuted him. Wrightson got in trouble with the law again, in 1814, when he beat and threatened a tax collector with a loaded pistol.[86] It wasn't nearly enough to end his career. John continued working at his controversial trade until his death, in the mid-1840s. Fifty years later, in the 1890s, local people were still telling stories about him, which they uttered with a still living sense of 'unconscious awe'.[87]

Cunning-folks' fees depended on what they thought their clients could afford. They were seldom cheap and could be astronomical. Take the renowned Devonshire wizard, Benjamin Baker, known variously as 'old Baker', 'conjuror Baker' and 'Doctor Baker'. Like many others in the trade, Benjamin followed his father Richard, a farmer and 'unsocial drunkard', into the cunning-craft.[88] For a year, throughout 1822, the young conjuror treated Elizabeth Bryant, a bewitched lady we've already met, who with her mother and sister brutalised their witch in the Somerset village of Wiveliscombe.[89] Benjamin began his therapy by confirming that Elizabeth was indeed bewitched. Next he helped identify the culprit by giving vague clues ('She's a dark haired woman who walks past your door', 'She'll call at your house tomorrow', that sort of thing).[90] Finally, and most importantly, the wizard prescribed magical cures. They included protective amulets, special pills, herbs to be burnt on the fire, and a powdered concoction that Elizabeth was supposed to drink while someone else read aloud the 68th psalm and the Lord's Prayer. As an astute and sensitive therapist, Baker would have known the value of professing expertise in as many specialisms as possible. But it didn't come cheap. 'Doctor' Baker charged £10 for his treatments. It was a vast sum for a working-class woman like Elizabeth. In Somerset, where she lived, it would have taken her the best part of a year to earn that sort of money.[91]

EVIL TRADITIONS

How, exactly, did witches sow sorcery and manifest magic? There was a multitude of methods, many old, a few novel, and most broadly similar to forms of witchery found across the globe. Witchcraft, in this respect, was an evolving tradition of evil.

Most obviously, witches worked by torturing figurines representing their victims.[92] Symbolically attacking effigies, or 'voodoo dolls' as they're often known today, is probably the oldest, most widespread and enduring type of magic in human history. Magical figurines have been used for various reasons, from binding gods and demons to healing, but effigies intended for supernaturally harming people were employed as long ago as Egypt in 1200 BC, Babylonia in *c.* 700 BC and Greece in 400 BC, to take a few recorded examples.[93] In early nineteenth-century Britain, much effigy magic was imaginary in the sense that alleged witches never attempted it. Yet some people really did try to harm their enemies in this way. Ironically, some of those enemies were alleged witches, bewitched by their victims as revenge. Usually, figurines were stuck with pins, burnt, melted, or left to rot and wither, though sometimes they were symbolically hanged too.[94] Dolls made for this purpose could be highly artistic, even life-like, to make sure spells hit their targets. This was the case in 1821, in the London district of Moorgate. A fortune-teller was the target. A disgruntled neighbour made, and then hanged from the window, a doll elaborately dressed up as a witch, wearing a high-rimmed pointy hat, with a birch-wood broom and holding a miniature pack of cards.[95] It may have been intended just to humiliate the fortune-teller, but the doll probably had more sinister connotations too.

Witches were supposed to be able to shapeshift into the form of sneaky, semi-nocturnal animals like cats and hares.[96] The most powerful sorcerers also commanded non-human servants of their own. Known as familiars, these minions secretly unleashed mischief on behalf of their wicked masters. Ann Izzard, a reputed witch from Great Paxton in Cambridgeshire, was in 1813 accused of possessing 'a white cat, and all sitch as that', a furtive reference to animal and impish familiars.[97] During the same year, Britain's newspapers reported on a Staffordshire woman who kept a toad in her garden, with the goal of feeding it the Bread of the Sacrament after church on Sunday, to transform the creature into a 'valuable familiar spirit'.[98] Whether or not the rumour was true, it spoke to the sort of genuine fears that made people take unusual precautions. Since at least the thirteenth century, builders had been concealing dead and dried cats in the fabric of houses, usually behind plaster panels or in wall cavities or roof spaces, and beneath floorboards.[99] Quite why remains a mystery because there is no accompanying written evidence to explain the strange practice. The undoubted expert is the archaeologist Brian Hoggard, who has calculated that 6 per cent of the cats discovered were placed in hunting poses, sometimes with the additional prop of a target rat. This suggests they were conceived of as a sort of magical pest control. However, as Hoggard notes, given that the cats were usually put in the same sorts of household locations as other magic-repelling objects, they were probably conceived of as vermin hunters on a spiritual plane. Plausibly, they were meant to hunt witches' familiars.

Servant familiars are an elemental witchcraft idea, found throughout history and in societies across the world, from Europe to Africa to South Asia.[100] However, between the period of the witch trials and the early twentieth century, animal familiars appear to have been particularly prominent in British witchcraft, and especially in East Anglian witchcraft.[101] It's unclear why, though one can advance several plausible explanations. The British were great keepers of pets, and perhaps the notion of an animal familiar chimed with this predilection. If normal folk enjoyed keeping dogs and cats, why shouldn't witches do something similar, albeit in a much darker form? Moving on to a more robust argument, during the early modern era, British artists and writers created some extremely memorable depictions of these satanic servants, which probably helped embed the idea in British culture for generations to come. Familiars figured in the opening scene of Shakespeare's *Macbeth* (1606) and in many popular witch trial pamphlets and woodcuts.[102] These tropes were recycled, throughout the eighteenth and early nineteenth centuries, by a succession of plays, chapbooks, journals and newspaper articles.[103]

Above all, British Protestantism nourished the idea of familiars, through the archaic language of the English Bible. The greatest English Bible, the King James Authorised Version (1611), had been produced under the patronage of a famously witch-conscious monarch, James VI of Scotland and I of England. He had been a victim of witchcraft, helped to prosecute the apparently responsible witches, and even wrote a pamphlet about the dark art.[104] Given its patron's interests, is it surprising that the King James

Version contained frank condemnations of witchery? There were no quibbles about whether the Hebrew word *kasaph* should be translated as 'seer', 'diviner' or 'poisoner', as most scholars now believe it should.[105] Instead, *kasaph* became 'witch', as in 'Thou shalt not suffer a witch to live' (Exodus 22:18). Witches featured strongly in the King James Bible and so, through a similar process of translation, did familiars. The King James Version contained no fewer than fifteen references to 'familiar spirits'. The most notorious was the Witch of Endor, a sorceress who possessed a familiar spirit of her own. There were plenty of other mentions. Leviticus, the third book of Moses, explicitly banned these ungodly servants:

> Regard not them that have familiar spirits, neither seek after wizards, to be defiled by them: I am the LORD your God. (Leviticus 19:31)

> A man also or woman that hath a familiar spirit, or that is a wizard, shall surely be put to death: they shall stone them with stones: their blood shall be upon them. (Leviticus 20:27)

As with *kasaph* and 'witch', some theologians thought the translators had made a mistake by translating the Hebrew words *haaoboth* and *aoub* into 'familiar spirit'. The real meaning, apparently, was more like 'serpent'. 'There is not any leading or remote idea in the word, which could possibly authorise them to give such a translation,' complained John Bellamy, in his 1818 translation of the Bible.[106] His words didn't make much impact. Throughout the early nineteenth century, most Bibles used the traditional translation, and many contained commentaries endorsing the idea that familiars were real and dangerous.[107]

* * *

New technologies facilitated novel types of magic by allowing sorcerers to create updated spells. For example, some people in the early nineteenth century thought witches worked by keeping toads under glass and watching the animals slowly die.[108] Glassware became a major (though still expensive) consumer product during the eighteenth century, so this sinister method was likely a recent imagining.[109] The use of glass was new, but toads had links with sorcery and demons dating back to at least the 1300s, and found widely in places as various as France, Italy, Holland, the Balkans and the Basque Country, as well as in Britain.[110] The idea may have grown out of several of the amphibian's associations during the medieval period, including the strong connection between toads and female sexuality, and the fact that some physicians regarded toads as a cure-all wonder drug, ideally to be eaten as part of the patient's daily diet.[111] More likely, the fact that some toads were poisonous, and that since the Roman period their blood and lungs had been regarded as noxious enough to kill, may have been enough to create their witchy connotations, given that witchcraft was often conceived of as a mystic form of poisoning.[112]

Sorcery was conveyed through seemingly friendly gestures, like gift giving. In 1809 a farmer from Hoo (Kent) concluded that his poultry flock had been bewitched through a duck given to him by a friend.[113] Spreading magical misfortunes via gifts was a long-standing witchcraft idea, current in Europe since at least the early modern era.[114] It implied that evil was contagious, a sort of occult disease. It also portrayed witches as fantastically disingenuous figures, the epitome of anti-social values, fakers who made community life impossible by pretending to aid their neighbours while secretly destroying them. This fantasy of witches as the supreme misanthropes was expressed through another of their techniques: sowing evil through customary words and phrases like greetings, farewells and compliments.[115] Magic could also be spread by poisoning food – another pervasive idea, found across the world and in Europe since the period of the witch trials. In 1818, a defendant at the Bow Street magistrates' court (London) claimed two women had bewitched him 'by means of some stuff which they put into some tea'.[116]

Any contact with witches was dangerous. Even their gaze was harmful. The evil eye, the souring power of a hateful or envious look, is usually associated with the Mediterranean world, but something like it existed in Britain. So explained Thomas Hudson, a young man from Leeds. In 1828 he was brought before the town's court for assaulting his neighbour, Susannah Ormond.[117] Hudson claimed that Susannah 'possessed the power of witchcraft', prompting an extended interrogation. 'Now then, you stupid fellow,' began the magistrate, trying to impress the mayor sitting beside him, 'do you deny having assaulted this woman?' Hudson did not, but felt his conduct was justified because: 'She's done all the mischief; and let her deny it if she can! She's the cause of it and I'm the sufferer.' 'The cause of what?' asked the magistrate, feigning ignorance. Witchcraft was the answer: 'I feel it in me,' Hudson continued, 'it burns like fire.' Scratching Susannah only provided temporary relief. 'When she stares at me, it comes back again,' the young man explained, excitedly. Victims of sorcery like him really did suffer, but from stress rather than magic. Within the medical literature, it is now 'generally accepted that psychological stress can cause or worsen physical pain', inducing ailments from migraines to back pain, ulcers, colitis, skin irritations and more.[118] When Thomas Hudson said he was burning up every time his witch looked at him, he was saying he was in agony, using what, for centuries, has been a common metaphor in the language of pain.[119] His pains, the burning, originated in the alarmingly stressful thought that witches' eyes really do convey evil power.

Perhaps the greatest evil tradition was the idea of family witchcraft. The notion that sorcery runs in the family was at least several centuries old, probably much more ancient, and has been found across the world.[120] Whether parents formally instructed their children in the dark arts or merely passed on evil temperaments, it is unclear how witches were felt to transmit their powers. Either way, once acquired, witchcraft reputations were dangerous and hard to shake.

The Izzards, of Great Paxton in Cambridgeshire, suffered more than most. Twice in May 1808 Ann Izzard, a grandmother of about sixty years of age, was dragged from her home, stripped, beaten and repeatedly cut by a huge mob of her fellow villagers.[121] The local constable offered no protection and apprehended none of her assailants, though eventually nine of Ann's neighbours were jailed.[122] Given this limited justice, it's not surprising the witch-hating locals continued to abuse the Izzards. In 1812, as she walked home from the pub, Ann's daughter Ruth was hit with a stick and thrown in a ditch by a woman who yelled about bewitchment while calling her 'one of Nan Izzard's imps'. The perpetrator received a week in jail. A year later old Ann Izzard suffered again, this time with abuse by a woman who threatened to throw her in the pond because she was an 'old witch' who kept a familiar.[123]

INDULGENT MAGISTRATES

In early 1800s Britain, witches were brazenly abused because their assailants felt justified in their actions, not just morally, but legally. 'I'll be damned if

I don't murder her, for there's no law to hang me,' Robert Northover bellowed as he battered the reputed witch Elizabeth Parsons.[124] He didn't really believe that he could legally kill her, but he certainly thought witchcraft was a crime punishable by law. 'I'll not leave the room till the old hag's down in prison,' Robert yelled, before calling on the town constable to arrest her. He wasn't alone in expecting the authorities to help when witchcraft was afoot. In 1812 a man 'of decent appearance' from Westminster (London) petitioned the Southwark magistrates to punish his neighbour for witchcraft. With great formality he asked the JPs to 'cite the magician before his tribunal, and ... inflict such pains and penalties upon him, as should prevent him from disturbing society in the future'.[125]

Citizens even arrested sorcerers, or tried to. In 1812, Chester's sheriff court heard how three men (Samuel Jones, William Jones and Thomas Speed) had taken a reputed witch, Jane Johnson, into custody.[126] Claiming her as their prisoner, and brandishing a paper they maintained was an arrest warrant, the men took Jane from the cottage she shared with her husband and kept her away the whole night, before releasing her the next day. They took her to the village of Ruabon, home of a famous cunning-man, and put her up at an inn. The innkeeper explained how Jane had been put under his care 'on account of being a witch' and that 'she was kept in custody ... by virtue of a warrant'. Even if the arrest was a ruse, it was clearly plausible enough for both Jane and the innkeeper to go along with it. But it may not have been a ruse. During Jane's incarceration, the kidnappers ordered that she should be given any food or assistance she desired. There was a sense of due process, and Jane's would-be prosecutors seem to have thought that they were acting properly by arresting her. They returned her to her husband the following day, presumably after discovering that the authorities disagreed.

What gave people the impression that magistrates and policemen would prevent witchcraft and punish witches? Was this conviction born of nothing more than the lingering folk-memory of the witch trials? Were early nineteenth-century witchcraft believers wholly out of touch with the reality of the law? In a word: no. Parliament officially decriminalised witchcraft in 1736: in theory, the law was unambiguous. In practice, officials responsible for actually implementing the law sometimes gave the impression that witchcraft was still a crime, albeit not a capital one. As we've already seen, local constables could be highly permissive of violence against witches. At

Great Paxton in 1808, Bridport in 1824 and Wickham Skeith in 1825 they stood idly by while alleged witches were mobbed, scratched or swum. At Abergavenny, in 1827, the constable played a leading role in the mobbing. Doubtless many other similar episodes went unrecorded.

Some JPs admonished witchcraft believers or patiently explained to them that the idea of sorcery was nothing more than a delusion.[127] Other Justices, however, took a very different line. Incredible as it may seem, during the early nineteenth century there were a few whose actions endorsed the idea that there was something in witchcraft. In 1826 a correspondent wrote to an Edinburgh paper to complain about the treatment of an old housekeeper who had been lacerated about the face on account of being a witch.[128] When the case came to court the magistrate bound over the assail-ants to keep the peace. But the Justice also bound over the alleged witch and her employer, despite the fact that they were guilty of no infringement. That judgment implied that the JP thought the witch had done something wrong, but occasionally his colleagues went further. When, in 1812, a petitioner asked the Southwark magistracy to arrest an alleged witch, the magistrate promised to comply with his request.[129] Far from remonstrating with the complainant or deriding his foolish convictions, the presiding Justice instead advised him to 'rest satisfied, that no effort in his power should be wanting to prevent the evil spirit from troubling him in the future'.

Were those the words of a busy magistrate, who humoured a complainant to get rid of him quickly? Perhaps, but another possibility is worth enter-taining. There were some in positions of authority who, though they did not themselves believe in witches, thought there was a case for preserving witch-craft belief among others, especially the poor. This expeditious line of thinking emerged from the governing classes' anxieties about what happens to popular revolts when they combine with secularism (as in the later stages of the French Revolution, when both the aristocracy and churches were violently attacked).

One proponent of this curious mindset was the Rev. John Anderson, Presbyterian minister to the parishes of Stronsay and Eday, on Orkney in the Scottish Northern Isles.[130] The ordinary islanders, Anderson observed in his chapter of the *Statistical Account of Scotland* (1795), were credulous enough to practise 'an inferior species of witchcraft' and give credit to fairies and ghosts.[131] The Reverend had come across many striking and recent examples of this credulity, but was in no rush to banish it. Its negative consequences, he felt, were unimportant in comparison to the positive effects a supernatural cosmology had in sustaining religious belief. Atheism and irreligion were the real enemies. They were new and radically dangerous to the status quo of Church and state.[132] It was better to leave the people in their superstitious ignorance, because their beliefs about witches and ghosts nourished their more general religious convictions.

Even at the dawn of the nineteenth century, some highly educated and well-placed people felt, on balance, that witchcraft belief ought to be indulged and sustained. This surprising discovery prompts an obvious question: who else thought witchcraft was worth believing in?

SHY DEMONOLOGISTS

Demonology, a genre of scholarly books about sorcerers, devils and spirits, lost its intellectual prestige around the dawn of the eighteenth century.[133] No longer could judges or eminent clergymen write learned treatises about witches, ruminating in fine philosophical detail about diabolical compacts or night-time revels. After the waning of the witch trials, it would have been career suicide for an esteemed public figure to concoct that sort of text. Nevertheless, well into the nineteenth century occult tomes continued to appear, catering to the numbers of literate people who nursed nagging anxieties about witchcraft. You could still read about who witches were, what they did and how they could be combated. But by the early 1800s it was a bit more difficult than hitherto, requiring forays into historical literature or the purchasing of anonymously authored books about the black art.

Republished historical works served as textbooks for practical magic. Several – perhaps as many as a dozen – editions of the early seventeenth-century botanist Nicholas Culpeper's *Complete Herbal*, which featured remedies for witchcraft, were published between 1800 and 1830. Numerous sixteenth- and seventeenth-century witchcraft tracts were reprinted too.[134] Among the most notorious was *Satan's Invisible World Discovered*, a compendium of hauntings, bewitchments and devilry written by the professor of philosophy at Glasgow University, George Sinclair, in 1685. According to one critic, during the 1820s it still had an 'extensive circulation' among the peasantry of Scotland.[135] There were also freshly compiled examples of this

33

strange genre, where history's greatest hauntings and bewitchments were briskly told, over a few pages, in an easy-to-read chapbook format.[136] Thus, in 1803, a Scottish publisher produced the snappily titled: *History of Witches, Ghosts, and Highland Seers: Containing Many Wonderful Well-attested Relations of Supernatural Appearances, Not Published before in Any Similar Collection. Designed for the Conviction of the Unbeliever and the Amusement of the Curious.*

Early nineteenth-century booksellers sold lots of high- and low-brow demonology. In 1819 in London, George Lackington was advertising 226 titles under the heading of 'Astrology, Alchemy, Magic, Witchcraft, &c', a fairly substantial portion of his catalogued stock.[137] Antiquaries and historians were obviously intrigued by esoteric tomes, but so too were people who wanted to understand or even wield witchery. James Heaton, a nonconformist preacher who, during the 1820s, wrote two attestations to witchcraft's reality, cited historical demonologists like William Perkins, Thomas Fuller and Henry More.[138] Heaton warned his readers not to engage in the 'curious arts and occult sciences', but some individuals undoubtedly used old texts as guides to profane magic. John Harries (*c.* 1785–1839), Wales' most renowned conjuror, likely did so.[139] His so-called 'book of incantations', now held by the National Library of Wales, contains two printed almanacs, a litany of spells and astrological calculations, details of his clients' accounts, and – tellingly – a London bookseller's catalogue.[140]

The most prolific shy demonologist was Peter Buchan. His *Witchcraft Detected and Prevented; or, the School of the Black Art Newly Opened* went through at least three editions during the 1820s.[141] A compilation of spells, charms and recipes 'gleaned from the works of the ancients', Buchan claimed his book was produced 'more with a view to amuse than to be put in practice'.[142] Nonsense: *Witchcraft Detected and Prevented* was clearly supposed to serve as a manual of magic. With almost two hundred individually indexed procedures, it told its readers how to do everything from charming away headaches to removing witchcraft. J.S. Forsyth's *Demonologia; or, Natural Knowledge Revealed* (1827) contained a similar catalogue of astrological techniques, lucky days and talismans. Outwardly an exposé of ancient and modern superstition, the work's formatting shows it was aimed at readers wanting a practical guide to magic. Its cover and table of contents flaunted the arcane knowledge contained inside. The author's decision to reveal only his initials also suggests he was well aware of the controversial uses his text would be put to.

Beyond instructive magical texts, various books and pamphlets defended the propriety of believing in witches. Romantic poets including Robert Burns, William Wordsworth and Lord Byron portrayed superstition as a commendable mindset, conducive to imaginative flights of fancy.[143] Methodists like John Wesley and his successors thought witchcraft was an important credo because it demonstrated the truth of the Bible and the veracity of Christianity.[144] Joanna Southcott (1750–1814), a milkmaid turned prophet and one of the most popular writers of her generation, saw witches as a more practical concern. She published dozens of prophecies, strange visions rendered in rough verse, selling over 100,000 copies between 1801 and 1816 alone.[145] Within were occasional references to witchcraft, Satan's minions, and evil powers.[146] It wasn't just for literary effect. From her upbringing in rural Devon, Joanna was thoroughly convinced that witches were 'wicked people, who are in a league with the devil'. Her followers occasionally wrote to her, saying they were bewitched and asking for help. To one couple with bedevilled animals, Joanna suggested they write 'Holiness to the Lord' on a piece of parchment, and place it inside their horses' bridles. Apparently, it worked.[147]

CRITICS MUSTER

There were plenty of critics too, ready to denounce anyone who believed in the dark arts. To some degree though, it was ever thus. The Kentish gentleman Reginald Scot published his classic exposé of 'witches and witchmongers', *The Discoverie of Witchcraft*, way back in 1584. Even then, his arguments were 'not all that new'.[148] Since the early 1700s, didactic literature had been warning the servant-employing classes about superstitious matrons and nursemaids, who were sure to transmit all sorts of weird fears to their charges.[149] On a more learned level, in the appendix to his *Observations on Popular Antiquities* (1777), the antiquarian John Brand had condemned witchcraft as ridiculous, castigated the former laws against it as a 'disgrace', and quoted the renowned seventeenth-century scientist and sceptic Francis Bacon to reinforce the point.[150] Some evangelists wrote tracts and delivered sermons to similar effect.[151]

As the eighteenth century gave way to the nineteenth, sceptics continued to rehearse familiar arguments against occult beliefs.[152] Then, around the

1820s, something changed. Journalists hardened their stance on witchcraft, largely because newspaper readers demanded they repudiate local outbreaks of superstition.[153] Of course, we should not exaggerate the effects of newspaper diatribes. Even when they tried to undermine witchcraft, journalists could unintentionally foster it by spreading information about the location and identity of cunning-folk.[154] Still, it's striking how suddenly witchcraft became the focus of newspaper exposés and hostile commentary. Previously it had only been reported when it led to crime, cruelty or disorder.[155] Yet during the 1820s, ordinary bewitchments became newsworthy. To take one example, in 1825 the *Bath Chronicle* thought it was worth publishing a cynical note about a bewitched farmhouse one hundred miles away, in Peters Marland (Devon), purely on account of the disasters said to be taking place there.[156] It was certainly a sensational story, involving cream-jugs leaping from the kitchen table, reap-hooks launching themselves around the room, and knives flying at the family. But witchcraft wasn't just covered because it made for thrilling copy. Relatively privileged Britons, the types who made up the bulk of newspaper subscribers, were developing new anxieties about the credulous tendencies of the masses. 'The idea that ignorance and superstition make men tractable,' as the *Morning Chronicle* put it in 1824, was fading.[157] Order and stability would be better served by educating the people, so they didn't credit fallacies of all types, whether supernatural or not. For the sake of property and liberty, witchcraft, along with its allied 'popular superstitions', needed to be dethroned.

* * *

At the dawn of the nineteenth century, did only poor and uneducated folk credit witchcraft? Many historians seem to think so. Owen Davies has done more than anyone to show how the 'educated discourse on witchcraft and magic never entirely declined'.[158] Yet even his generalisation, that British elites put the 'popular belief in witchcraft' under particular duress from the late eighteenth century, does not quite capture the evidence presented here.[159]

During the early 1800s, too many well-heeled people endorsed the reality of witchcraft for it to be classified as a popular belief. And even if superior sorts didn't themselves believe, they invariably sympathised with those who did. In the wake of the French Revolution, nervous magistrates and skittish parsons regarded the harms emanating from witchcraft as meagre compared to its benefits in reinforcing religion. Magic, according to their analysis, fostered order and stability.

This changed during the 1820s. Magical states of mind had always been controversial, but in this period sceptical detractors became particularly fervent and numerous. In his rustic satire 'The Parish' (c. 1820–7) the 'peasant poet' John Clare noted the disappearance of two stock village characters: the old-school farmer and the old-school parson, who 'always quoted the Witch of Endor as a knockdown to unbelievers in witchcraft'. In real life, similar developments were under way. One sign of this was the changing way newspapers reported on witchcraft. Previously witchy happenings were covered if they caused violence or unrest. Now, legal or not, the very existence of people who believed in the reality of spells and curses was a cause for concern. Witchcraft, a notion that until quite recently had been seen as conducive to religious orthodoxy and social stability, was increasingly labelled as a dangerous popular superstition.

THREE

TOUGH SUPERSTITIONS
1830–60

Convincing people to discard their 'superstitions' is difficult, frustrating and often impossible. Persuade, encourage, cajole, explain, mock, shame, dissect, inspire and admonish. You can do all that and worse. It rarely changes minds.

The trouble is, our ideas are precious possessions. They express our identities. They signify our loyalties. They grow out of our upbringings and experiences, meaning that revising our convictions can be like renouncing part of ourselves. If we rehearse our thoughts, they can become stubbornly familiar, as if stuck in our minds. Ideas generally are tough; but willed beliefs, deliberately forced or summoned convictions about things we *want* to be true, are particularly resilient. They can relate to political ideologies or to cultural shibboleths or to profound supernatural powers like spirits, witches, omens, fate, faith healing, intervening angels and strange gods. Whatever the case, faith-based mindsets are powerful indeed.

Transforming true believers into uncertain doubters takes skill, trust, respect, empathy and luck. The difficulties are evident today, all over the world. Scientists struggle to convince large numbers of Europeans and Americans that anthropogenic climate change isn't a hoax.[1] 'Deprogramming' initiatives, official counselling regimes aimed at cultists and violent Islamic extremists, are no more than moderately successful.[2] Broadly targeted 'counter-narratives', designed to refute terrorist ideologies, achieve even less and may well be totally ineffective.[3]

*   *   *

Persuasion problems were familiar to the early Victorians, the generations of people who lived between about 1830 and 1860. They, of course, were not troubled by man-made climate change, cults or terrorism. Their persuasion problem was different, though to their minds still serious. It related to what they called 'popular superstition.' Writers, clergymen, lecturers, journalists and a distinct sub-section of self-educated artisans – these high-minded people became alarmed by the thought that many of their fellow Britons sincerely believed in the existence of occult powers like ghosts, astrology, luck and especially witchcraft.

Popular superstitions were, in the view of their detractors, intellectual anachronisms. Obviously, they had no place in the glorious new world of railways, factories, newspapers, steam engines and telegrams. Popular superstitions weren't just wrong, but ungodly and even dangerous. They encouraged fantastical thoughts. They corrupted the pure spirit of rational Christianity. Worst of all, they filled ordinary people's minds with extravagant rubbish, taking up the space where edifying ideas and sober knowledge should be. Indirectly, popular superstitions made Britons vulnerable to the promises of demagogues, radicals and revolutionaries – the sorts of chancers who periodically overturned governments on the European continent. That, at any rate, was what many well-to-do early Victorians feared.

What to do about the problem of popular superstition? In an era of very small government (it consumed around 5 per cent of annual national income compared with over 40 per cent today) an official response was unlikely. Private social activism filled the gap. This meant writing, lecturing, sermonising and – most controversially of all – directly confronting believers in witches and ghosts.

Disappointingly, witches were not easily debunked. Millions of early Victorians – probably a majority – continued to believe. Scepticism handed down from on high wasn't well received by those below, not least because it was often filled with insulting phrases about the 'deluded multitude'. But there was also something tough about the credo of witchcraft belief. Certain thought processes and intellectual reference points made it resilient to criticism.

The great challenge to magic came not from rationalist crusaders, but from the police. More and better law enforcement bore down on violence against witches, discouraging vigilantes and making counter-witchcraft practices less physically aggressive. It proved impossible to eradicate the idea of sorcery and the strange fascination it exercised. Yet during the 'age of reform', as it has been called, Britain's police were at least able to pacify witchcraft's most ferocious expressions.

OUTRAGE IN OXFORDSHIRE: THE CASE OF THE 'LITTLE TEW GHOST'

In November 1838 tumult erupted at Little Tew, Oxfordshire. The cause was none of the usual 1830s suspects. Not Chartism, the political movement for democratic reform. Not the arrival of workhouses with the New Poor Law. Not even the enclosure of common land. Something very different disturbed this remote hamlet: mysterious happenings, at an otherwise ordinary cottage.

Odd noises, weird voices and bizarre accidents had become regular parts of life for the unfortunate inhabitants. Some locals said it was witchcraft. Others thought a ghost was present, a restless spirit looking for absolution. Sceptics called the disturbances a fraudulent farce. Either way the exploits of the 'Little Tew ghost', as it was soon known, became a chief topic of conversation in the village and the surrounding area too. Within months, hundreds of people came to witness the strange happenings for themselves.[4]

The unquiet cottage was part of a partitioned farmhouse belonging to Exeter College in Oxford. An old widower lived there with a newly married couple, Ann and Thomas Hall, and their infant child. Ann bore the brunt of the haunting. Aged 21, she'd been working in service at the nearby village of Chipping Warden, but left when she began having fits. Implying witchcraft, Ann said they had started when she offended a Roma fortune-teller, who predicted she would lose her job within two months. Sure enough, she did. Shortly afterwards Ann married a blacksmith named Thomas Hall and gave birth to a daughter.[5] Probably she felt pressured into the union since, like around half of women from her background, Ann was already pregnant when she wed.[6]

In a way, it was just another workaday Victorian haunting. Oxfordshire saw similar happenings in Bicester (1848), Witney (1855), Beckley (1857), Deddington (1869) and Horspath (1873).[7] Ghosts haunted towns and cities too. Rumours of their appearance inspired inquisitive crowds to gather in Chelsea in 1853, Southwark in 1868 and Westminster in 1874, to take a few London examples.[8]

But the Little Tew ghost was unusually well documented. Investigators wrote to the local papers, recounting extraordinary things they'd witnessed at Ann and Thomas Hall's cottage, a pseudo-exorcism, for instance. Half a dozen Baptists met in the cottage, to read aloud from the Gospel of St John, sing and pray, to drive out whatever malevolence festered there. The 'evil thing' merely mocked them, discordantly parodying their hymns and prayers. Then the haunting developed new features. Cries and screeches began, like a wailing cat. Ann's wedding ring and door key were lost then found, hidden in strange places around the house. When she took her medicine (a sedative?), the ghost would throw it on the floor. At mealtimes, the diners were disturbed by what sounded like a cockerel crowing. At night, there was such a racket that Ann and Thomas Hall couldn't sleep together in peace. Unoccupied chairs spontaneously fell over. All the while, Ann Hall collapsed into prolonged fits.

April 1839, six months after the haunting began, and there was still no sign of its end. No imposture had been detected. Rumours of evil spirits and black magic continued to swirl. The Hall's cottage had witnessed more exorcisms, more strange voices using blasphemous and obscene expressions, and more tables and chairs moving around as if they were alive. But what really troubled one local paper, the *Oxford Chronicle*, was the 'number of persons [who] are persuaded of the truth of these statements'. No 'respectable individuals' were willing to credit the genuineness of the haunting, yet in a way that only made the situation more alarming. The Little Tew ghost, it seemed, was corrupting the minds of the humble villagers. The poor, easily influenced, prone-to-revolting masses of Oxfordshire were being enraptured by wild ideas. Animated by this paranoid thought, the local newspapers urged their readers to sift the scandal and expose its true nature.

Most visitors to the Halls' cottage went out of curiosity. A few thought the events were religiously significant. And then there was a rump of sceptical investigators. Occupying fairly honourable positions in society, these doctors, tenant farmers and artisans were convinced they were dealing with a hoax. They went to great lengths to substantiate their suspicions. A group of farmers, thinking that Ann Hall imitated the evil spirit, hired a ventriloquist in an (unsuccessful) attempt to prove how it worked.

Half a century later, the truth finally emerged. The Rev. Edward Marshall, priest of the neighbouring parish of Sandford St Martin, discovered that Ann Hall eventually 'confessed her cheating'.[9] A publican from the village had 'paid so much per week to the ghosts and its friends to keep up the delusion' – presumably because she was doing brisk business catering to ghost-watching tourists.

As for Ann, she earned some much-needed money. But she must have got something else out of the affair. Ann was a serial haunter – a repeatedly bewitched woman. It happened when she was working as a maid. Then when she was a young mother, in Little Tew. Then again when the family moved to Hook Norton, another nearby village. The family relocated to Enstone. Again Ann's ghost followed. Why?

Ann was clearly troubled, if not disturbed. Decades later, a neighbour confessed to a local folklorist that Ann Hall, although nice, was 'always very strange'.[10] But there was more to it than that. Ann's hauntings had a rational, though perhaps subconscious, aspect. She used them, strategically, to leave a job and move back home to Little Tew, then to protest covertly about her home life. That's why the 'ghost' hid her wedding ring and stopped her and Thomas from sleeping together. Ann lived in an environment, and at a time, of little choice. A rural, working-class woman like her couldn't get divorced. In any case, she couldn't afford to live alone. If Ann was fundamentally unhappy, there were many things she couldn't say or do about it. But she could speak, and act, through the medium of witchcraft and spirits. Even here, she had to act within certain conventions. There were also risks within the unstable and always slightly crazy domain of magic. All the same, for marginalised people like Ann Hall, witches and ghosts could be strangely useful.

CURSING, IRISH AND OTHERWISE

The summer of 1854 was a worrying one. Drought parched much of the countryside. Cholera ravaged London. In the Crimea, Britain and its ally

France were at war with Russia. From Ireland many thousands were emigrating, mainly to Britain and America, fleeing the devastation of the Potato Famine that had begun almost a decade earlier, in 1845. The linguist George Borrow wanted to escape the bad news. So he took a holiday, a walking tour of Wales.

In *Wild Wales*, his classic travelogue of the journey, Borrow flaunted his mastery of the notoriously difficult Welsh language, while describing the picturesque places he saw and intriguing people he met. His strangest encounter happened on the road between Merthyr Tydfil and Caerphilly, market towns in South Wales. At Troedyrhiw, a village in the Rhondda Valley, lying beneath heather-covered hills that were starting to be heavily mined for coal, Borrow saw a bedraggled woman, trudging towards him: 'She seemed between forty and fifty, was bare-footed and bare-headed, with grizzled hair hanging in elf locks, and was dressed in rags and tatters.'

When the fearful figure got within ten yards of George Borrow, she stopped. Suddenly she threw herself forward, rolling head over heels three times. Then she stood bolt upright, raised her right arm, and cried: 'Give me an alms, for the glory of God!'

George Borrow said he doubted whether giving her alms would glorify God. But sensing a good story, he offered a donation in return for her tale. She obliged, introducing herself as Johanna Colgan, 'a bedivilled woman from the county of Limerick', in south-west Ireland. Johanna had lost everything after falling victim to a beggar's 'evil prayer', or curse. She'd been a smallholder and the proud mother to two strapping adult sons, until a malicious mendicant muttered the words '*Biadh an taifrionn gan sholas duit a bhean shalach!*' – a Gaelic curse meaning 'May the Mass never comfort you, you dirty queen!' Soon her animals and farm were gone, while Johanna took to drink and was abandoned by her sons. Ever since, she'd wandered Ireland, then England and Wales, looking for her child who had enlisted in the army. Walking in her rags, without shoes, a coat, or even a scarf for her head, she barely kept herself alive by threatening to curse whomever she met, using the same formula that had been her downfall. This amazing story, told by a desperately needy and also quite intimidating woman, elicited a shilling from Borrow. Shouting 'Hoorah!' Johanna went on her way.[11]

Travelling across Wales during the dry summer of 1854, George Borrow constantly encountered Irish people. They were camped on the green at

Chester, the ancient city on the English side of the border. They were sleeping rough under walls near Holyhead, on the Isle of Anglesey. At Ruthin locals bemoaned the Irish who 'at present infest these parts'.[12] Irish immigration had exploded in the wake of the Great Potato Famine of 1845–9, with perhaps 1.5 million people fleeing death and disease during those years alone.[13] Most went to the United States, though many settled in Britain too, such that by 1861 around 3.5 per cent of the mainland's population was Irish born. Because they concentrated in certain towns and cities, it seemed like more. One in nine Mancunians was Irish, one in five Liverpudlians and a similar proportion of Glaswegians.[14]

Irish migrants brought Irish magic with them. It made the news when it caused trouble: when, for example, Irish women fought about whether a sterile wife should be shunned, because she was unlucky.[15] In South Wales, in 1858, a local magistrate didn't know what to do when an Irish woman who'd been bitten by a dog insisted that the animal needed to be killed for her wound to heal.[16] But Irish magic wasn't just disruptive. It could be useful too, for people trying to survive in a foreign land. Tramps and Travellers earned a few pennies by telling housewives' and servant girls' fortunes, though they might get shooed off if someone else was at home, and there was also a small risk of being prosecuted for vagrancy or fraud.[17] 'Crass me hand with silver, an' I'll tell you your wish, an' what's past, an' what's to be.'[18] Supernatural healing was also valuable. Irish Travellers diagnosed diseases using special Irish names, and sold cures revolving around the symbolic use of gold (in Britain, silver was more typically used in magical healing).[19] In urban Manchester, Liverpool, London and Glasgow, one way Irish communities forgot their cares was by telling tales of home, about banshees and fairies (respectfully known as 'the wee folk'), the fantastical creatures that haunted the Emerald Isle's countryside.[20] Irish thieves even tried to get out of trouble by telling the police that they'd been given their stolen goods by the fairies.[21] Caught red-handed, it was probably worth playing dumb.

And then there were the famous Irish curses. During the early Victorian era, the Irish were notorious for swearing, turning the air blue with obscenities. They were also known for cursing, for using maledictions to smite their enemies.[22] It was part of the disparaging 'Paddy' stereotype, but it also rested on elements of truth. Johanna Colgan, the cursing beggar whom George Borrow met in South Wales in 1854, was not a singular character. In Ireland

and abroad, Irish beggars routinely uttered curses, often in Irish Gaelic for extra effect.[23] Beggars threatened to unleash maledictions to elicit money from people they met, to protect themselves, and simply as a cathartic release, if they were ill-treated. Patrick Donovan for instance, originally from County Cork, unloaded on the City of London's magistrates in 1848, when they confiscated his money and jailed him for a fortnight, for begging. As he was removed from the Mansion House court, Patrick 'amused himself by pouring out some hearty Irish maledictions.'[24]

It wasn't just beggars. The priest's curse, the malediction of the clergy of the Roman Catholic Church, was much feared in Ireland, where it was used to smite sinners, attack Protestant missionaries and intimidate Unionists during elections.[25] Occasionally, in mainland Britain's Irish neighbourhoods, the priest's curse was also heard. Throughout the early 1850s, reports circulated that in Islington and 'certain localities of the metropolis', Irish Catholic priests were hampering National Schools run by Protestant churches. Like their colleagues on the island of Ireland, the priests were using maledictions to deter local Catholic parents from enrolling their children, cursing from the altar anyone who dared defy them. 'The curse of God shall rest upon them, body and soul, living or dead.' 'If he curses me, no man or woman is allowed to speak to me,' complained one Londoner, about the social consequences of a priest's curse. Clerical maledictions also had real psychological, if not magical, power. Apparently, one cursed family felt unable to properly move, as if they were nailed to the floor, until their priest absolved them.[26]

The 'widow's curse' was another malediction that was well known on both sides of the Irish Sea. In Britain, it was most often uttered in court. Not only by Irish people, it must be said. In 1848, when London's Bow Street magistrates fined a boy for throwing stones at people, his mother called down her widow's curse on them.[27] But if Irish migrants were convicted of crimes, there were sometimes frightful scenes as they threw curses at magistrates, juries and prosecutors. In 1836 a down-and-out Irish widow, Eliza Thorrington, stole knives, forks, spoons, a petticoat and a Bible from Witham workhouse in Essex. When she was sentenced to three months in jail, Eliza pronounced her widow's curse on the workhouse master but not on the magistrates, who she said she couldn't blame for finding her guilty.[28] Eliza's scruples reflected an important subtlety about cursing. The Irish strongly distinguished curses from witchcraft and *piseogs*, as evil spells were sometimes called in Gaelic. Cursing and witchcraft were both occult attacks. But witchcraft harmed anybody, whether good or evil, nasty or nice. Cursing, on the other hand, was a *just* form of supernatural harm. It only afflicted guilty parties. If curses were pronounced on innocent people they'd miss, quite possibly rebounding on the curser.[29]

Irish folk knew dozens, maybe hundreds, of lyrical curses.[30] Some were silly, jokey and ironic like 'bad scran to you' and 'hard feeding to you'. Others were almost serious, angry and aggressive utterances such as 'high hanging to you'. Sincere Irish curses, uttered with deadly intent, were different again. They tended to be longer and much gorier: may God pour down his vengeance; may the devil be your guide; may every misfortune attend you and your family; may you be struck blind and deaf; may your children go wild; may the water you drink boil in your bowels; may the marrow come out through your shin bones; may you die without a priest; may hungry dogs be disgusted by your carcass, this I pray. That sort of thing. Mixing religion and magic, prayer and spell, was characteristic of Irish curses, whether they were uttered by priests, beggars, widows or others.

Among the British, it didn't really catch on. 'May the green grass grow before your doors,' usually taken to mean may you have neither friends nor visitors, was an 'old Irish malediction' that had become fairly well known in England by the 1820s.[31] Generally though, the Irish style of cursing remained confined to Irish people. Most Brits never heard about it, or if they did it was only fleetingly, when they fell victim to an Irish imprecation. You could pay a cunning-man or a wise-woman to teach you about spells and witchcraft. But you could only learn to curse like an Irishman or Irishwoman by spending lots of time in the confidence of Irish people. There was some intermarriage, of course, and some co-working between British and Irish folk. Yet during the nineteenth century, the Irish were notorious for living in close-knit neighbourhoods with migrants of similar extraction.[32] Ordinary Britons didn't keep their company enough to really immerse themselves in the wordy world of Irish magic.

Among the English, Lowland Scots, and even Celtic peoples like the Welsh and the Highlanders, the distinction between cursing and witchcraft was less pronounced. In Wales, for example, between the late eighteenth and mid-nineteenth centuries, a scandalously popular cursing well named

Ffynnon Elian, near the village of Llanelian yn Rhos, sustained a lucrative business in evil magic for the owners of the land on which it was situated.[33] Some patrons used Ffynnon Elian to punish thieves and cheats, though it's obvious that what occurred at the well went far beyond justified cursing, to much more vicious and selfish magic. Until the early modern period, the English had regarded curses as a distinct species of harmful magic, which only afflicted wrongdoers.[34] But by the nineteenth century, curses and witchcraft were merging into a general category of black magic. Perhaps, in Ireland, the distinction between cursing and witchcraft was kept alive by the heavy participation of Catholic parish priests. Perhaps, too, a justice-based form of harmful magic was particularly needed in Ireland, where the police and magistrates were heavily biased in favour of the Protestant minority, to the detriment of the Catholic majority.

Whatever the reasons, Britain possessed weaker cursing traditions than Ireland. Yet during the nineteenth century, there were still faint echoes. Book curses, maledictions written inside a tome's front and rear covers, promising doom to thieves, had been used since as far back as the medieval period, if not earlier.[35] Occasionally, they were still employed during the nineteenth century. Years ago, I bought an old Bible. With a nice embossed leather cover, it was published by the Society for the Promotion of Christian Knowledge in 1833. It had been awarded to a young man named Amos Grubbs, of Black Bourton in Oxfordshire, in 1836. Inside, on the front and back covers, it was full of Amos' writing. Like most people, he used his Bible to record when his close relatives were born and died. He also practised his handwriting. Clearly, Amos thought his Bible was precious. We can deduce this because he secured it with two traditional and well-known curses, written out in cursive, in the back: 'Steal not this book my dearest friend for fear the gallows should be your end', and 'Steal not this book for fear of shame, for you see the owner's name'.

It was a special Briton who cursed with all the solemnity, vehemence and theatre of an Irishman or Irishwoman. They would need to be angry, outraged even. They would have to possess a sense of history and, more importantly, knowledge of biblical curses. They would also have to be rather dramatic and comfortable with ritual. In all, they would need to be someone like the Rev. Carter Moore. Son of a clergyman, graduate of St John's College, Cambridge, and holder of numerous curacies (the office of a junior parish priest), the Rev. Carter Moore certainly knew his Bible. He was also prickly, quarrelsome and combative. During the years he served as curate of Flordon, Norfolk, between 1848 and 1852, there was never a time when the Rev. Carter Moore wasn't on bad terms with his neighbours. His troubles escalated in the spring of 1852 when the village postman roughed him up. Naturally, the Reverend wanted to prosecute. But a local magistrate, Mr William Gwyn, knew better. He wrote to the hot-headed young priest's father, telling him that his son ought to leave the village, where he was causing trouble. When the Rev. Carter Moore found out, he was furious. He vowed revenge.

It happened early in the evening, on Sunday 13 March 1852. Standing on the platform of Flordon railway station, dressed in his full canonicals, was the Rev. Carter Moore. He was waiting for the 5 o'clock train. On board was his enemy, William Gwyn JP. The train pulled in. The magistrate alighted, handed over his ticket to the stationmaster and began getting into his carriage. Then he saw the curate. 'I curse you,' the Rev. Carter Moore began, 'I curse your wife; I curse your children; I curse all you have – may your children be fatherless and vagabonds, and beg their bread.' Other travellers saw and heard everything. It made the national news, across Britain and Ireland. The scene was undoubtedly terrible: William Gwyn, the magistrate, said he felt his 'life even would not be safe'. Later, the Rev. Carter Moore was arrested. When the Bishop of Norwich found out, the curate was sacked too (though he salvaged his career, working as a chaplain and a curate in other parts of the country).[36] It was a highly unusual case – a clergyman who destroyed his reputation and lost his job, all for a curse. But it also illustrated the violent and sometimes destructive emotions that were roused when harmful magic was at play.

THE DRIVE AGAINST 'POPULAR SUPERSTITION'

Never was the public status of witchcraft belief lower than during the early Victorian period: never was it seen as more of a problem. Decades earlier, an articulate minority publicly testified to the reality of sorcery, citing Wesley and the Witch of Endor, depicting it as an article of Christian faith that sustained Church and state, order and property. No longer. By the 1830s those arguments had vanished from public discourse.[37]

Shorn of any positive associations, witchcraft was instead decried as a dangerous delusion. Along with other superstitions, it needed to be eradicated. 'The pretended art of witchcraft,' as the *Leeds Herald* proclaimed in 1830, 'justly merits public exposure.'[38] 'It is the duty of every member of society to expose ignorance and credulity,' chimed another critic, in 1855.[39] It may well have been everybody's duty, but the supporters of this drive against popular superstition came from a narrow range of backgrounds. Most were members of the respectable middle classes – clergymen, writers and lecturers – as well as working-class autodidacts. The chief vehicle for their campaign was the newspaper.

Like railways, newspapers were icons of the early Victorian era, and with good reason. Growing literacy, steam-powered printing and reduced taxation led to an explosion in newsprint, with 415 titles established between 1830 and 1855 alone.[40] Remote regions, like the Highlands, North Wales and East Anglia, now boasted their own journals. In the middle of the century, Devon possessed no less than thirteen.[41] Provincial news-sheets covered a bewildering array of topics, from agricultural markets to literary reviews, politics and humour. Superstition was a familiar theme and 'witchcraft in the nineteenth century' a cliché heading.

Journalists reporting from the assize courts and petty sessions highlighted witchcraft belief's connection with crime. Readers also submitted their own anecdotes about superstition's lamentable consequences in towns and villages nationwide. At least 260 separate witchcraft stories were published between 1830 and 1859, with many recycled dozens of times by editors stealing their competitors' best copy. Justified on the grounds of combating credulity, these reports usually began with outrage and concluded by asking responsible residents to use their influence to disabuse people of fallacious ideas. Inevitably, believers were mocked as 'dupes', 'fools', 'quacks', 'the worse for beer' and so on.

Few editors worried about whether, by committing them to print, they might inadvertently lend credence to witchcraft stories. In 1857 the *Suffolk Chronicle* told its readers it had received 'a communication which we feel bound to reject, because the effect might be to encourage superstition,'[42] but its scruples were unusual. Extraordinary rumours, about bewitched animals climbing trees, bedevilled people stricken with incurable ailments, and witches destroyed by powerful cunning-folk, were gladly recycled, so long as they were prefaced by critical remarks. Supernatural tales were too engrossing to be censored entirely.

Journalists attacked witchcraft, but across the early Victorian media it was pilloried. In town halls, assembly rooms and mechanics' institutes, public lecturers denounced superstition's unworthy influence.[43] In the literary world, reviewers blasted authors who broached the theme without making it absolutely clear that witchery was bunk. The Rev. S. Blair's fireside tale of a vengeful conjuror, for instance, was criticised for spreading credulity after its publication in The English Journal in 1841.[44] Writers about magic were expected to approach their subject from an extravagantly hostile angle, even great figures like the novelist Sir Walter Scott, whose celebrated Letters on Demonology and Witchcraft (1830) presented a thorough critique of history's most pervasive superstitions. Aimed at a family audience and illustrated by the famous caricaturist George Cruikshank, the first edition sold over 13,000 copies.[45] Scott structured his text around sceptical arguments.[46] The reference to witchcraft in Exodus was actually a mistranslation of a Hebrew word meaning 'poisoner', not 'witch'. Ideas about diabolical pacts, marks, Sabbaths and maleficium also lacked biblical authority. 'There is not,' Scott surmised, 'a word in Scripture authorising us to believe that such a system existed.'[47]

Beyond demanding that the media showcase their ideas, campaigners intent on debunking superstition typically resorted to one of three strategies. A brave, rather confrontational minority pressed their neighbours to repudiate witchcraft and other such notions. John Harris (1820–84), an autodidact poet and Methodist from Camborne, Cornwall, spent nights alone in the parish churchyard to disprove local tales about wandering ghosts.[48] Harris also tried to destroy the reputation of 'an old wizard' living nearby, by mocking his powers and interfering with his supposedly magical objects.

A second, less antagonistic approach to eradicating credulity was better schooling. Critics thought this a hopelessly optimistic plan, given the legions of great and learned historical figures who took the occult seriously – Napoleon, Lord Byron, Lord Castlereagh and the late Alexander I of Russia to name a few.[49] Undeterred, proponents of the superstition-smashing qualities of education asked 'our ruling classes [to] look into this matter of witchcraft' and implored Parliament to establish a school system that would ensure 'witchcraft and astrology shall no longer be permitted in England'.[50]

The third and probably most common practical step taken by opponents of witchcraft involved churchmen. It was their job, practically everyone agreed, to uproot supernatural credulity and replace it with pure and rational Christianity: when elderly women were attacked; when supposedly bewitched people put on extravagant public performances; when cunning-folk sold outrageous cures to gullible clients. Whenever such events came before the public eye, the cry usually went out for the local parson to do his duty by putting a stop to the disgraceful proceedings.[51] To be fair, many did.[52] 'I am so decided an enemy of anything bordering on superstition,' declared one Devonshire clergyman, 'I shall never entertain the slightest degree of reluctance, publicly and privately, to reprobate the fraud, and expose the fanaticism.'[53]

In Presbyterian Scotland, critics of witchcraft called upon 'every minister to root out of the minds of his hearers every vestige of such a belief'.[54] Believers should taste the same opprobrium as other sinners like drunkards and fornicators. Shamed, chastised, and denied the church privileges, they would soon abandon their dark predilections, apparently.[55]

In Wales, where Anglicanism was being eclipsed as the majority religion, nonconformists led the charge. Methodists provided most of the impetus behind the demolition of the notorious cursing well, Ffynnon Elian, in the parish of Llanelian yn Rhos, in 1829 (though the stream was diverted and the well soon rebuilt, on a neighbouring property).[56] English dissenters too saw it as their duty to eradicate witchcraft. At Stickney Methodist Chapel in 1841, one William Small preached 'against this foolery' – the rumour that a local woman was a witch.[57] At a higher institutional level, dissenters fought superstition by orchestrating missions not just to 'heathens' of Africa and India, but to the British masses too. 'Charms and superstitious observances for the cure of diseases, the prevention of witchcraft, and the insurance of good luck,' it was said, 'appear to be more deeply rooted in the minds of many than the most vital and impressive truths of holy writ.'[58] Unlike their eighteenth-century forebears, Victorian nonconformist clergymen utterly rejected the idea that witchcraft was still at work in the world.[59]

Liberals and dissenters used witchcraft's currency to embarrass their Tory and Anglican opponents, whom they blamed for entrenching superstition. The basis of this charge revolved around the opposition of Anglicans and Tories to nonconformist chapels and schools.[60] For political reasons, liberals and dissenters were the most outspoken rationalists, but commentators from across the spectrum agreed that superstition was dangerous. Fallacious supernatural beliefs, it was said, made the rural poor vulnerable to the approaches of revolutionaries, demagogues and agitators.[61]

The sense that superstition fostered rebellion was exaggerated but not baseless. The supernatural flickered in some types of popular protest. In 1838, the introduction of the New Poor Law provoked an uprising in Kent led by the pseudo-religious prophet 'Sir William Courtney', which resulted in the deaths of nine agricultural labourers.[62] The rising, journalists agreed, was fuelled by 'sheer fanaticism, a sort of superstitious madness'.[63] Anonymous threatening letters, sent to hated farmers and landlords, were often written in a style that echoed the language of curses and prophecy.[64] In Wales, some of the rick burners and animal maimers who participated in the Rebecca Riots of 1839–43 swore supernatural oaths in blood.[65]

There was a germ of truth in the idea that superstition inspired popular revolt. Yet it was not the reality of working-class dissent, but a fantasy of insurrection driven by heady credulity that made magical attitudes appear threatening. From a European perspective, early Victorian Britain looked like an island of stability in a sea of unrest. From the domestic point of view, things didn't seem so peaceable. The arson and machine breaking in Captain Swing's name (1830–1), the riots in Bristol and Nottingham engendered by the first Reform Bill's failure (1831), the violent protests against the New Poor Law (from 1837), the Rebecca Riots (1839–43), the deeply intimidating, armed, nocturnal mass meetings of early Chartism (1838) and the disastrous Newport Rising (1839) were just some of the more clearly defined hostilities that haunted the imaginations of middle-class Britons. More generally, cities were feared as the homes of sedition, disease and the godless masses. In the countryside, animal maiming was common, while enclosure continued to inspire localised outbreaks of disorder, like the Otmoor riots in Oxfordshire (1829–35).[66]

Popular revolt seemed, if not imminent, then perfectly possible. Tellingly, during the 1820s and 1830s the satirist George Cruikshank shifted his focus from corpulent royals and cynical politicians to the unruly masses.[67] Fears of revolt and revolution may have been overblown.[68] Nonetheless, these anxieties propelled the drive against popular superstition. In an age of real and perceived unrest, the eradication of witchcraft was thought of as tending towards the improvement, and pacification, of the populace.

A RESILIENT CREED

Whatever their motives, anti-witchcraft crusaders generally failed to convince. In 1834, journalists were unable to persuade a St Ives family that their daughter was not really bewitched: 'Our efforts were in vain to dispel the illusion of the parents'.[69] Reporting on a possession case from Somerton in 1835, another journalist noted how anyone who voiced doubts was described as 'a sceptic who don't believe the scriptures'.[70]

Magistrates presiding over the trials of witchcraft vigilantes seldom induced the persecutors to disbelieve in sorcery.[71] 'It may seem very clear to you, but it is true,' retorted a defendant from Hull, insisting that he'd attacked a woman who genuinely was an 'old witch'.[72] 'If they had seen as much,' replied another witch-scratcher to the JPs berating him, 'they would believe it too'.[73] Clergymen were equally ineffective. In 1850 the Rev. Gillett of Runham, Norfolk, discovered two of his parishioners attributed their pigs' deaths to witchcraft. Suspecting poison, and wanting to prove it, Gillett demanded the animals be dissected. But the owners refused. Their 'superstitious fears ... prevented this from being done', the bemused parson told a friend.[74] In 1841 the Lincolnshire village of Stickney was unsettled by the rumour that a local woman had bewitched her neighbours' cows. 'So strong was this feeling,' reported a local newspaper, 'that it was quite out of the power of the clergyman and the better-informed inhabitants to dispel it'.[75] Rather than wilting under the glare of rationalist scrutiny, witchcraft was remarkably resilient.

Witchcraft stuck partly because it was a willed conviction. In moments of crisis, people deliberately repressed their doubts and forced themselves to credit the existence of witches and the powers of cunning-folk. James Rudge, a clergyman from Devon, understood this mentality.[76] His work brought him into contact with bewitched people who sought relief from conjurors like Mr Perry – a cunning-man based in the fishing town of Dawlish. Herbal remedies, bottled medicines and magical rituals were at the heart of Perry's cures, along with an indispensable prerequisite: his patients 'must have faith'. Without sincere belief, the therapies would fail. The Rev. Rudge discovered how powerfully people could muster up a faith in magic when a family from his parish went to Perry for deliverance from witchcraft. Rudge confronted them, but didn't persuade. 'When superstition has taken hold of the mind,' he reflected, 'common sense and argument have no auditors to hear, and no power to convince!' Believing in witchcraft was a last, desperate throw of the dice, when conventional remedies failed. Once people resolved to credit sorcery and conjurors, the time for counter-arguments was over.[77]

For some, witchcraft belief was a willed conviction; for others, it was a plausible persuasion. They cited an impressive range of authorities to defend their view that witches and wizards really existed. Chief among these was the Word of God itself. Sceptics, as we have seen, argued that the biblical references to witchcraft were mistranslations, and that crediting wizardry and magic was anything but Christian. Such interpretations made little impression upon witchcraft believers. Doubting witchcraft, they insisted, meant disbelieving in the eternal and holy testament of the Bible.[78] As the mother of a supposedly bewitched child told some incredulous journalists, in 1834: 'The power of sin prevails on the earth – we read in the Bible that there were witches in the old days, and there were then so there are now.'[79]

It is unclear why Christianity fuelled scepticism in some and belief in others. Perhaps the arguments about biblical mistranslation were unfamiliar to witchcraft believers. Circulated in the popular media by both itinerant lecturers and celebrated writers like Sir Walter Scott, by the standards of the time they were not obscure propositions. It's true that mass elementary schooling, and with it mass literacy, did not emerge until the later nineteenth century. (During the early 1840s, one-third of men and almost half of women married in England and Wales were unable to write their own names.)[80] And the cost of attending a public lecture, never mind the expense of buying a big book like Scott's *Letters on Demonology*, was clearly beyond many early Victorians. (The families of agricultural labourers, the largest single occupational group, were typically so poor that they survived on a diet described as 'enforced vegetarianism'.)[81]

Still, we should be wary of picturing witchcraft believers as just ignorant and stupid. Rather than being born of vulgarity, their conviction that the scriptures testified to witchcraft's reality may also have been supported by a flourishing variety of Christianity known as evangelicalism, or 'Vital Religion'. Exhilarating but exacting, evangelicalism stressed the individual sinner's personal relationship to God through their apprehension of the scriptures. Originating with the Methodist movement of John Wesley and George Whitfield, by the nineteenth century it had spread to other nonconformist sects, the Church of England and even Roman Catholicism too.[82] For this reason, one historian names the years between 1800 and 1900 'the Evangelical century'.[83]

Rather than prioritising baptism or church attendance, evangelicals believed that sinners needed to grow their faith through self-examination and Bible study.[84] This partly explains why the production and distribution of Bibles became so important during the nineteenth century: Oxford University Press alone was printing over a million a year by 1860.[85] Seriousness and plain speaking were central to the evangelical temperament, as was a refusal to meekly defer to conventional wisdom.[86] Perhaps this disposition, along with the stress on a personal road to God through the scriptures, gave witch-craft believers the confidence they needed to reject counter-arguments and interpret the sacred text literally.

The truth, after all, was there in black and white, in the Authorised Version of the King James Bible found in almost every home. Chapter 22 of Exodus plainly commands: 'Thou shalt not suffer a witch to live.' Chapters 19 and 22 of Leviticus make the same point. Deuteronomy, the fifth book of Moses, contains similar divine injunctions: 'There shall not be found among you any one that maketh his son or daughter pass through the fire, or that useth divi-nation, or an observer of times, or an enchanter, or a witch.' Most notorious of all, the second book of Samuel recounts how, on the eve of battle, Saul, King of the Israelites, visited the Witch of Endor, inducing her to summon the ghost of the prophet Samuel. In the New Testament, the gospels describe no witchcraft but do recount several cases of demonic possession. A sorcerer named Simon Magus is mentioned in the Acts of the Apostles, while in his letter to the Galatians Paul names witchcraft among the works of the flesh.[87] All told, in the translation of the King James Bible used by the early Victorians, there were at least seventeen direct references to witchcraft and sorcery.

It didn't help that images of witchcraft enlivened many nineteenth-century Bibles. They were some of the best pictures, far too interesting to leave out. Charles Knight's pictorial Bible of 1836, for instance, reproduced Salvator Rosa's *Saul and the Witch of Endor* (c. 1688).[88] Beneath the image, a note expressed regret that belief in familiar spirits and necromancers 'lingers perhaps in some of the dark corners even of our own land'. Inconsistently, it then described the Witch as a 'cunning woman' and called some supernatural interpretations of the passage 'highly respectable'.

After the Bible, the second major corroborating authority for witchcraft was the testimony of others. Parents, grandparents, friends, neighbours and workmates – even, in some cases, trusted servants: their accounts of witches and wizards, cunning-men and wise-women, insidiously moulded the minds of younger generations. Old legends connected sorcery with local landmarks. In Oxfordshire it was said that a witch created the Rollright Stones, in the north of the county, by petrifying a king and his army.[89] Other stories were more plausibly historical. In Devon and Somerset, memories of the witch trials were kept alive throughout the nineteenth century and well into the twentieth, by village tales about evil-doers condemned to death for their crimes.[90] But most witchcraft stories described events from a generation or two ago: housewives cursed by the maledictions of mumbling beggars; decrepit crones shape-shifting into hares or foxes; precious children withered by the evil eye; horses unsettled, cows killed by infernal arts, young brides having fits, and witches finally destroyed by retaliatory magic. Those themes recurred again and again in stories told across the length and breadth of Britain.[91]

The fascination that witch tales exercised over their hearers owed much to the skill of the storytellers. Mastering the art was not easy. 'It took only seven days for the Almighty to make the earth; man was two hundred years making the Fens but it took three hundred years to make a good story teller,' was a saying in East Anglia.[92] There were rewards for accomplished narrators: esteem, prestige, maybe even beer and a smoke, if the venue was a village pub. W.H. Barrett, one of the last great storytellers from Cambridgeshire, learnt his craft at the knee of able forebears including:

one woman, Granny Hall, who, when she was over ninety could make one's flesh creep with tales of ghouls, witches and ghosts. She could recite tales of black magic, giving such a realistic account that people used to say that she was nothing more than a witch herself.[93]

Skilful storytellers knew how to draw their audiences in by speaking quietly. They knew how to change pace, and when to slowly drag out the spine-tingling parts of their tales. They used accents to give power to dialogue, and gestures for humour or emphasis. Sometimes there was a twist. An account of the ridiculous escapades of an over-eager believer might end by hinting that sorcery really was at work.[94] These techniques made witchcraft stories compelling.

'Silly and superstitious tales,' one commentator wrote in 1834, 'keep alive the lingering folly of imbecile minds.'[95] He was right that witchcraft tales did more than amuse and entertain. Repeated exposure inculcated anxieties in the minds of some listeners, in spite of their better judgement. 'I have sat talking of witch & ghost stories over our cups on winter nights till I felt fearful of going home,' the poet John Clare recalled of his youth in rural Northamptonshire. 'Tho I always felt in company a disbelief in ghosts [and] witches,' he explained, 'when I was alone in the night my fancys created thousands.'[96] Unable to shake the mental habits born of regularly hearing witchcraft and ghost stories, Clare's almost instinctive fears were not unique. As a child, autobiographer James Burn spent many a winter's night in 'the chimney nook of a moorland farmhouse . . . [where] tales of ghosts, witches and fairies, would go round until bed time'.[97] His mother was an ardent believer, and though Burn eventually doubted witchcraft's reality, he had to admit: 'Since I have attained manhood . . . it has frequently required all the little philosophy I possessed to keep the invisible agents of the other world from regulating my affairs.' The battle between his formal scepticism and intuitive belief, he candidly acknowledged, 'is sometimes little better than a drawn one'.[98]

Along with the Bible and village stories, an abundance of popular literature testified to magic's reality. Chapbook biographies of the Tudor prophet Mother Shipton were commonplace during the early Victorian period.[99] Modern editions of seventeenth-century compendiums like Nicholas Culpeper's *Complete Herbal* (first published in 1653) and William Lilly's *Christian Astrology* (first published in 1647) could also be found on book-stalls at county fairs and on bookshelves in many homes.[100]

Most popular of all were astrological almanacs, such as those produced by renowned stargazers like Raphael and Zadkiel. Their circulation expanded during the nineteenth century, thanks to increasing literacy rates and advances in printing. Raphael's *Prophetic Messenger*, first published in 1826, boasted that it could tell farmers when to buy and sell crops and cattle.[101] Worthy alternatives to this prophetic astrological tradition gained little traction. The *Illustrated London Almanac*, founded in 1845, replaced astrology with astronomy and meteorology but never captured more than a modest, middle-class audience.[102] By contrast *Zadkiel's Almanac*, which looked to the heavens to foresee events in politics and the weather, was a bestseller. (Its prediction, in 1861, of ill-health for the Prince Consort caused sales to leap when Albert did indeed die of typhoid.) Astrologers like Raphael and Zadkiel did not specifically endorse the reality of witchcraft. Even so, by postulating the existence of uncanny forces and esoteric powers they probably made the notion of malign magic appear more plausible. That, at any rate, was what some contemporaries thought. 'They are the writers who keep alive the stamina of superstition, fortune-telling, and witchcraft in the minds of the ignorant portion of the world,' judged one critic.[103]

Bewitched people, looking for guidance in their plight, were sometimes able to draw upon instructional texts. Not grimoires: those comparatively expensive and lengthy manuals of magic were popular in nineteenth-century France but unavailable in Britain.[104] Established publishers, wary of scandal, refused to deal in them. Yet out in the provinces, away from the scrutiny of London literary opinion, small-time printers did occasionally produce witchcraft-themed pamphlets and chapbooks. This shocked one journalist who, in 1839, bemoaned how: 'It is an actual fact, that in the fairs of Devonshire ... [are] sold, at this day, *charms against witchcraft*!'[105] Being ephemeral, provincial, and in some eyes immoral, only a handful of these self-help pamphlets now survive. One, written by the Exeter cunning-man 'Dr' Tuckett, was published in Devon during the 1830s. Entitled 'A Receipt for Ill-wishing', it was described by a writer for the *The Quarterly Review*, who purchased a copy from Tavistock Market.[106]

Dr Tuckett's recipe contained five methods for combating witchcraft. The first cured bewitched cattle. Take salt in your hand and throw it over each cow, beginning at the head and ending at the tail, while saying the words: 'As the servant Elisha headed the waters of Jericho by casting salt therein, so I hope to heal this my beast, in the name of God the Father, God the Son, and God the Holy Ghost. Amen.' If that doesn't work, there's a more powerful rite. Mix a little of the cow's hair and blood with salt and gunpowder, stuff it in a bladder, and incinerate it on a fire made of green ashen wood. As it burns, pronounce these words: 'I confine all evil and enemies of mine and of my cattle into the fire for ever, never to hurt me nor mine for ever, in the name of God the Father, God the Son, and God the Holy Ghost. Amen.' The pamphlet outlined three more aggressive techniques for dealing with entrenched cases of witchcraft. If a beast died, for instance, its owners were advised to remove the heart 'as soon as you can', before sticking it with pins, placing it in the chimney, and roasting it every day for a fortnight. Bewitched people should also read the first thirteen verses of chapter 28 of Deuteronomy every morning, and strictly 'no more'.

PROGRESS FOR THE FEW, WITCHCRAFT FOR THE MANY

Occult beliefs were frequently depicted as peasant superstitions. In truth though, sorcery troubled early Victorians from all sorts of backgrounds.

Rural workers sometimes saw their misfortunes as being set in train by witches, as did paupers, those too old to work and people simply described as 'poor'. So did farmers (male and female), blacksmiths, brick-makers, butchers, carpenters, colliers, journeymen labourers, fishermen, publicans, ladies' maids, housekeepers, jewellers, stable-keepers and brewers, to name a few occupations. Apart from farmers and their families, few middle-class witchcraft believers were named in newspaper reports from the period (except in the West Country, widely acknowledged to be England's most witch-ridden region, where commentators complained about otherwise 'respectable' people consulting conjurors and fearing witches).[107]

The ability to read and write did not stop people fearing witchcraft, as we can see from a letter sent to the Mayor of Yarmouth in 1834, asking him to prosecute a 'witch' living in the nearby town of Lowestoft.[108] Neither did city living. In 1831 a man from Westminster, living within sight of Parliament, tried to shoot his neighbour – a woman who, he claimed, had bewitched him for the previous four years.[109] The following year a young woman asked the Southwark magistrates to prosecute an elderly lady who, being 'nothing more or less than an old witch', had put 'a spell on her'.[110] There were also attempts to get witches arrested at Clerkenwell in 1842 and Hackney in 1858.[111]

Beyond London, witchcraft assaults and allegations occurred throughout the country. Mobs intimidated witches in Newcastle in 1835, Middlesbrough in 1853 and Wolverhampton in 1856.[112] Spellcasters were scratched or attacked in Edinburgh, Bristol and Hull.[113] Manchester, Plymouth and Liverpool were home to conjurors making their living by telling fortunes and diagnosing witchcraft.[114] Three cunning-folk from Leeds were prosecuted in the years

1856 and 1857 alone.[115] Durham – 'episcopal and collegiate Durham' – in 1859 reportedly possessed no fewer than four wise-women.[116] As one commentator observed, magic was not 'confined to the people of rural districts' but prevailed 'to a great extent in the large manufacturing towns'.[117]

From diagnosis to cure, witchcraft was dealt with communally and collectively. Friends, relatives and neighbours were usually the first to voice suspicions about evil magic poisoning someone's life. When, in 1849, a woman from Plymouth was bedridden by a mysterious illness that baffled the town's doctors, her sister suggested she was bewitched and persuaded her to consult Agnes Hill, the local wise-woman.[118] Similarly, after pigs belonging to a man from Woodhurst (Huntingdonshire) sickened, several villagers recognised witchcraft and counselled him to roast one to death to save the rest.[119] Outside help was vital when it came to devising methods for repelling witchcraft. In 1843, after a brewer from Peterborough concluded that his kit was afflicted, a local razor grinder proposed he 'burn the witch' by sticking a red-hot manure-fork inside.[120] Samuel Bartingale, a small-time landlord from Ely, ailed following his decision to evict a suspected witch from one of his properties. His 'neighbours met in the sick man's chamber, and solemnly deliberated upon the matter', resolving to nail a horseshoe to his door.[121]

As well as proposing cures, friends of seriously ill people took them to visit cunning-folk or even consulted conjurors on their behalf.[122] Sometimes they insisted the cunning-person's prescription was followed to the letter, even if the patient disagreed.[123] Vigilantes who scratched their witches occasionally acted in concert, too.[124] Others carried out their crimes alone, but did so on the advice of their neighbours.[125]

Locals were pushed to take sides, as bewitched people gathered support to intimidate their witches. This was done successfully in May 1840 at the Cornish fishing port of Newlyn. The crew of a boat named the *Broom* found themselves unable to land a decent catch. Attributing this spate of ill-luck 'to the evil wishes of a simple young woman of the place', the fishermen attempted to break her spell by burning a pile of fish on the quayside, 'amid the cheers and the huzzas of the assembled multitude'.[126] However, people claiming to be bewitched could not count upon the automatic support of their communities. Accusations had to be credible, and actions proportionate, especially if violence was involved. So discovered Sybil Baynum, an elderly woman from the Welsh village of Llanddewi, who in September 1837 tried to stab her neighbour, 25-year-old Elizabeth Walker, with a pen-knife.[127] Baynum accused Elizabeth and her recently deceased mother of killing cows with witchcraft. Her plan failed because a group of gleaners protected Elizabeth from the elderly woman's attacks.

The easiest way to counteract witchcraft threats was with defensive charms. Horseshoes, nailed to the doors of houses, cottages and outbuildings, were commonly used. Few sources explain why, but it is possible to venture some plausible reasons. Since ancient times, iron had been thought to repel malign supernatural beings, and horses were considered to be unusually sensitive to occult influences. However, according to a popular ballad of the 1850s, the explanation went back to the legend of St Dunstan, a tenth-century Abbot of Glastonbury.[128] Dunstan was once asked to re-shoe a strange horse. Noticing the rider's cloven hoof, and realising at once that he was the devil, he nailed the shoe to the Evil One instead, and removed it only after he promised not to harm dwellings bearing a horseshoe.

As noted in the previous chapter, archaeological research has uncovered a fascinating range of items and strategies used by householders to keep witchcraft at bay, including mummified cats placed in walls, shoes (an expensive commodity during the nineteenth century) concealed in roofs, and ritualistic marks carved into plaster, wooden panels and beams.[129] Outside the home, objects used to repel baleful magic included amulets made of rowan tree and red thread, written prayers and passages of scripture (often partly in Latin) pinned inside clothing, small bags of herbs and other mystical ingredients worn close to the body, and naturally occurring holed stones.[130]

A more taboo but also more effective way to defeat a witch was to act like one. Beyond the cornucopia of defensive rites, people intent on returning evil for evil tried to harm or even kill their malefactors with magic. The aim of this strategy was bluntly explained by a conjuror from Somerset, who assured a client: 'The party who had bewitched him would in return be overlooked.'[131] Cursed animals were still sometimes ritualistically incinerated, in the belief that the fire would be transmitted down the responsible witch's supernatural tendrils, forcing him or her to relinquish his or her unholy grip.[132] Scalding hot metal was plunged into bewitched milk, butter and beer for similar reasons. According to a commentator from north-east Scotland, stabbing bedevilled milk with a fork and cutting it with a knife was the 'equivalent to performing the same operation on the body of some unlucky witch'.[133] Boiling a bottle filled with bent pins, thorns and the urine of a spellbound person was supposed to attack the responsible witch or wizard's bladder.[134]

Most bloodthirsty of all, stabbing and roasting an animal heart was believed to threaten the witch's life. Biblical readings and prayers to the Trinity usually preceded such rituals, yet their aim was a long way from the New Testament ideal of turning the other cheek. Like black magic, these rites were invariably carried out in secret and in silence at the witching hour (midnight), when occult forces were most potent.[135] Success, however, was uncertain. The wickedest witches were thought to be uniquely resistant to retributive counter-magic, as if their malignity vaccinated them against occult attacks. According to a conjuror named William Wiggett, his supernatural afflictions were not as effective against 'persons [who] were very wicked'.[136] Like the diviners from 1960s and 1970s Normandy studied by the anthropologist Jeanne Favret-Saada, early Victorian cunning-folk represented themselves as engaging in mortal struggles with witches, in order to save their helpless clients.[137] It 'would be either death or glory', predicted James Tunnicliffe, alias the 'Bromley wizard', on the eve of a great magical duel.[138]

Most alleged witches did not even try to cast spells, never mind succeed in doing so. But some beggars still solicited donations by threatening to curse reluctant donors.[139] Those who did so crudely were occasionally prosecuted for obtaining money under false pretences, like Jonathan Fudge from Blackmore Vale (Dorset), who offered to 'take off the witchin' from his neighbours if they would only 'cross his hand with silver'.[140] Most extorters were subtler, saying just that their donors 'might regret' not giving something away.[141] In Bideford (Devon), one couple used threats of witchcraft to secure themselves poor-relief.[142] More lucratively, Martha More of Montrose made a small fortune from her uncanny reputation. In fishing villages around Anstruther, on Scotland's eastern coast, she begged cod and other articles from fishermen, who thought it unlucky to refuse her. When Martha died in 1849 a search of her cottage uncovered £157 in cash, including a bag containing 2,000 sixpences, and another with over 1,000 shilling pieces.[143]

Many cunning-folk undertook nefarious rites on behalf of their clients, to silence witnesses, punish thieves or torment love and business rivals. In 1833 a man from Oswestry, Shropshire, paid a conjuror to bewitch a woman who stole his watch.[144] In 1835 a woman from Burnham, Buckinghamshire, commissioned a cunning-woman to 'witch' the tongues of the local constable and a lodger, to prevent them from revealing her plan to poison her husband.[145]

Evil witchcraft was practised privately too. Probably its most common form was image magic. From Somerset to Scotland, clay figurines were stabbed with pins before being submerged in streams or rivers.[146] As they washed away, the victim's vitality was supposed to wither, until they finally died. In Yeovil, in 1854, workmen draining a pond found, at the bottom, a bottle containing three dolls impaled with black pins and marked with the sign of Saturn. A piece of paper inside identified the effigies as police officers from the town, and called for their 'sudden destruction, legal and moral'.[147] Other evil-doers carried charms designed to give them the power 'to spell people's things'.[148] A few used animal sacrifices. In 1838, a woman from the Essex village of Rivenhall was imprisoned for two weeks for killing her vicar's black cat, which she boiled alive 'with all due and dread solemnities' in order to afflict some Roma people.[149] Toad bones, thought to confer dark powers, were put to similar uses.[150] Spoken spells and wicked wishes were another alternative, for those without the time or means to procure powerful arcane objects.[151] In early Victorian Britain – in the most urban, industrial and scientifically advanced nation on earth – knowledge of magic's finer subtleties abounded.

CONJURORS AND CONSTABLES, MAGISTRATES AND MAGIC

Their trade was illegal, yet cunning-folk remained central to the British culture of magic. The 1736 Witchcraft Act had prescribed the pillory or a year's imprisonment for anyone guilty of 'pretenses' to witchcraft. The 1824 Vagrancy Act further outlawed 'using of any subtle craft ... to deceive and impose',[152] and made doing so punishable by ordinary magistrates, with a £25 fine or three months' hard labour. Still, during the 1830s and 1840s neither of those laws impinged greatly on conjurors, who were typically ignored by local authorities.

Wise-women operated in Lancashire, one critic complained in 1843, 'with the perfect cognisance of the magistrates'.[153] Throughout western

England, Wales and Scotland too, concerned citizens complained about known cunning-folk going unprosecuted.[154] In the lax legal environment, many wizards did not even feel obliged to hide their identities behind a second trade like tailoring or shoemaking. According to a correspondent from Lincolnshire, cunning-folk – 'long-fingered superstition mongers', he called them – had stalls at the weekly markets.[155] The situation was similar in Devon, where the self-styled 'Dr' Tuckett advertised his curative recipes in pamphlets sold at country fairs.[156] By 1842 his reputation was so great that a namesake, Nicholas Tuckett of Exeter, was being inundated with people looking for help against witchcraft. He had to put a notice in the local paper, telling 'his country friends he is no conjuror'.[157]

Sago Jenkinson, wise-man of Hull, was so esteemed that his surgery was 'crowded to excess' from morning till evening during every day of the week.[158] Summoned to appear before the town's magistrates in 1844, Sago went in military attire, in a long grey coat and a Prussian cap, decorated with gold lace. Commercial acumen, as well as eccentricity, lay behind his striking persona. Like most cunning-folk, he marketed his magical services with gossip. By wearing unusual clothes, filling their consulting rooms with amazing arcana, and spreading stories about their supernatural powers, wise-men and -women increased their fame and attracted clients. James Murrell (*c.* 1780–1860) of Hadleigh (Essex), wore iron goggles, carried a whalebone umbrella, kept semi-nocturnal hours, maintained aloof relations with his neighbours, and boasted 'I am the Devil's master'.[159] Mrs Ruth, from Rochdale, persuaded locals that she commanded nine familiar spirits.[160] Sarah McDonald, a white witch living in London's Bethnal Green during the 1850s, bribed her neighbours to spread stories about her magical prowess.[161]

Sincere cunning-folk were somewhat tolerated, but magistrates dealt harshly with shameless embezzlers. The difficulty was that fraudulent spell-breakers were hardest to catch. In 1841, two Roma fortune-tellers bamboozled an elderly man from Bradworthy (Devon) into giving them £53 to cure him of witchcraft. They'd fled the area by the time their victim came to his senses and reported them.[162] If they'd been caught after stealing such a large sum they would almost certainly have been tried under the draconian 1736 Witchcraft Act, like Elizabeth Small – an elderly Rom who cajoled a man into paying £28 for a magical cure, and robbed him of a further £25. For this she was jailed for a year with hard labour.[163]

Conjurors who charged less and acted somewhat conscientiously were tried under the more lenient 1824 Vagrancy Act. Like Mr Faulkner, a blind cunning-man from Bilston near Wolverhampton, who was charged with imposing upon one Mrs Waring. He had diagnosed her as bewitched and prescribed a combination of dried berries, sticks tied up in the shape of a cross, and a charm of the Lord's Prayer, all for the modest sum of 5 shillings.[164] When the magistrates asked how he made his living, Faulkner replied: 'By doing good after this manner.' It was an impertinent response, but the JPs offered to drop the charge if he returned the money and ceased his trade. After some grumbling, he agreed and was released.

Most clients refused to support prosecutions against cunning-folk. They were grateful, and afraid. 'We will have nothing to do with the law,' insisted one farmer, when asked to testify against a wise-woman who cured him of witchcraft.[165] In 1843, at the Cornwall Assizes, another 'intelligent and respectable-looking farmer' had to be subpoenaed to force him to tell the court about his consultation with a conjuror. Even then, he complained 'that he should not have preferred any charge'.[166] Such difficulties probably discouraged magistrates from more actively employing the laws available to them.

Occasionally, journalists goaded the authorities into action. In 1843 Mr Stainton, a renowned wise-man from Louth, a Lincolnshire market town, fell victim to the *Lincolnshire Chronicle*'s campaign to avenge an elderly housekeeper, who'd been accused of witchcraft and assaulted.[167] Calling for the wise-man's prosecution, the paper claimed he advised the assailant to draw blood. Louth's JPs responded by promptly arresting Stainton, but during his trial it became apparent that he had not actually counselled violence: the idea had come from another client, who spoke with the attacker as she waited for her consultation. Nevertheless Stainton was charged under the 1824 Vagrancy Act with selling charms against witchcraft, jailed for three months, and fined. The *Lincolnshire Chronicle* professed itself well pleased with the scourging of this 'pest to society'.

Around the middle of the nineteenth century, professional policing began mildly to disrupt the established culture of magic. Fears of crime, riot and revolution had overcome Britain's historic resistance to a paid, uniformed constabulary. Beginning with the Metropolitan Police Act of 1829 and ending with the County Police Act of 1856, legislation provided for the establishment of new forces, first in the towns and later in the countryside.[168] As a result, more disciplined and less indulgent police officers replaced the part-time parish constables who had previously been responsible for keeping the peace. Raw police manpower also grew, from somewhere in the region of 10,000 in England and Wales in 1842, to almost 20,000 in 1861, making it easier for the authorities to apprehend and prosecute certain offenders, including those implicated in the commercial practice of magic.[169]

Cunning-folk started to find themselves in court because of the 'interference of the police', rather than only at the instigation of disgruntled customers.[170] In 1853, for example, a wizard from Liverpool named Richard Parkinson was jailed for three months on the basis of evidence gathered by a local policeman who 'received information respecting the manner in which the prisoner obtained his livelihood'. After interrogating one of the cunning-man's clients, the officer searched his property, where he found a crystal ball, astrological charts and a book explaining 'how to cure witchcraft in man or beast'.[171] A year later, police from the West Yorkshire town of Wakefield devised an elaborate ruse to apprehend a cooper, James Clark, who was making a living as a conjuror.[172] The wives of two officers were sent to Clark to have their fortunes told. As they walked upstairs to the wizard's consulting room, he asked whether they would care to buy a sixpenny box of pills. Both did, and Clark provided their readings gratis. This exchange was evidently designed to ensure that, in the eyes of the law, Clark was guilty of selling medicines, not telling fortunes. It didn't work. After the readings, which included some mention of bewitchment, the wizard was arrested for obtaining money under false pretences.

Critics protested that cunning-folk were still being treated too leniently. Their concerns came to the fore in 1856 with the sensational trial of William Dove, an eccentric and probably insane farmer from Leeds who was ultimately hanged for murdering his wife with poison.[173] In court, Dove accused an astrologer, Henry Harrison, with whom he had many dealings, of planting the idea in his mind, by predicting his wife's death. Subsequently, the *Morning Advertiser* and many other newspapers called for conjurors, fortune-tellers and astrologers to be dealt with more severely: to be awarded, upon their conviction, nothing less than penal servitude or transportation to the colonies.[174]

It was certainly correct that, as currently constituted, the law was only able to modestly limit Britain's magical economy, rather than suppress it entirely.

Even with growing numbers of policemen, compiling evidence was always difficult and often impossible. In 1856, for example, a charge of obtaining money under false pretences against an Exeter wise-man 'could not be legally sustained', while 'some technical difficulties' prevented Hull's magistrates from convicting a witchcraft-diagnosing fortune-teller.[175] As before, prosecutions failed because clients refused to cooperate. North Walsham, a Norfolk market town of some 3,000 souls, was during the late 1850s home to four conjurors. 'How should it be otherwise?' asked one exasperated resident. 'Can it be expected that a woman who fears a "cunning" man more than she fears God will have nerve enough to speak out and divulge the doings of such people?'[176]

The forces of law and order were more successful at curbing attacks on witches. Magistrates began dealing more harshly with the perpetrators. In 1851 JPs from Woodbury, in Devon, fined a woman 15 shillings and imprisoned her for a fortnight for assaulting a beggar who threatened to curse her. To a reporter for the *Exeter Flying Post*, it seemed as though 'the Bench fined the defendant for believing in witchcraft, and not for the assault, the evidence being that no more violence was used than necessary in removing the complainant'.[177] With more policemen maintaining the Queen's peace, it became easier to arrest and prosecute witchcraft vigilantes. We can see this occurring on a local level in the testimony of a Devon JP, who in 1852 wrote that he had fined four people for assaulting witches during only 'the last few months'.[178]

Nationally, cases of witchcraft-related violence reported by the press increased almost four-fold, with eight occurring in the 1830s, eighteen in the 1840s and thirty-one in the 1850s.[179] Britain's magistrates and police were clearly more willing and better able to punish witch-attackers. However, the increase in reported cases also reflected the rapid expansion of provincial journalism and better coverage of the petty sessions.[180] Newspapers were more likely to notice outbreaks of witchcraft belief, violent or not. During the same period, the number of stories about witchcraft involving no legal action or criminality more than doubled, with twenty-two appearing in the 1830s, forty-five in the 1840s and fifty in the 1850s. These modest numbers remind us that, although newspapers are indispensable historical sources, the Victorian press never documented more than a fraction of what Britain's witchcraft believers thought and did.

Despite more attentive magistrates and better policing, violence haunted witches for decades to come. At least vigilantes now generally acted alone. By the 1850s, professional policing had almost entirely eradicated communal attacks against supposed sorcerers. Crowds still gathered for the purpose, as in Middlesbrough in 1853 and Easthorpe (Essex) in 1858.[181] However, local officers dispersed them before any harm could be done. Sadly, though, the law was unable to completely protect vulnerable people living in the most remote communities. In 1858 a 'half-witted' woman and reputed witch from the Devonshire village of Otterton was induced from her cottage by a large group of villagers, who set upon her and stabbed her in several different places.[182] Despite 'every exertion' by the local police, the perpetrators went unpunished, no doubt because the victim was unable to say who they were and her neighbours were unwilling to.

By the 1850s, Britain's magistrates and police firmly identified with the plight of alleged witches. Unlike some of their predecessors a generation earlier, the law's representatives were unwilling to tolerate outbreaks of superstitious violence. No longer would JPs bind over both alleged witches and their attackers to keep the peace. No longer would constables ignore duckings, mobbings or scratchings. Limited police manpower meant that many witchcraft vigilantes still escaped justice. A lack of compelling evidence and ineffective medical regulation also resulted in many cunning-folk continuing to work at their lucrative craft. Nonetheless, witchcraft believers now expected only hostility, rather than help, from those in power. Consequently, they stopped asking magistrates to prosecute witches. During the 1830s journalists recorded six appeals of this nature (13 per cent of the total number of witchcraft stories reported during the decade). In the 1840s seven requests for aid against witches were reported (8 per cent of the total). Over the course of the 1850s, however, only two similar requests were recorded (a mere 1.5 per cent of the total).[183] Finally, more than a century after witchcraft's decriminalisation, Britain's authorities were unwilling to pander to people who took black magic seriously.

SPELLBOUND OR MESMERISED?

Witchcraft belief was sometimes described as 'pagan' and 'primitive', 'barbarous' and 'medieval'. Those intemperate words reflected the stridency of sceptics during the early Victorian period, but they revealed little about the thinking of witchcraft believers themselves. Though adopted by some subsequent historians,[184] terms like 'pagan' perpetuate the fiction that witchcraft belief was essentially an archaic and outmoded intellectual system. In reality, the concept of sorcery was dynamic and evolving, mingling ancient archetypes with avant-garde terminology and ideas. This was particularly so during the 1840s and 1850s, when witchcraft theory began to incorporate some of the precepts of a comparatively new and controversial science: mesmerism.

Based on the theories and techniques of Austrian doctor Franz Anton Mesmer (1734–1815), mesmerism briefly appeared in Britain during the 1780s, and then again during the 1820s.[185] The therapy was just a passing fad until 1837, when it was imported for a third time by an enterprising French demonstrator, the self-styled 'Baron' Charles Dupotet.[186] Speaking before elegant audiences in drawing rooms in expensive parts of London, mesmerists like Dupotet claimed to possess the ability to manipulate a potent but invisible 'universal fluid'. Named 'animal magnetism', this fluid flowed through all matter, with important consequences. Controlling it gave mesmerists the power to heal, fixate and manipulate receptive subjects into states of unusual lucidity and even clairvoyance. With stylised gestures, theatrical arm movements, extreme concentration and sustained eye contact, mesmerists purported to induce these extraordinary effects. Mesmerism was vigorously advocated by Dr John Elliotson (1791–1868) of University College Hospital and, by the 1840s, mesmeric demonstrations regularly featured on the provincial lecture circuit. Despite some notorious exposés, including of Dr Elliotson himself in the summer of 1838, the nearly new science piqued the interest of a raft of distinguished figures, including the scientist Alfred Russel Wallace, Bishop Samuel Wilberforce and the author Charles Dickens.[187]

Adepts of mesmerism, keen to give their discipline historical credentials, claimed that witches were actually unconscious magnetisers. So maintained Mr Hall, a mesmerist lecturer who toured the north of England in 1844.[188] The *Bradford Observer*, for one, was convinced.[189] 'Looking at the wonders of mesmerism,' it observed, 'we are able to believe some of the otherwise incredible stories that are recorded of the ancient witches and wizards.' The powers of modern mesmerists were 'no doubt possessed by men of old, and might sometimes have been exerted by them unconsciously'. Speaking to members of the Brighton Mechanics' Institute in 1844, Mr J. Vernon likewise argued that 'the details of the effects produced by witchcraft would answer admirably for a description of Mesmeric effects'.[190] Victims of demonic possession, who suffered with fits, spoke in tongues and exhibited unnatural strength, were also retrospectively diagnosed as having been under the sway of animal magnetism rather than sorcery.[191]

Of all the aptitudes imputed to witches and wizards, their ability to leave people fascinated or spellbound invited the most striking comparisons with mesmerism. Local stories told how both maleficent witches and beneficent cunning-folk like John Wrightson of Stokesley could freeze to the spot those who cast doubt upon their powers until, terrified at their inability to move, they adopted a more respectful attitude. Tales like these moved the folklorist William Henderson to identify Wrightson as a 'natural clairvoyant' who practised 'something like electro-biology'. The striking similarities between witchcraft, mesmerism and – later – spiritualism caused not a few Victorians to re-evaluate traditional magic. Perhaps witchcraft was more than peasant credulity. Perhaps, as a correspondent to the *Evening Mail* put it in 1857: 'Rejection of the subject as mere superstition of the vulgar is proof, not of enlightenment, but, of insufficient knowledge – of ignorance of the deeper arcana of nature's book.'[192]

While enthusiasts argued that witches were unconscious mesmerists, horrified critics suggested the contrary. Mesmerists, they claimed, were nothing more than devotees of the dark arts. In 1852 villagers from Swineshead, Lincolnshire, were accused by the *Stamford Mercury* of harassing a travelling mesmerist, calling him 'a dealer in the occult science of witchcraft'.[193] The brevity and vagueness of the report make it rather suspect, but to its credit similar claims were made elsewhere. According to a commentator from Market Drayton, in Shropshire, numerous townsfolk believed an itinerant clairvoyant was 'really in league with the powers of darkness'.[194]

It was not just the uneducated masses who interpreted mesmerism as a species of malign magic. At Caithness, on Scotland's northern tip, a clergyman was committed to an asylum after declaring that he was under attack from enemies who dealt in witchcraft and mesmerism. He thought the two forces were synonymous, as one witness told the sheriff court: '[He fears certain parties] are labouring to put him to death, or to inflict serious injury on his person by means analogous to mesmerism, or witchcraft which he seems to consider as manifestations of the same power.'[195] Though used to justify a

madman's incarceration, this interpretation of mesmerism as a malign supernatural force had some theological backing.[196] In 1842, at St Jude's church in
Liverpool, the evangelical clergyman Hugh McNeile denounced mesmerism
as an example of 'satanic agency', heralding the coming of the Antichrist. While
the urbane *Gentleman's Magazine* mocked his sermon as a 'piece of foolery',
others heeded McNeile's warning.[197] In a pamphlet of 1848, for example, George
Corfe, a surgeon and cleric at Middlesex Hospital, described mesmerism as the
'devil's chicanery'.[198] Mesmerism and witchcraft, new occultism and old diab-
olism, were becoming conflated.

* * *

Early Victorian witchcraft was intricate, ferocious and widespread. Intricate
because it encompassed a myriad of occult techniques, drew on a rich lore
and incorporated subtle ideas about – for instance – the protective power of
evil. Ferocious because, ultimately, it was designed to prevent and cause
death: witchcraft was a form of controlled but pitiless aggression. And widespread because, by the standards of the majority, it was not cranky or eccentric to take sorcery seriously. Friends, neighbours and relatives were typically
the first to suggest that someone might be suffering from an occult affliction.
Despite the scorn poured on 'superstition' by journalists, lecturers, autodidacts and clergymen of every denomination, communities stood together
against supposed evil-doers. Magic remained the province of the many.

Witchcraft's vivid, vital qualities mean that it is impossible to accept the
characterisation of an earlier generation of historians, who maintained that
during the early Victorian era only a 'lingering belief' remained.[199] Given the
evidence considered in this chapter, it is also difficult to entirely agree with
Owen Davies' more cautious and certainly much more informed assessment,
that 'the relevance of witchcraft as an explanation for misfortune was no
doubt diminishing fairly quickly in … rapidly growing urban areas'.[200]
Throughout Britain, in villages and hamlets, quiet market towns and in great
industrial cities, belief in its reality abounded. As a writer for the *Saturday
Review* put it in 1857: 'In every quarter of England we find, not the lingering
and moribund, but the active influences of witchcraft at work.'[201]

Disbelief in witchcraft, though more prevalent than during the Georgian
era, continued to be a minority persuasion. Yet while they were comparatively

few in number, early Victorian sceptics were noisy and outspoken, confident and conspicuous. If nothing else, they successfully imposed their views on the respectable media – on newspapers, literature, sermons and public lectures. But they failed to move the minds of the masses. Sectarian conflicts and anxieties about plebeian disorder fuelled the drive against 'popular superstition', making early Victorian witchcraft deniers unusually ardent. Writing, as some historians do, about the disdainful attitudes of 'nineteenth-century elites' or 'educated Victorians' obscures the peculiar intensity of disbelievers in witchcraft during the 1830s, 1840s and 1850s.[202] It is important to recognise this, and not just for the sake of getting the history of these decades right. Scholars of secularisation and religious decline often take the category of disbelief for granted, as if its content is obvious and unchanging. In reality, disbelief in the supernatural is a highly variable mindset, with resonances and characteristics that shift over fairly short periods of time.

We can see this process at work during the later decades of the nineteenth century, when even doubters began to see a dark poetry in witchcraft belief. No longer did it appear to be a superstition requiring urgent eradication. Instead, witchcraft was increasingly conceived of as a species of 'folklore' – as something erroneous but also authentic, ancient and traditional. Perhaps this change in the outlook of disbelievers was made possible by the waning of physically aggressive counter-witchcraft techniques, along with the demise of general fears about revolution and popular revolt. The trend identified in this chapter, of violence against supposed witches being gradually curtailed by growing law enforcement, gathered pace during the later Victorian period. Witchcraft theory also continued to modernise, by further absorbing pseudo-scientific terminology and ideas from new types of occultism. The next chapters explore these developments.

FOUR

SECRET BELIEFS
1860–1900

There is a strong and unshaken belief in evil human
influences – in what is known as witchcraft. It is, probably,
not too much to say that this belief is found in every town and
village in England. Though that is difficult of proof, for
people conceal their thoughts on such a subject.

> *The Cornishman*, 15 February 1894

INVESTIGATING WITCHCRAFT WITH THE FOLKLORISTS

Witchcraft was deceased or in its death throes. This platitude was heard a
lot towards the nineteenth century's end. Journalists claimed belief in evil
magic was 'obsolete', 'dead', 'died out', 'exploded' or 'completely extinct'.[1] It
had 'gone to other planets'.[2] Even in remote regions like the Scottish
Highlands, sorcery had 'died away', apparently.[3]

Superstition's recent demise was an important theme in Thomas Hardy's
novels and short stories. Written between the 1860s and 1890s, they were set a
generation or three previously, in pre-1840s southern rural England, when
ordinary folk credited all sorts of oddities, from the healing power of touching
a hanged man's neck to the dreadful potency of ill-wishing. The implication:
common manners were very different during those 'old-fashioned days'.[4]

To be fair, the common people agreed, or seemed to, when asked. And they were asked about witchcraft and magic, more so than ever before, by inquisitive amateur scholars calling themselves 'folklorists'. Folklorists were typically well-heeled and well-read men and women, whose newfangled hobby involved scouring the countryside for what they (often wrongly) supposed were traces of ancient paganism contained within the populace's speech, stories and beliefs.[5] Undertaking this blend of anthropology and speculative history in a stuffy, highly stratified society like Victorian Britain entailed certain difficulties. Ordinary rural people didn't really like talking about haunted houses, fairy forts, unlucky activities (playing or working on Sundays), healing charms and omens. Richard Jefferies, a writer on rustic affairs, warned would-be folklorists not to bother because: 'Not one word of superstition, or ancient tradition, or curious folk-lore, can a stranger extract.'[6]

Investigating witches and wizards, surely the most intriguing folkloric characters, was hardest of all.[7] It just wasn't realistic to expect an easy candour between gentleman or lady scholars and informants who might normally call them 'Sir' or 'M'lady', while doffing their caps. Barriers of suspicion, mistrust, shyness and self-consciousness had to be overcome.[8] But with tact and persistence, after several repeat visits and perhaps a bribe of alcoholic drinks or a few pennies, some informants relented. Finally they began telling eerie tales about local women and men with dark powers, usually characters from a generation ago, who'd long since departed this world. The details were fascinating, yet these yarns also contained a disappointing subtext.[9] This negative message was articulated by one of the characters in *Lark Rise to Candleford*, Flora Thompson's fictitious but strongly autobiographical account of life in Oxfordshire and Buckinghamshire, in the heart of rural England, during the 1880s. Asked about witches, the protagonist's mother replied: 'They seem to have all died out.'[10]

Folklorists quietly disagreed with each other about whether witchcraft and magic really existed as genuine supernatural powers. A few were believers of sorts, eccentrics who wearied their relatives by demonstrating the incantations necessary to make a fruit-tree bear, a journey prosper, or to avert the evil eye.[11] Many didn't quite know where the truth lay. The critic Andrew Lang thought the evidence for 'abnormal events' like ghosts and spells was 'much on a par with that for anthropological details', and outlined his thesis in leading periodicals like *Longman's Magazine*, *Contemporary*

Review and *Blackwood's Magazine*.[12] Charles Leland, a sometimes unreliable American expert on Romany culture, was much bolder, insisting in print that 'magical power' was 'innate in all men and women', though it wasn't entirely clear what he meant.[13]

Other folklorists were sceptical elitists. Take Edward Clodd (1840–1930), a banker, proponent of the theory of biological evolution and devotee of the great agnostic scientists Charles Darwin and Thomas Huxley. According to Mr Clodd's chauvinistic thinking, magic was characteristic of the childhood of the world, attractive to the 'lower races' of mankind and to 'foolish and ignorant' folk in out-of-the-way places.[14] He obviously disagreed with those among his colleagues who sincerely thought it was worth knowing which spells averted evil and which attracted good fortune. Yet despite their differences, Victorian folklorists agreed about two things, as did most literate commentators. First, whether it was true or false, witchcraft possessed a shadowy romance and rustic wholesomeness, preferable to the trashy urban culture of music halls and the popular press.[15] Second, like all folklore, witchcraft was quickly retreating in the face of advancing civilisation. Hence the need to hurry into the countryside and begin the gargantuan task of documenting the remaining 'pagan survivals'.

Rapid change, an effervescence of new technologies and ideas, made witchcraft's demise appear eminently plausible. How could magic be relevant in late Victorian Britain, in the homeland of the foremost international power, from whence was directed the largest empire the world had ever known? Surely, primeval notions about malefic supernatural forces couldn't be taken seriously by people whose culture was awash with newness, from the 'new woman' to Art Nouveau to the 'new journalism'?[16]

Above all, witchcraft seemed destined to be killed by affluence. Food was getting cheaper, for reasons ranging from imperialism to the invention of refrigeration, meaning that most working people now regularly ate meat, if only a little. Overcrowding was common, but real wages were increasing, partly because workers were better educated and organised. A national system of schooling had finally been established in 1870 and was fully funded by the state from 1891. By that time, provincial technology colleges were bringing higher scientific learning to almost 10,000 men and women annually.[17] Some intellectuals were estranged from institutional Christianity, yet new churches and chapels were springing up everywhere, especially in industrial cities that once looked like hotbeds of godlessness. Sewers and domestic running water vastly improved public sanitation, particularly in towns: by the 1870s, 80 per cent of Manchester houses had at least one tap.[18] Private travel was enhanced by the late nineteenth-century bicycle boom. Public transport was faster too, with the world's first underground metropolitan railway established in London in 1863, and the first underground electric railway in 1890. Homes were now heated and lit by coal and gas, rather than the logs and candles of ages past. However, apart from aristocratic country houses, domestic electricity would have to wait until the twentieth century.[19] Parliamentary reforms in 1867 and 1884 meant around two-thirds of men could now make themselves heard through the ballot box, greatly augmenting the moral legitimacy of Britain's political system.[20] In another sign of affluence, working people were routinely taking annual holidays at seaside resorts like Blackpool and Margate. And this is to say nothing of the explosion of mass consumer products, from patent medicines to tinned food to branded soap.

There were certainly times when new ways of doing things discredited old witchcraft beliefs, as in 1871 when villagers from Slapton in Devon began whispering about the local mill being bewitched. Apparently everyone residing there sickened or suffered an untimely death. The latest owner, Mr Willing, had been killed by fever just a few months after moving in. Soon his wife died too, leaving nine orphaned children, two of whom were feverish. But contrary to village rumour, it wasn't witches' work. On learning of the Willing family's sad fate the local authorities, the Kingsbridge Board of Guardians, dispatched a sanitary inspector to investigate. He analysed a water sample from the mill's well, using a microscope to zoom in on the microbial content. Frankly, it was disgusting. The water was teeming with faeces and bacteria from the surrounding drains, the cause of diseases like typhoid, which had killed Prince Albert in 1861. There was no dark magic here: no curse blighting the mill. The problem was one of hygiene and sanitation, which the Kingsbridge Guardians solved by closing the well.[21]

Inexplicable misfortunes, plausibly blameable on witchcraft, were diminishing. But only slightly. Despite the scientific advances and improvements in public health, life remained brutally hard. Want abounded, especially among the old and sick, as social investigators like Jack London discovered when they began exploring Britain's ruined underworld, towards the nineteenth century's end.[22] Studying York, ostensibly a charming ancient city, Benjamin Seebohm Rowntree calculated that almost 30 per cent of the residents were seriously impoverished.[23] Huge numbers were constantly hungry and cold. Bread, dripping, tea, a little bacon and an occasional bit of butcher's meat were their dietary staples. Given the lack of calories, vitamins, minerals and other essential nutrients, it's no wonder sickness was rife. Average life expectancy had increased over the course of the nineteenth century, from just under 40 to around 50.[24] Yet when Edward VII ascended to the throne in 1901, still more than one in ten children were dying before their first birthday.[25] Other misfortunes proliferated too, harrying the human lot as they always have and probably always will. Unemployment, financial difficulties and business failures were routine, especially during recessions. Family disputes and ill-fated romances were also depressingly common, among rich and poor alike.

Troubles like these might be seen as obstacles on life's path, as ordinary travails, fated tests, character-building challenges or everyday annoyances. But if they arrived in clusters, misfortunes could be disorientating and amenable to mysterious interpretations. In moments of crisis, plenty of people in the late Victorian era were willing to countenance what they would normally dismiss. For the desperate, frustrated and confused, witchcraft no longer seemed wholly ridiculous. Perhaps someone wished them ill. Maybe, behind their diverse maladies, was a curse or spell.

British folklorists seriously underestimated how many people embraced uncanny suspicions when times were bad. This is evident from the period's newspapers. It is not journalistic commentary, which was marred by the same lazy platitudes about superstition's demise, that provides the most revealing sources but rather what we might call 'breaking-news reports', about people who thought sorcery really was at work in Britain's towns, hamlets and villages. Cunning-folk and fortune-tellers, prosecuted for selling magical cures. Assault trials of vigilantes who'd attacked supposed witches. Coroners' inquests into bewitched suicides. Fines for abusive language, levied on people who'd threatened alleged spell casters. Desertion and divorce proceedings, where husbands accused their wives of diabolical dealings. Slander cases and civil suits involving witchcraft allegations. Anecdotes about farmers suffering losses and blaming them on evil magic. Stories about disturbed houses and unquiet cottages, with witchery-induced poltergeist activity.

In the forty years between 1860 and 1899 Britain's newspapers published at least 462 separate reports about recent or current outbreaks of witchcraft. The 1860s had the highest number (162), but there were around 100 cases each in successive decades. The decline from the 1860s was partly the result of decreasing attacks on witches, in response to the continued expansion of rural policing. Witch-scratching, a centuries-old technique of breaking spells by drawing blood, was largely suppressed. Nonetheless, the vitality of late Victorian witchcraft is striking. The cases reported in the press reflected a tiny portion of what was going on unremarked, but they show that black magic was virtually everywhere. In the witchy West Country, of course, and the notoriously superstitious Highlands of Scotland. Likewise in London, Leeds, Sheffield, Manchester, Wakefield, Bolton, Blackburn and countless other towns. In agricultural districts, but also the north-east coalfields and the smoky manufacturing towns of the West Midlands. Perhaps it was somewhat reduced, compared to previous generations. Yet witchcraft still abounded in the urban environment of the late nineteenth century.

What about the contemporaries who said differently? Their testimonies should be either challenged or reinterpreted. The rural folk, who told stories about local witches from generations past, have been misunderstood. Rather than sincerely arguing witchcraft was dead, they were pursuing a diver-sionary strategy familiar to anthropologists.[26] As a Cornish journalist observed in 1894 regarding witchcraft: 'People conceal their thoughts on such a subject.'[27] Partly because they felt embarrassed, but also because it was a secret body of knowledge: when charms or rites were spoken about, they lost their effect.[28] Mostly because witches possessed supernormal hearing and didn't like being talked about. If you had an inkling witchcraft existed, the safest thing to do was to keep quiet or whisper about witches from long ago, who were safely dead and in the ground. As an old lady from Devon explained, it was 'not right to talk of such things'.[29]

The folklorists who insisted witchcraft was dying were rehearsing tired clichés, rather than engaging with the reality of their contemporaries' lives. But I don't want to treat the folklorists too harshly. They underestimated witchcraft, especially urban witchcraft, but they also undertook uniquely detailed investigations into the culture of working people living in Britain's countryside. Thankfully, folklorists recorded words, stories, sayings and atmospheres that no one else did. To understand late Victorian witchcraft,

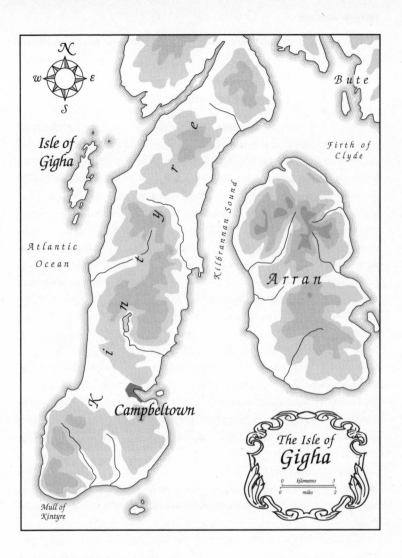

N

W · E

S

Bute

Isle of
Gigha

Firth of
Clyde

Atlantic
Ocean

Kilbrannan Sound

Arran

Campbeltown

Mull of
Kintyre

The Isle of
Gigha

0   kilometres   3
0   miles   2

we need to combine the results of folklore with the evidence of the news-paper archive. Such is the approach of this chapter.

WITCH HARES IN THE WESTERN ISLES

Spring 1862, and James Smith was beginning another long day's work on his farm. Today though, he saw something different as he stepped from his cottage into the morning half-light. Something unexpected. Across the yard, by the stable door, stood a woman. James called out to her in Scottish Gaelic, the main language on his home island of Gigha, asking what she was doing and telling her to get away. Perhaps she was a thief. More likely a beggar. Maybe even a vandal planning mischief. Whatever the case, James knew she shouldn't be lingering, unattended and uninvited, near his valuable livestock. To threaten her, he knelt down and reached for a tool. Yet when he looked up, the woman had gone. All he could see, in the field beyond, was a hare pacing through the dewy grass. James whistled for his dog and told it to chase, but the hare easily bounded out of reach, escaping into the daybreak.[30]

James Smith first told that story when he was rather the worse for drink, to revellers in a tavern near his home on Gigha, a small island lying off Scotland's west coast. His performance produced a powerful reaction. Some listeners were too afraid to hear it unfold in full. 'For God's sake hold your tongue,' said Archibald MacDonald, a fellow farmer, 'you're making my hairs creep.' Others thought the tale intriguing or important enough to be worth repeating to their friends, relatives and workmates. In the days that followed, James himself retold it at least four times, to farmers, Church elders, the local ferryman and a fisherman's family. Before long the rumour about the mysterious woman who transformed herself into a hare on James Smith's farm was the talk of Gigha and its 460 or so inhabitants.[31]

Why did the people of Gigha find the tale captivating yet disturbing? Modern readers, looking back from the vantage point of the early twenty-first century, might well regard it as boring or even pointless. The story's strangeness, our inability to intuitively grasp its appeal, reminds us it was generated by an alien culture, with its own assumptions, symbols and prior-ities.[32] Unlike us, the men and women of Gigha, gathered round the tavern's open fire, mugs of ale in hand, instantly understood the tale. To them, its meaning was obvious. James Smith had seen a witch, a witch who transcended her frail body's limitations by transforming herself into that most elusive animal: the hare. In time, it would be much debated whether James named the woman who so ostentatiously flaunted her occult powers. But the islanders who retold his tale were sure of her identity. She was Catherine McGougan, the notorious local malefactor.

Some said Catherine caused half of the misfortunes befalling her neighbours. As fishermen and farmers, they lived precarious lives, dependent on nature's unpredictable bounty, pitched against the vagaries of the waves and elements, remote from the comforts of the mainland. Perhaps the idea of witchcraft helped make their experiences more intelligible, meaningful and bearable. Psychological research has shown that humans find uncertainty acutely stressful.[33] By implying that evil happenings didn't necessarily occur randomly, but had a greater cosmic purpose, witchcraft may have provided a strange sort of comfort. If the witch did it, there was no need to face the painful truth that success, even life and death, were significantly determined by incalculable chance.[34]

It's possible to imagine why superstition appealed to people living dangerous lives, yet it's harder to understand why the denizens of Gigha suspected Catherine McGougan particularly. She hardly fitted the stereotype of what Owen Davies has termed an 'outsider witch': an ugly, aged, embittered, impoverished spinster.[35] A woman in her late fifties, Catherine was certainly mature by the standards of the mid-Victorian era, when people aged under 15 made up more than a third of the population.[36] But Catherine was also married, affluent and the respectable mother of five children. She and her husband rented their farm for around £150 a year – as much as a London clerk working in the civil service earned annually, and almost five times what James Smith, who devised the witch hare story, paid for his smallholding.[37] Catherine, a woman of means, had little to gain from her reputation. Not being a beggar, she didn't need to be held in ill repute to make her rounds more lucrative, though perhaps she got better business deals from her nervous neighbours. On the other hand, to be thought a witch on a small island like Gigha must have been deeply isolating. One can only speculate, but the solace of genuine friendship may have been unknown to her.

Catherine McGougan was clearly hurt by her reputation for witchcraft. Rather than meekly accepting her neighbours' innuendos, she was determined to prove she wasn't a mischievous shapeshifter. In February 1863, a year after the story about her transforming into a witch hare first began to circulate, Catherine reported its author to the nearest sheriff court, in Campbeltown. Invoking the law was not an easy option because Campbeltown was over 25 miles away, on the mainland. To get there Catherine traversed Gigha itself (which had 5 miles of serviceable road), before paying the ferryman to take her on the 2-mile crossing to the fishing village of Tayinloan. She then made her way south for a further 19 miles, towards the southern tip of the Kintyre peninsula. As well as being geographically distant this was also a culturally alien area of Highlands, where the Scots language predominated, unlike on Gigha and the other Western Isles where, as one commentator noted in 1845, 'Gaelic is the language generally spoken.'[38] Given that she was a substantial farmer's wife, we can assume Catherine travelled by horse. But hers would still have been a wearying, weather-dependent journey, taking at least an entire day in each direction. After arriving, no doubt exhausted, wet through and frozen, in Campbeltown, Catherine served a summons against James Smith, accusing him of slander, and demanding £200 in damages on account of his tale exposing her to 'the ridicule, scorn and contempt of her neighbours, associates, and parishioners'.

'The grounds of the present action may seem sufficiently absurd, but though the time has gone when witchcraft was generally believed in . . . there are still places where the superstition remains in full force.' So pronounced Thomas Cleghorn, Sheriff of Argyle, respecting the summons. Over the course of more than a year, he and his court heard a stream of appeals and counter-appeals on behalf of Catherine and her accused, James Smith. The eminently patient sheriff ultimately decided the case hinged on whether Catherine's reputation for practising the dark arts was harmful enough to warrant damages. Was a suspected witch on Gigha really the object of deep and genuine opprobrium? The *Statistical Account* of the island, a venerable source of information published a decade and a half earlier, in 1845, suggested not. Far from bemoaning the residents' superstitions, it noted, 'the habits of the people are improving', praising the fact that, of all the 460 residents of Gigha, none but twenty or thirty elderly folk were illiterate.[39]

After interrogating several witnesses from the island, Sheriff Cleghorn came to a different view. Gigha was rife with credulity, and Catherine had suffered greatly. James Smith's story about the witch hare 'did in fact cause much injury to her feelings and ... tended in such a community to bring her character into bad repute'. Consequently, the court ordered James to pay Catherine £10 along with the costs of the proceedings. Though well below the £200 she demanded, for James this was a hefty sum, amounting to four months' rent for his farm. Ultimately though, Catherine was denied even this compensation. James's attorney made a successful appeal to a senior court in Edinburgh, after discovering the 1736 Witchcraft Act not only abolished the crime of witchcraft but also decreed 'no prosecution, suit, or proceeding shall be commenced ... for charging another with any such offence'. The law was unambiguous: under no circumstances could a penalty or sanction be applied for accusing someone of witchcraft.

Catherine McGougan's suit failed, but the legal documents it generated reveal much about the variable nature of witchcraft belief on Gigha and beyond. Witnesses from the island were asked if they believed in witchcraft, whether they considered Catherine a witch, and whether they thought witches could transform into hares. Those questions produced a host of conflicting responses. James Smith claimed not to believe in witches, but when pressed on their ability to shapeshift gave an agnostic answer: 'Well I can't say – in Gigha, some believe it, some not'. By contrast, a local fisherman told the court, 'I believe there are such things as witches', but doubted their capacity to assume animal form ('I don't believe myself they can'). Donald MacDonald, a farmer, timorously confessed, 'I would not like to keep company with a person that was supposed to be a witch', but refused to answer any other questions about their proclivities, saying repeatedly, 'I cannot give any account of that'. Another farmer, Archibald MacDonald, denied the reality of witchcraft altogether, though he also confessed to being frightened by James Smith's witch hare story. Even on a small island like Gigha, therefore, witchcraft was contested and disputed. People broadly classified themselves as believers or doubters, yet not all believers were alike, nor all disbelievers. Within the camps of faith and doubt, there was plenty of scope for idiosyncrasy and individuality.

To be accused of witchcraft on Gigha was evidently dismal. On that little island, a reputation for the dark arts would have been inescapable. At least on the mainland, one could travel to find anonymity and peace in another place. Yet in other ways witchcraft on Gigha was similar to witchcraft elsewhere. Take the ancient and transcultural notion of the witch hare. Across Scotland, in the Highlands and Lowlands, among Gaelic speakers and users of Scots or English, it was a commonplace that witches could transform themselves into hares. Stories about witches, who assumed the form to suckle milk from cows or lead hunters on a merry chase before escaping with an incriminating wound, were told throughout the counties of England, Wales, the Isle of Man and Ireland, too.[40] Similar narratives have been recorded in Denmark, southern Norway, south-western Sweden, Austria and Germany.[41] As well as being widespread, the idea of the witch hare was old: it figured in some seventeenth-century English witch trials, though the notion is probably older still.[42] It was also long-lasting: 'The hare is linked all over Britain with witches, and there are few people who have not come across this association,' wrote two folklorists in 1972.[43]

Why hares? Fast, elusive and seldom tamed, hares were seen as distinctly sinister creatures. It's tempting to connect their unnerving reputation with their scream, which sounds like a child's cry. Yet the stigma attached to hares was probably a legacy of ancient cultural associations, rather than the animal's inherent physiological qualities. At the time of the Roman invasion, the people of Britain reportedly had a taboo against eating hares.[44] These uncanny associations may have been intensified by the arrival of Christianity, since in the Book of Deuteronomy Moses condemns hares as unclean. In medieval Europe, they were regarded as unlucky, and church wall paintings sometimes depicted the devil in the form of a hare.[45] Some people carried around hare's feet as curative charms against colic (internal pain). But the hare's sinister reputation persisted into the nineteenth century and beyond. According to a well-known though not necessarily widely believed folkloric idea, pregnant women who encountered hares gave birth to children with harelips. More seriously, fishermen considered 'hare' an unlucky word, under no circumstances to be spoken at sea.[46]

We should not get overly fixated on hares, because witches were thought to transform themselves into other animals too. Foxes, cats and white rabbits were alternate forms adopted by British witches, according to stories told in many villages and hamlets. By contrast, among the fishing communities on Canada's eastern shores some sailors were said to possess uncanny powers that allowed them to transform into seals.[47] According to the tribal peoples of nineteenth-century India, witches travelled at night by riding on or morphing into tigers and other forest beasts.[48] Throughout much of sub-Saharan Africa, on the other hand, witches were (and are) strongly associated with hyenas, snakes, crocodiles and cats.[49] Local fauna and folklore determined which animals were connected with sorcery. But across the world, witches were credited with powers that allowed them to change shape, travel incognito, move quickly and sow their mischief without being discovered.[50]

REGIONAL WITCHCRAFT

Witch hares haunted a vast territory: the countryside of the British Isles and northern Europe. Other aspects of witchcraft varied considerably, not just between countries, but across Britain's regions. Even the words for it differed drastically. Terms like 'overlooked', 'ill-wished', 'bewitched', 'cursed', 'witchcraft' and 'witch' were known just about everywhere. Yet they were not used equally often or in quite the same ways. Around Huddersfield, in woollen-producing West Yorkshire, 'witch' was applied to both male and female sorcerers, and could also mean a textile machine.[51] In Cornwall, England's most westerly county, 'ill-wished' and 'ill-wishing' were the primary expressions for witchcraft, whereas words like 'bewitched' and 'bewitch' were less common.[52]

Beyond the generic terms, Victorian Britons knew legions of regional expressions and dialect words for black magic. In Somerset and Devon, 'begaged' meant bewitched, while 'wishtness' denoted the result of witchcraft or the evil eye. To put it in the common parlance, a Somersetian who thought witchcraft afflicted his daughter might say something like: 'I calls it a proper wishtness ... the doctors can do her no good.'[53] On the other side of England, 300 miles east-north-east from the rolling pastures and blustery moorlands of the West Country, in the remorselessly flat Cambridgeshire Fens, 'tudded' meant bewitched. (As in: 'I'll say it again: that pig's tudded.'[54]) The word, as the folklorist Enid Porter later noted, probably had its origin in the frequent use of toads and familiars in East Anglian witchcraft. 'Overseen', used in the Cotswolds to mean bewitched, and 'he-witch', the Lancashire word for a wizard, were less obscure.[55] In Swaledale, North Yorkshire, 'carlin', literally meaning a female peasant, also denoted 'old woman' and 'witch', illustrating how British witches were stereotypically elderly crones. This cliché, found in some other countries but not everywhere around the world, was also discernible in the Yorkshire term 'hagging', which meant practising witchcraft (a 'hag' was a derogatory term for an old woman). 'Deeavlement' possessed similarly witchy connotations in Swaledale, and hinted at the dark art's satanic connection.[56]

Scotland probably had the most colourful witchcraft words – aptly, given its position as a centre of intense witch-hunting between the fifteenth and eighteenth centuries. Then and throughout the nineteenth century, in the Lowlands and among speakers of Scots elsewhere, witches' spells were gingerly referred to as 'cantrips'.[57] The word literally meant 'tricks', but in the context of witchcraft it implied much more, without tempting fate by being specific about the horrid details. Those horrid details included weather magic, raising storms and dispelling winds, to frustrate the god-fearing fisher-folk. (Thankfully, cunning-folk in Scotland offered to ensure good conditions and abundant shoals, provided the sailors were willing to pay for them.)[58] During the period of the witch trials, storms were occasionally blamed on witches, and that continued to be the case in the coastal regions of Victorian Scotland, though not elsewhere in Britain.[59]

Above all, Scottish witchcraft revolved around the malefic escapades of dairy witches. These leeches magically siphoned milk from their neighbours' cattle, taking the best bits, the 'freet' or 'profit' in the Scottish expressions, meaning the cream and buttermilk needed to make cheese, leaving just watery remains, if anything.[60] Sorcerers were blamed for drying up cows and stopping butter from churning throughout Britain; yet nowhere was the theme so prominent and elaborate as in Scotland. In the Highlands, Lowlands and on the Isles, there were troves of tales about these nasty folk. Malefactors' spells might involve touching or raking the victim's grazing grass, while whispering an incantation:

Gather in, gather in,
Cream and milk and cheese,
Gather in, gather in,
Stop not till I please.

Rural Scots knew innumerable anti-witchcraft techniques for righting afflicted cattle, too many to list in fact. Distinctively, these magical cures often featured silver, in the form of coins or rings placed in pails of water, over which charms were muttered.[61]

Fearing milk witches were holding back agricultural progress, some Scottish local authorities tried to dispel farming superstitions. In 1893 Banff County Council, in the north-east, established twenty-three dairy instruction centres, to teach scientific agriculture through lectures and demonstrations. The council was optimistic about its work, proclaiming: 'The use of the thermometer has dispelled the belief in witchcraft, and all other supernatural influences.'[62] Armed with their new thermometers, and aware of how milk's temperature strongly influenced its ability to be churned into butter, maybe Banffshire's farmers were less inclined to attribute dairy mishaps to witchcraft. But it was pure fantasy to suggest that witchcraft belief was dead. Scottish smallholders still experienced troubles aplenty, behind which the dread hand of magic plausibly lurked. In 1893 the sheriff court at Oban heard how a local farmer had been accused of using his evil eye to make another farmer's beast trip on the road.[63] In 1899, news reached the papers that a woman from the Highland parish of Latheron, in Caithness, believed a witch had dried up her cow.[64] During the same year, milk-stealing witchcraft was the cause of a fracas on the Isle of Lewis.[65] The scope of mysterious misfortunes was shrinking, slightly, but magical suspicions remained.[66]

In the Gaelic-speaking regions of Scotland, the Highlands and most of the Western Isles, the words for witchcraft were obviously different. *Buidseach* was Gaelic for 'black witch', the sort of malefactor who might raise a storm or drive away the herring to frustrate the fishermen, or use magic to steal milk from their neighbour's cow.[67] *Rosad* meant a 'spell' or 'mischance' put on an object like a gun, to make it misfire.[68] *Sian* referred to supernatural armour conjured by witches, usually to guard animals but sometimes to protect people too.[69] The words for witchcraft were different again on the Shetland Islands, 150 miles north of John o'Groats on Scotland's north-eastern tip, and almost 300 miles west of Norway. Reflecting the archipelago's historic connection with Scandinavia, on Shetland a witch-like woman was a *trullascud*, a compound of troll (the characteristic evil creature of Norwegian folklore) and *skudtm,* meaning elf-shot (an idea from fairy lore).[70] More plainly, on the Shetland Isles, a witch was also called a *luckie.*[71]

*   *   *

In other ways, witchcraft varied less between places than we might expect. Across Britain there was an abundance of urban witchcraft, even during the era of redbrick suburbs, gothic civic buildings and municipal socialism. Ill townsfolk were as capable as rustics of convincing themselves that magic lay behind their troubles. Bewitched urbanites noted in the press during the 1890s alone included a Lancashire mill worker, a Leeds market seller, a Yeovil omnibus driver and a Southport joiner.[72] Zooming out to take a more general view, in the later Victorian era, witchcraft was reportedly at work in towns as various as Hertford, Merthyr, Plymouth, Warwick, Ely, Wells, Whitby, Norwich, Warrington, Swansea, Oxford, Ipswich, Hastings, Stockton-upon-Tees, Durham, Bilston in Staffordshire, Sheffield, Bath, Dudley, Barnsley, Cardiff, Wakefield, Manchester, Blackburn and Bolton.[73]

There were even witches in the British Empire's bustling metropolitan capital, London – quite a lot of them, in fact. Evil magic was cited as the cause of a mental illness in Lambeth during 1861.[74] Letters threatening witchcraft were sent by a man living in Knightsbridge in 1862. A woman from Clerkenwell sought the magistrates' protection in 1863, because she was considered a witch and the local boys threw stones at her.[75] In 1870 a witch was reported to Thames Police Court for using magic to kill a hen.[76] The Southwark Justices were asked for help with witchcraft in 1876.[77] Fears about black magic resulted in the prosecution of Margaret Birmingham, from Bermondsey, in 1895. She'd attacked her neighbour, Eleanor, whom she blamed for making her little baby ill. As Margaret told the bemused magistrate: 'She's a witchcraft, that's what she is.'[78] In 1899 a labourer from Fulham was jailed for drunkenly beating his wife, whom he called 'a Devil' and accused of bewitching him.[79] London's dangerous, cramped, claustrophobic living conditions, it seems, were rather conducive to occult suspicions.

Although it figured everywhere, witchcraft was more widely believed in by the denizens of certain regions, particularly by the people of East Anglia, the West Midlands, North Yorkshire, the Scottish Highlands and Islands, and the West Country. In Norfolk, noted one commentator in 1894: 'The belief in witches and witchcraft is as strong as when the notorious Hopkins drove such a roaring trade as a witch-finder. Imps are still dreaded. The cauldron of the weird sisters still bubbles.'[80]

In Cornwall 'almost every house, homestead, or farm yard' had 'some mysterious legend of witch or wizard', a local writer observed in 1870.[81] No one could live in neighbouring Devon and mix with its population 'without finding a general belief in witchcraft still existing, and old customs and superstitions in full swing', it was said in 1867.[82] Devon folk credited witchcraft 'with all the credulous faith of the middle ages', claimed another.[83] Of all Britain's counties, Somerset probably had the most witchery. One (anonymous) Somerset parish was home to no fewer than five witches, a newspaper correspondent claimed.[84] To make the point numerically and generally, of the 462 witchcraft outbreaks reported by Britain's newspapers between 1860 and 1899, 201 occurred in the West Country. In 1901, the counties of Dorset, Devon, Cornwall and Somerset had a combined population of 1.65 million, out of a total of 37 million for Britain as a whole.[85] This meant the West Country created 43.5 per cent of the witchcraft cases, from only 4.5 per cent of the people.

Why was the West so extraordinarily witchy? The obvious answers, isolation and rusticity, are unconvincing. After all, witchcraft troubled townsfolk too, and Britain's other rural areas were not harried by witchcraft as much as the West Country was. Dorset, Devon, Somerset and Cornwall didn't possess radically different social and economic structures, sufficient to explain the extreme currency of witchcraft in those counties. Instead, it seems more likely that memory, myth, legend and tradition conjured a uniquely uncanny atmosphere in the West. Historians remain unsure of the extent of witch prosecutions in the West Country during the period of the trials, because few of the judicial records survive.[86] However, the latest research on the extant documentation suggests the region saw a good deal of witch persecution.[87] Western England may, in fact, have witnessed more witchcraft during the sixteenth and seventeenth centuries than Essex, the county that previous generations of historians regarded as the epicentre of English magic. The folklorist Enid Porter once observed that witchcraft belief persisted longest in regions 'where there is much evidence of it from the past'.[88] In the Victorian West Country, stories were still told of local witches tried and executed centuries ago.[89] These tales, this abundant history and powerful tradition of maleficent magic, probably explain why witchcraft figured disproportionately in the minds of West Country folk.

WITCH VILLAGES AND CURSING WELLS

Witchcraft differed from one region to the next, but it also varied over much shorter distances. Certain desolate, inhospitable or generally ominous locations were known as the favoured haunts of witches. Prolley Moor in

Shropshire was a notorious meeting place for practitioners of the dark arts, as was Locharbriggs hill in Dumfriesshire.[90] Tinkers Hole, a wood near Ostend in Essex, was said to be 'devil-haunted'.[91] Pendle Forest, a few miles from Burnley, had connections with black magic going back to the Lancashire witch trials of 1612, when ten people from the area were convicted of murder by witchcraft. 'Two hundred years have since passed away,' wrote one investigator in 1867, 'and yet the old opinions survive.'[92] Throughout the forest, the farmers were known for striving to:

Chase the evil spirits away by dint
Of sickle, horse-shoe, and hallow flint.

Every British county had a few witch villages, where wicked traditions echoed down the generations, or were supposed to. Around the mid-nineteenth century Weobley Marsh in Herefordshire was called a 'witch-ridden' place,[93] while Monzie in Perthshire was 'long and widely known for its witches'.[94] Reputations like these were often so well established they were expressed in local proverbs, adages and odes. Of Orcop, in Herefordshire, it was said that 'There'll always be nine witches from the bottom of Orcop to the end of Garway Hill as long as water runs.'[95] 'Welford for witches, Binton for bitches' was a rhyme about two Warwickshire villages.[96] A similar verse described the distinguishing features of four Norfolk places:

Beeston babies, Sheringham ladies,
Weybourne witches, Salthouses ditches.[97]

In Somerset it was a cliché that 'the Devil's in Frome and cannot get out'.[98] Inverkip and nearby Dunrod Castle, in Renfrewshire, were similarly infamous. 'In Inverkip the witches ride thick, and in Dunrod they dwell,' ran a local proverb.[99] Auchencrow, in east Berwickshire, 'had an evil reputation as the resort of witches', expressed in the maxim 'in the toun o' Auchencraw, where the witches bide'.[100]

Were these ditties, and the ideas behind them, taken seriously? There is evidence to suggest they were. During the 1870s, before a sketching trip to a Warwickshire village with a reputation for witchcraft, the author Elinor Mordaunt was implored by a servant 'with tears in his eyes, not to go there, for it was "fair swarmin' wid' witches" '.[101] An extreme reaction, but not wholly exceptional. Throughout the nineteenth century Canewdon, in south-east Essex, was an ill-reputed village. The folklorist Eric Maple was told carriers avoided it 'if possible, for fear of having the wheels of their wagons bewitched'.[102]

The most fearsome witchcraft locations were Welsh. They were places worth travelling many miles for – two cursing wells, where evilly inclined people laid deadly imprecations upon their enemies. For reasons lost to history, both the wells were dedicated to the Roman Catholic evangelist Saint Elian, who built some of Wales' first churches, during the fifth century.[103] One of Saint Elian's cursing wells was located near Llaneilian on Anglesey, the largest island in the Irish Sea, located just off the North Welsh coast, and accessible by road and rail after Thomas Telford completed his Menai suspension bridge in 1826.[104] The more notorious Welsh cursing well was situated in the parish of Llanelian yn Rhos, on the Denbighshire–Caernarfonshire border, near the coast of North Wales.

For centuries St Elian's well, known in Welsh as Ffynnon Elian, was used for healing. Yet during the later eighteenth century, it acquired darker associations.[105] Persons wishing ill upon their enemies would inscribe their victims' initials on pebbles, parchment or lead tablets, before solemnly immersing these offerings. Devised by various keepers of the well, who made a handsome living from owning or occupying the property on which it was situated, these practices made the power of witchcraft available to all. On several occasions, the neighbourhood's outraged churches and magistrates attacked the well and prosecuted its keepers. In 1814 the walls enclosing the well house were destroyed. In 1826 the Justices forbade use of the well. In 1829 the local Methodists celebrated the demolition of the entire structure, well house and all. Shortly after, an enterprising neighbour, a tailor named John Evans, diverted the water source to his cottage garden and established himself as the new keeper. Not until the 1850s was his trade in evil magic finally ended, after Mr Evans renounced his wicked ways and joined the Baptists.[106]

By the mid-Victorian era there was no longer a keeper of St Elian's cursing well. Yet the superstition refused to die. During the 1860s a visitor to the remains of Ffynnon Elian 'noticed corks with pins stuck in them, floating in the well'.[107] Presumably these were intended to direct malevolent forces at unfortunate persons. 'The ill fame of Ffynnon Elian,' another commentator confirmed in 1870, 'continues even to this day.'[108] Tales about the cursing well were still being told, through the nineteenth century and beyond, with folklorists recording some of the yarns.[109] Critics had long blamed Ffynnon Elian's popularity on the superstitious mindset of the 'peasantry of the neighbourhood.'[110] In reality, a broader spectrum of people used St Elian's curse, including individuals from England and Ireland, according to the last keeper of the well. Apparently, some of these had been the 'best people in the land in terms of wealth and education.'[111] The well inspired a sort of magical tourism, which is revealed in other sources. Ffynnon Elian featured in many nineteenth- and twentieth-century guidebooks to the region, including James Halliwell's *Notes of Family Excursions in North Wales* (1860).[112] He condemned the 'barbarous custom of invoking the presiding saint to injure an enemy'. Tellingly, though, Halliwell described the well's location and the various ceremonies typically enacted to induce a curse.[113] His readers might find this information useful, and perhaps not just out of antiquarian curiosity.

Menacing locations, where witches roamed and curses mustered, defy easy classification. They obviously contradict the archaeologist Christopher Tilley's theory, about the terrain of western capitalist countries being 'desanctified' – stripped of mystical and supernatural associations characterising the premodern landscape.[114] The idea that the early modern period witnessed a 'secularisation of space' is similarly unhelpful. Also problematic is the terminology of more sensitive scholars, who are alive to the persistence of holy landscapes long after the Reformation. Alexandra Walsham's *The Reformation of the Landscape* is a wonderful book, which shows how religious strife caused once sacred spaces – wells, rocks, ruined chapels and monasteries, wayside crosses – to be 'resanctified', 'reconfigured' and recreated, rather than being purged entirely of Christian connotations.[115] Categories like 'sacred', 'holy' and 'sanctified' are apposite in this context, but not for the domain of witchcraft. The terms are religious rather than magical, too positive and too evocative of personal control. Given the dark associations clinging to parts of Britain, it probably makes more sense to speak of the witch-ridden villages, bedevilled outcrops, damned fields and haunted landscapes. For people learned in witchcraft, seemingly innocuous terrains could be nerve-wracking, threatening, even terrifying.

WHO WERE THE WITCHES?

Witches didn't figure in every case of witchcraft. The 462 newspaper reports about outbreaks of witchcraft in Britain between 1860 and 1899 involved 502 victims, split precisely evenly between the genders. Yet there were only 311 identifiable witches. Around 150 cases, about a third of the total, lacked or didn't identify witches at the time of reporting.

This underlines something important about the procedural nature of cursing and bewitchment. It started with victims, who concluded their sufferings were unusual enough to be caused by malign magic. When that decision was made, the search for culprits began. In other words, people did not simply see someone who they believed to be a witch, and then look around for illnesses and disasters that were his or her doing. Quite the reverse: witchcraft accusations were voiced towards the end of the process, after it was decisively concluded that black magic was at work. Not infrequently, the witches were never found.

Discovering witches wasn't easy. Presumably they were characters the victim saw regularly, individuals with reasons to be envious or embittered. Some bewitched people were certain they knew who was responsible. Others weren't sure, so firmed up their suspicions with the expert help of cunning-folk and fortune-tellers. These professional magicians provided vague and quizzical guidance, rather than definitive answers. They'd say things like the witch was the next person to call at the house, or a man with grey hair, or a black woman.[116] Or they'd diagnose their customers as victims of numerous witches, like the Exeter wise-woman who gravely informed a client that no fewer than three witches, all women, were 'working' on her son.[117]

Visualisation techniques were sometimes used. Cursed people were made to spend minutes staring at a broken egg, slowly floating through a glass of warm water. Or they were settled over a bowl of liquid, and told to peer inside. Had they, perhaps, seen faces? Another more desperate and dangerous way to unveil malefactors was by attacking them with magic. Making a witch-bottle or roasting an animal's heart over the fire could force responsible witches to beg for mercy, or in other ways reveal themselves. If someone came to the door or was heard groaning during the ceremony, or if they were seen the next day with suspicious injuries, this was a sign of guilt. It didn't always happen, but identifying the witch was essential for an effective cure. Ultimately, it was up to the cursed person to make the final decision.

In theory, practically anyone could be a witch. During the 1880s, suspicions fell on at least two newspaper sellers from the West of England.[118] As during the period of the witch trials, gift givers were at risk if they bestowed charity on troubled folk at sensitive times.[119] Even clergymen, God's representatives on earth, weren't safe from suspicion. One Sunday early in 1893, a parish church in rural Worcester witnessed a shocking scene. As the worshippers filed down the aisle after service, a woman leapt at the vicar, scratching his face with her nails. She believed he'd bewitched her, and was trying to break the spell by drawing blood. 'The scene was ludicrously serious,' a bystander observed. Generously, the vicar didn't prosecute.[120] He wasn't the only clergyman suspected of being a witch. In Chew Magna church, Somerset, during the winter of 1898, Harriet Filer said she'd like to shoot the Rev. John Galbraith because he wouldn't leave her alone. Upon enquiry, it transpired Harriet believed the parson had 'overlooked' her family.[121]

Witchcraft grew out of envy and bitterness, it was supposed.[122] Witches were therefore likely to be people who had frequent but fraught contacts with their bedevilled victims – usually neighbours, though disgruntled employees or colleagues were obvious candidates too. In 1865 a farmer from Somerset sacked a labourer, accusing him of witching his body and livestock.[123] The following year a farrier from Nottinghamshire chided a fellow farm servant for bewitching the horses.[124] At Bury, Lancashire, a dyer dismissed his 16-year-old servant girl on account of witchcraft.[125] The lodge keepers of Taunton Hospital were discharged, in 1880, for blaming witchcraft on a nurse.[126] Business rivals might be witches, especially on the coasts of Scotland, where fishermen charged each other with using witchery to steer fish into their nets.[127] Occasionally, cunning-folk and fortune-tellers were accused of spreading evil by their paranoid clients.[128] That's why William Hillman, a blacksmith and white witch from Ottery in Devon, was scratched with the steel tip of his customer's walking stick during the summer of 1881.[129]

Family was a source of conflict as well as comfort. This explains why so many witches were closely related to their victims. Over one in ten of the witches identified in the late Victorian press were relatives (34 of 311). Husbands sincerely accused wives: in 1893 Henry Websdale, a horse driver for the local council in Lowestoft, Suffolk, abandoned his wife of twenty-six years, the mother of his five children, because he thought her witchcraft was behind his chronic insomnia.[130] At Brierley Hill magistrates' court, in 1894, Mr Ailfort also accused his wife of being a witch. Looking for his watch, he'd broken into her box of personal possessions and discovered a drawing of Satan's face, surrounded by other mystical characters. It was clearly meant for evil purposes.[131] During the 1890s Mrs Carpenter, of Blagdon in Somerset, found herself accused by her husband of bewitching him seven times. Amid the acrimony, Mrs Carpenter's neighbours disowned her.[132] Desperate to break spells by drawing their witch's blood, men scratched their mistresses as well as the mothers of their children, as Edward Lewis, a miner from Wolverhampton, did to Mary Ann Thomas.[133] William Jefford, a labourer from Charlton Horethorne in Somerset, was bound over to keep the peace in 1885, for beating his wife. Nothing had gone right since his marriage, William complained, because his mother-in-law had bewitched him.[134]

Family witchcraft went beyond husbands versus wives. Women blooded their sisters-in-law, like the lady from Durham who did so in the winter of 1867, before saying, 'I am satisfied ... she will witch me no more.'[135] Aunts attacked nieces in the name of witchcraft, as in the Welsh town of Merthyr in 1868.[136] Sons scratched mothers, sincerely believing they'd bewitched them.[137] In Norwich in 1887, Arthur Cropp was charged with using threatening language against his mother, whom he accused of witching him so he was unable to find work.[138] (She pleaded for clemency on his behalf, and the case was dismissed.) Stepsons attacked their stepmothers, for similar reasons.[139] Adult grandchildren assaulted frail grandparents, almost killing them in one case.[140] Charles Tellbrook, 27, an ex-solider living in Westminster, was convicted of attempted murder and given penal servitude for cutting his grandmother's forehead with a razor, then severely beating her. When arrested Charles explained he 'did not want to kill the old lady outright', only 'see her blood' so she'd 'not possess power over him'.[141] Lucy Denny, of Hardingham in Norfolk, suffered months of abuse from her in-laws during the mid-1860s, culminating in a public beating. None of the neighbours helped her, though some saw what was occurring.[142] Occasionally, parents accused their children of colluding in black magic.[143] In 1886, a farmer from Barnstaple in Devon disinherited his daughters because he believed they'd bewitched eczema into his hand.[144]

If they couldn't think of haters or enviers, cursed people settled on other candidates. People with sight-related disabilities were sometimes said to possess the evil eye and were blamed for local mishaps.[145] But the most obvious suspects were nasty characters who actually boasted they were witches. These blackguards revelled in their wicked reputations, making all sorts of ugly claims.[146] Old Mary Perry, from the West Midlands town of Wednesbury, told people she kept a toad in a jar, feeding it on bread and soil, giving her the power to bewitch.[147] Mary Whitaker, of Walford in Herefordshire, insisted her powers came from a black wand. It could make the villagers walk up the hill on their heads, backwards, Mary claimed. And if she stuck the wand in her garden, no one could enter. No one tried. Instead, Mary's neighbours wore protective charms, made by the local cunning-man.[148] The witch of Brixham, Devon, was a similar character, with a 'black stick' and a sharp tongue. Understandably, she was blamed for causing a local baby's death, in 1862.[149] Elizabeth Smith was the terror of the Norwich suburb of Cotton, during the early 1880s. She boasted of being a witch, threatening her neighbours that she could make them crawl home if she was so inclined.[150]

With their magical threats, witches really were dangerous. In the seventy years since the publication of '"Voodoo" Death', a classic article by the physiologist Walter B. Cannon, scientists of various kinds have explained how magical acts can and do kill people who are seriously afraid of them.[151] Put simply, a pointed bone, effigy or spell can trigger a person's 'flight or fight' response in an extreme way, perhaps because, in the past, they've inadvertently honed the neural pathways associated with fear, from continuous use. For some, the thought of being attacked with magic unleashes a massive release of adrenaline and stress hormones, inducing symptoms ranging from loss of appetite to vascular collapse, cardiac lesions and arrhythmias, and sometimes death.

The thought of being bewitched inspired a range of distressing health problems. It kept people awake at night and gave them splitting head-aches.[152] At worst, victims of sorcery took their own lives.[153] The horror witchcraft summoned is well illustrated by events in Exeter during the summer of 1892. Sarah Short, a married woman known for witchcraft, living in Horwell's Court, hung two effigies on her outside wall, facing towards the house of her neighbours. These neighbours blamed Sarah for bewitching them, so they must have been horrified to see the witch attacking their bodies with image magic. Angry and alarmed, one night in July, following too many ciders, they tried to shame Sarah into stopping by yelling abuse from the street.[154] They were cautioned for this breach of the peace, but the local magistrates didn't underestimate the impact of Sarah's actions, strongly warning her to desist. The JPs knew she was scaring her neighbours witless.

Witches were terrifying figures partly because they purveyed satanic power. Their victims were explicit about this, saying they were under assault from 'the devil and his angels'.[155] Less directly, bewitched people claimed they felt burning sensations or smelt of brimstone, when under magical attack.[156] The idea of diabolic witchcraft was an old one, formulated by the demonologists of the medieval period, perhaps with deeper roots in ancient Mesopotamian conceptions of demons.[157] By the late Victorian era, those intellectual origins were long forgotten. Cursed people learnt about witches' relationship with Satan from oral culture, from hushed stories about malefactors who'd dealt with the devil, thereby gaining special abilities and purses of bedevilled money.[158] Cunning-folk and fortune-tellers said similar things, when teaching their clients about witchcraft. In 1893 a fortune-teller from Devon told two women with sick pigs they were ill-wished by someone who'd sold their soul to the devil in return for powers to do evil while on earth.[159] But the witches' chief ally, the devil, had rivals. As the occult scene developed, towards the close of the nineteenth century, there emerged new ideas about the origins of witches' powers. In 1895 a woman from Coalville, Leicestershire, was jailed for beating a lady who she claimed had witched her, using the techniques of spiritualism.[160]

A minority of witches cultivated evil reputations, but most alleged sorcerers didn't deserve their notoriety. Innocent of occult crimes, these scapegoats were often scandalously ill-treated by their neighbours and families. Like Susan Sullock, an old woman from Colaton Raleigh in Devon, scratched for witchcraft in July 1860, not for the first time.[161] Or Mrs Cloak, a market worker from Plymouth, accused of witchcraft by her estranged husband, repeatedly attacked, but not before her spouse encouraged a mob of boys to follow her home, calling her 'witch'.[162] Occasionally husbands took the beating meant for their witch wives.[163] Thankfully, with the increasing numbers of policemen on Britain's streets, attacks on witches were declining. During the 1860s, the press reported 48 witchcraft-related assaults; by the 1870s the figure had fallen to 22, for the 1880s it was 20, and just 15 witchcraft fracases were noted during the 1890s. The threat of prosecution, rather than waning belief, was responsible for this decrease. As the curate of Heywood in Wiltshire drily put it, reputed witches were no longer ducked or beaten 'not because the will to do so is absent' but because vigilantes feared being fined.[164]

Witchcraft vigilantes found ways around the stricter standards of law enforcement. They jeered, swore, insulted, boycotted, jostled, and even threw dirt in a witch's face in one case – anything nasty, that kept just below the threshold needed for a prosecution.[165] And then there were the few bewitched people who no longer cared about the fines or punishments. Desperate, half-mad, consumed by hatred, they were prepared to do anything to stop the torment – even kill. 'Dummy', a deaf and dumb fortune-teller from Sible Hedingham in Essex, died of pneumonia in 1863 after a group of villagers pushed him into a ditch, because he'd cursed a local woman.[166] Ann Tennant, an elder of the Warwickshire village of Long Compton, expired in a pool of blood on the turnpike road in September 1875, after being stabbed with a pitchfork by a man who accused her of witchcraft.[167] In 1888 a fortune-teller from East Lambrook, Somerset, was killed by a fellow who thought she'd bewitched him.[168] In 1894 George Wiseman, a confectioner from Eastbourne in Sussex, was shot, wounded and very nearly murdered by a labourer who accused him of 'carrying on the power of wizardism or witchcraft' using a kind of mesmerism.[169] Dr Edward Havens, Lord of the Manor of East Donyland, Essex, relentlessly beat his wife Louisa. For six months he kept her prisoner in her bedroom, punching her in the face and body, pulling out clumps of her hair and even flashing his revolver, implying she'd soon be shot. All the while, Edward accused Louisa of bewitching him, their daughter and half the village. Louisa only escaped by chance, after calling to two policemen passing by the manor house. In the autumn of 1898, she was granted a separation order.[170]

This all sounds relentlessly vindictive. We can at least take comfort in the alleged witches who rejected, in magnificent style, the evil reputations ascribed to them, most commonly with words. Speaking almost to a script, though it must have hurt, they tried to laugh at their accusers, mock their beliefs and deny witchcraft's very existence. 'She did not hold with such things herself' was the formal language Susan Ford used in court in 1895, when explaining how her suicidal son believed himself bewitched (by her,

Susan failed to mention).[171] 'Go along man. You are the biggest fool I have known in my life' was how a father from Totnes reacted when his son accused him of witchery. 'I would let all the folks in the world bewitch me if they like,' he added.[172] Others took a tougher approach, perhaps ensuring they were never again publicly slandered. On the Isle of Unst in 1883, Andrina Johnston lashed a fisherman with a rope, because he'd said she'd bewitched his boat. The obviously very tough lady was fined 5 shillings.[173] Miss Passmore, from the Devon town of Barnstaple, may sound like a dainty figure. But when she was publicly accused of practising witchcraft in 1893, Miss Passmore roughed up the woman who said it. The magistrates sympathised, dismissing the assault charge brought against her.[174] Harriet Perkins, an elderly widow living in an almshouse in Long Sutton, Lincolnshire, was too old to meet violence with violence when a farmer's wife broke her wrist in a scuffle about evil magic. But Harriet was at least able to obtain some financial compensation, £4, in return for not bringing a prosecution.[175]

WOMEN AND WITCHCRAFT

Such were the witches of Victorian Britain. About them, a crucial point still needs to be made. They were predominantly, overwhelmingly, but not exclusively, women. Of the more than 300 sorcerers identified in newspaper reports between 1860 and 1899, almost 9 out of 10 (87 per cent) were female. Victorian witches were almost as stereotypically female as witches had been in England during the period of the witch trials, when women comprised around 90 per cent of the accused.[176]

This represents an extraordinary continuity in the history of magic between the era of the Tudors and the Stuarts and the reign of Queen Victoria. The historian Christina Larner's dictum about witch-hunting in Europe *c.* 1450–1700 can be easily applied to nineteenth-century England, Scotland and Wales. Whether in the 1500s or 1800s, British witchcraft 'was not sex-specific but it was sex-related'.[177]

Why, if you were unlucky enough to be deemed a witch, was there an almost 90 per cent chance you would also be a woman? An obvious place to start is with the theories of radical feminists, campaigners like the nineteenth-century suffragist Matilda Joslyn Gage, the twentieth-century anti-pornography activist Andrea Dworkin, and the scholars responsible for compiling the recent *Routledge International Encyclopedia of Women*.[178] They interpret witch-hunts as femicide or gynocide, killing of women because they are women, and see hostility to witchcraft as a facet of male domination, designed to attack females who refuse to conform to subordinate roles in the patriarchal system.[179] In the historian Marianne Hester's words, witchcraft accusations are: 'Ongoing mechanisms for social control of women ... a means of recreating the male status quo.'[180]

Some Victorian witches were independent women, who headed house-holds of children and grandchildren, or who lived alone and never married.[181] On average though, Victorian witches were no more independent or unorth-odox than Victorian women at large. In fact, judging by their personal lives, Victorian witches were rather less so. Of the 270 or so female witches referred to in the newspaper accounts, I managed to trace the marital status of 66, by linking them to the decennial census. Of the witches in this cohort, 12 per cent were single, roughly the same as for the female population generally.[182] A further 21.2 per cent of witches were widowed, while two-thirds (66.6 per cent) were married. Among the population as a whole, married women outnumber widowed and single women three to two.[183] Among the witches, the same figure was two to one. This means, contrary to the stereotype of the spinster sorcerer, that married women were over-represented as witches. Independent women were less likely to be accused of witchcraft, rather than more.

Radical feminist interpretations of witchcraft break down when we look closely at the people who accused women of practising sorcery. Half of the imputers were female. Of them, a fair minority were the sisters, daughters, nieces, aunts, cousins and in-laws of the women they accused. In the period of the witch trials, females made up almost half of the witnesses in court, though it has been suggested they were stage-managed by powerful men and so played only 'passive' roles in the process.[184] The Victorian women who accused and attacked witches certainly weren't passive. These modern witch-hunters brimmed with furious anger. Anne Brewer, from Merthyr in Wales, punched her niece in the face. The reason: Anne thought the niece had used mysterious powders to bewitch her daughters.[185] Bewitched people weren't troubled by nonconforming women. They were outraged by witch-craft. We can hear this in their words. 'She is one of them that can do things,' a Monmouthshire woman Mary Robins nervously said about her hated neighbour, Jane Ruddick.[186] Mary meant Jane was a witch, with the ability to kill with magic, if she pleased. 'You have had power over me long enough, and now I will be revenged,' muttered a sickly old man from the river-port Barnstaple, before he bloodied the lady he believed to be his witch.[187]

Women didn't preponderate among witches because they were victims of a cryptic form of social control. That's one explanation ruled out, but it leaves the vital question unanswered: why were most witches women? Here it is helpful to consider one of the many theories developed by scholars of the early modern European witch trials. Women, they suggest, were more often accused of witchcraft as they tended to be involved in the sort of tense, conflict-laden situations that brought sorcery to mind. This was because, compared to men, women were generally poorer, marginalised, and more likely to resort to verbal aggression rather than physical violence.[188]

This interpretation of witchcraft, as an outgrowth of poverty, has more purchase on the Victorian evidence. True, women's lives were improving during the late nineteenth century. There was a growing range of potential jobs (school teaching and clerical work, especially), and first-wave feminists were making the case for female political rights (women gained votes in local elections in 1869, although a property qualification meant they only formed somewhere between 12 and 17 per cent of the electorate).[189] Despite these gains, before the twentieth-century women's revolution dented traditional gender roles, most females endured extremely difficult existences. They earned considerably less than men, even for the same work, received worse education, and were limited by powerful social conventions. If her husband died, a wife didn't receive the old-age benefits he'd accrued with a trade union or friendly society.[190] This helps to explain why women formed the majority of paupers, perhaps as many as three-quarters.[191] Low wages meant that even fully employed widows could be practically destitute if they had children and grandchildren to support. If they weren't destitute, female-headed households were generally much poorer than male-headed households.[192] In an era of minimal state welfare (only 2.5 per cent of British people received poor relief in 1900), many thousands of women survived by seeking charity, or begging and borrowing from their neighbours, friends and relatives.[193] They were forced to put themselves in testy and desperate face-to-face situations that generated ill-feeling. So when troubled people concluded they were bewitched and looked around for the culprits, impoverished women were good candidates for witches.

As in the era of the witch trials, during the Victorian age some women survived in difficult circumstances by turning to sorcery: Harriet Hills, for example, a deformed woman from the Sussex seaside town of Hastings. Before she died, in 1892, Harriet lived for thirty years in the Hastings workhouse, where she enjoyed the rare privilege of being 'free from annoyance from the other inmates'. How did a decrepit woman avoid being bullied or robbed, by the tough folk she shared the workhouse wards with? Well, the other women didn't dare interfere with Harriet or her things because she was known as a witch who would curse anyone she crossed.[194] Harriet Hills certainly wasn't the only woman who used magic to protect herself. In 1862 Louisa Lewis, from the Somerset town of Frome, threatened to blood and bewitch a neighbour who'd beaten her children.[195] In 1873, at the South Molton petty sessions, Sarah Jane Loosemore was cautioned for threatening William Smith that she'd bewitch him if he didn't marry her or make her his housekeeper.[196] Beyond these anecdotes, the main reason women used witchcraft was to help them beg and extort. It worked for mendicants like Mary Ann Jones, who on 19 April 1894 called at the house of Mrs Bramley, near Henley Common in Surrey. She received bread and meat but Mary wanted money too, so threatened to witch Mrs Bramley if she didn't give her some. (Mrs Bramley gave her 1 shilling, but she also went to the police, and Mary received a week's hard labour.)[197]

Poverty and hardship explain why some Victorian witches were women. But these factors certainly don't account for all the cases. Some witches were respectable and lived in comfortable circumstances, with servants or family businesses employing numerous people.[198] Emotional power was a second reason why women were deemed witches. As in the era of the witch trials, women's authority within their families, including their ability to make or break their adult children's romantic relationships, led them into fractious encounters that festered into witchcraft suspicions.[199] In 1868 Hannah Down of Kingsbury, Somerset, was accused of witchcraft by a man who'd been romancing her daughter. Hannah had intervened to ensure the relationship was broken, so when the man fell ill, concluded it was sorcery and looked around for a suspect, she was an obvious candidate.[200] Another interfering mother who made herself look like a witch was Anne Bowerman, of Halberton in Devon. During the early 1860s she warned a girl who rejected her son's marriage proposal that 'there would be a death among them very shortly'. And there was: the girl's new husband did indeed expire soon after their wedding.[201]

So far we've looked at the minor, less significant reasons why witches were overwhelmingly women. The main reason lies elsewhere. It relates to the one thing that most of the women witches of Victorian Britain had in common: age. The youngest witch was 16, a servant girl accused by her master. The oldest was an impressive 90. But the majority of Victorian witches were middle-aged, not old by our standards, but certainly mature by the young demographic profile of the Victorian population. Of the 270 or so female witches mentioned in the newspaper accounts, I managed to establish the age of 80 of them. They were, on average, 55 years old: a similar age to Catherine McGougan, the shapeshifting witch of Gigha, whom we met in the case study.

In trying to explain why witches were invariably older women, it's tempting to conclude that they built up evil reputations over the course of longish lifetimes. Some witches undoubtedly did so, to devastating effect.[202] Yet not all witches were people of long-time ill repute, resulting from settled lives in stable communities. Suspicions fell on newcomers too, like Ellen Bowers, an Irishwoman living with her husband in the huts erected for the railway navvies building the Garsdale section of the (now unbelievably picturesque) Settle to Carlisle line. In 1874 Ellen was set upon by a fellow navvy and his wife, who hit her about the head with a poker, while accusing her of bewitching some pigs.[203]

Raw stereotyping was the reason why most witches were older females. The Victorians possessed a distinct image of witches being not just women but old women. The stereotype was there in promises made by cunning-folk, who persuaded their clients they were bewitched and said they'd 'completely annihilate the old witch' who was behind their troubles.[204] The phrase 'damned old witch' was on the lips of witchcraft vigilantes like John Davies, a brewer from Stratford-upon-Avon who cut the face of 58-year-old Jane Ward in the autumn of 1867.[205] But the term wasn't applied rigorously. Women were deemed to be 'old witches' even if they weren't old, like Lucy Denny, called an 'old witch' by her father-in-law and her neighbours, despite the fact that she was only 35.[206]

Why, exactly, was the Victorian witch stereotype an older woman? It was undoubtedly a robust stereotype, inherited from the past and with a long history behind it, stretching back until at least the period of the witch trials.

In part, it grew out of the idea that domestic magic fell within the female sphere of life, a domain over which wives and mothers had primary responsibility.[207] If women were the experts in magic then surely witches, who were unmatched in uncanny death dealing, were more likely to be female? Additionally, and in a way that is difficult to precisely fathom, the old female witch stereotype had a sexual component – a strange connection with erotic fantasies.[208]

During the era of the witch persecutions, witches were fantastical figures who 'broke every rule' by disregarding the laws of nature and conventional morality.[209] They did things normal folk couldn't but might secretly like to. Witches moved at unnatural speed. They acquired valuables without working. They defeated enemies with just a look or a word. And they partook in ecstatic sex.[210] In the Victorian period witches continued to be thought of as wild characters, though one wouldn't always know about their erotic activities from reading the work of nineteenth-century British folklorists and journalists. More so than their relatively liberated French colleagues, British writers heavily censored popular culture's sexual themes. In France, for example, scholars could describe the magical spells supposed to make a man impotent (tying a knot in a rat's tail, for instance).[211] Not so in Britain, where such things went unsaid, even in the more permissive atmosphere of the late nineteenth century. Occasionally though, something illicit slipped through, a suggestive fragment which points to a culture of bawdy storytelling, involving tales of extraordinary sensual escapades. In the Oxfordshire village of Stanton St John, at the close of the nineteenth century, people still whispered about a witch named Betty Cann, who'd lived a riotous life a generation earlier: 'Some of the older boys and men would go and look in at her window, or through the keyhole, and said as a fact that the old woman was dancing half-naked, and her old chairs were dancing too.'[212] We can learn a huge amount about witchcraft by combining the Victorian newspaper archive with the folklore record. Unfortunately, there's a void where the magic of sex should be.

*   *   *

Like today, during the later nineteenth century investigating witchcraft was extremely difficult. People who credited cursing, who believed in its reality and power, were reluctant to talk candidly about it. Partly because it was embarrassing to openly endorse a widely mocked idea. Partly because the enquirers asking about it, the folklorists, were remote and intimidating. Mostly because of a vague, unnerving feeling. You shouldn't talk about magic, not frankly and frivolously. Spells and charms stopped working if you told people about them. Utterances had an even worse effect on the devil and his agents, the witches. They might appear, or get angry, if loose-lipped individuals started blabbering about their malefic escapades. Don't speak of bad things: it makes them more likely to happen.

Because people who believed in witches didn't like talking about them, it's all too easy to underestimate late Victorian witchcraft, and to imagine the domain of evil magic was severely diminished, or had disappeared altogether, by the end of the nineteenth century. Attacks on witches certainly became much rarer from the 1870s. As the most conspicuous manifestations of witchcraft belief vanished, commentators settled into complacent mantras about magic being the province of savages and rustics.

But witchcraft was alive and potent. Witch-scratchings had waned through more active law enforcement, not decaying occult suspicions. Yes, everyday life was becoming more comfortable. True, the scope of mysterious misfortunes was contracting though only slightly. In hard times, in moments of dizzying despair and disorientating stress, uncanny fears swelled in many hearts. Not just among the obvious candidates – the denizens of the Highlands, the Western Isles of Scotland, the West Country and the marshes of East Anglia – but even in urban and industrial environs, magic flourished. Even in London, the Imperial metropolis. There was less witchery than in previous generations, but not greatly so. And when it appeared, witchcraft remained desperately serious, a vital and deadly matter.

Many of the events we've encountered in this chapter have been harmful, vindictive and violent. Given these destructive qualities, we might ask why something as damaging as witchcraft has made its way so persistently into human civilisation. How has it so often taken root, if it was so negative? Part of the answer, I think, is that witchcraft was not only damaging. The belief system conferred beneficent and beneficial effects on some of the people who managed to adhere to it. Unwitching, the process of removing witchcraft, was therapeutic and psychologically soothing, in times of great trial. Being attacked by black magic was undoubtedly traumatising. But with a cure came enormous relief. As we shall see in the next chapter, the primary benefit of witchcraft was in the healing.

FIVE

HEALING BLACK MAGIC
The unwitchers of late Victorian Britain

> So I went to the cunning-man, and he was very mysterious like.
> Cyril Thornton, *Conyers Lea* (London, 1862), p. 82

What distinguished cunning-folk from the other magicians of British history, like fortune-tellers and astrologers?

I used to think it was their ability to fight witchcraft. Repelling witches, I supposed, was something done by cunning-folk and by cunning-folk alone. Other professional magicians had different, less combative concerns. Among historians working on this topic, I was not unique in holding this view.[1] I must admit, though, I was wrong. It was actually revealed several decades ago, by Keith Thomas in *Religion and the Decline of Magic*, that during the period of the witch trials cunning-folk were not the only curers of witchcraft.[2] Others have reinforced the point that, during the seventeenth century, astrologers like William Lilly diagnosed and prescribed remedies to stop evil magic.[3]

It was similar during the nineteenth century. The Victorian newspaper archive provides abundant evidence that cunning-folk were not the only witch-busters. Urban fortune-tellers offered similar services. Like Harriet Gilbert of Wolverhampton, prosecuted in 1886 for diagnosing bewitchment and selling a defensive charm.[4] Or Catherine Gradwell of Bolton, jailed in

1899 after telling a client her family was bewitched, and recommending a magic potion of frogs, 'dragons' blood' (tree resin) and quicksilver.[5] Among agricultural communities, folk veterinarians known as 'cow doctors' and 'horse doctors' were occasionally called upon to remove witchcraft, if animals were afflicted.[6] Some beggars also claimed to have the ability to unwitch, as did Roma fortune-tellers. Because unwitching was not undertaken exclusively by cunning-folk, this chapter explores the work of a wider group of magicians, whom we might call the 'unwitchers' of later Victorian Britain.

Unwitchers combined the traits of magicians, business people and therapists. Crafty entrepreneurs but also spiritual healers, they probably helped their clients psychologically if not financially. But before making general remarks based on a wide range of cases, it seems apt to look at how the qualities of entrepreneur, magician and therapist were embodied in the life of an individual unwitcher. So we turn to the biography of Alexander Henderson, whom one journalist mistakenly designated 'the last Aberdeenshire Warlock'.

AN ABERDEENSHIRE WARLOCK: ON THE TRAIL OF ALEXANDER HENDERSON, ALIAS 'YOUNG SKAREY'

In Scotland, it was not unusual for cunning-men to be called 'warlocks'.[7] Darkly awesome figures, they were envisaged as being more powerful but also more dangerous than 'canny-women', females with special expertise in fighting butter witches, the stealers of milk and spoilers of butter feared by farmers throughout the north.[8] After all, it was not God who gave warlocks their powers, or not only God. Their lord was Beelzebub, Satan, the Dragon, the Angel of the Bottomless Pit. 'The Deil', as nervous Scots called him, made pacts with warlocks, accepting their souls in exchange for a tiny share of his terrible power.[9] According to some, warlocks couldn't set a foot in church for seven years after making their dark bargains.

Alexander Henderson, the Aberdeenshire Warlock, lived most of his life in a one-room cottage near the village of Meikle Wartle.[10] He clearly wasn't the wealthiest warlock in Scotland. He wasn't the most celebrated, either. That accolade went to the Willox family, a clan of wizards from Tomintoul in Banffshire, famed for possessing a magical crystal given to them by a mermaid, and a special leather girdle stolen long ago from a kelpie (water spirit).[11] Henderson, the 'warlock of Wartle', as some knew him, was notable for another reason. By chance, he became one of the best-documented professional magicians in Victorian Britain.

As well as featuring in the decennial census, Alexander Henderson was the topic of numerous local stories. Like a surprising number of cunning-folk, when he died he received an obituary in a local paper. Unusually, two local journalists interviewed Alexander during the autumn of 1879, resulting in four lengthy biographical articles. By then the warlock was over 80 years old, still practising the mystic arts and working as a cobbler too, his first trade. A short and slightly stooped man, who'd obviously been handsome in his youth, he had a furrowed face and 'expressive blue eyes', always glinting with humour. Inviting his interviewers to rest awhile by his fire, smoke a pipe of tobacco and take a drink, Alexander finished repairing a pair of shoes. He wore a sleeved waistcoat, rough tweed trousers, a leather apron and, though it was nowhere near bedtime, a red and blue striped nightcap. As he stitched, stories, epigrams and quotations from the King James Bible fell from his lips. His hearers found it impossible not to be impressed. A 'wonderful old man' was before them. But strangely, and sadly from our point of view, when the talk concluded, Alexander wouldn't pose for a photograph.

Actually, his refusal wasn't odd. Being a warlock meant treading a narrow, difficult, precarious path. People like Alexander cultivated reputations for knowing 'more than they ought', as the saying went. It helped to draw the attention of potential clients. Cunning-folk also needed to evade the clutches of the authorities, who prohibited making financial gains out of 'pretenses' to magic. Alexander had to be clever, sneaky, tricky, imposing, convincing, theatrical and difficult to pin down. The documents describing his life reflect, above all, his ability to perform different identities and roles, as the situation required.

The contradictions began with his birth. When he was interviewed in 1879, Alexander said he was born precisely on 19 September 1791, in the Glens of Foundland. But the 1881 census records Alexander as being born around 1796, some five years later. Whether or not he exaggerated his age slightly to seem a little more venerable, Mr Henderson certainly experienced a terrifically long life by the standards of his time, enjoying many years of 'almost unbroken good health' before departing this world during the unusually snowy December of 1888, having exceeded his ninetieth birthday. Alexander's father was the tenant at Skares Farm, from whence he got the nickname 'Auld Skarey', which Alexander inherited in the form of 'Young Skarey'. Sadly, soon after his son's birth, Henderson senior went down in the world, becoming a travelling fish seller, and making money on the side by selling charms and magical services. With few pennies to spare, Alexander received little formal education. But the naturally bright and inquisitive lad learnt his letters anyway, becoming a keen reader. Needing to support himself as early as possible, he was apprenticed young to be a shoemaker, a venerable artisanal trade practised by many autodidacts. He spent several years working as a cobbler in Aberdeen. But then a travelling theatre company came to town. When they left Alexander went with them, lured away by the romance of life on the road.

In 1821 Alexander had had enough of roving and moved back to Aberdeenshire. In the county of his birth, known for its dairy farms and fishing communities, he set up as a shoemaker, practising his father's second trade as a warlock on the side. Travelling players had to quickly strike deals whenever they arrived in a new place, and perhaps these skills helped Alexander persuade a local laird to give him a plot of land, apparently rent free, at the Drum of Wartle. His new home was a tiny settlement near the village of Meikle Wartle, little more than a few cottages scattered around a crossroads. Alexander himself built his one-roomed cottage. The journalists who interviewed him in the autumn of 1879 called it a 'rude edifice' blessed with a vegetable plot, large enough but only one storey high, with its door and most of its windows facing out to the road. Inside was a scene of 'picturesque confusion'. A bed lay in the corner. Books sat on windowsills. Bottles served as candleholders. The only stools faced a peat fire, guarded by nothing but rocks to stop the embers flying. Unlike the Scottish Highlanders, and in common with most Aberdeenshire folk, Henderson the warlock was a speaker of Doric, a regional dialect of lowland Scots, which in turn was not quite a separate language from English, but different enough to be no mere dialect either.[12] Had you met Alexander, that bright autumn day, you'd probably have understood him, just.

For three-quarters of a century Alexander Henderson lived a humble yet independent life, at the Drum of Wartle. He told the journalists he'd a prodigious memory, which during his days with the players allowed him to memorise 260 lines in one session, by reading them through just twice. Given the biblical quotations always upon his lips ('it would be difficult to meet with one who has a more extensive acquaintance with his Bible, or who can quote Scripture texts more glibly'), it seems likely Alexander was telling the truth. But it's harder to trust the other things he said that day, particularly when he assured the journalists: 'There's nae sic a thing as witchcraft, tho' some fowk believ't.' Could the warlock of Wartle, famed miles around for his occult powers, really disbelieve in the reality of sorcery?

Almost certainly not. Maybe Henderson vacillated from scepticism to belief and back again, making himself credit uncanny powers during the moments when he was actually doing magic. This was the sort of thing that cunning-folk asked their clients to do. Or perhaps, when he professed scepticism, Alexander was misleading the two nosey gentlemen who were prying into his sensitive, clandestine work. He admitted he knew the 'horseman's words', secret terms acquired during his roving days, giving him power over the best of the farm animals. He also understood which herbs hindered or helped a cow's ability to give milk.

It hardly matched the grand claims made about Alexander in local stories. Reputedly, the warlock of Wartle removed witchcraft from people and beasts, aiding farmers and their wives in desperate times, when butter refused to churn, horses grew agitated and cows dried up. As well as locating stolen or lost property, he laid restive ghosts and troublesome 'deils' (devils), using obscure hieroglyphics in his rituals and drawing protective circles around the terrified householders. Anyone who cheeked Henderson, who said his professed abilities were 'rubbish' and nothing else, could expect their cynicism to be repaid with an uncanny punishment of the warlock's devising. But there was a tale about a couple of jokers who fooled Alexander one evening by begging him to go to their friend's house several miles away, where his expertise was apparently needed. Alexander duly set out. When he finally arrived, in the dead of night, the household was abed, neither expecting nor welcoming his visit.

By the time Alexander Henderson died, late in 1888, experts on Scottish culture like the Rev. Walter Gregor, a founding member of the Folklore Society and local resident, were insisting that witchcraft was fast disappearing, scared away by the 'scream of the railway whistle'.[13] Living conditions in Aberdeenshire, like those across most of Britain, were certainly improving. Even this remote north-eastern county, once the heartland of the Picts, the site of more ancient standing stones than anywhere else, was feeling the impact of modern ways and manners.[14] Since the opening of the Aberdeen railway in 1850, much more beef and other local agricultural products were being sold in London.[15] A herring-processing industry had sprung up on the North Sea coast, fed by steamships and an international market for cured fish.[16] In another sign of increasing civilisation, farm servants, the least experienced and worst-paid workers, were becoming politically articulate, forming their own trade union in the spring of 1872 to agitate for better wages and conditions.[17] Probably they were better fed and housed than their colleagues in England. A survey conducted in 1900 found Aberdeenshire folk to be unusually tall, standing on average at 5 ft 9 in.[18] This was likely a result of a diet that included very little meat but lots of milk, oatcakes, vegetables, broth, porridge and potatoes, washed down with plenty of brose (an oatmeal drink, flavoured with honey or whisky, if you're lucky).[19]

For all the advances and relative comforts, we shouldn't exaggerate the degree of ease prevailing in north-eastern Scotland, during the late Victorian era. Poverty remained widespread, work was limited, and in the 1880s agricultural prices began to fall because of competition with farmers from Australasia and South America.[20] Droves of youngsters emigrated, well into the twentieth century. Despite the opening up of new markets and the arrival of new industries, the people of Aberdeenshire lived hard and uncomfortable lives, particularly the Irish Travellers who traversed the county, but also many settled residents. To take a nasty illustration: until at least the 1920s rural areas were blighted by repeated outbreaks of typhoid fever, a terrible disease which brought death after weeks of diarrhoea and intestinal perforations.[21]

When northern Scotland's folklorists and journalists said witchcraft was dying or 'exploded', we should be wary.[22] Perhaps it was diminishing, but a steady flow of newspaper reports prove that concerns about the occult were far from extinct. During the 1880s there were still bewitched farmers and housewives who accused their neighbours of stealing milk by uncanny means.[23] In 1883 a woman from Inverness caused a local scandal by claiming she was the victim of a 'corp creagh', a clay image used for maleficent magic.[24] In the Highland county of Ross-shire, the following year, an entire township was deemed bewitched when three cows died in the wake of a quarrel, caused by the tenants driving away Travellers who'd stopped to graze their horses.[25] In 1885 another Ross-shire township was the site of similar accusations, this time against a couple of local residents, who were said to have used witchcraft to kill 13 of the 34 beasts kept by the tenant farmers.[26]

Witchcraft suspicions undoubtedly persisted in late nineteenth-century Aberdeenshire. Across the county, stories about shapeshifters and ill-wishers continued to be told, with vigour and much insistence on their truth. According to one anecdote, a servant girl from Strachan, ordered by her master to skin a hare, refused on the grounds that 'it micht be somebody's granny!'[27] Throughout the nineteenth century and beyond, rowan trees were planted near farmhouses and carefully cultivated, in the belief that they'd ward off evil occult influences.[28] But the best way we can deduce the persistence of witchcraft in this region is from the late career of Alexander Henderson himself. During his twilight years before his death in 1888, to a degree that 'would surprise many', he was consulted by grateful clients, who journeyed great distances to hear his diagnosis and subject themselves to his therapies. These farmers and their wives, godly but suspicious people, neither easily fooled nor free with their money, clearly got something of value from the warlock of Wartle. As the journalist who wrote his obituary noted: 'Skarey's services were apt to be regarded as useful.'[29]

CUNNING-FOLK

The history of witchcraft is partly a capitalistic tale of money-making and entrepreneurship, satisfied customers and egregious frauds. This is because, in times of crisis, when conventional remedies failed and dark forces seemed to be at play, desperate people gladly paid for expert help. Demand for unwitching services, for professional assistance in diagnosing and curing witchcraft, remained strong throughout the nineteenth century. Some commentators even suggested it was increasing, as better policing stopped bewitched people from healing themselves by ritualistically attacking their witches.[30]

An exaggeration, but undoubtedly there were lucrative opportunities for entrepreneurs with a feeling for magic, medicine and human psychology. As well as being financially attractive, this line of work offered an unusual kind of status and autonomy. Being an unwitcher was a sole-trader or consultant type of role, suitable for independent self-starters who thrived on new challenges. Had there been a job advert it would have asked for someone passionate about magic, with a good deal of verbal dexterity including a talent for riddling, an appreciation of time management, preferably the ability to write (knowledge of Latin an advantage), charisma, emotional resilience, stamina, strong interpersonal skills, along with the capacity to lead, problem solve, plan and inspire.[31] A flair for publicity was important, to generate a client base. Still more vital was a detailed knowledge of the law. To succeed in this difficult but profitable industry you needed more than a mastery of the occult sciences. You also had to be canny, observant, unscrupulous, confident to the point of intimidating and very difficult to get the better of.

Beyond those general qualities, the unwitchers of later Victorian Britain were a varied lot. The wealthiest and most prestigious were cunning-folk.[32] Typically though not exclusively male, cunning-folk possessed a wide array of magical skills, including the ability to tell fortunes, draw astrological charts, cast love spells, find stolen goods, heal animals and people, and cure witchcraft. Some wielded magic for evil, to harm their clients' enemies. Most claimed their powers came from the Abrahamic God or his antagonist, the devil. Susannah Bond, the Plymouth white witch, told her clients 'God had sent her to do all the cures.'[33] A cunning-man arrested in the Devon town of Dawlish in 1890, by contrast, implied satanic connections by menacingly saying he knew 'Jack the Ripper', the unidentified Whitechapel murderer.[34]

Whether their powers came from heaven or hell, cunning-folk were masters of an elaborate Christian white magic, which used scriptural readings, Latin biblical phrases, and even physical Bibles to empower its rituals. Yet their frame of magical reference extended far beyond Christianity. Cunning-folk's consulting rooms brimmed with arcana – skulls, books, manuscripts, herbs, crystal balls, robes and perhaps even unique occult artifacts. The wise-woman of Templecombe, Somerset, was known for her black wand.[35] Mention has already been made of the Willox family's magic crystal and leather girdle.[36] These objects were used in rituals conducted in the consulting room, but if the situation seemed sufficiently dire and lucrative enough, cunning-folk might propose their most expensive service: travelling to their clients' homes to work magic, often spending the night, occasionally staying for the week.[37] Another line of income came from making and selling herbal concoctions and other potent items such as written charms, healing amulets and witch-bottles.[38]

Cunning-folk plied their trades just about everywhere, in the countryside, towns and even industrial cities, during the mid-Victorian period. Writing in 1862, a folklorist from Leeds claimed to know three or four wise-men, all of whom were 'above mere fortune-tellers', and who, 'up to a very few years ago, carried on a thriving business'.[39] In western England, cunning-folk could be found in town on certain weekdays, selling their wares in the marketplace or offering consultations in the semi-privacy of an inn.[40] Three were touting for clients in Penzance, on the tip of Cornwall, one market day in the spring of 1869.[41] At Stalbridge, a town in Dorset, a local cunning-man held an annual 'toad fair' during the 1870s, where people thronged the streets, jostling with each other to buy his magic bags, containing one of the animal's limbs, which protected against scrofula and the evil eye.[42] In 1889 the *Western Morning News* complained about a cunning-man living in the Devon countryside who'd established an office in the market town of Launceston, and who went monthly to Okehampton, on the edge of Dartmoor, for consultations.[43] His professional routine was not unusual, across Somerset, Cornwall and Devon, where cunning-folk called regularly at particular villages.[44] Billy Brewer (*c.* 1815–90), a cunning-man from Taunton in Somerset, was known to work the settlements around the moors 'for weeks together', staying at his clients' homes, where he was apparently given the best bed, in the belief that luck followed the wise-man's presence.[45] Cunning-folk made similar rounds at the opposite end of Britain, in Caithness, on the north-east tip of Scotland, where they travelled between villages on the coast, offering to cure animals and summon fair winds for the fishermen.[46]

By the later nineteenth century, magnetism, mesmerism and the mystique of science were influencing some cunning-folk. A few enacted magic with ostentatiously modern pseudoscientific paraphernalia, or said they did. William Chambers of Wells drove out witchcraft by burning drugs bought from the pharmacist, and – he said – by consulting a mysterious but unspecified 'instrument'.[47] Nothing matching that description was found when the police raided his offices in 1898, but the cunning-man did possess numerous fortune-telling books, along with a list of over 200 clients. John Harper, a white witch from West Down in Devon, used manganese and iron rods in his cures, with bits of paper attached to the ends bearing the names of planets. In court in 1877, Harper's advocate explained how the rods worked: 'The patient was to take the piece of manganese between the finger and thumb, and by striking it with the rod, either end, being the positive or the negative as the case may be, would emit or would bring into force some electric current.' The court was not impressed. Harper was jailed for a month (though his sentence was later quashed).[48] Mary Ann Ivey of Pool, Cornwall, told her clients a Roma fortune-teller had taught her how to cure ill-wishes, and claimed to possess a special machine, with a face and hands like a clock, which consumed particular 'chemicals'. The unscrupulous unwitcher probably owned no such machine, but she showed what she said was its box to a suspicious client in 1880. Mary was eventually reported to the police and imprisoned for three months, but not before she used talk of her box to elicit £40 from one female customer.[49]

Cunning-folk were big characters, notorious among their neighbours, known throughout their counties and beyond. When they died, they were among the few notables to receive obituaries in the local press.[50] They were well known because they cultivated their reputations to attract clients. As in earlier periods, cunning-folk made themselves conspicuous by dressing flamboyantly. John Collander cut an eccentric figure in the Devon town of Newton Abbot, during the 1860s, by wearing medals and a 'profusion of long ringlets'.[51] Bell Royal, an elderly wise-woman from Caithness, wore petticoats on the bottom, a man's vest and coat on the top, and a thick moustache on her lip.[52] Until his death in 1890 Billy Brewer, the Somerset wiseman and pipe-maker by trade, was recognised 'all the county round', with his numerous rings, Inverness cloak and a sombrero hat, from whence tumbled his dishevelled grey wig.[53]

Magicians like Billy Brewer encouraged talk about their mystic powers by spreading stories about their dealings with the devil and familiar spirits. But few cunning-men or wise-women spoke too openly or brashly about their abilities. It would have been dangerous folly, and not just because of the risk of prosecution. Frank talk about magic tempted God and fate. Riddles and hints, innuendo and obscurity were the proper ways of communicating about this mysterious domain. An enigmatic mode of discourse became second nature to James Stacey, ostensibly a miller but really a cunning-man from South Petherton in Somerset. He did his rounds at night, garnering an unsavoury reputation in the process, so much so that villagers from West Chinnock mobbed him one evening in January 1883. The unwitcher summoned nine of them for assault but his prosecution failed because he couldn't stop riddling, to the exasperation of the magistrates. (When they asked about his profession, Stacey replied: 'What I do do I do do, the same as you. You can't do any more if you wish to.')[54] Cunning-folk saw themselves as presiding over a necessarily secret body of knowledge. When charms or rites were plainly spoken about, they lost their effect.[55]

Medical pretensions and legal threats also made cunning-folk talk obscurely about their work. When speaking to census recorders and the compilers of local trade directories they were doctors, nurses, physicians, herbalists or veterinarians. Others passed themselves off as farmers, if they owned a smallholding, or as artisans like stonemasons or shoemakers.[56] A few had the temerity to advertise themselves, in provincial newspapers, as 'planet rulers', 'casters of nativities' and 'professors' of astrology.[57] Critics – journalists, clergymen and magistrates – dismissed them as quacks and cheats, swindlers and frauds. Mockers, joking in private with their friends, derided them as 'piss prophets' and worse. But most people whispered in more respectful tones, especially those who'd heard tales about their mystic powers or met these invariably intimidating persons as they did their rounds. Ordinary folk called them clever-men, wise-women and cunning-folk. In Devon and much of the West of England, they were 'whitwitches'.[58] In Cornwall, they were 'pellers', probably a derivation of repellers – persons able to repel evil magic.[59] In Wales, particularly, they were conjurors. In Scotland, as already noted, they were known as 'warlocks' and 'canny-women', as well as 'wizards', 'skilly-wives', 'spae-wives' and 'those who know'.[60]

Even during the final decades of the nineteenth century, many cunning-folk earned good livings. A wise-woman visiting the Scottish village of Avoch, in 1864, received a hen in payment for charming a cow, a piece of silver and a dram of whisky for bringing good winds to the fishermen, and dinner and lodging for telling fortunes and wishing ill upon a client's enemy.[61] During the 1860s and 1870s the so-called 'Conjuror of Troedlone', Llanidloes, was known throughout mid-Wales, with clients from Cardiganshire, Breconshire and Radnorshire. From curing cursed fields, bewitched cattle, sterile women and such like, he earned enough money to buy a horse and trap, and reroof his house.[62] Susannah Bond, a wise-woman from Plymouth, was financially secure enough to afford a servant and assistant.[63]

A few cunning-folk made huge sums, notably Edward Manning, 'surgeon' and 'doctor' as he styled himself, 'wizard Manning' as his neighbours knew him. He died in 1876, at the impressive age of 84, a dominant figure in the Northamptonshire village of Croughton. With an estimated £35,000 in cash and a 170-acre farm employing at least fourteen people, Wizard Manning's holdings placed him among the 36,000 greatest landowners in England. And it had all been got by magic. Beginning in 1819, aged 27, Edward had taken up the family trade, becoming like his father and brother a 'water doctor'. This meant combining the archaic medical technique of urine scrying with herbalism and more obviously supernatural remedies, in order to heal the unwell and cure the bewitched. During his 57-year career Manning successfully evaded prosecution, and though he was occasionally named in court cases and denounced by the local press, he died with a considerable local reputation. His herd of pigs were said to be his familiars, and there was something uncanny about the 'gaunt, black horse on which he was accustomed to visit outpatients'. Some said it possessed more knowledge than ought to be found in nature. When it and the wizard went out riding, 'his fiery little eyes glancing suspiciously in every direction', the people of Croughton quickly got out of the way. Apparently, even the pompous parish clerk 'cared not to meet the uncanny couple after sundown'.[64]

Admittedly, other cunning-folk endured wretched lives. None more so than 'Old Dummy', who died of pneumonia in 1863 after the villagers of Sible Hedingham, Essex, threw him in a stream. Deaf, dumb and homeless, 'Dummy' scratched a living by begging and telling fortunes, in the process making himself the terror of the neighbourhood.[65] 'Whistler' Brown, a respected wise-man from the same county, was scarcely better off, ending his life as a resident of the Risbridge Workhouse.[66] Doing magic for a living was not a particularly easy job for James Pullan, a wise-man from Otley, West Yorkshire. He nearly destroyed his marriage by carrying on his occult business against the wishes of his wife. She complained that he stayed up all night working with his 'witchcraft instruments', and that she was forced to endure all sorts of awkward callers looking to have their fortunes told, property located, beasts cured and the like. In 1873 they fought, and James even tried (unsuccessfully) to have her prosecuted for assault.[67]

Cunning-men and wise-women led difficult lives, not least because they had to compete for clients with magicians who offered similar services at a fraction of the price. Those competitors are the subjects of the next section: fortune-tellers.

FROM CARDS TO CURSES: FORTUNE-TELLING

Cunning-folk were not the only professional unwitchers selling their services to the late Victorian public. Most bewitched people would have found it cheaper and easier to consult fortune-tellers, many of whom also diagnosed and combated witchcraft.

The downside was that fortune-tellers offered less impressive therapies, lacking the sort of elaborate Christian white magic practised by cunning-folk. Mostly women, fortune-tellers pursued their subtle arts just about everywhere, in rural villages and market towns, in smart neighbourhoods to genteel clients, in poor areas to humble folks, in great industrial cities and in new seaside resorts like Blackpool and Skegness. Notionally the Vagrancy Act of 1824 prohibited their work, though the law was never fully or systematically enforced. Held back by only modest legal encumbrances, as the nineteenth century drew to a close there was a discernible increase in the practice and public profile of this type of magic, which critics derided as 'signs and products of decadence'.[68]

By 1900 it was estimated that Britain contained as many as 30,000 'astrologers, diviners, and quacks of all kinds'.[69] Along with becoming more prevalent, fortune-telling was evolving into a more professional occupation, with its own periodicals like *Palmist's Review* (from 1889), an annually compiled *Directory of Character Readers* (from 1894) and supporting institutions such as the Chirological Society of London.[70] Customers came from all social classes but fortune-tellers were notorious for catering to female servants, the largest category of women workers during the Victorian period. Dealing from a pack of cards or peering into a crystal ball, fortune-tellers offered their clients tantalising answers to life's most pressing questions. How long would they remain in their current job? Were their friends really true? When would they set up a home of their own, and where? Would they travel, perhaps even emigrate? How many children might they have? How long would they live? Would they or their relatives ever get well? And most common of all: what sort of man would they marry?

Beyond unveiling the future, fortune-tellers offered other useful magical services. For romantically frustrated customers, they might attract or infatuate the objects of their affections, usually by burning mystical powders over a fire while muttering incantations. For victims of crime they could locate stolen goods, by revealing details of the criminal's identity. Unwitching therapies too were sold by fortune-tellers like Marian Wood of Halifax, who like many of her colleagues worked with cards and a crystal, and claimed to be overwhelmed with clients when she was prosecuted for a fourth time, in July 1880. On that occasion, she was arrested after informing a customer that her family was bewitched by a grey-haired man, and offering to make a potion that would 'kill or cure' her husband.[71] Mary Ann Harvey, alias 'Brown Nell' of Dudley, provided similar services. She'd enjoyed a decade-long career as a fortune-teller, working largely using cards, by the time she was prosecuted in December 1881, for diagnosing a police informant as bewitched, and offering to break the spell for an additional sixpence.[72] The smoky manufacturing towns of the West Midlands were home to many people like her, as were other urban centres including Salford, Manchester, Durham, Sheffield and Ipswich.[73] If they were unlucky enough ever to find themselves in court, these fortune-tellers claimed to be leading virtuous lives. Elizabeth Elwell, 72, a well-dressed fortune-teller of considerable standing in Wednesbury, West Midlands, maintained rather implausibly that she gave away her earnings in charity to beggars.[74] In reality, though they provided services of much perceived value, there was an unseemly side to fortune-telling. Some practitioners claimed to possess the power to bewitch, laying deadly curses on their clients' enemies, unwanted spouses or relatives. In 1862 Alice Vicars, a fortune-teller from Manchester, asked for £1 in return for using witchcraft to kill her client's husband.[75] In 1860, a wise-woman from Bacup, Lancashire, was accused of offering to bewitch a child.[76]

Abortion, which before 1967 was not available legally, was the most dangerous service provided by Victorian fortune-tellers.[77] Not all undertook this risky work, punished more severely in Britain than anywhere else in Europe, but those who did tended to use concoctions of their own devising, combining them with card readings and perhaps even talk of witchcraft. So discovered Emily Andrew, a recently married young woman from Barnsley, South Yorkshire, who in 1889 caught the train to Rotherham to consult a fortune-teller named Annie Jones. At her rooms in Pigeon Lane, the fortune-teller produced a pack of cards and asked her client to cut them three times. Having seen women like Emily before, with unexpected pregnancies, Annie sensed what was wanted, but approached the point through the cards, interpreting them as meaning: 'You must not return to your husband; he cohabits with another woman – he is a deceiver and will kill you.' She handed over a bottle of medicine, prepared with ingredients from the pharmacist, saying it had helped many in Emily's condition. But to pay for it, Emily must pawn her wedding ring (the fortune-teller's little daughter was charged with taking it to the pawnbroker). For a little more money, Annie offered to 'witch' Emily's husband to stop him talking. Emily agreed, but on her train journey home she had a change of heart, threw the bottle of 'noxious substance' out of the carriage window, and went to the police. For breaching the Vagrancy Act of 1824 by telling fortunes, Annie was jailed for a month. The charge of trying to procure an abortion could not be proved.[78]

Like all magicians, fortune-tellers improvised, seized the moment, and used their intuition. But they also worked with specific techniques and according to general principles. These they acquired from relatives, experience, the oral tradition and literary sources. Grimoires, elaborate spellbooks popular in Europe and America, were too taboo for British publishers before the decadent final decades of the nineteenth century. By 1899 the environment was liberal enough to permit the publication of *Consult the Oracle*, a 200-plus page compendium of knowledge about 'the unseen world', from fighting witchcraft and the evil eye to the prevention of dreams, written by a mysterious fellow named Gabriel Nostradamus. Published by C. Arthur Pearson, one of Britain's three big publishers, *Consult the Oracle* became a bestseller, going through three editions in ten months.[79]

Before the 1890s, would-be magicians learnt their craft by purchasing fortune-telling manuals. These cheap pamphlet guides to a limited range of occult arts formed what was apparently the third most popular genre in British publishing (following the Bible and almanacs).[80] Often with no acknowledged author, churned out by London publishers like W.S. Fortey of Bloomsbury, perhaps with a few splashes of colour on their crudely illustrated covers, they were used by professional fortune-tellers like Sabina Lee of Brighton. Arrested in July 1885, Sabina was found in possession of several dubious publications, including the notorious *Norwood Gypsy's Fortune Teller*.[81] Named after a Roma group living on the outskirts of London, the *Norwood Gypsy's Fortune Teller* explained how to tell a husband's character from his hair-type (black = 'stout and healthy, but apt to be cross and surly'; red = wild, artful, loving and deceitful). The guide also revealed how to predict someone's fate from their moles, how to see a future spouse in an apparition or dream, and how to divine a person's destiny by reading their palm. The *Norwood Gypsy's Fortune Teller* got close to describing how to do maleficent witchcraft, with its spell to detect whether a sweetheart intended marriage. An unmarried woman was to borrow a pen-knife, without explaining why, acquire the blade bone of a shoulder of lamb, and before bed every night, for nine consecutive nights, stab the bone while repeating the rhyme:

Tis not this bone I mean to stick,
But my lover's heart I mean to prick,
Wishing him neither rest or sleep,
Til he comes to speak.

After nine days the victim would appear, asking for something to bind a wound. One can imagine how this ritual, with its mysterious rhyming spell, principles of sympathetic magic and emphasis on regularity, could have been adapted for darker uses.[82]

From wealthy cunning-folk to wandering fortune-tellers, British magicians had practised palmistry since at least Tudor times. Crystal balls were also used by well-heeled occultists during the early modern period, though they became much more widespread in the Victorian era, when mass production made them more affordable. In the meantime, other ancient methods of divination waned, such as the technique of placing shears in a sieve while two people held a handle each, watching how the shears moved as questions were posed.[83] Notorious during the 1500s, this cumbersome rite was replaced, over the eighteenth and nineteenth centuries, by more convenient divinatory methods like card reading.

Thought to originate either in China or India, playing cards have their first European references in Italy and Switzerland during the 1370s.[84] But it was not until much later, with advances in printing technology, that card reading became the indispensable skill of modern fortune-tellers. The first British guide to the art was published around 1730.[85] Over a century and a half later, in 1893, it was clear to the *Pall Mall Gazette* that, of all the modes of divination, 'probably more faith is placed' in cartomancy, fortune-telling with cards.[86] Tellingly, three of the seven pages of the *Norwood Gypsy's Fortune Teller* (1861) were devoted to divination with cards, using an ordinary gaming pack of fifty-two cards, made up of four suits. Those wanting to know their life's course were instructed to select a card representing themselves (the significator), then surround that card by laying the rest of the deck out in rows of eight. After the cards were turned over, those touching the significator were taken to be particularly telling. Generally, spades boded ill, with the nine, 'the worst card in the whole pack', portending illness and loss of wealth.

Decks designed explicitly for fortune-telling, usually about thirty-two cards, lacking suits but bearing written warnings and symbolic images, had been in use since at least the late 1700s.[87] Yet the tarot, an evocative deck of picture cards and suits, did not arrive in Britain until a century later. Originating as a gaming deck in fifteenth-century Italy, by the eighteenth century French, German and Swiss versions were being produced. The number of cards and the images upon them varied, but all tarot decks were made up of a smaller set of trump cards bearing the most resonant archetypes (the chariot, the tower, the wizard, the fool, in some occult-orientated decks), and a larger set of four suits. Widely used in Alsace and the Franche Comté, as well as Switzerland and Germany, during the 1860s tarot decks were 'known only as curiosities in London and Paris'.[88] This changed largely because of the later Victorian occult revival. In 1888 Samuel MacGregor Mathers, occultist and founder member of the Hermetic Order of the Golden Dawn, an elite magical society, published the first English guide to the deck and its use in fortune-telling.[89] By the late 1890s London's fortune-tellers, catering to genteel clients in smart parts of town, were using the tarot.[90] Among the half-dozen clairvoyants and palmists advertising on the front page of the *Morning Post* in 1898 was 'Lachesis', a 'scientific and institutional palmist' who, during the autumn season, occupied rooms on Old Bond Street, where she conducted readings with tarot cards.[91] Yet it was not until the 1910s, after the occultist A.E. Waite published his interpretation of the deck in collaboration with the African-American artist Pamela Colman Smith, that the tarot became the staple of provincial fortune-telling.

Fortune-tellers didn't just reveal what would come to pass. They also used magic to bring their predictions about, or to change them. Adelina Westernoff, working in Chesterfield in 1888, informed one client that her husband would die but told her not to worry because she'd marry another, rich man.[92] To induce this Adelina 'put a wish' on the men and constructed a well-known love charm, costing 3 shillings. It began with a purchase of so-called dragon's blood (a tree resin) from the druggist. This was combined, in a corked bottle, with a pin-stabbed heart-shaped piece of paper, bearing her name, and some mysterious powder, all to be carried around by her breast. The fortune-teller also gave her client three pieces of paper to burn, containing various love spells.

Fortune-telling was a 'profitable industry' from which it was possible to make a good wage.[93] Silver worth £30 was found among the belongings of Mary Ford, a fortune-teller and reputed witch, when she was admitted to Exminster Asylum in 1860.[94] Ann Fare, a widow from Cullompton in Devon, was able to maintain her children and grandchildren by revealing the future, discovering stolen goods, and curing witchcraft for clients rich and poor.[95] During the 1860s and early 1870s 'respectably dressed persons' were often seen calling at her little house, openly and publicly patronising her illegal business, in a smart country town that was home to two clergymen, one of whom was a magistrate. Ann worked her esoteric trade despite being illiterate (her surname was spelled differently in the censuses of 1871 and 1881), and following a tough upbringing, one consequence of which was that she didn't know exactly when she was born (1819 or 1820). For over a decade the local authorities left her undisturbed, but this changed in 1873 when Ann made the mistake of greedily overcharging a young client with an interfering mother, who not only demanded that Ann return the money but also reported her to the police. After serving three weeks in Exeter jail, Ann went back to Cullompton, officially working as a laundress, probably selling esoteric services on the side.

Like cunning-folk, fortune-tellers were sharp, clever, tough, quick and intuitive. But in late Victorian Britain, there was a final category of professional magicians who cultivated those qualities to an even greater degree: Roma people.

ROMA GO 'DUKKERIN'

Roma fortune-tellers, who were almost exclusively women, were prolific unwitchers. They were among the tens and perhaps hundreds of thousands of itinerants who spent their springs, summers and autumns travelling around Britain, living outdoors, sleeping in tents or caravans, cooking on open fires. As winter fell, most Roma people rented rooms in town. When the first signs of spring appeared, they gathered their belongings and got back on the road.[96]

Travellers, commonly called 'tinkers' and found especially in Scotland, were itinerants of Gaelic or Irish extraction. The Roma were different. Victorians usually called them 'gypsies'. The name is now controversial because, as late nineteenth-century scholars recognised, the Roma did not actually come from Egypt, as the name 'gypsies' implied. Instead, Roma people were descended partly from ancestors who over many centuries had made a long migration from India to Europe.[97] First arriving in large numbers in England around the year 1500, and in Scotland a little earlier, they initially endured heavy persecution. By the 1700s, a fair degree of mixing and inter-marriage had occurred with the host population of 'gorgios', the Romany word for settled people.[98] By the end of the nineteenth century there were an estimated 20,000 to 25,000 Roma, formed into various regional groups or highly extended families such as the Woods, Williams and Joneses of Wales, and the Boswells and Bucklands of England.[99]

As those British-sounding names suggest, Roma were not a remote or insular people. Their culture bore marks of its ancient eastern origins, from the musical scales Roma played on their fiddles to the Sanskrit-like Romany language.[100] But Roma were also nimble and open to change, attuning them-selves to life in the regions of Scotland, England and Wales where the various Roma groups spent most of their time. One indication of this was the fact that, by the later nineteenth century, Romany people often spoke several languages, including regional variants of both English and Romany, and an Anglo-Romany hybrid called *pogadi jib*.[101] Roma people's willingness to adapt was also evident in their famous caravans, or 'vardos'. These colourful wagons, pulled along by piebald horses, were not ancient modes of habitation. Rather, they were adopted from around the 1850s, following the example of travelling theatre companies. Vardos were great vehicles for selling services out of, at camps or fairs.

During the later nineteenth century, Roma people were increasingly both romanticised and controlled. Scholars like Charles Leland, and the others who formed the Gypsy Lore Society in 1888, cherished Romany culture, particularly its exotic components. At the same time, as the era of mass poli-tics and tabloid journalism dawned, politicians like George Smith led campaigns to drastically alter Roma people's semi-nomadic way of life.[102] In this challenging environment, Roma people survived by occupying niches, sharpening shears and doing other metalwork, toiling as seasonal agricultural labourers, hawking goods, begging, and entertaining with music, song and dance.[103] Occasionally they stole. Above all, Roma women made money by providing magical services, from money multiplication to unwitching to fortune-telling. 'I am afraid that too frequently they carry their wares about with them merely as a blind,' sighed Rodney Smith (1860–1947), a notable Roma evangelist, 'the occupation of most of them is fortune-telling'.[104] Magical work of this kind had a special name, in Romany. To go about telling fortunes, multiplying money, casting blessings and curing curses, for settled people or gorgios, was to go *dukkerin*.[105]

When outsiders asked, as they increasingly did during the second half of the nineteenth century, Roma people said the days of making good livings from *dukkerin* were over. 'Everyone can tell fortunes these times,' complained one Romany woman during the early 1850s, to the Rev. Francis Hindes Groome a sympathetic scholar. 'Even the lowest Irish tell fortunes now – for sixpence!'[106] About fifty years later, an elderly Welsh Rom named Saini Wood gave another reason for the alleged decline of *dukkerin*: 'All the old Gypsies are dead now and the young ones cannot tell fortunes so well. They are only half-breeds.'[107] These remarks, driven by either nostalgia, intergenerational rivalry or a wish to mislead nosey gorgios, were far from candid. In reality as many experts on Roma culture agreed, fortune-telling was far from dead.[108] Rodney Smith, a Roma and evangelical Christian convert, actually thought that his people were depending on fortune-telling more than ever, because other work was drying up.[109]

Dukkerin also remained important for Roma fortune-tellers' clients, who sought them out at fairs and big public events like the Ascot and Epsom horse races, where crossing a palm with silver might just result in a very special tip.[110] People who feared something was amiss in their lives, who wanted suspicions confirmed or destinies foretold, also consulted Roma women in their camps. This was possible, during the later nineteenth century, because Romany people still came to town. The commons they'd once occupied were either disappearing or, after 1876, were subject to bye-laws prohibiting Travellers.[111] But there were still parks, wastelands and fields where Roma people could pitch their tents, tether their horses and kindle their fires for a while.

Thus, during the autumn of 1869, a band of Roma folk arrived on the outskirts of Chesterfield. The Derbyshire market town of about 12,000 people was in the midst of a house-building boom that would leave it encircled by redbrick villas and terraces. Suburban civilisation was taking root. Perhaps this intensified the exotic cachet of the roaming Roma, when their wagons rolled up and a full-blown camp soon appeared. So many locals went to see the tents and have their fortunes told, paying an admission fee just to enter the camp's perimeter, that one journalist concluded the working folk of Chesterfield must have been 'bewitched'.[112]

In fact, they were the customers of a well-run commercial operation. It was probably conducted by a band calling themselves the 'Epping Forest Gypsies', who toured England and the Scottish borders between the early 1860s and mid-1870s, providing music and fortune-telling, trotting donkeys and much else besides.[113] At Bath, they hired the Assembly Rooms, charging a guinea a head for admission. At Bristol, after taking an astounding £126 in the first half hour, the camp gates had to be closed for fear of overcrowding.[114]

Other Roma bands were similarly commercial, if less slick and successful. In Hartlepool, a fishing and shipbuilding town on the north-eastern English coast, some Roma pitched on the recreation grounds during the spring of 1878. Two friends, Ellen Elliot and Caroline White, both labourer's wives, paid them a visit. Probably they thought it was better to go together, more fun and safer from chicanery. These ladies were not going to fall prey to the wiles of clever fortune-tellers. A mother and daughter team, Eva and Caroline Gray, thought they could make some money by assuring Ellen her husband was bewitched, so that 'she would be a widow in three months' unless she paid them to take 'the witching' off.[115] A horrified Ellen reported the Roma women to the police, but they escaped prosecution by promising the magistrates they'd leave town. That was fortunate because Roma fortune-tellers were usually treated harshly, if the authorities went to the trouble of apprehending them. In 1881, for instance, Ellen Lovell received a month's hard labour for charging a bit of food and a few pennies to unwitch a Dudley lady.[116]

Roma fortune-tellers were notorious for getting clients by calling, unannounced and uninvited, at their homes. After setting up their tents in a suitable spot, Roma women would set out to earn money, notionally by selling pegs and other household odds to the local settled population, really by using magic. These tough, clever and seasoned hawkers were hard to refuse. A Rom's curse might await someone who sent them away empty handed. Mary Williams, living in a tent in the Rhondda Valley in South Wales during

January 1883, was an intimidating figure who used threats of witchcraft to elicit £5 10 shillings from a local servant girl, who in turn stole it from her master. Apprehended and charged with fraud, Mary avoided prosecution because her victim claimed to be bewitched, and was unwilling to attend trial to testify against her.[117] Similar events occurred two years later in Presteigne, also in Wales, when two Roma women called on Hannah Probert, saying they wanted to tell her fortune. They left with 2 shillings and two loaves of bread, after threatening the girl they'd bewitch her.[118]

More typically, Roma women elicited money by predicting their clients' doom unless they acted quickly. Thus, in February 1881, a Roma fortune-teller named Eliza Manley called at a well-to-do house in Torquay, on the Devonshire coast. Predictably, she was answered by one of the young servant girls, Elizabeth Rogers. Eliza first asked Elizabeth whether she'd like to buy any brushes or pictures, to prepare for her forthcoming marriage. Receiving a negative reply, the hawker made a more ominous offer. 'I want to speak to you a minute,' she said in hushed tones, adding that Elizabeth looked 'not like a girl bewitched, but you are overlooked'. After asking for a shilling, Eliza asked whether the maid would give her a further 10 shillings in return for 'doing her good'. This was a clever way of implying an unwitching cure without strictly saying so, thus remaining outside the reach of the law. Eliza went back for more money, which she promised to return but did not. Elizabeth reported her to the police, but Eliza escaped prosecution by saying the money had been a loan, which she had every intention of returning. 'The prisoner had been sailing very near the wind,' concluded the presiding magistrate, 'but had managed adroitly to keep within the law.'[119]

Roma people really believed in witchcraft, in the mystic capacity of certain individuals to bestow misfortunes on their enemies and blessings on their friends. There were Romany words for it: a sorceress or witch of this sort was a *chovihani*. And *chovihanis* could be either Roma or settled folk. Throughout the nineteenth century and beyond, Roma told stories about ill-luck dogging people who carelessly offended *chovihanis*. Carnival men saw their steam engines destroyed and wagons seized. Other Travellers found their wagons broke down when they encountered notorious witches. As well as fearing black magic, Roma people credited the beneficent powers of cunning-folk like Joshua Loveridge of Towcester, about whom they told many strange stories.[120] But because they believed in some magic doesn't

mean they believed in it all. As Roma people occasionally admitted, to themselves and to their closest settled friends, the magic they sold to the gorgios
was mostly impressive nonsense.[121] One trick was to draw a charm, ostensibly to provide magical protection against witchcraft or some misfortune,
full of invented zodiac-style characters, with a box of text in the centre saying
something like '*Borra dinala se gauge ate patsen ta kerla kava koskaben
langay*', a Romany phrase meaning, in English: 'Great fools are women to
believe that this does them good.'[122] In spite of these frauds, Roma fortune-
tellers insisted their clients were not ill-treated. The gorgios who paid them
to do magic were 'fools' but also 'poor things', encumbered with work and
troubles. They deserved a moment of happiness, from a spell or fortune told.

Roma women had a special patter for the settled folk who entered their
tents or caravans, seeking mystic guidance and magical assistance. 'Come
in, my rei, and welcome, if you're not afraid to sit by the poor Gipsy ... Let
me tell your fortune, my pretty.'[123] Aside from this characteristic blend of
threat and flattery, the techniques Roma people used when they went
dukkerin were surprisingly modern and rarely distinguishable from those of
settled fortune-tellers. There was little of obviously eastern or ancient origin,
though this didn't stop some scholars from theorising a huge role for Roma
people in spreading magic around the world.[124] The more humdrum reality
was that many Roma used cards, mostly playing decks but occasionally
picture cards made for divining the future. Like settled fortune-tellers, they
must have adopted the method relatively recently. Roma people also learnt
magic from the acknowledged experts: cunning-folk. One Roma girl told
the Rev. Francis Hindes Groome that a wise-man from Aldershot had taught
her how to bewitch someone by sticking pins through a piece of red cloth
and burning it.[125] Cunning-folk sometimes diagnosed people as bewitched
by examining the bubbles in a glass of water, or by breaking an egg into the
solution and watching its movements. Roma too adopted this method, like
Rosanna Price, who was fined 20 shillings in 1887 for imposing on Eliza Ray
of Cardiff. Rosanna elicited 2 shillings and 6 pence worth of cash and articles by assuring Eliza her husband was bewitched and offering a cure, a
diagnosis she made by cracking an egg into a tumbler of hot water, and
adding three pieces of silver.[126]

Though Roma fortune-tellers learnt some tricks from cunning-folk, like
all magicians they also improvised their own eccentric rituals. Mrs Manley,

who in 1884 called at the home of Maria White, a dairyman's wife, worked with an uncanny book. After making sure no one else was at home, the fortune-teller asked whether Maria was ill, and told her that she had 'enemies' (implying witches), but that she knew a spell to defeat them. As so often in Roma unwitching cures, this involved 'borrowing' certain articles from the house, including a cheese, the largest coin, other silver. To complete the spell, Mrs Manley produced a book from her bag, and told Maria to lay the silver on certain marks. She promised to return the money the next day, but when she failed to do so the police were called.[127]

What made Roma people powerful fortune-tellers wasn't their store of ancient or eastern magic. There was no such store, or it wasn't used when they went *dukkerin* for gorgios. Roma women succeeded as fortune-tellers because their clients had confidence in them as inheritors of strange abilities and uncommon capacities. Above all, Roma fortune-tellers excelled because they were fantastic actors, well-practised storytellers, skilled with words, intimidating and inventive, fast thinking, with a strong sense of theatre and drama. Using these qualities, and a combination of threats and promises, they could elicit huge sums. Take the elaborate fraud perpetrated in 1887 by Beatrice Smith on Henry Fairbanks and his wife Mary. According to the prosecution, the Roma woman 'succeed in clearing the house out', taking bedding, clothes, silk handkerchiefs, butter, a couple of ducks, beds, a watch worth £3 and cash amounting to £1 8 shillings. She got this money by promising to rule Mary Fairbanks' planet, to ensure she'd receive a large inheritance, and by threatening to bewitch the couple so as to kill the master and make their cows lactate blood. The fraud, carried out over a period of weeks, involved sending forged letters to the couple, purporting to be from the court of chancery. For her crimes Beatrice was given three months in jail.[128]

UNWITCHING AS MENTAL HEALTH CARE

Cunning-folk and fortune-tellers, whether Roma or settled, were clever marketers and canny hoodwinkers. Yet it would be wrong to define these controversial figures entirely by their negative traits. Whatever one thinks of their professional ethics, however one feels about their supernatural claims, cunning-folk and fortune-tellers were more than just deceivers. There is, in fact, reason to think they provided their clients with something genuinely valuable: a useful service, a form of psychological healing which, before the twentieth century, was not readily available elsewhere. But to understand this service we'll need to evaluate the historical evidence in light of recent medical research exploring the relationships between religion, spirituality and human health.

The study of the bearing of religion and spirituality upon health has 'exploded since the mid-1990s', with scholars conducting a dizzying number of experiments and writing thousands of research papers. Around 80 per cent relate to the impact of religion and spirituality upon mental health.[129] As one might expect, consensus eludes this relatively new and multidisciplinary domain of enquiry, where studies vary greatly in quality, and precise definitions of religion and spirituality remain elusive. Nonetheless, academics working in fields as diverse as psychiatry, nursing, behavioural science, neuroscience, sociology and anthropology increasingly agree about a basic if controversial point. Religion and spirituality, it seems, *tend* to benefit mental health, making people better able to cope with adversity, enhancing hope and self-esteem, reducing anxiety, protecting against depression and improving wellbeing.[130]

Not only does a religious or spiritual disposition guard, somewhat, against melancholia. Sufferers of anxiety and depression may benefit from spirituality-based coping therapies, developed according to recognised psychological theories. A small but growing number of randomised controlled trials are finding 'statistically significant benefits' from using faith- or spirituality-based treatments for certain mental illnesses.[131] A notable example is faith-adapted cognitive behavioural therapies (CBT), a type of psychotherapy first devised in the 1970s, based on identifying and challenging dysfunctional patterns of thinking.[132] When treating depression, faith-adapted CBTs have been found more effective than no treatment, and in some instances more effective than secular CBTs too.[133] Neuroscientists provide complementary insights. In 2017, scientists at Columbia University published the results of magnetic resonance imaging (MRI) scans of the brains of 106 participants judged to be at familial risk of depression. As in previous studies, patients who attached a high degree of importance to religion and spirituality tended to be less afflicted by depression. MRI, however, allowed the neuroscientists to identify neural concomitants of this protective spiritual disposition: a thicker cerebral cortex and larger pial surface area.[134]

These revelations regarding the generally positive relationship between spirituality and mental health challenge us to re-evaluate the work of cunning-folk and fortune-tellers. Might their unwitching techniques have functioned, on some level, as psychiatric therapies that relieved their clients' feelings of depression, melancholy, despair and malaise? To put it another way, in times of great crisis, did unwitching serve as a cryptic form of mental health care?

Treating depression and mental illness was obviously not the stated aim of unwitching. None of the participants understood it in these terms. But they didn't need to possess an explicit understanding of unwitching's psychological healing function for it to have that effect. Cunning-folk and fortune-tellers undoubtedly dealt with many depressed and distressed clients. Their customers had serious and long-standing problems, from illnesses to unemployment, relationship breakdowns to financial crises. They'd tried conventional remedies, met with their chapel ministers and church parsons, paid vets or physicians or hospitals, yet still found themselves suffering. Medical research bears out the common-sense point that depression correlates with ill-health and financial pressure, as well as genetic and other factors.[135] This explains why, during the nineteenth century, bewitched people felt intense melancholia.

Some bewitched folk endured pains so overwhelming that they ended their own lives, or tried to. We can see this in the steady stream of coroner's inquests into the suicides of people who thought they were victims of sorcery. People like Harriet Bartle, of an unhappy couple from Lowestoft in Suffolk, who'd been treated by the doctor and who carried around charms against witchcraft in her handkerchief, but ultimately killed herself in January 1887.[136] William Scagell, 42, from Ashburton in Devon, a farmer, husband and father of five, hanged himself in 1885, thinking he was under the spell of witchcraft.[137] Jane Reece, a bewitched farmer's wife from Newton Abbot, cut her throat in 1883.[138] John Pope, also from Devon, committed suicide in an Exeter jail, where he was incarcerated for cattle stealing. He thought he was bewitched, had got no relief from conventional magical remedies like horseshoes, and had recently learnt of his wife's death.[139] Susannah Collins, 48, a mother to eleven children, killed herself in 1878, firmly believing that she was spellbound.[140] Rachael Grice, a cabinetmaker's wife from Shropshire, hanged herself during the mid-winter of 1870, thinking she was bewitched and destined for ruin.[141] Elizabeth Allen, a 72-year-old widow, strangled herself in June 1889, with a lace fastened to her old iron bed. She thought she was bewitched because she'd been suffering from a long illness and had not been able to find a cure.[142] It would be easy to multiply similar sad experiences many times over.

Bewitched people might well have benefited from some form of mental health care. But is there evidence that cunning-folk and fortune-tellers provided psychological healing, through their unwitching therapies? Not in all cases. Visiting a white witch from Taunton did not save Elizabeth Miffin, a 22-year-old groom's wife who drowned herself during the spring of 1874.[143] Likewise William Turner, a father of six, killed himself on the railway line near Bow Station, in Devon, despite having seen a conjuror about his bewitchment.[144] Consulting with cunning-folk evidently didn't mollify those people's despair. But because unwitching therapies did not always provide effective mental health care does not mean they never did. In the contemporary world, orthodox medical treatments for depression are not always effective. Antidepressant drugs and talking therapies are associated with better outcomes, but do not help all patients or even most, according to some studies.[145] Similarly, cunning-folk and fortune-tellers did not succeed in making every one of their apparently bewitched clients better able to cope with his or her tribulations. However, it seems likely they helped in some cases.

I say this because, like contemporary psychotherapists, unwitchers urged their clients to abandon negative thought patterns. They were simply not permitted to be dejected, depressed, melancholic, negative or morbidly fatalistic. Of the people who implored them to work their magic, cunning-folk and fortune-tellers demanded one thing above all: have faith. Believe, force yourself – if necessary – to believe in my power to make impossible things come to pass. Quiet your doubts and misgivings. Absolutely: you will be cured and your troubles will end. Fed by the correct mindset, magic can hurt or even kill. And evil can be returned, many times over, by those who know. The *Norwood Gypsy's Fortune Teller*, the cheap guide to some basic occult rites, described the prerequisite state of mind for successful magic as 'most seriously and earnestly wishing'. A French cunning-man, prosecuted in 1890 for imposing on people from the Devon town of Dawlish, was more explicit when he told a potential customer he could help if 'he believed in witchcraft and had faith in him'.[146] An Essex labourer, interviewed in 1888 about the secretive world of witchcraft and magic, made the same point. 'Faith is a wonderful thing,' he said, when describing how his wife had been healed by a cunning-man. The journalist interviewing him agreed that cunning-folk offered a type of 'faith healing'. But it was not the sort of faith healing someone might experience one night at a religious rally or spiritualist meeting, a single encounter, a momentary epiphany that one would be cured, an intense feeling that faded as quickly as it arrived. Unwitching was a sustained form of faith healing, taking place over a prolonged period of weeks and months. Its patients, if they can be so described, were asked to maintain a new and more optimistic way of thinking, to practise this positive form of cognition so it became embedded in their minds.

Not everyone could believe their troubles originated in witchcraft. It was difficult to have perfect faith in something like that, and harder still to credit a wise-man or fortune-teller with the power to put things right. To help the believing process along, to ensure their clients adopted more optimistic states of mind, unwitchers used confidence-building techniques, many of which have been mentioned already. Cunning-folk were particularly skilled confidence builders. They began the moment they met new customers. Like Mr Fall, the 'forecaster or weather-prophet' in Thomas Hardy's novel *The Mayor of Casterbridge*, wizards amazed their callers with advanced knowledge of their names and business.[147] This was how 'Dr' John Thomas, a cunning-man from Cornwall, astonished an apprentice sailor from the fishing port of Penryn, in 1873. Using cold-reading, good guesses and a little inside information, Dr Thomas revealed not just the man's name, but that he'd recently almost drowned, had fallen out with a Swedish captain years earlier, and was on disagreeable terms with a fellow named James.[148] After making some remarkable prophecies, cunning-folk changed tack, shocking their new clients into acquiescence with warnings they were in mortal danger. Dr Thomas, for instance, grimly assured the apprentice sailor he met in 1873 that a woman whose name began with 'A' wanted him drowned, and was working magic for this purpose. Susannah Bond, a wise-woman from Plymouth, also predicted disaster if her clients didn't act quickly.[149] Some fortune-tellers gave their clients a more specific prognosis, saying if they didn't believe in and fight the witchcraft that was upon them, they'd go nearly mad.[150] 'You're only just in time to be saved from utter ruin' was the thrust of the message.[151]

Was this a strategy designed to ensnare reluctant customers? One might imagine so. Yet a closer look at the evidence points to another explanation. Most new customers were already exceedingly committed to hiring their chosen cunning-person, well before they'd heard his or her spiel. Clients were motivated enough to travel huge distances, like the farmer's wife from Kellas in northern Scotland who went 40 miles to consult the sister 'of the far-famed Willox';[152] or the farmer from Bakewell in Derbyshire, who in 1881 journeyed 18 miles north-east, to Sheffield, to consult a cunning-man.[153] People travelled as far as 60 miles to see Miss Hay (d. *c.* 1890), a canny-woman from Inverness, whose reputation stretched from Moray to John O'Groats.[154] Billy Brewer, a famous Somerset wizard living in Taunton, had customers from as far away as Cardiff, in South Wales.[155] In 1866, three respectable Welsh women hired the landlord of the Nelson Inn, Penydarren, to drive them on a four-hour round trip to consult the wise-woman at Penderyn.[156] And there is more evidence of exceedingly committed, enthusiastic customers. Some wrote to cunning-folk, showering them with desperate entreaties. The following phrases, far beyond ordinary pleasantries, are from a letter sent to a Norfolk cunning-man, in 1871:

> My Dear friend Mr Covell ... please Mr Covell put a stop to them ... please dear friend stop her from doing us any harm ... please do all you can for us ... God bless you for ever and ever.[157]

When they told their customers that time was short, they must act immediately or die, cunning-folk weren't catching clients. At this stage in proceedings, they didn't need to do that. Unwitchers used dramatic declarations for different, more therapeutic reasons. They were portraying personal troubles as part of a grand cosmic battle. The effect, perhaps the intention, was to make their clients hyper-determined, instilling in them feelings of resolve and purposefulness. For someone beset by melancholy, this could be an electrifying, transformative experience.

There were other reasons why distressed and depressed people may have found unwitching cathartic. Like contemporary psychotherapists, cunning-folk and fortune-tellers forced their customers to face their problems, to discuss them openly and frankly. Bewitched people were supposed to tell all, about their friendships and relationships, living conditions, health, business concerns, working lives, accidents and prospects. As one wise-woman's client put it in court, they discussed 'everything'.[158] To draw out this deeply personal information, the magicians used their cards and crystal balls, as well as so-called 'cold-reading' techniques. Subtly, cunning-folk and fortune-tellers probed and prompted and nudged, until their clients finally voiced their worst fears. Bewitched people knew they would be called upon to do something like this, something confessional, as we can see from the letters they wrote to cunning-folk, when they couldn't visit in person. Professor Owen Davies has studied letters sent to Billy Brewer, of Taunton, which were published in a local paper after the magician's death.[159] Billy's clients wrote at length about their diverse problems, from illnesses to insomnia, tax bills, an inability to stop spending money, to clothes that had gone yellow in the wash. Very reasonably, Davies views Billy Brewer as acting like something of an 'agony uncle'.[160] His cathartic counselling was certainly not unusual. Letters sent to Benjamin Covell, a cunning-man from the Norfolk village of Shipdham, reveal similar conventions, of clients confessing their innermost anxieties. Semi-literate and phonetically spelled, the letters were sent by people who were in debt, too poor to eat or heat their cottages, living in overcrowded conditions, with rents due, suffering chest pains, banned from visiting their sweethearts, unable to sleep, lacking regular or any work, and so on. Presumably, Mr Covell's clients described their troubles in relentless detail so the cunning-man could devise the best supernatural solution. Jeanne-Favret Saada, when studying bewitched people in 1960s and 1970s Normandy, noticed how usually reticent folk revealed everything to their unwitcher, so the magician would 'know where to aim his blows'.[161] The goal was magical, not psychotherapeutic. Nonetheless, unwitching entailed self-revelatory conventions similar to clinical techniques for relieved distress and depression.

Unwitching likely activated ill people's placebo response. For clarity's sake, the placebo effect can be defined as an elevated form of the human body's self-healing function, caused by expectations surrounding what should be a physiologically inert treatment. Observed by physicians for millennia, studied in clinical trials from as early as 1799, the placebo effect remains an important though still dimly understood topic for medical research.[162] Since the 1960s, several studies have tentatively pointed to the existence of 'enhanced placebo effects', where practices with elaborate rituals or high technology tend to activate more powerful placebo responses, in comparison with more mundane techniques like swallowing a pill.[163] These tentative speculations can, I think, be plausibly applied to the impressive unwitching rituals and remedies devised by cunning-folk and fortune-tellers. Miss Hay (d. c. 1890), the Scottish cunning-woman from Inverness, 'displayed a very considerable amount of ingenuity in her charms and counter enchantments', a local journalist noted. One cure for witchcraft involved transferring the disease afflicting her customer to an animal, usually a chicken, with Miss Hay foretelling when the poor beast would expire, and using poison to bring her predictions about.[164] More typically, unwitching rituals occurred at the stroke of midnight, with doors and windows barred shut, as the smell of incense wafted through the air, in complete silence except for the sound of a crackling fire and a solemnly pronounced incantation.[165] Clients were instructed 'not to speak to anyone' about their predicament, or when the rituals were under way.[166] Some unwitchers asked the patients themselves, rather than their relatives, to pass them the money.[167] Ritualistic objects, others insisted, were only to be handled with the left hand.[168] Protective charms had to be worn right next to the victim's body, underneath their clothes and in contact with the skin. But they could never be shown to others, or spoken of, or allowed to touch the floor, or turned upside down, depending on the instructions of the particular cunning-person.[169]

Magic was exacting, theatrical and deeply symbolic. Taking part in it could be a heady and exciting experience. Too exciting, according to one report from 1883. After consulting a 'white witch', a farmer and his brother had become obsessed with the idea they were 'overlooked' by their own mother, to the point that one became suicidal and the other was removed to the county lunatic asylum.[170] This, however, was an exceptional incident, as to a lesser extent were the court cases described in the newspapers, resulting from disgruntled clients calling the police. Satisfied customers told other stories. When they were challenged about why they'd done something so odd as visit a cunning-man or a fortune-teller, and why they'd paid a fat sum for the privilege, these people struggled to explain. Eventually, they tended to say something like it 'did them good'.[171] Did this generic expression refer to a real form of healing, perhaps of a psychological character? Among anthropologists, it's something of a truism that ritualistic activity has therapeutic effects. The point has been made by scholars with expertise on societies as diverse as Haiti, Mexico, Siberia and rural France, though in a vague and circumscribed way, without elaborating on the nature of the therapeutic effects.[172] Admirable and understandable as this restraint once was, it is less justified in light of recent scientific research on depression, talking therapies and the relationship between mental health and spirituality. Plausibly, in a roundabout and unconscious way, the unwitchers of Victorian Britain helped at least some of their depressed clients climb out of the sloughs of despond.

WHY UNWITCHING WORKED

Thousands, probably tens of thousands of Victorians enriched themselves by selling a special type of magic, dedicated to fighting witches and stopping the misfortunes they caused. Most of Britain's 10,000 or so Roma women were capable of *dukkerin*, a mystical line of work that included counter-acting witchcraft. Some, perhaps many, of the estimated 30,000 quacks and fortune-tellers were also prepared to blunt curses and repel evil wishes. Combating witchcraft came naturally to cunning-folk, the real experts, of whom there were likely hundreds, though it's difficult to be sure. Unwitching was a substantial part of a niche but important service industry, dedicated to providing magical solutions for personal problems. To the surprise of some commentators, this industry remained profitable, even in Imperial Britain, even in the era of telegraph wires, public sanitation, mass politics for men, universal state-funded schooling, redbrick universities, mass-market consumer goods, tinned food, telephones, electric lighting, bicycles, internal combustion engines and the rest. If a trade in magic could happen then and there, it could happen anywhere.

The semi-secret, somewhat illicit magical services industry flourished for several reasons. By the close of the nineteenth century, the British state consumed around 10 per cent of annual national income; yet though it was becoming more powerful, in the decadent atmosphere of the late Victorian age Britain's government was unwilling to fully suppress the trade in super-natural services. Nor were the authorities capable of doing so. Cunning-folk and fortune-tellers were slippery tricksters, convincing actors, clever folk conditioned to operate in the shadows, renegades who were used to staying just beyond the reach of the law. They were also impressive figures, the sort of people you might try in desperate times. They clearly had a feeling for magic, but in most cases this was derived less from knowledge or study and more from intuition, quick wits, a sense of theatre, an attachment to drama, a liking for ritual and a talent for ominous patter.

Ultimately, what sustained these modern magicians were appreciative and enthusiastic customers. Did any real, tangible benefits accrue to the people who implored cunning-folk and fortune-tellers for help? The historical evidence demonstrates:

1. Cunning-folk and fortune-tellers had some troubled, depressed, melancholic clients.
2. The unwitching techniques devised by cunning-folk and fortune-tellers had similarities with contemporary psychotherapeutic methods for treating depression. In both cases, clients were taught to abandon dysfunctional thought processes and adopt optimistic, empowered states of mind.
3. Generally, cunning-folk and fortune-tellers had grateful customers, convinced of their power to 'do them good'.

We'll never have sufficiently detailed historical evidence to make a definitive judgement, and in the absence of that evidence it is up to readers to speculate. For my part, I think these mystic hucksters pulled some of their clients out of pits of despair and dejection by leading them into make-believe worlds of good and evil magic. Unwitching, in this analysis, functioned as a cryptic form of mental health care, which made some very unhappy people better able to cope with their disasters.

SIX

OCCULTISTS STUDY DARK ARTS
1850s–1900

> The extent to which the belief in witchcraft has grown during
> the last few years is incredible, especially amongst the people
> who move in the fast Society set.
>
> *Illustrated Police Budget*, 20 May 1899

Witchcraft didn't just trouble unsophisticated folk and under-educated clots.
Not by any means: not during the later nineteenth century. This was a spectacularly creative era for the theory and practice of magic.[1] Numerous well-
read, intelligent, rich, articulate, often politically radical Britons became
seriously interested in esoteric forces and supernatural powers, in what,
during effusive moments, they referred to as 'anomalous phenomena', 'the
other world', 'spiritual manifestations' and 'occult sciences'.[2] It would have
been extraordinary if their thoughts had never turned to magic's dark side.

FROM CRISIS OF FAITH TO OCCULT REVIVAL

The occult revival of the later Victorian period surprised many commentators. Understandably, they expected the later 1800s to be years of secularism
and science, not magic and mysticism. This was because, around the 1840s

and 1850s, Britain's small but influential intelligentsia had been beset by 'honest doubts', as they were called at the time, about the literal truth of the Bible.[3] German textual criticism showed that much of the sacred text was myth. Geology and biology revealed things about the age of the earth and the nature of its life forms that could not be squared with traditional Christian theology. With infidelity abroad and the gospels under attack, it was easy to assume that well-schooled Britons would automatically dismiss more incredible notions concerning occult powers and supernatural beings. Surely, no intelligent person took witchcraft seriously?

'Any educated man' would automatically deny 'a real instance of witchcraft at the present day', without needing to look at the evidence.[4] So presumed Baden Powell, Professor of Geometry at Oxford and theologian of rather advanced views. He was writing in 1860. Five years later William Lecky, a celebrated Irish historian, elaborated the point. Disbelief in supernatural powers had been deeply inculcated into the minds of modern educated Europeans, not by definite arguments, Lecky maintained in his *History of the Rise and Influence of the Spirit of Rationalism* (1865), but because of a change in mood brought about by advances in science, art, philosophy, theology and industry.[5] Progress had made it easy, inevitable even, for learned people to disbelieve in witchcraft, ghosts, hell, miracles and all the other gross errors of the past.

Yet it was not so. Just as rationalism's victory seemed assured, in the years following the publication of Charles Darwin's *On the Origin of Species* (1859), the zeitgeist shifted. Already, by 1863, one commentator was complaining: 'Supernaturalism and sensationalism are the appointed and leading dogmas of the day.'[6] Another put it less grandly, noting: 'A taste for the supernatural has greatly augmented of late among the educated classes of society.'[7] Strange dynamics were at work in British culture, a third and more perceptive critic noted: 'While scepticism and unbelief are gaining in one direction, what seems to be the grossest credulity and superstition are making their appearance in the other.'[8] Partly these remarks referred to the rise of spiritualism.

SPIRITUALISM AND EVIL MAGNETISM

Spiritualism originated in 1840s America, at a haunted farmhouse in upstate New York.[9] Leased to the Fox family, in 1848 it was apparently disturbed by the ghost of a pedlar who'd been murdered many years before. His spirit

140

began communicating with two of the Fox daughters, Margaret and Kate, through a series of knocks and raps. Or so they said.

There was a long history of similar noisy hauntings. Think of the Tedworth Drummer of 1662–3 (investigated by members of Charles II's court) and the Cock Lane Ghost of 1762 (ditto by Georgian London's literati).[10] Yet in the enterprising atmosphere of 1840s America, and under the management of their elder sister Leah, the Fox girls became spiritualism's first mediums. They and their imitators asked questions of spirits on behalf of the paying public, receiving replies in the forms of knocks, automatic writing and so-called 'table turning'. In 1888, in a $1,000 newspaper exclusive, Margaret Fox revealed that she and her sister had actually faked the raps by cracking their joints.[11] Widely reported in the US and covered in Britain too, the long-term impact of the revelation was minimal.[12] Spiritualism was too well established on both sides of the Atlantic. This was partly because it had a strong female appeal. Unusually for the Victorian period, spiritualism was an area of public life in which women led.[13]

Spiritualism arrived in Britain late in 1852, with the American medium Maria Hayden.[14] Although 'no great celebrity', her spirit-rapping séances were soon entertaining parties of nobles, ladies, officers and other elegant Londoners.[15] Critics guffawed, yet spiritualism quickly gained more professors, from humble drawing-room mediums and clairvoyants to the Davenport Brothers, a pair of American showmen. They toured Britain during the 1860s, astonishing and often outraging audiences with their 'cabinet séances', where musical instruments played and wooden objects whirled overhead, while the brothers themselves remained tied within a cupboard.[16] The extraordinary displays pained serious enquirers into the 'realm of twilight', who found their interests better catered to by a rich body of new occult literature. Works of supernatural history and theory, claiming spiritualism had existed in all cultures and ages, were written by famous and even distinguished figures, including the medium D.D. Home, the utopian socialist Robert Dale Owen, and the scientist Alfred Russel Wallace.[17] Their books portrayed witches not as diabolic agents but as unconscious mediums.[18] Witches were natural clairvoyants, friends of the benevolent spirit world, unfairly persecuted by the churches and their ignorant neighbours.

Spiritualism was not only about contacting the spirits of the dead. Yes, its main purpose was reconnecting with relatives who'd passed to the other side,

141

or conversing with great figures like Plato, Napoleon and Thomas Paine.[19] But healing was also an important part of the movement.[20] Spiritualist healers did not need to be mediums, though most were. Typically, their therapies began with demonstrations of diagnostic clairvoyance, where they identified what was wrong while the patients remained quiet. This could be done in person, by scrutinising the colour of a patient's spirit aura, or remotely, by meditating on some of his or her hair.[21] After the diagnosis, there might be a biblical reading – one of the verses about healing from Corinthians, perhaps. The right atmosphere achieved, the cure could now begin.

A few spiritualist healers prescribed herbal or homoeopathic remedies, in the form of lotions and pills.[22] Most, however, borrowed their cures from the mesmerists of the early Victorian era. Like mesmerists, spiritualist healers claimed they were conduits for magnetic forces with powerful curative properties. They cured the sick, in other words, by channelling benevolent magnetism. Often through mesmeric passes, by dramatically moving their hands around the afflicted limb or area. Or with 'insufflation', when the healer exhaled air pregnant with beneficent magnetism onto the patient's body. Occasionally, through a handkerchief, the patient inhaled the air.

Beneficent, 'good' or vital magnetism healed. Did this mean there were such things as 'bad' or harmful magnetism, which did the opposite? During the 1860s, spiritualists on both sides of the Atlantic invoked concepts of 'bad' and 'evil' magnetism to explain wars, famines and destruction.[23] Great calamities were increasing, they said, caused by a negative magnetic atmosphere, which in turn emanated from humanity's growing penchant for lust, avarice and violence. The initial focus was political and social, yet from the 1870s spiritualist healers began employing the terms of 'bad' and 'evil' magnetism more precisely and personally. Spiteful, nasty people were said to emit harmful spiritual forces, to which sensitive spiritualist mediums were uniquely vulnerable. The 'bad magnetism' flowing from ill-disposed or untrusting individuals could disrupt séances and even cause mediums physical pain, argued Charles Glass, a spiritualist and outspoken advocate of democratic reform.[24]

'Bad magnetism' harmed ordinary people too. An American proponent of magnetic healing warned his readers to 'keep away from the people who cause an involuntary shudder to creep through your frame when you come near them'.[25] Similar ideas circulated Britain, where they reflected the particular concerns of middle-class spiritualists. In 1882 *Light*, a spiritualist newspaper, cited 'good' and 'evil magnetism' to explain why refined houses emanated a calm atmosphere, whereas poor neighbourhoods had a 'jarring, painful effect'. Worst of all were busy omnibuses and railway carriages: 'Places of torture to the individual whose soul is growing prematurely too refined for the present condition of human life on our planet.'[26] Frequent commuters will know the feeling.

Spiritualist healing, with its pseudo-magical concepts of good and evil magnetism, was a fringe form of health care. How fringe is unclear. Emma Hardinge, one of early Victorian Britain's most renowned spiritualist healers, created enough of a reputation to take her talents on tour, in 1871, to America.[27] Moving from the celebrated to the ordinary, in the early 1880s the phrenologist James Burns was able to draw up a list of twenty London-based spiritualist healers for the magazine *Medium and Daybreak*.[28] This almost certainly underestimated their number. Like all unlicensed and esoteric medics, spiritualist healers were vulnerable to prosecution under the 1824 Vagrancy Act and the 1858 Medical Act. In 1876 the newspapers were awash with reports on the trial of Mrs Chandos Leigh Hunt, a mesmeric healer. These risks made spiritualists secretive. Generally they didn't advertise, attracting clients through word of mouth only.

THEOSOPHY AND INDIAN WITCHES

Notions of spiritual healing and supernatural harm figured more prominently in theosophy. This new religion was dedicated to cultivating its adherents' mystic powers. Founded in New York in 1875 by the Russian Helena Blavatsky (1831–91) and her collaborator Henry Olcott, theosophy was initially conceived of as a sort of reformed spiritualism.[29] Spiritualists didn't work through the spirits of the dead, Blavatsky maintained, but by harnessing misunderstood elemental powers. Theosophy's founders moved to India in 1879, from which point they gave the new religion a distinctly eastern hue.[30] Blavatsky claimed to be communing with the 'Masters' or 'Mahatmas', a brotherhood of immortal Buddhist monks living in the mountains of Tibet. Purportedly, they informed her how one might spiritually evolve and thereby gain access to awesome occult abilities.

The London Lodge of the Theosophical Society was founded in 1878. From 1887 it had the honour of hosting Madame Blavatsky herself, after she moved to Britain. By then the powers of eastern spirituality were familiar to readers of the movement's literature, textbooks like *Esoteric Buddhism* as well as the journal *The Theosophist*. Indian witches possessed genuine malefic abilities, it was said: '*All* natives, of whatever caste are well aware of these terrible powers and too often do they avail themselves of it.'[31] The occult journal *Borderland*, aimed at the general reading public rather than dedicated theosophical initiates, agreed.[32] It claimed there was 'no reasonable doubt' that sorcerers living in the Indian hills possessed 'certain powers of the dark side of magic, or sorcery'. As with all witches, their dark faculties originated in 'the evil magnetism of a hostile will'.[33]

Indian black magicians attacked British theosophists with evil magic. So maintained 'Nizida', pen-name of a theosophist who wrote a guide to 'the astral light', the transcendental force that was allegedly the basis of all occult powers.[34] Theosophy, according to Nizida's thinking, was a 'spiritual science' capable of elevating the human psyche to the levels necessary to end worldly injustices, from animal cruelty to misogyny to undemocratic government. Mastering the 'astral light' required theosophists to evolve spiritually, shedding their hatreds, wicked passions and carnal desires, elevating their souls to a higher moral plane. This would make them capable of marvellous feats like astral travel, where they could project ethereal versions of themselves onto different continents and even other planets.

Spiritually evolved theosophists were protected from black magic. This was important. As Nizida explained to her readers: 'Sorcery and witchcraft are by no means imaginary things, nor are they the follies of mere superstition.' Using the 'magnetism of evil' or the 'poisonous magnetism of an evil thought', black magicians caused illnesses, conjured delusions, summoned hallucinations, and even induced unwanted infatuations (a strangely recurrent theme in Nizida's theosophical handbook). Europe had plenty of malefactors but India was worse, being peopled with 'large numbers of black magicians'. Adepts of theosophy were particularly vulnerable because the most capable Indian wizards travelled abroad in astral form, attacking persons 'seeking occult knowledge'. 'They are a very dangerous element in the world,' Nizida warned, 'and are the cause of more evil than can be imagined.' For a budding theosophist, it must have been scary but exciting to imagine that, as they honed their powers, they would engage in cosmic battles with fearsome magi.[35]

BLACK MAGIC AND THE GOLDEN DAWN

Witchcraft and magic figured more in theosophy than they did in spiritualism, but for some late Victorian occultists it still wasn't enough. One of the dissatisfied was Anna Kingsford (1846–88), a mystic Christian and visionary who used chloroform to amplify her dreams.[36] She was also a social reformer, feminist, animal rights campaigner, vegetarian, and one of Britain's first qualified female doctors, with a medical degree from Paris. Between 1883 and 1884 this impressive esotericist was president of the Theosophical Society's London branch. Yet she never accepted the emphasis on eastern occultism and the pronouncements of the 'Mahatmas'.[37]

Anna Kingsford preferred western and 'hermetic' magical traditions.[38] She'd encountered these as a student in France, partly from reading the scholar Éliphas Lévi's *Dogme et rituel de la haute magie* (1854–6), partly too from befriending devotees of *occultisme*, the new trend among avant-garde Parisians of the 1870s.[39] Unmoved by Hinduism, left cold by Buddhism, Kingsford focused instead on western mysticism, from the ancient Jewish Kabbalah to Neoplatonism, the Latin works of Hermes Trismegistus, and European spell books like the fifteenth-century *Key of Solomon*, as well as the more modern ideas of the Rosicrucians, Swedenborg and spiritualism. Stifled by the Theosophical Society's emphasis on eastern esotericism, in 1884 Anna Kingsford founded a western-focused sub-branch called 'The Hermetic Society', reflecting her special occult interests.

Anna Kingsford's enthusiasms included witchcraft, black and white. She noted in a diary entry of 1881: 'There has always been the unholy art of the wizard, the art of "black magic," that of the man who sought to produce miraculous effects by evil means.'[40] Theosophists expected their spiritual evolution to protect them from magical malefactors, but Dr Kingsford used her occult powers to smite others, or tried to. She reconciled this with her mystical Christianity and commitment to high moral standards by arguing that whereas black magic was motivated by selfish desires, white magic stemmed from altruistic sentiments. According to this way of thinking, white magic included willing the death of evil people.

Evil people like the physiologists Paul Bert and Claude Bernard, and the father of germ theory Louis Pasteur. As vivisectionists, those French scientists enraged Kingsford by cutting and dissecting live animals. To stop them she wrote pamphlets, orchestrated demonstrations, and attempted magical murder. 'The will *can* and *does* kill,' Kingsford noted in her diary, without specifying whether she'd used particular magical rites beyond intense concentration. She credited herself with killing Claude Bernard (d. 1878) and Paul Bert (d. 1886), yet Pasteur was her undoing. He'd been ill but Anna was worse, with pneumonia and tuberculosis. In the privacy of her diary, she attributed her ill-health either to her curse rebounding or to the judgement of 'karma', ironic given her preference for western magic. 'It is not yet over and will, I suppose, only cease with my life,' she wrote in April 1887. In a way, she was right. Ten months later Anna died, suspecting her 'occult projections' were the ultimate cause.[41]

Maleficent witchcraft had less influence on the Hermetic Order of the Golden Dawn.[42] A highly exclusive and secret society, founded in London during the year of Anna Kingsford's death (1888), it soon opened temples in Paris, Edinburgh and more humble locations like the Yorkshire mill town of Bradford and the Somerset coastal resort of Weston-super-Mare. Like the theosophist Madame Blavatsky, the Golden Dawn's leaders claimed they were receiving mystic communications from superhuman cosmic agencies, the 'secret chiefs'. And as before, these communications provided instructions to aid the spiritual evolution of the Golden Dawn's initiates (over 300 of whom had been admitted to the London Lodge by 1896). Distinctively, this was knowing and ironic. The 'secret chiefs' didn't really exist, but were symbolic devices.

Following the secret chiefs' advice, the Golden Dawn's initiates practised ceremonial magic of a western orientation, not to change the world, but to induce feelings of spiritual and intellectual exaltation: to enter higher states of consciousness.[43] In the evenings after work, solicitors, actors, doctors, writers, clerks and other young middle-class professionals gathered in curtained rooms to perform solemn rituals. Using sacred manuscripts, wearing ceremonial robes, chanting and exalting, presenting offerings and so on. Consciousness raising was their goal, so whether alchemy, summoning demons, necromancy, angel evocation, divination or any other magic worked or not, in a practical sense, was irrelevant. 'Whether these alleged occurrences are to be accepted as substantiated facts is not the question on which the enlightened mystic desires to insist,' was how one senior member put it.[44]

The Golden Dawn thus put western-style ceremonial magic to the fairly distinctive end of 'spiritual' development as opposed to material gain'.[45] Yet it would be wrong to completely exclude practical magic from the story. Take

Arthur Edward Waite, who joined the order in 1891, wrote several important occult books and ultimately brought tarot cards to Britain. He certainly bemoaned the 'intellectual weakness', 'superstition' and 'frivolities' associated with utilitarian spell-slinging.[46] Yet Mr Waite's literary output provided knowledge about historical black and white magic to well-to-do readers, detached from the largely oral culture of vernacular folk magic. His *Book of Black Magic and Pacts* (1898) was the first serious history of grimoires (spell books), though at £2 2 shillings each, the first edition's 500 copies were expensive.[47] Waite is regarded as being among the most sceptical members of the Golden Dawn, regarding magic's practical efficacy. Yet even he believed that powerful individuals could affect others, through the influence of will and 'magnetism'.

Samuel MacGregor Mathers, a co-founder of the Golden Dawn, published the first English editions of the *Key of Solomon* and the *Lesser Key of Solomon*, two important grimoires. Mathers believed in the reality of maleficent magic enough to caution: 'Let him who, in spite of the warnings of this volume, determines to work evil, be assured that evil will recoil on himself and that he will be struck by the reflex current.'[48] Someone who didn't heed the warning was Aleister Crowley, 'the great beast', notorious hedonist and focus of various rumours and exaggerations. Crowley joined the Golden Dawn in 1898 and soon aided the order's destruction by publishing its secret manuscripts. Among his associates were sincere believers in the reality of black magic, such as the paranoid and probably mentally ill George Montagu Bennet, 7th Earl of Tankerville (1852–1931), who thought his mother was trying to destroy him with witchcraft.[49] Later in the twentieth century, Crowley himself ritually cursed at least one former pupil, and was rumoured to have laid several other imprecations, with deadly consequences.[50] Whether or not those tales were true, their existence underlines an important point. When it came to the domain of magic, the notion of maleficent witchcraft was always nearby.

CHRISTIAN SCIENCE: A NEW WITCHCRAFT

In 1887 reports began appearing in the British press about a new health-focused religion currently causing controversy in the United States.[51] Christian Science was the creation of a formerly poor and fragile New Englander named Mary Baker Eddy (1821–1910). It promised its devotees nothing less than deliverance from all ills, bodily and social.[52] Ailments, Mary

Baker Eddy suggested in *Science and Health* (1875), her manual of Christian Science, were ultimately mental creations – the physical manifestations of negative and harmful thoughts. Copiously citing the King James Bible, occasionally referencing electricity, psychology, spiritualism and other modern notions, Baker Eddy explained that because illness was ultimately willed, usually by oneself though occasionally by others, wellness lay within everyone's grasp.[53] With enough training, sick people could cure themselves, not with physical treatments but by thinking healthily, in accordance with the principles of Christian Science. There was even hope for people unable bring themselves to the correct mental state. They could be made whole by the intervention of a qualified Christian Scientist, either in person or remotely.

Christian Science's doctrines of mental influence and mental healing had a dark side. If thinking healthily induced healing in oneself and others, what were the consequences of jealousy, envy, spite and hatred? Mary Baker Eddy would later try to downplay it, but for years she was preoccupied, obsessed even, with the danger of malicious animal magnetism (or MAM, as it was known for short).[54] Her disgruntled pupils and clients, she suggested, were using their mental powers to harm herself, her husband and even her Church. The notion that evil thoughts and ill-will caused real illnesses sounded, to some critics, suspiciously like traditional notions of sorcery and maleficent magic, albeit rendered in a novel pseudo-scientific parlance. For this reason Frank Podmore, a psychical investigator, described malicious animal magnetism as the 'New Witchcraft'.[55]

To British journalists in the late 1880s, Christian Science looked like a dangerous racket. The American courts were investigating the untimely deaths of Christian Scientists who'd dismissed their doctors and trusted to a 'mental cure'. Meanwhile, Mary Baker Eddy was making a fortune selling her books and lecture courses to would-be healers, who travelled the country doing the same to prospective patients, in a sort of spiritual pyramid scheme.

What the British press failed to notice about Christian Science was its feminism, which contributed much to its niche appeal.[56] As well as being controlled by female leaders, Christian Science was animated by a feminist theology, which elevated female imagery and designated woman as 'a higher ideal of God than man'.[57] Christian Science was feminist in its enmities as well as its enthusiasms. Baker Eddy hated mesmerism, not least because it was practised almost exclusively by men.[58] She reviled orthodox medicine for similar reasons. This resonated with some first-wave feminists, the rebellious women on both sides of the Atlantic, usually middle or upper middle class, who were agitating for greater educational and occupational opportunities, as well as the vote. To these women, Christian Science held out the prospect of professional power and of regaining control over their health, by wresting it back from the masculine medical profession.

Christian Science arrived in Britain during the gloomy summer of 1888, with the Whitechapel murders haunting London.[59] It was imported by Henrietta Lord, an alumna of Girton College, Cambridge, one of the first British women to receive a university education, among the first to exercise a measure of the state's executive power by serving as a Poor Law Guardian, and an early translator of the Norwegian playwright Henrik Ibsen.[60] A path-breaking feminist, Henrietta discovered Christian Science while travelling in America. In 1886 she purchased a magazine dedicated to female advancement, *Woman's World*, which was already committed to the radical new religion.

Henrietta Lord began delivering lectures on Christian Science's 'mental cure' in London, mostly to affluent ladies.[61] She was conscious of her new credo's failings, such as the 'ignorance and avarice' of Christian Science's American leaders, who were mostly concerned with 'money making'.[62] Despite her scruples, Henrietta was soon touting a range of Christian Science courses and cures to fashionable Londoners, costing from as little as £1 to as much as £20 – more than their housemaids would have earned in a year.[63] She also published a textbook under her pen-name Frances Lord, *Christian Science Healing* (1888), which outlined her interpretation of Mary Baker Eddy's obscure theology, and instructed would-be healers how to pique the interest of a new class of potential patients ('a common likeness of its members must be found ... all are seeking Satisfaction'). In her manual, Henrietta did not use the term 'malicious animal magnetism' or its abbreviation (MAM). But she presented mental attacks as genuine and dangerous: 'A malicious person may "will" out of your mind certain bodily ills.'[64] Ignoring this dark theme would have been foolhardy. Henrietta knew from experience that many potential Christian Scientists were concerned about evil occult influences. 'Students always ask,' she noted, 'cannot we do harm as well as good?'[65]

The *St James's Gazette*, a fashionable London paper, mocked Henrietta's manual. The *Morning Post* was less harsh, calling it 'curious, and in its way interesting'.[66] Quoting Spinoza, Bede and the Acts of the Apostles,

J.H. Newman, the gospels and even Hindu texts like the Bhagavad Gita, this first British incarnation of Christian Science spoke to highly educated people who were ill, unhappy, frustrated and dissatisfied. Promising health of body, peace of mind, and knowledge of truth, Henrietta Lord knew her audience was comprised mainly of affluent rebels. She therefore directly addressed herself to agnostics, atheists, freethinkers and those who had explored eastern religions, instructing them to 'lay aside your theory of Darwinian Evolution'. She used the example of women's recent advancement to illustrate the transformative potential of Christian Science. The choice of simile says a lot about her preoccupations, and the concerns of her audience.

The history of Christian Science shows how occult influences, both evil and benign, troubled some of Victorian Britain's most sophisticated, politically progressive and avant-garde people. But how many were brought within the fold of this radical, new, health-focused religion? During the 1890s, other women who had encountered Christian Science while travelling in America began tutoring groups in London, Brighton, Bedford and even the Welsh health resort of Llangammarch Wells.[67] Yet in each case the number of patients, or students, appears to have been in the low single digits. In November 1897, with the approval of Mary Baker Eddy's American mother Church, Britain's (and Europe's) first Christian Science Church was opened, in a former synagogue on Bryanston Street, Marylebone, London. At the dedication service about 300 people were present, a figure that probably reflects the smaller number of committed Christian Scientists, rather than the larger figure of those who briefly experimented with the 'mental cure'.[68]

BAPHOMET AND PAGANISM

During the later nineteenth century, at the fringes of respectable enquiry, scholars began to reshape and reinterpret magic. They did this by creating new, highly potent images of witches and their allies. Initially, these new interpretations of witches and devils were merely theoretical. In time though, after decades of cultural incubation, the motifs became markers of personal identity, as well as the focus of novel magical practices and religious rituals.

Take the figure of Baphomet, the androgynous horned deity with cloven hoofs, wings, a woman's body and a goat's head, marked by the sign of the pentagram.[69] It was drawn and named by the French occultist Éliphas Lévi, to illustrate his extremely influential *Dogme et rituel de la haute magie*, where Baphomet sat proudly on the frontispiece of volume two of the expanded second edition (1861). The name came from the insalubrious history of the Knights Templar, the warrior monks accused of numerous heresies, including worshipping a vile god called Baphomet. The image drew on many sources, including the half-human half-beast gods of ancient Egypt, medieval depictions of Satan as a goat or cloven-footed horn-headed man, and eighteenth-century tarot cards showing the devil with wings.

Lévi's concept of Baphomet was more expansive and ambiguous than the Christian devil. For Lévi, Baphomet was a universal figure, embodying good and evil, light and dark, male and female, reason and sensuality, destruction and creation, separation and amalgamation. The terror of all religions, the great agent of magic, 'le fantôme de toutes les épouvantes' (ghost of all fears), Baphomet had worshippers throughout history and in all nations.[70] Perhaps he had them still. According to Lévi, Baphomet's devotees did not conceive of him as Satan, the evil devil. Rather, they regarded Baphomet as the ancient god of the natural world: Pan.

Éliphas Lévi unveiled the image of Baphomet, accompanied with a few suggestive remarks, in 1854. Five years later another French historian, Jules Michelet, extended the idea. Witches, he argued, were neither Satanists nor sorcerers, but mystic physicians and devotees of ancient paganism. Not the paganism of Hellenic Greece or Imperial Rome, the focus of the curriculums at Britain's public schools. The witches' creed was imagined to be something more primal. An underground cult suppressed by Europe's Churches. A sensual nature religion dedicated to fertility, born in dark forests and amid stone circles, ruled by druids or perhaps even a female priesthood. This thesis arrived in Britain in 1863, in a translated and highly censored edition of Michelet's *La Sorcière: The Witch of the Middle Ages*. 'Written by a maniac,' was how one reviewer described it.[71] Another thought it 'a medley of rhapsody and reason ... a useless book.'[72] 'No more objectionable work could have been selected for translation,' judged the *Morning Post*: 'Deplorable but brilliant.'[73] Even in its redacted form, Michelet's text was not the sort of thing one would want falling into the hands of servants. Never mind his allusions to wild sex. What would the working classes make of Michelet's suggestion that modern Europeans should replace gloomy Christianity with a new nature religion, more conducive to humanity's need for liberation?[74] Even its translator admitted that the book was only suited to sophisticated enquirers, who'd abandoned denominational Protestantism as a result of biblical criticism and the rest.

Initially, the practising magicians of Victorian Britain did not really embrace the conception of the devil as Pan and witchcraft as paganism. By the 1880s there were signs that a few theosophists and middle-class occultists were beginning to do so. In 1886 *The Globe*, a notable London newspaper, made fun of what it called 'Anglo-Buddhism', a collection of esoteric ideas entertained by the rather advanced people of London and Oxford, including notions about 'Baphomet and Witches' Sabbaths'.[75] By the 1890s, there were reports about Baphomet or Satan worship taking place in Paris.[76] Shortly afterwards, the ceremonial magician Aleister Crowley adopted the persona of Baphomet when undertaking his most controversial conjurations.

Rather than avant-garde occultists, it was amateur British scholars who endorsed the idea that witches were pagans. The thesis became central to the work of folklorists, and was most fully and fancifully elaborated by the American Charles Leland. In 1891, at the International Folklore Conference at London's Burlington House, Leland received 'loud applause' when he laid out his new theory, about the survival of a sort of shamanic witchcraft in Tuscany, in northern Italy.[77] Witches weren't devil worshippers, Leland claimed, but individuals who inherited the power to travel abroad in ethereal form at night, in order to do battle with genuinely evil powers. In 1899 he published the thesis in *Aradia, or the Gospel of the Witches*.[78] This creative but unscholarly book went on to be a core text of Wicca, the neo-pagan nature religion founded by Gerald Gardner around the mid-twentieth century.

The interpretation of witchcraft as a pagan survival was persuasive, romantic and misleading. Witchcraft, understood as evil magic or malicious conjuration, was a human universal rather than a distinctive feature of the pre-Christian era. When later Victorian folklorists classified working-class people's supernatural cosmology as 'pagan', they obscured the Christian motifs saturating vernacular British magic. Cunning-folk saw their powers as divine gifts from the Abrahamic God, and used words from the Latin Bible in their written charms. Magical rites often involved biblical readings, witchcraft was understood in terms of the scriptural injunctions against sorcery, and witches were thought to be servants of the Christian devil. What is true is that some magical symbols had very ancient origins: the hexafoil for instance, six 'leaves' within a circle, which featured in medieval church architecture and modern British folk magic, was very old indeed. However, the folklorists who portrayed witchcraft as a pagan survival went much further than this, in some cases into the realm of fake scholarship and outright falsification.

STRIDENT CHRISTIANS REVIVE DEMONOLOGY

The late Victorian occult revival energised Christians. Some regarded communicating with disembodied souls (spiritualism) as positively diabolical, a revival of ancient sorcery.[79] In 1891, at Eastbourne Town Hall, the Rev. C.B. Cooper warned his audience that spiritualism was a form of satanic witchcraft, reborn to tempt the modern world:

> One of the sins of the flesh is witchcraft. The Witch of Endor had wonderful power, and it has gone on ever since. St. Paul would not have warned the Galatians against that sin of witchcraft if it did not exist. Witchcraft is of the devil. I know that in the Middle Ages many people were burned as witches who were not witches at all. Still there are certain persons – mediums – who have the power to give themselves over to evil spirits. It is an awful system. May the Lord preserve us from it.[80]

Appalled by the rise of both occult and secular worldviews, a tiny but growing number of clerics reacted by espousing extremely severe interpretations of Christianity. The Rev. Thomas Millington's *Signs and Wonders in the Land of Ham* (1873) was a history of the ten plagues of Egypt, which vouched for their veracity despite an absence of any corroborating evidence beyond the Old Testament. He insisted on the reality of witchcraft and sorcery too, 'or God would not have warned his people so solemnly against them'.[81] It pained the *Morning Post* to find a clergyman 'calmly recognising witchcraft', but he was not a solitary figure.[82] The Rev. Frederick George Lee (1832–1902), vicar of All Saints church in Lambeth and an extreme Anglo-Catholic, wrote a slew of mysterious-sounding tomes arguing for the unqualified reality of 'historical Christianity', miracles, angels, witches, devils, ghosts and all. Lee's *Glimpses of the Supernatural* (1875) was 'highly entertaining' and seriously told so as to 'make the flesh creep', one reviewer conceded. But the book could not rise above the limitations of its genre: it was clearly 'a really typical instance of opposition to modern materialism taking refuge in a wide belief in the supernatural'.[83]

An increasingly indulgent atmosphere permitted the re-emergence of something like demonology. Scoffers and sceptics were clearly becoming more sanguine. Thus the *London Daily News* reminded its readers: 'Superstition ... has large claims upon the toleration of political rule and upon the charity of social criticism.'[84] With the stigma of superstition waning slightly, believers became freer with their views. A few wrote to their local papers, testifying to the reality not just of spiritualism, but of old-style sorcery and magic too.[85] Others, in the mechanics' halls and assembly rooms of provincial Britain, challenged orators who dismissed witchcraft as nothing more than a 'popular superstition.'[86] In 1862, when one Dr Ash lectured on 'witchcraft and superstition' to residents of Launceston, Cornwall, a 'very warm discussion followed', with an audience member insisting 'there were witches in the days of old and there were witches in our day'.[87] In 1872, the Rev. R.G. Buckley spoke about witchcraft at the Eversholt Reading Room, Bedfordshire, insisting it was a 'superstition' based on the 'the most puerile evidence'. This was contradicted by the event's chairman, another local clergyman, who 'declared his inability to arrive at the same conclusion' because witchcraft's reality was acknowledged in the Holy Scripture.[88] In some cases, even lecturers edged towards endorsing the reality of occult forces. On the Isle of Mull, in 1869, the Rev. D. Macfarlyen was unsure 'whether witchcraft had its origins in man, or in something beyond man'.[89] At Edinburgh's Philosophical Institute in 1872, attendees at a talk on 'demonology' were informed that 'the great facts underlying sorcery had never yet been told'.[90]

At Buckenham, Norfolk, in the winter of 1896, the Rev. G. Elwin lectured on witchcraft. He catalogued the many references to it in the Bible, underlined how God prohibited malefic work, and reassured his audience: 'The devil could not harm anyone without God's permission.'[91] A generation previously, the address would have caused a minor local scandal, for rehearsing the traditional Christian arguments in favour of witchcraft's reality. But in the more open-minded 1890s, it passed without comment.

* * *

During the second half of the nineteenth century, avant-garde occultists revived, refreshed and reinterpreted witchcraft. Witches reappeared theoretically, in serious books, learned articles, sermons and lectures. But what they were, none could agree. Portrayed variously as pagans, magicians, fools, emitters of evil magnetism, and devil worshippers, in rarefied circles witches became many things indeed.

Mystic interpersonal harm mattered deeply to the late Victorian occult revival. Some learned magicians used the traditional language of sorcery, and attempted to practise or combat the dark arts. Others reinterpreted occult interpersonal attacks. Notably, spiritualists, theosophists and Christian Scientists developed a jargon about 'evil', 'malicious' and 'bad' magnetism that resonated long after the nineteenth century. Malicious magic was given new, sophisticated and scientific-sounding names, more suited to the modern world.

Witchcraft thus became a little more prominent, in British highbrow and middlebrow culture. From non-existent in the 1850s, it had become a niche interest by the 1890s. The revival, however slight, is worth ruminating on. The French anthropologist Olivier Roy notes a paradox of secularisation, where general religious decline brings forth extreme spiritualities at the margins.[92] To put it another way, as aggregate religiosity falls across a society, there is a rise in the number of people adhering to vivid spiritualities, where the supernatural is ever present and instantly accessible.

Roy regards this as a distinctive feature of the contemporary western world, and thinks it helps explain the rise of terroristic jihad. Perhaps it does: but Roy's history is wrong. The later nineteenth-century occult revival is a good example of this strange dynamic at work: of religious decline engendering radical spiritualities, at the fringes. The 'crisis of faith', which beset some of the British intelligentsia during the 1840s and 1850s, made the occult revival possible. It created seekers estranged from the faith of their forefathers, thirsty to drink at new fountains of knowledge. More importantly, by undermining the idea of Christian orthodoxy to which all should subscribe, the crisis of faith liberated mystically minded people to explore new domains.

From the 1860s, British opinion makers grew more tolerant of radical spiritualities. This tolerance, which has slowly grown until the present day, is a key theme in the modern history of magic. But as we'll see in the next chapter, it was not driven just by events at home, in Britain. Experiences abroad, in the vast territories of the British Empire, also made some Britons wonder whether witchcraft deserved a second look.

SEVEN

GONE NATIVE
Witchcraft in the British Empire and beyond

Does education cure a person of superstition? From Enlightenment philosophers like Adam Smith to contemporary social workers, many commentators have suggested that it does.[1] Apparently, the more schooling someone has, the more they're exposed to the rational arts and sciences, the less they'll imagine that supernatural forces permeate everyday life. They'll know better, think critically, and be unwilling to attribute inexplicable events to magical causes.

A sensible, attractive argument. Sadly though, it doesn't accord with reality. With every year, it seems, more academic research is revealing that formal education alone is not powerful enough to create sceptics. Witness the surveys of sub-Saharan African opinion, which find over 50 per cent of secondary school graduates claiming to believe in witchcraft, and almost as many university attendees.[2] No wonder two neuroscientists studying the 'paranormal mind' deduce that supernatural thinking is 'largely resistant towards education.'[3]

Under certain circumstances, in particular environments and atmospheres, even the most learned people can begin to believe. Take Edward Evans-Pritchard. This Oxford- and LSE-educated scholar pioneered the sub-field of cultural anthropology, with his now classic text *Witchcraft, Oracles and Magic among the Azande* (1937). While researching his book,

Evans-Pritchard lived for a year or so with the Azande tribal farmers inhabiting the sparsely populated savannahs of southern Sudan. Focusing particularly on their witchcraft beliefs and practices because of their deep importance to the Azande, during his immersive fieldwork, something odd happened to Evans-Pritchard.[4] Despite his western upbringing and elite education, he too started to think in terms of witchcraft, becoming a sort of temporary believer. 'I had no difficulty using Zande notions as Azande themselves use them,' was how he later put it, without specifying whether or not he'd adopted these ideas deliberately.[5]

Evans-Pritchard was not alone. During the nineteenth and early twentieth centuries many Britons had similar, mentality-shifting experiences. Expatriates, particularly those living in the colonies of the British Empire, were notorious for succumbing to weird ideas and undergoing strange changes of heart. Ensconced in exotic climes, living among unfamiliar peoples, exposed to alien belief systems, colonists were even said to become more occult minded. Reams have been written about the culture, politics and economics of modern imperialism. But amid this plenty, the stereotype of the credulous colonist and the superstitious settler has not been investigated.[6] Doubtless this is because imperial historians assume that white Britons viewed the world through coldly secular eyes, dismissing native magic as contemptible humbug. As we shall see, the truth was different.

There were certainly a lot of expatriates, during the first age of globalisation, in the heyday of the European empires. The 1880s, a particularly mobile decade, saw some 2.5 million people sail from the UK to extra-European destinations, with around 500,000 making the return journey.[7] A significant minority sought new lives for themselves in the United States. But many more headed for the colonies of the rapidly growing British Empire, especially the white settler societies of New Zealand, Australia, Canada and South Africa. Smaller numbers went to places where Europeans were far less numerous, such as West Africa, India, the Caribbean and Malaysia. For Anglo-Saxons especially, foreign opportunities abounded. By the time Edward VII ascended to the throne in 1901, his empire encompassed almost a quarter of the globe and 400 million people, only 41.5 million of whom lived in the British Isles.[8]

Colonial Britons didn't suddenly become devout believers in exotic magic. Settlers, administrators, missionaries, district officers, traders, soldiers and others liked to see themselves as vastly more rational than the superstitious natives. Foreign notions about witchcraft were, they often said, 'all a delusion' and 'simply farcical'.[9] Privately though, expats were less dismissive. Whether they lived in India or Africa, the antipodes or the Caribbean, time abroad changed them, subtly and unexpectedly. Eventually, some began asking themselves whether the locals were not totally wrong about the reality of the occult. Walter Bagehot, one of the Victorian era's greatest commentators, noted this peculiar émigré outlook: 'Every sort of European resident in the East, even the shrewd merchant and the "post-captain", with his bright, wakeful eyes of commerce, comes soon to believe in witchcraft, and to assure you, in confidence, that there "really is something in it"'.[10]

'Something in it' was almost a cliché, the sort of tentative, highly quali-fied endorsement of native notions that colonists used, if they managed to overcome their feelings of self-consciousness.[11] 'I am not such a fool as to assert there is nothing in "witchcraft", nor would I endorse the view that witchcraft murders are instances of childish barbarisms.'[12] So wrote Joshua Flood, a legal expert at the Colonial Office, in a letter to the Governor of Tanganyika, East Africa, in 1937. Flood's letter was a rare instance of an official publicly expressing his supernatural sentiments. Usually, personal sources give us a more candid view of what, for some, was an embarrassing, disgraceful way of thinking. Among the best of those sources are the diaries and private papers of Dr Stanley George Browne (1907–86).

BAPTIST MEETS WITCH

In the morning, Browne went to the river. There he could forget the leprosy, malaria, smallpox and sleeping sickness – the horrific illnesses blighting people he met every day.

This was a deadly place. But it was also sublime, he reflected, mean-dering down the banks of the Congo, beside the mile-wide muddy waters, under the canopy of an equatorial rainforest, in the heat and humidity, with a thousand insects humming all around. Today though, he would not enjoy this tropical environment alone. Coming towards him, through the under-growth, was a figure. A woman, he could now see, who was moving oddly. Was she skipping? And something else. From head to toe, she was covered with the local marker of innocence – white chalk.[13]

When they met, he asked her why. She explained that her people had long suspected her of using witchcraft to make them ill. She'd endured this reputation until recently, when their accusations became fiercer. To dispel them, she'd consented to undergo the ordeal of the poison oracle. It meant drinking a dangerous concoction, made from the bark of the *nkasa* tree.[14] People who threw it up were deemed innocent. Those who responded differently (that is, died) were declared to be witches.[15]

A vicious revelatory system presided over by tribal leaders, the poison ordeal had been outlawed by the Belgian colonial government for at least a generation. Yet amid the Congolese people's intense fear of witches and understandable suspicion of their white overlords, the imperial authorities struggled to suppress it fully. In 1894 a missionary working in what was then a diabolically exploited part of Africa saw an 'epidemic of accusations of witchcraft', with several people dying from the poison ordeal in the month of December alone.[16] Thankfully the woman chalked in white, who underwent the same ordeal half a century later, didn't share their fate. She survived, and now everyone in her clan said she'd committed no crime.[17]

Dr Stanley Browne was a celebrated medical missionary hailing from Britain, and made Belgian-ruled Africa his home for almost two and a half decades, between 1936 and 1959. Needless to say, Dr Browne frequently encountered Congolese people who fervently believed in witchcraft. The first time he left his mission station at Yakusu to visit tribes living in the forest, he was greeted by a powerful 'witch doctor', or *nganga* (meaning 'medicine man').[18] With seventeen wives and eighty-three children in train, he was an awesome figure, wearing a headdress of parrot feathers, a leopard-skin girdle jangling with shells and beads, and a necklace made of leopard's teeth decorated with soot and sticky resin, and resplendent with two monkey tails dangling down his back. Patients at Dr Browne's infirmary often wore charms and fetishes crafted by this man – carved pieces of wood painted with the blood of a chicken, or special nutshells fastened around their ankles. Once, a woman arrived at the missionary hospital terrified she was about to die, because outside her hut she'd discovered blood and chicken bones – the ingredients of a malicious spell.[19]

One might think that such experiences would convince a foreigner that African witchcraft was a blend of arrant nonsense and dangerous superstition, especially someone like Dr Stanley Browne, a world-renowned expert on leprosy, Fellow of the Royal College of Physicians, author of numerous academic books and articles, and bearer of advanced degrees from universities in Britain and Europe. Browne's official biography certainly portrayed him as a relentless enemy of superstition, who used Christianity and medical science to fight witchcraft belief and the witch doctors who propagated it.[20]

The missionary's gleaming image did not correspond with grim reality. In his private diary (now held by the Wellcome Collection, in London), Dr Browne revealed his inner thoughts, which amounted to a limited belief in the world of African magic. Congolese witches worked through a combination of herbalism, psychological suggestion and a genuine ability to control dark mystic powers, Stanley Browne thought. Or, as he put it in his diary, they spread their evil by: '1. Subtle poisons. 2. Hypnotism. 3. Unknown psychic means.'[21] Because Dr Browne thought some witches genuinely embodied spiritual evil, he opposed the colonial laws designed to suppress witch doctors. After all, by detecting the authentic 'spiritual power' of witches, the medicine men were doing important work.

It might sound remarkable that a highly educated European physician thought like this, but Dr Browne was not alone. In the nineteenth-century Transvaal, in what would later become a province of British South Africa, German missionaries harboured similar sentiments.[22] In 1932 none other than Dr John Aglionby, the Anglican Bishop of Accra (capital of the Gold Coast, now Ghana), warned journalists not to dismiss the reality of African witchcraft. As he recuperated in his Kent garden from a bout of malaria, he insisted: 'It is not possible that such an unholy sway can be maintained by fraud alone.'[23] The domain of African occultism was undoubtedly awash with error, superstition and criminality. Yet to some godly minds, it also contained an element of truth – a dark revelation about the reality of supernatural evil in this world, as well as the next.

SUPERSTITION AND IMPERIALISM

'The phenomena of witchcraft in the heathen world are too numerous to be explained away.' So insisted a reader of the *Worcester Chronicle*, in a letter sent to the paper in 1861.[24] There was something bitterly ironic about Europeans finding themselves affected or in some way touched by the magic of the peoples whose lands they colonised. Ironic because, according to imperial dogma, the opposite was destined to happen: white colonists would bring rationalistic outlooks to the distant corners of the globe.

Imperialism may have been 'primarily a money making concern', as George Orwell put it, but like other European empires, the British Empire was also supposedly a civilising mission, designed to improve the earth's primitive tribes and emancipate its savage peoples.[25] Missionaries, government officials, industrialists and adventurers claimed that the spread of British rule over foreign lands would curtail native violence, superstition and irrationality, replacing those destructive habits with the rule of law, free trade, Christianity and science. This ostensibly altruistic but actually self-serving way of thinking has been called a 'fully encoded discourse of Orientalism', though it was actually applied to the world well beyond the orient.[26] European commentators of every political permutation espoused it, from critics of some aspects of colonialism like the London-based Aborigines' Protection Society to thoroughly oppositional figures like Karl Marx.[27] As a jobbing journalist in 1850s London, Marx claimed that, for all the misery the East India Company had brought to the Indian subcontinent, British imperialism was ultimately a progressive force because it smashed patriarchal village communities, the alleged foundations of 'Oriental despotism' that shaped Indians into an 'unresisting tool of superstition'.[28] It was not until the close of the nineteenth century that more fundamental critiques of imperialism emerged, particularly after journalists revealed the horrors perpetrated in the Belgian Congo. Even then, the British Empire continued to be portrayed benignly until at least the outbreak of the Second World War.[29]

Britain's civilising mission to the world masked a self-interested policy, but it was not entirely disingenuous. As well as fighting slavery (but only after it was abolished in the British Empire in 1834), the colonial authorities made some effort to suppress certain magical practices and to stop indigenous people from executing alleged witches. Politicians in London occasionally gave impetus to the campaign against destructive superstition. In 1883, after hearing about a series of massacres on the West African island of Sherbro, Under-Secretary of State for the Colonies Evelyn Ashley wrote to the local chiefs through whom British rule was mediated, ordering them not to execute people found guilty of witchcraft.[30] Ashley was clearly concerned about the alleged witches' plight, though his response of sending a threatening letter reflected his lack of power to do much about it. Elsewhere, it was not humanitarian sympathy but political expediency that motivated colonial attacks on indigenous magical traditions. From the Caribbean to Africa, magical practitioners were often at the forefront of anti-colonial resistance. At the same time, some colonists established cordial relations with local people, by sharing medicines, food and scraps of land. Africans, Australian Aboriginal people, Māoris and others reciprocated by using their supernatural traditions to heal ailing settlers. For once sceptical people, these encounters with exotic magic could be truly mind-altering.

THE OCCULT IN THE OUTBACK

Even by the sickly standards of nineteenth-century Australia, Bangate Station was a bad place to fall ill. Workers had been known to quit good jobs at the massive sheep ranch on the plains of New South Wales solely because it lacked proper medical facilities. During the 1890s, the nearest doctor lived 80 miles away. The closest railway station was the same distance again. Getting there took four days, assuming, of course, one had access to an experienced coachman who knew how to guide his horses down the rough bush roads.

Without professionally qualified physicians, when someone fell ill at Bangate Station, other arrangements had to be made. This happened frequently. Along with 138,000 sheep, the ranch's 250 acres were home to hundreds of people, including the proprietor, his wife and occasional parties of well-heeled guests. A large body of rather less affluent white labourers drove and sheared the animals, sleeping in draughty shacks under corrugated iron roofs. Most numerous of all was a clan of Aboriginal people, members of the Euahlayi tribe.[31] A few worked inside the master's house as servants, while others cared for the sheep.

Regardless of class, race or gender, if someone ailed on Bangate Station, Katie Parker took charge. The wife of the owner, Mr Langloh Parker, Katie ran the station while her husband was away, negotiating sales of wool and mutton. When he was at home, she took responsibility for the house, feeding the workers and treating the sick. Drawing on experience and an old medical manual, Katie issued prescriptions from her stock of patent medicines. If they were lucky, her patients also received extra rations of tobacco. But when a serious illness struck, Mrs Parker always consulted a certain Aboriginal woman, someone she called 'our witch-woman'.[32]

Her real name was Bootha. Aged over 60, she was a *wirreenun*, a shaman who in an altered state of consciousness communed with other-worldly spirits, seeking their guidance on how to heal, harm and change the weather. Her people, the Euahlayi, generally selected males to undergo the long induction into the shaman's craft.[33] But somehow Bootha had acquired a trove of magical expertise and a reputation to match. At Bangate Station, the Aboriginal people told the whites stories about her wonderful cures, her mysterious pets and her supernatural ability to summon rainfall onto the arid landscape.

Like other *wirreenuns*, Bootha did much of her magic with poles, which she carved, painted and imbued with the power of spirit animals (totems). One stick, strategically planted in the ranch owner's garden, warded off the malicious spirits of the dead. Another was supposed to keep away the spirits emanating from the sunset at the close of each day. Two further poles stopped alligators from swimming in the water tank.[34] But most impressive of all was Bootha's stick for predicting death. Many at Bangate Station became firm believers in this inauspicious upright when, one afternoon, while 'the air was quite still', it fell in the direction of the master's house. Hours later, news arrived that the cook's mother had just died.

Katie Parker once asked Bootha to help cure a female guest, a white girl named Adelaide, who'd become unaccountably pale and exhausted. Clearing the furniture from the centre of the room, where the invalid lay in repose, the shaman squatted down and began muttering to the spirits in an 'unintelligible dialect'. 'Presently her voice ceased,' Katie Parker remembered, 'and we heard from beside her a most peculiar whistling sort of voice, to which she [Bootha] responded, evidently interrogating. Again the whistling voice from further away.' Two recently deceased Aborigines had made contact, but they would not say what was wrong with the girl. A third was called and supplied the answer: Adelaide was ill because she'd bathed in the shade of a taboo tree, the Minggah, which was only to be touched by the shamans themselves. As this final spirit made its revelation, Katie Parker saw Bootha's lips move. Bootha, or the spirit, explained how a swarm of spirit bees had attacked Adelaide's liver, stinging and covering it with a waxy substance. Remarkably, the patient admitted that she'd swum in a pool beneath the shade of the special tree. And strangely, her back was indeed inflamed near the liver. Bootha told the girl to consume nothing hot and to take a long cold drink before bed, assuring her that she would be better in the morning. After rubbing Adelaide's wrists and mumbling an incantation, she left.

Katie Parker couldn't deny it: her patient 'looked a better colour the next morning, and rapidly recovered'. But was there any reason to think Bootha's cure was genuinely supernatural? Most of the time, Mrs Parker thought not. In an unpublished memoir, she claimed the old shaman was no more than 'a good physician and a ventriloquist'.[35] Apparently, the reason she regularly asked Bootha to make it rain and to cure the sick was to elicit ethnographic material for her path-breaking book, *The Euahlayi Tribe* (1905). Yet it's possible Mrs Parker had additional motivations. In 1899 she wrote a note for the Society for Psychical Research, an illustrious London outfit dedicated to investigating purported occult activity, where she presented Bootha in a less dismissive light.[36] We'll probably never know exactly what Katie thought about the old Euahlayi shaman, but if she was tempted – occasionally, fleetingly – to believe Bootha's magic might counter the hardships of outback life, Mrs Parker would not have been alone.

Since they first landed in Australia in 1788, European colonists had been borrowing from the Aboriginal people. Desperately short on medical supplies, settlers soon learnt to use their herbal teas and plant-based salves.[37] It's often assumed that Europeans shunned Aboriginal supernatural therapies, but this may not have been the case. Some colonists undoubtedly believed in magic, like the German immigrants who brought to Australia copies of the notorious spell book known as the *6th and 7th Books of Moses*.[38] Witchcraft accusations were made by people like Gotfried Hoffmann, who in 1854 was sentenced to hard labour by South Australia's Supreme Court, for feloniously wounding Mary Ann Wressel, who he said bewitched his cows and pigs.[39] British settlers protected their new homes with apotropaic objects used in Europe: with shoes concealed in roofs, mummified cats placed between walls, and ritual markings.[40]

By the 1890s, when Katie Parker was asking Bootha to heal the workers and bring rain to her farm, 'occultism' was 'in the air', with residents of Australia's great cities attending séances, having their fortunes told, and consulting clairvoyants.[41] In 1912 Mr W.G. Couch wrote to the Ballarat police to complain: 'I am under witchcraft, and am robbed at every turn I take. Even my camp has been robbed.'[42] The techniques Aboriginal people used to bewitch others were widely known among Australia's white settlers. Newspapers used the phrase 'pointing the bone', correctly assuming that their readers would know this term referred to a shaman using a human shinbone to direct harmful powers.[43] In this uncanny atmosphere, it seems perfectly possible that Katie Parker credited Bootha's powers more than she liked to admit.

What of Bootha herself – why did she use her magic to help elites like Katie and Langloh Parker, who owned so much of New South Wales? Clearly the old shaman did it to survive, to receive food, blankets, tobacco and clothes from the ranch owners. But she also had more emotional and less instrumental motivations. Her shamanism expressed her people's independence, and sometimes Bootha used it to bemoan the life the Euahlayi had come to lead. Once, after the ranch owners offended her, she refused to call for rain on their behalf. On another occasion, Bootha told Katie Parker that her rain magic had failed because the spirits disliked the white people, who were responsible for driving away the emus, possums and kangaroos that formerly made up the 'black fellow's food'.[44]

Colonial commentators claimed that white Australians 'never had to face the troubles of witchcraft'.[45] In reality, settlers brought mysticism from Europe and learnt to believe in certain aspects of Aboriginal magic. But superstitious settlers were not just found in Australia. Across the British Empire, everyday life seldom matched up to the complacent rhetoric about credulity being the peculiar province of non-white people. From India to Africa to the Caribbean to New Zealand, magical beliefs were surprisingly contagious.

MĀORIS AND *MAKUTU*: WITCHCRAFT IN NEW ZEALAND

Witchcraft figured in the white invasion, or colonisation, of New Zealand. In 1830 the country's two islands were home to just 300 Europeans, whom the 50,000 or so Māoris called 'Pākehās'. Huge numbers of settlers soon arrived, particularly after New Zealand was annexed to the British Empire in 1840. By the 1880s, half a million people of European extraction lived there.[46]

Early apologists for the invasion claimed British rule would civilise the Māori and other indigenous people by extinguishing their barbarous customs and gross superstitions like slavery, cannibalism, infanticide and

165

the killing of witches.[47] It was true that the Māori regarded witchcraft, which they called *makutu*, as a major cause of misfortune.[48] Yet, if anything, European immigration enhanced rather than reduced the place of *makutu* in Māori life, at least initially. White settlers brought sicknesses – influenza, whooping cough, typhoid, tuberculosis, cholera and more. By the 1840s Māori communities were so devastated that the German traveller and physician Ernest Dieffenbach thought they might soon die out altogether.[49] Little wonder many Māoris blamed *makutu* for their plight.[50] Little wonder they called British missionaries '*he iwi makutu*' – people who cast witchcraft.[51] In the privacy of their diaries, exasperated clergymen seethed. They wanted to make converts. Instead, they were 'very frequently' accused of killing Māoris with witchcraft. In 1835, when taking part in a prestigious tribal gathering, the Rev. Henry Williams actually had his cloak torn by an angry chief, who accused him of '*makutuing* people'.[52]

Although retributive magic and curative incantations abounded, Māori chiefs claimed the right to execute people of their own race whom they judged responsible for bringing death with *makutu*.[53] During the 1840s one observer claimed that murders of supposed witches were becoming 'less frequent' in the coastal regions where Māoris and Europeans lived closely.[54] This may have been overly optimistic. Between 1845 and 1872 many Māoris fought back against the Pākehās, in what are now known as the New Zealand Wars.[55] Wary of alienating more indigenous locals, the British authorities found it expedient to ignore witch-killings or else treat the perpetrators very leniently.[56] In 1859, a tribal court at Kawakawa ordered the execution of a suspected sorcerer. The government's response went no further than dismissing the chief from his salaried position as an assessor.[57] Between 1875 and 1877 Māori tribunals sentenced at least three people to death for *makutu*. The colonial government made no attempt to punish the executioners.[58]

Around the turn of the twentieth century, this changed. With the Māoris now comprising just 5 per cent of New Zealand's total population, they were in no position to oppose the state's monopoly on the use of force. Along with more purposeful policing, Christianity and public education initiatives largely put an end to the practice of killing witches.[59] However, belief in *makutu* was far from extinct. Emulating Britain's domestic laws against pretend witchcraft, in 1893 the colonial authorities prescribed hard labour for individuals claiming to 'exercise or use any kind of witchcraft, sorcery, enchantment, or conjuration'.[60] In 1907, as New Zealand gained Dominion status, its government went further by issuing the Tohunga Suppression Act, which aimed to quash Māori supernatural healers known as *tohunga* (literally translated as 'expert' or 'adept').[61] White officials and educated Māoris too were worried about the emergence of new-style *tohungas*, often younger than their venerable predecessors, who eclectically combined herbalism, Christianity and Māori magic.[62] State-funded Māori newspapers mocked the idea of *makutu*, and some commentators even tried to substitute it with the notion of *mate Māori* – 'Māori illness', meaning an esoteric sickness that was not caused by the evil magic of another person.[63] Ultimately though, the culture of *makutu* was curtailed and changed by these initiatives, not destroyed.

British settlers, far from bringing enlightenment, often found themselves acquiring new supernatural fears from Māoris. The defiantly independent inhabitants of Te Urewera, a tract of dense forest and rugged hills on the North Island, were notoriously great witches.[64] When they travelled to the coast, other Māoris dared not refuse their requests, in case they used *makutu* in revenge. White immigrants picked up this unnerving idea and took it seriously, according to Dr Dieffenbach in 1843.[65] None more so than the Pākehā Māori, the runaway sailors, mutinous soldiers and fugitive convicts who joined Māori communities, had their faces tattooed, and embraced tribal culture.[66] Kimble Bent (1837–1916) affiliated with the Māoris of South Taranki after deserting from his army regiment, eventually becoming a healer and caster of *makutu*.[67]

The experiences of Frederick Manning (1812–83), a Pākehā Māori of Anglo-Irish origin, illustrate how someone previously unfamiliar with Māori magic might start to believe in it. In his memoirs, Frederick recalled his first uncanny encounter with a *tohunga*, an old man with one eye, who muttered mysterious incantations while giving him pieces of ritual food. 'I remember I felt a curious sensation at the time, like what I fancied a man must feel who had just sold himself, body and bones, to the devil. For a moment I asked myself the question whether I was not actually being then and there handed over to the powers of darkness.'[68] It's hardly surprising Frederick Manning felt bedevilled, as the *tohunga* may well have been trying to injure him with black magic, using the standard *makutu* method of reciting a spell while the victim ate.[69]

More conventional colonists also learnt, in some way, to believe in *tohungas* and fear *makutu*. When they were displaced from their ancestral lands, Māoris marked their departures with magic, aiming bitter maledictions at the new occupiers. This was particularly so when white settlers built farms or roads on *wahi tapu*, or sacred ground.[70] After Māori-owned land in Waikato was seized during the New Zealand Wars, local *tohungas* reportedly stood on the confiscation boundary line and cursed the land appropriated by the covetous Pākehās.[71] It may have been scant comfort to the dispossessed, but fears about Māori curses genuinely haunted the minds of at least some European incomers. White farmers occasionally blamed their inability to prosper on Māori witchcraft, and even the newspapers used phrases like 'a *makutu* seems to be upon the land' when reporting on agricultural failures.[72] In 1924, farmers from the North Island told a government minister that *makutu* was blighting the area.[73] Among other things, they blamed it for unfinished road improvements.

If this sounds unlikely, consider the tribulations of the North Island's Rangiriri highway, which opened in 1925.[74] Marred by obstacles and obstructions, including the relocation of an old Māori graveyard, it took three years to construct just 17 miles. Reporting from the scene, a journalist described how the builders thought the delays were owed to black magic: 'The men on the job speak mysteriously of "makutu". Sometimes it is with bated breath, sometimes a twinkle may be detected in the eye, but the purport is the same – the Rangiriri job has been under a potent spell.'

In 1929, a burst reservoir on Mount Eden was blamed on an elderly lady who, years earlier, cursed the area.[75] And by the eve of the Second World War, *makutu* had become such a widely known and regularly used word in New Zealand that one etymologist thought it 'may be regarded as incorporated in the English Language'.[76]

SLAVERY AND SORCERY: *OBEAH* IN THE CARIBBEAN

On Jamaica, Barbados and the other tropical islands comprising the British Caribbean, the colonial authorities regarded anything savouring of witchcraft as politically perilous. Between the 1840s and 1870s developments in coal-powered shipping halved the time it took to travel there from England, from about six weeks to three. The world was shrinking, yet maintaining order remained paramount for the Anglo-Caribbean's dominant white minority.[77] Making up just 2–3 per cent of the 1.6 million population, they looked with suspicion on the mixed race people who comprised about a fifth of the populace, and with fearful contempt on the black majority, the descendants of slaves whose ancestors had been kidnapped from Africa to work on coffee and sugar plantations.[78]

Jamaica's government had long tried to shore up the island's plantation society by prohibiting a type of syncretic magic known as *obeah*. Proscriptions against it began in 1760, following an uprising orchestrated by a man named Tacky. He led slaves in revolt by giving them charms and powders designed to protect them in battle, binding them together with secret oaths, and helping them poison their white masters.[79]

An *obeah* man, Tacky was a gifted practitioner of a versatile and morally ambiguous form of supernatural power. Developed by plantation slaves, *obeah* blended West African rituals with herbalism, Islam, Christianity and even a smattering of British folk magic.[80] Its songs, dances, battle charms and animal sacrifices to powerful spirits were reminiscent of supernatural rites practised by people across sub-Saharan Africa. But though scholars seldom mentioned it, other facets of *obeah* had European roots. To discover a thief's identity, *obeah* men and *obeah* women placed a key in a Bible, bound and suspended the book by a piece of thread, and watched the way it turned while suspects read from the 50th psalm.[81] The technique was very similar to the Bible and key method of divination that had been used in Britain since at least the seventeenth century.[82] Commenting on *obeah* practitioners, one colonial doctor was surely right when he noted that Bible and key divination had 'been taught them by the whites'.[83] The same was true of '*obeah* bottles', which were buried on landholdings to protect crops from light-fingered intruders. While they were put to different uses, materially *obeah* bottles were much like the witch-bottles used in Britain, containing nails, bent pins and, as a contemporary who'd examined one put it, 'A conglomeration of substances of which I can give no correct statement.'[84]

The heirs to several diverse supernatural traditions, *obeah* men and *obeah* women claimed numerous extraordinary powers. Purportedly, they could bewitch and unwitch, heal, fascinate, charm, tell fortunes, detect stolen goods, protect their clients' homes, discover fortunes, reveal unfaithful lovers, command spirits (called 'duppies') and more.[85] Apologists for white dominance maintained that *obeah* had so 'retarded the moral improvement of the blacks' as to render them 'unfit for the common occupations of life'.[86] Yet *obeah* didn't just trouble Afro-Caribbean people. After the abolition of slavery in 1834, Jamaican whites continued to blame *obeah* for causing unusual deaths, and worried about the influence that *obeah* men and *obeah* women seemed to have over the black majority.[87]

Obeah's connection with black liberation was suggested by the example of Haiti. There, a voodoo rite began the slave uprising of 1791, which ultimately overthrew white rule and established the New World's first black republic. To stop the spirit of magic-inspired liberation from afflicting Jamaica, a law of 1856 extended the prohibitions on *obeah* beyond oath taking and poisoning to persons who practised *obeah* in any way. Henceforth, they could expect hard labour and the lash.[88] The blanket law was meant for peacetime. In periods of crisis, *obeah* was pitilessly suppressed. After martial law was declared during the Morant Bay rebellion of 1865, an alleged *obeah* man was summarily tried and shot. Another was killed for possessing an *obeah* stick (painted yellow and black, with a snake's carved head) and a cursing object known as an '*obeah* baby' (described as a 'hideous wooden doll').[89]

In these repressive conditions, Afro-Caribbean people generally concealed *obeah* from the white people.[90] The forbidden topic was not spoken about openly or candidly, visitors noted.[91] For most white commentators, it was axiomatic that *obeah* was only practised by black and coloured West Indians – by 'the silly negroes', as the *London Evening Standard* patronisingly put it.[92] These commentators further defined *obeah* as a sort of pretend witchcraft, owing what genuine potency it possessed to natural poisons and the power of mental suggestion.[93] Such was the white elite's official, public view.

Privately, some whites thought *obeah* had real occult qualities. 'Obeah is ... dreaded almost as much by the whites as by the black people,' one writer observed, in a short story of 1899, and he was probably right.[94] Giving evidence to a House of Commons inquiry over a century earlier, in 1789, a Jamaican planter confessed that he not only allowed his ailing slaves to be treated by *obeah* men, but that he'd procured their services for himself too.[95] He was not a singular figure. According to the novelist and social reformer Charles Kingsley, early nineteenth-century Jamaica was home to plenty of respectable white men and women who half-believed in the powers of *obeah* men.[96] Kingsley claimed such superstitious fears had disappeared from the minds of white Jamaicans by the 1870s, yet he was wrong about the spread of scepticism. In 1888 the Irish botanist Edith Blake, a regular visitor to the Bahamas and an attentive observer, noted 'a secret belief in obeahism' among all of the islanders, including the whites.[97] Plantation owners certainly used *obeah* to frighten their black neighbours.[98] To do this, they would conspicuously hire *obeah* men to 'let go plenty crimbo' – to cast spells and make charms in their fields, hoping this display would scare away thieves from stealing crops.[99]

Obeah wasn't just important to the black, white and mixed heritage people of the Caribbean. Its influence extended to the thousands of Indian migrants who arrived as indentured labourers following the abolition of slavery in 1834–8.[100] South Asians were particularly concentrated in Guyana and Trinidad, though smaller numbers settled across many other islands. Like the rest of the Caribbean's peoples, they soon began to draw on *obeah* when they fell strangely ill, needed to divine the future, felt they were bewitched, or wanted to visit harmful magic upon their enemies.[101] Becoming centrally involved in the practice of *obeah* was difficult but not impossible, when communities living alongside each other began witnessing different rituals, festivals, habits and customs.[102] In time, spiritually attuned people of South Asian heritage became *obeah* men and *obeah* women, thereby adding various Hindu, Islamic and South Asian concepts to the already diverse supernatural tradition. On Trinidad, some famous *obeah* men were also Hindu priests, or Brahmins. In rooms filled with images of Hindu and other deities, they conducted their consultations while sitting in impossible yoga positions, back straight, legs crossed, head fixed and hands clasped.[103]

With the waning of colonialism during the twentieth century, *obeah* gradually came out into the open. On Jamaica, prosecutions against people who practised this rich style of magic began to fade around the time all adults won the right to vote, in 1944. Revealingly, the last conviction occurred in 1964, two years after independence.[104] *Obeah* remained stigmatised, on Jamaica and elsewhere, not least because of the influence of evangelical Christianity. But that stigma too diminished, in subsequent decades. Partly this was thanks to the efforts of the Jamaican prime minister Edward Seaga, who insisted that *obeah* was a type of faith healing and part of the Caribbean's precious cultural heritage.[105] Technically, *obeah* remained illegal on Jamaica, but the prohibitions against it were removed in Anguilla (in 1980), Barbados (1998), Trinidad and Tobago (2000), and St Lucia (2004).[106] In less than half a century, *obeah*'s official status had been utterly reversed. Reflecting this change, in 1981 the people of Jamaica's wedding gift for Prince Charles and Lady Diana was an *obeah*-influenced painting by local artist Mallaci 'Kapo' Reynolds (1911–89), named *Shining Spring*.[107]

BEYOND COLONIAL POWER: WITCHCRAFT AND WITCH-HUNTING IN INDIA

India was the 'jewel in the crown of England', according to the novelist and serial prime minister Benjamin Disraeli. This gem of a territory was first mined by the East India Company, a multinational corporation powered by its own army, civil service, and a trade monopoly on eastern goods and spices.[108] Beginning in the 1610s with a few scattered coastal trading bases, from the 1750s the company rapidly expanded its dominion, deploying its forces against the Maratha Empire, winning direct control of large parts of southern and eastern India, and indirectly governing much of the rest of the subcontinent through hundreds of client dynasties.

Crucially, political power brought the ability to tax.[109] Local levies were used to fund the thousands of white soldiers, clerks, hill station administrators, district officers, magistrates and others who pursued lucrative careers in this part of the orient, along with numerous indigenous subordinates.[110] Yet, under the influence of political philosophers like James Mill, theorising from his London study, the East India Company's ambitions grew beyond commerce and careerism. As the eighteenth century gave way to the nineteenth, the company sought to remodel Indian society and culture, purging it of superstitions and barbarisms, refashioning Asia in the image of modern Europe.[111]

In theory, the world of witchcraft and magic was very much part of this colonial reform programme. 'We need to be very severe upon similar absurdities in Asia,' insisted Horace Wilson, regarding witchcraft and astrology, in his expanded edition of James Mill's *History of British India* (1840).[112] In the regions of the Indian subcontinent under its control, the East India Company had actually been trying to stop alleged witches from being killed since as early as the 1790s, sixty years after the crime of witchcraft had been struck from the British statute book. The company's initiatives began after a tribunal of Sutar people convicted and executed five women for witchcraft on the basis of several ordeals, one of which involved watching to see which bags of rice would be eaten by ants. Government proclamations decreed that anyone who killed *dakans*, as witches were called in Gujarati, would be deemed guilty of murder.[113]

Edicts alone did little to stop the gratuitous violence meted out to people like Chautee Hoomlo, an elderly woman from Chakdara village, on the banks of the Swat River, in the western province of Gujarat. In 1846 Chautee's neighbours hung her upside down from a tree and roasted her to death over a fire, after accusing her of using magic to cause a bull to break its leg.[114] Possibly more Indian women were killed for practising malign magic than were immolated as *satis* after being widowed, though it's difficult to be sure because our quantitative knowledge of nineteenth-century Indian witch-hunting rests on the uncertain approximations of colonial officials and commentators.[115] The Rev. J. Long, for instance, maintained that between 1800 and 1823 2,500 witches were put to death in the region of Mhow alone.[116] This was an implausibly high figure. The first census for Mhow cantonment (1881) recorded the local population as being 27,227 people.[117] Even if Mhow's residents attributed nearly every calamity to witchcraft, as several of India's aboriginal tribes reportedly did, the imputation that almost 10 per cent of the population were killed as witches over a twenty-three-year period seems vastly exaggerated.[118] More realistic was the estimate of Major-General Sir John Malcolm, a senior British official in central India, who on the basis of 'tolerable figures' calculated that between 1793 and 1823 at least a thousand women had been put to death as witches in the large area under his command.[119]

Revelations about the scale of Indian witch-hunting, however approximate, prompted the colonial authorities explicitly to ban the practice.[120] Difficult to enforce at the best of times, in moments of rebellion this prohibition was ostentatiously transgressed by tribes living in India's forests and mountains. When the Santals of eastern India rose in arms in 1855, they killed not only moneylenders but also women suspected of witchcraft.[121] After the East India Company's sepoy regiments mutinied in 1857 similar events unfolded elsewhere. The Kols of Uttar Pradesh seized the opportunity presented by the breakdown in authority and killed all the suspected witches they could find.[122] So did the Hos people of Singhbhum.[123] Order was eventually restored, this time under direct British rule, but after that the colonial courts dealt leniently with witch-hunters and witch-killers.[124] Without serious sanctions, the attacks continued. Women accused of witchcraft in Gujarat suffered 'often very serious' consequences, a local political advisor noted in 1873.[125] Murder and mutilation were rife. Some witches had their eyes burnt out to prevent them casting the evil eye. Encouragingly, a folklorist claimed that by 1894 it was rare for witches to be killed for causing cholera, because the disease was now more often attributed to Kali, the Hindu goddess.[126] Even so, in rural and tribal India the practice of witch-killing persisted up to and beyond independence in 1947. It continues to this day. A United Nations report found evidence of 25,000 witch-killings across India between 1987 and 2003, though the actual figure is apparently 'much higher'.[127]

Before its demise in 1858, the East India Company made some effort to punish witch-killers. It did almost nothing to change the attitudes that inspired them by challenging witchcraft belief more generally. Notionally, in the territories over which it claimed dominion, the company prohibited various commercial occult activities, including pretending to be a wizard or witch, pretending to avert hail or make rain fall, pretending to use magic to discover stolen goods, and 'falsely pretending to be possessed of supernatural Powers'.[128] But these proscriptions were rarely put into practice, so much so that some officials didn't know of their existence. This was why, in 1839, senior magistrates in the Bengal Presidency, the largest subdivision of British India, briefly contemplated initiating laws against pretend witchcraft, before deciding 'that it would be inadvisable to annex any punishments by law to the profession of the act of sorcery'.[129] Like other authorities across British India, lawmakers in the presidency were clearly afraid of creating discontent by 'outraging native prejudices'.[130] And with good reason. Magical practitioners of various kinds played important roles in the lives of people across the subcontinent. A survey of the Behar region of eastern India found a vast number of 'low people, called Ajha', who were paid to cast out devils, cure serpent bites, and heal bewitchments.[131] Ajhas typically specialised in one of those areas, like spiritual healers elsewhere. The Gond people of north-western India employed a class of priests named Baigas to protect them from misfortune-sowing evil spirits and hostile local gods.[132] Terrestrial witches, who were often said to use their malefic powers to consume their victims' livers, were dealt with by another type of occultist.[133]

Following the rebellion of 1857, the East India Company was dissolved and its responsibilities transferred to a branch of the British government. From Disraeli to Queen Victoria, Britain's governing classes agreed that the mutiny had been caused by misrule, by the East India Company's crass attempts to force India into a European mould. The new regime, the Raj, would embody a quite different ethos. It would venerate rather than vandalise local traditions, treasuring rather than traducing the ancient customs of South Asia.[134] Renouncing her government's right to interfere with native religions, Queen Victoria proclaimed this approach in 1858, assuring her Indian vassals: 'We declaim the right and desire to impose our convictions on any of our subjects.'[135]

Colonial magistrates now made little effort to prosecute professional Indian magicians. Not least this was because some senior Raj officers were deeply sympathetic to what they saw as oriental spirituality. 'In no other time or country,' claimed Sir Alfred Lyall, 'has witchcraft ever been so comfortably practised as it is now in India under British rule.'[136] Sir Alfred, who at various points in his career was Home Secretary to the Government of India and Chief Commissioner of the North West Provinces, was an enthusiastic student of Hindu philosophy and an admirer of the 'Eastern mind'. Unsurprisingly, he was sanguine about the freedom given to magical practitioners and supernatural healers of all kinds.[137] As he put it in 1884: 'So long as a witch keeps to white, or even to grayish magic, it would be unfair that an impartial magistracy should prosecute him hastily because he is a bit of an impostor.'[138]

Judging by the conversations recorded in colonial memoirs, Indians assumed that their British superiors would dismiss and decry the idea of witchcraft.[139] Ayahs, South Asian nursemaids employed by European expatriates, occasionally entertained their white charges with local tales of demons, witches and wizards.[140] But like indigenous people elsewhere, Indians were generally reluctant to discuss witchcraft with British adults. As one district officer put it: 'If you ask a Mirzapur hillman if there are any witches in his neighbourhood, he will look around furtively and suspiciously, and even if he admits he has heard of such people, he will be very reluctant to give much information about them.'[141] No doubt talking openly about witches was thought to be dangerous – likely to provoke the malefactors. But another reason for reticence was that South Asians expected a hostile response from their European interlocutors. Even under the tradition-treasuring Raj regime, some whites mocked or denigrated eastern magic. Richard Hodgson, a member of the Society for Psychical Research, besmirched Indian conjurors and those who credited them with super-normal powers, observing that snake charmers and their ilk worked entirely and 'unquestionably [by] conjuring tricks'.[142] Yet this cynic was still open to the possibility that Hinduism gave its adherents access to psychic laws unknown to western folk.

Other Europeans fell deeply under the spell of Indian mysticism. Major Wardlow, commander of Seoni in central India during the early nineteenth century, reportedly denied the existence of witchcraft before finally becoming convinced of its reality after falling ill and being cured in myste-rious circumstances.[143] Something similar happened to Signor Bruzzesi, an Italian artist living in Bengal at the turn of the twentieth century. He started believing in Indian witchcraft after witnessing a friend being cursed, then healed.[144] This friend, an administrator on a rural hill station, had suffered shooting pains on the right side of his body, in what appeared to be a severe case of rheumatism. Hospital treatments under European doctors didn't help. In desperation a native physician was consulted, followed by an astrol-oger. He diagnosed that the ailing man was a victim of black magic, trans-mitted by a brownish powder scattered around his office chair and a *yantra*, a geometric diagram used by Hindus to channel cosmic forces. After being subjected to an exorcising ceremony at the hands of another healer, the ill man recovered. Unnervingly, fourteen months later, a *yantra* with the victim's name inscribed on a piece of lead foil was unearthed near the steps to his office, just as the astrologer had predicted.

The strange story, describing the all too real power of eastern witchcraft and Hindu cursing, was one of many retold in the pages of *The Theosophist*, a magazine of oriental philosophy, art, literature and occultism. Established in 1879 and published out of Madras, by 1907 it was selling a respectable 2,700 copies a month, mostly to adepts of a radical new religion.[145] Theosophy was based on the claim that human beings could develop vast supernatural powers, enabling them to change the weather, heal or harm, communicate at great distances, summon spirits, and even reach immortal perfection.[146] To achieve those feats theosophists needed to evolve spiritually, kindling the divine spark present in everyone into a raging spiritual fire. And the way to do

1. Magic and superstition inspired artists during the Romantic movement of the late eighteenth and early nineteenth centuries. This painting, by Swiss-born and London-based Henry Fuseli, illustrates a scene from John Milton's *Paradise Lost*. It depicts a wicked rite, the imminent sacrifice of a child, at night on a stone altar, surrounded by dancing hags and the sound of drums. A deathly, blue-skinned witch holds the little boy's leg. In the foreground, a knife looms. In the sky, the Greek goddess Hecate (the 'night hag') appears – the deity responsible for witchcraft and magical incantations.

2. This spooky painting depicts a witchy woman and a hare – an animal frequently associated with witchcraft – at the stone circle near Castle Fraser, Aberdeenshire.

3. Forsaken by God and attacked by the Philistines, Saul, king of the Israelites, implored the Witch of Endor (left) to summon the ghost of the prophet Samuel to advise him. Images like this one, from 1 Samuel 28, featured in many nineteenth-century bibles.

4. A dimwitted farm worker enters the hayloft and uncovers an astonishing scene: over a brazier, amidst plumes of smoke, two burly witches conjure familiar spirits.

5. Across northern Europe, witches were believed to have the capacity to transform themselves into hares and other nocturnal animals. Malefactors across the world were and are credited with similar powers.

6. Alleged witches were threatened and attacked throughout the nineteenth century. The below image portrays the killing of Ann Tennant, from Long Compton in Warwickshire, in 1875.

7. The cunning-man will see you now. In this illustration, customers wait outside a cunning-man's consulting room. Inside, the conjuror instructs his client amidst all sorts of arcana and a boastful sign about the 'greatest astrologer in the world'.

Great News to the Afflicted !!!

To all who are afflicted with Diseases, let them be ever fo ftubborn or long ftanding, or if given up bv Phyficians, or turned out of Hofpitals incurable, fhall, with the help of GOD, be radically Cured, by James Hallett, the original Curer of all Difeafes.

Cancers, King's Evil, Scrofula and Scorbutic Eruptions, Sore Heads, Scald Heads, Deafnefs and Roaring Noife in the Head, Blindnefs and Bad Eyes, Defeafes of the Head, Brains, and Nerves, Palfy, Apoplxey, Lethargy, Convulfions, Frenzy, Vertigo, inveterate Head Ache, deplorable Nervous Diftempers Malancholy in men, and Vapours in Women, Billous cafes, Debility, Indigeftion, Goughs and Goulds, Lownees of Spirits Lofs of Appetite, all Impurity of the Blood, Relaxation, Rheumatic and outher Gouts, Yellow, Red, and other Jaundice, Agues, Afthma, and all Difeafes of the Lungs, Exulcerated Lungs & Livers, ftrengthens the Liver, the Memory made good, White Swelling in the Knee, St. Anthoney's Fire, St. Vitce's Dance, Corns either hard or foft, and a certain Difeafe, whether frefh or thirty years ftanding, Cured by Herbs only, Weus of all fizes, and all outher difeafes on tedious tormenting, Cured by James Hallett, the original Curer of all difeafes.

He may be feen at his New Houfe three doors from the Waggon and Lamb, Weft-Gate, Chichefter, every Wednefday and Thurfday morning until 10, and Saturday until 3 o'clock. To be feen at No. 8 Halfway-houfe, on Srturday evening, Sunday Monday and Tuefday, until 11 o'clock, Thurfday evening and Friday, until 11 o'clock.

A Univerfal Ointment for the Chilblains and Chap Hands, that will Cure them in a few hours if not Broke, and au other Ointment that will foon cure them if Broke.

Ladies and Gntleman waited on at their own Houfes, on the fhorteft notice.

** Nativities caft for the Cure of Witchcraft and other Difeafes that are hard to be cured,

8. 'Great News to the Afflicted!!!' begins this handbill advert for James Hallett, a self-styled 'Mathematician and Astrologer' and 'Curer of all Diseases'. Hallett was based in Chichester, Sussex, during the late eighteenth and early nineteenth centuries. Like other cunning-men, he offered many services including 'Nativities cast for the Cure of Witchcraft'.

9. Many magicians cured witchcraft, or were willing to try. In Scotland, a 'spae wife' was a woman who sold or traded occult services including fortune telling and witchcraft cures.

10. The wise-woman of Ilchester, Somerset, charming away foot-and-mouth-disease among cattle.

11. The last cunning-folk. Evan Griffiths, a Welsh conjuror (top), and George Pickingill (below), an Essex cunning-man, were among the last of Britain's traditional cunning-men, who made their living by selling Christianity-infused white magic. Their craft waned for many reasons, but mostly because the British state waged war on 'quackery' during the early twentieth century. From around the 1980s, neo-pagans selectively revived the cunning-craft, minus its historic Christian components.

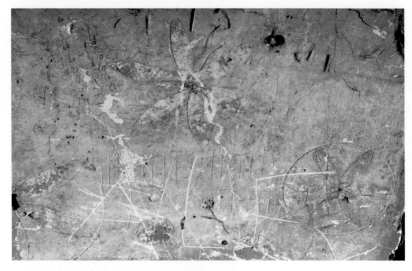

12. Hexafoils were magical markings used to protect buildings from evil and occult influences such as witchcraft. These examples were created in about 1900 to cover the interior walls of a barn at Pratt Hall, Derbyshire.

13. Magical materials. There were many ways to counteract witchcraft. Animals' hearts stuffed with pins were used to attack enemies, particularly witches. Sometimes they were roasted at midnight while spells were muttered and biblical passages read. Pieces of rowan tree bound with red wool were one of the very many remedies believed to provide protection against the influence of evil magic.

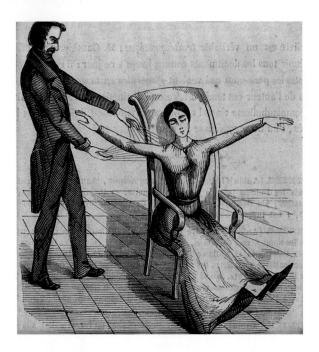

14. Mesmerism, a form of esoteric healing, first appeared in Britain during the late eighteenth century and influenced how people thought about magic, particularly from the 1830s. Was witchcraft actually a form of malicious animal magnetism?

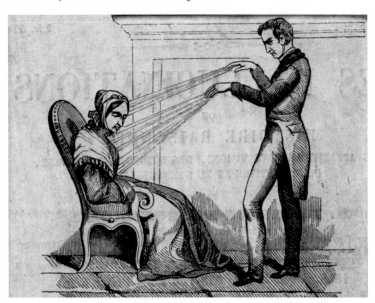

15. From devil to Pan: the figure of Baphomet, as imagined by the French occultist 'Éliphas Lévi' in 1854.

16. A medicine man from Gazaland (modern day Zimbabwe and Mozambique) wearing a fur headdress and an elaborate necklace made partly from animal teeth. Throughout the colonies of the British Empire, magicians such as he had a surprising influence on many white colonists.

17. The still-tended grave of the occultist Dion Fortune, creator of the witchcraft-like concept of psychic attack, and a portrait of her antagonist Lillias Hamilton.

18. The return of the exorcists: Rev. Christopher Neil-Smith conducts an exorcism in London, *c*. 1974.

19. 'Step inside, if you dare!' The Museum of Witchcraft and Magic in the lovely Cornish village of Boscastle has become perhaps the most successful independent museum in the UK. It is a unique resource for anyone with an interest in strange spells and peculiar powers.

20. A portrait of the creator of Wicca, Gerald Gardner, surrounded by his ceremonial artifacts in the Museum of Witchcraft.

21. Poppets and voodoo dolls collected or quite possibly created by the founder of the Museum of Witchcraft, Cecil Williamson.

Bogus Faith or Spiritual Healers

Faith or spiritual healers offer their services to people who may have:
- business problems
- marital disputes
- poor health
- friends or relatives in poor health or
- difficulty finding matrimonial partners for their children

They will:
- advertise their services through local and national radio, newspaper adverts and flyers which are delivered door-to-door
- omit to mention the cost at the outset
- claim to be spiritual healers who can cure illnesses and other problems
- claim to have many years of experience as successful healers and say they provide a 100% guarantee of positive results
- claim that money given to them will be returned to their victims many times over and threaten those who do not pay with curses and black magic.

Leicestershire
Police

22. Witchcraft updated: since the 1970s, there's been a surge in spiritual healers making money from curing black magic. Some charge huge sums, others advertise on niche radio stations and in newspapers, and many have websites and trade online.

this was by penetrating the inner mysteries of oriental occultism.[147] Specifically, according to the founder of the movement Helena Blavatsky (1831–91), theosophy was dedicated to following the teachings of 'the Masters', a brotherhood of immortal Buddhist monks living in Tibet. Perhaps the idea seemed somewhat plausible, at the close of the nineteenth century, because the mountain kingdom to the north-west of India was closed to outsiders, refusing all contact with the British government until 1904.[148] Conveniently, Madame Blavatsky was able to communicate with the Masters through the medium of psychic letter writing. She, apparently, was the conduit through which they conveyed their extraordinary wisdom to the world.

The Theosophical Society, founded by Blavatsky and her collaborator Henry Olcott in New York in 1875, had initially been designed to reform spiritualism.[149] According to the duo, spiritualist mediums did not, as most of them claimed, commune with the spirits of the dead. Rather, séance-room feats were just one example of gifted people's capacity to control elemental forces and occult powers. In 1879, Blavatsky and Olcott transplanted the Theosophical Society to India, where they reoriented its focus to a threefold mission designed to establish: (i) a universal brotherhood of humankind; (ii) the special virtues of oriental spirituality; (iii) the necessity of comparative religion. Theosophy, the already controversial occult movement, became even more countercultural, espousing an ethos that was decidedly anti-racist, anti-secularist, anti-Christian and anti-imperialist. The suspicious Raj authorities promptly put Blavatsky and Olcott under surveillance, though they could not stop the Theosophical Society from attracting a myriad of alternative thinkers, including feminists, socialists, artists and Indian nationalists (Asian and European).[150] After reading communications apparently sent by the Masters (or Mahatmas), Allan Hume, a former Indian civil servant, was inspired to co-found the Indian National Congress in 1885.[151] That party, under Gandhi's direction, would go on to lead the Indian independence movement.[152]

Critics attacked theosophy's portrayal of Hinduism and Buddhism as eccentric, misleading and deeply flawed.[153] It may well have been, but by venerating the idea of oriental spirituality, theosophy inspired occultists back in Britain to re-examine European mystical traditions, stimulating the field that would become known as 'western esotericism'. A numerically small movement driven by a feeling for eastern magic, theosophy sparked important political and cultural developments, in India and beyond.

THE CURSE OF A CONTINENT? WITCHCRAFT IN AFRICA

Witchcraft, along with slavery, was the 'curse of Africa'. So announced Dr David Livingstone, the celebrated missionary and explorer, to a bustling Hull lecture hall, in the autumn of 1864.[154]

Like Dr Livingstone, European commentators on the 'Dark Continent' routinely claimed that witchcraft was central to the lives of Africans, whether they lived in the rainforests of the Congo, the savannahs of Sudan, or the highlands of Kenya. Indeed, that Africa was a uniquely 'witch-bound' place was a colonial cliché.[155] Adventurers told tales of how, in lands where whites had never before trod, they'd subdued hostile natives by playing on their uncanny fears, using unfamiliar technology like guns or paraffin lamps to pretend that they possessed vast supernatural powers.[156]

Such stories raised gasps and smiles. Yet few European writers on Africa doubted the seriousness of local people's occult ideas. 'Witchcraft plays the chief part in the daily life of all African natives,' contended the *Pall Mall Gazette*'s special correspondent from Zambezi, in 1895: 'To witchcraft they attribute every ill that befalls them.'[157] Writing from Northern Rhodesia in 1923, another colonialist thought witchcraft was the 'ever-present tragedy of village life in Africa'.[158] Magic and witchcraft were 'continually in the native mind', observed Lord Hailey, in a celebrated survey of inter-war Africa.[159] Mary Kingsley, an irrepressible Victorian traveller who documented West African occult beliefs during the 1890s, dissented from this assessment, though just a little. She estimated that 60 per cent of all deaths were attributed to witchcraft.[160] The Rev. John Weeks came to a similar conclusion about the Congolese Boloki people, with whom he'd lived for three decades. They, apparently, recognised three causes of death: someone else's witchcraft, one's own witchcraft and the will of God.[161] However, for other tribes, like the Azande of South Sudan and the Batlhaping of South Africa, witchcraft was utterly ubiquitous, pervading daily life, causing practically all deaths, sicknesses and misfortunes.[162] So, at least, thought the anthropologists who studied those groups, during the early decades of the twentieth century.

Were Africans really so obsessed with witchcraft? Not for some historians. They are suspicious of the sources quoted above, seeing them as little more than 'colonial assertions', as exercises in derogatory stereotyping designed to justify the subordination of indigenous peoples.[163] To some extent their cynicism is merited. Inadvertently, European missionaries may well have amplified Africans' witchcraft fears, by discrediting the ancestor spirits to whom, formerly, misfortunes were also ascribed.[164] Without mentioning this, colonialists used the stereotype of the wild African witchcraft believer, of the superstitious savage, as a riposte to anti-imperialists back in the UK, who questioned whether it was proper for Britain to rule over territories as diverse as the Gold Coast in the west, Natal in the south, and Kenya in the east. Superstitious Africans, imperialists argued, needed the cool rationality of British rule. This was true during the late nineteenth-century Scramble for Africa, when a handful of European empires conquered most of the continent, dividing it up into thirty new colonies and protectorates under the guise of bringing civilisation, acquiring 110 million new subjects, and leaving just two independent states.[165] Amid the 1879 Zulu war, advocates for annexing Zululand to the British Empire justified their ambitions by highlighting Zulu King Cetshwayo's witch-hunting.[166] How, colonialists asked their fellow Britons, could these injustices be allowed to continue?

Following the Second World War, the empire's defenders continued to use stereotyping to denigrate African independence movements. In 1957, when the House of Commons debated South Rhodesia's (now Zimbabwe) white-dominated electoral system, opponents of black suffrage dwelt on the power that witchcraft had over the population.[167] Similar arguments were deployed during the Kenyan Mau Mau uprising of the 1950s. Formerly suppressed documents have begun to reveal that Kenya's colonial government fought the rebellion with a systematic campaign of torture, mass arbitrary detention and forced labour.[168] But the regime's supporters also waged a propaganda war, denying legitimacy to the Kikuyu tribe by obscuring the real social and economic ills behind their rising. Apparently, Mau Mau was unrelated to the living conditions of a quarter of the Kikuyu, 250,000 people squatting on farmsteads in the so-called 'White Highlands'.[169] Because Mau Mau supporters swore deadly oaths, apologists for white dominance argued that rebellion was entirely derived from an African appetite for witchcraft, superstition and savagery. The 'squalid secret society' was a 'deadly amalgam of witchcraft [and] debased politics', pronounced the *Dundee Courier* in 1953, but the message was not just conveyed by sympathetic journalists.[170] Spokesmen for white farmers toured provincial towns, speaking at rotary clubs, making the point that Mau Mau was 'based on witchcraft'.[171] On the whole, the British government agreed. Mau Mau was a 'shadow of witchcraft, savagery and crime', Oliver Lyttleton, Colonial Secretary, assured the House of Commons, in 1952.[172]

The stereotype of the superstitious African was undoubtedly cultivated for political reasons. Yet it was also true that the continent's people strongly believed in witchcraft. Magic words and occult terminology varied enormously from place to place, of course, and from people to people. The Pedi in the Transvaal of southern Africa called witches *baloi*.[173] Over 1,000 miles north, among the Luda, Lwena and Luchazi of Northern Rhodesia, *uloji* was the term for baleful magic, *mukayi* meant protective rites, *wanga* denoted the physical materials used in sorcery, while *muloji* translated as 'witch'.[174] Another thousand miles north, the Sudanese Dinka used *apeth* to denote witchcraft.[175] The words for witchcraft differed across Africa, but the belief system's general concepts were not so varied. Often, witches were said to control evil familiars, cavort naked with their comrades at night, and eat the flesh of the dead. As in Europe, Asia and the Americas, in Africa witches were thought to be able to shapeshift into animals, temporarily becoming crocodiles or hyenas in order to travel incognito or lie in wait for their victims.[176] Distinctively, in many of the sub-Saharan parts of the continent, witches were believed to possess a special organ, similar and close to the gall bladder. Called *mangu* by the Azande of south Sudan, this organ was either inherited or grown by evil conjuring and supposedly gave sorcerers a host of malefic abilities.[177]

When Europeans made significant incursions into Africa, during the later nineteenth century, the continent's peoples were combating witchcraft in various ways. Relatively benign techniques included counter-magic, witchcraft-cleansing practices, fines and ostracism, with suspected witches being sent to live in dedicated areas. Violent solutions included murder, enslavement, the poison-drinking ordeal and judicially sanctioned executions.[178] Exploring Portuguese Angola during the 1860s, Oxford drop-out William Reade witnessed several witch trials, in which the accused confessed their crimes, recalling in minute detail where they stored their evil-sowing witchpowder.[179] Major Elliott, a British resident among the Thembu people of southern Africa, judged that during the 1870s they and their neighbours (the Pondos, Bomvanas and Galekas) killed around 400 people for being witches.[180] In the 1880s a commission of the Cape Colony's government lamented that the Pondomise people 'generally killed' individuals accused of using witchcraft to cause illnesses, after torturing them with fire and insects.

Mere colonial aspersions, one might protest. But a similar point, about the prevalence of witchcraft-related violence, was made by John Mensah Sarbah (1864–1910). He was an intellectual from the Gold Coast, graduate of Taunton College Somerset, member of Lincoln's Inn, and one of the first black Africans to be called to the Bar.[181] As a co-founder of the Aborigines' Rights Protection Society and spokesperson for the Gold Coast's chiefs, he was no meek colonial collaborator. Nevertheless, Mensah Sarbah chided his own Fanti people for the way they treated suspected witches. 'So much annoyance, mischief, and injury is caused by the reckless imputation of witchcraft,' he observed, 'that many a woman has been known to commit suicide, unable to bear the disgrace of a false imputation.'[182] Pastor Mojola Agbebi (1860–1917), a Nigerian who founded the country's first indigenously led church, also acknowledged the frequently deadly consequences of African witchcraft. At the first Universal Races Conference, held in London in 1911, he told delegates that, in tropical Africa, maleficent witches were 'more or less visited with the death penalty'. As a pan-Africanist and racial segregationist, he saw a harsh approach to witchcraft as characteristic of African culture. For Pastor Mojola, the problem was not witch-killers but Europeanised Africans who wanted to alter the traditional African social system.[183]

From a British point of view, African magic nurtured not just violence but rebellion. The culprits here were medicine men, priests, diviners (often female), rain-makers, spirit mediums and prophets (of both sexes).[184] These varied figures, whom the whites often crudely lumped together as 'witch doctors', seemed to be 'the greatest power in the land'.[185] It was easy to claim they embodied Africa's traditional, archaic culture, since some rejected European goods entirely, and refused to perform their rituals in the presence of whites.[186] Yet in areas where there had been considerable missionary activity, there were also healers and mediums who were not so implacably hostile to western culture, and who infused their work with broadly Christian ideas.[187]

Whatever their approach, as providers of services ranging from divination to ancestor worship to witch-finding, spiritual practitioners were highly valued within African society, even revered. Whenever an uprising broke out against British rule, they seemed to be involved, encouraging the natives with visions of victory, blessing their weapons and arming them with protective charms.[188] This occurred in the Xhosa-occupied lands of Britain's Cape Colony, where during 1856 and 1857 a prophet named Nongqawuse encouraged her cattle-farming people to slaughter 300,000 of their livestock, foretelling that the sacrifice would inspire Africa's ancestral spirits to drive the British into the sea.[189] Spirit mediums fomented the 1896 and 1897 rising of Rhodesia's Ndebele and Shona peoples, not least by assuring them that the white men's bullets would turn to water.[190] An impressed British soldier thought the 'witch doctors' were wonderful ventriloquists, particularly a woman in the Mazo Valley, who bellowed battle cries in the midst of the mêlée, with a voice that seemed to descend from the heavens.[191] Because they were so threatening, after Cecil Rhodes' South Africa Company defeated its indigenous opponents, it hanged two of their most influential spirit mediums, Mbuya Nehanda and Sekuru Kaguvi, burying their bodies in secret graves in an ineffective attempt to erase their memory.[192]

Given these challenges to colonial rule, one can begin to understand why Lord Hailey, author of an important 1930s survey of the continent, saw witchcraft as 'the outstanding problem of the lawgiver in Africa'.[193] Britain's colonial regimes had long tried to suppress its many guises. From the 1830s, treaties with the Xhosa contained clumsily worded provisions against both pretend witchcraft and witchcraft accusations. After the 1870s, the Cape Colony began enacting somewhat more tightly defined laws, to a similar effect.[194] On the Gold Coast, in western Africa, two popular witch-finding techniques were outlawed in 1874: the poison ordeal, and the 'corpse carrying', where a dead person's body was held aloft by his or her relatives, in the expectation that it would direct them to the responsible witch.[195] By the 1920s, almost every British African colony had gone further, totally prohibiting witchcraft accusations of any sort, as well as proscribing the practice of magic, black and white.[196] Northern Rhodesia's laws were particularly harsh, punishing witch-accusers with three years' imprisonment, twenty lashes and a £50 fine, and witch doctors with seven years' imprisonment, twenty-four lashes and a £100 fine.[197] Kenya's ordinance of 1918 was milder, specifying that 'any person who holds himself out to be a witch doctor' was liable to a year's incarceration, though in 1925 the maximum sentence was increased to five years.[198] Tanganyika's laws made no explicit reference to witch doctors, but specified that anyone who claimed to wield 'occult power or knowledge' would be fined £50 and jailed for a year. Those pretending to be maleficent witches would receive seven years.[199]

These laws, known as the African witchcraft ordinances, were spectacularly unpopular. True, they criminalised the widely reviled practice of malign magic, but they did so in a way that made the crime almost impossible to prove in court.[200] By also outlawing witch-finding, an activity regarded as imperative to individual and social welfare, the statutes outraged most Africans.[201] 'One of the chief complaints against our rule,' a magistrate from Rhodesia noted, 'is that (in native eyes) we punish the conscientious man who discovers a witch.'[202] Some colonists also opposed the ordinances, which they saw as 'the most conspicuous instance of the superimposition of the white man's law and opinion, without any consideration of the African's view.'[203] Worse, they were largely ineffective. Aware that any knowledge they imparted might bring trouble, black Africans generally concealed information about witchcraft from the white community.[204] Perhaps counter-witchcraft practices became some-what less violent. In the wake of the witchcraft ordinances, they certainly became more hidden, covert and 'furtive', as one anthropologist put it.[205]

Even if magistrates managed to uncover evidence of the vast but concealed world of operative magic, the English wording of the witchcraft ordinances did not precisely match up to the infinitely various terminology of African supernaturalism, making the laws difficult to apply. In early twentieth-century South Africa, female diviners appear to have been dealt with stringently.[206] Elsewhere, officials ignored everyday examples of thera-peutic magic, which seemed to do no real harm, and were too numerous to be stopped anyway.[207] Tanzania's 1928 witchcraft ordinance allowed prose-cutions only with the consent of the governor, thus ensuring the legislation was little used. Indeed, towards the end of the colonial period Tanzania's regime tried to win its people's loyalty by using state funds to finance witch-finders and witch-cleaners, in certain areas.[208] Across British Africa, the anti-witchcraft laws were generally reserved for scandalous cases that the colonial authorities felt unable to ignore, like the 1931 murder of Mwaiki, a Kamba woman from Kenya who was beaten to death by a mob.[209] Sixty men received death sentences for their involvement. It says a lot about the limits of the colonial campaign against witchcraft that, eventually, every one of those punishments was commuted.

In the newspapers, courtrooms and debating chambers of colonial Africa, witchcraft was maligned as native nonsense.[210] But when they encountered witchcraft and magic privately, in their personal or working lives, at least some white expatriates found it difficult to sustain a dismissive attitude.

African ritual performances were extremely compelling, even for Britons with a scientific education like Richard Freeman, a medical officer in the Gold Coast. On a diplomatic expedition to the territories north of the colony in 1889, he witnessed a dance venerating the African deity Sakrobudi. It was part of a recently founded witchcraft eradication movement, designed to provide protection against evil occult powers. Seventy men and women, arranged by age, dressed in ceremonial kilts and coloured anklets, formed an incomplete circle. Slowly rotating according to a steady ('hypnotic' was the word Freeman used) rhythm, the dancers were periodically seized as if possessed. In the circle's centre was a man wearing a huge wooden mask, painted red and white and bearing horns so it looked like the head of a giant antelope.[211] While the dance continued he performed various deliverance rites, running to and from an adjacent building, occasionally kneeling on the ground. Witnessing this had a powerful influence on Richard Freeman, the medical officer. The 'strange and weird performance', he recalled, 'had quite an uncanny effect'.[212]

Africans were renowned for their tendency to mislead white questioners about religion and the occult[213] – understandably, given that Europeans were not above hectoring them for their 'heathen immorality'.[214] Despite the communication barriers that must inevitably have arisen in such circumstances, after living with black servants for many years, most settlers would have heard rumours about the dark work of witches. These tales inspired strange daydreams for Karen Blixen, a Kenyan coffee farmer, who found herself fantasising one night that the hyenas she heard howling were actually witches on the prowl.[215] Elspeth Huxley (1907–97), whose childhood was spent in a very similar environment on a Kenyan coffee plantation, heard about and indeed witnessed the effects of witchcraft on Kikuyu farm labourers. Judging by her autobiography, she and her British family tentatively believed that African magic was not entirely imaginary. Elspeth once asked a witch doctor to make her pet duiker (a small antelope) a charm to protect it against a python.[216] In dangerous times, other Europeans put themselves under the care of native healers.[217] Lieutenant Colonel H.F. Trew, Deputy Commissioner of the South African Police in the years following the First World War, recalled meeting a farmer who'd lost four oxen and, in desperation, consulted a well-known *kraal*, who did indeed tell him where to find his beasts.[218] An Englishwoman who grew cotton and tobacco in the Eastern Transvaal did something similar when she paid a witch doctor to discover the location of her pony. The rite succeeded, she informed readers of the *Western Morning News* in 1938.[219]

'Some things cannot be explained,' mused T.E. Dorman, reflecting on the weird things he'd seen while working as an education officer in Northern Rhodesia during the 1950s. Even after half a century of British rule, with its roads, hospitals, schools and agricultural schemes, witchcraft remained a powerful force in African society. The education officer himself once met a witch doctor whose powerful aura of evil made him 'feel cold even in the heat of the tropics'. More traumatically, an African clerk serving under Mr Dorman had died believing that he'd been bewitched. A horrible event like that could be pure coincidence or an illustration of the force of psychological suggestion. But as the years passed, Mr Dorman found himself becoming less cynical, and less convinced by secular interpretations of witchcraft. 'No one who has been in Africa for any length of time scoffs at witchcraft and dismisses it out of hand,' he candidly admitted.[220]

Naïve cadets, fresh to the topics, full of ambitious plans for modernising the continent and its peoples, might disbelieve. But after spending decades in Africa, more experienced colonial officials thought differently. Old hands like these were tempted to take seriously the dark powers so feared by the locals. Take the Rev. Edwin Smith and Captain Andrew Murray Dale, who together studied the witchcraft beliefs of the Ila-speaking peoples of Northern Rhodesia, during the 1910s. 'At risk of ridicule,' they admitted to readers of their book, 'we profess that we believe there is really something behind the intense conviction.'[221] Or take Frank Melland, a Fellow of the Royal Anthropological Institute and magistrate for the Kasempa District of Northern Rhodesia between 1911 and 1922. He saw witchcraft as 'the poisonous creeper that spreads over Africa and impedes all progress'.[222] But he was uncertain about whether it was really practised: 'I do not know: it may be, but I doubt it.'[223] Melland's musings were partly stimulated by the work of Margaret Murray, an eccentric Egyptologist at work back in London, who contended that a genuine pagan witch cult survived in pre-modern Europe, underground and in secret. 'For some time I have had a suspicion, and reasonable ground for the suspicion,' the Rhodesian magistrate reflected, 'that there may be a class of professional and hereditary witches behind the scenes: men (and women) who habitually provide the means to bewitch, or impart the necessary knowledge to the layman to enable him to carry out his desires.' Melland went so far as to say that, in Africa, it was probable that there was a guild of master witches who inducted the more casual malefactors by supplying them with the means to do harm.[224] His paranoid ideas, born both of time in Africa and of reading Margaret Murray, made this magistrate publicly question the colonial witchcraft ordinances. 'Before condemning the whole order of witch-doctors,' he reminded readers of his book, 'it would seem that more evidence is required as to the existence or non-existence of the witches.'[225]

BRINGING MAGIC BACK

Witchcraft and magic had a bearing on British imperialism, and a place in the lives of Britons living abroad. More often than not, the largest empire the world had ever known found itself unable to stop native peoples from harming supposed sorcerers. In the African and the Indian countryside particularly, the world of witchcraft remained untamed and dangerous. When they prohibited witch-finding and witch-killing, the imperial authorities acted from mixed motives, to justify their presence in foreign lands and to preserve innocent human lives. Ultimately though, by challenging destructive superstitions, Britain's colonial governments alienated the people they aspired to rule, exploit, and tutor in the ways of western civilisation.

After spending years abroad, some British expatriates also began to regret the colonial laws against witchcraft and magic. They were impolitic, betraying a distinct lack of sympathy for native culture. But there was another, sinister and unsettling reason. Hearing uncanny stories, witnessing occult rituals, and meeting apparently bewitched people raised questions in the minds of at least some expats. Was there 'something in it'? Not a few settlers, missionaries and officials discovered that their scepticism was a weak veneer, an ineffective inoculation against the weirdly beguiling, strangely familiar occult ideas they learnt from the locals. A key theme of this book is the growing tolerance for unorthodox supernaturalism, which steadily grew in Britain from the mid-nineteenth century onwards. This libertarian process, this proto-multicultural development, was accelerated by the uncanny experiences of Brits abroad, during the heyday of the British Empire.

EIGHT

WITCHCRAFT'S DECLINE
1900–1960s

In this book, I've criticised other scholars for overstating witchcraft's decline and for calling it too early. But that doesn't mean black magic persisted at a constantly high level throughout the modern epoch, from the mostly rural world of two centuries ago, until the technologically abundant present day.

There was indeed an era of substantial decay – a time when sorcery dwindled from a widespread concern to a fringe fear. Britons cherished oodles of fads, fancies and superstitions. Increasingly though, witchcraft wasn't one of them. Few now allowed themselves to credit the black art or believe their misfortunes somehow originated in the machinations of malevolent magicians. Most people never even considered the idea. Wise-men and cunning-women had disappeared. Across the countryside, in the hamlets and villages, folk no longer congregated as they once did, passing time with stories, retelling great yarns about generations past, scaring themselves with talk of local witches.

Witchcraft undoubtedly declined. But it did so remarkably recently: between the early 1900s and the 1960s. This may surprise some readers. I can almost see foreheads furrowing and eyebrows rising, incredulously. We must, however, follow the sources – the newspapers, folklore reports, autobiographies, oral histories, archaeology and medical literature. Frankly, this evidence suggests that witchery faded as a popular belief during a familiar period, much of which remains within living memory, an era beginning with Edwardian imperial grandeur and suffragette radicalism, and ending with the swinging sixties. When deference collapsed and truly democratic politics arrived, in the form of universal suffrage for men (1918), votes for women (1918 and 1928), and the mass disobedience of the General Strike (1926).[1] When a huge welfare state was constructed, thanks to legislation like the National Insurance Act (1911) and the National Health Service Act (1946), pulling millions out of crushing poverty. When, consequently, the state became vastly more invasive and expensive, growing from around 10 per cent of Britain's economic output in 1900, to 40 per cent in 1960.[2] An epoch punctuated by two astonishingly destructive world wars, the first of which killed hundreds of thousands of British men and ushered in Irish independence, while the second doomed thousands of civilians and the British Empire. An often austere period that nonetheless ended in a golden age, a post-war economic boom when white goods proliferated and a distinct youth culture exploded onto the scene.

This chapter explains when and where British witchcraft diminished. It also tries to answer the much more difficult question of why. Decay, however, is not the only theme. Witchcraft ebbed, in its traditional, folkloric, loosely Christian formulation. Yet it never died out entirely. Partly this was thanks to the efforts of avant-garde occultists. These supernatural explorers reinterpreted the idea of mystic interpersonal harm, rendered it in modern language, and thereby made it resonate with at least some of their contemporaries. No novel rephrasing of witchery was as potent as Dion Fortune's concept of 'psychic attack'.

UNDER PSYCHIC ATTACK: HOW VIOLET FIRTH BECAME DION FORTUNE

This is the story of one of twentieth-century Britain's most influential occultists. Not the most notorious, Aleister Crowley, the great beast, the wickedest man alive. Unlike him, Dion Fortune (1890–1946) did not fascinate journalists, novelists and (later) bands like Led Zeppelin.[3] But as the author of at least seventeen unashamedly middlebrow books, Dion Fortune was more read and better understood than Crowley. His writings, largely self-published, sold dismally.[4] Her occult novels and guidebooks, published commercially, were 'well known' and by the 1930s 'arousing a good deal of attention'.[5] Fortune founded a cabbalistic society, the Fraternity of the Inner Light. She helped create a European-flavoured magical tradition known as 'western esotericism'.[6] Her work on Glastonbury, the Somerset town, did much to enhance its reputation as a place fizzing with supernatural power.[7]

Dion Fortune was also a key figure in the modern history of witchcraft. By developing the idea of 'psychic attack' she rendered, in modish terminology, the notion that some human misfortunes stem from black magic.

The tale begins with a girl, Violet Firth. Born in 1890 at Llandudno, a coastal town in North Wales, she was no ordinary Welsh lass. Violet belonged to the Firth dynasty, a clan of wealthy steel magnates. From humble beginnings in early Victorian Sheffield, by the end of the nineteenth century they had joined Britain's upper middle class. Being a Firth meant that Violet enjoyed a fine childhood of expensive clothes, spiral staircases, golf courses, fetes and London society. Aged 10 she met the Queen's daughters, Princesses Helena and Victoria, not for the last time.[8]

Rich and socially connected, Violet Firth was gifted too. Arthur, her father, ensured she was reading canonical literature from a young age, including poetry by Tennyson, Macaulay, Pope and Dryden.[9] Aged 13 she published her first book, a collection of clever nature poems, which sold an impressive 3,000 copies in a year.[10] At 16 Miss Firth wrote a second volume, *More Violets*.[11] Meanwhile, she became a minor media sensation. Violet, the 'schoolgirl prodigy' and 'clever child', was the focus of admiring newspaper features, where her handwritten poems were reproduced facsimile, along with her picture.[12] Some said, for her age, Violet was more talented than Emily Brontë.[13] Surely, young Miss Firth was destined for success.

Violet was destined for success, but not in a way anyone expected: not in the pleasant art of nature poetry, not in the respectable sphere of upper middle-class life. Miss Firth took an unconventional path, into the other world of esoteric societies and occult publishing. Why? Aleister Crowley, the notorious ceremonial magician, embraced a decadent occult lifestyle partly as a reaction against his austere Christian upbringing, among a family of Plymouth Brethren. Not so Violet Firth. Her interest in 'the Unseen' was only a slight legacy of her affluent childhood. Following her mother, during her teenage years Violet became a Christian Scientist. The female-centric healing religion would have familiarised her with the concept of malicious animal magnetism: the unnerving idea that spiteful folk emit vicious mental forces, injuring their enemies.

Violet Firth's occultism began elsewhere. Chiefly, in a horrible encounter and its aftermath. It occurred at Studley Horticultural and Agricultural College, where Violet enrolled aged 20. A women-only institution, set in an old country house in rural Warwickshire, Studley catered to girls who were 'unsuited to town life'.[14] Subtly, that meant the college was a good place for individuals experiencing minor emotional problems, though it also provided a certificated education in a plausible field. Like Violet, the students were genteel ladies, daughters of solicitors, merchants and ministers, who'd been to expensive private schools.[15] Mornings were for classroom teaching. During afternoons students worked in the dairy or outside, on the estate's market garden. It was a practical education, involving plenty of exercise and fresh air.

Unfortunately, the college was financially distressed. To improve its management and medical credentials, the governors appointed a formidable new warden: Dr Lillias Hamilton (1858–1925). Lillias was a tough, powerful, imposing woman. Students never forgot her 'extraordinary', 'unpredictable' and 'indomitable spirit'.[16] One of Britain's first female doctors, Miss Hamilton was educated at Cheltenham Ladies' College, the London School of Medicine for Women, and in Brussels, Vienna and Stockholm.[17] She joined the Royal College of Physicians in 1890 before leaving for India, where she became physician in charge of Dufferin Hospital, Calcutta. Next, Lillias moved to Afghanistan, a fragmented but irrepressibly independent nation, after receiving the distinction of being summoned by the Emir himself. For three years she served as the Emir's personal physician, an extraordinary achievement given that in his kingdom many women were confined to their homes.[18] War eventually forced Dr Hamilton to leave, and in 1906 she became warden of Studley College, from where she campaigned as a forceful but non-militant feminist, agitating for women to receive the vote along with better education and employment.[19] She was heroic too. In 1915, as war set the Balkans aflame, Lillias went to Montenegro as part of a medical relief team.[20]

'I have never seen a more devoted set of teachers and students,' recalled one visitor to Studley College, the American astronomer John Brashear.[21] The students had more mixed memories, particularly of Dr Hamilton. She had an 'interesting and vital personality', one observed, euphemistically.[22] Others were franker about the 'forceful' woman. Reportedly, Lillias 'never took "no" for an answer'.[23] Many of the girls 'did not understand her – she was certainly eccentric'.[24] Dr Hamilton's correspondence confirms the picture of an exceedingly intimidating lady. Writing to her brother, Major Claude Hamilton, she began with the sentence: 'I cannot imagine how you have been so idiotic.'[25]

Violet Firth fell victim to Dr Hamilton's temper. Not initially: Violet's studies went well, so after graduating she remained at Studley to work in the poultry department. Yet in 1913 she had a shattering confrontation with the warden. In her autobiographical writings, Violet remembered Dr Hamilton as a bully who hinted she'd acquired dark magical powers while working in India.[26] It's tempting to dismiss this claim as pure imagination, but there's evidence to suggest otherwise. Dr Hamilton wrote, but never published, an eerie-sounding novel called *Powers that Walk in Darkness*. Lillias' sister was a member of the Society for Psychical Research, and during the 1880s both women made a small contribution to *Phantasms of the Living*, a huge research project into spectral appearances.[27] As we've seen in the previous chapter, it was a cliché for British colonists to find themselves thinking there was 'something in' witchcraft, after spending time abroad. It's plausible that Lillias said something about exotic supernatural powers, which Violet interpreted as a magical boast.

Dr Hamilton was known for mistreating her colleagues. Violet helped the victims, once refusing to testify against a former staff member who sued the college for unpaid wages. Eventually though, she resolved to leave Studley. Others told her to go without announcement. Wanting to act properly, Violet delivered a letter of resignation to Lillias. At this, the warden demanded a meeting.

It lasted four hours. Violet prepared a speech, which she never had the chance to give. Instead, Lillias dominated. Staring fixedly into Violet's eyes, she said: 'You are incompetent, and you know it. You have no self-confidence, and you have got to admit it.'

It was Violet's first job. She was in her early twenties, perhaps with a minor depression. But the former child prodigy could summon up confidence. Violet denied Dr Hamilton's accusations. The warden didn't argue or shout. She glared. And repeated her charges. Violet protested. So it continued. 'You are incompetent, and you know it. You have no self-confidence, and you have got to admit it.' Again and again. For four hours. Between ten in the morning and two in the afternoon. 'She must have said these two phrases several hundred times,' Violet recalled, 'why I did not pursue the obvious remedy of taking refuge in flight I do not know.'[28] Eventually, she began 'to feel unreal'. Dizzy, with hysteria looming, desperate to escape (who can blame her?), Violet admitted her incompetence. She had no self-confidence. And with that, Violet left the warden's office. She went to her room, lay on her bed, and slept for thirty hours straight.

Violet's health collapsed. She was now powerfully depressed, even outside the toxic atmosphere of Studley College. Lacking energy, unable to rest or concentrate, her mind raced. 'My body was like an electrical battery that had been completely discharged,' she remembered. Naturally, the doctors were sent for. They prescribed a sedative (bromide).

It didn't help. Nor, really, did psychotherapy. Fed partly by the traumas of the Great War, the mid- to late 1910s saw an upsurge of medical interest in psychological dysfunction, or 'neurosis'.[29] Desperate to understand her condition, Violet studied this young area of medicine at a clinic in London. Many of the early psychiatrists' patients felt persecuted by occult powers akin to witchcraft. Conolly Norman, an alienist mentioned in James Joyce's *Ulysses*, even wrote a paper about the 'paranoiacs of to-day who entertain the very common delusions of mystic influence'.[30] Nonetheless, most schools of psychiatry and psychotherapy curtly dismissed such 'delusions', without really probing their nature. For Violet, the field was beset by other problems too. As someone who was not entirely at ease with the sensual side of life, she felt Freudian psychoanalysis overstated the significance of unconscious sexual impulses, though Violet had to admit that Freud's theories hinted at the human mind's hidden depths. Jungian analytical psychology, more mystical and attentive to the idea of the occult, had some appeal. Ultimately, Violet found the entire domain of psychotherapy unsatisfying.

In her depleted state, Violet finally found relief in occultism. She was not alone. The stresses of the Great War had invigorated superstitions of all kinds.[31] Good luck charms abounded, the folklorist Edward Lovett showed in his writings and object collections.[32] Books of prophecy appeared, like Ralph Shirley's *Prophecies and Omens of the Great War* (1915). Supernatural rumours were widely credited, notably a tale about angels interceding on behalf of the Allies at the Battle of Mons in 1914.[33] During the decades after the war, popular interest in spiritualism peaked, fuelled partly by the endorsements of bereaved parents like the scientist Oliver Lodge. By 1937, Britain's Spiritualists National Union was affiliated with no fewer than 520 local societies.[34] Though niche, the practice of ceremonial magic was becoming a little more prevalent within elite circles. In London, people like the Austrian occultist Julius Kohn published books about 'the real black magic', explaining how to muster supernatural powers by emulating the world's most mystical peoples, from the Māoris to the Roma. 'Black Magic [is] not a joke to be trifled with,' Kohn assured his readers in 1921.[35]

In this prophetic atmosphere, one could experiment with supernatural ideas and rituals without being deemed an incorrigible eccentric. Violet Firth, however, went far beyond mere dabbling. She immersed herself in the solemn world of esoteric societies, becoming a dedicated occultist, an adept of the 'secret science' of magic. In recognition of her change in orientation, she took a new name. Violet Firth became Dion Fortune. It was not exactly a rejection of her upbringing and heritage. The name Dion Fortune was derived from the Firth family motto: *deo non fortuna* (God, not luck).

It took a while for Dion Fortune to settle on a brand of magic that chimed with her sensibility. First she was mentored by a genteel occultist. Then, in 1919, she joined the Alpha et Omega lodge of the Golden Dawn, a successor to the secret society founded in 1888.[36] Next she became involved in theosophy, though Dion never really connected with its brand of eastern magic, preferring western esotericism and Christian mysticism.[37] To facilitate these occult interests, in 1922 Dion Fortune founded her own magical society: the Fraternity of the Inner Light. Around the same time she purchased two properties: the Chalice Orchard, in Glastonbury, and 3 Queensborough Terrace, in the heart of London. In April 1927 she married Thomas Penry Evans, a Harley Street doctor.[38] It had taken years, but she now felt at home.

At last, Dion Fortune understood what had happened to her about a decade and a half earlier, when she was working at Studley College. Dr Hamilton, the warden who brought on her depression, wasn't a conventional bully. She was a master of malicious thoughts and occult powers. Violet Firth, as she'd then been known, was the victim of nothing less than a 'psychic attack'.

'Psychic attack' wasn't a term coined by Dion Fortune. It had been used since the beginning of the twentieth century by psychiatrists and neurologists, to describe symptoms associated with epilepsy and neurosis.[39] Occultists adopted the concept in the 1910s, to denote interpersonal harm by uncanny means, from black magic to malicious magnetism.[40] But it was Dion Fortune who elaborated on it. Exhaustion, depression, nightmares, constant feelings of fear, unease and oppression: these were the surest signs of psychic attack. One's problems might have mundane explanations, of course. Misattributing ordinary illness to the supernatural is all too tempting. Acknowledging this risk, one must be open to the possibility that extraordinary influences are at work in everyday life. Frankly, psychic attacks 'are far commoner than is generally realised'.[41]

Evil-doers wander among us, Dion Fortune warned in one of her most successful books *Psychic Self-defence* (1930): trained magicians, members of Black Lodges who've taken the 'left hand path' of death-dealing and destruction, other wicked people, spiteful bullies with powerful minds who unintentionally emit noxious thoughts, and magical beings, discarnate entities, demons from the Pit, disembodied souls unwilling to leave the earthly plane.[42] Accidental or not, whether caused by humans or supernatural creatures, psychic attacks are devastating. Victims suffer frayed nerves, mental breakdowns, disturbed sleep and stranger symptoms. Poltergeist activity in their homes. Bruising and marks on their bodies. Trails of slime in their gardens. Odd footprints in the snow. Inexplicable outbreaks of fire. Weird sounds, clicks and the ringing of 'astral bells'.

Reading this, reviewers thought the theories outlined in *Psychic Self-defence* sounded like an updated version of witchcraft. True, there was more emphasis on mental ailments and less on the sorts of physical misfortunes traditionally ascribed to malign magic. Even so, Dion Fortune's concept of 'psychic attack' overlapped significantly with witchcraft, understood as interpersonal harm by uncanny means. 'Witchcraft and magic still survive, although perhaps in newer forms and different forms,' noted the *Sheffield Independent*, in a 1931 review of *Psychic Self-defence*.[43] With her notion of psychic attack, Fortune had rendered black magic in a modern idiom, blending esoteric ideas with psychological and psychiatric terms like 'sympathy', 'subconscious' and 'suggestion'. Racy subject matter was presented with a sober, subdued tone. In Fortune's 'amazing book', wrote a critic: 'All the paraphernalia of the magic of the Dark Ages is tricked out in pseudo-scientific language, with a fine show of distorted logic.'[44]

It was a fair point. The witches of the Middle Ages were psychic attackers, Dion claimed. A clear statement, but Miss Fortune could have been more precise about the nature of psychic attacks. Sometimes she described them as natural forces, varieties of mental influence that were in no sense uncanny. Then, a few paragraphs later, she gave a different impression, by writing of 'occult attacks' and using terms like 'supernatural' and 'supernormal' to warn about the dangers of 'the Unseen'. Worst of all, the great occultist barely explained how victims could defend themselves. Use 'common sense', she suggested: move house, break contact with the attacker, take baths of salted water, and say prayers ('I exorcise thee, creature of earth, by the living God').[45]

Inconsistency and a lack of instructions didn't stop Dion Fortune's *Psychic Self-defence* manual from selling well, within its limited genre. The book 'attracted some attention in interested circles' and contained 'a good deal of interest for serious students', one reviewer noted.[46] Between its first publication in 1930 and 1970, *Psychic Self-defence* went through at least twelve impressions (many more have been published since). No wonder contemporary magical practitioners regard it as a 'classic text'.[47] By explaining how occult attacks could be diagnosed, if not resisted, *Psychic Self-defence* became perhaps the most influential book by the woman who was probably modern Britain's leading occultist. Thus, among esoteric circles, maleficent witchcraft lived on.

WITCHCRAFT'S DECLINE: 1900-1930s

Between the 1900s and the early 1930s, a folksy version of black magic continued to be credited by lots of ordinary people. The *Taunton Courier* was right when, in 1921, it wrote of witchcraft: 'Such things are believed in today not simply by illiterate rustics in remote hamlets, but also by men and women living in our larger towns, who have had all the advantages of a Board School education.'[48]

For proof, consider the inquest held at the seaside resort of Scarborough in September 1904. It concerned the death of an infant from the town. In court, the child's mother sincerely explained that her baby had died because a neighbour bewitched it.[49] Similar feelings were evoked at an inquest in Taunton, Somerset's county town, over thirty years later in 1935. A woman's suicide, the court heard, grew out of her daughter's death and her own ill-health, both of which she attributed to the fact 'that there had been an ill-wish on the family'.[50]

Bewitched suicides, superstitious assaults, magical frauds and witchcraft accusations still made the news. By the early 1900s, however, the number of cases had dwindled considerably since the Victorian period. Alleged witches and ill-wishers were attacked at Grimsby (Lincolnshire) in 1911, Brixham (Devon) in 1913, Paignton (Devon) in 1919, Clyst St Lawrence (Devon) in 1924, and East Dereham (Norfolk) in 1940.[51] In 1916 a Somerset farmer shot dead a man he thought had bewitched his daughter and his horses.[52] At Tiptree (Essex) in 1908, a witch's husband was beaten after remonstrating with a man who threatened his wife and tried to get the village schoolchildren to throw stones at her.[53] At Burleston (Dorset) in 1917 and Glastonbury (Somerset) in 1925 supposed witches went on the attack after being provoked by months of malign rumours and innuendo.[54] Some bewitched people fell foul of the law by threatening their witches with violence – such as at Cotleigh (Devon) in 1905, Taunton (Somerset) in 1907, Tipton (Staffordshire) in 1926, and Langport (Somerset) in 1929.[55] Others were reprimanded for behaving in an offensive manner. In 1921, a man from Torquay (Devon) was summoned before the town's magistrates for spitting in the face of a woman who, he claimed, had cursed his seven children.[56]

Privately, magical fears haunted many hearts until around the outbreak of the Second World War in 1939. The residents of Horseheath, Cambridgeshire, were not unusual in being 'extremely courteous' to their neighbours, who were rumoured to control occult powers, during the 1910s.[57] Slad, in Gloucestershire, was during the 1920s home to a disabled beggar known as 'Albert the Devil', whose toxic gaze was thought capable of making women infertile and men impotent.[58] In 1924, rumours circulated in the Welsh coastal town of Aberystwyth that an ailing woman recuperating in the town had been killed by the evil eye.[59] Mathry, on the Pembrokeshire coast, was home to 'many people' said to possess 'the power of witchcraft', during the inter-war period.[60] With its witchy connections, the village was far from unique. No wonder two Welsh folklorists concluded, in 1926, that 'witchcraft lives and flourishes at the present day'.[61]

Superstitious suspicions motivated countryfolk from early twentieth-century Somerset to burn their cut hair, nails and removed teeth, to stop these potentially magical items falling into evil hands.[62] For the same reason Warwickshire people indulged in what one folklorist termed 'the repulsive habit' of licking blood from their wounds, rather than let it drop on the ground.[63] In rural Yorkshire, old-timers wore amulets of holed stones to keep black magic at bay.[64] At the Oxfordshire village of Deddington, during the 1920s, aged labourers fastened little bags of magical substances inside their clothes, for protection.[65] In the Quantock hills, during the 1930s and 1940s, locals carried rabbits' feet in their pockets as anti-witchcraft prophylactics.[66] Beyond the body, farmers still knew how to guard their buildings and produce from malefic powers. Written charms against witchcraft, containing passages of biblical Latin, were being purchased in Wales in the 1920s. Across Britain, evidence occasionally came to light of early twentieth-century people making witch-bottles to defeat evil spells, such as at Bottisham in Cambridgeshire in 1903.[67] Around the year 1900, the owner of a barn in the Derbyshire hamlet of Pratt Hall thought it was worth going to the trouble to cover the mortar of the interior walls with around eighty ancient apotropaic (evil-repelling) symbols known as hexafoils.

In a few villages, at the dawn of the twentieth century, witchcraft was rife. Take Long Compton in rural south Warwickshire, the heart of the English countryside. Home to about 600 people, with a post office, three chapels and a church, it lay 6 miles from the nearest railway station, in the Cotswold town of Moreton-in-Marsh. A mile beyond Long Compton, just over the brow of the hill, loomed the Rollright Stones, a defaced but still very impressive stone circle.

'There are enough witches in Long Compton to draw a wagon load of hay up Long Compton hill,' locals still said during the early twentieth century. It was a serious proverb. Investigating in 1912, the folklorist J. Harvey Bloom discovered Long Compton's villagers knew scores of creepy stories, which they eventually shared with him 'after much persuasion and with some fear of the consequences', tales about women and men from a generation ago.[68] Witches who'd been seen riding hurdles at night, and who'd sold their souls to the devil in return for dark powers. Evil folk, whose magic caused endless mischief, from madness to the inability to die, from domestic disasters to agricultural accidents. These stories made a powerful impression on the Rev. Harvey Bloom, who was unwilling to entirely dismiss witchery as a delusion. 'Did we but know their secrets,' he mused, 'modern science might well be the gainer.'[69]

Witchcraft, in early 1900s Long Compton, wasn't an archaism, a wicked thing confined to storytelling and the past. People blamed present-day misfortunes on black magic, up to and beyond the First World War. As one former resident remembered: 'Powerful interested in witches folk used to be in them days! If anybody were bad or a chimney pot fell off or some dire calamity befell, the witches was always to blame.'[70] Emma Wallington, a beggar living in a woodland hut on Long Compton's outskirts, was one reputed local witch, not entirely surprisingly.[71] There were plenty of others, including some who cultivated magical reputations for commercial ends. During the 1920s, a woman from the area earned her living partly by ill-wishing. She enacted her magic with spoken curses and by scratching her victims' initials into chestnuts which she roasted on the grills of her fire.[72]

A TWENTIETH-CENTURY WHITE WITCH: THE LATE CAREER OF MOTHER HERNE

White witches and cunning-men, canny-women and conjurors. Many worked their magical trades during the first three decades of the twentieth century. Gathering herbs by moonlight. Grinding out salves and ointments. Boiling up potions. Telling fortunes. Curing mysteriously ill beasts. Healing strangely afflicted people. Trickiest of all: diagnosing and repelling the evil eye, ill-wishing and witchcraft.

These services weren't just relevant to the remote past, to a lost world of primitive peasants. White witchery remained in demand, in Britain, throughout the Edwardian era, into the desperate times of the First World War, and even during the malaise-stricken inter-war years of extreme polit-ical ideologies, wireless radios and cinemas. It simply wasn't true that, by the close of the nineteenth century, the need for wise-men and cunning-women had vanished.[73] For proof, witness the occult career of Mother Herne.[74]

A little woman, raven-haired, skin weathered to the colour of parch-ment, with penetrating beady eyes. Born around the mid-nineteenth century, Mother Herne lived on the outskirts of Charlton Horethorne, a village near the Somerset–Dorset border, until her death in 1924. She had no less than three husbands over the course of her long life, with whom she lived in quite extraordinary circumstances, even by the eccentric standards of rural western England. In the shadow of Deadman's Hill (really), their lonely cottage struck one visitor as 'a suitable illustration for any child's fairy book'. Outside was a gate but no fence, a tied-up goat, several black hens and a black cat. Inside, mice scuttled, guinea pigs rustled, bottles clinked, herbs hung from low ceilings and a cauldron simmered over the open fire (again, really).

It was all part of the image that made Mother Herne famous in this area of the countryside. 'Who in these parts,' a journalist asked rhetorically in 1940, a full sixteen years after the old woman's death, 'has not heard of . . . Mother Herne?'[75] The reason she was so renowned? Mother Herne was one of the last, and greatest, of Britain's traditional white witches.

Mother Herne knew exactly how to behave to cultivate a wise-woman's reputation. Arriving at her cottage, visitors might find her leaning over the gate, with a cat perched on her shoulder. Before they could greet her, Mother Herne would say something extraordinary. A remark about who they were or why they'd come or what had recently happened to them, which she surely couldn't have known by normal means. Now, come inside, my dear, and sit by the fire.

In a thick Somerset accent, Mother Herne hinted, rhymed, riddled and implied. Rarely did she state outright precisely what was wrong, or what needed to be done to put it right. Conversing mysteriously, in an almost trance-like manner, she gave her clients plenty of scope to shape the discussion, to contribute to the narrative of what caused their ills and what would cure them. Talking like this also helped to keep Mother Herne within the law. If a person was foolhardy enough to report her to the authorities, she could always say something like: 'Why your honour, I never mentioned witchcraft, and I certainly never told the silly man to draw that woman's blood.' And she hadn't: not directly anyway.

Mother Herne was a qualified herbalist with a diploma and, it was said, formal training in nursing. She was certainly good at treating sprains and injuries. Yet Mother Herne's work went far beyond natural remedies, encompassing everything you'd expect of a white witch. Police numbers had surged since the beginning of the century, from around 40,000 in England and Wales in 1900 to 60,000 in 1930.[76] Despite the growth of law enforcement, Mother Herne's clients still asked for help detecting stolen and lost goods. Others requested aid for their suffering livestock – for pigs who refused to eat or cows with watery milk. Young women, especially, went to have their fortunes told. The wise-woman's technique was simple enough. Without announcing what she was going to do, she'd grasp her client's hand and turn it over so it opened upwards. Then, she'd slowly trace her long fingernail down the client's palm lines, while commenting on their prospects for love, wealth and health. During the First World War, Mother Herne's predictive skills became yet more relevant. Worried clients travelled from miles around to ask after the fate of their sons and friends, away doing battle in the muddy chaos of France and Flanders.[77]

Of all Mother Herne's gifts, the most difficult was unwitching. It wasn't something to be requested lightly. People endured long lists of sufferings, years of harrowing misfortunes, before they finally snapped and consulted the wise-woman. If someone asked Mother Herne whether their beast was overlooked, she might be candid enough to say 'bewitched he is . . . but you know the cure' (i.e. fetch the evil-doer's blood).[78] Coyer clients, nervous even to use witchcraft words, received more cryptic advice: 'You have a woman who visits you and she is bringing you bad luck, you must not let her into your house again.'[79]

Mother Herne liked to tell stories about her successful cures, and there's no doubt she was strikingly popular. Others from the area confirmed how, during the early 1900s, she was inundated with thousands of socially diverse clients, from the rural poor to farmers and even gentryfolk. 'I have seen gigs and pony carts by the dozen queued up outside her cottage,' remembered the folklorist Olive Knott, who'd had a consultation herself, and knew the great woman well.[80]

The white witch was fondly remembered after her death in 1924. 'I have never heard of an instance in which she attempted to do anything but help her fellows,' another local author recalled.[81] He knew from personal experience that Mother Herne had, on at least one occasion, given £2 of her own money to a man who came to her with dire financial difficulties.

There was, however, a dark side to the old lady's reputation. Some said she cursed with a stroke a local farmer, who'd prosecuted her son for poaching.[82] A worse fate awaited the man who challenged Mother Herne's livelihood. She conducted her white witchery successfully in the remote Somerset countryside, but Mother Herne could not completely evade the increasingly powerful medical profession. According to one story, a head-strong Irish doctor learned the wise-woman had stolen one of his patients. Furious, he rode over to Mother Herne's cottage, threatening that if the old herbalist didn't desist, he'd bring a prosecution. 'That's nothin' to what I shall do to thee,' Mother Herne retorted, 'think theeself lucky if thee's got home tonight wi' a broken neck.'[83] According to the story, the doctor did indeed fall from his horse, dying that very night.

THE WAR AGAINST QUACKERY

Mother Herne's confrontation with a qualified doctor may have been exaggerated or even invented. The broad scenario, however, was typical of the early twentieth century. Unscientific medical practitioners were assailed as never before by orthodox medics, and persecuted by the British state. Cunning-folk, along with unorthodox healers of all kinds, became victims of a 'war against quackery'.[84]

Quackery, meaning pretending to possess medical skill, is not conventionally associated with the early 1900s.[85] According to the distinguished historian of medicine Roy Porter, the 'long' eighteenth century, between the late 1680s and early 1840s, was the golden age of the quack. As a result of Victorian medical reforms, Porter contended, quackery suffered a 'gradual and partial eclipse'.[86]

In reality, that's not how British quackery declined. Unscientific medicine remained 'rampant', as one doctor complained, well after the Victorian age waned.[87] The quacks of the early 1900s were multitudinous, stretching from herbalists to bonesetters, water casters, faith healers, occultists, sellers of patent medicines, electricians (working with electricity) and cunning-folk. And they could be found practically everywhere. We can see this from a report of 1908, based on information supplied by some of the 1,600 Medical Officers of Health employed by local governments.[88] In the army town of Aldershot, the practice of medicine by those who were unqualified was 'large in extent, and could not very well be larger'.[89] Ebbw Vale, in Wales, was 'much infested by itinerant quacks'.[90] Newport hosted an 'enormous trade carried on in nostrums'.[91] At Stornoway, capital of the Western Isles, 'credulous islanders' were 'made a prey of by quacks'.[92]

To quash quackery, to curtail its outrageous prevalence, doctors began calling for 'rigorous repressive measures'. So great was the problem, nothing less than a 'crusade' would do.[93] Similar campaigns were already under way in Holland, Germany, Australia and elsewhere.[94] Why not Britain? With every passing year, the marvellous superiority of scientific medicine was becoming more apparent. From the discovery of blood groups and new vaccines, at the start to the twentieth century, to sulphonamides in the 1930s and antibiotics during the 1940s, doctors could now remedy a host of deadly and previously baffling diseases. Combined with the increased medical provision of the welfare state and growing affluence, scientific medicine caused the average Briton's life expectancy to surge from about 50 in 1900 to around 70 in 1960. The case of pneumonia, 'the old man's friend', is illustrative. It killed around 30 per cent of its victims until the advent of penicillin (discovered in 1928, mass-produced from 1941) drove its fatality rate down to 6 per cent.[95]

The war against quackery had selfish motives too. As a few doctors were prepared to admit, it was not just about providing patients with the most effective therapies. Competition within the medical profession was intensifying, as Britain's new redbrick universities trained ever more MDs. Patients were increasingly fought over, and salaries squeezed. 'Unqualified men are making more money than the qualified ones,' some grumbled.[96] Partly, the war against quackery was designed to improve the prospects of bona fide doctors, by quashing at least some of the competition.[97]

The British state, not doctors, was at the forefront of the war. For humanitarian reasons and for the sake of national efficiency, successive governments attacked quackery with a host of exacting new regulations. Between the Midwives Act of 1902 and the Pharmacy and Medicines Act of 1941, biomedicine's monopoly on health care was firmly established.[98] To take a few examples, nurses were subject to state registration in 1919, dentists in 1921, and in 1936 the British Medical Association established the Board of Registration of Medical Auxiliaries.[99] When herbalists, quackery's most respectable representatives, put forward a bill of registration in 1923, it was dismissed.[100] With new regulations abounding, Britain was becoming a more dangerous place for unqualified and unscientific healers.

THE LAST CONJURORS IN WALES

Urban cunning-folk began to struggle. They had plenty of willing customers, but there were more police too, and more laws prohibiting unqualified medical work. We can see this in the fortunes of 'conjurors' or *dyn hysbys*, as Welsh cunning-folk were known. Around the start of the twentieth century, a conjuror from Lampeter, a university town in south-west Wales, described the new stricter regime to the scholar John Humphreys Davies (1871–1926). He'd plenty of clients, at least several every day, until just a few years ago, when 'the old bobbies got fussing around'. Since then, the cunning-man sighed: 'I rarely get one.'[101]

Rural conjurors had it easier. The authorities closely watched the towns, but in the quiet of the countryside it was still possible to monetise magic. During the late 1920s a 'powerful wizard' was based at the village of Llangurig, Powys, who cured all manner of ailments, but especially mental illnesses.[102] An even more impressive wizard lived at Pwllheli, a market town on the Llyn Peninsula, whose clients reputedly came from as far away as America.[103] Throughout the 1930s, folklorists noted that conjurors were still plying their mysterious trade across much of rural Wales.[104] A reporter from the *Daily Express* confirmed this with an investigation conducted during the snowy December of 1932. Visiting out-of-the-way Welsh villages he met many people who, remarkably, were prepared to admit they'd suffered from the evil eye. Several of these informants had, in the recent past, called in wise-men to help them identify their witches and break their spells.[105]

Like their predecessors, the conjurors of the 1930s ruminated on mysterious books while making their diagnoses.[106] They broached the topic of witchcraft carefully, furtively, by speaking of 'evil-doers' and 'evil-wishers'. Conjurors created written charms and witch-bottles, to be placed in strategic locations around their clients' properties (some of which still survive in the collections of the National Library of Wales). Conjurors, in other words, were still masters of a Christian white magic, filled with prayers and biblical invocations, involving signs of the cross, but supplemented by a broader arcana of planetary symbols and occult words. They maintained the time-honoured rules for magic, not speaking about it, doing it secretly, locking doors before pronouncing charms, and so on. Conjurors worked at distance, sending magical items with messengers or by post. In the most desperate circumstances, they also attended their clients.

It didn't last. Conjurors, the final resort of desperately troubled people, disappeared during the post-war period. In March 1961 *The Times* reported that Wales' last *conjyr* was dead.[107] According to an ethnographer from the Welsh Folk Museum, the man in question was a 'combination of wizard and quack doctor', with a lucrative gift for lifting spells and curing cattle of the evil eye. Before his death some two years earlier this *conjyr* had, in accordance with tradition, named a successor; but his apprentice too had since passed away. For good or ill, conjurors had gone from Wales.

They'd left the rest of Britain too. Amid the austerity-escaping 1950s and the heady 1960s, commentators in western England suggested that white witches could still be found. On closer inspection though, the people in question turned out to be humble charmers rather than genuine cunning-folk like Mother Herne.[108] Finally, far later than many critics had anticipated, the ancient craft had been supressed.

Ironically, the cunning-craft disappeared around 1951, when the 1736 Witchcraft Act and anti-magic sections of the 1824 Vagrancy Act were repealed.[109] Those laws, prohibiting fraudulent 'pretenses' to witchcraft, had been the basis for the sporadic prosecution of a range of magicians, including cunning-folk. Increasingly, however, the statutes found new targets: spiritualists. The press regularly covered the prosecution of mediums like Helen Duncan, a Scottish medium, who in 1950 was convicted under the 1736 Witchcraft Act.[110] In the slowly liberalising atmosphere of twentieth-century Britain, it seemed retrograde and religiously intolerant that spiritualists should be treated so heavy-handedly. What's more, spiritualism had grown large enough to exert political influence, with several hundred thousand adherents by the 1940s. Sympathetic MPs agitated, and in 1951 the old Witchcraft and Vagrancy Acts were repealed. Under the new Fraudulent Mediums Act, no longer was it illegal to pretend to possess supernatural powers, so long as it was done for 'entertainment'. It came too late to help the last few cunning-folk. Their traditional brand of vaguely Christian white magic was beyond saving.

WITCHCRAFT'S COLLAPSE: 1940s–1960s

Witchcraft belief, already in decline, rapidly diminished from the 1940s. The modest flow of superstitious frauds, assaults, suicides and accusations reported in the press became a trickle, then just an occasional drip.

Even so, a measure of magic survived. During the so-called 'Phoney War' stage of the Second World War, early in 1940, as basic foods began to be rationed, a woman from Clifton in Lancashire killed herself believing she was bewitched.[111] The following year, in 1941, a group of Somerset Roma were prosecuted for cursing people who refused to buy their pegs.[112] Five years later, in 1946, a child neglect trial in Trowbridge, Wiltshire, heard how a local couple thought their little boy was bewitched by the neighbours (the parents tried to counteract this by throwing salt on the fire).[113]

By the 1950s, witchcraft had almost entirely disappeared from British news. Wednesbury, a West Midlands town, was home to an old woman who in 1951 told a rent tribunal she feared her sub-tenants had cast 'witchcraft and wishes' on her council house. They'd wished her dead, and she really believed it, the tribunal concluded.[114] In July 1955, two women from London asked Marylebone County Court for an injunction against their landlord, who for the last two years had been interfering with their flat, particularly the water and power supply. In court the landlord said the pair had bewitched his wife, causing her to behave erratically, through the medium of their cat.[115]

Quietly, among elders in some rural areas, oral storytelling kept a traditional conception of witchcraft alive. Old tales about decrepit hags, so vicious they'd bewitched their own children, were too fascinating to be entirely forgotten.[116] Thus, during the Second World War, residents of Seaton Ross, a village in the East Riding of Yorkshire, told tales about Peg Harper. She'd died almost a century earlier in 1853, but was remembered for bewitching carts and animals.[117] In the late 1940s, the old folk from around Shepton Mallet knew stories about Nancy Camel, a famous witch from the area who'd passed away well over a century earlier.[118] In 1950 'numerous legends' were circulating in the Norfolk villages of North and South Lopham, including one about witches being dunked in the pond at North Lopham.[119] Telling a tale like that was difficult, requiring a good memory, a sense of drama, clever voice work, gesticulations, and plenty of practice. Yet by the 1960s, the art of oral storytelling was dying. Younger generations, it seemed, no longer cultivated it.[120] The post-war youth preferred more passive, private and visual entertainments. Cinema attendances peaked in 1946 at 1,635 million a year, while the proportion of people with televisions in their homes rocketed between 1950 and 1960, from 4 per cent to 82 per cent.[121]

The years of war and austerity, the heyday of the British 'stiff upper lip', were animated by a distinctly unmagical ethos.[122] Cinema was dominated by urbane and economical productions, from thrillers like *The Third Man* (1949) to comedies such as *Kind Hearts and Coronets* (also 1949). Admittedly, a few movies depicted something as sensational as sorcery. *Wings of the Morning*, which showed at the Taunton Odeon in December 1945, concerned the dire results of a Rom's curse.[123] On the whole though, if films featured witchcraft at all it was as something silly, not serious. *I Married A Witch* was a 1943 comedy romance from Hollywood, a popular film containing light-hearted depictions of spellcraft. Similar themes soon appeared on television. *Bewitched*, a 1960s American sitcom, contained magic along with a few jabs at conventional housewifery, and was gentler still. This sort of mass media helped to ensure that, by the 1960s, words like 'witchcraft' and 'bewitched' were losing their previously fierce connotations. People now spoke about being 'cursed', if they felt they were suffering mystically derived misfortunes. The traditional language of witchcraft no longer had threatening resonances.

With old witch stories circulating less in the countryside, villages once notorious for housing large numbers of witches lost their evil reputations. As late as the 1940s, Somerset possessed a reputedly cursed mill at Crowcombe, along with a cursing well at Bishops Lydeard.[124] Canewdon, in south-east Essex, had a black reputation during the nineteenth century. Its ill-repute had largely dissipated by the mid-twentieth century, although as the folklorist Eric Maple warned in 1960: 'Even today, the feeling against it is not quite dead.'[125]

During the post-war era, the idea of sorcery barely figured in the average Briton's consciousness. Supernatural beliefs generally hadn't died. Occasionally, parents still burnt their offsprings' milk teeth, though now for luck and not to prevent evil-doers from acquiring the raw materials of spell-craft.[126] Many homeowners still nailed horseshoes to their doors. Good luck was the aim, not keeping off witches, as in the past. Plenty of older Scots possessed at least a smattering of witchcraft lore during the 1950s. They knew sayings like 'rowan-tree and red thread will put the witches to their speed'.[127] The same, however, could not be said of their younger relatives. The impression was confirmed by the anthropologist Geoffrey Gorer, who in 1950 surveyed 'English character' by sending questionnaires to 5,000 readers of *The People*. He asked whether they believed in ghosts (13 per cent of men and 21 per cent of women did), if they owned lucky mascots (about one in eight respondents), and whether they'd consulted fortune-tellers (44 per cent of people had, at least once in their life).[128] In all, Mr Gorer concluded that about a quarter of England's population held a view of the universe that could 'be designated as magical'. But he didn't bother to ask about witchcraft, cursing or harmful occult powers. Those ideas probably seemed ridiculously fringe, irrelevant even.

Magic, black and white, was deeply at odds with the zeitgeist of the 1940s and early 1950s.[129] Witchcraft was a heady, consciousness-altering belief system. Its adherents often willed it to be true, deliberately intensifying their faith by repressing doubts. Without faith, magic would surely fail. Such an extravagant way of thinking was deeply out of sync with the wartime ethos, cultivated by the propaganda of the Ministry of Information and embodied in media stretching from movies to political speeches.[130] 'Whatever happens, keep a stiff upper lip,' Churchill said in 1940, after the fall of France, during a secret session of the House of Commons.[131] Many people did. In this great age of emotional continence, when something went wrong, Britons didn't go on mind-bending trips where they made themselves believe they were bewitched. They behaved much more reasonably when adversity struck, as it frequently did amid the dark days of the Second World War, rationing and austerity. Britons followed the dictum of a subsequently famous, though at the time never-used propaganda poster. They kept calm and carried on.

Changing attitudes showed up in the child-rearing practices of the 'greatest generation', who came of age during the Second World War. When weaning their baby-boomer offspring, they generally didn't teach the little ones about witchcraft, in the traditional sense of black magic. Formerly, children heard stories about mystic death-dealers from the local area. They were warned to avoid certain evil-eyed characters. Alternatively, throughout the nineteenth and into the twentieth century, youngsters were encouraged to harass witches, presumably because juvenile vigilantes were unlikely to be prosecuted. This inculcation of children into the dark domain of witchcraft ceased sometime around the mid-twentieth century. We can see this from the work of Iona Opie and Peter Opie, husband and wife folklorists who during the 1950s surveyed the lore and language of 5,000 British schoolchildren. Kids knew legions of games, riddles, rhymes, seasonal customs, initiation rites and superstitions, many more than most adults would expect. Yet amid the 'strange and primitive culture' of childish folklore, the Opies found almost no trace of witchcraft. The exception was a harmless ditty from Scotland:

This is the nicht o' Hallowe'en
Where the witches can be seen,
Some are black and some are green,
And some the colour o' a turkey bean.[132]

In the dreams of children, witches had become silly figures, not the night-marish death-dealers of old.

The decline of Christianity, particularly Protestantism, aided witchcraft's collapse by removing one of its intellectual props. Church attendance had been falling since at least 1905, while between the 1920s and 1960s Britain's (particularly England's) religious atmosphere became more relaxed and less puritanical.[133] The Bible, formerly a great source of authority for the credo of witchcraft belief, was no longer widely admired or even well known. The devil, the old master of witches, wasn't much feared now (surveys suggested that three-fifths of Britons disbelieved both in the devil and in Hell, even in the loosest metaphorical sense).[134] According to a folklorist writing at the start of the twentieth century, believers in witchcraft from rural Berkshire 'constantly' justified their persuasion by citing the Old Testament story of the Witch of Endor.[135] In 1920s Norfolk, people made the same point: 'We all know there are witches. It is in the Bible. There was the Witch of Endor.'[136] Yet by the 1950s, the argument was seldom made and had probably been forgotten. In part this was because new biblical translations were appearing that made little or no mention of witches and familiar spirits. 'You shall not allow any sorceress to live' somehow didn't have the same urgent ring.[137] Witchcraft's supporting Christian mythology had disappeared.

Decline was the dominant trend. Yet a few embers of evil magic smoul-dered in the post-war world of white goods and state welfare. A mystic aura clung to horsemen, expert workers with equines, formerly the most precious things on Britain's roads and farms. Relatively few remained by the 1960s because of the uptake of motorcars and tractors.[138] Yet among the surviving horsemen there were some who genuinely created 'toad bones', in order to gain magical power over animals. It was done at the witching hour of midnight, by throwing frog or toad limbs into a river, and picking out any that floated upstream, against the current. It reeked of spellcraft, of devilry even, at least to outsiders. There were certainly mid-twentieth-century farm labourers who said they'd smelt brimstone when the horseman set to work.[139]

Probably the most consistent believers in malefic interpersonal influ-ences were fishermen operating trawlers out of Britain's ports, great and small. Practitioners of a dangerous and uncertain craft, many seafarers (though not all) clung to a litany of superstitions about dangerous words, unlucky actions and potent objects. Their taboos included deep aversion to whistling women (said to be witches, capable of conjuring winds) and cross-eyed people (known to possess the evil eye).[140] 'Among the seafaring population there are many who to this day still believe in the witch's power,' a folklorist of north-eastern Scotland had noted in the 1920s.[141] In the 1950s, one commentator thought that among Morayshire's fisherfolk, a 'considerable degree of superstition endures to the present day – if less openly than used to be the case'.[142] Around the mid-twentieth century, in the streets around Hull's docks and among the fishermen who worked them, stories were shared about evil-doers who whistled up the wind.[143]

After fisherfolk, the next most frequent witchcraft believers were West Country people. It was, however, hard to say how many westerners really feared evil magic. Sorcery was 'rapidly diminishing', 'virtually extinct' in most places, according to a Devon folklorist in 1965, only credited by the 'very old' in the view of an expert on Somerset.[144] The controversial folklorist Ruth Tongue was overstating it when she claimed, in 1965: 'The belief in witchcraft and fear of it is wide-spread, in Somerset.'[145] But certainly, the West Country continued to be a quietly witchy place. If you knew where to look and whom to ask, you could still find people burning effigies of their enemies. Or hammering nails into their footprints, to lame them. Or sticking pins into wax and animal hearts, for obvious reasons. Or pronouncing the old hate charm:

'Tis not this thing I wish to burn
But Mrs Priddy's heart I wish to turn.
Wishing thee neither to drink, sleep nor rest
Until thou dost come to me and do my request.[146]

Witchcraft didn't just persist, albeit much reduced, among horsemen, fishermen and in western England. Traces of black magic could be found just about everywhere during the mid-twentieth century, even in towns. To take a sinister example, at an insurance office in Birmingham, clerks sorting through an ex-colleague's belongings discovered an effigy of a woman impaled with pins.[147] Such anecdotes convinced the folklorist Christina Hole (1896–1985) that 'the darker aspects of magic are not forgotten'.[148] However, in Miss Hole's view, modern witchcraft had a new gentler quality. It was apparently 'no longer a terror even to those who believe in it'.[149]

An interesting hypothesis, but wrong. Witchcraft was far less widely credited – with that, none could disagree. Yet the few 1950s people who managed to believe in evil magic were just as unsettled by the idea as their forebears had been. Witchcraft remained a potent notion, capable of inspiring powerful psychosomatic and placebo responses. Note the testimony of a Devon doctor, who told a British Medical Association enquiry: 'The practice of magic, both white and black was widely spread in my Devon practice. I have had one definite death from witchcraft, or I suppose I should say suggestion.'[150] This was not a unique situation. Speaking to a journalist from the *Daily Herald* in 1956, a general practitioner from Holsworthy, a little market town towards the north Devon coast, claimed to know no less than six people who'd committed suicide because they thought they were bewitched. They might have done so anyway, he admitted: 'But it's terribly easy to persuade a nervous and insecure person that ill-luck was purposefully wished upon them.'[151]

What sort of events, what sort of magical insinuations, terrified people in 1950s Britain into unbearable insanity? A hint is provided by grim happenings in Horrabridge, Devon, towards the end of May 1956. One night, about ten o'clock, a well-organised crowd surged through the village, carrying a straw effigy. Holding a placard with the victim's name, it represented an unpopular local man who worked as a taxi driver and salesman. Bearing it aloft through the village to a nearby field, the crowd yelled and spat at the effigy, before burning it while dancing around, then throwing the remnants in the river.

The effigy-burning procession in Horrabridge, in May 1956, was a late example of an ancient rite. Found across Europe, in English it was usually known as 'rough music'. A pitiless form of 'psychic terrorism', as the social historian E.P. Thompson described it, communities used rough music to intimidate deviants in their midst.[152] The procession in Horrabridge had many symbolic components, but the attack on the effigy carrying a placard with the man's name might well have been interpreted as a magical assault. Questioned by a journalist, the target and his family tried to dismiss the rough music as 'just one of those things'. 'Oh, we're not at all worried. It was nothing.'[153] Maybe they weren't worried. Maybe it was nothing. But the continuing trickle of bewitched suicides suggests otherwise. During the 1950s and beyond, there were still a few people who were deeply traumatised by the thought of being supernaturally harmed.

WHY DID WITCHCRAFT DECLINE?

'The younger generation, of course, do not believe in witches. They are educated.' So ventured the *Somerset Herald*, in 1947.[154] With that remark, the paper recycled an obvious and clichéd explanation for witchcraft's decline: education. Britons, the *Somerset Herald* and many others suggested, were too well schooled to fear something as ridiculous as sorcery. Surely, no properly educated persons could regard black magic as anything other than folly, fantasy and poppycock?

In previous chapters, I've already cast doubt on this theory about formal education's superstition-smashing qualities. The comparative evidence, from places in the world where witchcraft is currently virulent, is particularly telling. Today, across much of sub-Saharan Africa, legions of university graduates, civil servants, politicians, doctors and other highly educated people believe, as one scholar notes, that 'witchcraft is an urgent and very harassing reality'.[155] A thorough grounding in maths, grammar, science, history, geography and even medicine has done very little if anything to stop them fearing evil magic.

The British evidence confirms the impression. For one thing, the chronology doesn't match, between the rise of schooling and the contraction of witchcraft belief. Universal state-funded education was established in Britain between the 1870s and 1890s. Yet witchcraft remained widely believed in until about 1900, and fairly common until the late 1930s, half a century after the great Victorian education reforms. It's also worth remembering the minority of well-educated British people who credited the reality of sorcery and supernatural powers: from the scientist Alfred Russel Wallace, to the doctor Anna Kingsford, to the colonists who found themselves starting to believe when ensconced in foreign lands. If education reduces one's propensity to believe in malign magic, it's not by much. Formal learning, in the form of more and better schooling, does not plausibly account for the decline of British witchcraft.

A better explanation for black magic's decline is the waning of unpredictable, life-shattering misfortunes. In recent years, historians like Owen Davies have identified people's growing comfort and control over their lives as the primary reason why witchcraft subsided.[156] This is a much more convincing argument, logically and empirically. Witchcraft, after all, was a method for coping with an overwhelming series of disasters. If devastating happenings became less common in people's personal lives, they would have less need to invoke a belief system involving curses and ill-wishes.

Witchcraft declined (moderately from the 1900s, rapidly from 1930s) at the same time as ordinary folk experienced big improvements in their living standards. During the first third of the twentieth century, working people still endured brutally hard lives. Especially in the countryside, families raised animals, dug allotments and kept cottage gardens, baked their daily bread, cooked on open fires, slept in overcrowded beds, collected water from rainfall or gathered it from wells, and relieved themselves in outdoor privies. Those everyday hardships did not begin to wane until the 1930s and later, with the arrival of household running water, domestic electricity, motorcars on country lanes, council houses and home radios.[157] During the 1940s, plenty of country cottages still lacked plug sockets, water taps and gas pipes.[158] By then, however, new technologies, from plastics to penicillin, were reducing the scope of illness. Ordinary Britons were experiencing fewer devastating misfortunes thanks also to the growth of the welfare state, pensions, enormous public housing programmes and the National Health Service.

Yet difficult-to-explain disasters still haunted the common lot: romantic frustrations, for example, as well as unemployment and business failures; hard-to-treat and often mortal conditions like cancer; accidents and, above all, mental illnesses. During the inter-war period, some folklorists claimed that people only used witchcraft to explain old-fashioned agricultural misfortunes, like horses going lame or cows falling ill. They were wrong. Other folklorists, working in 1920s Wales for instance, noticed how there were still folk who attributed nervousness, anxiety, melancholia, depression and financial problems to magic.[159] A few Welsh cancer sufferers, it was implied, attributed their ailments to evil occult influences.[160] Writing in 1961, the writer Olive Knott claimed to know a young couple from Somerset who were 'firmly convinced' their television was bewitched, because it broke down regularly each Saturday evening.[161]

This diminishes the explanatory power of the argument, outlined above, that witchcraft declined because mysterious misfortunes waned. Barely explicable disasters continued, on a smaller scale. People didn't stop suffering from heartbreaks, bankruptcy, cancers and mental illnesses. Rather, they largely (not totally) stopped attributing these misfortunes to the uncanny actions of individuals with evil eyes and black hearts.

Magic, it is worth remembering, can coexist with the latest technology, a dynamic economy and improving life chances. Look at contemporary sub-Saharan Africa, where witchcraft is ubiquitous despite credit cards, computers, telephones, the internet, growing wealth, modern medicine, entrepreneurialism, jobs in financial services and so on. Modernity, with its comforts and technologies, does not automatically destroy witchcraft.

Britain's dark world of evil magic withered, during the early twentieth century, for many reasons. People living less dangerous lives was undoubtedly a factor. So was the decline of oral storytelling, and the waning of popular Protestantism. More speculatively, the calm and determined demeanour of the 1940s and 1950s may have played a part. But what really diminished witchcraft was state power. Intense regulation of the market in health care made life impossible for cunning-folk, conjurors, wise-men, warlocks and the other figures we've met in this book.

Cunning-folk didn't just heal witchcraft by providing protective items or conducting cleansing spells. They also explained what witchcraft was, who witches were and how they accomplished their evil. They taught their clients the importance of faith and the principles of magic. In short, cunning-folk were crucial propagators of this belief system. Without them, it crumbled and was largely forgotten. It wasn't, as some scholars have suggested, a decline in witchcraft belief that killed the cunning-craft.[162] The opposite was true. The destruction of the cunning-craft, suppressed by an increasingly powerful and scientifically minded state, caused the decline of witchcraft among the population at large.

ROMA DOING LESS *DUKKERIN*, BUT STILL CURSING

Like cunning-folk, Roma fortune-tellers suffered too. Although sincere believers in occult powers, they were notorious for hoodwinking house-dwellers with theatrical but ultimately nonsensical rites. Cynicism didn't stop Roma fortune-tellers from being important magicians, itinerants who provided the British public with a range of esoteric services, from love divination to unwitching. However, this work became difficult during the increasingly regulated twentieth century. *Dukkerin*, as fortune-telling was known in the Romany language, never disappeared completely from Britain, but it became rarer.

Roma people were famously adaptive, good at filling economic niches, quick to respond to new opportunities. Perceiving a demand for fortune-telling among tourists at coastal holiday resorts, they pitched their tents. But already by the 1910s, commentators noticed how Roma were being driven from their old seafront spots in towns like Blackpool, only to be replaced by palmist boxes on the pier.[163] Some, like the Rom autobiographer Gordon Boswell's parents, abandoned *dukkerin* as ungodly behaviour when they converted to evangelical Christianity.[164] Most Roma fell victim to the interventions of local governments, keen to enforce bye-laws in order to rid their towns of these stigmatised freewheelers. With Roma compelled to camp on the boundaries of seaside towns, the most lucrative form of *dukkerin* became more difficult.

Some said *dukkerin* Roma were gone for good. In 1915 one journalist thought Romany people were 'fast disappearing' from Britain, driven to America by a wish to avoid the Great War.[165] During the 1930s, Traveller sympathisers continued to bemoan the 'passing of the gypsy', in the parlance of the time. Nomadism and *dukkerin* were, allegedly, part of a now impossible way of life. Modern civilisation's drab uniformity beckoned for all, Roma and gorgios (house-dwellers) alike.[166]

In reality, the Roma people hadn't disappeared. According to a 1964 survey 15,000 still lived in England and Wales, but this was an underestimate – the true figure may have been as high as 63,000.[167] However, in the post-war period Travellers were forced to abandon itinerancy, their traditional habit of living on the road, and settle on a hugely inadequate number of dedicated Traveller campsites. The main culprits were the 1959 Highways Act, which prohibited roadside camping, and the 1960 Caravan Sites and Control of Development Act, which allowed local authorities to close common land to Travellers.[168] Immediately, many did. Families who'd traversed rural Britain for generations found themselves threatened by the police if they dared pull their vans onto the verge, or served with dispersal notices if they camped on the commons.[169] 'Old England was a wonderful place,' recalled Gordon Boswell, looking back at life in the early twentieth century. 'Now,' he wrote in the late 1960s, 'it seems to me like a police state.'[170]

Hawking certainly became more difficult. But talk of *dukkerin*'s total disappearance was overstated. Roma women still called door to door, selling flowers and pegs, along with new items like doormats.[171] They dealt in mystic arts too, if they sensed the householder was receptive. Herbal cures were still worth knowing.[172] Fortune-telling remained popular. Some gorgios could even be manipulated into paying for good luck blessings.

Most lucrative of all was curse removal. But it was risky. Lillian Jones discovered this in 1940, when she was convicted of stealing £40, a gold watch and various other household goods from a brother and sister living near Aberdare, in Wales. With her daughters Lillian had enacted something like the old Roma *dukkerin* trick, saying the items contained a 'bad power', which would condemn the house and its inhabitants if they didn't clean it off.[173] Another convicted curse remover was Rosina Smith, who in 1950 stole £22 and a pair of earrings from a Birmingham woman. Rosina said she'd give the money to her grandmother to place 'under a planet', in order to remove a curse placed on the dupe by 'a dark-haired woman'.[174] In 1958 a Rom named Elizabeth Pearl Price (36) successfully prised £14 from a woman living at Langley Mill, Derbyshire, in return for removing a 'curse' from her house. Price was spotted by a patrolling police officer and arrested.[175] In 1959 Anna Lee was arrested in Dudley for claiming to cure a man's cancer with herbs. She had two previous convictions, one for taking money off local people to cure a curse (using a crystal), another for removing an evil spell.[176]

Romany people were *dukkerin* less frequently, yet they remained powerful casters of curses. For oft-despised people, it could be a helpful skill, even in the white heat of the 1960s technological revolution. In 1961, 60-year-old Prince Gypsy Lee, claiming to be heir to the throne of the Spanish and Irish Roma, caused a scandal by cursing Norfolk County Council, based at King's Lynn. First he'd been ordered to move his caravan from council-owned land on the quayside. A month later, he was refused a showground space at King's Lynn's annual fair, because the council had banned palmists and astrologers. In January Prince Lee spoke to the press, offering to break his curse at the next full moon, if the council left him alone to make a living. Lee claimed to have 'inherited the power of witch-craft from my father'.[177] The council did indeed let Gypsy Lee take part in the county fair, though apparently not because of the curse.[178] Yet curses did change some people's minds. In 1964, a scrap dealer from Dudley didn't remove Roma people from his land because of the threat of magical retribution. As he explained to the reporter from the *Birmingham Daily Post*: 'I really do believe that gipsies can put a curse on you. I know people who have been cursed with illness and they have been ill.'[179]

pagan witch cults and a magic murder

Between the 1920s and 1960s, a once eccentric interpretation of witchcraft went mainstream. Witchcraft, according to this reading, wasn't the practice of black magic. On the contrary, it was a pagan nature religion, an ancient cult, a fertility-worshipping secret society. It prevailed in Europe for millennia, first openly, then underground, until it was incinerated in fires stoked by the gloomy clerics of the Middle Ages.

This thrilling but empirically false thesis was developed by a handful of nineteenth-century writers. From the 1920s, however, it became well known and widely endorsed in Britain. Partly because it accorded with many of the period's assumptions and expectations.[180] Witchcraft as paganism was a conspiracy theory interpretation of history for an era awash with conspiracies, real and imagined, from the Bolsheviks to the Protocols of the Elders of Zion. The idea also fitted in with the widely accepted theory of Sir James Frazer, Cambridge anthropologist and author of *The Golden Bough*, that ancient religion was fertility-orientated.[181] Beyond the intellectual resonances, the notion that witchcraft was a pagan cult spread because of one extraordinary woman: the unbelievably energetic, maddeningly dogmatic, Margaret Murray.

Margaret Murray was a diminutive woman born in the mid-Victorian era. Despite possessing no formal academic qualifications, she managed, through personal connections, to become an academic at University College London, eventually rising to the rank of Professor of Egyptology. And though she was an Egyptologist, Murray established herself as one of the world's premier authorities on the history of witchcraft. Aside from some obscure articles, it began with *The Witch Cult in Western Europe* (1921), published by the august Oxford University Press. She'd discovered a 'hitherto unrecognized cult', Murray announced, devoted to a pagan fertility god. The scholarship was, frankly, untenable. To sustain her thesis, Murray completely ignored any evidence of 'operative witchcraft', meaning spells for good or evil, the overwhelming content of witchcraft. Focusing instead on 'ritual', the Egyptologist made her case for paganism with unjustified but confident assertions, by quoting out of context, and using inconsistent methods of interpretation.[182]

In lectures, interviews and an entry for the *Encyclopaedia Britannica* (1929), she belittled the folkloric evidence of contemporary British witchcraft.

Sticking pins in effigies, constructing counter-witchcraft charms and blooding supposed witches – these were nothing more than 'elementary spell-binding' and 'very simple, really'.[183] This was ironic, since there were occasions when Murray actually practised magic for evil, cursing an academic rival, and melting an effigy of Kaiser Wilhelm II during the First World War. She even received letters from bedevilled readers, begging her to unwitch them. Nonetheless, Murray used her public profile to argue that the pagan witch cult was what mattered.

Published by Oxford University Press, featured in the *Encyclopaedia Britannica* until the 1960s and largely ignored by her scholarly colleagues, what made Murray's witch-cult thesis really widely known was an unsolved murder. In 1945 Charles Walton, a 74-year-old labourer from Lower Quinton, Warwickshire, was found dead outside the village. In the shadow of Meon Hill, he'd been stabbed with a garden-fork, had his arms cut where he'd tried to defend himself, and had his throat slashed by a sickle. Police enquiries headed by the celebrated detective Robert Fabian ('of the Yard') went nowhere. In part because the officers quickly became convinced that this was somehow a witchcraft murder, on account of the fact that seventy years earlier, in 1875, Ann Tennant of nearby Long Compton had been killed for being a witch, also with a garden-fork. The investigation, moreover, was disrupted by Margaret Murray's presence. She, above all, was convinced that the murder was an echo of a fertility-orientated witch cult.

Margaret Murray continued to expound her witchcraft-as-paganism theory, in print and in the press. In 1950 she was interviewed for a front-page story by a journalist from the *Birmingham Daily Post*. Described as a 'scientist', she propounded her cranky thesis that 'witchcraft lives on', not just in the sense of black magic, but as a sacrificial cult, a descendant of pre-Christian religion. Charles Walton 'was one of the people sacrificed', she said, because he died in February: 'One of the four months in the year when sacrifices are carried out.'[184] Hearing these lurid remarks, the commendably sceptical *Daily Herald* sent a reporter to ask residents of Lower Quinton what they thought of the woman who 'accused most of them of believing in witchcraft', and of practising bloodcurdling pagan rites. The opinion of the village schoolmaster summed it up well: 'Tripe.'[185]

217

WICCA

At first, pagan witchcraft existed only as an idea, fear or fantasy. Around the middle of the twentieth century, however, it assumed a tangible reality. At last, it became a religion. Margaret Murray's pagan witch-cult thesis was combined with rituals drawn from sources as diverse as freemasonry, high Victorian occultism, eastern spirituality, nudism, Malayan knife-work and domestic folklore. The result was something unique. 'Wica' ('Wicca' from the 1960s) was the only codified religion to originate in Britain, ever, in history.[186] Its creator, or synthesiser, was a retired civil servant: Gerald Brosseau Gardner.

Born in 1884 into an expatriate middle-class family, Gerald Gardner was notable for his mischievous humour and glinting blue eyes.[187] After a largely school-free childhood he spent most of his working life managing planta-tions in Ceylon and Malaya, where, like a surprising number of colonists, he was deeply affected by the supernatural atmosphere.[188] Gerald began exploring the occult, first in the form of Malayan folklore, before turning to spiritualism and various forms of ritualised high magic, particularly after his return to England during the 1930s.

By the 1940s Gerald and at least one collaborator had begun formulating a religion of pagan witchcraft. Then an opportunity arose. In 1947 Gerald met Cecil Williamson, a filmmaker, entrepreneur and occult enthusiast.[189] Both men needed to make an income and both also owned huge personal collections of occult artifacts, some of rather dubious provenance, many acquired during travels around the now collapsing British Empire. The solution was obvious. Cecil and Gerald decided to go into business together, using the publicity from the repeal of the Witchcraft Act in 1951 to open a museum. The responsible-sounding 'Folklore Centre of Superstition and Witchcraft' would be based at Castletown, on the mystical Isle of Man. Initially, the venture was successful enough. Before long though, in 1953–4 the duo fell out, mostly because of Williamson's impatience with Gardner's distinctive interpretation of witchcraft as a still surviving pagan cult. Gardner took sole charge of the Castletown museum, from where he continued to propagate his religion, most notably, with his 1954 book *Witchcraft Today*.

In *Witchcraft Today* Gerald Gardner posed as an anthropologist who had discovered ancient witches' covens operating in rural England. Their cult was based on an unbroken oral tradition stretching back to the pre-Christian era. And, unlike the witches of myth, they eschewed hexing and harmful magic.[190] Instead, Gardner's witches were overwhelmingly focused on worshipping two deities: a Horned God (representing maleness and death) and a Moon Goddess (representing femininity, fertility and rebirth). On key dates in the year, Wiccans conducted magical rites, involving ceremonial swords, chanting, dancing and ritual nudity. They literally practised magic, Gardner claimed. Distinctively though, Wiccan witches aspired not to personal gain, but to venerate Old Gods and elemental powers.

Recordings survive of Gardner and his initiates participating in Wiccan rites.[191] The chants are impressive. Most last two or three minutes. Voices in unison. Slowly at first, tripping through tongue-twisting verses. Then gradually faster, louder, more urgent. A beat begins, hands slap, the voices are almost reaching for musical notes now. The key gets higher in pitch after every stanza. Then, with an abrupt cry, the spell ends.

Participating in Wicca was a heady experience. For some, it provided a refreshing alternative to the restrained, buttoned-up atmosphere of early 1950s Britain. Gardner himself stressed Wicca's power to bring peace, ease and 'psychological satisfaction'.[192] Yet almost from the outset, there were tensions, as with all new religions. Covens were soon established in Britain and across the Anglo-Saxon world by independent thinkers, mostly women. Some venerated Gerald Gardner as the fountainhead of the Wiccan tradition. Others had different leaders or priorities. Ritual nudity wasn't a necessary part of Wicca, one of Gardner's great collaborators Doreen Valiente later suggested.[193] Other pagan witches found the emphasis on collective religious rites stifling. Gardner's final book, *The Meaning of Witchcraft* (1959), put more emphasis on operative magic than his earlier Wiccan publications had done. Within Wicca, a movement for solitary spellcraft, for something more like witchcraft in the traditional sense, was gaining momentum.[194]

*   *   *

Witchcraft didn't die, during the early and mid-twentieth century. Between the Edwardian equipoise and the swinging sixties, there were always Britons who thought black magic was genuinely dangerous. Some people tried to protect themselves against it. Others, a malicious few, attempted to wield it. In the era of the welfare state, there was still a place for time-honoured horrors: image magic, sticking pins in effigies, stabbing hearts. Alternatively, avant-garde occultists renamed maleficent and beneficent magic, using terms like 'psychic attack' and 'psychic self-defence'. Witchcraft, as an idea, was evolving.

Witchcraft evolved, but it also declined. Steadily, to a minority credo, between about the 1900s and the 1930s. Rapidly, to a fringe persuasion, during the 1940s and 1950s. Witchery waned for several reasons, the balance of which must remain provisional. Tentatively, I think the main cause was an alliance between orthodox medicine and state regulation. Medical science, from vaccines to antibiotics, heavily reduced the scope of misfortune. The need for a misfortune-coping belief system waned commensurately. More importantly, as the British state grew, it suppressed unorthodox healers like cunning-folk, who'd traditionally taught people about witchcraft, as well as cured it.

Already in a depleted state, witchcraft was further diminished by cultural changes. The dwindling of popular Protestantism, between about the 1920s and 1960s, removed one of its major intellectual props. The decline of oral storytelling in the countryside played a minor role. The shrinking of witchcraft-related trades, like horse work and fishing, contributed. So did the settling of the Roma onto dedicated caravan sites, meaning they less often went *dukkerin*. The stiff upper lip ethos may even have played a part in witchcraft's decline, during the austere years of the Second World War and beyond.

This restrained situation was never likely to last. Magic could be tempting, freeing, transcendent and euphoric. It was always likely to entice those who felt confined by modern life. Hence the appeal of Wicca, from the 1950s. It was a sign of things to come. In the multicultural atmosphere of late twentieth-century Britain, magic was about to experience a revival.

nine

MULTICULTURAL MAGIC
1970–2015

On Thursday 14 March 1974 cinemas in London's West End began screening what some were calling 'the vilest and most repulsive film ever made'.[1]

The Exorcist, directed by William Friedkin and written by William Peter Blatty, was a close adaptation of the latter's bestselling novel. Loosely based on actual events, it told the story of Regan MacNeil, a 12-year-old girl possessed by an ancient demon, fruitlessly put through everything medical science had to offer, before being exorcised by two Roman Catholic priests, both of whom died in the process. A critical and commercial triumph, *The Exorcist* won four Academy Awards and became the second highest grossing movie in the UK during 1974 – a significant achievement given its '18' rating.[2] With an unforgettable depiction of a head-twisting, vomit-spewing demoniac, and a uniquely sincere tone, this instant classic took the genre of horror to a darker place.

For its creator, *The Exorcist* was not an exercise in shallow make-believe. A sincere Catholic, William Peter Blatty hoped it would persuade movie-goers of nothing less than the reality of demons and the existence of God and His angelic host.[3] In an era when only a shrinking minority of Britons were regular churchgoers, this theological message may well have been lost on most. But it ensured *The Exorcist* won some clerical admirers, including Fr Joseph Crehan, a senior Jesuit from London. Commissioned to review

The Exorcist for the *Daily Mirror*, his reaction could not have been more positive: 'I would like everyone over sixteen to see this film.'[4] Fr Crehan saw the movie as embodying profound but no longer widely accepted truths about the reality of supernatural evil and the duty of Christians to combat it. David Curnock, a captain in an Anglican outreach organisation named the Church Army, felt similarly. In a letter to the *Church Times* he confirmed from personal experience that: 'The demonic possession and exorcism sequences were, to a point, realistic.'[5]

Those public, apparently sincere reactions to *The Exorcist* illustrate an intriguing late twentieth-century development. It was becoming easier for respectable people to admit to believing in supernatural beings and esoteric powers, to say that devils and demons – even ghosts and curses – existed not just metaphorically or subjectively, but literally in this world at the present time. Britain, like much of Western Europe and North America, was increasingly multicultural, pluralistic and permissive. Minority religions and alternative faiths were growing. Occult beliefs and pseudo-magical practices were losing their taboo. 'Evil is . . . an active force, a living, spiritual being . . . it is a terrible reality, mysterious and frightening', Pope Paul VI had insisted in a speech of November 1972.[6]

It was not only Christians who expressed vivid supernatural beliefs. By the 1970s, novices wanting to hunt ley-lines or channel cosmic energies could learn how from books produced by dedicated metaphysical publishers and sold in specialist 'New Age' bookshops. The climate became more accepting in the 1980s, when spiritualist mediums began doing readings on regional television, and newspapers set up premium-rate horoscope phone lines, playing the pre-recorded insights of celebrity stargazers.[7] Conference halls across Britain hosted 'festivals of mind and body', exhibiting all sorts of mystical pursuits, from crystal healing to ufology, meditation, aura reading and palmistry. Esoteric therapies became fashionable at the highest levels of public life in the 1990s. Princess Diana told journalists she cured her nail biting habit with acupuncture, reflexology and aromatherapy.[8] In 1995 the clairvoyant Betty Palko claimed she'd put the princess in contact with the spirit of her deceased father, the late Earl Spencer. Buckingham Palace dismissed it as 'utter nonsense'. Yet in August 1997, residents of the Derbyshire village of Pilsley were shocked to see Diana arrive by helicopter to consult her favourite spirit medium, Rita Rogers.[9]

This dramatic shift in the threshold of acceptable public behaviour was bound to register in opinion polling. Back in 1950, when the American pollster Gallup asked Britons whether they believed in ghosts, about one in ten admitted they did. When the same question was posed in the 1970s the figure had more than doubled to one in five, by the early 1990s it was just under one in three, while 37 per cent of respondents claimed they thought houses could be haunted, when asked by Gallup in 2005.[10]

In comparison to ghosts, supernatural powers like sorcery were less widely credited. During the 1970s, around one in ten Britons said they believed in black magic. By the early 2000s, asked the slightly different question of whether they believed in witchcraft, around one in eight respondents confessed that they did.[11] The growing tolerance for magical beliefs doubtless contributed to the increase. So too did the more multicultural character of British society. Broken down on very broad ethnic and gender lines, a poll of 2008 found 16 per cent of respondents overall claiming witchcraft was real, rising to 19 per cent among women, and over a quarter among those from minority backgrounds: fairly low numbers, by international standards, but not exceptionally so.[12] Like the British, around an eighth of Canadian adults believed in witchcraft, or said they did.[13] The French were a little more credulous as were the Americans, just over a fifth of whom testified to witchcraft's reality.[14] But the most striking results came from sub-Saharan Africa, where of 10,000 people polled in 2009, more than half (55 per cent) admitted to believing in witchcraft.[15]

There is a problem with those results: a reason why we should be cautious about using them to make categorical claims about patterns of belief. In Britain, it was unclear what a question like 'Do you believe in witchcraft?' really meant. Since the fifteenth century, 'witchcraft' had sometimes been the name given to white magic, though more often it was used to denote a series of misfortunes caused by the supernatural powers of another person.[16] By the early 2000s, the already ambiguous terminology had become more muddled. Wicca – the ritualistic nature religion unveiled to the world by Gerald Gardner during the 1950s, and with at least 13,000 British adherents by 2011 – had given old words like 'witch' and 'witchcraft' new meanings. A witch could be an adherent of Gardnerian Wicca, or a follower of one of the rival traditions created during the 1960s and 1970s by occultists like Alex Sanders (1926–88). Other forms of witchcraft emerged in the 1990s, including hedge witchcraft, which portrayed witches as independent magical practitioners who were highly attuned to the natural world. Given the potential for confusion, it is little wonder that some people who traced their misfortunes to malign magic found new ways of describing their predicament. Rather than using the language of witchcraft they opted for terms like 'hexed', 'ill-wished', under 'psychic attack', 'jinxed' and – above all – 'cursed'.

A reader of the *Sunday People* used this language when she wrote to the paper's psychic counsellor and agony uncle in 2007. 'I think I have been cursed,' she began, 'both my parents died in a fire at home and while I was trying to deal with this my husband of twenty-six years ran off with someone and broke my heart.'[17] This chapter is about people like her. Despite living in a world rich with technology and information, they were bewildered by successive disasters. Like witchcraft believers in the past and across the globe, they fell ill and couldn't find a cure, or saw their romantic relationships collapse. They suddenly became accident-prone, lost their jobs, had runs of bad luck, or combinations of the above. Struggling to cope and desperate for a solution, they eventually concluded that curses were causing their troubles. They may well have done so in error, but their views were not exactly derived from ignorance.

In late twentieth- and early twenty-first-century Britain, it required serious effort to learn about this unnerving topic. People who thought they were cursed built up an understanding of their predicament by talking to friends and relatives, reading specialist books, doing research on the internet and consulting experts in so-called 'curse removal'. A litany of enterprising metaphysicians had filled the gap in the market created by the disappearance of traditional cunning-men and wise-women. They included African spiritualists, complementary therapists, *jinn*-removers, voodoo doctors, *obeah* men and women, spirit mediums, deliverance ministers and magical practitioners working within Wiccan and other traditions. In the tolerant atmosphere of multicultural Britain, magic was reborn in new and diverse forms.

THE EVOLUTION OF ENCHANTMENT: JOHN LUNDY'S CURSE

John Lundy was an agricultural worker with a penchant for vintage tractors and terrier dogs. Born in 1945, by the time the new millennium dawned this deeply religious man was living with his wife Mary and their adult son

Christian, in the sprawling village of Lamerton, west Devon. Like much of rural England it was experiencing a measure of gentrification, with barns and cottages converted into holiday homes for tourists visiting the nearby Tamar Valley and Dartmoor National Park. Despite the presence of a few affluent outsiders, Lamerton was home to families whose local connections went back generations. John Lundy belonged to one of those families.

So far so ordinary. In one respect though, John Lundy was exceptional. Between 2005 and 2014 he made himself among the best-documented witchcraft believers in British history. He did it by compiling a dossier of 200 hand-written pages, photographs, letters, legal documents, newspaper cuttings, religious literature, photocopies from books about local folklore and printed out webpages. He aimed to prove that his family's worst afflictions were caused by curses: curses laid by their long-time neighbours, the Fosters. Meticulously but repetitively, often in a rather disjointed way, John described how black magic almost destroyed his family. He outlined his theory of curses, recorded where he got his ideas from, and explained how he finally saved himself. Not wanting to waste his insights, John eventually donated his dossier to the Museum of Witchcraft and Magic, in the Cornish village of Boscastle, where it remains to this day.

It began with George Foster, a farmer. John Lundy did a great deal of work for him, over the years. After Mr Foster retired, he entered a local care home. Mary Lundy, a former nurse, began tending to him. John ran errands, collecting Foster's pension, driving to fetch his lady friend, and taking him to the local Conservative Club. Like many carers, John and Mary were unpaid and under-appreciated. Eventually, they became resentful and began withdrawing their help. Unfortunately, this prompted a confrontation.

George Foster, uninvited and unexpected, let himself into the Lundys' cottage. He demanded that John drive him to Tavistock, the nearby town. John refused. Mr Foster, who as he aged was becoming increasingly hot-tempered, became not just angry but positively incandescent. What he said is unclear. Compiling his dossier, John referred back to Mr Foster's outburst dozens of times, assiduously noting how at 6:30 p.m. on 21 October 2003, 'Foster cursed me.' But never once did he record exactly what Mr Foster said. Perhaps John thought it unimportant. More likely, whatever words George Foster uttered were so horrible, so terrifying, that John could not bring himself to repeat them. Maybe Foster wished him ill: probably he wished him dead.

But it was George Foster who died, three weeks after the altercation. Around the same time, disasters stuck John and Mary Lundy. She developed jaw abscesses, joint seizures and insomnia. John contracted infections, struggled to sleep, and felt his joints seizing up. Then he had a stroke, paralysing the right side of his body. With so many troubles arriving at once John began to wonder whether George Foster, in his fit of rage, had actually hexed his family. His suspicion became a conviction after he spoke with an old friend who had 'read a lot about witchcraft'. She asked after John's health and, hearing about his problems, said she'd once been cursed by a Rom. She also explained the three-fold law – a Wiccan ideal loosely inspired by the Buddhist notion of karma, which posits that whatever energy someone puts into the world, whether positive or negative, will be returned to them three times over. John Lundy was a sincere and serious Christian. Yet, instantly, he saw the mantra's relevance. George Foster had been killed by his own curse, which had rebounded on him with three times its initial strength.

John soon began re-evaluating the plight of his son, Christian. Five years earlier, after enrolling as a law student at Plymouth University, he'd suffered a severe, behaviour-altering brain injury. Several times he had gone missing from home, and once the police found Christian hundreds of miles away, in Sheffield, where he'd been attacked and robbed. After blaming drug use, the authorities later concluded that the young man was disturbed and tried to have him sectioned. John and Mary Lundy successfully challenged this move, but were left unsure about the precise nature of Christian's condition. Ultimately, John added it to the litany of misfortunes caused by George Foster's curse.

George Foster was dead, but his evil lingered. In late 2004 things started going wrong at the Lundys' cottage. Light bulbs fused constantly. The dog fell ill. At night, John and Mary heard strange noises coming from the walls. Fearing this was the work of George Foster's evil spirit, the Lundys discussed their problems with their vet. She referred them to Madeleine Walker, an ecologically minded therapist and esoteric healer from Somerset, described by John simply as 'the exorcist'. According to Madeleine's website, she offered services ranging from 'animal communication', to 'human empowerment', stress management, and 'house healing and space clearing'. After visiting the Lundys in Lamerton and conducting rituals to cleanse their home of evil entities, she told John that his terrier Bick had fallen ill because she was absorbing 'negative energy' aimed at her master.

John believed Madeleine saved his life by exorcising Foster's ghost and slowing his curse, though she was unable to stop it entirely. Madeleine also taught John about his condition, probably giving him the idea that curses are electrical in nature. In John's view, black witches like George Foster tampered with vital currents permeating and surrounding their victims' bodies. As he put it: 'What scum like Foster do is attack the aura – the electrical field of the body.' And again: 'What scum like the Fosters do is reverse the polarity of the body.'

Second-hand New Age spirituality, drawing on a long tradition of mystical pseudo-science, clearly informed John Lundy's outlook. At the same time, his understanding of the occult had deeper roots. Local folklore had long convinced him that magic permeates ordinary life. Even today one still meets with people from the West Country who have inherited charms for warts or bleeding. The taxi driver who drove me from the Museum of Witchcraft and Magic in Boscastle, where I studied John's dossier, mentioned in passing that his sister could charm warts. George Foster may have claimed a similar ability, since Lundy referred to him 'bragging about his powers'. Witchcraft remains a conspicuous part of Devon's and Cornwall's cultural heritage, with hundreds of regional books, from recently authored histories to reprinted Victorian ethnographies, keeping alive memories of nineteenth-century witches and wise-women. John Lundy himself learnt about Granny Boswell (*c.* 1817–1909), a Rom woman from the Cornish town of Helston, who was notorious for ill-wishing.[18] Her history persuaded him that 'black witchcraft and all that goes with it is not that unusual'. Conversations with people who had experienced magic's dark side reinforced the point. 'A friend of mine in Surrey had a curse or black witchcraft bestowed on him,' John recalled, 'I have no doubt Foster did the same thing.'

John Lundy blamed George Foster, 'an evil bastard', for throwing most of the curses that blighted his family. But John did not think Mr Foster acted alone. Like English witchcraft believers since at least the sixteenth century, John saw a propensity for engaging in the dark arts as in some sense hereditary.[19] And like witchcraft believers across the globe, he also thought that witches colluded with each other to realise their nefarious ambitions. Apparently, George Foster cursed Christian at the instigation of a local solicitor, who hated the Lundys because they'd accused him of malpractice. Mr Foster was also taught how to do black magic by his father-in-law Frank

Rogers, John conjectured. In turn, George Foster inducted his children into the black art, especially his eldest son, who had taken over the family farm.

By 2014 John Lundy's health (and handwriting) had improved markedly since he began writing his witchcraft dossier ten years earlier. Yet Mr Lundy was still suffering from ailments he attributed to the curse. His tongue, cheeks and teeth hurt. Mary Lundy's condition had also deteriorated, and she was admitted to the local hospital after growing thin and collapsing. The saving grace was Christian, whose mental state was finally starting to improve. 'We cannot express anything but delight,' John wrote in 2008, though he later added the depressing prediction: 'I have little doubt we will never have grandchildren as the vile act of black witchcraft very often makes people . . . sterile.'

According to John, curses damaged his family for at least a decade and a half. His sufferings were worsened by the incredulity, even mockery, he received when explaining his experiences to others. Given the biblical references to witchcraft and sorcery, John found the cynicism of members of the Anglican Church particularly egregious. The vicar of Lamerton had plainly stated that he could not believe George Foster laid a curse. Unsatisfied, John Lundy wrote to the Bishop of Exeter, who referred him to the Rev. Simon May, rector of nearby Whitchurch. He at least recognised the reality of malign magic – indeed, the Rev. May claimed to have been a victim of it himself. But after hearing John's story and looking at photographs of his injuries, he expressed doubts about black witchcraft being the cause. Upset by this, John stopped his annual donation to St Peter's church, Lamerton, and severed his life-long affiliation to the Church of England. One can only imagine his opinion of the local police, who dismissed his allegations and issued John with an anti-harassment notice, banning him from contacting his witches. 'The police turn their back on this,' John reflected, 'if you take anything relating to black witchcraft to court they would stand up and laugh at you.'

This explains why Lundy so thoroughly documented his sufferings. The Church, police, doctors and many of his neighbours saw him as a crank with a persecution complex. But John expected time to vindicate his views, musing, 'in my opinion the next 40 to 50 years will reveal more than I have written'. Whether or not his dossier contributes to a general re-evaluation of the occult, whether or not it convinces the authorities that his sufferings really were supernatural, John Lundy created a valuable historical document.

It vividly illustrates how the concept of maleficent magic evolved into a synthesis of old and new ideas, drawn from sources as diverse as local folklore, New Age spirituality and Wicca.

John Lundy's dossier reveals more than the changing character of this diffuse, eclectic and seductive belief system. Every page radiates anger and outrage. John clearly felt betrayed not just by the people who cursed him, but also by those who refused to accept that his plight was supernatural. His experiences may not be typical, but they raise the possibility that, during the contemporary period, the subjective experience of malign magic became more emotionally traumatic. Working-class Victorians who considered themselves bewitched could generally count upon the sympathy of many of their friends and neighbours, if not those in positions of power. By the early twenty-first century, with the waning of belief in witchcraft, such support networks had diminished though not disappeared entirely. People like John Lundy, who made it known that curses caused their problems, were lucky if they did not find themselves isolated or ostracised.

OLD STORIES AND ALTERNATIVE LIFESTYLES: WITCHCRAFT IN THE COUNTRYSIDE

Goathland is an upland village set in the midst of the beautiful but bracing North York Moors. Known nationally for being the place where the nostalgic television drama *Heartbeat* is filmed, locally Goathland has a reputation for something more sinister: witchcraft.

Stories have long been told about Nanny Peirson, a fearsome woman who took the form of a hare, bewitched people till they were bedridden, and whose glare was so malignant it turned milk sour.[20] Apparently, even the geese were scared of her. Writing in 1898, the folklorist Richard Blakeborough thought this 'witch of the old school' lived in the eighteenth century. But Peirson was and is a common name in Goathland, and it's probable that over the generations several women with the same surname acquired reputations for witchcraft, deservedly or not.[21] Nanny Peirson may well be a composite figure, created from anecdotes about various villagers living at different times, but her legend has proved to be a powerful one. In 1974 Kathryn Smith did fieldwork in Goathland as part of her doctoral studies. Among the residents she found 'evidence of belief in the witch and her powers up to the present day'.[22] Many could point out Nanny Peirson's old house, and some knew tales about her metamorphic powers. Interestingly, those stories included recent inventions as well as old yarns passed down by relatives or gleaned from local history books. For instance: a mysterious cat, believed to be the witch, had been seen near the property, where its ethereal presence was said to interfere with the house's electrics.

Practically everyone in Britain watched television during the 1970s: by the end of the decade, 99 per cent of households owned or rented a set.[23] Yet even in the 'television age', oral storytelling remained an important part of life and supernatural tales resonated with many people, especially in regions with strong folk traditions. Few appreciated this more than Kingsley Palmer, a scholar at Leeds University's Institute of Dialect and Folklife Studies. Between 1968 and 1970 he gathered oral stories about various folksy subjects from residents of Gloucestershire, Wiltshire, Dorset, Somerset, Devon and Cornwall – a large area of south-west England he romantically named 'Wessex'. Mr Palmer's research revealed that, within the corpus of everyday storytelling, certain supernatural themes were disappearing.[24] His informants seldom spoke about fairies, for example, whom they did not regard as credible beings. Ghosts, by contrast, were 'as strong as ever'. Tales about them circulated in almost every village and town.

Between the nearly extinct fairies and the ubiquitous ghosts were witches and curses. They certainly figured in the imaginations and conversations of some people from the rural south-west, and in Somerset particularly, where it was easy enough to find elderly folk willing to reminisce about 'old mother so and so, who used to live up the lane, and everyone thought she was a witch'.[25] At Wookey Hole, a limestone cavern on the southern edge of the Mendips, the local tourist industry played on the county's long-standing association with magic by directing visitors to an anthropomorphic stalactite, said to be a witch who was turned to stone by a monk's holy water.[26] Talk of witchcraft was not always light-hearted. Wadeford, on the east side of the Blackdown Hills, was home to a woman whose grandfather had been accused of bewitching someone from the neighbouring village.[27] Elsewhere, there were legions of similar anecdotes. Go to Somerset's rural parishes, wrote a local historian in 1977: 'Ask if anyone knows any stories of ghosts or witches, and with patience and tact one can discover a vast area of mythology and belief in the supernatural still going on.'[28]

Witch tales were spine-tingling, bizarre, funny, thought-provoking, tragic and grotesque. People told them because they were entertaining and interesting from a historical point of view. But these stories also spoke to nagging anxieties about the reality of harmful magic in the present. During the 1970s, rural communities across England were still home to a few alleged witches – to women and men who, in the estimation of at least a few locals, possessed evil occult powers. Ralph Whitlock, author of *The Folklore of Wiltshire* (1976), claimed to personally 'know of more than one alleged witch in Wiltshire today, and they are regarded with superstitious anxiety by their neighbours'.[29] Doris Jones-Baker, in *The Folklore of Hertfordshire* (1977), maintained that 'fear and dread of the power of witches to do evil, to lay harmful spells upon people and animals bringing sickness and death has not yet departed'.[30]

The same was true in East Anglia – in the Fenlands of Cambridgeshire and Norfolk. This once isolated region had been transformed by better roads, regular public transport, electric lights and television aerials protruding from almost every cottage's roof. At night though, peering through the window of the last bus home from Ely, staring into the thick marsh fog, the Fens did not look particularly civilised. So, at least, thought Enid Porter, curator of the Cambridge Folk Museum. She really was a consummate folklorist. Whether in the pub, at a bus stop, or after a talk she'd given to the Women's Institute, Porter seldom missed an opportunity to gently unearth information about seemingly extinct but actually still resonant supernatural beliefs. Mental health workers from the district assured her they cared for patients who believed the dark influence of witchcraft was upon them. From her own experiences, Porter knew that such anxieties remained part of rural life. She had at least one acquaintance from a Fenland village who was said by her neighbours to possess the evil eye.[31]

Among the best evidence we have about the persistence of magic, black and white, comes from Scotland. Writing in 1976, the folklorist Anne Ross had 'no doubt that belief in powers to work good and evil is still fairly widespread' in the countryside. From her work as an education officer on the Isle of Skye, she knew some Highlanders and Islanders still respected occult forces. One was Annie Fraser, from the Inverness-shire village of Kiltarlity. An inheritor of supernatural gifts from her parents and grandparents, she possessed a spell-lifting charm. It involved waking before sunrise, gathering water from a stream by the village cemetery, in a pail containing a silver coin and her wedding ring, and pronouncing the words: 'I, Mrs Fraser, sprinkle this water on [here she mentions her client's name]... in the name of the Father, Son and Holy Spirit I bless you and may all evil depart from you.'[32]

Another witchcraft-believing Highlander was Betsy Whyte (1919–88). The settled Traveller from Perthshire was a veritable compendium of magical lore. Betsy's autobiography, *The Yellow on the Broom* (1979), evoked an inter-war childhood peppered with supernatural incidents, such as when her infant nephew died after a jealous countrywoman 'put her eye on him'.[33] There were many others like Betsy: Scots born in the generation before the Second World War, who carried supernatural stories and memories acquired during their rural childhoods into the wealthier world of the late twentieth century. During the 1970s and 1980s, scholars at Edinburgh University's School of Scottish Studies collected hundreds of anecdotes about witchcraft from residents of the Highlands and Islands, despite the fact that it was not a subject that people really cared to talk about.[34] On Tiree, the most westerly of the Inner Hebrides, they heard about Factor MacLaren, a nineteenth-century land agent and master of the dark arts. Like wizards from England, France and eastern Canada, he was remembered for carefully guarding his collection of 'black books', and for his uncanny ability to seduce women.[35]

The notion of milk-stealing witches lived on too. Elderly Scots from Shetland and Orkney described evil-doers 'taking the profit' from their neighbours' cows.[36] Elsewhere tales were told about witches who shape-shifted and controlled the weather. Lizzie Ann Higgins (1929–93), a settled Traveller and retired fish filleter from Aberdeenshire, proved to be a gold-mine of such yarns when she was interviewed in 1986.[37] She discussed Donald, the wizard of Tarland, and his witch companion, who took the form of a hare, became invisible, and lifted the fog from the sea. Everything she recounted really happened, insisted Lizzie, who let it be known that she possessed clairvoyant and psychic gifts of her own – an inheritance from her father, she said.

Roma people and Travellers continued to be strongly associated with the occult, not least because some portrayed themselves as magical adepts. Oddly enough, it was still useful to be known as a controller of dark forces or mysterious powers. Studying Traveller communities in southern England, the anthropologist Judith Okely was told about a widow living on a designated Traveller site, who broke the strict taboo against keeping cats as pets.

She wanted her neighbours to think she was a *chovihani* – a witch – because this was a protective reputation for a woman living alone.[38] Magic was useful for others, too. As their nomadic lifestyles were made impossible and many Roma people struggled to find places to live, a few resorted to occult threats in desperate attempts to speed up the planning process. In 1978 a fortune-teller from Essex said he'd curse members of the Colchester town council if they refused to provide a site for Travellers by the end of the year.[39]

Other Roma invoked magic to protect their reputations and to dispense justice. That was why, in 1980, some Roma people from Hertfordshire publicly cursed the child killer Harry Davies.[40] But Travellers did not always put their occult powers to such noble ends. Roma beggars still muttered maledictions to solicit donations and sell their wares. In 1974 the *Daily Mirror*'s agony aunt received a letter from someone who'd been suffering from bad luck, and wondered whether it could be because she'd been cursed by a Rom after refusing to buy her lucky heather.[41] Writing in 1988, the Traveller historian David Mayall thought 'many people today' could tell a similar story.[42]

It was not meant to be like this: malign magic was not supposed to be part of modern life in the British countryside. Since the nineteenth century, folk-lorists had been announcing the imminent demise of superstitions like witchcraft, citing reasons as various as schooling, Christianity, industrialisa-tion, urbanisation, scientific medicine and the mass media. By the 1970s some scholars were pointing to a new corrosive trend, about to dissolve what remained of Britain's rural folklore: gentrification. Villages and hamlets were attracting unprecedented numbers of outsiders, intent on trading drab suburbs and congested towns for their own versions of arcadia.[43] In Berkshire, the opening of the M4 in 1972 was largely to blame for the arrival of various executives and middle-income professionals.[44] Cheap properties and clean air meant that the Welsh villages south of Cardiff and Swansea attracted fewer commuters but more pensioners, many of them English.[45] 'The present-day rural village has tended to take on the character of a dormitory for the nearby town, alongside a well-kept geriatric compound,' observed the folklorist and pioneering oral historian George Ewart Evans, himself an incomer to Blaxhall in Suffolk.[46] Writing in 1979, Evans thought strangers were diluting villages, displacing locals, and breaking the social and genera-tional bonds down which rural folklore was transmitted.

In reality, more than a few village newcomers also enjoyed tales about neighbourhood witches, some of which they gleaned from books. Eric Maple noted this trend as early as 1965, during his work on the notoriously witchy Essex village of Canewdon. Established inhabitants were reluctant to talk openly about sorcery, but Maple found that commuters to nearby Southend were 'far from reticent about the local tradition of witchcraft, much of which they have derived from purely literary sources'.[47] Critics of the changing countryside portrayed most new arrivals as affluent executives or withdrawn retirees, but Britain's villages were actually swelled by a diverse cohort of people, some of whom were decidedly countercultural. Hippies and eco-activists, along with a bewildering array of pagans, occultists, New Agers and other mystics, all valued the darkly poetic supernatural associations of areas like Cornwall, Somerset and East Anglia.[48] Far from destroying what remained of rural folklore, these people kept alive old ideas about witchcraft and magic by selectively incorporating them into their idiosyncratic cosmologies.

Cecil Hugh Williamson (1909–99) was an outsider who did more than anyone to invigorate Cornwall's tradition of witchcraft and magic.[49] A lifelong occultist and collector of esoteric objects, in 1960 he relocated his Museum of Witchcraft to the blustery inlet of Boscastle, a former fishing village on Cornwall's remote northerly coast. Cecil's interest in magic was far from academic. During the evenings, after the museum's doors closed for the day, he worked as a sort of pseudo-cunning-man, removing curses and breaking spells for people who asked him for help against evil powers. Judging by his notebook, Williamson fused modern ceremonial occultism, like that formulated by Aleister Crowley during the early twentieth century, with the folk magic he read about and personally encountered in the West Country. To stop bleeding or remove warts he used techniques similar to those utilised by historical wise-women and local charmers, though without any overtly Christian invocations. By contrast, to cure ill-wishing Williamson created a stately rite involving candles, a magic circle, trestles, and incantations about Lucifer and 'the God of Light'.

For decades, Cecil Williamson seems to have been the only local offering anything like an anti-black magic therapy. In the 1970s, Cornwall was undoubtedly home to numerous esoteric practitioners. But they worked in other areas, like the spiritualist Alan Williams, of St Austell, who, under the direction of a Native American spirit guide, purportedly conducted psychic surgery on his clients' bodies. Some folklorists claimed that 'white witches' could still be found in the county, but on closer inspection, these individuals turned out to be humble charmers, like Charlie Bennett, a retired builder living in Tintagel, who in 1974 still 'did a bit of charming' to get rid of warts for friends and neighbours.[50]

By the 1990s, that had changed and not just in Cornwall. Across rural Britain magical practitioners were selectively reviving the cunning-craft, often as a personal lifestyle choice, occasionally as an income-generating profession.[51] Some described themselves as a 'hedge witch' or 'traditional witch'. Others preferred more historical sounding titles like 'white witch' or 'wise-woman'. Either way, they tended to be neo-pagans disillusioned with Wicca's hierarchical coven structure and theological orientation towards the invocation of religious deities. Perhaps their sense of spiritual restlessness had been amplified by the historical research of Aidan Kelly and Ronald Hutton, which was making it clear that while Wicca was a fascinating and entirely legitimate belief system, it was not exactly the ancient fertility religion Gerald Gardner once claimed.[52] Whatever the case, thousands of women and some men too orientated themselves away from Wicca and towards the practice of solitary magic.

There was undoubtedly a spiritual dimension to these new types of modern witchcraft. At their core, however, were spells for almost every occasion and ailment: spells to ease the difficulties of everyday life; spells to attract lovers, provide magical protection, repel unwanted visitors, comfort teething babies and change the weather; spells to remove warts, stop bleeding, find lost property like misplaced passports and see into the future. Most of these spells were idiosyncratic and personal inventions. Others were reminiscent of the historical magic their authors encountered in places like the Museum of Witchcraft in Boscastle, and read about in folklore compendiums.[53] The modern witch's path was a mixture of learning and intuition, facilitated by the numerous guidebooks and journals that soon began to appear.

Like the wise-women of the past, hedge witches and traditional witches openly acknowledged the reality of misfortune-sowing curses. Rae Beth, for example, who coined the term 'hedge witch' in a manual of 1992, insisted that malicious supernatural influences like black magic and ill-wishing were 'all too common'.[54] Gemma Gary, a Cornish practitioner of Modern Traditional Witchcraft, reiterated the point in a guidebook of 2015. 'Age-old beliefs in the power of the curse and of ill-wishing,' she noted, 'are still very much alive.'[55] Some of her clients attributed their misfortunes to evil magic, and though most did not want to know who was responsible, they did want their hexes dispelled. Hedge and traditional witches devised a huge range of remedies. Some used powerful objects similar to those prescribed by historical cunning-folk, such as horseshoes nailed to doors, witch-bottles buried beneath hearths, or written charms sewn into small bags and worn close to the body. Others relied on herbal remedies like one recommended by Rae Beth, which involved reciting a charm while ritually burning rosemary, juniper and blackthorn leaves.[56] Whether new or old, genuinely historical or recently invented, during the era of the internet and the personal computer white magic experienced a rural revival.

VOODOO LONDON: MAGIC IN THE URBAN ENVIRONMENT

As the twentieth century drew to a close, magic reappeared in the urban environment too. Britain's towns and cities saw a boom in esoteric practitioners who made their living by selling unorthodox health care and unconventional wellbeing services. Some were secular, teaching meditation or mindfulness to stressed-out people. Many others claimed to be able to harness sacred powers and supernatural forces for the benefit of their clients, with the dubious proviso that it was all 'for entertainment only'.

Glastonbury, a once quiet country town in Somerset, became the centre of Britain's New Age scene after esoteric practitioners began exploiting its historical associations with pilgrimages and holy wells.[57] Developments in Kendal, a market town on the edge of the Lake District, were more typical. In the early 1970s just over 20,000 people lived there, many of whom were workers in tourism, agriculture, shoe manufacturing or papermaking.[58] Needless to say, Kendal in those years possessed no yoga teachers, no reiki healers, no modern white witches and no professional spirit mediums – no alternative therapists of any kind, in fact. Not so by the early 2000s. At least ninety-five mind–body–spirit practitioners had set up businesses in Kendal, according to social scientists from nearby Lancaster University. Every week those practitioners worked with around 600 locals, around 1.6 per cent of the population.[59]

Developments in Kendal were mirrored across the country. By the early 1980s, 7,800 alternative practitioners were estimated to be working in Britain, along with 20,000 religious or spiritual healers. Barely over a decade later, in 1995, the size of the so-called 'folk sector' had almost doubled, with 50,000 alternative practitioners and spiritual healers operating across the UK.[60] Many worked secretively, attracting clients by word of mouth rather than adverts in newspapers and business directories, so we should not expect those figures to be precisely accurate.[61] But if the estimates are broadly correct, on the eve of the new millennium Britain possessed around 60 per cent more alternative practitioners and spiritual healers than it did doctors working in general practice.[62]

Some alternative therapists were unable or unwilling to remove curses, but many were certainly prepared to try. So many, in fact, that by the beginning of the twenty-first century this controversial metaphysical service was probably more widely available than it had been since the late Victorian period. Anyone wanting it done could choose from an unprecedentedly diverse range of providers. On the reassuringly professional end of the spectrum, self-styled paranormal consultants offered to rid their clients' homes of unwelcome or evil presences like ghosts and curses.[63] Boasting websites, business cards and sometimes even a penchant for management jargon, these outfits took a self-consciously modernistic approach to their work. Alternatively, in larger towns and cities, spiritual healers offered expertise in all sorts of exotic traditions.

Modern metaphysicians differed in many ways. But they agreed about a fundamental fact. Successful magic requires belief. Pure, sincere and unquestioning belief, if possible. Forced, contrived and simulated belief, if necessary. Cassandra Latham-Jones, a 'village wise-woman' from Cornwall, would ask her clients 'whether they want to be healed', a deceptively simple question designed to coax them into a position of 'real willingness'.[64] Jimmy Lee Shreeve, a writer who created the persona of a voodoo priest named Doktor Snake, also thought it was crucial to adopt a believing state of mind. 'To execute magic successfully', he advised readers of his *Voodoo Spellbook*, 'we need to believe in it 100 per cent.'[65] David Devereux, former 'Senior Field Officer' at a paranormal services company named Athanor Consulting, regarded belief as similarly vital.[66] His clients found it difficult to shed their scepticism, but after years of working with magic Devereux easily embraced the perceptual changes – the 'shifts in world view' – others found jarring. He could 'believe something completely, absolutely and passionately for five minutes, then change to whichever belief is required for the next operation'.[67]

During the later twentieth century, new and exotic magical traditions took root. Probably the first of these was *obeah*. A corpus of charms and rituals designed to harness supernatural forces, either to harm or to heal, *obeah* was created in the Anglophone Caribbean by enslaved Africans and their descendants. Their empowering synthesis of West African folk magic and Christianity registered in the consciousness of white Britons as early as 1760, when *obeah* was banned in Jamaica after being implicated in a slave revolt known as Tacky's Rebellion. But it was not brought to Britain until after the Second World War, when around half a million West Indians emigrated to the UK.[68] British doctors, social workers and psychiatrists noticed how, Rastafarians aside, their Afro-Caribbean patients credited *obeah* with a dazzling array of malefic and beneficent functions.[69]

This morally ambiguous power could make or break fortunes, change the course of love, predict the future and sow misfortune. Ardent believers would scarcely talk about it, despite having grown up hearing 'duppy stories' – tales about the evil spirits, usually animals dressed in human attire, sent as a warning by a master of *obeah*. Even a tactful and experienced folklorist like Venetia Newall struggled to coax the Jamaicans she met in 1970s London, not all of whom were first-generation migrants, into sharing their knowledge of such happenings. When she finally built trusting relationships, she discovered that *obeah* was very much at work in the UK.[70] Certain laypeople were known for their uncanny affinities, but as always its chief exponents were *obeah* men and *obeah* women – gifted professionals who made their livings by shaping this versatile genre of magic.[71] A few had moved to Britain, where they found a ready market for their services in cities with large concentrations of West Indians. As in the Caribbean, they were paid to turn people's hearts in certain directions, smite the wicked and remove curses.[72] The actions of one of them can be glimpsed in a case described in the *British Medical Journal* in 1997, involving a 20-year-old woman from Trinidad who was admitted to a London hospital after refusing food and drink for several days. Conventional psychiatric treatment failed to ameliorate her condition, not least because she was convinced that she was under an *obeah* curse. After consulting someone the doctors described as a 'traditional healer', she began to eat and drink again, showing no further signs of mental illness.[73]

It was not just West Indians who imported previously unfamiliar magic to Britain. By 1971, over 460,000 people had arrived from the Indo-Pakistani subcontinent, including Sikhs from the Punjab, mostly Hindus from Gujarat, and mostly Muslims from Bangladesh and Pakistan.[74] As the initial waves of predominantly male migrants became established, their wives, parents, siblings, cousins and children joined them, so that by the late 1980s some 1.3 million South Asians were living in the UK.[75] Their beliefs in illness-causing *nazar* (the evil eye) and *bhut* (ghosts) certainly survived the transition from the rural east to the largely urban west. After living in Britain for several decades, many Hindus still saw weddings and pregnancies as perilous times, when *nazar* might strike the happy couple. Children were also thought to be uniquely vulnerable to the deadly effects of a jealous gaze, as a health visitor from London noted in 2005: 'All the [70] Gujarati households I know in Harrow are concerned, to a greater or lesser extent, about the protection of children from najar.'[76] To safeguard their offspring, Hindu parents said prayers after their birth, carefully avoided feeding them in front of others, tied protective black threads around their wrists, and used soot to make black marks (called *kohl*) around their infants' eyes. The latter was designed to make children look less attractive, less likely to excite envy. Knowledge of these pseudo-magical practices was passed down the generations, from elderly parents to their adult children. South Asian Hindus could also purchase professional help in the form of spiritual healers called *vaids*, 300 of whom were reckoned to be working in the UK by the beginning of the twenty-first century.[77]

Probably more common still were Muslim *hakims*, dispensers of a holistic folk medicine known as *unani tibb*.[78] They fought ill-health with herbalism and four-humour-style dietary advice based on the teachings of the ancient Greek physician Galen, recommending 'hot' substances like ginger and garlic for 'cold' conditions like asthma and respiratory infections. *Hakims* also created amulets containing Koranic verses, designed to protect their patients from *nazar* – the harmful gaze of someone filled with envy or love.

A third genre of spiritual healing, brought to Britain largely by South Asians, was *ruqyah*.[79] Undertaken by practitioners known as *raqis*, it used Koranic chanting to counteract *sihr* (black magic) and exorcise *jinn* (invisible supernatural beings credited with harming humans). Not all South Asians took these ideas seriously, but they did have a wide purchase, particularly among first-generation migrants. A study of South Asians living in 1980s Glasgow found most dismissing the evil eye-like concept of *nazar* as superstition. Yet scepticism was not universal: a significant minority (16 of 65 participants, or just under 25 per cent) believed that *nazar* was a dangerous power, which caused minor illnesses and was even blamed for bringing on a case of type 2 diabetes. Much greater levels of supernatural belief were recorded in a larger study (involving 111 participants) of Muslims living in Leicester. Four-fifths testified to the reality of *jinn*, three-quarters believed in the evil eye, while slightly under two-thirds of respondents thought black magic was a genuine force for evil. Beyond those abstract attestations of belief, around half of the Muslims surveyed thought that supernatural beings and powers caused illnesses in humans.[80]

It was not just South Asians or Muslims who, occasionally, were tempted by such ideas. Shopping around for a solution to their troubles, driven by desperation to try unorthodox therapies, people with no previous experience of Islam occasionally consulted Islamic spiritual healers. A reporter for the online media outlet *Vice* discovered this in 2015, when he experienced a *jinn* removal ceremony in Glasgow. 'I work with Muslims and non-Muslims alike,' explained the *raqi*, who charged £250 for the ritual, 'more and more people are getting into alternative healing.'[81]

At first, outside minority communities, little was known about the exotic magical traditions recent migrants had brought to Britain. Gradually though, between the 1980s and early 2000s, multicultural approaches to health care changed this. Counsellors and psychiatrists became aware of the serious health inequalities afflicting ethnic minority groups, some of whom suffered from rates of schizophrenia that were up to five times higher than the British average.[82] Understanding the experiences and outlooks of minority communities was clearly crucial to levelling such inequalities, so health care professionals began to investigate ideas about *obeah*, *nazar* and *jinn*. Rather than eradicating or denigrating supernatural concepts, this work aimed to provide orthodox medics with a better appreciation of the unfamiliar belief systems they might encounter when treating patients from minority communities.

'Cultural competence', as this exercise in empathy became known, was presented as an important weapon in the alienist's arsenal.[83] But, as a medicinal strategy for a multicultural society, it went beyond merely under-standing magical or faith-based interpretations of illness. Tentatively, some counsellors and psychotherapists started working with *obeah* women, *hakims* and *vaids* in order to care better for patients who worried that their maladies were of an occult nature. Partly to enable these collaborations, a charity named the Nafsiyat Inter-Cultural Therapy Centre was founded in London, in 1983.[84] By the 1990s it was no longer controversial to advocate combining biomedicine with so-called 'traditional' healing, especially in cases of mental illness, where there were realistic prospects of therapeutic benefits accruing from taking patients' supernatural fears seriously. An article in the *British Medical Journal* warned, in 1997: 'A doctor presented with someone claiming to have been bewitched may misdiagnose a para-noid disorder and treat the patient with antipsychotic drugs. Involving a traditional healer would be more appropriate.'[85]

Like the medical profession, the legal system was becoming less hostile to spiritual healers and magical practitioners. More were operating in Britain than at any time in recent history, yet very few were prosecuted for defrauding their clients. In theory, the 1951 Fraudulent Mediums Act protected the public from the designs of cynical magicians. In practice, it was difficult to apply because prosecutors needed to demonstrate that anyone accused of breaching its terms harboured a genuine 'intent to deceive'. Because the 1951 Act specifically prohibited 'telepathy, clairvoyance, or other similar powers', it was also unclear from its wording whether it outlawed other magical activities, like curse removal. Despite these difficulties, the Fraudulent Mediums Act was occasionally invoked. In 1975 five people were charged with offences under the act, while between 1980 and 1995 there were six prosecutions, five of which led to successful convictions.[86]

These were tiny numbers, given the tens of thousands of people employed in Britain's metaphysical economy. The law had become highly permissive, as Lord Lester of Herne Hill implied in a House of Lords debate of 1996, when he asked 'whether the Fraudulent Mediums Act 1951 is obsolete and should be repealed'.[87] Speaking for the Conservative government, Baroness Blatch conceded that there were few prosecutions under the act, though she thought it ought to remain in place as a safeguard. The Fraudulent Mediums Act remained on the statute book but only until 2008, when it was replaced by consumer protection regulations implementing the European Union's Unfair

Commercial Practices Directive.[88] Some psychics and spiritualists worried that the new regulations would lead to a crackdown.[89] The UK's advertising regulators certainly issued more stringent guidance to sellers of reputedly psychic and spiritual services.[90] They were told not to claim that their products possessed genuine supernatural efficacy, and to include disclaimers informing potential clients that undertakings like fortune-telling and curse removal were nothing more than confidence props or for entertainment purposes. These disclaimers had little impact on Britain's burgeoning metaphysical economy. As the author of a handbook for 'spiritual teachers' put it in 2012, the regulations 'do not seem to be as much of a challenge to mediums and psychics ... as was initially feared'.[91]

Curse removal, some argue, 'removes money, not curses'.[92] While most professional metaphysicians appear to have been sincere, magic remained as amenable to fraud as ever, and unscrupulous charlatans certainly took advantage. In 2006 Gina Stevenson of Leicester was jailed for fifteen months and ordered to pay £5,500 to former clients whom she defrauded of £56,000.[93] Using the name Sister Grace, she distributed flyers in Leicester city centre, claiming she could foresee the future and conduct psychic healing. A 53-year-old mother went to an initial £100 tarot reading session. In time, she was persuaded into giving away her life savings of £20,932 and borrowing £28,000 from the bank. Without that money, Sister Grace warned, a curse would kill her son and husband, and her daughter would never marry.

Sole-trading swindlers like Gina Stevenson devastated their clients. Large-scale supernatural scams perpetrated fraud on a shallower but wider scale. In 2006 the Office of Fair Trading (OFT) blocked the delivery of a morbid scam letter, which asked recipients to send £17 to prevent the death of a relative and ensure a lottery win.[94] Commendable as the regulator's actions were, the OFT lacked the resources to severely damage, never mind destroy, this vast industry. In 2006 alone, an estimated 170,000 Britons fell victim to unsolicited letters sent by fraudulent clairvoyants, with the average victim losing £240.[95] Claiming to be from gifted, internationally renowned psychics, these letters urged their readers to send money in return for powerful items that would attract good luck and repel evil. Prophesying the imminent arrival of a dreadful curse, the letters also promised great financial windfalls to those who acted quickly.

Supernatural fears and magical beliefs facilitated mass frauds, but they also had more dire consequences. During the first decade of the twenty-first century, the Black African population of England and Wales doubled, from just under half a million people to slightly fewer than one million.[96] Among the diaspora were spiritual healers like Malibu Faty. Born in Nigeria in 1957, he spent most of his life working in Western Sahara. Then Malibu noticed a lucrative opportunity to sell his supernatural services in Britain and so he moved to London.

In 2002 Malibu Faty was exposed by an undercover reporter working on the *Sunday Express*'s campaign against African spiritual healers operating in the UK.[97] An advert in *The Voice*, one of Britain's leading ethnic minority newspapers, caught the journalist's attention. He paid for a consultation at Malibu's Dulwich flat. The 'voodoo medicine man', as he described himself, had customers from across society. In his waiting room was a smartly dressed white woman. She explained how she hoped Malibu would use his powers to avenge her marital difficulties. 'If you want to destroy a person, you can use voodoo magic,' Mr Faty assured the *Express*'s reporter, 'but you can also use voodoo for love.' Surrounded by candles and orange drapes (the colour of Oshun, the river goddess of Malibu's Yoruba tribe, in Nigeria), with bits of orange peel pinned to the walls, Malibu told his new client to sit on the floor and stare into a long rectangular mirror. 'There is power within you but you don't know how to use it,' he said, 'I will give you that power.' Notionally the consultation cost £20, but Malibu charged £5,000 or more for special items, which, he promised, would provide phenomenal business success, total sexual power over women, and the ability to lay or cure curses. The vast sum was needed to pay for the creation of a powerful amulet, to be hung around the neck. It was so expensive because it contained a uniquely potent magical ingredient: a piece of human flesh.

One can only hope that Malibu Faty was lying. He claimed that, for £5,000, he could procure the finger of a ritually slaughtered African girl. Tragically, the type of corpse magic he referred to was (and is) only too real. Often going by the name *muti* – the Zulu word for medicine – it is more accurate to describe it as '*muti*-murder', since the general category of *muti* incorporates a wide range of healing and magical techniques, most of which are benign. Practised in southern Africa since at least the nineteenth century, *muti*-murder appears to have become more widespread during the late

243

twentieth and early twenty-first centuries.[98] Precise figures remain elusive, but it has been recorded across the subcontinent, in South Africa, Malawi, Zambia, Mozambique, Tanzania, Ghana, Kenya and Zambia. In 2008 alone, over 300 cases of ritual murder were reported to the Ugandan police, 18 of which resulted in prosecutions.[99]

Far from being a primitive hangover, this horrifying trade gained traction because of the specific conditions of late twentieth-century Africa. Murder often went unpunished. Healers selling human organs went unprosecuted. The AIDS epidemic presented very real terrors. Extreme economic inequality enabled rich people easily to pay for death.[100] Like Malibu Faty in London, African healers dealing in *muti* did not themselves kill, but gave minutely detailed orders for human flesh to specialist gangs. Virgins, children, the uncircumcised, albinos and the offspring of noticeably fertile parents were usually targeted, in the belief that their corpses contained larger amounts of supernatural power. Preferably, organs were removed while the victims were alive and conscious. Certain body parts were thought to have special potencies. Genitals for sex. Blood for vitality. Eyes for seeing the future. Tongues to romance and convince. Heads for business success. Breasts and body fat for good luck.

During the early twenty-first century, the trade in human body parts and the practice of *muti*-murder arrived in Britain. On 21 September 2001 the headless, armless, legless torso of a small boy was found floating in the Thames, near Tower Bridge.[101] Named 'Adam' by the Metropolitan Police, DNA analysis revealed that he grew up in southern Nigeria, between Ibadan and Benin City.[102] A post-mortem investigation showed that his stomach contained clay pellets and traces of the Calabar bean. Probably he'd been made to drink a potion before having his limbs removed and blood drained. As of 2018 his killers had not been detected. In all likelihood, Adam was trafficked into the UK so that his body parts could be harvested to meet the mercifully small but perhaps growing local demand for *muti*-amulets.

OUT OF AFRICA? WITCHCRAFT AND CHILD ABUSE

Victoria Adjo Climbié was born in Abobo, a densely populated suburb on the outskirts of Abidjan, capital of Ivory Coast, on 2 November 1991.[103] She died at 3:15 p.m. on 25 February 2000, in the Intensive Care Unit of St

Mary's Hospital, London, aged 8 years and 3 months. Hypothermia had caused Victoria's major organs to fail. One of the Home Office's most experienced pathologists, Dr Nat Cary, examined her body. He found Victoria malnourished, deformed and covered with 128 separate injuries, inflicted by both sharp and blunt objects. It was 'the worst case of deliberate harm to a child he had ever seen'.[104]

For months, Victoria had been pitilessly abused by Marie-Therese Kouao, her great-aunt and guardian, and a Londoner named Carl John Manning, her great-aunt's lover. Since arriving in Britain in April 1999, Victoria and Marie-Therese Kouao had been in frequent contact with social workers, doctors and other government employees. Few noticed the little girl's plight and none successfully intervened to stop it, despite well over a dozen opportunities to do so. This revelation inspired the Labour government to set up a public inquiry, chaired by Lord Laming. It excoriated social services across London for their repeated failings. The inquiry also revealed more about Victoria's killers and their preoccupation with supernatural evil.

Before Victoria's death, Marie-Therese called her a 'wicked child' and spoke to a friend about her being 'possessed by an evil spirit'. Victoria was taken to at least two different African-style Pentecostal churches, where the preachers confirmed she was possessed and recommended courses of prayer and fasting. One pastor asked Marie-Therese to bring Victoria to his church's weekly service for deliverance from 'witchcraft, bad luck and everything bad or evil'. During Victoria's final hours, Carl Manning attempted to do just that – to have her delivered from an 'evil spirit'. Previously, he recorded in his diary how it had been necessary to 'release satan from her bag' – a reference to Victoria, who for long periods was left tied up in a bag, lying in her own urine and faeces, in the bathroom of Manning's flat.

Lord Laming's report did not directly explore how far Marie-Therese Kouao and Carl Manning were motivated by their occult beliefs. Perhaps it was difficult to do so without being inflammatory or divisive. Some journalists were certainly discussing the references to witchcraft and spirit possession in light of wider anxieties about mass immigration, cultural change and political correctness.[105] Others suggested that Pentecostal and Black majority churches, with their demonological theology and deliverance services, bore much responsibility for Victoria's death. Representatives from those bodies indignantly pointed out that their congregations were large, law-abiding, and not at all inclined to the sort of cruelty exhibited by Marie-Therese Kouao and Carl Manning.[106] Nonetheless, experts in the fields of social work and law enforcement began to cite Victoria's murder as an example of 'faith based abuse', driven by 'religious beliefs'.[107]

There is undoubtedly some truth to that view. But rather than being the simple consequence of bad religion, Victoria's abuse grew out of a combination of African-style Pentecostalism with more general African attitudes to witchcraft. Marie-Therese absorbed those attitudes during her upbringing in Ivory Coast, where a Gallup poll of 2009 found 95 per cent of people crediting *sorcellerie* (French for witchcraft).[108] For comparison, across eighteen sub-Saharan countries an average of 55 per cent of interviewees claimed to believe, ranging from 80 per cent of Senegalese (the second highest rate) to 15 per cent of Ugandans (the lowest).

Stark as those figures are, they do not convey the intensity of modern sub-Saharan Africa's obsession with witchcraft. A better sense of this can be gleaned from the writings of anthropologists like Peter Geschiere, who spent much of the 1970s, 1980s and 1990s studying the Maka of eastern Cameroon. He found witchcraft thoroughly embedded in almost every aspect of their lives: 'Whatever subject I chose – agriculture, bridewealth, education – I always came up against witchcraft'.[109] Since the waning of French colonialism, village courts had begun convicting alleged witches, despite a lack of evidence. Politicians blamed project failures on witchcraft. Townsfolk accused business elites of using sorcery to amass wealth. Even football supporters attributed defeats to black magic.[110] Sensational witchcraft stories were not just conveyed by word of mouth, but also broadcast on the radio.[111] Wherever there was power, loss and misfortune, there was witchcraft. Geschiere had the impression that, over time, Cameroonians were becoming more preoccupied with the threat of witchcraft rather than less.[112]

Cameroon is 2,000 kilometres from Ivory Coast, where Victoria Climbié was born, but the people of both countries share similar fears. Ivory Coast's *tribunaux correctionnels* (correctional tribunals or local courts) convict witches, as one Dutch legal scholar discovered in 1999 when she observed eleven cases from the west of the country.[113] And like many people in sub-Saharan Africa, citizens of Ivory Coast credit witches with a dazzling array of malefic powers, some broadly similar to European witchcraft notions, others quite distinct. Invariably, evil-doers are said to possess a special organic substance, or organ, located in their abdomens.[114] Called *mangu* by the Azande of southern Sudan, *Kundu* by the Congolese and *djambe* by the Maka of eastern Cameroon, this substance enables witches to transform into rodents to destroy innocent people's crops, or hyenas in order to travel incognito, or snakes to do their enemies harm.[115] At night, in dreams and on a spiritual plane, whether in animal or human form, witches act like incorporeal vampires by eating the souls of their victims' organs. They might render a woman infertile by consuming the soul of her womb, or destroy a man's virility by castrating the spiritual counterpart of his penis.[116] If they siphon off enough life force, these soul-eaters can initiate illnesses or even kill. During the hours of darkness they are said to convene their secret society, meeting with each other to dance, feast on human flesh and drink human blood.[117]

Witches, in sub-Saharan Africa, are greedy predators who practise astral as well as literal cannibalism. Occasionally, they emanate their malice unintentionally.[118] Often they inherit their powers from their parents.[119] Usually they are women, but not always.[120] Unlike in historical Western Europe, where most witches were their victims' neighbours, in Africa they are invariably members of the victim's immediate or extended family.[121] Typically they are adults, usually elderly – but again, not always.[122] Whether so-called 'child witchcraft' in Africa is a contemporary invention continues to be debated, with most scholars and non-governmental organisations insisting that it is indeed a recent development.[123] In the Bangoua region of Cameroon during the 1950s children were 'frequently accused of witchcraft'.[124] Elsewhere, only in recent decades have children been routinely labelled as witches. The chief but not the sole cause of this disturbing development appears to have been the growth of independent Pentecostal churches, whose pastors readily identify children as being possessed. Those children usually have something special about them. Under pressure from the congregation, they often admit to having witched others.[125] Cures provided by the new Pentecostal churches typically involve prayer, fasting and the laying on of hands. Outside the churches, however, more traditional and violent cleansing practices are employed.

Victoria Climbié was a child who stood out because of her intelligence. This was partly why Victoria's parents agreed to let her be informally fostered by Marie-Therese Kouao, her great-aunt. In October 1998, just before Victoria's seventh birthday, her family received a visit from Marie-Therese, who lived in France but had returned to Ivory Coast for her brother's funeral. Marie-Therese told Victoria's parents she hoped to take a child back with her to France, where she would arrange for his or her education. Such informal kinship fostering was and is common in West Africa, usually because it has economic and other benefits for all parties. To give a sense of its normalcy: a study by the World Bank, carried out in Ivory Coast during 1985, found one-fifth of non-orphaned children aged between 7 and 14 living with surrogate parents.[126] In November 1998 Marie-Therese took Victoria to France on a passport bearing another girl's photo, and under the false name Anna Kouao.

For five months they lived in Villepinte, a remote Parisian suburb. Marie-Therese came under investigation for fraudulently claiming state benefits, so in April 1999 she relocated to London, where she had a distant relative. In May they moved into a hostel in Harlesden. By June there were clear signs that Victoria was being mistreated. Marie-Therese's relative was so concerned about the little girl's weight, scars and patchy hair that she made two anonymous calls to Brent Social Services. Around this time Marie-Therese moved in with a bus driver named Carl Manning. Victoria's abuse escalated, and from July onwards she was regularly beaten, her fingers cut, face burnt, and scalding water poured on her body. When Victoria's child-minder asked about these injuries Marie-Therese claimed they were self-inflicted, while at the same time imploring her to take Victoria 'for good'.

Presumably Marie-Therese tried to permanently transfer custody of Victoria to her child-minder because she thought the 'wicked child', as she called her, was a witch or controlled by an evil spirit. Perhaps, like people across sub-Saharan Africa, she was trying to ostracise or shun a girl who she thought was possessed.[127] Whether it was the investigation into benefit fraud, the difficulty they had finding decent accommodation or their generally impoverished lives, it is not clear what problems Victoria is supposed to have initiated. Marie-Therese later complained that she 'caused trouble for me', but the only specific misfortune she mentioned was Victoria's incontinence (in some parts of Africa, witches are said to be especially vulnerable to ill-health, disabilities and the attacks of other witches).[128]

The violence Marie-Therese and Carl Manning inflicted on Victoria was positively sadistic. Yet it was also broadly similar to some of the more malicious counter-witchcraft techniques employed in Africa where 'witches', as one scholar notes, 'are said to be permanently malevolent unless exorcised'.[129] Some West African cleansing practices involve symbolic or real aggression. Historically, the Beng of Ivory Coast smeared witches' faces with powdered chilli peppers, before chasing them into the forest.[130] Today, in neighbouring Ghana, suspected witches are subjected to a catalogue of brutality, including being choked, stripped, shaved, beaten and lynched, either for the sake of reprisal or to make them confess their crimes.[131] A particularly harrowing Ghanaian case of witchcraft abuse centres on an epileptic girl, who for eight years was barricaded in her room, denied human contact, fed scraps, seldom bathed and severely beaten.[132] Unlike Victoria Climbié, she was eventually rescued. That tragic difference aside, the parallels between their experiences are striking.

He had not meant to kill her, Carl Manning claimed during his trial for Victoria's murder, he only beat her because he thought she was possessed by the devil.[133] His barrister described Manning, of Tottenham, as a loner who, under the influence of an older foreign woman, was 'transformed . . . from a harmless nerd to a child killer'.[134] Marie-Therese obviously conveyed her understanding of child witchcraft, which she in turn derived from both Pentecostal Christianity and the West African tradition. But Carl Manning, a British citizen, also learnt about child spirit possession from the African-style Pentecostal churches he attended in London. Neither he nor Marie-Therese referred to the organic witchcraft substance, nor did they call Victoria a 'witch'. Instead, following Pentecostal theology, they translated those ideas into a broadly Christian idiom, describing the little girl as being possessed. Victoria's torturers appear to have accused her of behaving precisely like an African witch, by practising astral cannibalism, carrying out her actions at night and in dreams, and even having some sort of association with vicious supernatural animals.

Like vulnerable alleged witches across Africa, the brutalised and no doubt hectored Victoria confessed to being in thrall to the occult.[135] In February 2000 Marie-Therese took her to the Universal Church of the Kingdom of God, in Finsbury Park, to have her delivered. Upon entering, Victoria stood in the middle of the congregation shouting that she would eat them alive.[136] During a meeting with the assistant pastor she continued in this vein, saying 'she had a vision at night when the devil, in the form of a snake, told her to do these things and she was unable to stop. She said Satan

made her do it. She said she hated me because I prayed for people.'[137] The
pastor later recalled: 'She said it was satan ... Yes, I thought the child was
possessed. She said she liked doing evil, she liked doing it.'[138] He asked
Marie-Therese to bring Victoria back the following Friday, so he could
release the evil spirit. A day before the deliverance service was due to take
place, Marie-Therese phoned to say that Victoria was as cold as ice. She and
Carl Manning brought Victoria to the church. The pastors told them to take
her to hospital. Despite the best efforts of the staff at St Mary's, Paddington,
Victoria died the next day.

In the years following Victoria Climbié's death, witchcraft-related child
abuse became more common, though its exact scale remained uncertain.
Between 2000 and 2010 at least five children of African heritage were killed
in Britain by violence or neglect associated with them being labelled as
witches.[139] Reporting for the Department of Education, Eleanor Stobart
discovered that between 2000 and 2006 the authorities investigated at least
thirty-eight cases of abuse, involving forty-seven children, linked to accusations of witchcraft and possession.[140] Like Victoria Climbié, the victims were
typically beaten, starved, isolated and burnt by parents and guardians who
wanted to exorcise them of evil supernatural entities. And like Victoria
Climbié, most were children 'with a difference', who suffered from disabilities, nightmares, incontinence or another form of challenging behaviour.[141]
Slightly over a third came from the Democratic Republic of Congo – by any
standards, the world's centre of child witchcraft, where estimates suggest
that around 20,000 minors live rough on the streets of Kinshasa as a result
of being labelled witches.[142] All but one of the thirty-eight cases of abuse
analysed by Stobart involved families who were first- or second-generation
migrants.[143] Most were of sub-Saharan African heritage, but not all. Among
South Asian families, the Islamic concept of *jinn* possession figured in
several cases of child abuse. In October 2004 Samira Ullah, a three-month-
old baby, was killed after being swung against a wall by her delusional and
drug-addicted father, Sitab Ullah. The education officer from London
believed his child was controlled by a *jinn*.[144]

The murders of children like Victoria Climbié and Samira Ullah made
Britain's authorities more alive to violence inspired by supernatural beliefs.
Across the country, local government boards issued new guidelines. London
boroughs with high numbers of migrants of African origin, such as Hackney

and Tower Hamlets, also produced workshops and handbooks for social workers.[145] In 2005, London's Metropolitan Police established Project Violet specifically to investigate instances of belief-based child abuse.[146] It recorded twenty-three crimes of this nature in 2013, forty-six in 2014, and sixty during the first ten months of 2015.[147] In this new climate, once fierce advocates of multiculturalism and political correctness, like the former head of the Equality and Human Rights Commission Trevor Phillips, began to wonder whether Britain's tolerant atmosphere was in some sense responsible for the emergence of homegrown witchcraft-related child abuse. According to the anthropologist Jean La Fontaine, competition between independent Pentecostal churches in London had increased the number of children accused of witchcraft, with pastors playing on their apparent cleansing powers to attract adherents.[148] However, the violence parents and guardians meted out to 'London's witch children' resulted not from the teachings of the churches, but from older African ideas about the exorcising power of pain. Witchcraft-related child abuse was inspired by a destructive synthesis of modern religion and superstitious violence.

THE DELIVERANCE MINISTRY: A NEW DEMONOLOGY

During the 1970s, many friends of the churches pondered an existential question: was Britain still a Christian country? Hitherto 'Britain was or regarded herself as a Christian country', the historian Lord Blake mused in a House of Lords debate of 1977, but whether it continued to be so, was a question 'not entirely easy to answer'.[149]

True, most Britons vaguely thought of themselves as Christians. Many identified with Anglicanism if they lived in England, Presbyterianism if they were Scottish and the chapels if they were from Wales. But Christianity's more demanding public expressions were declining.[150] Regular church attendance was falling. So were the number of baptisms, confirmations, sanctified marriages and religious funerals. The increasingly permissive state had abandoned puritan Christian morality, legalising homosexuality and abortion, abolishing the crime of blasphemy and curtailing censorship of the arts. Especially in London and among younger generations, popular culture was more liberal and less saturated with traditional Christian values. At society's fringes, alternative faiths were rising. People of Afro-Caribbean heritage were powerfully attached to Christianity, yet other migrant groups were equally committed to world religions like Islam and Hinduism.

The permissive, pluralist and in many ways frightening new world threatened members of the Church of England. But it also drove them into action. Some Anglicans moved in the liberal direction of John Robinson, Bishop of Woolwich, whose secular theology denied the reality of the supernatural altogether.[151] Others took a very different course. Emboldened by the increasingly tolerant multi-faith atmosphere, they embraced fundamentalist worldviews that saw the hand of God and the handiwork of the devil in everyday events.

Writing in 1980, the Rev. Russ Parker, vicar of the Leicestershire town of Coalville, was probably right to warn his fellow Christians that 'the occult is gaining respectability', given the growing interest in New Age cults and ouija boards.[152] Beyond the genuine religious and cultural changes at work in British society, fundamentalist Christians were inspired by a heady fantasy of supernatural evil. Stories about black magic, devil worship and satanic rites became common currency in the 1960s, when tales of graves desecrated and church altars despoiled regularly featured in the press.[153] During the 1970s the rumours grew more menacing. By the late 1980s and 1990s largely unfounded allegations of children being subjected to ritual satanic abuse were sweeping Britain, Western Europe, Australia and the USA.[154]

Amid this panic, some members of the Church of England were drawn to the work of a prolific German Lutheran pastor, the Rev. Kurt E. Koch (1913–87).[155] His lectures and books, translated into English during the 1960s and 1970s, blended demonology and psychiatry into a new ecclesiastical activity he named the ministry of 'deliverance'.[156] In ancient Judaea, Jesus and his Disciples channelled the Holy Spirit to heal the sick and cast out devils. The deliverance ministry, as delineated by the Rev. Koch and his successors, went further. It confronted a vast occult fraternity – an extended family of darkness ranging from restless spirits to generational curses, evil presences, poltergeists, witchcraft, Satanism, ungodly soul ties and black magic. It would do so soberly and carefully, ensuring genuine mental illnesses were not misdiagnosed as occult afflictions. But when it encountered the forces of evil, the deliverance ministry would vanquish them with the ritual acts of Christian devotion: with prayers, blessings, biblical readings, fasting, the laying on of hands, anointing with oil (unction), taking communion and, if need be, with full-blown exorcisms.

It began in London – the epicentre of the permissive society. In 1970 Christopher Neil-Smith, the Anglican vicar of St Saviour's church in Hampstead, was granted permission by the Bishop of London to conduct exorcisms. Four years later he claimed to have undertaken no less than 2,000, as part of his campaign to rid people of poltergeists, witchcraft, evil spirits, demonic possession and satanic oppression.[157] Though unusually prolific, the Rev. Neil-Smith was not acting alone. The year 1974 saw the publication of the first manual by a UK author about 'the actual mechanics of casting out demons' – *But Deliver Us from Evil* by the Rev. John Richards.[158] In 1975 a clergyman from the West Midlands told journalists he undertook around ten exorcisms a month, largely to free local youths from the influence of ouija boards, witches' covens, satanic societies and other 'forces of evil'.[159] A few Christian mental health professionals also incorporated ministries of deliverance into their work, such as Dr Kenneth McAll, a consultant psychiatrist from Hampshire.[160]

Anglican leaders quickly realised the new deliverance ministry needed careful regulation. Scandal tarnished the movement as early as 1974 when Michael Taylor, from Ossett in West Yorkshire, murdered his wife the morning after receiving an all-night exorcism.[161] In court, Taylor's barrister argued that his client had been subjected to 'grotesque and wicked malpractices' by a clique of religious maniacs, who returned him to his family home 'with the spirit of murder in his head and unreason in his heart'. Tabloid newspapers like the *Daily Mirror* described the affair as 'like something from the middle ages'.[162]

Even close friends of the Church admitted that nocturnal exorcisms went too far.[163] With more direction evidently needed, in 1975 the House of Bishops issued guidelines specifying that ministries of deliverance should: (1) be conducted in collaboration with accredited doctors, psychotherapists or psychiatrists, (2) be done in a context of prayer and the sacrament, (3) occur without publicity and with the authorisation of a bishop, and (4) be followed by continuing pastoral care.[164] Anglican dioceses began producing their own directives and employing dedicated advisors on exorcism.[165] In part, this was for insurance reasons. 'No one, other than the Bishop and his two advisors, is insured to perform an exorcism,' warned one former advisor.[166] Further support came from the Society for the Promotion of Christian Knowledge, which in 1987 published 'the Church of England's definitive publication on exorcism', a handbook for Christian counsellors entitled *Deliverance: Psychic Disturbances and Occult Involvement*.[167] Compiled by Michael Perry, the former Archdeacon of Durham Cathedral, by 2012 the book had gone through two editions and four reprints, and had been admitted to the SPCK 'classics' range.

Its initial impetus came from within the Church of England – from bishops, vicars and other clerics who felt the world around them was beset by occult forces. Yet the deliverance ministry would have come to nothing if it were not for the existence of strong popular demand. The Rt Rev. Dominic Walker, Bishop of Monmouth, summed up the raw nature of this demand. 'People turn up on the vicarage doorstep, looking for help,' he wrote, 'they might feel possessed or cursed, might have experienced a ghost or some paranormal activity, might have been involved in the occult.'[168] Many had no prior connection with the Church. Desperate as they were, their requests for help could be depressingly utilitarian. As a bishop's advisor on deliverance explained to me, when I corresponded with him in 2016, most calls for assistance he received were 'not connected with a regular congregation. This can be tricky on occasions, as in this consumerist society, I have encountered people who shop around.' From interviewing a range of Anglican clerics, it's clear that most requests for help they received came from people who feared their homes were disturbed by ghosts or evil spirits. The typical solution involved blessing the property with prayers and holy water.[169]

Occasionally, Anglican ministers were (and are) called upon to deal with curses. 'People have come to me saying that they believe they have been cursed by someone, either in words alone or sometimes by pins being stuck into a doll-like representation of themselves,' recalled Canon Ken Gardiner, author of *The Reluctant Exorcist* (2002). Towards the start of his career, he responded by praying that the curse rebounded on the person who cast it. Later, Canon Gardiner concluded that his prayers did not embody the spirit of the Gospels and so began asking only that curses be lifted.[170] In his influential manual for deliverance ministers, Canon Michael Perry agreed that 'the malign influence of a curse should not be ruled out when a series of calamities afflicts an individual or a family, or if an illness persists for which there appears to be no cause and perhaps no medical diagnosis'.[171] To illustrate, he cited the case of a man in his fifties who experienced 'a series of unhappy events', including being made redundant. Apparently, his tribulations 'started following a malediction spoken by a gypsy'. Roma curses retained a prominent place within the cosmology of the deliverance ministry, as we can see from another handbook, written by the evangelical minister Russ Parker. 'Have you (or a family member) been involved with gypsies?' Parker asked his readers, in an appendix designed to help them identify occult influences on their lives: 'Has one hexed (cursed) you?'[172] Roma curses could blight organisations too. In 2001 the management at third division football club Oxford United, panicked by their team having lost thirteen of their last seventeen games, asked none other than the Bishop of Oxford to dissolve a Rom's malediction on their stadium.[173] The Rt Rev. Richard Harries obliged by administering a blessing.

From the 1990s, a cornucopia of international Pentecostal churches began practising deliverance in Britain. Compared with the Church of England, their approach to the ministry was far more public, ecstatic and frankly irresponsible. Take the Mountains of Fire and Miracles Ministry, founded in Nigeria in 1989. By 2012 it had opened at least eighty-three British branches, including one on the highly religious Shetland Isles.[174] Among the many publications written by its founder and General Overseer, Dr D.K. Olukoya, was a guidebook entitled *Overpowering Witchcraft* (1999). Disgracefully, it claimed that within many ordinary households disobedient and manipulative 'children are using the weapon of witchcraft' to harm their parents.[175]

Dr Olukoya's Mountains of Fire and Miracles Ministry was one of the most successful African-style Pentecostal churches to take root in Britain. Innumerable smaller churches followed its example. The London borough of Newham alone possessed, in 1999, seventy-two different Pentecostal congregations, 40 per cent of which had been founded since 1980.[176] Deliverance from supernatural evil, particularly from witchcraft and malign spirits, was among their primary functions. Many adherents were African migrants, struggling to create good lives for themselves in expensive London, worrying about the influences 'immoral' British youths were having on their offspring.[177] In times of trouble, they might be drawn to one of the regular deliverance services held at African-style Pentecostal churches. There, while emotive music played and worshippers held their hands aloft, the minister would demand that all curses, demons and evil spirits depart in the name of Jesus. In a rousing atmosphere, some among the faithful would step into the aisles or go to the front of the church in order to be healed through the laying on of hands. One or two congregants could start speaking in tongues or lose control of their bodies, writhing on the floor in the stereotypical manner of possessed people. Others might confess to occult involvement, whether in the form of practising witchcraft or playing with ouija boards, before renouncing their evil ties. None of this came for free. Typically, pastors charged hundreds of pounds or more, to cure the witchcraft they diagnosed in adults and – frequently – children.

The notion of child witchcraft was unique to the thinking of African-style Pentecostal churches, but intense supernatural fears were not. The 1980s saw the creation of non-denominational foundations like Ellel Ministries (est. 1986), which sold weekend healing retreats, based in country houses, to people from a wide range of backgrounds who wanted relief from spiritual oppression. Peter Horrobin, founder of Ellel Ministries and author of a huge textbook entitled *Healing through Deliverance*, propounded a conspiratorial worldview in which the personal figure of Satan literally reigned over much of the earth 'by placing ruling spirits over churches, schools, companies, organizations, etc'.[178] According to Horrobin, the devil commanded thousands upon thousands of fallen angels, and through them innumerable demons and evil spirits. To dispel any suspicion that he might be speaking metaphorically, Horrobin plainly wrote in his handbook: 'Demons are not just ideas or indefinable forces that operate from within the mind of man. They are living, functioning spiritual beings with a mind, characteristics and a will of their own that are dedicated to the service of Satan.'[179]

Like the authors of the *Malleus Maleficarum,* a notorious fifteenth-century demonological treatise, Peter Horrobin insisted on the reality of malign entities like the incubus ('an evil spirit that attaches itself to the sexuality of a woman').[180] His doubtless sincere views were vastly more extreme than those of Anglican deliverance ministers, but it would be a mistake to dismiss him as an unimportant crank operating at the fringes of religious life. His organisation, Ellel Ministries, achieved an international profile, with centres in at least twelve countries. Reports submitted to Companies House and the Charity Commission showed that between 2011 and 2014 its annual income averaged slightly above £3.7 million.[181] In 2013, Ellel Ministries' UK properties and estates alone were given a 'conservative valuation' of £6.4 million. Its publishing arm, Sovereign World, generated almost £260,000 in 2014, by selling books by Horrobin and other demonologists.[182]

Convinced demons were everywhere, some Christians engaged in a form of conduct known as 'spiritual warfare'.[183] Practised by laypeople but devised largely by evangelical and fundamentalist pastors, it was a religious lifestyle dedicated to detecting and defeating hostile preternatural beings. By attributing personal ills to non-human supernatural creatures, proponents of spiritual warfare were concerning themselves with what we might call 'witchcraft without witches'. A booklet published by Ellel Ministries entitled *Defensive Spiritual Warfare* (1996) ascribed the following afflictions to spiritual attacks by demonic powers: food allergies, lust, bad dreams, insomnia, anxiety, depression, self-doubt, anger, bitterness, pride and stress.[184] It also blamed demons for what, historically, was a classic sign of witchcraft: 'Sickness or physical conditions that have no medical reason or do not respond to medical treatment.'[185]

Beyond demons, an influential Cambridge-educated and Florida-based Pentecostal pastor named Derek Prince (1915–2003) popularised the idea that generational curses caused personal misfortunes. His archetype of an accursed person was synonymous with the historical notion of a bewitched individual: 'Success eludes him. His children are rebellious, his marriage under strain, accidents and illnesses routine.'[186] Yet for the Rev. Prince, evilly disposed people were only one, comparatively minor, source of curses. Negative words, uttered by authority figures, were another. People could even curse themselves, through self-condemnatory words and pessimistic attitudes. Above all, Prince believed curses originated in the sins of fathers and mothers, grandparents and ancestors. They were divine punishment for the infidelity, occultism, carnality and anti-Semitism of previous generations. Thankfully, accursed people could gain God's blessing by renouncing the sins of the past. After Prince formulated these ideas in the 1970s and 1980s, they became a mainstay of spiritual warfare and deliverance ministry literature.[187] Later authors added to the already long list of causes, arguing that curses result from sins as various as a penchant for rock music, sex outside marriage, exotic foreign objects and anything savouring of eastern religiosity (such as yoga).[188]

Its adherents had to live positively ascetic lives; even so, as a therapeutic system spiritual warfare had advantages. By attributing personal misfortunes to non-human supernatural entities it retained the emotional satisfaction of conventional witchcraft belief, and jettisoned the interpersonal difficulties. Spiritual warfare provided some feeling of control over a confusing series of disasters and held out the alluring possibility, as the Rev. Derek Prince put it, of 'freedom from pressures you thought you had to live with'. It did not entail a magical battle with a witch or a falling out with a real person. Historically, identifiable witches were often neighbours, but partly thanks to the growth of the welfare state during the second half of the twentieth century, few British people depended on their neighbours.[189] Some did not even know them: an investigation of 2012 estimated that 3.5 million Britons had never encountered their neighbours, not even on a single occasion.[190]

In a society where neighbourliness was vastly diminished, perhaps conventional witchcraft belief was less viable. Perhaps, for people inclined to attribute their worldly cares and troubles to supernatural evil, it was not plausible to implicate witches whom they had never met. Blaming disembodied demons, evil spirits and generational curses may well have been more suited to the norms of a somewhat anti-social society.

THE OCCULT ONLINE

Around the turn of the millennium, the internet began to play an increasingly important role in many British people's lives. One growth area was shopping: in 2000, just 0.8 per cent of total UK retail spending occurred online, but by 2004 the figure was 2.4 per cent (or £5 billion) and by 2013 it was 12.7 per cent.[191] Groceries, electronics and clothes began to be sold over the internet. So did magical items and supernatural services.

On 30 August 2012 eBay, one of the western world's premier online marketplaces, prohibited its users from selling spells, curses, blessings, tarot readings and prayers. The company explained that it was responding to persistent user feedback within the niche sub-category of 'intangible' metaphysical services. Conflicts between buyers and sellers were arising that could not be satisfactorily resolved.[192] People purchasing spells promising money, love or luck were finding themselves as poor, alone and unfortunate as ever. Some were crying fraud. The decision by eBay to ban all intangible metaphysical services from its website caused grumbling in Britain and America, with sellers, and a few buyers too, complaining that they were being unfairly victimised. Undeterred, in 2015 Etsy, another peer-to-peer online marketplace, went a step further. It prevented its users from selling anything purporting to have supernatural powers.[193] Those wanting weight loss amulets or ex-lover-shaped voodoo dolls or healing charms would henceforth have to look elsewhere.

Etsy and eBay acted to protect their reputations, not because regulators compelled them to. Rather than diminish the availability of supernatural services on the internet, their self-imposed crackdown just moved magic to other platforms. By the early 2010s, legions of esoteric entrepreneurs had set up personal websites to directly advertise and sell their wares. In April 2016 I explored the websites of thirty-five British-based metaphysicians, all of whom offered 'curse removal'.[194] They represented a bafflingly diverse and eclectic array of occult traditions. Brian, a psychic healer and reiki master, used a psychotherapeutic empowerment technique known as 'spirit release' to remove black magic, curses, witchcraft, voodoo and *jinns*. David, a white witch and medium, charged his online clients £45 for a standard single cast curse removal, and £75 for the purportedly more effective thrice cast curse removal. He was a good deal cheaper than Barbatoz, 'a High Master of the Black Arts', who charged the princely sum of £300 to remove curses with his dark magic. Laura, a tarot reader and online psychic, asked between £13.50 and £34 for personal readings, and offered a host of other rites, including curse removal. Kevin, a Wiccan and paranormal investigator based in Sussex, also touted a wide range of metaphysical therapies. A few healers included tiny disclaimers on their websites, stating that their work was for 'entertainment purposes only'. Most did not, clearly feeling no obligation to comply with consumer protection regulations.

Along with marketing occult services, the internet also reinforced magical ways of thinking. Discovering and purchasing specialist literature concerning everything from the deliverance ministry to *unani tibb* became easier. More importantly, the internet enabled fervent believers in the supernatural to connect with like-minded people from across the world. Whether it was neo-pagans treading the hedge witch's path or Christians practising spiritual warfare, people with fringe interests began to construct websites about their lifestyle choices.[195] Their aim was not so much to make money as to share stories and learn from others. As they engaged with self-selecting online communities, participants may well have had their supernatural beliefs subtly modified. In everyday life, our sense of what is normal and reasonable is often formed intuitively, by observing what others say and do. Uncon-sciously, by repeatedly encountering sentiments that chimed with their own, members of niche supernatural communities may have become more convinced that their interpretations of the world were entirely creditable and unquestionably reasonable. The internet thus reinforced its users' occult beliefs, inadvertently breeding new and more extreme forms of certainty.[196]

* * *

Between 1970 and 2010 Britain experienced a modest but sustained revival of magic. Ever more people tried to put supernatural powers to practical ends. Old taboos lost their force, making it easier for individuals to publicly admit to believing in the existence of paranormal powers. Beyond simple professions of faith, more people acted on their occult convictions by collaborating with the tens of thousands of spiritual healers, clairvoyants, deliverance ministers and other sellers of new esoteric services. Magical beliefs were not just more widespread, they were more fully expressed.

They were also more diverse. By the early twenty-first century, Britain's culture of magic ranged from rural folktales about ill-wishing Roma to *obeah*, from *muti* to *unani tibb*, from hedge witchcraft to *ruqyah*, from New Age spirituality to the deliverance ministry. Those fairly distinct genres of supernatural activity possessed different theories, practices and mythologies. But some laypeople moved easily between them, trying several in succession as they sought relief from their most intractable problems. Pure desperation undoubtedly propelled this experimentation with previously unfamiliar therapies. Yet it was also facilitated by fundamental conceptual or archetypal similarities. In one way or another, most supernatural therapies acknowledged the existence of curses, ghosts, the evil eye, possession and magically induced love.

Immigration contributed to the diversification and revival of magic. Mostly though, magic revived in Britain because it was allowed to. In an increasingly multicultural and multi-faith environment, the authorities – and public opinion too – became more lenient towards magical practitioners and their patrons. Too lenient, perhaps. The modern revival of magic can certainly be interpreted in terms of liberation and emancipation. Formerly proscribed, stigmatised and denigrated activities began to flourish once again, with emotional and spiritual benefits. But there were dark sides to the revival of magic, involving fraud, violence and child abuse.

CONCLUSION

WITCHCRAFT'S DECLINE AND RETURN

This book's broadest conclusion is that witchcraft, understood as black magic, is an enduring, erratic belief system. It can be therapeutic, but it's also apt to be fraudulent and dangerous. If it's not properly controlled, witchcraft will certainly do damage. Social activism and intellectual criticism are unlikely to help. Instead, the best way to control the weird world of black magic is by targeted government regulation.

*   *   *

Black magic comes from the night side of the human mind. It's a desperate thing, to imagine you're cursed. To think, in times of trouble, that your problems and pains have mystic, malevolent causes. A frightening idea, but empowering and rejuvenating too, perhaps. Witchcraft, curses, spells, hexes, maledictions – defeating these powers requires one thing above all: faith. If you believe enough, if you can summon up absolute conviction, then maybe your troubles will end. A magical battle is under way, and your main weapon is your mind. You can win, but only if you truly believe. You must.

Here, black magic becomes dangerous. Having true faith means crediting it all. It means knowing for sure that someone or something is mystically attacking you. An occult enemy, intent on your destruction, who has to be defeated. That idea can make people do terrible things. Some spend fortunes on spiritual healers. Others slander, mistreat, abuse, attack, fight or even kill.

The 'belief' dimension of witchcraft is too often overlooked in the media and in the specialist literature. Many scholars interested in the topic neglect to mention it at all. But to understand witchcraft, it's vital to appreciate that people drawn to this way of thinking don't always see being cursed as an ordinary idea, a conclusion reached solely on the basis of the facts. Rather, being cursed is an intuition, a faith-based mentality adopted against doubts and despite cynicism, a summoned conviction mustered by force of will. This helps to explain why witchcraft is difficult to dislodge and frequently destructive when left unchecked. Being faith-based, it's deeply emotional and hard to confute.

Witchcraft is a dynamic belief system that easily incorporates new ideas and adapts to new situations. A core endures: the notion of interpersonal harm caused by mystic means. Yet around this archetype, novel terms, theories and practices readily converge. Throughout its long history, witchcraft has always altered and developed. But it has been particularly mutable during the last two hundred years, as the pace of cultural and social change has quickened. Thus, the bedevilled people of Britain have gone from being 'bewitched' and 'overlooked' to being assailed by 'malicious magnetism', put under 'psychic attack' and – above all – 'cursed'.

Witchcraft, as we've seen, was widely feared across nineteenth-century Britain. Town dwellers fought over it. City folk accused each other of practising it. Even metropolitan Londoners ascribed their misfortunes – from unemployment to sickness – to black magic. So did the denizens of the countryside. And so, particularly, did people living in witchy regions like East Anglia and the West Country, and the residents of witch villages like Long Compton in Warwickshire. Most commoners believed in witchcraft's reality: secretly, a fair number of their social 'betters' did too. The Rev. William Ettrick, the witch-fearing parson we met in Chapter 2, was not a solitary figure.

The witches of the early 1800s faced the ignominy of being publicly abused and mobbed by their indignant neighbours. Until the final decades of the nineteenth century, individual attacks on witches, usually designed to break spells by drawing blood, were commoner still. To stop these outrages, sceptics tried to discredit witchcraft belief, especially between about the 1830s and 1860s, by arguing that it was unscientific and unbiblical. Overwhelmingly, they failed. Superstitious vigilantism wasn't ended by rational disputation. Nor was it much diminished by the growth of schooling and popular education. Attacks on witches were stopped by Victorian policing reforms, by an increase in police numbers and a more professional ethos.

Far from being anti-magical, many modern developments were compatible with witchcraft, or even conducive to it. The collapse of Christian orthodoxy, engendered by the mid-nineteenth-century crisis of faith, gave certain avant-garde characters leeway to explore the nether regions of the occult, including the murky domain of supernatural healing and harm. Victorian cities were claustrophobic and dangerous places, which bred occult suspicions. Science possessed a mystique and an esoteric jargon, which was easily co-opted into uncanny ways of thinking. Colonialism was supposed to civilise the inhabitants of savage climes: instead, suffering indigenes invoked witchcraft to explain their worsening plights. As for white expatriates, plenty found themselves strangely affected by the magically minded people and the uncanny atmospheres they encountered in India, Africa, the Caribbean and the Antipodes. Eventually, following years spent in foreign lands, they became less dismissive of witchcraft. Maybe there was 'something in it', after all.

For the entire nineteenth century, most Britons would have been prepared to believe in black magic, under properly dire circumstances. Across the land, thousands of professional magicians earned considerable sums by exploiting their customers' anxieties about witchcraft. Cunning-folk, wise-men, canny-women, conjurors, warlocks, fortune-tellers and Roma women – they taught desperate people what witchcraft was, and how to cure it. Much of their magical money-making was cynical, tricky, unethical or fraudulent. At the same time, there's reason to think the unwitchers of British history helped as well as swindled their clients. Depressed people, sinking beneath life's hardships, were dragged out of pits of despondency and ushered into make-believe worlds of witchery and magic. If they could only have faith, if they forced themselves to believe, their misfortunes might disappear.

Witchcraft's decline, from a majority belief to a fringe credo, occurred relatively recently, between the early and mid-twentieth century. It was partly driven by cultural changes: the decline of oral storytelling, the waning of popular Christianity and the rise of the 'stiff upper lip' ethos. Life was also getting easier, increasingly comfortable and less dangerous, thanks to the growth of the welfare state and massive advances in scientific medicine. Most of all though, witchcraft collapsed because the British state used regulation to eliminate the cunning-craft, the ancient trade of the white witches, who had previously propagated this belief system.

Just because witchcraft was vastly diminished, by the 1950s, didn't mean it had gone for ever. In the more liberal, libertine environment of the late twentieth century, black magic began to revive. Migrants from around the world imported exotic supernatural beliefs and practices into Britain, but that was not the only reason. With multiculturalism ascendant, it was difficult to distinguish between legitimate minority spiritualities and destructive superstitions. Alternative healers flourished once again, alongside a multitude of new curse removers, spirit mediums, exorcists, aura purifiers, energy cleansers and others. Drawn from a myriad of diverse traditions, like the cunning-folk of old these spiritual healers offered many esoteric services, from love spells to money magic, fortune-telling and exorcism. And, like the wise-men and cunning-women of British history, some modern metaphysicians taught their bewildered clients what it was to be attacked by evil esoteric forces, and how the power of belief could stem their troubles.

Believing in witchcraft and magic undoubtedly helps some people to cope with otherwise overwhelming problems like financial difficulties, illnesses and relationship breakdowns. Outside the realm of private spell-casting, however, witchcraft belief often inspires unacceptably destructive behaviour. Egregiously expensive curse removal services and scam letters or emails promising vulnerable people protection from black magic are only its lesser harms. Across the world, in the name of combating witchcraft, innocent people are heckled, humiliated, assaulted, mistreated and murdered.

Witchcraft-related human rights abuses are rife in the worst governed parts of sub-Saharan Africa, as well as in rural India and much of Melanesia. Yet in contemporary Britain too, witchcraft-related abuse is on the rise. Mercifully, superstitious killings, like that of Victoria Climbié in the year 2000, are rare, maybe one every year or two. Tragically, thousands of children annually are forced to endure violent or traumatising anti-possession rituals. In 2017, figures collated from English local authorities by the Department of Education recorded 1,460 incidents of 'faith-based abuse' against minors during the previous year, usually involving accusations of witchcraft or possession.[1] The figures represented a huge leap from the year before, reflecting a growing awareness of the problem among child protection agencies. The data released in 2018 recorded another increase. During 2017–18, 1,630 children in England were found to be suffering from abuse 'linked to faith or belief'. However, while London recorded 400 cases, Birmingham 106, Nottingham 68 and Surrey 60, dozens of other local authorities recorded none at all. In all likelihood, this means that the scale of witchcraft- and possession-related abuse in contemporary Britain is still significantly underestimated.

Looking back at history, can we learn anything about how to combat witchcraft's destructive consequences? Educational campaigns which explicitly try to debunk the concept of magic are likely to be ignored or resented by the target audience. After all, we're dealing with a faith-based mentality, rather than strictly rational thought. Some legal scholars suggest the UK should follow the example of African countries like the Democratic Republic of Congo, by prohibiting the branding of children as witches.[2] This might well help. Yet the problem of destructive superstition goes deeper than these difficult-to-uncover and therefore difficult-to-prosecute accusations. Witchcraft reached its lowest ebb in modern British history when the state clamped down on the market for alternative health care, with targeted regulation and more policing. Perhaps a similar campaign could be mounted today, against the most unscrupulous spiritual healers operating in Britain.

And so the history of witchcraft continues. Look around. See the New Age store, the esoteric section of the bookshop, the adverts for spiritual healers in free newspapers and on internet message boards. Look at the deliverance services held in local churches, the curse-removal products sold through online marketplaces, the flyers handed out by alternative healers in parts of London and elsewhere. Supernatural healing, and protection from supernatural harm, can be found practically everywhere – in Britain and across much of the world. We cannot assume this magic will wane as our technology advances and our lives (hopefully) improve. Indulged and ignored in the West, witchcraft – both black and white – is already undergoing a revival. How far that revival progresses, and what shape it assumes, depends in large part upon the way we elect to be governed.

ENDNOTES

I BLACK MAGIC IN MODERN TIMES

1. Ronald Hutton, *The Witch: A History of Witchcraft, Magic and Culture Fear, from Ancient Times to the Present* (New Haven, CT, 2017), Chapter 2. Christopher A. Faraone, 'Binding and Burying the Forces of Evil: The Defensive Use of "Voodoo Dolls" in Ancient Greece', *Classical Antiquity*, 10 (1991), pp. 165–205. Magali Bailliot, 'Roman Magic Figurines from the Western Provinces of the Roman Empire: An Archaeological Survey', *Britannia*, 46 (2015), pp. 93–110.

2. In Papua New Guinea, for instance, sorcery-related violence is apparently 'a huge social phenomenon'. Local newspapers reported that 147 witches were attacked between 2000 and 2006. No doubt much violence went unreported. See Jack Urame, 'The Spread of Sorcery Killing and Its Social Implications', in Miranda Forsyth and Richard Eves (eds), *Talking it Through: Responses to Sorcery and Witchcraft Beliefs and Practices in Melanesia* (Canberra, 2015), pp. 23–4. I make comparisons with contemporary India and Africa in subsequent chapters, so will not repeat the statistics here.

3. Beyond this book, for those wanting to read further about the modern history and anthropology of witchcraft in Western Europe, I particularly recommend the writings of Owen Davies, Ronald Hutton, Jeanne Favret-Saada, Willem de Blécourt and Jean La Fontaine, as well as more specialist works by Karl Bell, Andrew Sneddon, Richard Suggett and Jason Semmens. See Owen Davies, *Witchcraft, Magic and Culture: 1736–1951* (Manchester, 1999), and *Grimoires: A History of Magic Books* (Oxford, 2009). Ronald Hutton, *The Triumph of the Moon: A History of Modern Pagan Witchcraft* (Oxford, 1999), and *The Witch* (London and New Haven, CT, 2017). Jeanne Favret-Saada, *Deadly Words: Witchcraft in the Bocage*, trans. Catherine Cullen (Cambridge, 1980), and *The Anti-Witch*, trans. Matthew Carey (Chicago, IL, 2015). Willem de Blécourt, Ronald Hutton and Jean La Fontaine (eds), *The Athlone History of Witchcraft and Magic in Europe*, vol. 6: *The Twentieth Century* (London, 1999). Jean La Fontaine, *Witches and Demons: A Comparative Perspective on Witchcraft and Satanism* (New York and Oxford, 2016). Karl Bell, *The Magical Imagination: Magic and Modernity in Urban Britain 1780–1914* (Cambridge, 2012). Richard Suggett, *A History of Magic and Witchcraft in Wales* (Stroud,

2008). Andrew Sneddon, *Witchcraft and Magic in Ireland* (Basingstoke, 2015). Jason Semmens, *The Witch of the West: Or, The Strange and Wonderful History of Thomasine Blight* (Plymouth, 2004).

4. Jean La Fontaine, 'Satanism and Satanic Mythology', in de Blécourt, Hutton and La Fontaine (eds), *The Athlone History of Witchcraft and Magic in Europe*, vol. 6: *The Twentieth Century*, pp. 124–38. Sheila Fitzpatrick and Robert Gellately, 'Introduction to the Practices of Denunciation in Modern European History', *Journal of Modern History*, 68 (1996), p. 762.

5. Hutton, *The Witch*, p. xi.

6. James Rudge, 'Pretensions of the Bishops of Rome', *The Churchman*, July (1840), p. 282. *Western Times*, 11 January 1876.

2 BLOOD THE WITCH, SWIM THE WIZARD: 1800–30

1. Martin Joseph Naylor, *The Inanity of and Mischief of Vulgar Superstitions* (Cambridge, 1795), p. iii.

2. *Hereford Journal*, 21 May 1800.

3. *Leicester Chronicle*, 9 May 1829.

4. *Morning Chronicle*, 18 November 1808.

5. *Morning Post*, 7 January 1803.

6. *Jackson's Oxford Journal*, 14 June 1806. *Morning Chronicle*, 31 May 1804.

7. *Lancaster Gazette*, 31 March 1821.

8. For a good summary of the rate of witchcraft prosecution in Britain and Ireland, see Andrew Sneddon, *Witchcraft and Magic in Ireland* (Basingstoke, 2015), esp. Chapter 4.

9. Malcolm Gaskill, 'Witchcraft and Evidence in Early Modern England', *Past and Present*, 198 (2008), pp. 33–70. Ian Bostridge, *Witchcraft and its Transformations c. 1650–1750* (Oxford, 1997), pp. 185–91. Owen Davies, *Witchcraft, Magic and Culture: 1736–1951* (Manchester, 1999), pp. 1–2.

10. *Cheltenham Chronicle*, 12 September 1811.

11. *The Scots Magazine and Edinburgh Literary Miscellany*, 1 February 1818.

12. 'Witchcraft and Astrology', *Taunton Courier*, 18 March 1819, p. 2.

13. *The Times*, 25 March 1858. *Cheltenham Chronicle*, 28 December 1815.

14. James Paterson, *A Belief in Witchcraft Unsupported by Scripture* (Aberdeen, Edinburgh and London, 1815), p. i.

15. Ibid., p. 4.

16. Francis Young, *English Catholics and the Supernatural, 1553–1829* (Farnham, 2013), p. 163. J.F.C. Harrison, *The Second Coming: Popular Millenarianism 1780–1850* (London, 1979), esp. Chapter 3. William Gibson states that 'witchcraft was abandoned as implausible by the educated classes in the early eighteenth century': see *The Church of England 1688–1832: Unity and Accord* (London, 2001), p. 168. Stephen Mitchell seems to think that, by the early nineteenth century, only the 'populace' were given to witchcraft belief; see 'A Case of Witchcraft Assault in Early Nineteenth-century England as Ostensive Action', in Owen Davies and William de Blécourt (eds), *Witchcraft Continued: Popular Magic in Modern Europe* (Manchester, 2004), p. 24. A similar argument is implied in Roy Porter, *Enlightenment: Britain and the Creation of the Modern World* (London, 2001), pp. 207, 220–9.

17. E. Watts Moses, 'The Ettricks of High Barnes', *Antiquities of Sunderland and its Vicinity*, 20 (1932–43), pp. 9–15. For further biographical information see *Morning Post*, 23 January 1847. *Durham Chronicle*, 5 January 1838. *Brighton Gazette*, 28 January 1847. *Sunderland Daily Echo*, 25 January 1933.

18. William Ettrick's papers are divided between the wonderful Sunderland Antiquarian Society (which holds most of the diaries) and Tyne and Wear Archives. Special thanks to both for their help with my research. At Tyne and Wear Archives, I made particular use

of DF.ETT, Acc 839/222; DF.ETT, Acc 839/228; DF.ETT, Acc 2539/1; DF.ETT, Acc 2359/3. Some of the most important extracts from Ettrick's diary are printed in Christina Hole (ed.), *Witchcraft at Toner's Puddle, 19th C.: From the Diary of the Rev. William Ettrick* (Dorchester, 1964).

19. James Hardy, 'Wart and Wen Cures', *The Folk-Lore Record*, 1 (1878), p. 219. L.F. Newman and E.M. Wilson, 'Folk-lore Survivals in the Southern "Lake" Counties and in Essex: A Comparison and Contrast', *Folklore*, 62 (1951), p. 257. Roy Vickery, 'The Use of Broad Beans to Cure Warts', *Folklore*, 102 (1991), p. 240. Jennifer Chandler, 'Whiteness and Warts', *Folklore*, 105 (1994), p. 101.

20. Rev. W. Ettrick, *The Second Exodus; or, Reflections on the Prophecies of the Last Times, Fulfilled By Late Events and Now Fulfilling By the Scourge of Popery*, 2 vols (Sunderland, 1810).

21. David Cannadine, *Victorious Century: The United Kingdom, 1800–1906* (London, 2017), p. 63.

22. Tyne and Wear Archives, DF.ETT, Acc 2359/3: Memoranda book for 1823–8.

23. The reports from the *Suffolk Chronicle* and *Suffolk Herald* were widely reprinted. See *The Morning Chronicle*, 18 July 1825. *Coventry Herald*, 22 July 1825. *The Examiner*, 24 July 1825. *Caledonian Mercury*, 28 July 1825. There is also an account of the affair, apparently 'taken from the mouth of a respectable parishioner', in Robert Forby, *The Vocabulary of East Anglia* (London, 1830), vol. 2, pp. 391–2.

24. James Sharpe, *Instruments of Darkness: Witchcraft in England 1550–1750* (London, 1997), pp. 61–2.

25. Davies, *Witchcraft, Magic and Culture*, pp. 86–9. Sharpe, *Instruments of Darkness*, pp. 218–19, 282.

26. Forby, *The Vocabulary of East Anglia*, vol. 2, p. 391.

27. *The Morning Chronicle*, 18 July 1825. *Coventry Herald*, 22 July 1825. *The Examiner*, 24 July 1825. Also see Davies, *Witchcraft, Magic and Culture*, p. 112.

28. *Morning Chronicle*, 11 April 1827.

29. Watkins was sentenced to six months' imprisonment; the others to three. For the petition see National Archives – HO 17/58/13.

30. National Archives – HO 17/58/13.

31. The petition was indeed refused.

32. *Leeds Intelligencer*, 16 August 1802. *Staffordshire Advertiser*, 21 August 1802. *Devizes and Wiltshire Gazette*, 6 May 1824. *Yorkshire Gazette*, 19 August 1826. *Chester Chronicle*, 21 November 1828.

33. *Morning Chronicle*, 8 April 1823. *Devizes and Wiltshire Gazette*, 10 April 1823.

34. Simon Szreter and Graham Mooney, 'Urbanization, Mortality, and the Standard of Living Debate: New Estimates of the Expectation of Life at Birth in Nineteenth-century British Cities', *Economic History Review*, 51 (1998), p. 100.

35. Rosemary Rees, *Poverty and Public Health 1815–1948* (Oxford, 2001), p. 111.

36. When he moved from rural Northamptonshire to London, the so-called 'peasant poet' John Clare felt so nervous about 'meeting with supernatural [agents]' at night that he always tried to make sure a friend walked him home. See J.W. and Anne Tibble (eds), *The Prose of John Clare* (London, 1951), pp. 39–40, 44.

37. Szreter and Mooney, 'Urbanization, Mortality, and the Standard of Living Debate', p. 101. Also see Rees, *Poverty and Public Health 1815–1948*, p. 116.

38. Jane Humphries and Tim Leunig, 'Cities, Market Integration, and Going to Sea: Stunting and the Standard of Living in Early Nineteenth-century England and Wales', *Economic History Review*, 62 (2009), pp. 458–78.

39. For an excellent exposition of this point see Karl Bell, *The Magical Imagination: Magic and Modernity in Urban Britain 1780–1914* (Cambridge, 2012), pp. 45–50.

40. *Leeds Intelligencer*, 16 August 1802. *Staffordshire Advertiser*, 21 August 1802.

41. *Yorkshire Gazette*, 19 August 1826.

42. *Devizes and Wiltshire Gazette*, 6 May 1824.

43. John Jamieson, *Supplement to the Etymological Dictionary of the Scottish Language*, vol. II (Edinburgh, 1825), p. 349. 'Witchcraft', *Inverness Courier*, 22 November 1826, p. 4.

44. Sally Parkin, 'Witchcraft, Women's Honour and Customary Law in Early Modern Wales', *Social History*, 31 (2006), pp. 310–11. Keith Thomas, *Religion and the Decline of Magic: Studies in Popular Beliefs in Sixteenth- and Seventeenth-century England* (1971: London, 1991), pp. 633–4, 649. Mark Stoyle, 'The Road to Farndon Field: Explaining the Massacre of Royalist Women at Naseby', *English Historical Review*, 123 (2008), p. 912.

45. This is suggested in Barbara Rosen, *Witchcraft in England: 1558–1618* (Amherst, 1969), p. 19.

46. Eugene Fugle, 'Mesquakie Witchcraft Lore', *Plains Anthropologist*, 6 (1961), p. 34. Richard Gordon, 'Imagining Greek and Roman Magic', in Valerie Flint, Richard Gordon, Georg Luck and Daniel Ogden (eds), *The Athlone History of Witchcraft and Magic in Europe*, vol. 2: *Ancient Greece and Rome* (London, 1999), p. 237.

47. See 'The Ballads of Andri and the Hymns of Hallgrim', in Jacqueline Simpson (ed.), *Icelandic Folktales and Legends* (Berkeley and Los Angeles, CA, 1972), pp. 79–81.

48. *Yorkshire Gazette*, 19 August 1826. *Northampton Mercury*, 19 August 1826. *Morning Chronicle*, 8 April 1823. *Devizes and Wiltshire Gazette*, 10 April 1823; 6 May 1824.

49. *Cheltenham Chronicle*, 29 August 1811.

50. Robert F. Murphy, *An Overture to Social Anthropology* (Upper Saddle River, NJ, 1979), p. 175. Edward Bever, *The Realities of Witchcraft and Popular Magic in Early Modern Europe: Culture, Cognition, and Everyday Life* (Basingstoke, 2008), pp. 17–18, 156. For another somewhat similar historical case, see Ulinka Rublack, 'Pregnancy, Childbirth and the Female Body in Early Modern Germany', *Past and Present*, 150 (1996), pp. 92–3.

51. Young, *English Catholics*, p. 164.

52. 'Atrocious Act', *Cumberland Pacquet*, 12 July 1824, p. 1.

53. *Chester Courant*, 22 May 1810. *Lancaster Gazette*, 19 May 1810. *Cheltenham Chronicle*, 14 June 1810. *Hampshire Chronicle*, 9 January 1809. *Morning Chronicle*, 8 April 1823. *Devizes and Wiltshire Gazette*, 10 April 1823. *Westmorland Gazette*, 7 November 1818.

54. *Stamford Mercury*, 9 April 1819.

55. *Kent Gazette*, 4 September 1812.

56. *Chester Chronicle*, 21 November 1828. *Devizes and Wiltshire Gazette*, 6 May 1824. For the best study of hag-riding see Owen Davies, 'Hag-riding in Nineteenth-century West Country England and Modern Newfoundland: An Examination of Experience-centred Witchcraft Tradition', *Folk Life* 35 (1996–7), pp. 36–53.

57. 'Belief in Witchcraft', *Newcastle Courant*, 21 February 1829, p. 2. 'March of Credulity', *Cheltenham Chronicle*, 13 August 1829, p. 4.

58. *Chester Chronicle*, 21 November 1828.

59. *Royal Cornwall Gazette*, 12 May 1821.

60. M.K. Ashby, *Joseph Ashby of Tysoe 1859–1919: A Study of English Village Life* (London, 1974), p. 16.

61. 'March of Credulity', *Cheltenham Chronicle*, 13 August 1829, p. 4.

62. Robin Briggs, *Witches and Neighbours: The Social and Cultural Context of European Witchcraft* (London, 1996), p. 116.

63. 'Witchcraft and Astrology', *Taunton Courier*, 18 March 1819, p. 2. 'Superstitious Customs and Sayings', *London Courier and Evening Gazette*, 14 October 1825, p. 4.

64. 'Historical Notices of the Popular Superstitions, Traditions, and Customs of Tiviotdale', *The Scots Magazine* (June 1820), p. 536.

65. On which see the various excellent essays by Timothy Easton, Brian Hoggard, June Swann and others in Ronald Hutton (ed.), *Physical Evidence for Ritual Acts, Sorcery and Witchcraft in Christian Britain: A Feeling for Magic* (Basingstoke, 2016).

66. *Devizes and Wiltshire Gazette*, 10 April 1823. 'March of Credulity', *Cheltenham Chronicle*, 13 August 1829, p. 4. Also Tabitha Cadbury, 'Amulets: The Material Evidence', in Hutton

(ed.), *Physical Evidence for Ritual Acts*, pp. 118–208. Owen Davies and Timothy Easton, 'Cunning-folk and the Production of Magical Artefacts', in ibid., pp. 209–31.

67. Alex M. McAldowie, 'Personal Experiences in Witchcraft', *Folklore*, 7 (1896), pp. 309–10. 'Society of Antiquaries of Scotland', *Glasgow Herald*, 11 April 1893. Donald Wintersgill, *Scottish Antiques* (London, 1977), pp. 33–4. Jenni Calder, *The Wealth of a Nation in the National Museums of Scotland* (Edinburgh and Glasgow, 1989), p. 92. Calder maintains the term 'luckenbooth brooch' wasn't much used until the late nineteenth century. However, the name was used in the 1840s by R.R. M'Ian, *Gaëlic Gatherines; or The Highlanders: at Home, on the Hearth, the River, and the Loch* (London, 1845), p. 6. Jewellers appear to have advertised them as 'silver heart brooches' and 'Queen Mary brooches'. See 'Robert Naughten, Jeweller, Silversmith, & Manufacturer of Highland Ornaments', *Inverness Courier*, 24 July 1862, p. 1. For the 'fairy hearts' name see 'Queries: LX Brooches', *Northern Notes and Queries: or, The Scottish Antiquary*, vols 1 and 2 (1886–8), p. 150.

68. McAldowie, 'Personal Experiences in Witchcraft'. A nice image of a good example is included in M'Ian, *Gaëlic Gatherines*, p. 6.

69. 'Belief in Witchcraft', *Newcastle Courant*, 21 February 1829, p. 2. 'Witches' Spell of the Present Day', *Sherborne Mercury*, 4 October 1830, p. 2.

70. These stories had an enduring appeal. For examples, 'Scotch Notes', *Belfast Weekly News*, 26 March 1887, p. 8. 'Flora MacDonald: Story of Prince Charlie Relics', *The Scotsman*, 18 May 1937, p. 11. Interestingly, in America, luckenbooth brooches went on to influence the silver production of the Iroquois and other First Nations, where they became a symbol for bravery. On which, see 'Reviews', *Material History Bulletin*, 14 (spring 1982), pp. 92–3.

71. This apparently happened to a Scottish folklorist from Aberdeenshire, when he was a baby, during the early nineteenth century. See McAldowie, 'Personal Experiences in Witchcraft', pp. 309–10.

72. On these impulses in the atmosphere see G.M. Young, *Portrait of an Age* (1937: London, 2002), Chapter 2. Asa Briggs, *The Age of Improvement: 1783–1867* (1959: London, 1974), Chapter 4, part 4, 'The March of the Intellect', and Chapter 8, part 1, 'The Cult of Progress'. Also the various essays in T.C.W. Blanning and Peter Wende (eds), *Reform in Great Britain and Germany: 1750–1850* (Oxford, 1999).

73. Keith Thomas, *Man and the Natural World: Changing Attitudes in England 1500–1800* (London, 1983), pp. 144, 149, 159.

74. *Hampshire Chronicle*, 9 January 1809. *Manchester Mercury*, 28 April 1812.

75. *Chester Courant*, 22 May 1810. *Lancaster Gazette*, 19 May 1810; 18 August 1810. *Cheltenham Chronicle*, 14 June 1810.

76. *Glasgow Herald*, 19 June 1826. *Inverness Courier*, 21 June 1826.

77. Owen Davies, *Popular Magic: Cunning-folk in English History* (2003: London, 2007), pp. viii–x, 1–5. Willem de Blécourt, 'Witch Doctors, Soothsayers and Priests: On Cunning Folk in European Historiography and Tradition', *Social History*, 19 (1994), pp. 285–303.

78. Timothy R. Tangherlini, '"How Do You Know She's a Witch?" Witches, Cunning Folk, and Competition in Denmark', *Western Folklore*, 59 (2000), p. 280.

79. 'Witchcraft and Astrology', *Taunton Courier*, 18 March 1819, p. 2.

80. *Ipswich Journal*, 21 March 1801. *Hampshire Chronicle*, 16 November 1807. *Leeds Mercury*, 29 October 1808. *Hull Packet*, 1 November 1808. *Lancaster Gazette*, 18 November 1809. *Stamford Mercury*, 23 July 1813. *Bury and Norwich Post*, 28 July 1819. *Stamford Mercury*, 9 April 1819.

81. On the 1824 Vagrancy Act see Davies, *Witchcraft, Magic and Culture*, pp. 54–75.

82. North Yorkshire Record Office, MS QSB 1797 4/6; QSB 1797 4/8/1. J.C. Atkinson, *Forty Years in a Moorland Parish: Reminiscences and Researches in Danby in Cleveland* (London and New York, 1891), pp. 111–12.

83. *Yorkshire Gazette*, 9 November 1850. Ronald Hutton, *The Triumph of the Moon: A History of Modern Pagan Witchcraft* (Oxford, 1997), p. 88. William Henderson, *Notes on the Folklore of the Northern Counties of England* (London, 1879), pp. 215–18.

84. Atkinson, *Forty Years in a Moorland Parish*, pp. 114–24.

85. I explore this topic at length in Chapter 5. For now see Robert L. DuPont, 'The Healing Power of Faith: Science Explores Medicine's Last Great Frontier', *American Journal of Psychiatry*, 158 (2001), pp. 1347–8. Michael Lyvers, Norman Barling and Jill Harding-Clark, 'Effect of Belief in "Psychic Healing" on Self-reported Pain in Chronic Pain Sufferers', *Journal of Psychosomatic Research*, 60 (2006), pp. 59–61. Frederic A. Ailing, 'The Healing Effects of Belief in Medical Practices and Spirituality', *Explore*, 11 (2015), pp. 273–80.

86. North Yorkshire Record Office, MS QSB 1797 4/6; QSB 1797 4/8/1; QSB 1814 1/6/5.

87. Atkinson, *Forty Years in a Moorland Parish*, p. 110.

88. Richard Baker, alias old Baker senior, died in 1819, aged 70. For an obituary see 'Old Baker', in *Taunton Courier*, 22 April 1819, p. 6. For further reports on his son and successor, Benjamin, see 'Taunton', *Taunton Courier*, 2 July 1834.

89. *Morning Chronicle*, 8 April 1823. *Devizes and Wiltshire Gazette*, 10 April 1823.

90. 'March of Credulity', *Cheltenham Chronicle*, 13 August 1829, p. 4.

91. In 1814 a landowner from Dellington, Somerset, estimated that 'common wages in that neighbourhood' were 9 shillings a week. See *Report from the Select Committee of the House of Commons on Petitions Relating to the Corn Laws of this Kingdom* (London, 1814), p. 68.

92. *Westmorland Gazette*, 7 November 1818. 'Historical Notices of the Popular Superstitions, Traditions, and Customs of Tiviotdale', *The Scots Magazine* (June 1820), p. 534.

93. Natalie Armitage, 'European and African Figural Ritual Magic: The Beginnings of the Voodoo Doll Myth', in Natalie Armitage and Ceri Houlbrook (eds), *The Materiality of Magic: An Artifactual Investigation into Ritual Practices and Popular Beliefs* (Oxford, 2015), pp. 85–101. Ronald Hutton, *The Witch: A History of Fear, from Ancient Times to the Present* (New Haven, CT, 2017), p. 46. Erica Reiner, 'Astral Magic in Babylonia', *Transactions of the American Philosophical Society*, New Series, 85 (1995), p. 101. Christopher A. Faraone, 'Binding and Burying the Forces of Evil: The Defensive Use of "Voodoo Dolls" in Ancient Greece', *Classical Antiquity*, 10 (1991), esp. pp. 190, 196, 201.

94. 'Curious Remains of Popular Superstitions in Forfarshire', *The Scots Magazine* (February 1818), p. 116.

95. 'The Witch of Moorgate', *Evening Mail*, 3 September 1821. 'A Witch', *Stamford Mercury*, 7 September 1821. The victim of Mary Colder, the 'witch of Moorgate', Miss Walcot, her upstairs neighbour, made the doll.

96. 'Curious Remains of Popular Superstitions in Forfarshire', *The Scots Magazine* (February 1818), p. 116. Also see, for instance, the shapeshifting stories about early nineteenth-century witches in W.J. Monk, *History of Witney* ([Witney], 1894), p. 53.

97. *Cambridge Chronicle and Journal*, 16 June 1813.

98. 'Superstition', *Bristol Mirror*, 3 July 1813, p. 3.

99. On which see Brian Hoggard, 'Concealed Animals', in Hutton (ed.), *Physical Evidence for Ritual Acts*, pp. 106–10. Margaret M. Howard, 'Dried Cats', *Man*, 51 (1951), pp. 149–51. Finds of dried cats are sometimes mentioned in local folklore accounts: for instance Christine Bloxham, *Folklore of Oxfordshire* (Gloucestershire, 2005), p. 78, mentions a cat from a house in Wheatley, built in the 1930s. For concealed cats in the United States, with a review of the European evidence, see M. Chris Manning, 'The Material Culture of Ritual Concealments in the United States', *Historical Archaeology*, 48 (2014), pp. 52–83.

100. On which see the excellent discussion in Hutton, *The Witch*, Chapter 10. Also M.G. Marwick, 'The Social Context of Cewa Witch Beliefs', *Africa*, 22 (1952), p. 121. Isaac Schapera, 'Sorcery and Witchcraft in Bechuanaland', *African Affairs*, 51 (1952), p. 44. U.A. Casal, 'The Goblin Fox and Badger and Other Witch Animals of Japan', *Folklore Studies*, 18 (1959), esp. pp. 20–1, 24, 45, 67.

101. Sharpe, *Instruments of Darkness*, pp. 71–4. L.F. Newman, 'Some Notes on the History and Practice of Witchcraft in the Eastern Counties', *Folklore*, 57 (1946), pp. 23–4, 32–3.

The topic is explored from a Modern Pagan perspective by Emma Wilby, *Cunning Folk and Familiar Spirits: Shamanistic Visionary Traditions in Early Modern British Witchcraft and Magic* (2005: Brighton and Portland, OR, 2010).

102. Hutton, *The Witch*, pp. 273–7. Sharpe, *Instruments of Darkness*, pp. 71–4.

103. 'Pro Rege Lege et Grege', *Perthshire Courier*, 30 July 1830, p. 3. See the report on 'the new drama of The Witch-Finder', in 'Drury-Lane Theatre', *Morning Chronicle*, 21 December 1829, p. 3. For literary recycling, 'Extract from the Church Book at Bottesford', *Leicester Chronicle*, 8 April 1826, p. 4.

104. Sharpe, *Instruments of Darkness*, pp. 47–50. L. Normand and G. Roberts (eds), *Witchcraft in Early Modern Scotland: James VI's Demonology and the North Berwick Witches* (Exeter, 2000). Julian Goodare, 'The Framework for Scottish Witch-hunting in the 1590s', *Scottish Historical Review*, 81 (2002), pp. 240–50.

105. Jeffrey Burton Russell, *Witchcraft in the Middle Ages* (1974: Ithaca, NY, and London, 1984), p. 54. Robert Thurston, *The Witch Hunts: A History of the Witch Persecutions in Europe and North America* (3rd edn, Abingdon, 2009), p. 89. Malcolm Gaskill, *Witchcraft: A Very Short Introduction* (Oxford, 2010), p. 19.

106. John Bellamy (trans.) *The Holy Bible, Newly Translated from the Original Hebrew: with Notes Critical and Explanatory* (London, 1818), p. 333, n. 31.

107. Rev. John Brown, *The Self-interpreting Bible, Containing the Old and New Testaments* (new edn, Edinburgh, 1831), pp. 138, 321, 429, 479, 718.

108. *Yorkshire Gazette*, 19 August 1826.

109. For the best account of the manufacture and adoption of glassware see Maxine Berg, *Luxury and Pleasure in Eighteenth-century Britain* (2005: Oxford, 2007), pp. 117–26. Also Lorna Weatherill, *Consumer Behaviour and Material Culture in Britain: 1660–1760* (2nd edn, London and New York, 1998), pp. 28–30, 55.

110. William Monster, 'Toads and Eucharists: The Male Witches of Normandy, 1564–1660', *French Historical Studies*, 2 (1997), pp. 563–95. Michael D. Bailey, 'From Sorcery to Witchcraft: Clerical Conceptions of Magic in the Later Middle Ages', *Speculum*, 76 (2001), p. 970. Lucinda Cole, *Imperfect Creatures: Vermin, Literature, and the Science of Life, 1600–1740* (Ann Arbor, MI, 2016), pp. 27–34. William G. Pooley, 'Can the "Peasant" Speak? Witchcraft and Silence in Guillaume Cazaux's "The Mass of Saint Sécaire"', *Western Folklore*, 71 (2012), p. 101. T.P. Vukanović, 'Witchcraft in the Central Balkans, I: Characteristics of Witches', *Folklore*, 100 (1989), pp. 12–13. Douglas Gifford, 'Witchcraft and the Problem of Evil in a Basque Village', *Folklore*, 90 (1979), p. 14. Clive Holmes, 'Women: Witness and Witches', *Past and Present*, 140 (1993), pp. 67–8.

111. Renate Blumenfeld-Kosinskim, 'The Strange Case of Ermine de Reims (c. 1347–1396): A Medieval Woman between Demons and Saints', *Speculum*, 85 (2010), pp. 343–8. Fabián Alejandro Campagne, 'Demonology at a Crossroads: The Visions of Ermine de Reims and the Image of the Devil on the Eve of the Great European Witch-hunt', *Church History*, 80 (2011), pp. 472, 489–90. Francis B. Brévart, 'Between Medicine, Magic, and Religion: Wonder Drugs in German Medico Pharmaceutical Treatises of the Thirteenth to the Sixteenth Centuries', *Speculum*, 83 (2008), pp. 18, 37, 49.

112. Esther Cohen, 'Law, Folklore and Animal Lore', *Past and Present*, 110 (1986), p. 29. David B. Kaufman, 'Poisons and Poisoning among the Romans', *Classical Philology*, 27 (1932), p. 163. Diana Paton, 'Witchcraft, Poison, Law, and Atlantic Slavery', *William and Mary Quarterly*, 69 (2012), p. 240.

113. *Hampshire Chronicle*, 9 January 1809. This gift had, it seems, been in turn given to that friend by the 'witch'.

114. For witchcraft's association with gift-giving during the early modern period see Lyndal Roper, *Witch Craze: Terror and Fantasy in Baroque Germany* (New Haven, CT, and London, 2004), pp. 4, 77, 128, 171. Alison Rowlands, *Witchcraft Narratives in Germany: Rothenburg, 1561–1652* (Manchester and New York, 2003), pp. 153–4.

115. *Morning Chronicle*, 30 March 1829; 14 August 1829.

116. *Westmorland Gazette*, 7 November 1818.
117. *Leeds Intelligencer*, 13 November 1828. *Chester Chronicle*, 21 November 1828.
118. Gul Hwang et al., 'Influence of Psychological Stress on Physical Pain', *Stress and Health*, 24 (2008), p. 159. Bever, *The Realities of Witchcraft and Popular Magic*, esp. pp. 1–37.
119. Joanna Bourke, 'Languages of Pain', *The Lancet*, 379 (2012), pp. 2420–1; *The Story of Pain: From Prayer to Painkillers* (Oxford, 2014), pp. 53, 57, 79, 135, 150.
120. Deborah Willis, 'The Witch-family in Elizabethan and Jacobean Print Culture', *Journal for Early Modern Studies*, 13 (2013), pp. 4–31. Alison Rowlands, 'Witchcraft and Old Women in Early Modern Germany', *Past and Present*, 173 (2001), pp. 81–2. Per Zachrisson, 'Witchcraft and Witchcraft Cleansing in Southern Zimbabwe', *Anthropos*, 102 (2007), p. 39. Robert Gabriel Mac-Machado, 'Witchcraft and Witchcraft Cleansing among the Vasava Bhils', *Anthropos*, 105 (2010), p. 193. Hans Sebald, 'Franconian Witchcraft: The Demise of a Folk Magic', *Anthropological Quarterly*, 53 (1980), pp. 175–6.
121. *Norfolk Chronicle*, 2 December 1809.
122. Mitchell, 'A Case of Witchcraft Assault in Early Nineteenth-century England as Ostensive Action'. Davies, *Witchcraft, Magic and Culture*, pp. 49, 111–12, 195, 197.
123. *Cambridge Chronicle and Journal*, 16 June 1813.
124. *Devizes and Wiltshire Gazette*, 6 May 1824.
125. *Kentish Gazette*, 4 September 1812.
126. *Chester Chronicle*, 24 April 1812.
127. *Morning Chronicle*, 8 April 1823. *Devizes and Wiltshire Gazette*, 10 April 1823. *Chester Chronicle*, 21 November 1828.
128. *Morning Post*, 17 November 1826. *Inverness Courier*, 22 November 1826.
129. *Kentish Gazette*, 4 September 1812.
130. The fact that he made this point in a publication designed to give helpful advice to ministers and their families tells us something about his perception of its public interest.
131. John Anderson, 'United Parishes of Stronsay and Eday', in John Sinclair (ed.), *The Statistical Account of Scotland: Drawn Up from the Communication of the Ministers of the Different Parishes*, vol. 15 (Edinburgh, 1795), pp. 430–2.
132. Ibid., p. 432.
133. Stuart Clark, *Thinking with Demons: The Idea of Witchcraft in Early Modern Europe* (Oxford, 1999), pp. x, 684–5.
134. For instance, Walter Scott (ed.), *A Collection of Scarce and Valuable Tracts, on the Most Interesting and Entertaining Subjects* (London, 1810), p. 3. David Webster, *A Collection of Rare and Curious Tracts on Witchcraft and the Second Sight; with an Original Essay on Witchcraft* (Edinburgh, 1820).
135. 'Breaking the Spell', *Atheneum, or, Spirit of the English Magazines*, 2(9) (Boston, 15 July 1829), p. 300. At least one edition of *Satan's Invisible World* was published by the London printer James Clarke in 1814.
136. For an excellent discussion of this hitherto little-studied genre see Jonathan Barry, 'News from the Invisible World: The Publishing History of Tales of the Supernatural c. 1660–1832', in Jonathan Barry, Owen Davies and Cornelie Usborne (eds), *Cultures of Witchcraft in Europe from the Middle Ages to the Present* (Basingstoke, 2018), pp. 179–213.
137. *Lackington, Hughes, Harding, Mavor, and Jones's General Catalogue of Books in the Ancient and Modern Languages, and Various Classes of Literature: For the Year 1819* (London, 1819), pp. 335–43.
138. James Heaton, *Farther Observations on Demoniac Possession and Animadversions on Some of the Curious Arts of Superstition* (London, 1822), pp. 56, 58, 87–90.
139. On Harries see Richard C. Allen, 'Wizards or Charlatans, Doctors or Herbalists? An Appraisal of the "Cunning Men" of Cwrt Y Cadno, Camarthenshire', *North American Journal of Welsh Studies*, 1(2) (2001), pp. 68–85.
140. 'A Book of Incantations', National Library of Wales MS. 11117B, p. 24.

141. Peter Buchan's *Witchcraft Detected and Prevented; or, the School of the Black Art Newly Opened* (Peterhead, 1824). Owen Davies, *Grimoires: A History of Magic Books* (Oxford, 2009), p. 134.

142. Buchan, *Witchcraft Detected and Prevented*, p. iv.

143. See Arthur Palmer Hudson, 'The "Superstitious" Lord Byron', *Studies in Philology*, 63 (1966), pp. 708–21.

144. Henry Moore, *The Life of the Rev. John Wesley*, vol. 2 (London, 1825), p. 445. *Morning Chronicle*, 10 April 1823.

145. Sylvia Bowerbank, 'Southcott, Joanna (1750–1814)', *Oxford Dictionary of National Biography* (Oxford, 2004), http://www.oxforddnb.com/view/article/26050 (accessed 11 June 2014).

146. Joanna Southcott, *Letters and Communications of Joanna Southcott, Prophetess of Exeter; lately written to Jane Townley* (Stourbridge, 1804), pp. 78–9.

147. Joanna Southcott, *Astrology and Witchcraft* (Bradford, Wiltshire, 1853).

148. Walter Stephens, 'The Sceptical Tradition', in Brian P. Levack (ed.), *The Oxford Handbook of Witchcraft in Early Modern Europe and Colonial America* (Oxford, 2013), p. 117.

149. Celestina Wroth, ' "To Root the Old Woman Out of Our Minds": Women Educationists and Plebeian Culture in Late Eighteenth-century Britain', *Eighteenth-Century Life*, 30 (2006), pp. 48–73.

150. John Brand, *Observations on Popular Antiquities: Including the Whole of Mr. Bourne's Antiquitates Vulgares* (Newcastle and London, 1777), pp. 318–20. Paul Langford, *A Polite and Commercial People: England 1727–1783* (Oxford, 1989), p. 281.

151. Susan Pedersen, 'Hannah More Meets Simple Simon: Tracts, Chapbooks, and Popular Culture in Late Eighteenth-century England', *Journal of British Studies*, 25 (1986), pp. 91, 102.

152. John Brand, *Observations on Popular Antiquities: Chiefly Illustrating the Origin of Our Vulgar Customs, Ceremonies, and Superstitions*, ed. Henry Ellis (London, 1813), vol. 2, p. 367. Naylor, *Inanity and Mischief*, especially pp. iv, ix, 35, 40, 56. Paterson, *A Belief in Witchcraft Unsupported by Scripture*. I. Mann, *Saul's Visit to the Witch of Endor Considered* (Shipley, 1852), pp. 22–3, 6, 20–1. For biographical details of the Rev. Mann see 'Calendar of Letters, 1742–1831, Collected by Isaac Mann', *Baptist Quarterly*, 6 (1932), p. 39. Rev. W. Steadman, 'A Brief Memoir of the Late Rev. Isaac Mann', *The Baptist Magazine*, February 1832, pp. 45–9.

153. For some examples see *Jackson's Oxford Journal*, 31 July 1819. *Stamford Mercury*, 1 November 1822. *Exeter and Plymouth Gazette*, 26 May 1827.

154. Owen Davies, 'Newspapers and the Popular Belief in Witchcraft and Magic in the Modern Period', *Journal of British Studies*, 37 (1998), p. 152.

155. Davies, 'Newspapers', p. 142.

156. *Bath Chronicle and Weekly Gazette*, 1 December 1825. Among other things, 'the pestle and mortar fell from the chimney-piece, the cream-jug leaped from the table, a reap-hook flew at the leg of one of the family – a knife at another, and the whole contents of the pantry found legs and walked into the kitchen'. For similar reports see *Bath Chronicle and Weekly Gazette*, 10 November 1825. *North Devon Journal* 11 October 1827. *Morning Post*, 12 January 1825. *Bristol Mercury*, 29 August 1825. *Northampton Mercury*, 3 September 1825.

157. *Morning Chronicle*, 29 December 1824.

158. Davies, *Witchcraft, Magic and Culture*, p. 1.

159. Ibid., p. 77.

3 TOUGH SUPERSTITIONS: 1830–60

1. Kirsti M. Jylhä et al., 'Denial of Anthropogenic Climate Change: Social Dominance Orientation Helps Explain the Conservative Male Effect in Brazil and Sweden', *Personality and Individual Differences*, 98 (2016), pp. 184–7. Riley E. Dunlap, 'Climate Change Skepticism and Denial: An Introduction', *American Behavioral Scientist*, 56 (2013), pp. 691–8.

2. Bandar A. Alsubaie, 'Countering Terrorism in the Kingdom of Saudi Arabia: An Examination of the Prevention, Rehabilitation, and After-care Strategy (PRAC)', PhD thesis, University of New Haven (2016), esp. pp. 81–113, 180–200.

3. Kate Ferguson, *Countering Violent Extremism through Media Communication Strategies: A Review of the Evidence* (Partnership for Conflict, Crime and Security Research, 1 March 2016), p. 15.

4. This case study is based on a range of contemporary newspaper reports, later recollections, and folklore enquiries. Namely, Edgar Hewlett, *Personal Recollections of the Little Tew Ghost, Reviewed in Connection with the Lancashire Bogie, and the Table-talking and Spirit-rapping of the Present Day* (London, 1854). *Oxford University and City Herald*, 15 December 1838; 22 December 1838. *Oxford City and County Chronicle*, 6 April 1839. *Jackson's Oxford Journal*, 24 November 1883; 23 February 1884; 1 March 1884. Percy Manning, 'Stray Notes on Oxfordshire Folklore (Continued)', *Folklore*, 14 (1903), pp. 71–2.

5. Ann (Hannah) and Thomas married in May 1837. The 1841 Census records their daughter Mary's age as 4, meaning that Ann gave birth to her the same year.

6. In rural Kent, 40.7 per cent of brides were pregnant when they married. A further 9 per cent had already given birth. See Barry Reay, *Microhistories: Demography, Society and Culture in Rural England, 1800–1930* (Cambridge, 1996), pp. 180–1.

7. *Oxford City and County Chronicle*, 13 May 1848. *Jackson's Oxford Journal*, 26 May 1855. *Oxford City and County Chronicle*, 2 May 1857. *Jackson's Oxford Journal*, 25 September 1869. *Oxford Times*, 20 December 1873.

8. *Lloyd's Weekly Newspaper*, 11 September 1853. *Reynolds's Newspaper*, 11 September 1853. S.C. Williams, *Religious Belief and Popular Culture in Southwark, c. 1880–1939* (Oxford, 1999), p. 80. Owen Davies, *The Haunted: A Social History of Ghosts* (London, 2007), p. 91. Karl Bell, *The Magical Imagination: Magic and Modernity in Urban Britain 1780–1914* (Cambridge, 2012), pp. 201–3.

9. *Jackson's Oxford Journal*, 24 November 1883; 23 February 1884; 1 March 1884.

10. Manning, 'Stray Notes on Oxfordshire Folklore (Continued)', p. 72.

11. George Borrow, *Wild Wales: Its People, Language, and Scenery* (3rd edn, London, 1872), Chapter 55, pp. 326–31.

12. Ibid., pp. 11, 38, 66, 87–8, 338–9.

13. Roy Foster, *Modern Ireland: 1600–1972* (London, 1989), pp. 323–5.

14. *Census of the British Empire: Compiled from Official Returns for the Year 1861. With its Colonies and Foreign Possessions. Part 2: Scotland, Ireland, and the British Colonies* (London, 1864), p. 157. Donald M. MacRaild, *The Irish Diaspora in Britain, 1750–1939* (2nd edn, Basingstoke, 2011), esp. Chapters 2 and 3.

15. *Sheffield Independent*, 1 August 1840.

16. *Merthyr Telegraph*, 16 January 1858.

17. The Irish fortune-teller was so familiar to the Victorians that she became a stock character in art, literature and on the stage. See Anon., *Tim Doolan: The Irish Emigrant* (London, 1869), Chapters 13 and 14. For plays see *The Trafalgar Medal; or, The Irish Fortune-teller*, advertised in *The Morning Advertiser*, 18 June 1857. For some real-life cases see *Bedfordshire Mercury*, 8 February 1862. *Sunderland Daily Echo and Shipping Gazette*, 11 March 1885.

18. Miss Mason, *Kate Gearey; or, Irish Life in London. A Take of 1849* (London, 1853), pp. 29–30.

19. *Dundee Courier*, 16 December 1871. John H. Barbour, 'Some Country Remedies and Their Uses', *Folklore*, 8 (1897), p. 390. Niall Mac Coitir, *Irish Wild Plants: Myths, Legends and Folklore* (Cork, 2006), p. 123.

20. Lynn Hollen Lees, *Exiles of Erin: Irish Migrants in Victorian London* (Manchester, 1979), p. 188.

21. *The Globe*, 19 October 1860.

22. Borrow, *Wild Wales* (1872), p. 331.

23. The best primary source on this topic is *First Report from His Majesty's Commissioners for inquiring into the Condition of the Poorer Classes in Ireland, with Appendix (A) and Supplement* (House of Commons, 1835), esp. pp. 449, 525, 530, 537, 550, 565, 577, 628, 639, 648, 687.
24. *Morning Post*, 27 October 1848.
25. K. Theodore Hoppen, *Elections, Politics, and Society in Ireland: 1832–1885* (Oxford, 1984), pp. 212–13.
26. *Bell's Weekly Messenger*, 11 May 1850. *Morning Post*, 30 October 1851. *Norfolk Chronicle*, 18 March 1854.
27. *Lloyd's Weekly Newspaper*, 16 April 1848
28. *Chelmsford Chronicle*, 3 June 1836.
29. Ronald Hutton, 'Witch-hunting in Celtic Societies', *Past and Present*, 212 (2011), pp. 61, 63, 67. John O'Donovan, 'Folk-lore. No. II. On the Traditions of the County of Kilkenny', *Transactions of the Kilkenny Archaeological Society*, 1 (1851), p. 365.
30. The best account of these curses is William Carleton, 'An Essay on Irish Swearing', in *Traits and Stories of the Irish Peasantry* (2nd edn, Dublin, 1834), vol. 1, esp. pp. 348–9.
31. *Morning Chronicle*, 19 July 1823.
32. John Belchem, 'The Immigrant Alternative: Ethnic and Sectarian Mutuality among the Liverpool Irish during the Nineteenth Century', in Owen Ashton, Robert Fyson and Stephen Roberts (eds), *The Duty of Discontent: Essays for Dorothy Thompson* (London, 1995), pp. 231–50.
33. For the best account of the cursing well and its dark history see Richard Suggett, *A History of Magic and Witchcraft in Wales* (Stroud, 2008), Chapter 6.
34. Keith Thomas, *Religion and the Decline of Magic: Studies in Popular Beliefs in Sixteenth and Seventeenth-century England* (1971: London, 1991), pp. 599–611.
35. Marc Drogin, *Anathema! Medieval Scribes and the History of Book Curses* (New York, 1983). Kevin J. Hayes, *Folklore and Book Culture* (Knoxville, TN, 1997), esp. Chapter 7. Patricia Crain, *Reading Children: Literacy, Property, and the Dilemmas of Childhood in Nineteenth-century America* (Philadelphia, PA, 2016), pp. 116–17. Holbrook Jackson, *The Anatomy of Bibliomania* (Urbana and Chicago, IL, 2001), pp. 370–1.
36. *Norfolk Chronicle*, 24 April 1852. *Bury and Norwich Post*, 24 March 1852; 21 April 1852. John Venn and J.A. Venn (eds), *Alumni Cantabrigienses*, vol. 2, part 4 (Cambridge, 2011), p. 450. *Stamford Mercury*, 2 April 1852.
37. Only one really literary figure professed the reality of witchcraft, in an unreconstructed form, and then only in private: the Rev. Robert Stephen Hawker, poet, opium eater (admittedly, not unusual at the time) and 'one of the most superstitious Englishmen that ever lived'. Living in witchy western England, in the coastal Cornish parish of Morwenstow, Mr Hawker undoubtedly believed in witchcraft, blaming the death of one of his ewes on the evil eye. But his first biographer, the Rev. S. Baring-Gould, exaggerated when he claimed Hawker admitted 'without questioning, the stories he heard of witchcraft, and the power of the evil eye'. See 'A Plea for Superstition', *The Spectator*, 23 March 1896, p. 15. S. Baring-Gould, *The Vicar of Morwenstow: A Life of Robert Stephen Hawker* (New York, 1892), p. 161. Also C.E. Byles (ed.), *The Life and Letters of R.S. Hawker (Sometime Vicar of Morwenstow)* (Edinburgh, 1906), pp. 122–4. The letter in which Hawker attributes the sheep's death to the evil eye is quoted in Piers Brendon, *Hawker of Morwenstow: Portrait of a Victorian Eccentric* (London, 1975).
38. Reported in *Leeds Intelligencer*, 4 November 1830. *York Herald*, 6 November 1830.
39. *The Suffolk Chronicle*, 25 August 1855.
40. Martin Hewitt, *The Dawn of the Cheap Press in Victorian Britain: The End of the 'Taxes on Knowledge', 1849–1869* (London, 2014), p. 98.
41. *Hammond's List of London and Provincial Newspapers* (January, 1850), p. 8.
42. *Suffolk Chronicle*, 25 April 1857.
43. *Stamford Mercury*, 21 December 1838. *Exeter and Plymouth Gazette*, 20 April 1839; 14 November 1840. *Sussex Advertiser*, 8 February 1841. *Royal Cornwall Gazette*,

12 February 1841. *Wiltshire Independent*, 25 March 1841. *Bradford Observer*, 20 October 1842; 16 February 1843. *Bristol Mercury*, 15 October 1842.

44. *Hull Packet*, 14 May 1841. The paper was outraged by the fact 'that a clergyman should, directly or indirectly, inculcate a belief in the doctrines of second-sight, or witchcraft'.

45. Helen Groth, *Moving Images: Nineteenth-century Reading and Screen Practices* (Edinburgh, 2013), pp. 84, 98 n. 18.

46. Walter Scott, *Letters on Demonology and Witchcraft, addressed to J.G. Lockhart* (London, 1830), p. 3.

47. Ibid., p. 54.

48. John Harris, *My Autobiography* (London, 1882), pp. 6, 39, 42–5.

49. *London Standard*, 9 June 1838. *Nairnshire Telegraph and General Advertiser*, 22 September 1858. James Augustus St John, *The Education of the People* (London, 1858), p. 29.

50. *Liverpool Mercury*, 10 April 1857.

51. *The Oxford City and County Chronicle*, 7 October 1837. *Lincolnshire Chronicle*, 11 June 1841. *Exeter and Plymouth Gazette*, 26 February 1848. *Western Times*, 22 November 1851. For similar remarks, calling on the clergy as a body to apply themselves to the eradication of superstition see *Stamford Mercury*, 14 May 1841.

52. See, for instance, John Skinner, *The Journal of a Somerset Rector 1803–1834*, ed. Howard Coombs and Peter Coombs (Oxford, 1984), pp. 400–1.

53. *Exeter and Plymouth Gazette*, 9 May 1840.

54. J. Mitchell and Jn. Dickie, *The Philosophy of Witchcraft* (Paisley, 1839), p. 358.

55. Ibid., p. 358.

56. On which see Richard Suggett, *A History of Magic and Witchcraft in Wales*, Chapter 6.

57. *Stamford Mercury*, 5 March 1841.

58. *Bristol Mercury*, 20 July 1839.

59. For eighteenth- and early nineteenth-century attitudes see Michael Snape, *The Church of England in Industrialising Society: The Lancashire Parish of Whalley in the Eighteenth Century* (Woodbridge, 2003), pp. 51, 64, 65–6, 71. Owen Davies, 'Decriminalising the Witch: The Origin of and Response to the 1736 Witchcraft Act', in John Newton and Jo Bath (eds), *Witchcraft and the Act of 1604* (Leiden, 2008), p. 225. Jeremy Black, *Eighteenth-century Britain, 1688–1783* (2nd edn, Basingstoke, 2008), p. 139.

60. *Western Times*, 18 August 1838. For similar complaints see *Sussex Advertiser*, 16 August 1841. William Ferguson, *The Impending Dangers of Our Country; or, Hidden Things Brought to Light* (London, 1848), pp. 96, 111. *Western Times*, 13 June 1835.

61. As reported in the *Taunton Courier and Western Advertiser*, 29 May 1839; *Caledonian Mercury*, 27 May 1839; and *Newcastle Courant*, 31 May 1839.

62. Barry Reay, *Rural Englands: Labouring Lives in the Nineteenth Century* (Basingstoke, 2004), p. 146.

63. *The Champion and Weekly Herald*, 11 June 1838, p. 129.

64. E.P. Thompson, 'The Crime of Anonymity', in *Albion's Fatal Tree: Crime and Society in Eighteenth-century England*, ed. Douglas Hay et al. (New York, 1975), p. 303.

65. *Reports of the Commissioners of Inquiry into the State of Education in Wales, Appointed by the Committee of Council of Education. Part 1: Carmarthen, Glamorgan, and Pembroke* (London, 1847), p. 6.

66. Robert Lee, *Unquiet Country: Voices of the Rural Poor, 1820–1880* (Macclesfield, 2005), esp. Chapters 2, 3 and 4; J.E. Archer, *'By Flash and a Scare': Incendiarism, Animal Maiming and Poaching in East Anglia, 1815–70* (Oxford, 1990).

67. Anne L. Helmreich, 'Reforming London: George Cruikshank and the Victorian Age', in Debra N. Mancoff and Dale J. Trela (eds), *Victorian Urban Settings: Essays on the Nineteenth-century City and Its Contexts* (New York and London, 1996), pp. 157–8.

68. Harold Perkin, 'An Age of Great Cities', in Mancoff and Trela, *Victorian Urban Settings*, p. 7.

69. *Huntingdon, Bedford and Peterborough Gazette*, 9 August 1834.

70. *Oxford University and City Herald*, 3 January 1835.

71. See *Nottingham Review and General Advertiser*, 28 May 1841 ('The reasoning of the bench seemed to have no effect on her superstitious feelings'). *Bradford Observer*, 3 November 1842 ('he left the Court firmly convinced, no doubt, that he was "a witched man"'). *Norfolk Chronicle*, 13 May 1843.

72. *Hull Packet*, 26 July 1833.

73. *Lincolnshire Chronicle*, 15 October 1852.

74. David Bromwich (ed.), *The Diary and Memoirs of John Allen Giles* (Somerset Record Society; Taunton, 2000), pp. 287–8.

75. *Stamford Mercury*, 5 March 1841.

76. James Rudge, 'Pretensions of the Bishops of Rome', *The Churchman*, July 1840, p. 282. Also see *Exeter and Plymouth Gazette*, 9 May 1840.

77. During the 1970s the French anthropologist Jeanne Favret-Saada found similar mental processes at work among witchcraft believers in rural Normandy. See Favret-Saada, 'Unbewitching as Therapy', in *American Ethnologist*, 16 (1989), p. 47, and *Deadly Words: Witchcraft in the Bocage*, trans. Catherine Cullen (Cambridge, 1980), pp. 175–85.

78. For an early nineteenth-century memory of this way of thinking see James Burn, *The Autobiography of a Beggar Boy*, ed. David Vincent (London, 1978), p. 67.

79. *Huntingdon, Bedford and Peterborough Gazette*, 9 August 1834. For other examples see William Lovett, *The Life and Struggles of William Lovett, In His Pursuit of Bread, Knowledge, and Freedom* (London, 1876), p. 14. *John O'Groat Journal*, 18 November 1842.

80. W.B. Stephens, *Education, Literacy and Society, 1830–70: The Geography of Diversity in Provincial England* (Manchester, 1987), Appendix D, p. 322. It is important to remember that more people could read than could write. Moreover, the habit of reading aloud, in the home, the pub and even the public square, meant that even those who could not read felt some of the benefits of literacy.

81. Reay, *Rural Englands*, p. 77.

82. Boyd Hilton, *A Mad, Bad, and Dangerous People? England 1783–1846* (Oxford, 2008), p. 175. Callum Brown, *The Death of Christian Britain: Understanding Secularisation 1800–2000* (2nd edn, Abingdon, 2009), p. 42.

83. Brown, *The Death of Christian Britain*, p. 43.

84. Hilton, *A Mad, Bad, and Dangerous People?*, p. 181.

85. Francis Knight, *The Nineteenth-century Church and English Society* (Cambridge, 1995), p. 38.

86. On which see Noel Annan, *Leslie Stephen: The Godless Victorian* (New York, 1984), Chapter 5.

87. Chapter 5 verse 20.

88. *The Pictorial Bible; Being The Old and New Testaments According to The Authorized Version: Illustrated with Many Hundred Wood-Cuts*, vol. 2 (London, 1838), pp. 74–5.

89. B.H. Cowper, 'Oxfordshire Legend in Stone', *Notes and Queries*, 168 (15 January 1853), pp. 58–9.

90. Mrs Bray, *A Description of the Part of Devonshire Bordering on the Tamar and the Tavy* (London, 1836), vol. 2, pp. 277–8. R.L. Tongue, *Somerset Folklore*, ed. K.M. Briggs (London, 1965), pp. 585–6, 224.

91. Thomas Sternberg, *The Dialect and Folk-lore of Northamptonshire* (London, 1851), pp. 148–50. *Choice Notes from 'Notes and Queries': Folklore* (London, 1859), pp. 81, 177–8, 186. *Yorkshire Gazette*, 5 February 1853.

92. W.H. Barrett, *Tales from the Fens*, ed. Enid Porter (1963; London, 1969), p. x.

93. Ibid., p. xi.

94. For example see W.H. Barrett, *More Tales from the Fens*, ed. Enid Porter (London, 1964), pp. 133–6.

95. William Godwin, *Lives of the Necromancers: or, an account of the most eminent persons in successive ages, who have claimed for themselves, or to whom has been imputed by others, the exercise of magical power* (London, 1834), p. 465.

96. J.W. and Anne Tibble (eds), *The Prose of John Clare* (London, 1951), pp. 39–40.

97. Burn, *Autobiography of a Beggar Boy*, p. 66.

98. Ibid., p. 68.

99. Charles Mackay, *Memoirs of Extraordinary Popular Delusions*, vol. 1 (London, 1841), pp. 184.

100. See Tibble and Tibble (eds), *The Prose of John Clare*, pp. 39, 43–4. *Manchester Times*, 4 February 1854.

101. Owen Davies, *Witchcraft, Magic and Culture: 1736–1951* (Manchester, 1999), pp. 153–7.

102. Katherine Anderson, *Predicting the Weather: Victorians and the Science of Meteorology* (Chicago, 2005), pp. 57–76.

103. *Stamford Mercury*, 22 December 1837.

104. Owen Davies, *Grimoires: A History of Magic Books* (Oxford, 2009), pp. 131–8.

105. *Bell's New Weekly Messenger*, 22 September 1839.

106. *The Quarterly Review*, 59(118) (1837), pp. 297–9. Also see J. Henry Harris, *My Devonshire Book: in the Land of Junket and Cream* (Plymouth, 1907), pp. 131–2.

107. *Exeter and Plymouth Gazette*, 15 March 1845. *Wells Journal* 27 January 1855. *Sheffield Daily Telegraph*, 21 August 1856. *North Devon Journal*, 20 November 1851.

108. *Chelmsford Chronicle*, 31 January 1834.

109. *Bell's Life in London and Sporting Chronicle*, 16 January 1831.

110. *London Standard*, 21 August 1832.

111. *Evening Mail*, 4 February 1842. *Reynolds's Newspaper*, 21 November 1858.

112. *Newcastle Courant*, 11 April 1835. *York Herald*, 6 August 1853. *Wolverhampton Chronicle and Staffordshire Advertiser*, 27 August 1856.

113. *Hull Packet*, 26 July 1833. *Public Ledger and Daily Advertiser*, 4 March 1831. *Cheltenham Chronicle*, 4 August 1857.

114. *Bolton Chronicle*, 22 March 1845. *Liverpool Mail*, 24 December 1853. *London Daily News*, 30 December 1853. *North Devon Journal*, 30 November 1843.

115. *Yorkshire Gazette*, 13 June 1857.

116. *Durham County Advertiser*, 25 February 1859.

117. *Leeds Times*, 6 June 1857.

118. *North Devon Journal*, 30 November 1843. *Leicestershire Mercury*, 16 December 1843. For a similar case see *Taunton Courier and Western Advertiser*, 14 March 1832.

119. *Huntingdon, Bedford and Peterborough Gazette*, 12 October 1833.

120. *Cambridge Chronicle and Journal*, 22 April 1843.

121. *Cambridge Independent Press*, 14 March 1846. *Bury and Norwich Post*, 18 March 1846.

122. *Inverness Courier*, 17 February 1830. *Western Times*, 5 July 1834. *North Wales Chronicle*, 1 July 1834. *Western Times*, 4 June 1842; 11 June 1842.

123. *Bradford Observer*, 7 September 1843. *Hull Packet*, 7 June 1844.

124. *Public Ledger and Daily Advertiser*, 4 March 1831.

125. *Lincolnshire Chronicle*, 15 October 1852.

126. *West Kent Guardian*, 30 May 1840. Copied from the *Falmouth Packet*.

127. *Hereford Times*, 23 September 1837. *Morning Chronicle*, 27 September 1837. *Bristol Mercury*, 30 September 1837.

128. Edward G. Flight, *The True Legend of St Dunstan and the Devil; Showing How the Horse-shoe Came to be a Charm Against Witchcraft* (2nd edn, London, 1852).

129. On this fascinating theme see the essays collected in Ronald Hutton (ed.), *Physical Evidence for Ritual Acts, Sorcery and Witchcraft in Christian Britain: A Feeling for Magic* (Basingstoke, 2016).

130. *Elgin Courant, and Morayshire Advertiser*, 24 June 1853. *Nottinghamshire Guardian*, 1 April 1852. *Worcester Journal*, 27 August 1853.

131. *Wells Journal*, 10 February 1855.

132. *Worcester Herald*, 23 January 1830. *Huntingdon, Bedford, and Peterborough Gazette*, 12 October 1833. *Hereford Journal*, 12 February 1834. *Chelmsford Chronicle*, 19 December 1834. *Hereford Times*, 14 February 1834. *Royal Cornwall Gazette*, 22 May 1840.

133. *Stonehaven Journal*, 5 July 1853.
134. *Wells Journal*, 10 February 1855.
135. *Devizes and Wiltshire Gazette*, 5 December 1833.
136. *Norfolk News*, 26 April 1851.
137. Favret-Saada, *Deadly Words*, pp. 68–9, 74, 76, 8–9.
138. *Worcester Journal*, 20 March 1857.
139. *Hull Packet*, 26 July 1833. *Huntingdon, Bedford and Peterborough Gazette*, 9 August 1834.
140. *Salisbury and Winchester Journal*, 25 May 1844.
141. *Public Ledger and Daily Advertiser*, 4 March 1831.
142. *North Devon Journal*, 14 April 1836.
143. *Caledonian Mercury*, 8 October 1849. *Stonehaven Journal*, 9 October 1849.
144. *Chester Chronicle*, 26 April 1833.
145. *The Ipswich Journal*, 15 August 1835.
146. *Inverness Courier*, 3 May 1837. *Sherborne Mercury*, 24 March 1849. For another version of image magic see *Exeter Flying Post*, 6 March 1856.
147. *Dorset County Chronicle*, 14 September 1854.
148. *Shrewsbury Chronicle*, 25 June 1852.
149. *The Ipswich Journal*, 5 May 1838.
150. *Morning Post*, 4 November 1856.
151. *Blackburn Standard*, 23 December 1835. *John O'Groat Journal*, 21 November 1856.
152. Davies, *Witchcraft, Magic and Culture*, p. 54.
153. *Liverpool Mercury*, 30 June 1843.
154. *Western Times*, 8 February 1845. *North Wales Chronicle*, 26 October 1850. *John O'Groat Journal*, 15 May 1840. For a similar complaint from Bolton in 1851, see *Bolton Chronicle*, 12 April 1851.
155. *Stamford Mercury*, 14 May 1841.
156. *The Quarterly Review*, 59(118) (1837), pp. 297–9. Harris, *My Devonshire Book*, pp. 131–2. *Bell's New Weekly Messenger*, 22 September 1839.
157. *Western Times*, 5 March 1842.
158. *Hull Packet*, 7 June 1844.
159. Hutton, *Triumph of the Moon*, p. 87.
160. *Liverpool Mercury*, 30 June 1843.
161. *Morning Chronicle*, 2 September 1858.
162. *Western Times*, 26 June 1841.
163. *Worcester Journal*, 28 July 1842. *Royal Cornwall Gazette*, 29 July 1842.
164. *Wolverhampton Chronicle and Staffordshire Advertiser*, 14 July 1841.
165. *Manchester Times*, 19 July 1845.
166. See *Devizes and Wiltshire Gazette*, 6 April 1843.
167. *Lincolnshire Chronicle*, 9 June 1843; 16 June 1843.
168. Clive Emsley, *Crime and Society in England: 1750–1900* (2nd edn, Harlow, 1996), pp. 216, 225–33.
169. D.J.V. Jones, 'The New Police, Crime and People in England and Wales, 1829–1888', *Transactions of the Royal Historical Society*, 5th Series, 33 (1983), p. 154. K. Theodore Hoppen, *The Mid-Victorian Generation 1846–1886* (Oxford, 1998), p. 116.
170. *Salisbury and Winchester Journal*, 3 April 1852.
171. *Liverpool Mail*, 24 December 1853. *London Daily News*, 30 December 1853.
172. *Leeds Times*, 4 March 1854.
173. For a wonderful exploration of this trial see Owen Davies, *Murder, Magic, Madness: The Victorian Trials of Dove and the Wizard* (Harlow, 2005).
174. *Morning Advertiser*, 15 August 1856. *Wells Journal*, 23 August 1856. *Leeds Mercury*, 16 August 1856.
175. *Exeter Flying Post*, 6 March 1856. *Hull Packet*, 26 September 1856.

176. *Norfolk News,* 17 October 1857.
177. *Exeter Flying Post,* 24 July 1851.
178. 'Darkness in Devonshire', *Household Words,* 5(117) (19 June 1852), p. 325. For earlier, similar comments see *North Devon Journal,* 29 April 1851.
179. Overwhelmingly these were attacks on supposed witches, though a handful of cases were attacks *by* people accused of witchcraft.
180. Owen Davies, *A People Bewitched: Witchcraft and Magic in Nineteenth-century Somerset* (Bruton, 1999), p. 113.
181. *York Herald,* 6 August 1853. *Essex Standard,* 22 September 1858.
182. *Dorset County Chronicle,* 26 August 1858.
183. *Hull Packet,* 26 September 1856.
184. For example, James Obelkevich, *Religion and Rural Society: South Lindsey 1825–1875* (Oxford, 1976), pp. 280–7. K. Theodore Hoppen prefers the term 'semi-pagan attitudes': see *The Mid-Victorian Generation,* p. 464.
185. Paul Kléber Monod, *Solomon's Secret Arts: The Occult in the Age of Enlightenment* (New Haven, CT, 2013), pp. 304–13.
186. Alison Winter, *Mesmerized: Powers of Mind in Victorian Britain* (Chicago, IL, and London, 1998), pp. 42–6. On the early history of mesmerism see Robert Darnton, *Mesmerism and the End of the Enlightenment in France* (Cambridge, MA, 1968), esp. pp. 3–4.
187. Steve Connor, 'All I Believed is True: Dickens Under the Influence', *19: Interdisciplinary Studies in the Long Nineteenth Century,* 10 (2010), http://nineteen.cch.kcl.ac.uk/index. php/19/article/view/530. Winter, *Mesmerized,* pp. 57–8, 250–2. Michael Shermer, *In Darwin's Shadow: The Life and Science of Alfred Russel Wallace* (Oxford, 2002), pp. 177–8.
188. *Carlisle Journal,* 20 July 1844.
189. *Bradford Observer; and Halifax, Huddersfield, and Keighley Reporter,* 11 January 1844.
190. *Sussex Advertiser,* 17 December 1844. For similar remarks see *Leicestershire Mercury,* 14 September 1844. *Nottingham Review and General Advertiser,* 18 October 1844. *John O' Groat Journal,* 26 September 1851. *Aberdeen Herald and General Advertiser,* 27 December 1851. *Dumfries and Galloway Standard,* 2 July 1851.
191. 'A New Explanation of Old Superstitions', *Chambers's Edinburgh Journal,* New Series, 1(24) (1844), p. 382.
192. *Evening Mail,* 4 May 1857.
193. *Stamford Mercury,* 2 July 1852.
194. *Eddowes's Shrewsbury Journal,* 20 June 1855.
195. *John O'Groat Journal,* 20 December 1850. For a similar case see *North Devon Journal,* 26 February 1852.
196. Winter, *Mesmerized,* pp. 260–2.
197. *The Gentleman's Magazine,* New Series, 20 (August, 1843), p. 170.
198. Quoted in Winter, *Mesmerized,* p. 262.
199. George Kitson Clark, *Churchmen and the Condition of England: 1832–1885* (London, 1973), p. 147.
200. Davies, *Murder, Magic, Madness,* p. 29
201. 'Matthew Hopkins Wanted', *Saturday Review,* 3(74) (28 March 1857), p. 284.
202. Robert Lee, *Rural Society and the Anglican Clergy, 1815–1914: Encountering and Managing the Poor* (Woodbridge, 2006), pp. 32, 146. Bell, *Magical Imagination,* p. 119.

4 SECRET BELIEFS: 1860–1900

1. *Evening Star,* 2 February 1888. *Manchester Courier and Lancashire General Advertiser,* 13 June 1890. *Burnley Express,* 3 February 1887. *Northwich Guardian,* 22 September 1888. *Aberdeen Free Press,* 9 January 1888. *Lincolnshire Chronicle,* 1 February 1895.

2. *Essex Standard*, 10 March 1888.

3. *St James's Gazette*, 2 March 1888.

4. Thomas Hardy, 'The Withered Arm', in *Selected Short Stories and Poems* (Everyman edn, London, 1993), p. 45.

5. Mark Freeman, 'Folklore Collection and Social Investigation in Late-nineteenth and Early-twentieth-century England', *Folklore*, 116 (2005), pp. 51–65. Richard M. Dorson, *The British Folklorists: A History* (London, 1968). Gillian Bennett, 'Folklore Studies and the English Rural Myth', *Rural History*, 4 (1993), pp. 77–91. Ronald Hutton, *The Triumph of the Moon: A History of Modern Pagan Witchcraft* (Oxford, 2001), Chapter 7.

6. Richard Jefferies, *Red Deer* (2nd edn, London, 1892), p. 242.

7. J.C. Atkinson, *Forty Years in a Moorland Parish: Reminiscences and Researches in Danby in Cleveland* (London and New York, 1891), p. 58: 'I have often found it very difficult to get them to speak with any approach of unreserve on the topics which lie nearest to the very core of our most interesting folklore.'

8. 'Highland Superstitions', *Oban Times*, 30 January 1869.

9. Discussed at length in Thomas Waters, ' "They Seem to Have All Died Out": Witches and Witchcraft in Lark Rise to Candleford and the English Countryside, c. 1830–1930', *Historical Research*, 87 (2014), pp. 134–53.

10. Flora Thompson, *Lark Rise to Candleford: A Trilogy* (Oxford, 1947), p. 266

11. Charles Oman, *Memories of Victorian Oxford* (London, 1941), p. 5.

12. Those essays were collected in Andrew Lang, *Cock Land and Common-sense* (London, 1894). The quotation is from the introduction, pp. ix–x.

13. Charles Leland, *Gypsy Sorcery and Fortune Telling* (New York, 1891), Chapter 11. Leland's contemporaries certain thought he believed in the 'gipsy mysteries'. See, for example, *Bristol Mercury*, 21 March 1894.

14. Edward Clodd, *The Childhood of the World: A Simple Account of Man in Early Times* (London, 1874), pp. 75–7.

15. 'There is much that is romantic and poetical in these old superstitious beliefs', wrote the *Dundee Courier*, 28 December 1864. For similar remarks, *The Cornish Telegraph*, 13 March 1890. *Portsmouth Evening News*, 2 April 1890.

16. Margaret D. Stetz, 'The Late-Victorian "New Man" and the Neo-Victorian "Neo-Man" ', *Victoriographies*, 5 (2015), pp. 105–21. Alan McNee, *The New Mountaineer in Late Victorian Britain: Materiality, Modernity, and the Haptic Sublime* (Basingstoke, 2016). David Cannadine, *Victorious Century: The United Kingdom, 1800–1906* (London, 2017), p. 514. J.O. Baylen, 'The "New Journalism" in Late Victorian Britain', *Australian Journal of Politics and History*, 18 (1972), pp. 367–85.

17. G.R. Searle, *A New England? Peace and War 1886–1918* (Oxford, 2004), pp. 50, 626.

18. Note that, even on the eve of the First World War (1913), 62 per cent of homes in rural England still lacked piped water. See Shani D'Cruze, 'The Family', in Chris Williams (ed.), *A Companion to Nineteenth-century Britain* (Oxford, 2004), p. 265.

19. 'Electric Lighting in England', *Science*, 7 (1886), pp. 343–4. Julia M. Gergits, 'Housework and Domestic Technology', in Sally Mitchell (ed.), *Victorian Britain: An Encyclopedia* (London, 1988), p. 379.

20. Gareth Stedman Jones, *Karl Marx: Greatness and Illusion* (London, 2016), p. 487.

21. *Western Morning News*, 15 December 1871.

22. Jack London, *People of the Abyss* (London, 1903), esp. Chapter 21.

23. B. Seebohm Rowntree, *Poverty: A Study of Town Life* (London, 1908), pp. 111–18, 39.

24. Roderick Floud, 'Britain, 1860–1914: A Survey', in Roderick Floud and Deirdre McCloskey (eds), *The Economic History of Britain Since 1700* (Cambridge, 2002), p. 7. Dudley Baines and Robert Woods, 'Population and Regional Development', in Roderick Floud and Paul Johnson (eds), *The Cambridge Economic History of Modern Britain*, vol. II: *Economic Maturity, 1860–1939* (Cambridge, 2004), p. 38. Barry Reay, *Rural Englands: Labouring Lives in the Nineteenth Century* (Basingstoke, 2004), p. 94.

25. Reay, *Rural Englands*, p. 105. Daniel Dorling, *Unequal Health: The Scandal of Our Times* (Bristol, 2013), p. 54.

26. For anthropologists who have noticed this critically important fact see Jeanne Favret-Saada, *Deadly Words: Witchcraft in the Bocage*, trans. Catherine Cullen (Cambridge, 1980), pp. 9–11, 64–5, 81–2. Marc Simmons, *Witchcraft in the Southwest: Spanish and Indian Supernaturalism on the Rio Grande* (Lincoln, NB, 1980), pp. 118, 166. U.A. Casal 'The Goblin, Fox and Badger and Other Witch Animals of Japan', *Folklore Studies*, 18 (1959), p. 76. R. Howard, 'Emotional Psychoses among Dark-skinned Races', *Transactions of the Society of Tropical Medicine and Hygiene*, 3 (1910), p. 324. Nancy E. Levine, 'Belief and Explanation in Nyinba Women's Witchcraft', *Man*, 17 (1982), p. 262. Graham Dwyer, *The Divine and the Demonic: Supernatural Affliction and its Treatment in North India* (London, 2003), pp. 75, 80. Jean La Fontaine, *Witches and Demons: A Comparative Perspective on Witchcraft and Satanism* (New York, 2016), p. 118. The theme is discussed in Waters ' "They Seem to Have All Died Out" ', pp. 148–9.

27. *The Cornishman*, 15 February 1894. Regarding cases of unwitching and fortune-telling, 'people naturally wanted to keep them quiet', the Mayor of Chesterfield recognised, in 1888. See *Derbyshire Times and Chesterfield Herald*, 17 October 1888.

28. *Hertfordshire Express and General Advertiser*, 6 May 1865. *London Evening Standard*, 12 August 1868. Joseph Hammond, *A Cornish Parish: Being an Account of St. Austell, Town, Church, District and People* (London, 1897), p. 354.

29. *Litchfield Mercury*, 28 July 1882.

30. The case study is based on the witness statements and court proceedings contained in National Records of Scotland, MS. SC50/5/1863/1.

31. As one resident, a fisherman named James Wotherspoon, put it: 'the story was talked of through the whole island'. The 1861 Census recorded Gigha's population as being 460, a fall of 90 since the last census in 1851. See *Census of Scotland – 1861. Population Tables and Report* (Edinburgh, 1862), pp. 62–3.

32. An important point made brilliantly, three decades ago, by Robert Darnton. See *The Great Cat Massacre and Other Episodes in French Cultural History* (1984: London, 2001), pp. 77–8.

33. For instance, Archy O. de Berker et al., 'Computations of Uncertainty Mediate Acute Stress Responses in Humans', *Nature Communications*, 7 (29 March 2016), 10996.

34. Psychologists in South Africa contend that bewitchment involves people redirecting painful feelings. See Gavin Ivey and Terita Myers, 'The Psychology of Bewitchment (Part II): A Psychological Model for Conceptualising and Working with Bewitchment Experiences', *South African Journal of Psychology*, 38 (2008), pp. 75–94.

35. Owen Davies, *America Bewitched: The Story of Witchcraft after Salem* (Oxford, 2013), p. 69.

36. Searle, *A New England?*, pp. 45–6.

37. K.T. Hoppen, *The Mid-Victorian Generation: 1846–1886* (Oxford, 1998), p. 45.

38. *The New Statistical Account of Scotland*, vol. VII: *Renfrew–Argyle* (Edinburgh and London, 1845), p. 401.

39. Ibid.

40. Margaret Killip, *The Folklore of the Isle of Man* (London, 1975), pp. 56–7.

41. Bodil Nildin-Wall and Jan Wall, 'The Witch as Hare or the Witch's Hare: Popular Legends and Beliefs in Nordic Tradition', *Folklore*, 104 (1993), p. 67. Bernhard Baader, 'Hexe als Hase', in *Volkssagen aus dem Lande Baden und den angrenzenden Gegenden* (Karlsruhe, 1851), p. 50. Christa Agnes Tuczay, 'Witches and Devil's Magic in Austrian Demonological Legends', in Jonathan Barry, Owen Davies and Cornelie Usborne (eds), *Cultures of Witchcraft in Europe from the Middle Ages to the Present: Essays in Honour of Willem de Blécourt* (Basingstoke, 2018), pp. 38–40.

42. Alan Charles Kors and Edward Peters (eds), *Witchcraft in Europe, 400–1700: A Documentary History* (Philadelphia, PA, 2001), p. 376.

43. George Ewart Evans and David Thomson, *The Leaping Hare* (London, 1972), p. 142.

44. S. Ireland, *Roman Britain: A Sourcebook* (2nd edn, London, 1996), p. 19.

45. Jeffrey Burton Russell, *Witchcraft in the Middle Ages* (1972: Ithaca, NY, 1984), pp. 105, 246, 250.

46. 'Hare', in Jacqueline Simpson and Steve Roud, *A Dictionary of English Folklore* (Oxford, 2000), p. 166.

47. Barbara Rieti, *Making Witches: Newfoundland Traditions of Spells and Counterspells* (Montreal, 2008), p. 56.

48. W. Crooke, *An Introduction to the Popular Religion and Folklore of Northern India* (Allahabad, 1894), p. 354.

49. Norman N. Miller, *Encounters with Witchcraft: Field Notes from Africa* (New York, 2012), esp. pp. 86–91.

50. Ronald Hutton, *The Witch: A History of Fear, From the Ancient Times to the Present* (New Haven, CT, 2017), p. 264.

51. Alfred Easthmer, *A Glossary of the Dialect of Almondbury and Huddersfield* (London, 1883), p. 149.

52. M.A. Courtney and Thomas Q. Couch, *Glossary of Words in Use in Cornwall* (London, 1880), pp. 63, 89. Fred W.P. Jago, *The Ancient Language, and the Dialect of Cornwall, with an Enlarged Glossary of Cornish Provincial Words* (Truro, 1882), p. 194. M.A. Courtney, *Cornish Feasts and Folk-lore* (Penzance, 1890), pp. 139, 142.

53. Frederic Thomas Elworthy, *The Dialect of West Somerset* (London, 1875), pp. 56, 835. *Totnes Weekly News*, 18 February 1888. J.F. Palmer, *A Dialogue in the Devonshire Dialect* (London, 1837), p. 30.

54. W.H. Barrett, *More Tales From the Fens*, ed. Enid Porter (London, 1964), pp. 121, 135.

55. Richard Webster Huntley, *A Glossary of the Cotswold (Gloucestershire) Dialect* (London, 1868), p. 18. John H. Nodal and George Milner, *A Glossary of the Lancashire Dialect* (Manchester, 1875), p. 158.

56. John Harland, *A Glossary of Words Used in Swaledale, Yorkshire* (London, 1873), pp. 32, 85, 52.

57. John Mactaggart, *The Scottish Gallovidian Encyclopedia* (2nd edn, London and Glasgow, 1876), pp. 113–14. John Gregorson Campbell, *Witchcraft and Second Sight in the Highlands and Islands of Scotland* (1902: Glasgow, 1974), pp. 2, 5, 220. William Wilson, *Folk Lore and Genealogies of Uppermost Nithsdale* (Dumfries, 1904), pp. 14–20. Mrs Mary Mackellar, 'The Sheiling: Its Traditions and Songs', *Transactions of the Gaelic Society of Inverness*, 15: 1888–9 (Inverness, 1890), p. 167.

58. George Sutherland, *Folk-lore Gleanings and Character Sketches from the Far North* (Wick, 1937), pp. 49–50, 52, 60–2, 74. Campbell, *Witchcraft and Second Sight in the Highlands*, pp. 19–30. Alasdair Alpin MacGregor, *The Peat-fire Flame: Folk-tales and Traditions of the Highlands and Islands* (1937: Edinburgh and London, 1947), pp. 263–4.

59. On storms and witchcraft during the period of the trials see Lizanne Henderson, *Witchcraft and Folk Belief in the Age of Enlightenment: Scotland, 1670–1740* (Basingstoke, 2016), pp. 65, 68, 95–6, 220.

60. Sutherland, *Folk-lore Gleanings*, pp. 52–6, 58–9, 64, 70, 73. Campbell, *Witchcraft and Second Sight in the Highlands*, pp. 7–10. J.A. Macculloch, *The Misty Isle of Skye* (Edinburgh and London, 1905), p. 245. MacGregor, *The Peat-fire Flame*, pp. 262, 268. 'Shetland Superstitions', *Shetland Times*, 22 January 1898, p. 6. John Spence, *Shetland Folk-lore* (Lerwick, 1899), pp. 140–1.

61. 'Getting Even with a Witch', *Dundee Courier*, 23 June 1899. *Inverness Courier*, 19 September 1867.

62. *Banffshire Journal and General Advertiser*, 24 October 1893.

63. *Dundee Evening Telegraph*, 10 June 1893. *Edinburgh Evening News*, 10 June 1893.

64. 'Getting Even with a Witch', *Dundee Courier*, 23 June 1899.

65. *Edinburgh Evening News*, 30 November 1899. *Dundee Evening Telegraph*, 30 November 1899.

66. For more on this point see Henderson, *Witchcraft and Folk Belief in the Age of Enlightenment*, Chapter 8.

67. Campbell, *Witchcraft and Second Sight in the Highlands*, pp. 4–5.

68. Alexander Macbain, 'Highland Superstition', *Transactions of the Gaelic Society of Inverness*, 14: 1887–8 (Inverness, 1889), p. 251.

69. Macculloch, *The Misty Isle of Skye*, p. 249. Campbell, *Witchcraft and Second Sight in the Highlands*, p. 3. Macbain, 'Highland Superstition', p. 251.

70. Thomas Edmondston, *An Etymological Glossary of the Shetland and Orkney Dialect* (Edinburgh, 1866), p. 132. James Stout Angus, *A Glossary of the Shetland Dialect* (Paisley, 1914), p. 144.

71. Edmondston, *An Etymological Glossary of the Shetland and Orkney Dialect*, p. 68.

72. *Wigan Observer and District Advertiser*, 18 May 1894. *Yorkshire Evening Post*, 23 September 1891. *Western Morning News*, 5 April 1893. *Lancashire Evening Post*, 25 June 1897.

73. *Hertford Mercury and Reformer*, 21 July 1861. *Herts Guardian*, 21 July 1861. *Monmouthshire Beacon*, 11 February 1860. *Hereford Journal*, 8 February 1860. *Western Daily Mercury*, 23 December 1864. *Birmingham Daily Post*, 1 November 1867. *Cambridge Chronicle and Journal*, 4 April 1868. *Bristol Times and Mirror*, 20 April 1869. *Bradford Daily Telegraph*, 9 September 1874. *Norwich Mercury*, 4 July 1874. *Bradford Daily Telegraph*, 16 September 1876. *South Wales Daily News*, 17 August 1877; 17 October 1877. *Oxford Times*, 9 October 1886. *Evening Star*, 5 July 1888. *Essex Standard*, 5 July 1888. *Hastings and St Leonards Observer*, 30 January 1892. *Newcastle Daily Chronicle*, 10 February 1860. *Cardiff and Merthyr Guardian*, 11 May 1861. *Newcastle Daily Chronicle*, 2 March 1863. *Birmingham Daily Post*, 18 June 1864. *Staffordshire Advertiser*, 25 June 1864. *Sheffield Daily Telegraph*, 25 August 1866. *Bath Chronicle and Weekly Gazette*, 30 January 1873. *The County Express*, 17 December 1881. *Barnsley Chronicle*, 3 July 1886. South *Wales Echo*, 17 December 1887. *Yorkshire Evening Post*, 23 September 1891; 15 August 1892. *Western Morning News*, 5 April 1893. *Manchester Courier and Lancashire General Advertiser*, 23 August 1862. *The Globe*, 6 May 1863. *Blackburn Standard*, 23 May 1896. *Lancashire Evening Post*, 25 June 1897. *Daily Telegraph*, 13 January 1899.

74. *London Evening Standard*, 3 December 1861.

75. *Gravesend Reporter*, 15 August 1863.

76. *Lloyd's Weekly Newspaper*, 15 May 1870.

77. *London Daily News*, 9 September 1876.

78. *South London Press*, 26 October 1895.

79. *West London Observer*, 21 April 1899.

80. *Eastern Evening News*, 17 March 1894.

81. 'Jottings by Rambler', *Western Times*, 13 May 1870.

82. *Exeter and Plymouth Gazette*, 26 July 1867.

83. *Exeter Flying Post*, 14 May 1862.

84. *Western Daily Press*, 26 March 1894.

85. Figures calculated from *Census of England and Wales. 1901. Summary Tables* (London, 1903), p. 106.

86. James Sharpe, *Instruments of Darkness: Witchcraft in England 1550–1750* (London, 1997), p. 120.

87. See Mark Stoyle, *Witchcraft in Exeter: 1558–1660* (Exeter, 2017), and 'Witchcraft in Exeter: The Cases of John and Elizabeth Crosse', *Devon Notes and Queries*, 41 (2015).

88. Barrett, *More Tales From the Fens*, p. xv.

89. For some examples see R.L. Tongue, *Somerset Folklore*, ed. K.M. Briggs (London, 1965), esp. Appendix II.

90. Roy Palmer, *The Folklore of Shropshire* (Logaston, 2004), p. 148. Andrew Cheviot, *Proverbs, Proverbial Expressions, and Popular Rhymes of Scotland* (Paisley and London, 1896), p. 17.

91. Eric Maple, 'The Witches of Dengie', *Folklore*, 73 (1962), p. 180.

92. John Harland and T.T. Wilkinson, *Lancashire Folk-lore: Illustrative of the Superstitious Beliefs and Practices, Local Customs and Usages of the People of the County Palatine* (London, 1867), p. 164.

93. E.M. Leather, *The Folk-lore of Herefordshire* (London and Hereford, 1912), p. 53.

94. D. Macara, *Crieff: Its Traditions and Characters with Anecdotes of Strathearn* (Edinburgh, 1881), pp. 78, 178.

95. Quoted in Roy Palmer, *Herefordshire Folklore* (Logaston, 2002), p. 114.

96. Roy Palmer, *Folklore of Warwickshire* (London, 1976), p. 18.

97. Enid Porter, *The Folklore of East Anglia* (London, 1974), p. 163.

98. Tongue, *Somerset Folklore*, p. 214.

99. Cheviot, *Proverbs*, p. 202. Robert Chambers, *Popular Rhymes, Fireside Stories, and Amusements, of Scotland* (Edinburgh, 1842), p. 34.

100. George Henderson, *The Popular Rhymes, Sayings, and Proverbs of the County of Berwick; with Illustrative Notes* (Newcastle, 1856), pp. 53–60. Cheviot, *Proverbs*, p. 160. Chambers, *Popular Rhymes*, p. 5. Auchencrow is locally pronounced Edencraw.

101. Elinor Mordaunt, *The Garden of Contentment* (London, 1902), p. 90.

102. Eric Maple, 'The Witches of Canewdon', *Folklore*, 71 (1960), pp. 241–2.

103. For a brief outline of St Elian's legend see Robert Williams, *A Biographical Dictionary of Eminent Welshmen* (London, 1852), pp. 139–40.

104. W.O. Stanlet, 'Folk Lore: Superstition in Anglesey', *Notes and Queries*, 4th Series, 9 (30 March 1872), p. 256.

105. Marie Trevelyan, *Folk-lore and Folk-stories of Wales* (London, 1909), pp. 15–16. For an example of belief in the deadly efficacy of the well see David Hughson, *Cambria Depicta: A Tour Through North Wales: Illustrated with Picturesque Views* (London, 1816), pp. 391–2.

106. Richard Suggett, *A History of Magic and Witchcraft in Wales* (Stroud, 2008), pp. 130–1.

107. John Rhys, 'Sacred Wells in Wales', *Transactions of the Honourable Society of Cymmrodorion: Session 1892–93* (London, 1893), p. 3.

108. D.R. Thomas, *A History of the Diocese of St. Asaph* (London, 1870), p. 23.

109. Some of these are collected in Trevelyan, *Folk-lore and Folk-stories of Wales*, pp. 15–16.

110. Rice Rees, *An Essay on the Welsh Saints* (London, 1836), pp. 267–8. For similar remarks see Samuel Wilderspin, *Early Discipline Illustrated; or, The Infant System Progressing and Successful* (London, 1832), p. 177.

111. Quoted in Suggett, *A History of Magic and Witchcraft*, p. 132.

112. Other examples include *Black's Picturesque Guide to North Wales: New Edition* (Edinburgh and Chester, 1870), pp. 20, 37. *Panorama of the Beauties, Curiosities, and Antiquities of North Wales* (3rd edn, London, 1839), p. 40. *London and North Western Rail Tourist Guide to North Wales* (1909), p. 44.

113. J.O. Halliwell, in his *Notes of Family Excursions in North Wales, Taken Chiefly from Rhyl, Abergele, Llandudno, and Bangor* (London, 1860), pp. 63–5.

114. Christopher Tilley, *A Phenomenology of Landscape: Places, Paths and Monuments* (New York, 1994), esp. pp. 20–1. For commentary see John Bintliff, 'The Death of Archaeological Theory?', in J.L. Bintliff and M. Pearce (eds), *The Death of Archaeological Theory?* (Oxford, 2011), pp. 15–16. Nicola Whyte, *Inhabiting the Landscape: Place, Custom and Memory, 1500–1800* (Oxford, 2009), pp. 3–4.

115. Alexandra Walsham, *The Reformation of the Landscape: Religion, Identity, and Memory in Early Modern Britain and Ireland* (Oxford, 2011), pp. 151, 166, 184–6, 191–8, 210, 220, 226–8.

116. *John O' Groat Journal*, 24 September 1874. *Bradford Daily Telegraph*, 21 July 1880. *Dudley and District News*, 23 April 1881. *Nottingham Evening Post*, 21 April 1881.

117. *Western Times*, 28 January 1875.

118. *Western Gazette*, 11 November 1887. *Western Chronicle*, 20 January 1888.

119. Lyndal Roper, *Witch Craze: Terror and Fantasy in Baroque Germany* (New Haven, CT, and London, 2004), pp. 4, 77, 128. Alison Rowlands, *Witchcraft Narratives in Germany: Rothenburg, 1561–1652* (Manchester and New York, 2003), pp. 153–4. *Windsor and Eton Express*, 22 October 1864.

120. *Worcestershire Chronicle*, 21 January 1893.

121. *Western Daily Press*, 2 February 1898.

122. Percy Manning, 'Folk-Lore Miscellania', Bodleian Library MS. Top. Oxon. D. 192, p. 262; 'Stray Notes on Oxfordshire Folklore', *Folklore*, 13(3) (1902), pp. 289–91. Envy, spite and malice are universally associated with witchcraft. For some examples see Roper, *Witch Craze*, pp. 61–2, 230. Isak A. Niehaus, 'Witch-hunting and Political Legitimacy: Continuity and Change in Green Valley, Lebowa, 1930–91', *Africa: Journal of the International African Institute*, 63(4) (1993), p. 503.

123. *Western Gazette*, 1 September 1865.

124. *Evening Mail*, 29 October 1866.

125. *Manchester Evening News*, 4 January 1873. *Bolton Evening News*, 4 January 1873.

126. *Taunton Courier, and Western Advertiser*, 28 January 1880.

127. *Dumfries and Galloway Standard*, 19 September 1866.

128. *Newcastle Daily Chronicle*, 19 June 1866. *Shields Gazette*, 14 June 1866. *Morning Advertiser*, 11 November 1868.

129. *Western Times*, 8 July 1881.

130. *Lowestoft Journal*, 14 January 1893.

131. *Staffordshire Chronicle*, 22 December 1864.

132. *Bristol Mercury*, 24 April 1894. *Wells Journal*, 26 April 1894. *Shepton Mallet Journal*, 27 April 1894.

133. *Wolverhampton Chronicle and Staffordshire Advertiser*, 22 March 1865.

134. *Western Gazette*, 31 July 1885.

135. *Newcastle Daily Chronicle*, 11 December 1867.

136. *Cardiff and Merthyr Guardian*, 18 July 1868. *Chepstow Weekly Advertiser*, 18 July 1868.

137. *Western Times*, 6 October 1860. *Durham Chronicle*, 24 July 1868.

138. *Lowestoft Journal*, 10 December 1887.

139. *Exeter and Plymouth Gazette*, 22 June 1880. *Western Times*, 18 June 1880.

140. *Western Times*, 20 December 1862.

141. *Morning Advertiser*, 19 June 1862. *Lloyd's Weekly Newspaper*, 22 June 1862.

142. *Norfolk Chronicle*, 27 January 1866.

143. *South Eastern Gazette*, 26 April 1864.

144. *Exeter and Plymouth Gazette*, 28 May 1886. *Portsmouth Evening News*, 28 May 1886.

145. *Western Times*, 3 March 1860.

146. One wonders about the personality of old Will Groves, from Mare in North Devon, 'considered to be a very wicked wizard'. Sal Ley from nearby Marwood apparently kept a brood of toads. According to stories told in the 1890s, they took pride in their evil reputations. See 'Old North Devon Beliefs & Customs', *North Devon Journal*, 2 April 1896.

147. *Birmingham Daily Post*, 31 January 1862.

148. *Monmouthshire Beacon*, 1 June 1861. *Hereford Journal*, 29 May 1861.

149. *Western Daily Press*, 6 January 1862; 11 January 1862.

150. *Norwich Mercury*, 4 July 1883.

151. W.B. Cannon, ' "Voodoo" Death', *American Anthropologist*, 44 (1942), pp. 169–81. Esther M. Sternberg, 'Walter B. Cannon and "'Voodoo' Death": A Perspective from 60 Years On', *American Journal of Public Health*, 92 (2002), pp. 1564–6. Martin A. Samuels, ' "Voodoo" Death Revisited: The Modern Lessons of Neurocardiology', *Cleveland Clinic Journal of Medicine*, 74 (2007), Supplement 1, S8–16.

152. *Sheffield Daily Telegraph*, 25 August 1866. *Western Times*, 3 April 1899. Headaches are particularly likely to be caused by stress. See Juanita K.M. Berry and Peter D. Drummond,

'Psychological Generators of Stress-headaches', *Journal of Behavioral Medicine* (2017), pp. 1–13. Hiroe Kikuchi et al., 'Influence of Psychological Factors on Acute Exacerbation of Tension-type Headache: Investigation by Ecological Momentary Assessment', *Journal of Psychosomatic Research*, 79 (2015), pp. 239–42.

153. *Derby Daily Telegraph*, 25 January 1899. *Western Times*, 3 April 1899.

154. *Exeter and Plymouth Gazette*, 17 July 1897.

155. *Shields Daily Gazette*, 18 February 1890. Also *Birmingham Daily Post*, 18 June 1864. *Staffordshire Advertiser*, 25 June 1864.

156. *Eastern Evening News*, 17 May 1892.

157. Hutton, *The Witch*, esp. pp. 47–54.

158. For a tale of this type see 'The Witch's Purse', in Katherine M. Briggs and Ruth L. Tongue (eds), *Folktales of England* (London, 1965), pp. 57–9.

159. *East and South Devon Advertiser*, 20 May 1893.

160. *Leicester Chronicle*, 16 March 1895.

161. *Taunton Courier and Western Advertiser*, 18 July 1860. *Exeter and Plymouth Gazette*, 14 July 1860.

162. *Western Daily Mercury*, 23 December 1864.

163. *Western Times*, 30 May 1865. *Taunton Courier*, 31 May 1865.

164. Francis George Heath, *Peasant Life in the West of England* (London, 1881), p. 331.

165. *Western Gazette*, 3 January 1868. *Taunton Courier and Western Advertiser*, 8 January 1868. Heath, *Peasant Life in the West of England*, p. 331. *Shepton Mallet Journal*, 30 July 1869. *East Anglian Daily Times*, 17 September 1895. *Lowestoft Journal*, 21 September 1895. *Western Times*, 13 June 1865.

166. On this case see Owen Davies, *Witchcraft, Magic and Culture: 1736–195* (Manchester, 1999), p. 99.

167. *Bicester Herald*, 24 September 1875. *Banbury Advertiser*, 23 September 1875. *The Times*, 17 December 1875.

168. *West Somerset Free Press*, 31 March 1888. *Bristol Mercury*, 27 March 1888; 14 July 1888. *Taunton Courier, and Western Advertiser*, 18 July 1888.

169. *Eastbourne Gazette*, 13 February 1895.

170. That was Louisa's account of her sufferings, anyway. Given in court to make her case for a separation, so perhaps slanted to that end. Perhaps exaggerated. Yet her husband did not contest her version of events, adding no comment except that he had indeed beaten her. See *Evening Star*, 3 September 1898. *Eastern Evening News*, 5 September 1898. *Suffolk and Essex Free Press*, 7 September 1898. *Chelmsford Chronicle*, 9 September 1898.

171. *Shepton Mallet Journal*, 1 November 1895.

172. *Totnes Weekly News*, 18 February 1888.

173. *Shetland Times*, 27 October 1883.

174. *Western Morning News*, 15 September 1893.

175. *Lincolnshire Echo*, 15 June 1895. *Eastern Evening News*, 15 June 1895.

176. Sharpe, *Instruments of Darkness*, pp. 108, 114, 125, 169.

177. Christina Larner, *Enemies of God: The Witch-hunt in Scotland* (1981: Edinburgh, 2000), p. 92.

178. For an excellent evaluation of the many and varied feminist approaches to the history of witchcraft see Alison Rowlands, 'Witchcraft and Gender in Early Modern Europe', in Brian P. Levack (ed.), *The Oxford Handbook of Witchcraft in Early Modern Europe and Colonial America* (Oxford, 2013), pp. 449–67. Additionally, Mary E. Corey, 'Matilda Joslyn Gage: A Nineteenth-century Women's Rights Historian Looks at Witchcraft', *OAH Magazine of History*, 17 (2003), pp. 51–3.

179. Margaret Abraham, 'Femicide', in Dale Spender and Cheris Kramarae (eds), *Routledge International Encyclopedia of Women: Global Women's Issues and Knowledge* (Abingdon and New York, 2000), pp. 701–3.

180. Marianne Hester, 'Patriarchal Reconstruction and Witch Hunting', in Jonathan Barry, Marianne Hester and Gareth Roberts (eds), *Witchcraft in Early Modern Europe: Studies in Culture and Belief* (1996: Cambridge, 1999), pp. 288–9.

181. *Croydon's Weekly Standard*, 28 June 1862. *Bedford Times and Independent*, 1 July 1862. *Taunton Courier and Western Advertiser*, 18 September 1867. *Western Gazette*, 11 October 1867.

182. Michael Anderson, 'The Social Position of Spinsters in Mid-Victorian Britain', *Journal of Family History*, 9 (1984), p. 379, and 'The Social Implications of Demographic Change', in F.M.L. Thompson (ed.), *The Cambridge Social History of Britain 1750–1950*, vol. 2: *People and Their Environment* (1990: Cambridge, 1996), p. 28.

183. Hoppen, *The Mid-Victorian Generation*, p. 319.

184. Women comprised 47.68 per cent of witnesses on England's Home Circuit during the 1600s. See Clive Holmes, 'Women: Witness and Witches', *Past and Present*, 140 (1993), pp. 45–78.

185. *Cardiff and Merthyr Guardian*, 18 July 1868. *Chepstow Weekly Advertiser*, 18 July 1868.

186. *Monmouthshire Beacon*, 31 January 1874.

187. *Western Daily Press*, 4 May 1870. *North Devon Journal*, 26 May 1870.

188. Julian Goodare, 'Women and the Witch-hunt in Scotland', *Social History*, 23 (1998), pp. 292, 297, 303. Edward Bever, 'Witchcraft, Female Aggression, and Power in the Early Modern Community', *Journal of Social History*, 35 (2002), esp. pp. 962–75.

189. Jonathan Parry, *The Rise and Fall of Liberal Government in Victorian Britain* (New Haven, 1993), p. 234. Searle, *A New England?*, p. 63.

190. George R. Boyer and Timothy P. Schmidle, 'Poverty among the Elderly in Late Victorian England', *Economic History Review*, 62 (2009), p. 256.

191. James Winter, 'Widowed Mothers and Mutual Aid in Early Victorian Britain', *Journal of Social History*, 17 (1983), pp. 116–17.

192. Ian Gazeley and Andrew Newell, 'Poverty in Edwardian Britain', *Economic History Review*, 64 (2011), p. 63.

193. Boyer and Schmidle, 'Poverty among the Elderly in Late Victorian England', p. 249.

194. *Hastings and St. Leonards Observer*, 30 January 1892.

195. *Frome Times*, 21 May 1862. *Wiltshire Independent*, 22 May 1862.

196. *Western Times*, 10 October 1873.

197. *Sussex Agricultural Express*, 1 May 1894.

198. For a couple of examples, *Dorset County Chronicle*, 29 June 1865. *Bridport News*, 1 July 1865. *Birmingham Daily Post*, 31 January 1862. The article describes Mary Perry as 'old' but a trawl through the 1861 Census reveals she was in fact around 37 when the witchy events unfolded. The article also mis-spells her assailant's name (not unusual for such reporting, which was not based on written documents, but on what journalists heard in court), which was actually Mary Laren.

199. Raisa Maria Toivo, *Witchcraft and Gender in Early Modern Society: Finland and the Wider European Experience* (Abingdon and New York, 2008), p. 200.

200. *Western Gazette*, 3 January 1868. *Taunton Courier and Western Advertiser*, 8 January 1868.

201. *Tiverton Gazette*, 11 February 1862.

202. *Norwich Mercury*, 15 June 1861.

203. *York Herald*, 10 August 1874. *London Evening Standard*, 10 August 1874. *Bradford Observer*, 11 August 1874.

204. See the trial of Mary Pinning of Gainsborough, in *Stamford Mercury*, 12 October 1860.

205. *Birmingham Daily Post*, 1 November 1867. *Birmingham Daily Gazette*, 3 December 1867.

206. *Norfolk Chronicle*, 27 January 1866.

207. Malcolm Gaskill phrases this point well, writing of mid-1600s England: 'witchcraft was female power, and belonged to the female sphere of running a household: the image of

a witch tended to be that of a supremely disobedient and destructive mother or wife, and other women were thought to be the best detectors of such failings.' See Malcolm Gaskill, *Witchfinders: A Seventeenth-century English Tragedy* (2005: London, 2006), p. 48.

208. Goodare, 'Women and the Witch-hunt in Scotland', p. 307.

209. Roper, *Witch Craze*, p. 104.

210. The theme of witches using their powers to move at unnatural speed (relating to the period of the trials) is brilliantly dealt with in Robin Briggs, *Witches and Neighbours: The Social and Cultural Context of European Witchcraft* (London, 1996), pp. 108–11. In Europe, this theme persisted into the nineteenth century and beyond. For a Victorian story about a rapidly moving witch, an elderly woman who was able to teleport to the top of a tree, see Percy Manning, 'Stray Notes on Oxfordshire Folklore', *Folklore,* 13(3) (1902), pp. 290–1.

211. Noted in Ralph Gibson, *A Social History of French Catholicism: 1789–1914* (London, 1989), p. 135. Censorship remained a matter of dispute throughout the European folklore movement. See Alan Dundes, *Folklore Matters* (1989: Knoxville, TN, 1996), esp. pp. 116–17.

212. Manning, 'Stray Notes on Oxfordshire Folklore', p. 291.

5 HEALING BLACK MAGIC: THE UNWITCHERS OF LATE VICTORIAN BRITAIN

1. Owen Davies, *Witchcraft, Magic and Culture: 1751–1951* (Manchester, 1999), p. 215.

2. Keith Thomas, *Religion and the Decline of Magic: Studies in Popular Beliefs in Sixteenth- and Seventeenth-century England* (1971: London, 1991), pp. 377, 756.

3. Paul Kléber Monod, *Solomon's Secret Arts: The Occult in the Age of Enlightenment* (New Haven, CT, 2013), pp. 64–5.

4. *Tamworth Herald*, 16 October 1886.

5. *Daily Telegraph and Courier*, 13 January 1899.

6. *North Devon Journal*, 7 October 1886. In 1886 Mr Penhale, a 'celebrated horse doctor' from Devon, was reported to be helping a farmer who'd lost several horses and feared he'd be ruined by witchcraft. Standing in the farmer's barn, Penhale pointed to a stack of barley straw, said that's where the witch was located, and advised the farmer to replace it with hay.

7. Alexander Warrack and William Grant (eds), *A Scots Dialect Dictionary: Comprising Words in Use from the Latter Part of the Seventeenth Century to the Present Day* (Edinburgh, 1913). Entries for 'aploch' (p. 8), 'Hallowmas-rade' (p. 244) and 'variet' (p. 646). Louise Yeoman, 'Hunting the Rich Witch in Scotland: High-status Witchcraft Suspects and their Persecutors, 1590–1650', in Julian Goodacre (ed.), *The Scottish Witch-hunt in Context* (Manchester, 2002), pp. 112–14, 215. Anstruther Rhomson, *Eighty Years' Reminiscences* (London, 1904), p. 5. Joseph Grant, *Tales of the Glens with Ballads and Songs* (Stonehaven, 1869), pp. 63–81. *'Aberdeen Journal' Notes and Queries*, 7 (1914), p. 50.

8. Walter Gregor, 'The Witch', *Folklore*, 7 (1889), p. 281. Women 'versed in occult matters', who knew how to stop witches stealing milk from other people's cows, were frequent characters in Scottish witchcraft stories. See, in addition to the above, David Rorie, 'Stray Notes on the Folk-lore of Aberdeenshire and the North-east of Scotland', *Folklore*, 25 (1914), p. 344. Walter Gregor, 'Stories of Fairies from Scotland', *Folk-Lore Journal*, 1 (1883), pp. 57–8.

9. A helpful glossary of Scots vocabulary, including 'the Deil' and accented towards nineteenth-century usage, can be found in William Donaldson, *Popular Literature in Victorian Scotland: Language, Fiction, and the Press* (Aberdeen, 1986), pp. 173–81.

10. Unless otherwise stated, the sources used for Alexander Henderson's biography are 'Death of "Young Skarey", the Last of the Aberdeenshire Warlocks', *Aberdeen Free Press*,

19 January 1889. 'A Visit to an Aberdeenshire Warlock', *Herald and Free Press*, 28 June 1879; 5 July 1879; 12 July 1879; 19 July 1879. Thanks to the National Library of Scotland for help in tracking down these articles. Additional stories about 'Young Skarey' were recorded in *Aberdeen Press and Journal*, 15 January 1896.

11. *Inverness Courier*, 6 June 1867. James Thompson, *Recollections of a Speyside Parish* (1887: 2nd edn, Elgin, 1902), pp. 114–17. *Dundee Advertiser*, 17 May 1862. Alexander Macbain, 'Highland Superstition', *Transactions of the Gaelic Society of Inverness*, 14: 1887–8 (Inverness, 1889), p. 256. Florence Marian McNeil, *The Silver Bough*, vol. 1: *Scottish Folklore and Folk-belief* (1951: Edinburgh, 2001), p. 131.

12. William Alexander, *Rural Life in Victorian Aberdeenshire*, ed. Ian Carter (Edinburgh, 1992), p. 7.

13. Walter Gregor, *The Folk-lore of the North-East of Scotland* (London, 1881), p. 2. For a brief biography and extensive bibliography of Walter Gregor see David Buchan and Ian A. Olson, 'Walter Gregor (1825–97): A Life and Preliminary Bibliography', *Folklore*, 108 (1997), pp. 115–17.

14. T.M. Devine, 'Temporary Migration and the Scottish Highlands in the Nineteenth Century', *Economic History Review*, 32 (1979), p. 354.

15. J.H. Smith, 'The Cattle Trade of Aberdeenshire in the Nineteenth Century', *Agricultural History Review*, 3 (1995), pp. 114–18.

16. The nature and consequences of the herring industry's expansion are explored in Devine, 'Temporary Migration and the Scottish Highlands', esp. pp. 351–4, and T.M. Devine, 'Highland Migration to Lowland Scotland, 1760–1860', *Scottish History Review*, 62 (1983), pp. 148–9.

17. Gwenllian Evans, 'Farm Servant's Unions in Aberdeenshire from 1870–1900', *Scottish Historical Review*, 31 (1952), pp. 29–40.

18. J. Gray and J.F. Toucher, 'The Physical Characteristics of the Population of West Aberdeenshire', *Journal of the Anthropological Institute of Great Britain and Ireland*, 30 (1900), p. 87.

19. For an oral history-based account of a farm servant's diet see Ian Carter, 'Oral History and Agrarian History: The North East', *Oral History*, 2 (1974), pp. 37–8.

20. Peter Hillis, 'The Journal of James Wilson: An Insight into Life in North East Scotland Toward the End of the Nineteenth Century', *Agricultural History*, 86 (2012), esp. p. 8.

21. James P. Watt, 'Typhoid Carriers in Aberdeenshire', *Journal of Hygiene*, 22 (1924), pp. 417–37.

22. *Aberdeen Free Press*, 9 January 1888.

23. *Aberdeen People's Journal*, 10 July 1880. *Aberdeen Evening Express*, 25 June 1881; 11 February 1887.

24. *Glasgow Herald*, 18 December 1883. *Dundee Advertiser*, 18 December 1883.

25. *Edinburgh Evening News*, 28 July 1884. *Glasgow Herald*, 28 July 1884.

26. *Edinburgh Evening News*, 12 September 1885. *Glasgow Evening Post*, 26 September 1885.

27. Rorie, 'Stray Notes on the Folk-lore of Aberdeenshire and the North-east of Scotland', pp. 344–5.

28. Mary M. Banks, 'Folklore Notes from Scotland', *Folklore*, 45 (1934), p. 344. In 2017 I met a lovely lady from Guisborough, North Yorkshire, who told me she'd planted a rowan tree in her garden to repel her neighbour's evil eye.

29. 'Death of "Young Skarey", the Last of the Aberdeenshire Warlocks', *Aberdeen Free Press*, 19 January 1889.

30. *Edinburgh Evening News*, 12 September 1885. For more on the specific case mentioned in the article see *Glasgow Evening Post*, 26 September 1885.

31. Owen Davies's job advert is funnier than mine, and deserves repeating here: 'Only the following need apply: men and women with prior working experience outside the business, and entrepreneurial acumen. Must have competent literary skills, possess own books of the trade, herbal experience, good divinatory skills, practical knowledge of

conjuration, and intimate understanding of witchcraft. Working knowledge of astrology desirable. Own transport advisable. Formal dress optional. The candidate will work from home, but must expect to be on call at all times, and be prepared to work with animals. Lack of scruples no barrier. Start of employment: when sufficient numbers of people complain of bewitchment again.' See Owen Davies, *Popular Magic: Cunning-folk in English History* (London, 2003), pp. 196–7.

32. The best accounts of these fascinating characters, within the context of the British Isles, are Davies, *Popular Magic: Cunning-folk in English History*. Ronald Hutton, *The Triumph of the Moon: A History of Modern Pagan Witchcraft* (Oxford, 1999), Chapter 6. Richard Suggett, *A History of Witchcraft and Magic in Wales* (Stroud, 2008), Chapter 5. Andrew Sneddon, *Witchcraft and Magic in Ireland* (Basingstoke, 2015), Chapters 3 and 7. A trove of information about cunning-folk's spells and charms is collated in Jim Baker, *The Cunning-man's Handbook: The Practice of English Folk Magic 1550–1900* (London, 2013). Excellent accounts of individual cunning-folk include Jason Semmens, *The Witch of the West: or, The Strange and Wonderful History of Thomasine Blight* (Plymouth, 2004). Richard C. Allen 'Wizards or Charlatans – Doctors or Herbalists? An Appraisal of the "Cunning Men" of Cwrt Y Cadno, Camarthenshire', *North American Journal of Welsh Studies*, 1 (2001), pp. 67–85. For a European perspective see Willem de Blécourt, 'Witch Doctors, Soothsayers and Priests: On Cunning Folk in European Historiography and Tradition', *Social History*, 19 (1994), pp. 285–303.

33. *Exeter Flying Post*, 1 February 1865. *Exeter and Plymouth Gazette*, 3 February 1865.

34. *Western Times*, 30 September 1890.

35. *Western Gazette*, 9 May 1863.

36. *Dundee Advertiser*, 17 May 1862.

37. *Royal Cornwall Gazette*, 27 November 1863. *Lake's Falmouth Packet and Cornwall Advertiser*, 28 November 1863. *Torquay Times*, 25 July 1890.

38. For an excellent discussion see Owen Davies and Timothy Easton, 'Cunning-folk and the Production of Magical Artifacts', in Ronald Hutton (ed.), *Physical Evidence for Ritual Acts, Sorcery, and Witchcraft in Christian Britain* (Basingstoke, 2016), pp. 209–29.

39. Anon., *The Dialect of Leeds and its Neighbourhood, Illustrated by Conversations and Tales of Common Life* (London, 1862), p. 451.

40. During the 1870s Frederick Culliford, the wise-man of Crewkerne, went to Yeovil every market day, where he held consultations in a pub. From there he sold witch-bottles, filled with the patient's urine, thorns and a charm reading: 'As long as this paper remains in this bottle of water of mine, I hope Satan will pour out his wrath upon the person that has been privately injuring me . . . they shall not live for more than 90 days from this day, and no longer; and then go into Hell everlasting.' See *Western Times*, 24 June 1876. *Western Daily Press*, 24 June 1876. *Western Gazette*, 30 June 1876.

41. *Cornubian and Redruth Times*, 30 April 1869.

42. Francis George Heath, *Peasant Life in the West of England* (4th edn, London, 1881), pp. 338–9.

43. *Western Morning News*, 21 September 1889.

44. Lucretia Tatchell (1826–1908), a wise-woman from Somerton, in Somerset, regularly travelled to surrounding towns and villages. See *Western Gazette*, 12 June 1874.

45. *Taunton Courier*, 31 December 1890. *Exeter and Plymouth Gazette*, 30 May 1891.

46. George Sutherland, *Folk-lore Gleanings and Character Sketches from the Far North* (Wick, 1937), pp. 49–52.

47. *Taunton Courier, and Western Advertiser*, 17 August 1898.

48. *Exeter and Plymouth Gazette*, 14 August 1877. *Western Times*, 15 August 1877. Harper the 'white witch' had clients all over North Devon, one critic complained, including farmers who kept him on a yearly stipend in order to protect their cattle from being overlooked. See *Exeter and Plymouth Gazette*, 2 July 1878. The critic added that he often met the white witch 'carrying his tin of mysterious rods at his back'.

49. *The Cornishman*, 27 May 1880.

50. For Mary Vickers of Tottington in Norfolk, see *Bury Times*, 19 October 1867. For Miss Hay of Inverness, *Aberdeen Press and Journal*, 18 January 1890. For Billy Brewer of Taunton, *Taunton Courier*, 31 December 1890. For Edward Manning of Croughton, *Banbury Advertiser*, 20 January 1876.

51. *Western Daily Mercury*, 17 June 1863. *Exeter and Plymouth Gazette*, 19 June 1863.

52. Sutherland, *Folk-lore Gleanings and Character Sketches from the Far North*, p. 49.

53. *Exeter and Plymouth Gazette*, 30 May 1891. *Taunton Courier*, 31 December 1890.

54. *Western Gazette*, 26 January 1883.

55. *Hertfordshire Express and General Advertiser*, 6 May 1865. *London Evening Standard*, 12 August 1868.

56. James Pullan, a wise-man from Otley, West Yorkshire, was designated a stonemason on the censuses of 1861 and 1871. For a description of his real, occult profession see *Bradford Daily Telegraph*, 10 November 1873. James Stacey, a Somerset unwitcher, ostensibly worked as a miller. See *Western Gazette*, 26 January 1883.

57. *South Wales Echo*, 11 July 1888.

58. *Western Times*, 19 September 1873. Sarah Hewett, *The Peasant Speech of Devon. And Other Matters Connected Therewith* (2nd edn, London, 1892), p. 147.

59. This etymology was suggested in *Cornish Telegraphy*, 31 March 1869. Semmens, in his *Witch of the West*, is not quite sure of the meaning, but says the word was first used in 1865, and in common usage by the 1880s.

60. 'Eccentric Characters of Perth and Perthshire', *Dundee Courier*, 12 January 1883. *Aberdeen Press and Journal*, 15 January 1890.

61. *Aberdeen People's Journal*, 3 September 1864.

62. *Bucks Herald*, 8 March 1879.

63. *Exeter Flying Post*, 1 February 1865. *Exeter and Plymouth Gazette*, 3 February 1865.

64. *Banbury Advertiser*, 20 January 1876.

65. *Suffolk and Essex Free Press*, 13 August 1863. *Chelmsford Chronicle*, 21 August 1863; 28 August 1863; 11 September 1863.

66. *Essex Standard*, 24 April 1863.

67. *Bradford Observer*, 10 November 1873. *Bradford Daily Telegraph*, 10 November 1873.

68. 'Tarot and Crystal', *Pall Mall Gazette*, 4 April 1900.

69. 'Should Palmists be Prosecuted?', *Pall Mall Gazette*, 17 April 1900.

70. Davies, *Witchcraft, Magic, and Culture*, pp. 253–4.

71. *Bradford Daily Telegraph*, 21 July 1880.

72. *The County Express*, 17 December 1881.

73. *Wolverhampton Chronicle*, 4 July 1860; 22 March 1865. *Staffordshire Advertiser*, 30 June 1860. *Birmingham Daily Post*, 18 June 1864. *Manchester Courier and Lancashire General Advertiser*, 23 August 1862; 15 April 1865. *Newcastle Daily Chronicle*, 2 March 1863. *Derbyshire Times and Chesterfield Herald*, 26 March 1881. *Globe*, 8 September 1882.

74. *Wolverhampton Chronicle*, 4 July 1860. *Staffordshire Advertiser*, 30 June 1860.

75. *Manchester Courier and Lancashire General Advertiser*, 23 August 1862.

76. *Bury Times*, 10 March 1860.

77. For an extremely informative discussion about access to abortion among working-class communities, see Francesca Moore, ' "Go and See Nell; She'll Put You Right": The Wisewoman and Working-class Health Care in Early Twentieth-century Lancashire', *Social History of Medicine*, 26 (2013), pp. 695–714.

78. *Sheffield Evening Telegraph*, 17 October 1889.

79. For Arthur Pearson's role in the history of British publishing see Howard Cox and Simon Mowatt, *Revolutions from Grub Street: A History of Magazine Publishing in Britain* (Oxford, 2014), pp. 29–35 and Chapter 3.

80. Karl Bell, *The Magical Imagination: Magic and Modernity in Urban England 1780–1914* (Cambridge, 2012), p. 108.

81. *Brighton Gazette*, 8 July 1885.
82. Note the similarity with the following cursing incantation:

> It is not this heart I mean to burn,
> But the person's heart I wish to turn,
> Wishing them neither rest nor peace
> Till they are dead and gone.
> *Bath Chronicle and Weekly Gazette*, 22 February 1894

83. Thomas, *Religion and the Decline of Magic*, p. 253.
84. Laura A. Smoller, 'Playing Cards and Popular Culture in Sixteenth-century Nuremberg', *Sixteenth Century Journal*, 17 (1986), p. 184.
85. Baker, *The Cunning-man's Handbook: The Practice of English Folk Magic 1550–1900*, p. 127.
86. *Pall Mall Gazette*, 26 December 1893.
87. For a textual reference to fortune-telling cards, relating to the mid-nineteenth century, see Francis Hindes Groome, *In Gypsy Tents* (Edinburgh, 1881), p. 25. The British Museum has some nice examples of fortune-telling cards in its collection. Some of these decks were clearly aimed at wealthy people ('Card 21: have a vigilant eye upon your servants'). See, for instance, 'The Gipsey's Last Legacy, or New Pack of Fortune Telling Cards' (1806). Registration number: 1896,0501.1037.
88. *The Examiner*, 14 January 1865.
89. *Abergavenny Chronicle*, 12 April 1879. *Glasgow Herald*, 7 June 1888.
90. *St James's Gazette*, 1 September 1900, p. 5, notes 'the "tarot cards" so prevalent in Bond-street nowadays'.
91. *Morning Post*, 24 October 1898. For another tarot-using fortune-teller, *Morning Post*, 10 February 1900.
92. *Derbyshire Times and Chesterfield Herald*, 17 October 1888.
93. *St James's Gazette*, 12 January 1888.
94. *Western Times*, 3 March 1860.
95. *Exeter and Plymouth Gazette*, 24 January 1873. *Western Times*, 28 January 1873.
96. Sharon Bohn Gmelch, 'Gypsies in British Cities: Problems and Government Response', *Urban Anthropology*, 11 (1982), pp. 348–9.
97. On this topic the genomic history of the Roma is most revealing. See Isabel Mendizabal et al., 'Reconstructing the Population History of European Romani from Genome-wide Data', *Current Biology*, 22 (2012), pp. 2342–9. Bharti Morar, 'Mutation History of the Roma/Gypsies', *American Journal of Human Genetics*, 75 (2004), pp. 596–609.
98. David Mayall, *Gypsy-Travellers in Nineteenth-century Society* (Cambridge, 1988), p. 84.
99. See B.C. Smart and H.T. Crofton, *The Dialect of the English Gypsies* (2nd edn, London, 1875), esp. pp. vii–xxiii.
100. For an introductory exploration of the Romany people's Indian roots see Isabel Fonseca, *Bury Me Standing: The Gypsies and Their Story* (London, 1995), pp. 83–112.
101. Ginny Lapage, 'The English Folktale Corpus and Gypsy Oral Tradition', in Thomas Acton and Gary Mundy (eds), *Romani Culture and Gypsy Identity* (Hatfield, 1997), p. 22.
102. Colin Clark, ' "Severity Has Often Enraged but Never Subdued a Gypsy": The History and Making of European Romani Stereotypes', in Nicholas Saul and Susan Tebbutt (eds), *The Role of the Romanies: Images and Counter-images of 'Gypsies'/Romanies in European Cultures* (Liverpool, 2004), pp. 242–3.
103. Mayall, *Gypsy-Travellers in Nineteenth-century Society*, Chapter 3.
104. Rodney Smith, *Gipsy Smith: His Life and Work* (New York, 1902), pp. 24–5.
105. Charles G. Leland, *The English Gypsies and Their Language* (London, 1893), p. 88. George Borrow, *Romano Lavo-lil: Word-book of the Romany, or, English Gypsy Language* (London, 1907), pp. 195–203. *The Romany Rye: A Sequel to 'Lavengro'* (London, 1900),

pp. 45, 55–7, 62–5, 72–6. *Lavengro: The Scholar – The Gypsy – The Peasant* (New York, 1851), pp. 106, 375–6, 433–7.

106. Francis Hindes Groome, *In Gypsy Tents* (Edinburgh, 1881), p. 377 and Chapter 10, part 2.

107. M. Eileen Lyster, 'Taw and the Gozvalo Gajo', *Journal of the Gypsy Lore Society*, New Series, 2 (1908–9), p. 52.

108. Leland, *The English Gypsies*, p. vii. Gypsies had plenty of folk tales about fortune-telling, as Leland noted, showing its importance in their culture. See pp. 204–5, 215, 238. George Smith, *Gipsy Life: Being an Account of Our Gipsies and Their Children with Suggestions for Their Improvement* (London, 1880), p. 249.

109. Rodney Smith, *Gipsy Smith*, p. 225. The Rev. George Hall, *The Gypsy's Parson: His Experiences and Adventures* (London and Philadelpia, PA, n.d. [1915]), p. 107.

110. Groome, *In Gypsy Tents*, p. 377. Leland, *The English Gypsies*, pp. 68–9.

111. Somewhere in the region of 7.35 million acres of once common land was enclosed in England alone. See John Chapman, 'The Extent and Nature of Parliamentary Enclosure', *Agricultural History Review*, 35 (1987), p. 28. For the legislation limiting the gypsies' rights to camp, beginning with the 1876 Commons Act, see Mayall, *Gypsy-Travellers in Nineteenth-century Society*, esp. Appendix I.

112. *Sheffield Independent*, 6 October 1869.

113. Mayall, *Gypsy-Travellers in Nineteenth-century Society*, p. 56.

114. Eric Otto Winstedt and Thomas William Thompson, 'Gypsy Dances', *Journal of the Gypsy Lore Society*, New Series, 6 (1912–13), p. 25.

115. *Sunderland Daily Echo and Shipping Gazette*, 23 February 1878.

116. *Dudley and District News*, 23 April 1881. *Nottingham Evening Post*, 21 April 1881.

117. *Western Mail*, 4 January 1883. *South Wales Daily News*, 4 January 1883.

118. *Montgomeryshire Express*, 22 December 1885. In this case they were convicted of stealing and given four months hard labour each. For a similar case see *Wellington Journal*, 1 February 1896.

119. *Western Times*, 4 March 1881.

120. For some stories of this sort, told in a caravan on Abingdon Common, in about 1910, see Frank Stanley Atkinson and Eric Otto Windstedt, 'A Witch, a Wizard, a Charm', *Journal of the Gypsy Lore Society*, New Series, 5 (1911–12), pp. 269–79.

121. See Smith, *Gipsy Smith*, p. 25. 'The gipsies do not themselves believe this; they know that fortune-telling is a cheat.' Also J.W. and Anne Tibble, *The Prose of John Clare* (London, 1951), p. 38: 'I have heard them laugh over their evening fire at the dupes they have made in believing their knowledge in foretelling.'

122. Groome, *In Gypsy Tents*, p. 377.

123. Ibid., p. 330. Also 'Bulwer Lytton as a Romany Rye', *Journal of the Gypsy Lore Society*, 3 (1891–2), p. 219.

124. Charles Leland claimed that gypsies 'have done more than any race or class on the face of the earth to disseminate among the multitude a belief in fortune-telling, magical or sympathetic cures, amulets and such small sorceries as now find a place in Folk-lore'. See Charles Leland, *Gypsy Sorcery and Fortune Telling* (New York, 1891), p. xi.

125. Francis Hindes Groome, 'The Influence of the Gypsies on the Superstitions of the English Folk', in Joseph Jacobs and Alfred Nutt (eds), *The International Folk-lore Congress 1891: Papers and Transactions* (London, 1892), p. 295.

126. *South Wales Echo*, 17 December 1887.

127. *Bridport News*, 1 February 1884.

128. *Staffordshire Chronicle*, 14 January 1888.

129. Harold G. Koenig, 'Religion, Spirituality and Health: The Research and Clinical Implications', *ISRN Psychiatry* (2012), 2012. doi: 10.5402/2012/278730. For similar remarks see Eltica de Jager Meezenbroek et al., 'Measuring Spirituality as a Universal Human Experience: A Review of Spirituality Questionnaires', *Journal of Religion and Health*, 51 (2012), pp. 336–54.

130. Koenig's 'Religion, Spirituality and Health' provides a concise and statistical overview of this literature as it pertains to both mental and physical health. For some examples of studies finding that religion and spirituality either alleviate or inhibit psychological distress see Lisa Miller et al., 'Religiosity and Major Depression in Adults at High Risk: A Ten-year Prospective Study', *American Journal of Psychiatry*, 169 (2012), pp. 89–94. Elizabeth J. Krumrei et al., 'Jewish Spirituality, Depression, and Health: An Empirical Test of a Conceptual Framework', *International Journal of Behavioral Medicine*, 20 (2013), pp. 327–36. Linda B. Piacentine, 'Spirituality, Religiosity, Depression, Anxiety, and Drug-use Consequences During Methadone Maintenance Therapy', *Western Journal of Nursing Research*, 35 (2013), pp. 795–814. Dan Blazer, 'Religion/Spirituality and Depression: What Can We Learn from Empirical Studies?', *American Journal of Psychiatry*, 169 (2012), pp. 10–12. Nalika Unantenne, Narelle Warren, Rachel Canaway and Lenore Manderson, 'The Strength to Cope: Spirituality and Faith in Chronic Disease', *Journal of Religion and Health*, 52 (2013), pp. 1147–61. As noted, not all researchers find religiosity and spirituality have beneficent mental health effects. For a study associating supernatural beliefs with greater psychological distress, in the context of Taiwan, see Eric Y. Liu, Scott Schieman and Sung Joon Jang, 'Religiousness, Spirituality, and Psychological Distress in Taiwan', *Review of Religious Research*, 53 (2011), pp. 137–59.

131. Naomi Anderson et al., 'Faith-adapted Psychological Therapies for Depression and Anxiety: Systematic Review and Meta-analysis', *Journal of Affective Disorders*, 176 (May 2015), pp. 183–96. J.P.B. Goncalves et al., 'Religious and Spiritual Interventions in Mental Health Care: A Systematic Review and Meta-analysis of Randomized Controlled Trials', *Psychological Medicine*, 45 (2015), pp. 2937–49. George A. Hurst et al., 'Faith-based Intervention in Depression, Anxiety, and Other Mental Disturbances', *Southern Medical Journal*, 101 (April 2008), pp. 388–92. Sara L. Warber, 'Healing the Heart: A Randomized Pilot Study of Spiritual Retreat for Depression in Acute Coronary Syndrome Patients', *Explore*, 7 (2011), pp. 222–33.

132. The classic account of this approach is Aaron T. Beck, A. John Rush, Brian F. Shaw and Gary Emery, *Cognitive Therapy of Depression* (New York, 1979). For briefer accounts of the various features of CBT see Lee Hyder et al., 'Group, Individual, and Staff Therapy: An Efficient and Effective Cognitive Behavioral Therapy in Long-term Care', *American Journal of Alzheimer's Disease & Other Dementias*, 23 (2009), pp. 528–37.

133. Anderson et al., 'Faith-adapted Psychological Therapies for Depression and Anxiety: Systematic Review and Meta-analysis'.

134. Jie Liu et al., 'Neuroanatomical Correlates of Familial Risk-for-depression and Religiosity/Spirituality', *Spirituality in Clinical Practice*, 4 (March 2017), pp. 32–42.

135. 'Adverse employment change resulted in … significant increases in depression.' See David Dooley, Joann Prause and Kathleen A. Ham-Rowbottom, 'Underemployment and Depression: Longitudinal Relationships', *Journal of Health and Social Behavior*, 41 (2000), pp. 421–36. For the 'hardship–depression link', which apparently decreases with age in Anglo-Saxon countries, see Katia Levecque et al., 'Economic Hardship and Depression across the Life Course: The Impact of Welfare State Regimes', *Journal of Health and Social Behavior*, 52 (2011), pp. 262–76.

136. *Lowestoft Journal*, 8 January 1887.

137. *Totnes Weekly Times*, 14 February 1885. *Western Times*, 9 February 1885.

138. *Illustrated Police News*, 25 August 1883.

139. *Western Morning News*, 24 November 1880. *Portsmouth Evening News*, 24 November 1880.

140. *Exeter and Plymouth Guardian*, 25 November 1878.

141. *Shrewsbury Chronicle*, 14 January 1870.

142. *North Devon Journal*, 18 June 1889.

143. *Exeter and Plymouth Gazette and Daily Telegram*, 18 April 1874.

144. *Western Morning News*, 25 November 1870.

145. Whether counselling and medicinal treatments are similarly efficacious remains a matter of dispute within the medical literature. See Edward H. Wagner and Gregory E. Simon, 'Managing Depression in Primary Care: The Type of Treatment Matters Less Than Ensuring it is Done Properly and Followed Up', *British Medical Journal*, 322 (31 March 2001), pp. 746–7. For additional and important discussion, see the letters by Wai-Ching Leung, Andrew Martyn Thornett, David Curtis, Clair Chilvers and Michael Dewey, 'Antidepressants and Counselling for Major Depression in Primary Care', *British Medical Journal*, 323 (4 August 2001), pp. 282–3. Ingrid Torjesen, 'Acupuncture and Counselling Hasten Recovery from Depression', *British Medical Journal*, 347 (28 September 2013), p. 5.

146. *Western Times*, 30 September 1890.

147. Thomas Hardy, *The Life and Death of the Mayor of Casterbridge: A Story of a Man of Character* (London, 1997), Chapter 26.

148. *Royal Cornwall Gazette*, 6 September 1873. Dr Thomas died in 1874 while staying at a customer's house. See *West Briton and Cornwall Advertiser*, 26 February 1874.

149. *Exeter Flying Post*, 1 February 1865. *Exeter and Plymouth Gazette*, 3 February 1865.

150. *Reynolds's Newspaper*, 10 September 1882.

151. *Western Times*, 4 April 1871.

152. *Dundee Advertiser*, 17 May 1862.

153. *Derbyshire Times and Chesterfield Herald*, 26 March 1881.

154. *Aberdeen Press and Journal*, 15 January 1890.

155. *Taunton Courier*, 31 December 1890.

156. *Merthyr Telegraph and General Advertiser*, 24 February 1866.

157. I translate into standard English the original phonetic and semi-literate letter: 'My Dear Frend Mr Covel … Please Mr Covil to Put a Stop to Them … Please Dear to Stop Hir from Duing Hus any Harm … Pleas to Due Hall you Cand for Hus … God Bles u for ever and ever.' Norfolk Record Office: MC 167/1–3.

158. *Merthyr Telegraph and General Advertiser*, 24 February 1866.

159. Extracts from the letters were printed in *Taunton Courier*, 7 January 1891.

160. Owen Davies, *A People Bewitched: Witchcraft and Magic in Nineteenth-century Somerset* (Bruton, 1999), Chapter 3, part 1.

161. Jeanne Favret-Saada, *Deadly Words: Witchcraft in the Bocage*, trans. Catherine Cullen (Cambridge, 1980), p. 9, and *The Anti-Witch*, trans. Matthew Carey (Chicago, IL, 2015), p. 22.

162. The placebo-controlled trials of 1799 were conducted by Dr John Haygarth, at Bath General Hospital. See his report *Of the Imagination, as a Cause and Cure of Disorders of the Body; Exemplified by Fictitious Tractors, and Epidemical Convulsions* (Bath, 1800). For a good general account on the history and character of the placebo effect see Luana Colloca, Magne Arve Flaten and Karin Meissner (eds), *Placebo and Pain: From Bench to Bedside* (London and Waltham, MA, 2013).

163. A good introduction to this area of research is Ted J. Kaptchuk et al., 'Do Medical Devices Have Enhanced Placebo Effects?', *Journal of Clinical Epidemiology*, 53 (2000), pp. 786–92. Also Ted J. Kaptchuck, 'The Placebo Effect in Alternative Medicine: Can the Performance of a Healing Ritual Have Clinical Significance?', *Annals of Internal Medicine*, 136 (2002), pp. 817–25. For a study involving placebo effects and paranormal beliefs see Adam J. Rock, 'Randomized Expectancy-enhanced Placebo-controlled Trial of the Impact of Quantum BioEnergetic Distant Healing and Paranormal Belief on Mood Disturbance: A Pilot Study', *Explore: The Journal of Science and Healing*, 8 (2012), pp. 107–17.

164. *Aberdeen Press and Journal*, 15 January 1890.

165. *Torquay Times*, 25 July 1890.

166. *Western Times*, 10 November 1865; 15 November 1865.

167. *Western Daily Press*, 20 January 1881.

168. *Nottingham Evening Post*, 21 April 1881.

169. *Bristol Mercury*, 17 March 1883.

170. *Bristol Mercury*, 17 March 1883.

171. That phrase was used during a case from slightly outside this period. See 'Devonshire Witchcraft Case. Powder and the Lord's Prayer', *Exeter and Plymouth Gazette*, 15 May 1903. For similar remarks in the context of witchcraft, see 'The Herb Doctor in Trouble', *Western Times*, 15 August 1877. 'English Superstition', *Western Daily Press*, 25 September 1863. 'Witchcraft Extraordinary', *Bury and Norwich Post*, 25 February 1862. Also revealing is an interview conducted with some Essex labourers, about witchcraft and the power of the wise-man, 'The Essex Labourer, Drawn from Life', *Essex Standard*, 8 September 1888.

172. Favret-Saada, *The Anti-Witch*, pp. 11–12.

6 OCCULTISTS STUDY DARK ARTS: 1850S–1900

1. For a wide-ranging academic introduction to the history of spiritualism and the occult revival see the essays in Tatiana Kontou and Sarah Willburn (eds), *The Ashgate Research Companion to Nineteenth-century Spiritualism and the Occult* (London, 2012).

2. 'Extraordinary Revelations from the Other World', *North-Eastern Daily Gazette*, 6 October 1888. 'Alleged Visitors from "The Other World"', *Manchester Courier: Weekly Supplement*, 17 December 1892, p. 8. 'Extraordinary Spiritual Manifestations', *Dundee Courier*, 10 July 1869.

3. On which see Noel Annan, *Leslie Stephen: The Godless Victorian* (London, 1984), esp. Chapters 6 and 7. K. Theodore Hoppen, *The Mid-Victorian Generation: 1846–1886* (Oxford, 1998), Chapter 13. G.M. Young, *Portrait of an Age* (1936: London, 2002), esp. Chapters 11 and 17. Timothy Larsen thinks the scope and influence of the crisis of faith has been overstated in the past. He has a point, but I think he pushes it too far. See Timothy Larsen, *Crisis of Doubt: Honest Faith in Nineteenth-Century England* (Oxford, 2006).

4. Baden Powell, 'On the Study of the Evidences of Christianity', *Essays and Reviews* (London, 1860), p. 141.

5. W.E.H. Lecky, *History of the Rise and Influence of the Spirit of Rationalism in Europe* (London, 1865), vol. 1, esp. pp. vi–vii, vol. 2, p. 408.

6. *Dorset County Chronicle*, 30 April 1863.

7. H. Spicer, *Strange Things Among Us* (London, 1863), p. 2.

8. *Maidstone Telegraph*, 4 April 1863.

9. On spiritualism's origins and early American history, see Ann Braude, *Radical Spirits: Spiritualism and Women's Rights in Nineteenth-century America* (1989: Bloomington, IN, 2001), pp. 10–19. Simone Natale, *Supernatural Entertainments: Victorian Spiritualism and the Rise of Modern Media Culture* (University Park, PA, 2016), esp. Chapter 1. Bret E. Carroll, *Spiritualism in Antebellum America* (Bloomington, IN, 1997).

10. On which see Owen Davies, *The Haunted: A Social History of Ghosts* (Basingstoke, 2007), pp. 80–3.

11. 'Spiritualism Exposed: Margaret Fox Kane Confesses Fraud', *New York World*, 20 October 1888.

12. 'A Lady Spiritualist Confesses', *St James's Gazette*, 3 November 1888; *Tenby Observer*, 8 November 1888. 'How "Spirit-rapping" is Done', *East Aberdeenshire Observer*, 16 November 1888.

13. Alex Owen, *The Darkened Room: Women, Power, and Spiritualism in Late Victorian England* (London and Chicago, IL, 2004).

14. Georgina Byrne, *Modern Spiritualism and the Church of England: 1850–1939* (London, 2010), pp. 39–40. On spiritualism's history in nineteenth-century England, see, in addition to works cited later in this chapter, Logie Barrow, *Independent Spirits: Spiritualism and English Plebeians, 1850–1910* (London, 1986). Janet Oppenheim, *The Other World:*

Spiritualism and Psychical Research in England, 1850–1914 (Cambridge, 1895). Rhodri Hayward, *Resisting History: Religious Transcendence and the Invention of the Unconscious* (Manchester, 2007), pp. 34–44.

15. Henry Spicer, *Sights and Sounds: The Mystery of the Day: Comprising an Entire History of the American 'Spirit' Manifestations* (London, 1853), pp. 373–5. 'Spirit Manifestations Tested', *Scottish Guardian*, 22 March 1853. 'An Evening with Mrs. Hayden', *Berkshire Chronicle*, 27 August 1853.

16. *Jacksons Oxford Journal*, 10 December 1864. Antonio Melechi, *Servants of the Supernatural: The Night Side of the Victorian Mind* (London, 2008), p. 210. Ronald Pearsall, *The Table-rappers: The Victorians and the Occult* (Stroud, 1974), Chapter 6.

17. Robert Dale Owen, *Footfalls on the Boundary of Another World: With Narrative Illustrations* (London, 1860). D.D. Home, *Lights and Shadows of Spiritualism* (London, 1878). Malcolm Jay Kottler, 'Alfred Russel Wallace, the Origin of Man, and Spiritualism', *Isis*, 65 (1974), pp. 144–92.

18. For example, Alfred Russel Wallace, *On Miracles and Modern Spiritualism* (London, 1875), pp. 15, 207–8. Home, *Lights and Shadows of Spiritualism*, pp. 110–12, 153–4.

19. Melechi, *Servants of the Supernatural*, p. 239.

20. The best account of which is Owen, *The Darkened Room*, Chapter 5. Some spiritualists were uneasy about the healing side of the movement, fearing that charlatans might damage its reputation. See 'The Present Aspect of Spiritualism', *The Spiritual Magazine*, 2 (London, 1876) pp. 557–8. 'Paid Mediums', *Spiritual Scientist*, 5 (13 November 1876), p. 130.

21. Charles E. Glass, *Advanced Thought* (London, 1876), p. 149.

22. 'Charges Against a Spirit Medium', *Morning Post*, 8 October 1880.

23. Anon., *Further Communications from the World of Spirits, on Subjects Highly Important to the Human Family* (2nd edn, New York, 1861), p. 155.

24. Glass, *Advanced Thought*, p. 185.

25. Andrew Stone, *The New Gospel of Health: An Effort to Teach People the Principles of Vital Magnetism* (New York, 1875), p. 29.

26. 'Good and Evil Magnetism Contrasted', *Light*, 26 June 1886, p. 288.

27. *Liverpool Mercury*, 10 August 1871.

28. Owen, *The Darkened Room*, pp. 112–15.

29. Stephen Prothero, 'From Spiritualism to Theosophy: "Uplifting" a Democratic Tradition', *Religion and American Culture*, 3 (1993), esp. pp. 197–208. Also Joscelyn Godwin, *The Theosophical Enlightenment* (New York, 1994), pp. 277–306.

30. Godwin, *The Theosophical Enlightenment*, Chapter 15.

31. E.H. Morgan, 'Witchcraft on the Nilghiris', *The Theosophist*, 4(12) (September, 1883), pp. 320–1. B., 'Sickness and its Cure by Witchcraft', *The Theosophist*, 22(10) (July, 1901), pp. 599–605.

32. Founded by the celebrated journalists W.T. Stead in 1893, *Borderland* survived for four years before folding. See Joseph O. Baylen, 'W.T. Stead's "Borderland: A Quarterly Review and Index of Psychic Phenomena", 1893–97', *Victorian Periodicals Newsletter*, 4 (1969), pp. 30–5.

33. Rhoda Batchelor, 'Sorcerers of the Indian Hills: The Kurumbas of the Nilgiris', *Borderland*, 1(4) (July, 1894), pp. 477–9.

34. Nizida, *The Astral Light: An Attempted Exposition of Certain Occult Principles in Nature with Some Remarks Upon Modern Spiritualism* (2nd edn, London, 1892).

35. Ibid., pp. 99–106, 130, 144.

36. On whom see Alison Butler, 'Anna Kingsford: Scientist and Sorceress', in David Clifford, Elisabeth Wadge, Alex Warwick and Martin Willis (eds), *Repositioning Victorian Sciences: Shifting Centres in Nineteenth-century Scientific Thinking* (London, 2006), pp. 59–69.

37. Godwin, *The Theosophical Enlightenment*, pp. 343–4.

38. Probably the best scholarly account of western esotericism is Nicholas Goodrick-Clarke, *The Western Esoteric Traditions: A Historical Introduction* (Oxford, 2008).

39. Edward Maitland, *Anna Kingsford: Her Life, Letters, Diary and Work*, ed. Samuel Hopgood Hart (3rd edn, London, 1913), vol. 1, esp. pp. 276–7, 280, 371. Butler, 'Anna Kingsford: Scientist and Sorceress', p. 66.

40. Maitland, *Anna Kingsford: Her Life, Letters, Diary and Work*, vol. 2, p. 39.

41. Ibid., pp. 39, 291, 315.

42. There are several excellent accounts of the Golden Dawn, including Alison Butler, *Victorian Occultism and the Making of Modern Magic: Invoking Tradition* (Basingstoke, 2011). Ronald Hutton, *The Triumph of the Moon: A History of Modern Pagan* Witchcraft (Oxford, 1999), pp. 72–83.

43. About this the secret chiefs had a point, as research in academic fields from neuroscience to anthropology suggests that the human mind is prone to entering a three-stage altered state of consciousness, which can be induced by various means including pain, psycho-active substances and ritualistic activity. This literature is summarised and used to brilliant effect in David Lewis-Williams and David Pearce, *Inside the Neolithic Mind: Consciousness, Cosmos and the Realm of the Gods* (London, 2005), esp. Chapter 2.

44. Arthur Edward Waite, *The Occult Sciences: A Compendium of Transcendental Doctrine and Experiment* (London, 1891), p. 2.

45. Butler, *Victorian Occultism*, p. 149.

46. Waite, *The Occult Sciences*, p. 110.

47. Owen Davies, *Grimoires: A History of Magic Books* (Oxford, 2009), pp. 181–2.

48. S. Liddell MacGregor Methers, *The Key of Solomon the King (Clavicula Salomonis)* (London, 1889), p. vi.

49. Tobias Churton, *Aleister Crowley: The Biography. Spiritual Revolutionary, Romantic Explorer, Occult Master – and Spy* (London, 2011), pp. 129, 132, 393.

50. The most fully documented is the ritual curse Crowley cast in 1914 on his former pupil in the magical arts Victor Benjamin Neuburg (1883–1940). See Marco Pasi, 'Varieties of Magical Experience: Aleister Crowley's Views of Occult Practice', in Henrik Bogdan and Martin P. Starr (eds), *Aleister Crowley and Western Esotericism* (Oxford, 2012), p. 52 n. 75. The death of Crowley's doctor, barely a day after 'the beast' himself perished, inspired further curse rumours, on which see Richard Kaczynski, *Perdurabo: The Life of Aleister Crowley* (Berkeley, 2002), p. 549.

51. *St James's Gazette*, 8 July 1887; 13 December 1887. *Stamford Mercury*, 1 June 1888.

52. Claudia Stokes, 'The Mother Church: Mary Baker Eddy and the Practice of Sentimentalism', *New England Quarterly*, 81 (2008), pp. 438–40.

53. David L. Weddle, 'The Christian Science Textbook: An Analysis of the Religious Authority of Science and Health by Mary Baker Eddy', *Harvard Theological Review*, 84 (1991), p. 276.

54. Owen Davies, *America Bewitched: The Story of Witchcraft after Salem* (Oxford, 2013), pp. 95–8.

55. Frank Podmore, *Mesmerism and Christian Science: A Short History of Mental Healing* (London, 1909), pp. 270–1.

56. Rolf Swensen, 'Pilgrims at the Golden Gate: Christian Scientists on the Pacific Coast, 1880–1915', *Pacific Historical Review* (2003), esp. pp. 229–34.

57. Mary Baker Glover, *Science and Health* (Boston, MA, 1875), p. 249. On this theme see also Claire F. Gartrell-Mills, 'Christian Science: An American Religion in Britain, 1895–1940', DPhil. thesis, University of Oxford (1991), p. 48.

58. Cynthia D. Schrager, 'Mark Twain and Mary Baker Eddy: Gendering the Transpersonal Subject', *American Literature*, 70 (1998), p. 34.

59. As late as April 1888, the *Manchester Courier* thought Christian Science was 'so far, confined to the United States'. See *Manchester Courier and Lancashire General Advertiser*, 16 April 1888.

60. *South London Press*, 10 November 1883; 1 March 1884. Elizabeth Carolyn Miller, *Slow Print: Literary Radicalism in Late Victorian Print Culture* (Stanford, CA, 2013), p. 143. Leslie Ann Dovale, 'New Woman Theatre and the British Avant-garde, 1879–1925', DPhil. thesis, State University of New Jersey (2010), p. 13.

61. *St James's Gazette*, 1 September 1888.

62. Frances Lord, *Christian Science Healing: Its Principles and Practice* (London, 1888), p. ix.

63. John Burnett (ed.), *Useful Toil: Autobiographies of Working People from the 1820s to the 1920s* (London, 1976), p. 162.

64. Lord, *Christian Science Healing*, p. 238.

65. Ibid., p. 53.

66. *St James's Gazette*, 23 October 1888. *Morning Post*, 18 October 1888.

67. Gatrell-Mills, 'Christian Science: An American Religion in Britain, 1895–1940', p. 55.

68. Ibid., p. 60.

69. For a brief introduction to Baphomet, see Per Faxneld, ' "In Communication with the Powers of Darkness": Satanism in Turn-of-the-century Denmark, and Its Use as a Legitimating Device in Present-day Esotericism', in Henrik Bogdan and Gordan Djurdjevic (eds), *Occultism in a Global Perspective* (Abingdon, 2013), pp. 62–3. Michael D. Bailey, *Magic and Superstition in Europe: A Concise History from Antiquity to the Present* (New York, 2007), pp. 121, 227. For a more detailed consideration, see Julian Strube, 'The "Baphomet" of Eliphas Lévi: Its Meaning and Historical Context', *Correspondences*, 4 (2016), pp. 37–79.

70. Éliphas Lévi, *Dogme et rituel de la haute magie* (Paris, 1861), vol. 2, pp. 208–13, 101, 222–3, 301.

71. *Bath Chronicle and Weekly Gazette*, 4 December 1862.

72. *London Evening Standard*, 15 August 1863.

73. *Morning Post*, 3 August 1863.

74. J. Michelet, *La Sorcière: The Witch of the Middle Ages* (London, 1863), trans. L.J. Trotter, pp. 399–401.

75. *The Globe*, 6 September 1886.

76. *Glasgow Herald*, 14 May 1896.

77. 'Folk-lore Congress', *The Globe*, 5 October 1891, p. 5.

78. For a more detailed discussion see Hutton, *Triumph of the Moon*, pp. 141–8.

79. *Marylebone Mercury*, 20 February 1864. *Newcastle Journal*, 10 November 1864.

80. *Eastbourne Gazette*, 2 December 1891, p. 2.

81. Thomas S. Millington, *Signs and Wonders in the Land of Ham: A Description of the Ten Plagues of Egypt with Ancient and Modern Parallels and Illustrations* (London, 1873), p. 52.

82. *Morning Post*, 13 February 1874.

83. *The Graphic*, 17 April 1875.

84. *London Daily News*, 8 October 1872.

85. *Worcestershire Chronicle*, 18 September 1861. *Western Gazette*, 16 February 1866. *Bridport News*, 27 April 1867.

86. *Hull Packet*, 28 February 1862. *York Herald*, 22 December 1866. *Bridport News*, 20 April 1867. *East London Observer*, 19 February 1870. *Marylebone Mercury*, 16 April 1870.

87. *Launceston Weekly News*, 15 November 1862.

88. *Bedfordshire Times and Independent*, 1 October 1872.

89. *Oban Times, and Argyllshire Advertiser*, 23 January 1869.

90. *The Scotsman*, 30 November 1872.

91. *Norfolk Chronicle* 11 January 1896.

92. Olivier Roy, *Holy Ignorance: When Religion and Culture Part Ways* (London, 2010), trans. Ros Schwartz, esp. pp. 2–3.

7 GONE NATIVE: WITCHCRAFT IN THE BRITISH EMPIRE AND BEYOND

1. Charles L. Griswold Jr, *Adam Smith and the Virtues of Enlightenment* (Cambridge, 1999), p. 273. Michele B. Hill and Greg Brack, 'The Killing and Burning of Witches in South Africa: A Model of Community Rebuilding and Reconciliation', in Julie R. Ancis (ed.), *Culturally Responsive Interventions: Innovative Approaches to Working with Diverse Populations* (New York, 2004), p. 178.

2. A recent study of 19 sub-Saharan African countries finds that witchcraft belief has some correlation with education, though not sufficiently 'to support a simple version of "modernization" theory'. See Boris Gersham, 'Witchcraft Beliefs and the Erosion of Social Capital: Evidence from Sub-Saharan Africa and Beyond', *Journal of Development Economics*, 120 (2016), pp. 182–208.

3. Peter Brugger and Christine Mohr, 'The Paranormal Mind: How the Study of Anomalous Experiences and Beliefs May Inform Cognitive Neuroscience', *Cortex*, 44 (2008), p. 1293.

4. E.E. Evans-Pritchard, 'Some Reminiscences and Reflections on Fieldwork', *Journal of the Anthropological Society of Oxford*, 4 (1973), p. 3.

5. E.E. Evans-Pritchard, *Witchcraft, Oracles and Magic among the Azande* (Oxford, 1937), p. 541.

6. 'It is difficult to know their private opinions, they probably varied widely', one scholar contends, in a footnote about the attitudes of Kenyan colonial officials to witchcraft. See Richard D. Waller, 'Witchcraft and Colonial Law in Kenya', *Past and Present*, 180 (2003), p. 250 n. 26.

7. Stephen Constantine, 'Migrants and Settlers', in Judith M. Brown and William Roger Louis (eds), *The Oxford History of the British Empire*, vol. IV: *The Twentieth Century* (Oxford, 1999), p. 165.

8. Ronald Hyam, 'The British Empire in the Edwardian Era', in Brown and Louis (eds), *The Oxford History of the British Empire*, vol. IV: *The Twentieth Century*, p. 48.

9. 'A Conjurer and Conjuration', *The African Repository and Colonial Journal*, 23 (1847), p. 20. Waller, 'Witchcraft and Colonial Law in Kenya', p. 250 n. 26.

10. Walter Bagehot, *Physics and Politics* (New York, 1948), p. 97.

11. 'How much is there in it?' asked two Rhodesian ethnographers, regarding African witch-craft belief, before answering their question with a tentative affirmative. See Edwin W. Smith and Andrew Murray Dale, *The Ila-speaking Peoples of Northern Rhodesia* (London, 1920), vol. 2, p. 96.

12. Quoted in Katherine Luongo, *Witchcraft and Colonial Rule in Kenya, 1900–1955* (Cambridge, 2001), p. 134.

13. On the symbolic significance of white chalk in the Congo see 'White', in Molefi Kete Asante and Ama Mazama (eds), *Encyclopedia of African Religion* (London, 2009), vol. 1.

14. For some accounts of the poison oracle in later nineteenth-century Africa see Paul B. Du Chillu, *Explorations and Adventures in Equatorial Africa* (New York, 1861), pp. 256–7. Robert Christison, 'On the Properties of the Ordeal-bean of Old Calabar, West Africa', *The Pharmaceutical Journal*, 14 (1854), pp. 470–3. Henry Rowley, *Africa Unveiled* (New York, 1876), p. 124.

15. John D. Viccars, 'Witchcraft in Bolobo, Belgian Congo', *Africa: Journal of the International African Institute*, 19 (1949), p. 220.

16. George Hawker, *The Life of George Grenfell: Congo Missionary and Explorer* (New York, 1909), p. 352.

17. S.G. Browne, 'African Stories', Wellcome Library MS. WTI/SGB/B.11.3.

18. For observations on Congolese *nganga* see John H. Weeks, *Among Congo Cannibals: Experiences, Impressions, and Adventures During a Thirty Years' Sojourn amongst the Boloki and Other Congo Tribes* (London, 1913), Chapter 20.

19. Sylvia Duncan and Peter Duncan, *Bonganga: Experiences of a Missionary Doctor* (London, 1958), Chapters 1–5.

20. Ibid., p. 15.

21. S.G. Browne, 'African Stories', Wellcome Library MS. WTI/SGB/B.11.3.

22. See Peter Delius, 'Witches and Missionaries in Nineteenth-century Transvaal', *Journal of Southern African Studies*, 27 (2001), p. 433.

23. Thomas Waters, 'Maleficent Witchcraft in Britain since 1900', *History Workshop Journal*, 80 (2015), p. 116.

24. *Worcester Chronicle*, 18 September 1861.

25. The quotation is from George Orwell, 'Rudyard Kipling', in *Essays: Selected and Introduced by John Carey* (London, 2002), p. 399.

26. Edward Said, *Culture and Imperialism* (New York, 1994), p. 168.

27. On the Aborigines' Rights Protection Society see Felix Driver, 'Henry Morton Stanley and His Critics: Geography, Exploration and Empire', *Past and Present*, 133 (1991), p. 156. On the attitudes of European socialists and liberals to imperialism see Duncan Bell, 'Empire and Imperialism', in Gregory Claeys and Gareth Stedman Jones (eds), *The Cambridge History of Nineteenth-century Political Thought* (Cambridge, 2011), esp. pp. 865–73.

28. Karl Marx, 'The British Rule in India', *New York Herald Tribune*, 10 June 1853. Later in life Marx revised his view of communal landholding as unviable and undesirable. See Gareth Stedman Jones, *Karl Marx: Greatness and Illusion* (London, 2016), pp. 356–9, 568–9, 582.

29. Bernard Porter, *The Absent-minded Imperialists: Empire, Society and Culture in Britain* (Oxford, 2004), pp. 275–9.

30. *Hansard*, HC Deb. 26 July 1883, vol. 282 cols 543–4.

31. On whom, see K. Langloh Parker, *The Euahlayi Tribe: A Study of Life in Australia* (London, 1905). Also Robert S. Fuller et al., 'Star Maps and Travelling to Ceremonies: The Euahlayi People and Their Use of the Night Sky', *Journal of Astronomical History and Heritage*, 17 (2014), pp. 149–60.

32. Marcie Muir, *My Bush Book: K. Langloh Parker's 1890s Story of Outback Station Life* (Adelaide, 1982), pp. 91–100.

33. See 'Yualai', in Christina Pratt (ed.), *An Encyclopedia of Shamanism*, vol. 2: N–Z (New York, 2007), p. 555.

34. K.L. Parker, 'An Australian Witch', *Journal of the Society for Psychical Research*, 9 (1899), p. 71.

35. Muir, *My Bush Book*, p. 96.

36. Parker, 'An Australian Witch', pp. 69–71.

37. Philip Clarke, 'Aboriginal Healing Practices and Australian Bush Medicine', *Journal of the Anthropological Society of South Australia*, 33 (2008), pp. 3–24.

38. Ian Harmstorf and Michael Cigler, *The Germans in Australia* (Melbourne, 1985), pp. 77–8.

39. "Witchcraft in South Australia', *Perth Inquirer*, 8 March 1854.

40. Ian Evans, M. Chris Manning and Owen Davies, 'The Wider Picture: Parallel Evidence in America and Australia', in Ronald Hutton (ed.), *Physical Evidence for Ritual Acts, Sorcery and Witchcraft in Christian Britain: A Feeling for Magic* (Basingstoke, 2016), esp. pp. 243–50.

41. *Table Talk*, 9 June 1893; 23 June 1893.

42. 'Father Sought', *Riverine Herald*, 28 March 1912.

43. 'Pointing the Bone', *The Tumut Advocate*, 28 April 1925.

44. Muir, *My Bush Book*, p. 100.

45. *Telegraph* (Brisbane), 4 March 1895. For similar remarks see the *Daily News* (Perth), 3 February 1934.

46. On which see Michael King, *The Penguin History of New Zealand* (Rosedale, 2003), Chapter 12, esp. p. 193.

47. Charles Terry, *New Zealand, its Advantages and Prospects, as a British Colony; with a Full Account of the Land Claims, Sales of Crown Lands, Aborigines, etc. etc.* (London, 1842), p. 172.

48. Elsdon Best, 'Maori Magic: Notes upon Witchcraft, Magic Rites, and various Superstitions as Practised or Believed in by the Old-time Maori', *Transactions and Proceedings of the Royal Society of New Zealand*, 34 (1901), pp. 69–70. W.H. Goldie, 'Maori Medical Lore: Notes on the Causes of Disease and Treatment of the Sick among the Maori People of New Zealand, as Believed and Practised in Former Times, together with some Account of Various Ancient Rites Connected with the Same', *Transactions and Proceedings of the Royal Society of New Zealand*, 37 (1904), pp. 3–4, 22, 31–45.

49. Ernest Dieffenbach, *Travels in New Zealand; with Contributions to the Geography, Botany, and Natural History of the Country*, vol. 2 (London, 1843), p. 15.

50. Ibid., Chapter 2. Terry, *New Zealand, its Advantages and Prospects*, pp. 178–9.

51. D.E. Hanham, 'The Impact of Introduced Diseases in the Pre-Treaty Period: 1790–1840', MA thesis, University of Canterbury (2003), pp. 13, 79–90. Lachy Paterson, 'Government, Church and Māori Responses to Mākutu (Sorcery) in New Zealand in the Nineteenth and Early Twentieth Centuries', *Cultural and Social History*, 8 (2011), p. 177.

52. Lawrence M. Rogers (ed.), *The Early Journals of Henry Williams* (Christchurch, 1961), pp. 248, 261, 430.

53. Vincent O'Malley, *The Meeting Place: Māori and Pākehā Encounters, 1642–1840* (Auckland, 2012), pp. 193–4. Goldie, 'Maori Medical Lore', p. 35.

54. Dieffenbach, *Travels in New Zealand*, vol. 2, p. 17.

55. For an introduction to the New Zealand Wars see Philippa Main Smith, *A Concise History of New Zealand* (Cambridge, 2005), pp. 70–6.

56. Paterson, 'Government, Church and Māori Responses to Mākutu', p. 175.

57. Vincent O'Malley, 'English Law and the Maori Response: A Case Study from the Runanga System in Northland, 1861–65', *Journal of the Polynesian Society*, 116 (2007), pp. 8–9.

58. *The New Zealand Herald*, 16 November 1877.

59. Paterson, 'Government, Church and Māori Responses to Mākutu', pp. 186–8.

60. Malcolm Voyce, 'Maori Healers in New Zealand: The Tohunga Suppression Act of 1907', *Oceania*, 60 (1989), p. 103.

61. Derek A. Dow, ' "Pruned of its Dangers": The Tohunga Suppression Act 1907', *Health and History*, 3 (2001), pp. 41–64.

62. Voyce, 'Maori Healers', p. 101. Also 'Revival of Tohungaism', *New Zealand Herald*, 20 September 1905.

63. Paterson, 'Government, Church and Māori Responses to Mākutu', p. 186.

64. For a detailed history of this region, its people and their encounters with white settlers see Judith Binney, *Encircled Lands: Te Urewera, 1820–1921* (Wellington, 2009).

65. Dieffenbach, *Travels in New Zealand*, vol. 2, p. 59.

66. See especially Trevor J. Bentley, *Pakeha Maori: The Extraordinary Story of Europeans who Lived as Maori in Early New Zealand* (Auckland, 1999).

67. See James Cowan, *The Adventures of Kimble Bent: A Story of Wild Life in the New Zealand Bush* (London, Melbourne and Christchurch, 1911), pp. 327–9.

68. Anon., *Old New Zealand, a Tale of the Good Old Times; and a History of the War in the North Against the Chief Heke, in the Year 1845. By a Pakeha Maori* (London, 1876), p. 111.

69. On using food to convey *makutu* see Elsdon Best, *Spiritual and Mental Concepts of the Maori: Being Illustrations of Animism and Animatism* (Wellington, 1922), p. 32. 'The Hangi', *New Zealand Herald*, 8 October 1927. 'Native Intelligence', *New Zealand Herald*, 9 August 1872.

70. Evelyn Stokes, *Wiremu Tamihana: Rangatira* (Wellington, 2002), p. 119. 'A Maori Invocation', *Cromwell Argus*, 30 March 1936. 'A Debatable Land', *New Zealand Herald*, 13 September 1913.

71. 'Waikato Past and Present', *Otago Witness*, 6 November 1901.

72. 'Local Gossip', *New Zealand Herald*, 12 January 1924. 'Superstitious Settlers: "Makutus" in the North', *New Zealand Herald*, 7 January 1924. 'Abandoned Farms', *New Zealand Herald*, 22 January 1924.

73. 'Superstitious Settlers: "Makutus" in the North', *New Zealand Herald*, 7 January 1924.

74. 'Ideal Motor Road', *New Zealand Herald*, 24 April 1925.

75. 'Local Gossip', in *New Zealand Herald*, 24 August 1929.

76. Johannes C. Andersen, 'Maori Words Incorporated into the English Language', *Journal of the Polynesian Society*, 55 (1946), pp. 141, 153.

77. Compare the accounts of the journey in P.H. Cornford, *Missionary Reminiscences; or, Jamaica Retraced* (Leeds, 1856), p. 1, and Anon., *Letters from Jamaica: The Land of Streams and Woods* (Edinburgh, 1873), pp. 11–12.

78. For the demography of the British Caribbean see Dennis Arthur Brown, *The Political Economy of Fertility in the British West Indies: 1891–1921* (Kingston, 2000), pp. 29–32. On the salient role of racism in structuring Caribbean society see Bridget Brereton, 'Social Organization and Class, Racial and National Conflicts', in K.O. Laurence and Jorge Ibarra Cuesta (eds), *General History of the Caribbean*, vol. 4, *The Long Nineteenth Century: Nineteenth-century Transformations* (London, 2011), esp. pp. 338–41.

79. Sasha Turner Bryson, 'The Art of Power: Poison and Obeah Accusations and the Struggle for Dominance and Survival in Jamaica's Slave Society', *Caribbean Studies*, 41 (2013), p. 64. Randy M. Browne, 'The "Bad Business" of Obeah: Power, Authority, and the Politics of Slave Culture in the British Caribbean', *William and Mary Quarterly*, 68 (2011), pp. 455–6.

80. Diana Paton, *The Cultural Politics of Obeah: Religion, Colonialism and Modernity in the Caribbean World* (Cambridge, 2015), esp. pp. 28–30. Owen Davies, *Grimoires: A History of Magic Books* (Oxford, 2009), pp. 155–67. Jerome S. Handler, 'Slave Medicine and Obeah in Barbados, circa 1650 to 1834', *New West Indian Guide*, 74 (2000), pp. 59–63.

81. Anon., *Antigua and the Antiguans: A Full Account of the Colony and Its Inhabitants from the Time of the Caribs to the Present Day*, vol. 2 (London, 1844), p. 55. R.R. Madden, *Twelvemonth's Residence in the West Indies, During the Transition from Slavery to Apprenticeship*, vol. 2 (Philadelphia, PA, 1835), p. 70.

82. On which see G.D. Henderson, *Religious Life in Seventeenth-century Scotland* (Cambridge, 1937), pp. 12–13. Owen Davies, *Witchcraft, Magic and Culture: 1736–1951* (Manchester, 1999), p. 225.

83. Anon., *Antigua and the Antiguans*, p. 70.

84. Ibid., p. 54.

85. Browne, 'The "Bad Business" of Obeah', p. 459. Jane C. Beck, 'The Implied Obeah Man', *Western Folklore*, 35 (1976), pp. 23–33.

86. W.W. Wright, 'The British West Indies', *De Bow's Review*, 28 (1860), p. 209. James Maxwell, *Remarks on the Present State of Jamaica, with a Proposal of Measures for the Resuscitation of Our West Indian Colonies* (London, 1848), pp. 32–3.

87. Anon., *Letters from Jamaica*, p. 131. Bryson, 'The Art of Power', pp. 65–74.

88. *The Laws of Jamaica, Passed in the Nineteenth Year of the Reign of Queen Victoria* (Kingston, 1856), pp. 512–13.

89. *London Evening Standard*, 12 April 1866. John Gorrie, *Illustrations of Martial Law in Jamaica. Compiled from the Report of the Royal Commissioners, and Other Blue Books Laid Before Parliament* (London, 1867), p. 88.

90. Joseph Jones, *Medical and Surgical Memoirs: Containing Investigations on the Geographical Distribution, Causes, Nature, Relations, and Treatment of Various Diseases*, vol. 1 (New Orleans, 1870), p. 231. For more on this theme see Herbert T. Thomas, *Something about Obeah* (Kingston, 1891), p. 3.

91. 'Negro Life in Jamaica', *Harper's New Magazine*, 44 (1871–2), p. 558.

92. *London Evening Standard*, 12 April 1866.

93. Rev. David King, *The State and Prospects of Jamaica* (London, 1850), pp. 204–6.

94. 'Hobbling Mary', *Dundee Evening Telegraph*, 15 April 1899.

95. Quoted in Bryson, 'The Art of Power', p. 73.

96. Charles Kingsley, *At Last: A Christmas in the West Indies* (London, 1872), p. 289.

97. Edith Blake, 'In the Bahamas', *The Living Age*, 177 (2 June 1888), p. 539. Blake's article was first published in *The Nineteenth Century*.

98. R.R. Madden, *A Twelvemonth's Residence in the West Indies*, p. 72.

99. Hesketh J. Bell, *Obeah: Witchcraft in the West Indies* (London, 1893), pp. 2–5, 119.

100. Peter van der Veer and Steven Vertovec, 'Brahmanism Abroad: On Caribbean Hinduism as an Ethnic Religion', *Ethnology*, 30 (1991), esp. pp. 149–51. Lomarsh Roopnarine, 'East Indian Indentured Emigration to the Caribbean: Beyond the Push and Pull Model', *Caribbean Studies*, 31 (2003), pp. 97–134.

101. For a story about a person of Indian heritage falling ill and seeking the help of *obeah* men, see Prabha Jerrybandan, 'Unsilencing Hi(stories) of Indo-Caribbean Women: Re-writing and Re-presenting Self and Community', PhD thesis, Graduate Program in Education, York University, Toronto (2015), p. 161.

102. Paul Younger, *New Homelands: Hindu Communities in Mauritius, Guyana, Trinidad, South Africa, Fiji, and East Africa* (Oxford, 2010), pp. 67, 110.

103. Roslyn Roach, 'Obeah in the Treatment of Psychiatric Disorders in Trinidad: An Empirical Study of an Indigenous Healing System', MSc. thesis, Department of Psychiatry, McGill University (1992), esp. pp. 55–62.

104. Paton, *The Cultural Politics of Obeah*, pp. 274–6.

105. On Seaga's views see Edward Seaga, *My Life and Leadership*, vol 1: *Clash of Ideologies 1930–1980* (Oxford, 2009), p. 31. Patrick E. Bryan, *Edward Seaga and the Challenges of Modern Jamaica* (Jamaica, Barbados, and Trinidad and Tobago, 2009), pp. 3, 27, 133–4.

106. On which see the extremely useful Jerome S. Handler and Kenneth M. Bibly, *Enacting Power: The Criminalization of Obeah in the Anglophone Caribbean 1760–2011* (Kingston, 2012).

107. David Howard, *Kingston: A Cultural and Literary History* (Oxford, 2005), p. 202.

108. The company's India monopoly was removed in 1813, and its China monopoly in 1833.

109. For a brief breakdown of the East India Company's tax revenues see H.V. Bowen, *The Business of Empire: The East India Company and Imperial Britain, 1756–1833* (Cambridge, 2005), p. 5.

110. On the civil servants of British India see Cliver Dewey, *Anglo-Indian Attitudes: The Mind of the Indian Civil Service* (London, 1993), esp. Chapter 1.

111. Nick Robins, *The Corporation that Changed the World: How the East India Company Shaped the Modern Multinational* (London, 2012), pp. 187–90.

112. James Mill, *The History of British India. Fourth Edition, with Notes and Continuation by Horace Hayman Wilson*, vol. 1 (London, 1840), p. 492, n. 1.

113. Nancy Gardner Cassels, *Social Legislation of the East India Company: Public Justice versus Public Instruction* (New Delhi, 2010), pp. 72–3.

114. Ajay Skaria, 'Women, Witchcraft and Gratuitous Violence in Colonial Western India', *Past and Present*, 115 (1997), p. 109.

115. Ibid., p. 110.

116. Rev. J. Long, 'Five Hundred Questions on the Social Condition of the Natives of Bengal', *Journal of the Royal Asiatic Society*, 2 (1866), p. 49.

117. P.N. Shrivastav, *Indore* (Bhopal, 1971), p. 125.

118. W. Crooke, *An Introduction to the Popular Religion and Folklore of Northern India* (Allahabad, 1894), p. 349. R.M., 'Witchcraft in Bengal', ed. W. Schlich, *The Indian Forester: A Quarterly Magazine*, 1 (1875–6), pp. 318–20.

119. Malcolm, *A Memoir of Central India*, p. 213.

120. Shashank S. Sinha, '1857 and the Adivasis of Chotanagpur', in Biswamoy Pati (ed.), *The Great Rebellion of 1857 in India: Exploring Transgressions, Contests, and Diversities* (Abingdon, 2010), pp. 25–8.

121. Tanika Sarak, 'Gendering of Public and Private Selves in Colonial Times', in Douglas M. Peers and Nandini Gooptu (eds), *India and the British Empire* (Oxford, 2012), p. 307.

122. *Statement Exhibiting the Moral and Material Progress and Condition of India during the Year 1859–1860* (House of Commons, 1961), part 2, p. 8. Sinha, '1857 and the Adivasis of Chotanagpur', p. 27.

123. Biswamoy Pati, 'Beyond Colonial Mapping: Common People, Fuzzy Boundaries and the Rebellion of 1857', in *The Great Rebellion of 1857*, pp. 38–41.

124. Ajay Skaria, 'Shades of Wildness: Tribe, Caste, and Gender in Western India', *Journal of Asian Studies*, 56 (1997), esp. pp. 726–7, 732, 738–9.

125. E. West, 'Notes on Witchcraft and Demonology in Gujarat', *The Indian Antiquary*, 2 (January, 1873), pp. 13–14.

126. Crooke, *Popular Religion*, p. 92.

127. Soma Chaudhuri, 'Extending the Logical of Functional Explanations: A Theoretical Model to Explain the Victimization Process during an Indian Witch Hunt', K. Jaishankar and Natti Ronel (eds), *Global Criminology: Crime and Victimization in a Globalized Era* (London, n.d.), p. 315.

128. *Returns and Papers Presented to the House of Lords, pursuant to an Order dated 11th June 1852, and Ordered to be printed in Session, 1852, Relative to the Affairs of the East Indian Company* (London, 1852), pp. 390, 431.

129. Police Department Correspondence of the Governor of the Presidency of Fort William, Bengal (1839). British Library MS IOR/Z/E/4/16/S888, pp. 287–8.

130. The quotation is taken from an early nineteenth-century article on Indian colonial governance. See 'The British Empire in India', *The Gentleman's Magazine*, (July 1833), p. 3.

131. Montgomery Martin, *The History, Antiquities, Topography, and Statistics of Eastern India; Comprising the Districts of Behar, Shahabad, Bhagulpoor, Goruckpoor, Dinajepoor, Puraniya, Rungpoor, & Assam*, vol. 1: *Behar (Patna City) and Shahabad* (London, 1838), p. 139.

132. Crooke, *Introduction to the Popular Religion*, pp. 62–4. S.C. Bhatt and Gopal K. Bhargava (eds), *Land and People of Indian States and Union Territories*, vol. 15: *Madhya Pradesh* (Delhi, 2006), p. 42.

133. Crooke, *An Introduction to the Popular Religion*, p. 349.

134. David Cannadine, *Ornamentalism: How the British Saw Their Empire* (London, 2001), p. 41.

135. David Gilmour, *The Ruling Caste: Imperial Lives in the Victorian Raj* (London, 2007), p. 3.

136. A.C. Lyall, 'The Relation of Witchcraft to Non-Christian Religions', *The Fortnightly Review*, new series, 13 (1873), p. 445.

137. For Sir Alfred's oriental enthusiasms see Mortimer Durand, *The Life of the Right Hon. Sir Alfred Comyn Lyall* (Edinburgh and London, 1913), p. 164.

138. Alfred C. Lyall, *Asiatic Studies, Religious and Social* (2nd edn, London, 1884), pp. 96–8.

139. W.H. Sleeman, *Rambles and Recollections of and Indian Official*, vol. 1 (London, 1844), p. 90.

140. Maive Stokes, *Indian Fairy Tales: Collected and Translated* (Calcutta, 1879), p. v.

141. Crooke, *Popular Religion and Folklore of Northern India*, pp. 348–9.

142. Richard Hodgson, 'Indian Magic and the Testimony of Conjurers', *Proceedings of the Society for Psychical Research*, 9 (1893–4), p. 363.

143. Sleeman, *Rambles and Recollections*, vol. 1, p. 90.

144. 'Sickness and its Cure by Witchcraft', in H.S. Olcott (ed.), *The Theosophist: A Magazine of Oriental Philosophy, Art, Literature & Occultism*, 22 (Madras, 1901), pp. 599–605.

145. A. Ganesan, *The Press in Tamil Nadu and the Struggle for Freedom: 1917–1937* (Delhi, 1988), p. 46.

146. A.P. Sinnett, *The Occult World* (3rd edn, London, 1883), pp. 2–3, 15.

147. A.P. Sinnett, *Esoteric Buddhism* (London, 1885), pp. xii–xiii. Henry S. Olcott, *Theosophy: Religion and Occult Science* (London, 1885), esp. pp. 214–15.

148. Dawa Norbu, *China's Tibet Policy* (Richmond, 2001), p. 155.
149. Stephen Prothero, 'From Spiritualism to Theosophy: "Uplifting" a Democratic Tradition', *Religion and American Culture*, 3 (1993), esp. pp. 197–208.
150. Mark Bevir, 'Theosophy and the Origins of the Indian National Congress', *International Journal of Hindu Studies*, 7 (2003), p. 106. Joy Dixon, *Divine Feminism: Theosophy and Feminism in England* (Baltimore, OH, 2001), p. 3. Judith M. Brown, *Gandhi's Rise to Power: Indian Politics 1915–1922* (Cambridge, 1974), p. 135.
151. Bevir, 'Theosophy and the Origins of the Indian National Congress', p. 110.
152. Brown, *Gandhi's Rise to Power*, p. 135.
153. For a brief account of which see Dixon, *Divine Feminism*, pp. 4–5.
154. *Hull Advertiser and Exchange Gazette*, 21 September 1864.
155. Note the title of Frank Melland's book: *In Witch-bound Africa* (London, 1923).
156. Francis Galton, *The Art of Travel; or, Shifts and Contrivances in Wild Countries* (5th edn, London, 1872), p. 1. Elspeth Huxley, *The Flame Trees of Thika: Memories of an African Childhood* (London, 1959), pp. 26–30.
157. 'The Natives of Africa', *Pall Mall Gazette*, 19 November 1895.
158. Melland, *In Witch-bound Africa*, p. 195.
159. Lord Hailey, *An African Survey: A Study of Problems Arising in Africa South of the Sahara* (London, 1938), p. 295. Also Waller, 'Witchcraft and Colonial Law in Kenya', p. 241.
160. Mary Kingsley, *West African Studies* (London, 1899), p. 209.
161. Weeks, *Among Congo Cannibals*, pp. 314–15.
162. Evans-Pritchard, *Witchcraft, Oracles and Magic*, p. 63. George W. Stow, *The Native Races of South Africa. A History of the Intrusion of the Hottentots and Bantu into the Hunting Grounds of the Bushman, the Aborigines of the Country* (London, 1905), p. 458.
163. Danielle N. Boaz, 'Witchcraft, Witchdoctors and Empire: The Proscription of African Spiritual Practices in Britain's Atlantic Colonies, 1760s–1960s', PhD thesis, University of Miami (2014), pp. 25–6, 78–9, 112–17.
164. Ronald Hutton, *The Witch: A History of Fear, from Ancient Times to the Present* (New Haven, CT, and London, 2017), p. 30.
165. For a vivid account of this process see Thomas Pakenham, *The Scramble for Africa: 1876–1912* (London, 1991).
166. *Hansard*, HC Deb. 27 May 1879, vol. 246, cols 1371. Also *Hansard*, HL Deb. 15 August 1882, vol. 273, cols 1803–7.
167. *Hansard*, HC Deb. 25 November 1957, vol. 578, col. 896.
168. David M. Anderson, 'Mau Mau in the High Court and the "Lost" British Empire Archives: Colonial Conspiracy or Bureaucratic Bungle?', *Journal of Imperial and Commonwealth History*, 39 (2011), pp. 699–716.
169. John Lonsdale, 'Mau Maus of the Mind: Making Mau Mau and Remaking Kenya', *Journal of African History*, 31 (1990), p. 394. Luongo, *Witchcraft and Colonial Rule*, pp. 159–60.
170. 'The Real Story of Mau Mau', *Dundee Courier*, 18 February 1953. 'Kenya – A Beautiful Country with a Great Future', *Portsmouth Evening News*, 27 October 1952. *Hartlepool Northern Daily Mail*, 20 November 1952.
171. *Fife Free Press and Kirkcaldy Guardian*, 14 April 1956. 'The Terror of Mau Mau: Kenya Farmers Talk to Matlock Rotarians', *Belper News*, 4 March 1955.
172. 'Mau Mau Will Not Turn Us Out', *Portsmouth Evening News*, 7 November 1952. *Hansard*, HC Deb. 7 November 1952 vol. 507, col. 458.
173. Delius, 'Witches and Missionaries in Nineteenth-century Transvaal', p. 433.
174. C.M.N. White, 'Witchcraft, Divination and Magic among the Balovale Tribes', *Africa*, 18 (1948), pp. 82–4.
175. Godfrey Lienhardt, 'Some Notions of Witchcraft among the Dinka', *Africa*, 21 (1951), p. 303.

176. A. Werner, *The Natives of British Central Africa* (London, 1906), pp. 168–9. Smith and Dale, *The Ila-speaking Peoples of Northern Rhodesia*, vol. 2, pp. 90–6. Alexander William Mitchinson, *The Expiring Continent: A Narrative of Travel in Senegambia, with Observations on Native Character, the Present Condition and Future Prospects of Africa and Colonisation* (London, 1881), p. 13. David Lan, *Guns and Rain: Guerrillas and Spirit Mediums in Zimbabwe* (Berkeley, CA, 1985), pp. 35–6. James Stevenson-Hamilton, *The Low-veld: Its Wild Life and Its People* (London, 1929), pp. 220–6. Lienhardt, 'Some Notions of Witchcraft among the Dinka', pp. 306–8. White, 'Witchcraft, Divination and Magic among the Balovale Tribes', pp. 84–5.

177. Evans-Pritchard, *Witchcraft, Oracles and Magic*, p. 21.

178. For a uniquely learned summary of witchcraft in Africa and beyond see Hutton, *The Witch*, Chapter 1, esp. pp. 23–35.

179. William Winwood Reade, *Savage Africa: Being the Narrative of a Tour in Equatorial, South-western, and North-western Africa* (London, 1864), p. 256.

180. Henry F. Norbury, *The Naval Brigade in South Africa During the Years 1877–78–79* (London, 1880), p. 24.

181. S. Tenkorang, 'John Mensah Sarbah, 1864–1910', *Transactions of the Historical Society of Ghana*, 14 (1973), pp. 65–78.

182. John Mensah Sarbah, *Fanti Customary Laws: A Brief Introduction to the Principles of the Native Laws and Customs of the Fanti and Akan Districts of the Gold Coast, with a Report of Some Cases Thereon Decided in the Law Courts* (2nd edn, London, 1904), p. 114.

183. Pastor Mojola Agbebi, 'The West African Problem', in G. Spiller (ed.), *Papers on Interracial Problems Communicated to the First Universal Races Congress, Held at the University of London, July 26–29, 1911* (London, 1911), pp. 346, 343.

184. For a classic account of Zimbabwean spirit mediums, which contains some material on the colonial period, see Lan, *Guns and Rain*.

185. 'The Natives of Africa', *Pall Mall Gazette*, 19 November 1895.

186. On this point see Lan, *Guns and Rain*, esp. pp. 143–5, 232.

187. Sean Redding, 'Women as Diviners and as Christian Converts in Rural South Africa, c. 1880–1963', *Journal of African History*, 57 (2016), p. 374.

188. G.S. Hofmeyr, 'King William's Town and the Xhosa, 1854–1861: The Role of a Frontier Capital During the High Commissionership of Sir George Grey', MA thesis, University of Cape Town (May 1981), pp. 10, 48–9.

189. Robert Giddings, *Imperial Echoes: Eye-witness Accounts of Victoria's Little Wars* (London, 1996), p. 162.

190. Terence Ranger, *Revolt in Southern Rhodesia, 1896–97: A Study in African Resistance* (Evanston, IL, 1967), p. 217.

191. 'Life in South Africa', *Thetford and Watton Times*, 24 October 1896.

192. Arthur Keppel-Jones, *Rhodes and Rhodesia: The White Conquest of Zimbabwe 1884–1902* (Kingston and Montreal, 1983), p. 477. Blessing-Miles Tendi, *Making History in Mugabe's Zimbabwe: Politics, Intellectuals and the Media* (Bern, 2010), p. 94. Tanya Lyons, *Guns and Guerilla Girls: Women in the Zimbabwean National Liberation Struggle* (Trenton, 2004), p. 72.

193. Hailey, *An African Survey*, p. 295.

194. Boaz, 'Witchcraft, Witchdoctors and Empire', pp. 25–6. Redding, 'Women as Diviners and as Christian Converts in Rural South Africa', pp. 367–89.

195. Natasha Gray, 'Witches, Oracles, and Colonial Law: Evolving Anti-witchcraft Practices in Ghana, 1927–1932', *International Journal of African Historical Studies*, 34 (2001), p. 340.

196. Boaz, 'Witchcraft, Witchdoctors and Empire', p. 20.

197. George Orde-Browne, 'Witchcraft and British Colonial Law', *Africa: Journal of the International African Institute*, 8 (1935), p. 481.

198. Luongo, *Witchcraft and Colonial Rule in Kenya*, p. 92. C. Clifton Roberts, 'Witchcraft and Colonial Legislation', *Africa*, 8 (1935), p. 488.

199. Orde-Browne, 'Witchcraft and British Colonial Law', p. 482.

200. Luongo, *Witchcraft and Colonial Rule*, p. 104.

201. Waller, 'Witchcraft and Colonial Law in Kenya', pp. 244–5.

202. Melland, *In Witch-bound Africa*, p. 198.

203. Orde-Browne, 'Witchcraft and British Colonial Law', p. 484.

204. Melland, *In Witch-bound Africa*, pp. 8–9. Karen Blixen, *Out of Africa* (1937: London, 2001), pp. 123–6.

205. C.W. Hobley, 'Some Reflections on Native Magic in Relation to Witchcraft', *Journal of the Royal African Society*, 33 (1934), pp. 243, 246.

206. Redding, 'Women as Diviners and as Christian Converts in Rural South Africa', p. 376.

207. Hobley, 'Some Reflections on Native Magic', p. 245. Luongo, *Witchcraft and Colonial Rule in Kenya*, p. 104. Donald Cameron, 'Native Administration in Tanganyika and Nigeria', *Journal of the Royal African Society*, 36 (1937), p. 28.

208. Simeon Mesaki, 'Witchcraft and the Law in Tanzania', *Internal Journal of Sociology and Anthropology*, 1 (2009), pp. 134–5.

209. See Luongo, *Witchcraft and Colonial Rule in Kenya*, Chapter 5.

210. Roberts, 'Witchcraft and Colonial Legislation', p. 489.

211. Richard Austin Freeman, *Travels and Life in Ashanti and Jaman* (Westminster, 1898), pp. 148–52.

212. Ibid., p. 152. Also quoted in John Parker, 'Witchcraft, Anti-witchcraft and Trans-regional Ritual Innovation in Early Colonial Ghana: Sakrabundi and Aberewa, 1889–1910', *Journal of African History*, 45 (2004), p. 399.

213. As Richard Freeman put it: 'African natives are as a rule extremely reticent on the subject of their religious beliefs, and if pressed for information usually deliberately mislead their questioners.' See Freeman, *Travels and Life in Ashanti and Jaman*, p. 148, also p. 249.

214. Huxley, *The Flame Trees of Thika*, pp. 48, 54.

215. Blixen, *Out of Africa*, p. 126.

216. Huxley, *The Flame Trees of Thika*, pp. 83, 151–60, 191.

217. Quoted in Delius, 'Witches and Missionaries in Nineteenth-century Transvaal', p. 433.

218. H.F. Trew, 'Black Magic in Africa', *The Graphic*, 13 September 1930.

219. 'From Africa to Barnstaple', *Western Morning News*, 29 August 1938.

220. T.E. Dorman, *African Experience: An Educational Officer in Northern Rhodesia* (London, 1993), pp. 33, 132–4, 148.

221. Smith and Dale, *The Ila-speaking Peoples of Northern Rhodesia*, vol. 2, p. 96.

222. Melland, *In Witch-bound Africa*, pp. 183–4

223. Ibid., p. 196.

224. Ibid., p. 202.

225. Ibid., p. 203.

8 WITCHCRAFT'S DECLINE: 1900–1960s

1. Ross McKibbin, *Classes and Cultures: England: 1918–1951* (Oxford, 1998), pp. v, 68–9, 385, 528–36, and his *Parties and People: England 1914–1951* (Oxford, 2010), pp. vi–viii.

2. The figures are very difficult to calculate and thus remain approximate. For data and a discussion see Roger Middleton, 'The Size and Scope of the Public Sector', in S.J.D. Green and R.C. Whiting (eds), *The Boundaries of the State in Modern Britain* (1996: Cambridge, 2002), esp. p. 62.

3. W. Somerset Maugham's novel *The Magician* (1908) was inspired by Aleister Crowley.

4. Alan Richardson, *Aleister Crowley and Dion Fortune: The Logos of the Aeon and the Shakti of the Age* (Woodbury, MN, 2009), p. 62.

5. 'Barbara's Budget', *Western Daily Press*, 26 November 1938, p. 10. 'Writer's Sheffield Associations', *Sheffield Daily Telegraph*, 7 March 1939. 'Dion Fortune', *Western Mail*, 13 February 1939.

6. For early uses of the term see Rudolf Steiner, *The Way of Initiation: or, How to Attain Knowledge of the Higher Worlds* (London, 1909), p. 34. Eugène Lévy, *Mrs Besant and the Present Crisis in the Theosophical Society* (London, 1913), p. xiv.

7. The best accounts of Dion Fortune are Gareth Knight, *Dion Fortune and the Inner Light* (London, 2000). Alan Richardson, *The Magical Life of Dion Fortune: Priestess of the Twentieth Century* (London, 1987). Ronald Hutton, *The Triumph of the Moon: A History of Modern Pagan Witchcraft* (1999: Oxford, 2001), pp. 180–8. I rely on these biographies, unless otherwise noted.

8. 'Woman's Sphere', *The Sphere*, 14 July 1900, p. 64. Violet presented a bouquet to the dignitaries, not for the last time: 'Charity Fair at Sheen House', *Morning Post*, 10 July 1901, p. 2. 'The Fete at Sheen House', *Illustrated London News*, 20 July 1901.

9. 'Music and Poetry: The Achievements of Two Clever Children', *Birmingham Gazette and Express*, 24 November 1904, p. 7.

10. Entitled *Violets*. 'Echoes of the Day', *Lincolnshire Echo*, 14 November 1904. 'Poetess at Thirteen', *St James's Gazette*, 14 November 1904, p. 6.

11. 'Books and Booksellers', *London Daily News*, 7 July 1905. 'Child-verse', *The Bystander*, 14 March 1906, p. 548.

12. 'Music and Poetry: The Achievements of Two Clever Children', *Birmingham Gazette and Express*, 24 November 1904, p. 7.

13. 'A Schoolgirl Prodigy', *The Sphere*, 8 July 1905, p. 46.

14. 'Doctors' Visit to Studley', *Birmingham Gazette*, 28 July 1911, p. 6.

15. Alison Light, *Common People: In Pursuit of My Ancestors* (2014: Chicago, IL, 2015), p. 51.

16. 'Notes about Dr. Hamilton, by D.M. Garstang (c. 1971)', in Gaskell, Correspondence re LH with former Studley Students, Wellcome Collection, PP/Ham/D2.

17. 'Dr. Lillias Hamilton: Lady's Adventurous Career', *Western Morning News*, 10 January 1925.

18. 'The Armitstead Lectures: Dr. Lillias Hamilton', *Dundee Courier*, 28 November 1898, p. 5.

19. 'Educated Women in Factories. Address by Dr. Lillias Hamilton', *Leamington Spa Courier*, 5 March 1915, p. 7.

20. 'Dr. Lillias Hamilton off to Montenegro', *Birmingham Daily Mail*, 4 June 1915, p. 4.

21. John A. Brashear, *A Man Who Loved the Stars* (1924: London, 1988), p. 173.

22. 'Letter from M.W. Gubbins, to E. Gaskell, 26th of Jan 1970', Wellcome Collection, PP/Ham/D2.

23. 'Letter from K.M. Lewis to E. Gaskell, 5th February 1970'. 'Notes about Dr. Hamilton, by D.M. Garstang (c. 1971)', Wellcome Collection, PP/Ham/D2.

24. 'Letter from Miss M.E. Rotherham O.B.E. to E. Gaskell, 22nd January 1970', in Wellcome Collection, PP/Ham/D2.

25. 'Letter from Lillias Hamilton to Claude Hamilton, 11th January 1911', in Hamilton, Letters to Claude, Wellcome Collection, PP/Ham/B6.

26. Dion Fortune, *Psychic Self-defence: A Study in Occult Pathology and Criminality* (1930: London, 1974), p. 12.

27. Edmund Gurney, Frederic W.H. Myers and Frank Podmore, *Phantasms of the Living*, vol. 2 (London, 1886), p. 656.

28. Fortune, *Psychic Self-defence*, p. 15.

29. Richard Overy, *The Morbid Age: Britain between the Wars* (London, 2009), Chapter 4. Rhodri Hayward, *The Transformation of the Psyche in British Primary Care: 1880–1970* (London, 2015), p. 53.

30. Conolly Norman, 'Modern Witchcraft: A Study of a Phase of Paranoia', *Journal of Mental Science*, 51 (1905), pp. 117–18.

31. See Owen Davies, *A Supernatural War: Magic, Divination and Faith during the First World War* (Oxford, 2018).

32. Edward Lovett, *Magic in Modern London* (London, 1925). See also S.C. Williams, *Religious Belief and Popular Culture in Southwark c. 1880–1939* (Oxford, 1999), pp. 22, 54, 58, 70, 74. Several British museums possess objects collected by Mr Lovett, most notably the Wellcome Collection.

33. David Clarke, 'Rumours of Angels: A Legend of the First World War', *Folklore*, 113 (2002), pp. 151–73. Paul Fussell, *The Great War and Modern Memory* (1975: Oxford, 2000), pp. 115–16.

34. Jennifer Hazelgrove, 'Spiritualism after the Great War', *Twentieth Century British History*, 10 (1999), pp. 405–6.

35. J.K., 'The Real Black Magic Revealed without Mystery (London, 1921)', published typescript, Wellcome Collection MS. 3126, xii.

36. Susan Johnston Graf, *Talking to the Gods: Occultism in the Work of W.B. Yeats, Arthur Machen, Algernon Blackwood, and Dion Fortune* (Albany, NY, 2015), pp. 103–4.

37. Ibid., p. 109. In 1926 Violet was preaching to the Bath Lodge of the Theosophical Society. See 'Free Church News', *Bath Chronicle*, 4 September 1926, p. 22.

38. 'Marriages', *Sheffield Daily Telegraph*, 11 April 1927, p. 3.

39. Dr R. von Krafft-Ebing, *Text-book of Insanity, Based on Clinical Observations, for Practitioners and Students of Medicine*, trans. Charles Gilbert Chaddock (Philadelphia, PA, 1904), pp. 123–4, 170, 486.

40. Magus Incognito, *The Secret Doctrine of the Rosicrucians: Illustrated with the Secret Rosicrucian Symbols* (London and Chicago, IL, 1918), p. 216.

41. Fortune, *Psychic Self-defence*, p. 10.

42. Ibid., p. 35.

43. 'Witchcraft and Magic', *Sheffield Independent*, 9 March 1931, p. 4.

44. 'Dracula Authenticated', *Western Morning News*, 22 December 1930, p. 2.

45. Fortune, *Psychic Self-defence*, pp. 172–6.

46. 'From the Beyond', *Aberdeen Press and Journal*, 31 October 1932, p. 2.

47. David Devereux, *Memoirs of an Exorcist* (London, 2006), p. 222.

48. *Taunton Courier and Western Advertiser*, 27 July 1921.

49. *Sunderland Daily Echo*, 26 September 1904. *Manchester Guardian*, 26 September 1904.

50. *Western Daily Press*, 18 November 1935.

51. *Stamford Mercury*, 20 January 1911. *Sheffield Daily Telegraph*, 14 January 1911. *Western Times*, 9 December 1913; 29 March 1919. *The Times*, 9 December 1924. *Western Daily Press*, 9 December 1924. *Hull Daily Mail*, 6 January 1941.

52. *Wells Journal*, 11 August 1916. *Western Times*, 27 October 1916. *Tamworth Herald*, 5 August 1916.

53. *Essex Newsman*, 8 August 1908.

54. *Western Gazette*, 4 January 1918; 29 January 1926.

55. *Western Times*, 7 September 1905. *Exeter and Plymouth Gazette*, 8 September 1905. *Derby Daily Telegraph*, 5 September 1905. *Manchester Guardian*, 13 January 1926; 11 June 1929. *The Times*, 13 January 1926. *Western Daily Press*, 11 June 1929.

56. *Nottingham Evening Post*, 5 August 1921.

57. Enid Porter, *Cambridgeshire Customs and Folklore* (London, 1969), p. 163.

58. Laurie Lee, *Cider with Rosie* (1959: London, 2002), p. 35.

59. For this and other anecdotes see L. Winstanley and H.J. Rose, 'Scraps of Welsh Folklore, I', *Folklore*, 37 (1926), pp. 163–73.

60. L. Winstanley and H.J. Rose, 'Welsh Folklore Items, III', *Folklore*, 39 (1928), p. 172.

61. Winstanley and Rose, 'Scraps of Welsh Folklore, I', p. 163.

62. George Sydenham, 'The Vulgar Errors and Superstitions of West Somerset in Their Relation to Medicine', *British Medical Journal*, 10 November 1900, pp. 1366–7.

63. F.W. Bennett, *Tiddyoody Pie* ([n.d., c. 1930]), p. 90.

64. Some of which were collected by the folklorist Edward Lovett. See Horniman Museum, 'Black and brown coloured holed stone threaded through with a length of short twine. Used as a charm against witches' (1912). Object: 12.196, http://www.horniman.ac.uk/object/12.196.

65. Mollie Harris, *A Kind of Magic: An Oxfordshire Childhood in the 1920s* (1969: Oxford, 1983), pp. 15, 114.

66. Ruth Tongue, *Somerset Folklore*, ed. Catherine Briggs (London, 1965), p. 86.

67. *Nottingham Evening Post*, 3 February 1903. *Western Gazette*, 29 May 1903.

68. J. Harvey Bloom, *Folk Lore, Old Customs and Superstitions in Shakespeare Land* (London, [n.d., c. 1929]), p. 96.

69. Ibid., p. 91.

70. Sheila Stewart, *Country Kate* (Kineton, 1971), p. 43.

71. Ibid., p. 78.

72. Bennett, *Tiddyoody Pie*, pp. 90–1.

73. As suggested by James Obelkevich, *Religion and Rural Society: South Lindsey 1825–1875* (Oxford, 1976), p. 291.

74. Unless otherwise noted, this account of Mother Herne is based on Olive Knott, *Witches of Wessex* (Sturminster Newton, [n.d. c. 1961), pp. 6–8. Rodney Legg and Olive Knott, *Witches of Dorset* (Wincanton, 1974), pp. 33–9. An excellent account of Somerset cunning-folk, including Mother Herne, can be found in Owen Davies, *A People Bewitched: Witchcraft and Magic in Nineteenth-century Somerset* (Bruton, 1999), Chapters 2 and 3.

75. 'Somerset Stories and Customs', *Western Gazette*, 29 November 1940, p. 5.

76. These figures are frustratingly absent from many, if not most, histories of British policing. Some quantifiable solace can be found in Joe Hicks and Grahame Allen, *A Century of Change: Trends in UK Statistics since 1900* (House of Commons Library Research Paper 99/111, 21 December 1999), p. 14. For a provincial breakdown of the 1920s statistics see *Report of the Royal Commission on Police Powers and Procedure* (London, 1929), pp. 137–40.

77. H.W. Brown, 'A Witch Doctor', *Somerset County Herald*, 7 July 1926, p. 10. Also 'A 20th Century White Witch', *Somerset County Herald*, 21 September 1940, p. 2.

78. Legg and Knott, *Witches of Dorset*, p. 37.

79. Memories of Mother Herne persisted as late as 2014, when a local man named George Dite, from Charlton Horethorne, began to investigate. George began his valuable work after reading Owen Davies' superb account of nineteenth-century popular belief, *A People Bewitched*. The tales and tidbits he uncovered reveal Mother Herne to have been a quick-witted and sharp-tongued woman, as well as a gifted healer, a detector of stolen goods, an infallible predictor of the future, and a wielder of uncanny powers. The quotation comes from an anecdote involving George's aunt Maud and her husband, who farmed a smallholding near the village. After a year of misfortune Maud consulted Mother Herne, who told her: 'you have a woman who visits you and she is bringing you bad luck, you must not let her into your house again.' Maud followed this advice, though it meant turning away her old friend, and sure enough life on the farm got better.

80. Legg and Knott, *Witches of Dorset*, p. 38.

81. H.W. Brown, 'A Witch Doctor', *Somerset County Herald*, 7 July 1926, p. 10. Also 'A 20th Century White Witch', *Somerset County Herald*, 21 September 1940, p. 2.

82. This was another anecdote collected by George Dite, in 2014, the story told of a local farmer and keen shooter. He resolved to prosecute Mother Herne's son, whom he found illegally catching rabbits in his field. When she found out Mother Herne ominously foretold that if the farmer went ahead with his case he would never shoot again. True to form, when the trial day came the farmer suffered a stroke, spending the rest of his life in a wheelchair.

83. Legg and Knott, *Witches of Dorset*, p. 38.

84. 'The War against Quackery', *British Medical Journal*, 28 September 1907, pp. 836–7.

85. For an enlightening discussion of the definition of 'quackery', based on legal rulings, see Leonard Le Marchant Minty, *The Legal and Ethical Aspects of Medical Quackery* (London, 1932), pp. xiii–xvi.

86. Roy Porter, *Health for Sale: Quackery in England 1660–1850* (Manchester, 1989), p. 228.

87. 'Quackery and Female Complaints', *British Medical Journal*, 27 May 1911, p. 1240.

88. *Report as to the Practice of Medicine and Surgery by Unqualified Persons in the United Kingdom* (London, 1910), p. 2.

89. Ibid., p. 31.

90. Ibid., p. 38.

91. Ibid., p. 45.

92. Ibid., p. 63.

93. Harrison Mitchell, 'Ambulance Classes as Opportunities for Erecting the Best Bulwark against Quackery', *Supplement to the British Medical Journal*, 18 January 1908, p. 18. 'The War Against Quackery', *British Medical Journal*, 5 October 1907, p. 940. Reflecting its readers' priorities, in 1911, the *British Medical Journal* devoted an entire issue to the 'monster' of 'quackery'. See *British Medical Journal*, 1(2630) (27 May 1911), pp. 1289–90.

94. 'The War Against Quackery', *British Medical Journal*, 13 January 1906, p. 100.

95. Roy Porter, *The Greatest Benefit to Mankind: A Medical History of Humanity* (New York, 1997), p. 457.

96. 'Medical and Dental Quackery', *British Medical Journal*, 13 June 1908, pp. 1456–7. For similar complaints, 'Quackery', *British Medical Journal*, 12 October 1901, p. 1115.

97. Anne Digby, *Making a Medical Living: Doctors and Patients in the English Market for Medicine, 1720–1911* (Cambridge, 1994), pp. 19–20.

98. On which see Francesca Moore, ' "Go and See Nell; She'll Put You Right": The Wisewoman and Working-class Health Care in Early Twentieth-century Lancashire', *Social History of Medicine*, 26 (2013), pp. 695–714. P.S. Brown, 'The Vicissitudes of Herbalism in Late Nineteenth- and Early Twentieth-century Britain', *Medical History*, 29(1) (January 1985), pp. 71–92.

99. Gerald Larkin, *Occupational Monopoly and Modern Medicine* (London and New York, 1983), pp. 18, 19.

100. Ibid., p. 20.

101. John Humphreys Davies' account of the meeting was published posthumously. See J.H. Davies, 'Collecting Welsh Books', *Transactions of the Honourable Society of Cymmrodorion: Session 1940* (London, 1941), p. 146.

102. Winstanley and Rose, 'Welsh Folklore Items, III', p. 174.

103. Ibid., pp. 177–8.

104. 'Uwchaled, A Ramble in Clun Forest', *The Welsh Outlook*, 17 (1930), p. 281. Miss R.M. Evans, 'Folklore and Customs in Cardiganshire', *Cardiganshire Antiquarian Society*, 12 (1937), p. 57. C.J.S. Thompson, *The Hand of Destiny: Everyday Folklore and Superstitions* (1932: London, 1995), p. 289.

105. 'Farmers Appeal to Wizard to Rescue Them from "Evil Eye" ', *Daily Express*, 27 December 1932.

106. The material for this paragraph comes from a particularly good folklore report: Dr W.Ll. Davies, 'The Conjuror in Montgomeryshire', *Collections, Historical & Archaeological relating to Montgomeryshire and Its Borders*, 45 (1938), pp. 158–66.

107. *The Times*, 14 March 1961.

108. 'The "White Witch" Saves Foal', *Daily Herald*, 25 May 1956. Owen Davies, 'Charmers and Charming in England and Wales from the Eighteenth to the Twentieth Century', *Folklore*, 109 (1998), p. 41.

109. For an excellent discussion of the legislative process that led to the passage of the 1951 Fraudulent Mediums Bill see Owen Davies, *Witchcraft, Magic and Culture: 1736–1951* (Manchester, 1999), pp. 61–75.

110. On whom see Malcolm Gaskell, *Hellish Nell: Last of Britain's Witches* (London, 2001).

111. 'Goiter Sufferer's Obsession', *Hull Daily Mail*, 13 January 1940, p. 3.

112. 'Alleged Thefts by Gipsies', *Somerset County Herald*, 10 May 1941, p. 5.

113. 'Parents Feared Their Boy Was Bewitched!', *Sunday Post*, 13 October 1946, p. 2.

114. 'Woman Who Fears "Witchcraft Wish" in Her Council House', *Birmingham Gazette*, 28 February 1951, p. 5.

115. 'My Wife Is Bewitched by Cat, He Says', *Daily Herald*, 8 July 1955.

116. For some tales of this order see Margaret Eyre, 'Folk-lore of the Wye Valley', *Folklore*, 16 (1905), esp. p. 172.

117. 'A Yorkshire "Witch"', *Newcastle Weekly Chronicle*, 23 March 1940, p. 1.

118. 'Nancy Camel's Hole', *Somerset Herald*, 12 April 1947, p. 2.

119. 'The Weavers and Wonders of Lopham', *Norfolk and Suffolk Journal and Diss Express*, 25 August 1950, p. 4.

120. W.H. Barrett, *Tales from the Fens*, ed. Enid Porter (1963: London, 1969), pp. x–xi.

121. Peter Clarke, *Hope and Glory: Britain 1900–1990* (London, 1996), p. 250. Paul Addison, *No Turning Back: The Peacetime Revolutions of Post-war Britain* (Oxford, 2010), p. 56.

122. On the peak of the stiff upper lip see Thomas Dixon, *Weeping Britannia: Portrait of a Nation in Tears* (Oxford, 2015), pp. 69, 205.

123. 'Next Week's Films', *Somerset County Herald*, 1 December 1945, p. 4.

124. 'Crowcombe Mill', *Somerset County Herald*, 9 January 1943, p. 2. 'Tragic Spell to Break', *Wells Journal*, 25 December 1942, p. 1. Tongue, *Somerset Folklore*, p. 219.

125. Eric Maple, 'The Witches of Canewdon', *Folklore*, 71 (1960), p. 241.

126. Christina Hole, 'Notes on Some Folklore Survivals in English Domestic Life', *Folklore*, 68 (1957), p. 414.

127. 'Witchcraft', *Aberdeen Press and Journal*, 11 February 1950, p. 2.

128. Geoffrey Gorer, *Exploring English Character* (New York, 1955), pp. 263–9.

129. For remarks on 'still-prized stiff-upper-lippedness' see David Kynaston, *Austerity Britain: 1945–1951* (London, 2007), p. 304. Also David Kynaston, *Family Britain: 1951–1957* (London, 2009), p. 515. Robert Murphy, *British Cinema and the Second World War* (London, 2000), pp. 6–7. Jessica Mann, *The Fifties Mystique* (Sheffield, 2012), p. 22. Brian Harrison, *Seeking a Role: The United Kingdom 1951–1970* (Oxford, 2009), p. 374.

130. On which see David Welch, *Persuading the People: British Propaganda in World War II* (London, 2016).

131. Winston S. Churchill, *Secret Session Speeches*, compiled by Charles Eade (London, 1946), p. 11.

132. Iona Opie and Peter Opie, *The Lore and Language of Schoolchildren* (Oxford, 1959), p. 274.

133. S.J.D. Green, *The Passing of Protestant England: Secularisation and Social Change c. 1920–1960* (Cambridge, 2011), esp. Chapters 4 and 8.

134. Gorer, *Exploring English Character*, p. 252.

135. L. Salmon, 'Folklore in the Kennet Valley', *Folklore*, 13 (1902), p. 427.

136. Quoted in Mark R. Taylor, 'Norfolk Folklore', *Folklore*, 40 (1929), p. 130.

137. James Moffatt's new translation of 1926, revised in 1935, referred to the 'Witch of Endor' (she is the 'woman of Endor' in some more recent translations), but did not mention familiar spirits or witches in the context of the Old Testament injunctions against ungodly behaviour. Being a 'sorceress' was condemned though. James A.R. Moffat, *The Bible: James Moffatt Translation* (1935: San Francisco, 1995), pp. 86, 344.

138. Alun Howkins, *The Death of Rural England: A Social History of the Countryside Since 1900* (London, 2003), p. 152.

139. George Ewart Evans, *Horse Power and Magic* (London, 1979), esp. pp. 106–8. Also pp. 9, 97, 100–5, 128.

140. Christina Hole, 'Superstitions and Beliefs of the Sea', *Folklore*, 78 (1967), p. 185.

141. J.M. McPherson, *Primitive Beliefs in the North-east of Scotland* (London, 1929), pp. 286–9.

142. 'Strange Stories from the North-east', *Aberdeen Evening Express*, 21 June 1952, p. 4.

143. Alec Gill, *Superstitions: Folk Magic in Hull's Fishing Community* (Beverley, 1993), pp. 30–3. For background see esp. pp. 8–14.

144. Ruth E. St Leger-Gordon, *The Witchcraft and Folklore of Dartmoor* (London, 1965), pp. 132, 135. 'Somerset Witch Beliefs', *Somerset County Herald*, 21 March 1942, p. 2.

145. Tongue, *Somerset Folklore*, p. 65.

146. Ibid., pp. 75–6, 85, 87, 89.

147. Katherine M. Briggs, 'Christina Hole: An Appreciation', *Folklore*, 90 (1979), p. 7.

148. Christina Hole, *A Mirror of Witchcraft* (London, 1957), p. 17.

149. Christina Hole, *Witchcraft in England* (London, 1966), p. 215.

150. British Medical Association, *Divine Healing and Co-operation between Doctors and Clergy* (London, 1956), p. 34.

151. 'Black Witchery Can Lead to Murder', *Daily Herald*, 7 June 1956, p. 6.

152. See E.P. Thompson, 'Rough Music Reconsidered', *Folklore*, 103 (1992), p. 20.

153. 'Black Witchery Can Lead to Murder', *Daily Herald*, 7 June 1956, p. 6.

154. 'Witchcraft', *Somerset County Herald*, 14 June 1947, p. 2.

155. E. Oduwole, 'The Relevance of Occult and Paranormal Phenomenon in West Africa in the Era of Globilisation', in Josephat Obi Oguejiofor and Tobias Wendl (eds), *Exploring the Occult and Paranormal in West Africa* (London and Berlin, [n.d. c. 2012]), p. 116.

156. Owen Davies, *America Bewitched: The Story of Witchcraft after Salem* (Oxford, 2013), p. 207. Also Davies, *Witchcraft, Magic and Culture*, Chapter 6, esp. pp. 280–93. Hutton, *Triumph*, p. 110.

157. Selina Todd, *The People: The Rise and Fall of the Working Class* (London, 2015), pp. 112, 152–5.

158. A good record of the lack of modern amenities in rural life, even after the Second World War is W.J. Turner, *Exmoor Village: A General Account* (London, 1947).

159. T. Gwynn Jones, *Welsh Folklore and Folk-Custom* (London, 1930), p. 126.

160. Winstanley and Rose, 'Welsh Folklore Items, III', pp. 174–8.

161. Knott, *Witches of Wessex*, p. 28. Also Legg and Knott, *Witches of Dorset*, p. 60.

162. Owen Davies, *Popular Magic: Cunning-folk in English History* (2003: London, 2007), pp. 187–8.

163. 'Dukkering', *The Globe*, 4 April 1911, pp. 1–2.

164. Silvester Gordon Boswell, *The Book of Boswell: Autobiography of a Gypsy*, ed. John Seymour (1970: London, 2012), pp. 17, 19, 24, 27.

165. 'The Gipsies in Time of War', *Sunday Post*, 7 March 1915, p. 5.

166. 'The Passing of the Gypsy', *Worthing Herald*, 9 May 1931. 'The Secret People', *The Sphere*, 2 July 1892, p. 6.

167. Judith Okely, *The Traveller-Gypsies* (Cambridge, 1983), p. 22. Donald Kenrick and Sian Bakewell, *On the Verge: The Gypsies of England* (Hatfield, 1995), p. 11.

168. Becky Taylor, *A Minority and the State: Travellers in Britain in the Twentieth Century* (Manchester, 2008), p. 114. Jake Bowers, 'Gypsies and Travellers Accessing their Own Past: The Surrey Project and Aspects of Minority Representation', in Michael Hayes and Thomas Action (eds), *Travellers, Gypsies, Roma: The Demonisation of Difference* (Newcastle, 2007), p. 25. Okley, *The Traveller-Gypsies*, p. 22.

169. For examples from Kent see Simon Evans, *Stopping Places: A Gypsy History of South London and Kent* (Hatfield, 2004), Chapters 3 and 4.

170. Boswell, *The Book of Boswell*, p. 33.

171. Netta Cartwright, *The Many Lives of Zillah Smith: An English Romany* (Oxford, 2014), p. 51.

172. On the gypsies' continuing knowledge of herbal remedies see ibid., p. 12.

173. 'Your Home is Bewitched', *Daily Herald*, 22 February 1940, p. 3. ' "Spell" on House: Story in Theft Case', *Western Mail*, 22 February 1940, p. 9. Mrs Jones lived in a new bungalow

on the outskirts of Merthyr. In court she described herself as an antique dealer (a conventional gypsy self-description, during this period), and said she'd been asked to put a curse on the house by gypsies.

174. '"Curse on a House" Story', *Birmingham Daily Gazette*, 23 September 1950, p. 3.

175. She went back a second time, when she was seen, and claimed the curse would kill the victim's husband. See 'Had Money "to Remove a Curse" Allegation', *Birmingham Daily Post*, 24 October 1958, p. 5.

176. 'Gipsy's "Mean Trick" on Woman', *Birmingham Daily Post*, 29 January 1959, p. 7.

177. 'My Curse . . . by Prince Gipsy Lee', *Daily Herald*, 25 January 1961.

178. 'The Gipsy Beats the Council He Cursed', *Daily Herald*, 27 January 1961.

179. 'Man Feared the Gipsies' Curse', *Birmingham Daily Post*, 16 May 1964, p. 7.

180. Jacqueline Simpson, 'Margaret Murray: Who Believed Her, and Why?', *Folklore*, 105 (1994), p. 92.

181. For an excellent discussion of how Frazer's thesis was received see Mary Beard, 'Frazer, Leach, and Virgil: The Popularity (and Unpopularity) of the Golden Bough', *Comparative Studies in Society and History*, 34 (1992), pp. 203–24.

182. For a detailed discussion see Simpson, 'Margaret Murray: Who Believed Her, and Why?', pp. 90–2. Hutton, *Triumph*, p. 362.

183. *Surrey Mirror*, 2 March 1934.

184. 'Midland "Black Magic" Murders?', *Birmingham Gazette*, 2 September 1950, p. 1.

185. 'Witchcraft? It's Rubbish', *Daily Herald*, 5 September 1950, p. 3.

186. Ronald Hutton's *The Triumph of the Moon* is a magnificent account of Wicca's origins, and comes thoroughly recommended. Also very enlightening, particularly because it continues until the early 2000s, is Ethan Doyle White, *Wicca: History, Belief, and Community in Modern Pagan Witchcraft* (Eastbourne, 2016), Chapters 2–7.

187. For instance, Gardner's 'strong sense of humour' was mentioned in a brief account of him in *The Sphere*, 21 April 1962, p. 107.

188. Doreen Valiente, *An ABC of Witchcraft Past and Present* (1973: Washington, 1986), p. 152. G.B. Gardner, *The Meaning of Witchcraft* (London, 1959), Chapter 1.

189. On the very fascinating Cecil Williamson see Steve Patterson, *Cecil Williamson's Book of Witchcraft: A Grimoire of the Museum of Witchcraft* (London, 2014), esp. pp. 119–47. Hutton, *Triumph*, pp. 208–9, 218–19, 242–4.

190. This point is explored in Ethan Doyle White, '"An' it Harm None, Do What Ye Will." A Historical Analysis of the Wiccan Rede', *Magic, Ritual, and Witchcraft*, 10 (2015), pp. 142–71.

191. Several recordings exist in the archive of the Museum of Witchcraft and Magic, Boscastle. Many of these can also be found on the internet.

192. Gerald Gardner, *Witchcraft Today* (London, 1954), esp. Chapter 1.

193. Valiente, *An ABC of Witchcraft*, p. 156.

194. Wiccan authors responded to the demand for spellcasting. See Paul Huson, *Mastering Witchcraft: A Practical Guide for Witches, Warlocks, and Covens* (New York, 1970). Huson's book is overwhelmingly concerned with operative magic rather than religious devotion.

9 MULTICULTURAL MAGIC: 1970–2015

1. *Daily Mirror*, 7 March 1974.

2. Sian Barber, *The British Film Industry in the 1970s: Capital, Culture and Creativity* (Basingstoke, 2013), p. 73. Sue Harper and Justin Smith, *British Film Culture in the 1970s: The Boundaries of Pleasure* (Edinburgh, 2012), p. 210.

3. See William Peter Blatty, *If There Were Demons, Then Perhaps There Were Angels: William Peter Blatty's Own Story of the Exorcist* (Suffolk, 1999).

4. *Daily Mirror*, 7 March 1974.

5. '"The Exorcist" Spreads "Fear & Alarm"', *Church Times*, 29 March 1974, p. 12.

6. Quoted in S.T. Joshi (ed.), *Icons of Horror and the Supernatural: An Encyclopedia of Our Worst Nightmares*, vol. 1 (Westport, CT, and London, 2007), p. 33. Moshe Sluhovsky, *Believe Not Every Spirit: Possession, Mysticism and Discernment in Early Modern Catholicism* (Chicago, IL, and London, 2007), p. 56.

7. Nicholas Campion, *Astrology and Popular Religion in the Modern West: Prophecy, Cosmology and the New Age Movement* (London, 2016), p. 132.

8. *Daily Express*, 1 October 1990, p. 3.

9. *Daily Express*, 2 February 1995, p. 7; 13 August 1997, pp. 1–2; also 14 August 1997, p. 2.

10. Owen Davies, *The Haunted: A Social History of Ghost* (Basingstoke, 2007), p. 241. Brian Harrison, *Finding A Role? The United Kingdom 1970–1990* (Oxford, 2011), p. 372. Gallup, 'Paranormal Beliefs Come (Super)Naturally to Some', 1 November 2005, http://www.gallup.com/poll/19558/paranormal-beliefs-come-supernaturally-some.aspx (accessed December 2018).

11. Ipsos MORI, 'Survey on Beliefs', 31 October 2007, https://www.ipsos.com/ipsos-mori/en-uk/survey-beliefs (accessed January 2019).

12. Clive D. Field, 'Witchcraft', 25 August 2010, http://www.brin.ac.uk/witchcraft/ (accessed January 2019).

13. Gallup, 'Paranormal Beliefs Come (Super)Naturally to Some'.

14. Owen Davies, 'Witchcraft Accusations in France, 1850–1990', in Willem de Blécourt and Owen Davies (eds), *Witchcraft Continued: Popular Magic in Modern Europe* (Manchester, 2004), p. 127. David W. Moore, 'Three in Four Americans Believe in Paranormal', 16 June 2005, http://www.gallup.com/poll/16915/three-four-americans-believe-paranormal.aspx (accessed December 2018).

15. Bob Tortora, 'Witchcraft Believers in Sub-Saharan Africa Rate Lives Worse', 25 August 2010, http://www.gallup.com/poll/142640/witchcraft-believers-sub-saharan-africa-rate-lives-worse.aspx (accessed December 2018).

16. On the usage of the words 'witch' and 'witchcraft' during the early modern period see Karen Jones, 'Witchcraft and Magic in Kent, 1396–1543', in Sheila Sweetinburgh (ed.), *Later Medieval Kent, 1220–1540* (Woodbridge, 2010), p. 190.

17. *Sunday People*, 9 December 2007. For an earlier example of such usage see *Daily Mirror*, 21 August 1974.

18. On Granny Boswell see M.R.T., 'Some Personal Experiences', *Folklore*, 47 (1936), pp. 399–400.

19. Keith Thomas, 'The Relevance of Social Anthropology to the Historical Study of English Witchcraft', in Mary Douglas (ed.), *Witchcraft Confessions and Accusations* (1970: London, 2004), p. 51.

20. The name is spelt variously as 'Peirson', 'Pierson' and 'Pearson'. For stories about Nanny Peirson's escapades see Richard Blakeborough, *Wit, Character, Folklore and Customs of the North Riding of Yorkshire* (London, 1898), pp. 192–4. Marlon Atkinson, *Legends of the North York Moors: Traditions, Beliefs, and Folklore Customs* (Clapham, 1981), pp. 27–8. Eileen Rennison, *Yorkshire Witches* (Stroud, 2013).

21. Blakeborough, *Wit, Character, Folklore and Customs*, p. 192.

22. Kathryn C. Smith, 'The Role of Animals in Witchcraft and Popular Magic: With Special Reference to Yorkshire', in J.R. Porter and W.M.S. Russell (eds), *Animals in Folklore* (Norwich, 1978), p. 100.

23. See http://www.barb.co.uk/resources/tv-ownership/ (accessed October 2016).

24. Kingsley Palmer, *Oral Folktales of Wessex* (Newton Abbot, 1973), pp. 104, 131–49.

25. Kingsley Palmer, *The Folklore of Somerset* (London, 1976), p. 65.

26. Ibid., p. 69.

27. Ibid., p. 61. Also Palmer, *Oral Folktales*, p. 115.

28. E. Sigmund, *Avon and Somerset Witchcraft* (St Ives, 1977), pp. 5–6.

29. Ralph Whitlock, *The Folklore of Wiltshire* (London, 1976), p. 111.
30. Doris Jones-Baker, *The Folklore of Hertfordshire* (London 1977), p. 114.
31. Enid Porter, *The Folklore of East Anglia* (London, 1974), pp. 16, 154.
32. Francis Thompson, *The Supernatural Highlands* (London, 1976), pp. 52–3. During the early 2010s residents of Kilarlity still remembered how Annie told fortunes and used her special ritual to heal ailments that could not be cured by medical science. See 'Boblainy Forest Community Archaeology Project: Local Knowledge and Local Questions' (2015), pp. 20–1. As of June 2016 this document can be accessed through the website: http:// www.archhighland.org.uk.
33. Betsy Whyte, *The Yellow on the Broom* (Edinburgh, 1979), pp. 4, 12, 24–5, 41–2, 59–60, 62, 64, 90, 95–6, 130, 131–2.
34. Anne Ross, *Folklore of the Scottish Highlands* (London, 1976), pp. 69–70. As of June 2016, these recordings can be listened to through the website Tobar an Dualchais (Kist o Riches): http://www.tobarandualchais.co.uk/en/ (accessed December 2018).
35. www.tobarandualchais.co.uk/fullrecord/65142/1 (accessed December 2018).
36. For instance, www.tobarandualchais.co.uk/fullrecord/61511/1; www.tobaranandualchais. co.uk/fullrecord/64955/1; http://www.tobaranandualchais.co.uk/en/fullrecord/67530/5; www.tobaranandualchais.co.uk/fullrecord/86143/1 (all accessed December 2018).
37. http://www.tobaranandualchais.co.uk/en/fullrecord/82160/99 (accessed December 2018).
38. Judith Okely, *The Traveller-Gypsies* (1983; Cambridge, 1998), p. 96.
39. *Daily Express*, 19 October 1978, p. 23.
40. *Daily Mirror*, 13 June 1980.
41. *Daily Mirror*, 21 August 1974.
42. David Mayall, *Gypsy-Travellers in Nineteenth-century Society* (Cambridge, 1988), p. 6.
43. Trevor Wild, *Village England: A Social History of the Countryside* (London, 2004), p. 152.
44. On which see J.K. Bowers and P.C. Cheshire, *Agriculture, the Countryside and Land Use: An Economic Critique* (London, 1983), pp. 46–7.
45. Alun Howkins, *The Death of Rural England: A Social History of the Countryside since 1900* (London, 2003), pp. 178–9.
46. George Ewart Evans, *Horse Power and Magic* (London, 1979), p. 9.
47. Eric Maple, 'Witchcraft and Magic in the Rochford Hundred', *Folklore*, 76 (1965), p. 218.
48. On this theme, from a European perspective see Jeremy MacClancy, *Alternative Countrysides: Anthropological Approaches to Rural Western Europe Today* (Manchester, 2015).
49. On whom see Steve Patterson, *Cecil Williamson's Book of Witchcraft: A Grimoire of the Museum of Witchcraft* (London, 2014). The charms and spells I refer to below can be found on pp. 27–41.
50. Michael Williams, *Supernatural in Cornwall* (St Teath, 1974), pp. 40–6.
51. For example, Cassandra Latham-Jones, *Village Witch: Life as a Village Wisewoman in the Wilds of West Cornwall* (Oxford, 2013). 'Spellcraft for Hedge Witches', *The Hedge Wytch*, 29 (February 2005), p. 8. Marian Green, *A Witch Alone* (London, 1991).
52. Aidan Kelly, *Crafting the Art of Magic* (Woodbury, MN, 1991). Ronald Hutton, *The Pagan Religions of the Ancient British Isles: Their Nature and Legacy* (Oxford, 1991), esp. pp. 330–8.
53. For a personal introduction to this approach see Latham-Jones, *Village Witch*, esp. pp. 60–82.
54. 'Spellcraft for Hedge Witches', p. 8.
55. Gemma Gary, *Traditional Witchcraft : A Cornish Book of the Ways* (London, 2011), p. 30.
56. 'Spellcraft for Hedge Witches', p. 11.
57. On which see Ruth Prince and David Riches, *The New Age in Glastonbury: The Construction of Religious Movements* (New York and Oxford, 2000), esp. p. 64. Based on their work in the 1990s the authors found that, of Glastonbury's 7,500 residents, around 500 were adherents of New Age spiritualities.

58. The population was 21,572 according to the 1971 Census.
59. Paul Heelas, 'Challenging Secularization Theory: The Growth of "New Age" Spiritualities of Life', *The Hedgehog Review* (spring 2006), p. 47.
60. Cecil G. Helman, *Culture, Health and Illness* (5th edn, London, 2007), pp. 109–10.
61. Ronnie Moore and Stuart McClean, 'Folk Healing in Contemporary Britain and Ireland: Revival, Revitalisation or Reinvention?', in Ronnie Moore and Stuart McClean (eds), *Folk Healing and Health Care Practices in Britain and Ireland: Stethoscopes, Wands and Crystals* (New York and Oxford, 2010), p. 6.
62. Helman, *Culture, Health and Illness*, pp. 109–10.
63. For the autobiography of someone who did this sort of work see David Devereux, *Memoirs of an Exorcist* (London, 2006).
64. Latham-Jones, *Village Witch*, pp. 112, 96.
65. Doktor Snake, *Doktor Snake's Voodoo Spellbook* (New York, 2000), p. 11.
66. Devereux, *Memoirs*, p. 32.
67. Ibid., p. 24.
68. Not all stayed permanently. Thus the number of West Indians living in Britain was 302,970, according to the 1971 Census.
69. Sharon-Ann Gopaul-McNicol, *Working with West Indian Families* (New York and London, 1993), pp. 47, 111–12, 144, 147. Roland Littlewood and Maurice Lipsedge, *Aliens and Alienists: Ethnic Minorities and Psychiatry* (3rd edn, London, 1997), pp. 175, 203. Nathaniel Samuel Murrell, 'Obeah: Afro-Caribbean Religious Medicine Art and Healing', in Patsy Sutherland, Roy Moodley and Barry Chevannes (eds), *Caribbean Healing Traditions: Implications for Health and Mental Health* (Hove, 2014), p. 70.
70. Venetia Newall, 'Some Examples of the Practice of Obeah by West Indian Immigrants in London', in *Folklore*, 89(1) (1978), p. 32.
71. In 2002 Mark Lambie, a notorious London gang leader, was jailed for kidnap and torture. At his trial, his victims and fellow gangsters intimated that Lambie's power over *obeah* made him 'untouchable' – that it had enabled him to escape arrest and even death. See Steven Morris, 'Powerful Leader Jailed for Kidnap and Torture', *Guardian*, 21 May 2002, https://www.theguardian.com/uk/2002/may/21/stevenmorris (accessed December 2018).
72. Newall, 'Some Examples of the Practice of Obeah', pp. 37–8.
73. Simon Dein, 'Mental Health in a Multiethnic Society', *British Medical Journal*, 315 (23 August 1997), p. 473.
74. Paul Addison, *No Turning Back: The Peacetime Revolutions of Post-War Britain* (Oxford, 2010), pp. 234–5.
75. Ceri Peach, 'Three Phases of South Asian Emigration', in Judith M. Brown and Rosemary Foot (eds), *Migration: The Asian Experience* (Basingstoke, 2004), p. 39.
76. Alison M. Spiro, 'Najar or Bhut – Evil Eye or Ghost Affliction: Gujarati Views about Illness Causation', *Anthropology & Medicine*, 12 (2005), p. 64.
77. Helman, *Culture, Health and Illness*, p. 111. Siobhan E. Laird, *Anti-oppressive Social Work: A Guide for Developing Cultural Competence* (London, 2008), p. 67.
78. On *hakims* and *unani tibb* see Waqar Ahmad, 'The Maligned Healer: The "Hakim" and Western Medicine', *Journal of Ethnic and Migration Studies*, 18 (1992), pp. 521–36. Rajinder Singh Bhopal, 'The Inter-relationship of Folk, Traditional and Western Medicine within an Asian Community in Britain', *Social Science & Medicine*, 22 (1996), pp. 99–105. Sophie Gilliat-Ray, *Muslims in Britain: An Introduction* (Cambridge, 2010), p. 128. For an English manual written by a Leicester-based *hakim* see Muhammad Salim Khan, *Islamic Medicine* (Abingdon, 1986).
79. Simon Dein and Abdool Samad Illaiee, 'Jinn and Mental Health: Looking at Jinn Possession in Modern Psychiatric Practice', *The Psychiatrist*, 37 (2013), pp. 290–3.
80. Najat Khalifa et al., 'Beliefs about Jinn, Black Magic and the Evil Eye among Muslims: Age, Gender and First Language Influences', *Journal of Culture and Mental Health*, 4 (2011), pp. 68–77.

81. Nick Chester, 'I Went to an Islamic Exorcism in the Back of a Glaswegian Nail Salon', *Vice*, 2 May 2015, https://www.vice.com/en_uk/read/i-went-to-an-islamic-exorcism-in-the-back-of-a-glaswegian-nail-salon-293.

82. George Fink (ed.), *Stress Consequences: Mental, Neuropsychological and Socioeconomic* (San Diego, CA, and Oxford, 2010), p. 27.

83. See, for example, G. Hussein Rassool, 'Cultural Competence in Counseling the Muslim Patient: Implications for Mental Healthcare', *Archives of Psychiatric Nursing*, 29 (2015), pp. 321–5. Joseph E. Trimble, 'Bear Spends Time in Our Dreams Now: Magical Thinking and Cultural Empathy in Multicultural Counselling Theory and Practice', *Counselling Psychology Quarterly*, 23 (2010), pp. 241–53.

84. On which see Aisha Dupont-Joshua (ed.), *Working Inter-culturally in Counselling Settings* (Hove, 2003), pp. 1–4. Jafar Kareem and Ronald Littlewood (eds), *Intercultural Therapy: Themes, Interpretations and Practice* (2nd edn, London, 1999).

85. Dein, 'Mental Health in a Multiethnic Society', p. 473.

86. The statistics come from answers given to written questions submitted by Members of Parliament. See *Hansard*, HC Deb. 20 March 1979, vol. 964, col. 511W. *Hansard* HL Deb. 13 January 1997, vol. 577 cols 14–5WA.

87. *Hansard*, HL Deb. 10 December 1996, vol. 576, col. 89WA.

88. Specifically, it was replaced by the Consumer Protection from Unfair Trading Regulations 2008.

89. Caroline Davies, 'Psychic Crackdown on the Cards', *Guardian*, 6 April 2008, https://www.theguardian.com/uk/2008/apr/06/eu (accessed December 2018).

90. For details see Giles Crown, Oliver Bray and Rupert Earle (eds), *Advertising Law and Regulation* (2nd edn, Bloomsbury, 2010), pp. 621–2.

91. Dee Apolline, *The Spiritual Teacher's Handbook: A Practical Guide to Teaching, Facilitating and Leadership in a Spiritual Context* (Winchester, 2012).

92. Karen Stollznow, *Language, Myths, Mysteries and Magic* (Basingstoke, 2014), p. 16.

93. *Telegraph*, 12 July 2006. *Mirror*, 12 July 2006. *Daily Star*, 12 July 2006.

94. Simon Moon, 'Death-threat Scam is Blocked', 26 January 2006, http://www.thisismoney.co.uk/money/bills/article-1596185/Death-threat-scam-is-blocked.html.

95. '"Clairvoyant" Conmen Reap Millions by Preying on Weak and Vulnerable', *The Observer*, 25 February 2007.

96. Peter J. Aspinall and Martha J. Chinouya, *The African Diaspora Population in Britain: Migrant Identities and Experiences* (Basingstoke, 2016), p. 12.

97. *Sunday Express*, 3 November 2002, p. 19.

98. Paul Osifodunrin, 'Crime, Murder, and the Religious Body in Late-colonial Lagos', in Saheed Aderinto and Paul Osifodunrin (eds), *The Third Wave of Historical Scholarship on Nigeria* (Newcastle, 2012), pp. 308–12. Anne Digby, *Diversity and Division in Medicine: Health Care in South Africa from the 1800s* (Bern, 2006), p. 323. Bonny Ibhawoh, *Imperial Justice: Africans in Empire's Court* (Oxford, 2013), esp. pp. 92–6.

99. Theodore Petrus, 'Cultural Beliefs, Witchcraft and Crimes in South Africa', in Kim Sadique and Perry Stanislas (eds), *Religion, Faith and Crime: Theories, Identities and Issues* (Basingstoke, 2016), p. 154. John Alan Cohan, 'The Problem of Witchcraft Violence in Africa', *Suffolk University Law Review*, 44 (2011), p. 866.

100. Louise Vincent, 'New Magic for New Times: Muti Murder in Democratic South Africa', *Health and Nutritional Problems of Indigenous Populations*, special issue ed. Kaushik Bose, *Studies of Tribes and Tribals*, 2 (2008), pp. 43–53.

101. For the best discussion of this tragic case see Jean La Fontaine, *Witches and Demons: A Comparative Perspective on Witchcraft and Satanism* (New York and Oxford, 2016), pp. 59–71.

102. 'Muti – The Story of Adam', *Independent*, 2 August 2003, http://www.independent.co.uk/news/uk/crime/focus-muti-the-story-of-adam-98821.html (accessed December 2018).

103. For an account of Victoria's short life, see: 'For Anna, the Promise of a New Life Ended in Pain, Fear and Filth', *Guardian*, 13 January 2001.

104. Lord Laming, *The Victoria Climbié Inquiry* (2003), p. 36.

105. For example, 'The Cowards Who Watch Black or Brown Girls Die in the Name of Racial Harmony', *Daily Express*, 15 January 2001.

106. Afe Adogame, *The Public Face of African New Religious Movements in Diaspora: Imagining the Religious 'Other'* (Farnham, 2014), pp. 267-8.

107. Melanie Phillips, 'Issues of Ethnicity', in Kate Wilson and Adrian James (eds), *The Child Protection Handbook: The Practitioner's Guide to Safeguarding Children* (3rd edn, Philadelphia, PA, 2007), p. 157.

108. Tortora, 'Witchcraft Believers in Sub-Saharan Africa Rate Lives Worse'.

109. Peter Geschiere, *The Modernity of Witchcraft: Politics and the Occult in Postcolonial Africa* (Charlottesville and London, 1997), p. 27.

110. In 2014, while playing for Tottenham, Ghanaian footballer Emmanuel Adebayor blamed his goal drought on his mother performing 'juju' on him. See *Daily Mirror*, 1 December 2014.

111. Geschiere, *The Modernity of Witchcraft*, esp. pp. 2-15.

112. Ibid., p. 21.

113. Veerle van Gijsegem, 'Criminal Law of French Origin and Criminal Behavior of African Occult Origin: The Modernity of Witchcraft Trials in the West of the Republic of the Ivory Coast', *Comparative Studies of South Asia, Africa and the Middle East*, 26 (2006), pp. 191-202.

114. Daniel A. Offiong, 'Witchcraft among the Ibibio of Nigeria', *African Studies Review*, 26 (1983), pp. 111-12. Geschiere, *The Modernity of Witchcraft*, p. 13.

115. Sheila S. Walker, 'Witchcraft and Healing in an African Christian Church', *Journal of Religion in Africa*, 10 (1979), pp. 127-38. G. Parrinder, *West African Psychology: A Comparative Study of Psychological and Religious Thought* (Cambridge, 1951), p. 164.

116. On which see Elizabeth Ischei, *Voices of the Poor in Africa* (Martlesham, 2004), pp. 154-6.

117. Walker, 'Witchcraft and Healing', p. 127. Van Gijsegem, 'Criminal Law of French Origin', p. 198.

118. Van Gijsegem, 'Criminal Law of French Origin', p. 197.

119. Parrinder, *West African Psychology*, p. 164.

120. Adam Ashforth, *Witchcraft, Violence, and Democracy in South Africa* (Chicago, IL, 2005), p. 11. Human Rights Watch, *Violence against Women in South Africa: The State Response to Domestic Violence and Rape* (New York, 1995), p. 23. Robert A. LeVine, 'Witchcraft and Sorcery in a Gush Community', in John Middleton and E.H. Winter (eds), *Witchcraft and Sorcery in East Africa* (London, 1963), p. 254.

121. Geschiere, *The Modernity of Witchcraft*, pp. 25, 34, 42-3.

122. Ibid., p. 50.

123. Leethen Bartholomew, 'Child Abuse Linked to Beliefs in Witchcraft', *Transnational Social Review*, 5 (2015), p. 193. Leo Ruickbie, ' "Child Witches": From Imaginary Cannibalism to Ritual Abuse', *Paranthropology* 3(3) (2012), p. 14.

124. Robert Brain, 'Child-witches', in Mary Douglas (ed.), *Witchcraft Confessions and Accusations* (London, 1970), p. 161.

125. Jennifer Badstuebner, ' "Drinking the Hot Blood of Humans": Witchcraft Confessions in a South African Pentecostal Church', *Anthropology and Humanism*, 28 (2008), pp. 8-22. Van Gijsegem, 'Criminal Law of French Origin', p. 200. Brain, 'Child-witches', pp. 165-70. Ashforth, *Witchcraft, Violence, and Democracy in South Africa*, pp. 77-80.

126. Martha Ainsworth, *Economic Aspects of Child Fostering in Côte d'Ivoire*, World Bank Working Paper (Washington DC, 1992), p. 1.

127. Alma Gottlieb, 'Witches, Kings, and the Sacrifice of Identity; or, The Power of Paradox and the Paradox of Power among the Beng of the Ivory Coast', in W. Arens and Ivan Karp (eds), *Creativity of Power: Cosmology in Action in African Societies* (Washington DC, 1989), p. 250.

128. Audrey Gillian, 'For Anna, the Promise of a New Life Ended in Pain, Fear and Filth,' *Guardian*, 13 January 2001, https://www.theguardian.com/uk/2001/jan/13/child protection.society7 (accessed January 2019). Geschiere, *The Modernity of Witchcraft*, p. 44.

129. Mensah Adinkrah, *Witchcraft, Witches, and Violence in Ghana* (New York and Oxford, 2015), p. 95.

130. Gottlieb, 'Witches, Kings, and the Sacrifice of Identity', p. 249.

131. Adinkrah, *Witchcraft, Witches, and Violence in Ghana*, pp. 10, 82, 178, 223, 240. Ischei, *Voices of the Poor in Africa*, pp. 154–6.

132. Adinkrah, *Witchcraft, Witches, and Violence in Ghana*, p. 262.

133. *Daily Express*, 14 December 2000.

134. 'Manning "Nerd" Besotted with Older Woman Turned into Child Killer', *Guardian*, 13 January 2001.

135. For accounts of the experiences and confessions of alleged witches from West Africa see Karen Palmer, *Spellbound: Inside West Africa's Witch Camps* (New York, 2010), esp. pp. 63–6.

136. Gillian, 'For Anna'.

137. Jeevan Vasagar, 'The Exorcists', *Guardian*, 15 January 2001, https://www.theguardian. com/world/2001/jan/15/religion.uk (accessed July 2016).

138. Gillian, 'For Anna'.

139. Prospera Tedam, 'Witchcraft Branding and the Abuse of African Children in the UK: Causes, Effects and Professional Intervention', *Early Child Development and Care*, 184 (2014), pp. 1403–14.

140. Eleanor Stobart, *Child Abuse Linked to Accusations of 'Possession' and 'Witchcraft'* (London, 2006), p. 8.

141. Ibid., p. 15.

142. See Filip de Boeck, 'At Risk, as Risk: Abandonment and Care in a World of Spiritual Insecurity', in Jean La Fontaine (ed.), *The Devil's Children – From Spirit Possession to Witchcraft: New Allegations that Affect Children* (Abingdon, 2009), pp. 129–50. Aleksandra Cimpric, *Children Accused of Witchcraft: An Anthropological Study of Contemporary Practices in Africa* (Dakar, 2010), pp. 14–15.

143. Stobart, *Child Abuse Linked to Accusations of 'Possession' and 'Witchcraft'*, p. 24.

144. Emile Secker and Yasmin Rehman, 'Possession or Oppression: Witchcraft and Spirit Possession Accusations as a Form of Ritual Abuse of Children and Women', in Yasmin Rehman, Liz Kelly and Hannana Siddiqui (eds), *Moving in the Shadows: Violence in the Lives of Minority Women and Children* (London, 2016), pp. 144–5. 'Father Jailed for "Possessed Baby" Murder', *Guardian*, 22 December 2005, https://www.theguardian. com/uk/2005/dec/22/ukcrime1.

145. Stobart, *Child Abuse Linked to Accusations of 'Possession' and 'Witchcraft'*, p. 27.

146. On which see Robert Pull, ' "Project Violet": Addressing the Practice of Faith and/or Belief Based Ritualistic Related Abuse of Children', in La Fontaine (ed.), *The Devil's Children*, pp. 179–88. La Fontaine, *Witches and Demons*, pp. 121–2.

147. ' "Witchcraft" Abuse Cases on the Rise', www.bbc.co.uk/news/uk-34475424 (accessed August 2016).

148. La Fontaine, *Witches and Demons*, esp. Chapter 7.

149. *Hansard*, HL Deb. 18 May 1977, vol. 383, cols 707–8.

150. On Christianity's late twentieth-century decline see Callum G. Brown, *Religion and Society in Twentieth-century Britain* (Harlow, 2006), Chapters 6 and 7.

151. For an outline of Robinson's controversial book *Honest to God* and the reaction it provoked see Brown, *Religion and Society*, pp. 224, 232–3.

152. Russ Parker, *The Occult: Deliverance from Evil* (Leicester, 1989).

153. See *The Times*, 18 March 1963. Hutton, *The Triumph of the Moon: A History of Modern Pagan Witchcraft* (Oxford, 1999), p. 267.

154. Bill Ellis, 'The Highgate Cemetery Vampire Hunt: The Anglo-American Connection in Satanic Cult Lore', *Folklore*, 104 (1993), pp. 13–39. Richard Jenkins, *Black Magic and Bogeymen: Fear, Rumour and Popular Belief in the North of Ireland 1972–74* (Cork, 2014), pp. 42, 249–54.

155. Kurt Koch, *Christian Counseling and Occultism* (Grand Rapids, MI, 1965), and *Occult Bondage and Deliverance: Advice for Counselling the Sick, the Troubled and the Occultly Oppressed* (Lahr-Dinglingen, 1970). For Koch's biography see Bill Ellis, *Raising the Devil: Satanism, New Religions, and the Media* (Lexington, 2000), p. 15. Owen Davies, *Grimoires: A History of Magic Books* (Oxford, 2009), pp. 252–4. For the general background to Koch's work see Monica Black, 'Miracles in the Shadow of the Economic Miracle: The "Supernatural '50s" in West Germany', *Journal of Modern History*, 84 (2012), esp. p. 846.

156. Notably Koch, *Christian Counseling*.

157. *Daily Express*, 13 March 1974; 15 March 1974. See also *Daily Mirror*, 28 February 1972.

158. John Richards, *But Deliver Us From Evil: An Introduction to the Demonic Dimension in Pastoral Care* (London, 1974). Connie Ho Yan Au, *Grassroots Unity in the Charismatic Renewal* (Eugene, OR, 2011), p. 102.

159. *Church Times*, 21 March 1975.

160. R. Kenneth McAll, 'The Ministry of Deliverance', *Expository Times*, 86 (July 1975), pp. 296–8.

161. Probably the fullest single account of the gruesome affair is Brian McConnell, *The Possessed: True Tales of Demonic Possession* (London, 1995), Chapter 12.

162. *Daily Mirror*, 24 March 1975.

163. *Church Times*, 4 April 1975.

164. David McDonald, 'The Role of the Psychiatric Advisor in the Ministry of Deliverance', Royal Society of Psychiatry publications archive. See http://www.rcpsych.ac.uk

165. Michael Perry, *Deliverance: Psychic Disturbances and Occult Involvement* (London, 2012), pp. 1–2. Neal Milner, 'Giving the Devil His Due Process: Exorcism in the Church of England', *Journal of Contemporary Religion*, 15 (2000), pp. 248–69.

166. 'Deliverance Ministry', *New Directions*, 163 (December 2008).

167. Milner, 'Giving the Devil', p. 250.

168. *Church Times*, 20 July 2012, p. 24.

169. Richards, *But Deliver Us From Evil*, pp. 213–14.

170. Ken Gardiner, *The Reluctant Exorcist: A Biblical Approach in an Age of Scepticism* (Watford, 2015), p. 138.

171. Perry, *Deliverance*, p. 70.

172. Parker, *The Occult*, p. 156.

173. *Church Times*, 16 November 2001, p. 10.

174. Paul Gifford, 'Evil, Witchcraft, and Deliverance' in the African Pentecostal Worldview, in Clifton R. Clarke (ed.), *Pentecostal Theology in Africa* (Eugene, OR, 2014), p. 112.

175. D.K. Olukoya, *Overpowering Witchcraft* (Lagos, 1999), p. 68.

176. Greg Smith, 'East London Is No Longer Secular: Religion as a Source of Social Capital in the Regeneration of East London', *Rising East: The Journal of East London Studies*, 4 (1999), p. 137; 'Religious Organisations in Newham in 1998–99', in *Directory of Religious Groups in Newham* (3rd edn, London, 1999). La Fontaine, *Witches and Demons*, p. 102.

177. For the best account of these churches and their congregations see La Fontaine, *Witches and Demons*, pp. 102–13.

178. Peter J. Horrobin, *Healing through Deliverance* (3rd edn, Lancaster, 2008), p. 80.

179. Ibid., p. 100.

180. Ibid., p. 533. On incubi and the *Malleus Maleficarum* see Christopher S. Mackay (ed.), *The Hammer of Witches* (Cambridge, 2009), pp. 121–39.

181. 2011: £4,029,119. 2012: £3,998,211. 2013: £3,633,384. 2014: £3,200,915. Ellel Ministries is registered as The Christian Trust under charity number 1041237 (in the UK) and SCO 38860 (in Scotland). A summary of its accounts can be accessed through the websites of the Charity Commission and Scottish Charity Regulator.

182. The Christian Trust, 'Annual Report and Consolidated Financial Statements for the Financial Year ended 30 December 2014', p. 18. Available through Companies House (Company registration number: 02883771).

183. Like the deliverance ministry, spiritual warfare emerged during the 1970s. For one of this movement's earliest texts see Michael Harper, *Spiritual Warfare* (London, 1970).

184. Tom Marshall, *Defensive Spiritual Warfare* (Tonbridge, 1996), pp. 17–18.

185. Ibid., p. 17. Also Horrobin, *Healing through Deliverance*, pp. 314–39. Ed Robert, *Spiritual Warfare* (Tonbridge, 2002), pp. 37–41. Chester Kylstra and Betsy Kylstra, *An Integrated Approach to Biblical Healing Ministry* (Lancaster, 2007), p. 220. Martin Israel, *Exorcism: The Removal of Evil Influences* (London, 1997), Chapter 7.

186. Derek Prince, *Blessing or Curse: You Can Choose* (3rd edn, Ebbw Vale, 2006), pp. 18–19.

187. Kylstra and Kylstra, *An Integrated Approach to Biblical Healing Ministry*, Chapter 3. Larry Huch, *10 Curses that Block the Blessing* (New Kensington, PA, 2006), Chapters 7 and 8.

188. Horrobin, *Healing Through Deliverance*, pp. 421–39.

189. Emily Cockayne, *Cheek by Jowl: A History of Neighbours* (London, 2012), p. 211.

190. 'Knock, Knock. Who's There? Dunno: Britain's Disappearing Neighbourliness', *Independent on Sunday*, 8 April 2012.

191. Colin Come, *Introduction to E-business* (London, 2006), p. 328. Fabio Musso and Elena Druica, *Handbook of Research on Retailer–Consumer Relationship Development* (Hershey, PA, 2014), p. 130.

192. BBC News, 'Sale of Tarot Readings and Spells Banned on eBay', 20 August 2012, http://www.bbc.co.uk/news/technology-19323622 (accessed November 2016).

193. Sam Thielman, 'Spells Broken: Etsy Bans Sale of "Metaphysical Services"', *Guardian*, 18 June 2015, https://www.theguardian.com/technology/2015/jun/18/etsy-ban-metaphysical-services (accessed December 2018).

194. That is to say, websites of curse removers with UK-based domain names.

195. The sub-field of internet folklore is still in its infancy, but for an excellent account of how spiritual warfare flourishes online see Robert Glenn Howard, 'Crusading on the Vernacular Web: The Folk Beliefs and Practices of Online Spiritual Warfare', in Trevor J. Blank (ed.), *Folklore and the Internet: Vernacular Expression in a Digital World* (Logan, UT, 2009), esp. pp. 159–74. On internet folklore more generally see Trevor J. Blank, *Toward a Conceptual Framework for the Study of Folklore and the Internet* (Boulder, CO, 2014).

196. On this point see Howard, 'Crusading on the Vernacular Web', pp. 162–3.

CONCLUSION: WITCHCRAFT'S DECLINE AND RETURN

1. The figures are from the Department for Education's 'Children in Need Census'. As of 2019 they were collated at: https://www.gov.uk/government/statistics/characteristics-of-children-in-need-2016-to-2017; https://www.gov.uk/government/statistics/characteristics-of-children-in-need-2017-to-2018 (accessed January 2019).

2. Perhaps by amending the criminal law to make it an offence to incite harm against a child.

SELECT BIBLIOGRAPHY

mAnUSCRIpT SOURCES

Wellcome Library, Euston Road, London
MS. 3126. 'The Real Black Magic Revealed without Mystery (London, 1921)' by J.K.
MS. 8568. Pharmacist's Scrapbook belonging to Lewis Herbert Llewellyn of Bridgewater, Somerset.
MS. PP/Ham/B6. Letter from Lillias Hamilton to Claude Hamilton, 11 January 1911.
MS. PP/Ham/D2. Correspondence and notes regarding Dr Lillias Hamilton.
MS. WTI/SGB.B.11/3. 'African Stories' by S.G. Browne.

National Archives, Kew, London
ASSI 11/33. Assizes, Midland Circuit, Crown Minute Books.
ASSI 13/6. Witness statements for the coroner's inquest into the death of Ann Tennant, 17 September 1875.
HO 17/58/13. Petition and letters relating to the sentencing of William Watkins.

British Library, Euston Road, London
MS. IOR/Z/E/4/16/S888. Police Department Correspondence of the Governor of the Presidency of Fort William, Bengal (1839).

National Records of Scotland, Edinburgh
MS. GD268/139/25-6. Letter from D. Stewart, of Tain, to James Loch MP. 26 June 1845.
MS. SC50/5/1863/1. Action for damages by Catherine Galbreath, alias Kate Ian, of Gigha, against James Smith.

National Library of Wales, Aberystwyth
MS. 11117B. John Harries' 'Book of Incantations'.

Bodleian Library, University of Oxford
MS. D. Dew. Diary of George James Dew.
MS. Top. Oxon. D. 192. Percy Manning, 'Folk-Lore Miscellania'.

Oxfordshire History Centre, Oxford
MS. P1/1/M53/4. Typed notes of Frank Cull, on Oxfordshire folklore.

Norfolk Record Office, Norwich
MC 167/1-7. Letters to Mr Covell, wise-man of Banningham.

Tyne and Wear Record Office, Newcastle
Memorandum books and personal papers of the Rev. William Ettrick, particularly:
DF.ETT, Acc 2539/1. Memorandum book for 1815–16.
DF.ETT, Acc 2539/2. Memorandum book for 1817.
DF.ETT, Acc 2359/3. Memorandum book for 1823–8.

Sunderland Antiquarian Society, Douro Terrace, Sunderland
Diaries of the Rev. William Ettrick.

North Yorkshire Record Office, North Allerton
QSB 1797 4/6. Bill of Indictment for John Wrightson of Stokesley.
QSB 1797 4/8/1. Quarter Sessions Examination for John Wrightson of Stokesley.
QSB 1814 1/6/5. Bill of Indictment against John Wrightson of Stokesley.

Walsall Local History Centre, West Midlands
MS. 1497/1 'Personal horoscope of Cedric Edwin Sleigh'.
MS. 1497/1/1 'Birth chart of Cedric Edwin Sleigh'.
MS. 1497/1/2 'Horoscope of Cedric Edwin Sleigh'.

Museum of Witchcraft and Magic, Boscastle, Cornwall
Dossier of John Lundy of Lamerton, Devon, describing his curses (*c.* 2007–14).

Warwickshire County Record Office, Warwick
CR 1077/4. Minute book of the Long Compton Congregational Church.
CR 1892, 1. 'Account of a Witchcraft Murder in Long Compton.'

Private collection
'Recollections of Ivy Hallywell, of Bank Green Farm, Fox Lane, Millthorpe, Cordwell Valley.'
    Composed *c.* 1970s/1980s.

SELECT SECONDARY SOURCES

Adinkrah, Mensah, *Witchcraft, Witches, and Violence in Ghana* (New York and Oxford, 2015).
Ahmad, Waqar, 'The Maligned Healer: The "Hakim" and Western Medicine', *Journal of Ethnic and Migration Studies*, 18 (1992), pp. 521–36.
Allen, Richard C., 'Wizards or Charlatans, Doctors or Herbalists? An Appraisal of the "Cunning Men" of Cwrt Y Cadno, Carmarthenshire', *North American Journal of Welsh Studies*, 1(2) (2001), pp. 68–85.
Anderson, Naomi et al., 'Faith-adapted Psychological Therapies for Depression and Anxiety: Systematic Review and Meta-analysis', *Journal of Affective Disorders*, 176 (May 2015), pp. 183–96.

Armitage, Natalie and Houlbrook, Ceri (eds), *The Materiality of Magic: An Artifactual Investigation into Ritual Practices and Popular Beliefs* (Oxford, 2015).

Ashforth, Adam, *Witchcraft, Violence, and Democracy in South Africa* (Chicago, IL, 2005).

Badstuebner, Jennifer, ' "Drinking the Hot Blood of Humans": Witchcraft Confessions in a South African Pentecostal Church', *Anthropology and Humanism*, 28 (2003), pp. 8–22.

Bailey, Michael D., 'From Sorcery to Witchcraft: Clerical Conceptions of Magic in the Later Middle Ages', *Speculum*, 76 (2001), pp. 960–90.

—— *Magic and Superstition in Europe: A Concise History from Antiquity to the Present* (New York, 2007).

Baker, Jim, *The Cunning Man's Handbook: The Practice of English Folk Magic 1550–1900* (London, 2013).

Barrow, Logie, *Independent Spirits: Spiritualism and English Plebeians, 1850–1910* (London, 1986).

Barry, Jonathan, Davies, Owen and Usborne, Cornelie (eds), *Cultures of Witchcraft in Europe from the Middle Ages to the Present* (Basingstoke, 2018).

Barry, Jonathan, Hester, Marianne and Roberts, Gareth (eds), *Witchcraft in Early Modern Europe: Studies in Culture and Belief* (1996: Cambridge, 1999).

Bartholomew, Leethen, 'Child Abuse Linked to Beliefs in Witchcraft', *Transnational Social Review*, 5 (2015), pp. 193–8.

Bell, Karl, *The Magical Imagination: Magic and Modernity in Urban Britain 1780–1914* (Cambridge, 2012).

Bennett, Gillian, 'Folklore Studies and the English Rural Myth', *Rural History*, 4 (1993), pp. 77–91.

Bentley, Trevor J., *Pakeha Maori: The Extraordinary Story of Europeans Who Lived as Maori in Early New Zealand* (Auckland, 1999).

Bever, Edward, *The Realities of Witchcraft and Popular Magic in Early Modern Europe: Culture, Cognition, and Everyday Life* (Basingstoke, 2008).

—— 'Witchcraft, Female Aggression, and Power in the Early Modern Community', *Journal of Social History*, 35 (2002), pp. 955–88.

Bhopal, Rajinder Singh, 'The Inter-relationship of Folk, Traditional and Western Medicine within an Asian Community in Britain', *Social Science & Medicine*, 22 (1996), pp. 99–105.

Black, Monica, 'Miracles in the Shadow of the Economic Miracle: The "Supernatural '50s" in West Germany', *Journal of Modern History*, 84 (2012), pp. 833–60.

Blank, Trevor J. (ed.), *Folklore and the Internet: Vernacular Expression in a Digital World* (Logan, UT, 2009).

Bogdan, Henrik and Djurdjevic, Gordan (eds), *Occultism in a Global Perspective* (Abingdon, 2013).

Bogdan, Henrik and Starr, Martin P. (eds), *Aleister Crowley and Western Esotericism* (Oxford, 2012).

Bostridge, Ian, *Witchcraft and its Transformations c. 1650–1750* (Oxford, 1997).

Briggs, Robin, *Witches and Neighbours: The Social and Cultural Context of European Witchcraft* (London, 1996).

Brown, Callum G., *The Death of Christian Britain: Understanding Secularisation 1800–2000* (2nd edn, Abingdon, 2009).

—— *Religion and Society in Twentieth-century Britain* (Harlow, 2006).

Brown, Judith M. and Louis, William Roger (eds), *The Oxford History of the British Empire*, vol. IV: *The Twentieth Century* (Oxford, 1999).

Browne, Randy M., 'The "Bad Business" of Obeah: Power, Authority, and the Politics of Slave Culture in the British Caribbean', *William and Mary Quarterly*, 68 (2011), pp. 451–80.

Brugger, Peter and Mohr, Christine, 'The Paranormal Mind: How the Study of Anomalous Experiences and Beliefs May Inform Cognitive Neuroscience', *Cortex*, 44 (2008).

Bryson, Sasha Turner, 'The Art of Power: Poison and Obeah Accusations and the Struggle for Dominance and Security in Jamaica's Slave Society', *Caribbean Studies*, 41 (2013), pp. 61–90.

Butler, Alison, 'Anna Kingsford: Scientist and Sorceress', in David Clifford, Elisabeth Wadge, Alex Warwick and Martin Willis (eds), *Repositioning Victorian Sciences: Shifting Centres in Nineteenth-century Scientific Thinking* (London, 2006), pp. 59–69.

—— *Victorian Occultism and the Making of Modern Magic: Invoking Tradition* (Basingstoke, 2011).

Byrne, Georgina, *Modern Spiritualism and the Church of England: 1850–1939* (London, 2010).

Campion, Nicholas, *Astrology and Popular Religion in the Modern West: Prophecy, Cosmology and the New Age Movement* (London, 2016).

Cannadine, David, *Ornamentalism: How the British Saw Their Empire* (London, 2001).

—— *Victorious Century: The United Kingdom, 1800–1906* (London, 2017).

Cannon, W.B., ' "Voodoo" Death', *American Anthropologist*, 44 (1942), pp. 169–81.

Clark, Stuart, *Thinking with Demons: The Idea of Witchcraft in Early Modern Europe* (Oxford, 1999).

Davies, Owen, *America Bewitched: The Story of Witchcraft After Salem* (Oxford, 2013).

—— *Grimoires: A History of Magic Books* (Oxford, 2009).

—— 'Hag-riding in Nineteenth-century West Country England and Modern Newfoundland: An Examination of Experienced-centred Witchcraft Tradition', *Folk Life*, 35 (1996–7) pp. 36–53.

—— *The Haunted: A Social History of Ghosts* (London, 2007).

—— *Murder, Magic, Madness: The Victorian Trials of Dove and the Wizard* (Harlow, 2005).

—— *A People Bewitched: Witchcraft and Magic in Nineteenth-century Somerset* (Bruton, 1999).

—— *Popular Magic: Cunning Folk in English History* (London, 2003).

—— *A Supernatural War: Magic, Divination, and Faith during the First World War* (Oxford, 2018).

—— *Witchcraft, Magic and Culture: 1736–1951* (Manchester, 1999).

Davies, Owen and De Blécourt, Willem (eds), *Witchcraft Continued: Popular Magic in Modern Europe* (Manchester, 2004).

De Blécourt, Willem, 'Witch Doctors, Soothsayers and Priests: On Cunning Folk in European Historiography and Tradition', *Social History* 19 (1994), pp. 285–303.

De Blécourt, Willem, Hutton, Ronald and La Fontaine, Jean (eds), *The Athlone History of Witchcraft and Magic in Europe*, vol. 6: *The Twentieth Century* (London, 1999).

De Jager Meezenbroek, Eltica et al., 'Measuring Spirituality as a Universal Human Experience: A Review of Spirituality Questionnaires', *Journal of Religion and Health*, 51 (2012), pp. 336–54.

Dein, Simon and Illaiee, Abdool Samad, 'Jinn and Mental Health: Looking at Jinn Possession in Modern Psychiatric Practice', *The Psychiatrist*, 37 (2013), pp. 290–3.

Delius, Peter, 'Witches and Missionaries in Nineteenth-century Transvaal', *Journal of Southern African Studies*, 27 (2001), pp. 429–43.

Dorson, Richard M., *The British Folklorists: A History* (London, 1968).

Douglas, Mary (ed.), *Witchcraft Confessions and Accusations* (1970: London, 2004).

Drogin, Marc, *Anathema! Medieval Scribes and the History of Book Curses* (New York, 1983).

Dwyer, Graham, *The Divine and the Demonic: Supernatural Affliction and its Treatment in North India* (London, 2003).

Emsley, Clive, *Crime and Society in England: 1750–1900* (2nd edn, Harlow, 1996).

Evans-Pritchard, E.E., 'Some Reminiscences and Reflections on Fieldwork', *Journal of the Anthropological Society of Oxford*, 4 (1973).

—— *Witchcraft, Oracles and Magic among the Azande* (Oxford, 1937).

Faraone, Christopher A., 'Binding and Burying the Forces of Evil: The Defensive Use of "Voodoo Dolls" in Ancient Greece', *Classical Antiquity*, 10 (1991), pp. 165–205.

Favret-Saada, Jeanne, *The Anti-Witch*, trans. Matthew Carey (Chicago, IL, 2015).

—— *Deadly Words: Witchcraft in the Bocage,* trans. Catherine Cullen (Cambridge, 1980).

Forsyth, Miranda and Eves, Richard (eds), *Talking it Through: Responses to Sorcery and Witchcraft Beliefs and Practices in Melanesia* (Canberra, 2015).

Freeman, Mark, 'Folklore Collection and Social Investigation in Late Nineteenth- and Early Twentieth-century England', *Folklore*, 116 (2005), pp. 51–65.

Gaskill, Malcolm, *Hellish Nell: Last of Britain's Witches* (London, 2001).

—— 'Witchcraft and Evidence in Early Modern England', *Past and Present*, 198 (2008), pp. 33–70.

—— *Witchcraft: A Very Short Introduction* (Oxford, 2010).

—— *Witchfinders: A Seventeenth-century English Tragedy* (2005: London, 2006).

Gersham, Boris, 'Witchcraft Beliefs and the Erosion of Social Capital: Evidence from Sub-Saharan Africa and Beyond', *Journal of Development Economics*, 120 (2016), pp. 182–208.

Geschiere, Peter, *The Modernity of Witchcraft: Politics and the Occult in Postcolonial Africa* (Charlottesville and London, 1997).

Godwin, Joscelyn, *The Theosophical Enlightenment* (New York, 1994).

Goodare, Julian, 'The Framework for Scottish Witch-hunting in the 1590s', *Scottish Historical Review*, 81 (2002), pp. 240–50.

Goodare, Julian (ed.), *The Scottish Witch-hunt in Context* (Manchester, 2002).

Goodrick-Clarke, Nicholas, *The Western Esoteric Traditions: A Historical Introduction* (Oxford, 2008).

Gray, Natasha, 'Witches, Oracles, and Colonial Law: Evolving Anti-witchcraft Practices in Ghana, 1927–1932', *International Journal of African Historical Studies*, 34 (2001), pp. 339–63.

Green, S.J.D., *The Passing of Protestant England: Secularisation and Social Change c. 1920–1960* (Cambridge, 2011).

Handler, Jerome S., 'Slave Medicine and Obeah in Barbados, circa 1650 to 1834', *New West Indian Guide*, 74 (2000), pp. 57–90.

Handler, Jerome S. and Bibly, Kenneth M., *Enacting Power: The Criminalization of Obeah in the Anglophone Caribbean 1760–2011* (Kingston, 2012).

Harrison, Brian, *Finding a Role? The United Kingdom 1970–1990* (Oxford, 2011).

Hayward, Rhodri, *Resisting History: Religious Transcendence and the Invention of the Unconscious* (Manchester, 2007).

Hazelgrove, Jennifer, 'Spiritualism after the Great War', *Twentieth Century British History*, 10 (1999), pp. 404–30.

Henderson, Lizanne, *Witchcraft and Folk Belief in the Age of Enlightenment: Scotland, 1670–1740* (Basingstoke, 2016).

Holmes, Clive, 'Women: Witnesses and Witches', *Past and Present*, 140 (1993), pp. 45–78.

Hoppen, K. Theodore, *The Mid-Victorian Generation: 1846–1886* (Oxford, 1998).

Howkins, Alun, *The Death of Rural England: A Social History of the Countryside Since 1900* (London, 2003).

Hudson, Arthur Palmer, 'The "Superstitious" Lord Byron', *Studies in Philology*, 63 (1966), pp. 708–21.

Hutton, Ronald, *The Pagan Religions of the Ancient British Isles: Their Nature and Legacy* (Oxford, 1991).

—— (ed.), *Physical Evidence for Ritual Acts, Sorcery and Witchcraft in Christian Britain: A Feeling for Magic* (Basingstoke, 2016).

—— *The Triumph of the Moon: A History of Modern Pagan Witchcraft* (Oxford, 1999).

—— *The Witch: A History of Fear, from Ancient Times to the Present* (New Haven, CT, and London, 2017).

Ivey, Gavin and Myers, Terita, 'The Psychology of Bewitchment (Part II): A Psychological Model for Conceptualising and Working with Bewitchment Experiences', *South African Journal of Psychology*, 38 (2008), pp. 75–94.

Jenkins, Richard, *Black Magic and Bogeymen: Fear, Rumour and Popular Belief in the North of Ireland 1972–74* (Cork, 2014).

Khalifa, Najat et al., 'Beliefs about Jinn, Black Magic and the Evil Eye among Muslims: Age, Gender and First-language Influences', *Journal of Culture and Mental Health*, 4 (2011), pp. 68–77.

Knight, Francis, *The Nineteenth-century Church and English Society* (Cambridge, 1995).

Koenig, Harold G., 'Religion, Spirituality and Health: The Research and Clinical Implications', *ISRN Psychiatry*, vol. 2012.

Kontou, Tatiana and Willburn, Sarah (eds), *The Ashgate Research Companion to Nineteenth-century Spiritualism and the Occult* (London, 2012).

La Fontaine, Jean, *Witches and Demons: A Comparative Perspective on Witchcraft and Satanism* (New York and Oxford, 2016).

La Fontaine, Jean (ed.), *The Devil's Children – From Spirit Possession to Witchcraft: New Allegations that Affect Children* (Abingdon, 2009).

Lan, David, *Guns and Rain: Guerrillas and Spirit Mediums in Zimbabwe* (Berkeley, 1985).

Larkin, Gerald, *Occupational Monopoly and Modern Medicine* (London and New York, 1983).

Larner, Christina, *Enemies of God: The Witch-Hunt in Scotland* (1981: Edinburgh, 2000).

Lee, Robert, *Rural Society and the Anglican Clergy, 1815–1914: Encountering and Managing the Poor* (Woodbridge, 2006).

—— *Unquiet Country: Voices of the Rural Poor, 1820–1880* (Macclesfield, 2005).

Levack, Brian P. (ed.), *The Oxford Handbook of Witchcraft in Early Modern Europe and Colonial America* (Oxford, 2013).

Lewis-Williams, David and Pearce, David, *Inside the Neolithic Mind: Consciousness, Cosmos and the Realm of the Gods* (London, 2005).

Luongo, Katherine, *Witchcraft and Colonial Rule in Kenya, 1900–1955* (Cambridge, 2001).

MacClancy, Jeremy, *Alternative Countrysides: Anthropological Approaches to Rural Western Europe Today* (Manchester, 2015).

Mac-Machado, Robert Gabriel, 'Witchcraft and Witchcraft Cleansing among the Vasava Bhils', *Anthropos*, 105 (2010), pp. 191–204.

Manning, M. Chris, 'The Material Culture of Ritual Concealments in the United States', *Historical Archaeology*, 48 (2014), pp. 52–83.

Miller, Norman N., *Encounters with Witchcraft: Field Notes from Africa* (New York, 2012).

Monod, Paul Kléber, *Solomon's Secret Arts: The Occult in the Age of Enlightenment* (New Haven, CT, 2013).

Monster, William, 'Toads and Eucharists: The Male Witches of Normandy, 1564–1660', *French Historical Studies*, 2 (1997), pp. 563–95.

Moore, Francesca, '"Go and See Nell; She'll Put You Right": The Wisewoman and Working-class Health Care in Early Twentieth-century Lancashire', *Social History of Medicine*, 26 (2013), pp. 695–714.

Moore, Ronnie and McClean, Stuart (eds), *Folk Healing and Health Care Practices in Britain and Ireland: Stethoscopes, Wands and Crystals* (New York and Oxford, 2010).

Murrell, Nathaniel Samuel, 'Obeah: Afro-Caribbean Religious Medicine Art and Healing', in Patsy Sutherland, Roy Moodley and Barry Chevannes (eds), *Caribbean Healing Traditions: Implications for Health and Mental Health* (Hove, 2014).

Natale, Simone, *Supernatural Entertainments: Victorian Spiritualism and the Rise of Modern Media Culture* (University Park, PA, 2016).

Niehaus, Isak A., 'Witch-hunting and Political Legitimacy: Continuity and Change in Green Valley, Lebowa, 1930–91', *Africa: Journal of the International African Institute*, 63(4) (1993), pp. 498–530.

Nildin-Wall, Bodil and Wall, Jan, 'The Witch as Hare or the Witch's Hare: Popular Legends and Beliefs in Nordic Tradition', *Folklore*, 104 (1993), pp. 67–76.

Normand, L. and Roberts, G. (eds), *Witchcraft in Early Modern Scotland: James VI's Demonology' and the North Berwick Witches* (Exeter, 2000).

Obelkevich, James, *Religion and Rural Society: South Lindsey 1825–1875* (Oxford, 1976).

Oppenheim, Janet, *The Other World: Spiritualism and Psychical Research in England, 1850–1914* (Cambridge, 1985).

Overy, Richard, *The Morbid Age: Britain between the Wars* (London, 2009).

Owen, Alex, *The Darkened Room: Women, Power, and Spiritualism in Late Victorian England* (London and Chicago, IL, 2004).

Palmer, Karen, *Spellbound: Inside West Africa's Witch Camps* (New York, 2010).

Paterson, Lachy, 'Government, Church and Māori Responses to Mākutu (Sorcery) in New Zealand in the Nineteenth and Early Twentieth Centuries', *Cultural and Social History*, 8 (2011), pp. 175–94.

Paton, Diana, *The Cultural Politics of Obeah: Religion, Colonialism and Modernity in the Caribbean World* (Cambridge, 2015).

—— 'Witchcraft, Poison, Law, and Atlantic Slavery', *William and Mary Quarterly*, 69 (2012), pp. 235–64.

Patterson, Steve, *Cecil Williamson's Book of Witchcraft: A Grimoire of the Museum of Witchcraft* (London, 2014).

Pooley, William G., 'Can the "Peasant" Speak? Witchcraft and Silence in Guillaume Cazaux's "The Mass of Saint Sécaire"', *Western Folklore*, 71 (2012).

Porter, Bernard, *The Absent-minded Imperialists: Empire, Society and Culture in Britain* (Oxford, 2004).

Prince, Ruth and Riches, David, *The New Age in Glastonbury: The Construction of Religious Movements* (New York and Oxford, 2000).

Reay, Barry, *Rural Englands: Labouring Lives in the Nineteenth Century* (Basingstoke, 2004).

Redding, Sean, 'Women as Diviners and as Christian Converts in Rural South Africa, c. 1880–1963', *Journal of African History*, 57 (2016), pp. 367–89.

Rieti, Barbara, *Making Witches: Newfoundland Traditions of Spells and Counterspells* (Montreal, 2008).

Roper, Lyndal, *Witch Craze: Terror and Fantasy in Baroque Germany* (New Haven, CT, and London, 2004).

Rowlands, Alison, *Witchcraft Narratives in Germany: Rothenburg, 1561–1652* (Manchester and New York, 2003).

—— 'Witchcraft and Old Women in Early Modern Germany', *Past and Present*, 173 (2001), pp. 50–89.

Roy, Olivier, *Holy Ignorance: When Religion and Culture Part Ways*, trans. Ros Schwartz (London, 2010).

Said, Edward, *Culture and Imperialism* (New York, 1994).

Samuels, Martin A., ' "Voodoo" Death Revisited: The Modern Lessons of Neurocardiology', *Cleveland Clinic Journal of Medicine*, 74 (2007), Supplement 1, S8–16.

Searle, G.R., *A New England? Peace and War 1886–1918* (Oxford, 2004).

Sebald, Hans, 'Franconian Witchcraft: The Demise of a Folk Magic', *Anthropological Quarterly*, 53 (1980), pp. 173–87.

Semmens, Jason, *The Witch of the West: Or, The Strange and Wonderful History of Thomasine Blight* (Plymouth, 2004).

Sharpe, James, *Instruments of Darkness: Witchcraft in England 1550–1750* (London, 1997).

Simmons, Marc, *Witchcraft in the Southwest: Spanish and Indian Supernaturalism on the Rio Grande* (Lincoln, NB, 1980).

Simpson, Jacqueline (ed.), *Icelandic Folktales and Legends* (Berkeley and Los Angeles, CA, 1972).

Simpson, Jacqueline, 'Margaret Murray: Who Believed Her, and Why?', *Folklore*, 105 (1994), pp. 89–96.

Skaria, Ajay, 'Women, Witchcraft and Gratuitous Violence in Colonial Western India', *Past and Present*, 155 (1997), pp. 109–44.

Smith, Kathryn C., 'The Role of Animals in Witchcraft and Popular Magic: With Special Reference to Yorkshire', in J.R. Porter and W.M.S. Russell (eds), *Animals in Folklore* (Norwich, 1978), pp. 96–110.

Snape, Michael, *The Church of England in Industrialising Society: The Lancashire Parish of Whalley in the Eighteenth Century* (Woodbridge, 2003).

Sneddon, Andrew, *Witchcraft and Magic in Ireland* (Basingstoke, 2015).

Spiro, Alison M., 'Najar or Bhut – Evil Eye or Ghost Affliction: Gujarati Views about Illness Causation', *Anthropology & Medicine*, 12 (2005), pp. 61–73.

Stobart, Eleanor, *Child Abuse Linked to Accusations of 'Possession' and 'Witchcraft'* (London, 2006).

Strube, Julian, 'The "Baphomet" of Eliphas Lévi: Its Meaning and Historical Context', *Correspondences*, 4 (2016), pp. 37–79.

Suggett, Richard, *A History of Magic and Witchcraft in Wales* (Stroud, 2008).

Tangherlini, Timothy R., '"How Do You Know She's a Witch?": Witches, Cunning Folk, and Competition in Denmark', *Western Folklore*, 59 (2000), pp. 279–303.

Thomas, Keith, *Religion and the Decline of Magic: Studies in Popular Beliefs in Sixteenth and Seventeenth-Century England* (London, 1971).

Toivo, Raisa Maria, *Witchcraft and Gender in Early Modern Society: Finland and the Wider European Experience* (Abingdon and New York, 2008).

Vincent, Louise, 'New Magic for New Times: Muti Murder in Democratic South Africa', in *Health and Nutritional Problems of Indigenous Populations*, special issue ed. Kaushik Boses, *Studies of Tribes and Tribals*, 2 (2008), pp. 43–53.

Voyce, Malcolm, 'Maori Healers in New Zealand: The Tohunga Suppression Act of 1907', *Oceania*, 60 (1989), pp. 99–123.

Vukanović, T.P., 'Witchcraft in the Central Balkans I: Characteristics of Witches', *Folklore*, 100 (1989), pp. 9–24.

Waller, Richard D., 'Witchcraft and Colonial Law in Kenya', *Past and Present*, 180 (2003), pp. 241–75.

Walsham, Alexandra, *The Reformation of the Landscape: Religion, Identity, and Memory in Early Modern Britain and Ireland* (Oxford, 2011).

Waters, Thomas, 'Belief in Witchcraft in Oxfordshire and Warwickshire, c. 1860–1900: The Evidence of the Newspaper Archive', *Midland History*, 34 (2009), pp. 98–116.

—— 'Magic and the British Middle Classes: 1750–1900', *Journal of British Studies*, 54 (2015), pp. 632–53.

—— 'Maleficent Witchcraft in Britain Since 1900', *History Workshop Journal*, 80 (2015), pp. 99–122.

—— '"They Seem to Have All Died Out": Witches and Witchcraft in Lark Rise to Candleford and the English Countryside, c. 1830–1930', *Historical Research*, 87 (2014), pp. 134–53.

White, Ethan Doyle, '"An' it Harm None, Do What Ye Will." A Historical Analysis of the Wiccan Rede', *Magic, Ritual, and Witchcraft*, 10 (2015), pp. 142–71.

—— *Wicca: History, Belief, and Community in Modern Pagan Witchcraft* (Eastbourne, 2016).

Wilby, Emma, *Cunning Folk and Familiar Spirits: Shamanistic Visionary Traditions in Early Modern British Witchcraft and Magic* (2005: Brighton and Portland, OR, 2010).

Williams, S.C., *Religious Belief and Popular Culture in Southwark, c. 1880–1939* (Oxford, 1999).

Willis, Deborah, 'The Witch-family in Elizabethan and Jacobean Print Culture', *Journal for Early Modern Studies*, 13 (2013), pp. 4–31.

Winter, Alison, *Mesmerised: Powers of Mind in Victorian Britain* (Chicago, IL, and London, 1998).

Wroth, Celestina, '"To Root the Old Woman out of Our Minds": Women Educationists and Plebeian Culture in Late Eighteenth-century Britain', *Eighteenth-Century Life*, 30 (2006), pp. 48–73.

Young, Francis, *English Catholics and the Supernatural, 1553–1829* (Farnham, 2013).

Zachrisson, Per, 'Witchcraft and Witchcraft Cleansing in Southern Zimbabwe', *Anthropos*, 102 (2007), pp. 33–46.

MAPS AND ILLUSTRATIONS

maps

1. The British Isles with key places of witchcraft and magic mentioned in the text.
2. The British Empire showing dominions and major shipping routes.
3. The Isle of Gigha.

ILLUSTRATIONS

1. Henry Fuseli, *The Night-hag Visiting Lapland Witches*, 1796. Courtesy of the Metropolitan Museum of Art, New York.
2. James Giles, *The Weird Wife o' Lang Stane Lea*, 1830. © Royal Scottish Academy of Art and Architecture.
3. The witch of Endor conjures up the ghost of Samuel at the request of Saul, who lies petrified on the ground. Engraving by W. Raddon, 1811, after B. West. Courtesy of the Wellcome Collection, CC BY.
4. Thomas Rowlandson, *Witches in a Hay Loft*, 1807. Courtesy of Boston Public Library.
5. *The Witch Hare of Berry*, 1852. Chronicle / Alamy Stock Photo.
6a. 'Attempt to Drown a Supposed Witch' from the *Illustrated London Police News*, 1 July 1876.
6b. 'Killing a Supposed Witch' from the *Illustrated London Police News*, 1 January 1876.
7. An engraving after a drawing by Edmund Fitzpatrick. From William Carleton, *The Evil Eye; or, the Black Spectre*, Dublin, 1860, p. 272. Courtesy of the British Library.
8. An advert for the practice of James Hallett, a quack. Courtesy of the Wellcome Collection, London, CC BY.
9. A 'spae wife' (fortune-teller). Engraving by J.A. Wright after T. Stothard, *c.* 1829. Courtesy of the Wellcome Collection, London, CC BY.
10. The wise-woman at Ilchester, Somerset, charming away foot and mouth disease among cattle. From *The Day's Doings*, vol. 3, 9 December 1871, p. 321. Credit: Chronicle / Alamy Stock Photo.

11. Two conjurors, Evan Griffiths, 1928, and George Pickingill, early twentieth century. Courtesy of the National Library of Wales and the Folklore Society.

12. Hexafoils on the walls of a barn at Pratt Hall, Derbyshire.

13. A seagull's heart stuck with pins and a Rowan tree cross bound with red wool, both early twentieth century. Courtesy of Scarborough Museums Trust and the Wellcome Collection, CC BY.

14. Mesmerists using animal magnetism on female patients, 1845. Courtesy of the Wellcome Collection, London, CC BY.

15. Baphomet. Illustration from Éliphas Lévi, *Dogme et Rituel de la Haute Magie*, vol. 1, Paris, 1861.

16. A Gazaland medicine man wearing an elaborate necklace and headdress, *c.* 1910. Courtesy of the Wellcome Collection, London, CC BY.

17a. The grave of Dion Fortune (née Violet Firth). Courtesy of Robert B. Osten, 2011.

17b. James Peter Quinn, portrait of Lillias Hamilton. Courtesy of the Wellcome Collection, London, CC BY.

18. Rev. Christopher Neil-Smith conducting an exorcism, London, *c.* 1974. Trinity Mirror / Mirrorpix / Alamy Stock Photo.

19. The Museum of Witchcraft and Magic, Boscastle, Cornwall, 2018.

20. A portrait Gerald Gardner, creator of Wicca, surrounded by his ceremonial artifacts in the Museum of Witchcraft, 2018.

21. Poppets and voodoo dolls in the Museum of Witchcraft, 2018.

22. A warning poster issued by Leicestershire Police in 2018.

ACKNOWLEDGEMENTS

Thank you indeed, everyone who has helped me write this book. There are so many of you, and you've helped me in all sorts of direct and indirect ways. Blessings upon you: sincerely, thank you.

My experience of working with everyone at Yale University Press London has been outstanding. Thanks also to the many archivists, librarians and scholars across Britain and beyond who have made my research possible. As a student, Simon Green's teaching was inspirational. The excellent research of Ronald Hutton and Owen Davies laid the basis for my own work. The staff and volunteers at the Sunderland Antiquarian Society were especially welcoming, as was everyone at the Museum of Witchcraft and Magic in Boscastle. Thanks also to my colleagues and students, both current and former.

My family has been incredibly supportive, for a very long time. Thank you to you all, for everything. Latterly, Anne and David Betts did invaluable – though I fear rather dreary – work proof-reading the text. I'm extremely grateful. Any errors remaining are, naturally, their fault. (Joking.)

Above all, I want to thank Helen Betts, who over many years has been amazingly patient and helpful. This book could not have been written without Helen. It is dedicated to her.

INDEX

Note on British places. Cities and islands are listed separately. Towns and villages in England and mainland Scotland are listed under their historic (pre-1974) counties. Welsh towns and villages are listed under 'Wales'.

Aberdeenshire: 10, 23, 232; Meikle Wartle, 107–12
Aboriginal people, 162–5
abortion: service provided by fortune-tellers, 119–20; legalised, 251
acupuncture, 222
'Adam', victim of *muti*-murder, 244
Africa, sub-Saharan: African laws prohibiting witchcraft and witchcraft accusations, 159, 161, 182–3, 186, 265; African-style Pentecostalism and the deliverance ministry, 255–6; allegations of superstition used to justify colonialism, 160–2, 178–80; characteristics of alleged witches, 247–50; child witchcraft; 247–50, 256; concept of witchcraft in comparative perspective 20, 27, 84–5, 158–60, 178–86, 246–7; enslaved Africans develop *obeah*, 169, 238; influence of African magic on European colonialists, 158–60, 183–6; magical and spiritual traditions of African origin in the UK, 6, 243–51; migration of Africans to the UK, 243; *muti* and *muti*-murder, 243–4; prevalence

of witchcraft belief, 2, 156, 178–81, 211, 213, 223, 246–7; treatment of alleged witches, 158–62, 180–1, 247–50; 'witch doctors' and spiritual practitioners, 159, 181–2, 184–6, 243–4
Afro-Caribbean people: 168–72; migration to the UK, 238; *obeah* in the UK, 238–9
Agbebi, Mojola (Nigerian Baptist minister), 181
agnosticism, 75, 150
AIDS, 244
Albert, Prince Consort, 58, 76
alder tree, 21–2
alternative practitioners, 237
America, United States of: American clients of Welsh quacks and conjurors, 203; American movies and television shows make witchcraft look silly, 205–6; American online marketplaces prohibit selling metaphysical services, 258–9; availability of grimoires, 120; currency of witchcraft belief, 223; disbelief in anthropogenic climate change, 38; impact of American agricultural imports, 111; incubator of evangelical ideas about

America *(continued)*
  'spiritual warfare' and generational curses, 257; Irish and British emigration to America, 43–4, 157; origin of Christian Science, 147–50; origin of spiritualism, 140–3; origin of theosophy, 143; Roma emigration to America, 214
amulets, 12, 22, 25, 61, 133, 197, 239, 243–4, 259
Angels of Mons, 192
Angola, 180
Anglesey, Isle of, 44, 91
Anguilla, 171–2
antibiotics, 202, 220
antiquaries, 9, 34, 35, 92
apocalypse, 13
Aradia, or the Gospel of the Witches (1899), 152
Argyll: Campbeltown, 82; Oban, 87
aromatherapy, 222
astrology, 34, 50, 57–8, 66, 106, 113, 116, 172, 176, 215, 222
astral light (theosophical concept), 144
asylums, 70, 123, 136
atheism, 13, 33, 150
aura (esoteric concept), 142, 222, 227
Australasia: colonisation, 157, 164–6; rumours of satanic ritual abuse, 252; traditions of witchcraft and magic, 20, 162–8
autodidacts (working class), 49, 50, 109
Azande people, 156–7, 178

Babylonia, 26
Bacon, Francis, 35
Baker, Benjamin, 25
Balkans, 29
Banffshire: 86–7; Tomintoul, 107
Bangate Station, 162–5
Baphomet, 150–3
Barbados, 171–2
Basque Country, 29
Bath, 36, 88, 126
Batlhaping people, 178
Bedfordshire: Bedford, 150; Eversholt, 154
begging, and magic, 14, 20, 43–6, 62, 67, 107, 101, 117, 125, 196, 198, 233
belief, importance in magic, 8, 24–5, 38, 53–4, 132–3, 237–8, 261–5
Bennet, George Montagu, 7th Earl of Tankerville, 147
Bernard, Claude, 145–6
Berkshire, 208, 233

Bert, Paul, 145–6
Berwickshire: Auchencrow, 90
Beth, Rae (hedge witch), 235–6
Bhagavad Gita, 150
Bible: biblical curses and book curses in, 47–8; and Christian Science, 148; cited as evidence of the existence of witchcraft, 28, 53–5, 154, 208; cunning-folks' knowledge of the Bible, 109–10, 113, 152, 203; debates about witchcraft and Hebrew mistranslations, 28, 50, 54, 262–3; declining popular knowledge of the Bible 208; influence of German biblical criticism, 139–40, 152; modern biblical translations soften the concept of maleficent witchcraft, 208, 228; reality of witchcraft and witches' familiars strongly asserted by the King James Version, 27–8, 54–5; sales, 55; spiritualist healing uses biblical readings, 142; use in *obeah*, 169; use in remedies for witchcraft, 12, 22, 24, 61–2, 113, 197, 203, 252; witchcraft images in illustrated Bibles, 55
Birmingham, 209, 215, 265
black magic: and accidents, 15, 20, 193–4, 197, 224, 226; and animals, 12–13, 19, 20, 23, 29, 53, 58–9, 61, 97, 111–12, 196, 226, 231; aversion to talking about, 7, 73–4, 78, 164, 170, 175–6, 183, 225; and compliments, 29; concept, 1–2, 7–8, 14, 19–20, 53–4, 68–71, 142–54, 159–60, 165–8, 169, 176, 180, 223–4, 225–9, 237–40, 245–51, 256–8; and crop failure, 11–12, 247; and death, 19–20, 61, 145–6, 178, 185, 195, 197, 224–9, 232; and ghosts, 40–2, 226–7; and gifts, 29, 94; and mental illness, 14, 20, 193–4, 197; mockery of the idea, 9, 49–50; and physical illness, 11–12, 14, 20, 21, 60, 76, 88, 101, 132, 135, 144, 148, 166–7, 176–7, 196, 224–9, 231, 257; prevalence of belief, 10, 16–18, 59–61, 71, 78, 88–92, 178–81, 185–6, 195–8, 204–12, 223, 231–6, 238–40, 252, 254–6; quantification of cases reported in the press, 49, 67–8, 78, 88–9, 93–4, 97–100; and spoiled food, 11–12, 20, 29, 61–2; used to threaten, 20; victims as heart of the belief system, 7–8
Blatty, William Peter (author), 221–2
Blavatsky, Helena (occultist), 143–4, 176–7
blessings and benedictions, 21
Blixen, Karen (author), 184

blood: bleeding stemmed by charms and spells, 227, 234–5; blood drunk by witches in Africa, 247; blood and *muti*-murder, 244; discovery of blood groups, 201–2; drawn to break spells or enchantment 16–21, 30, 53, 65, 78, 94–5, 101, 262; drawn to swear oaths, 52; in milk as a symptom of bewitchment, 129; precautions taken against blood falling into witches' hands, 196–7; used in spells, 29, 58, 159, 244

Board of Registration of Medical Auxiliaries, 202

Boloki people, 178

book curses, 47

Bootha (Aboriginal shaman), 162–5

Boswell, Gordon (Roma writer), 214

Bradford, 18, 69, 146

Brahmins, 171

brain, physiology and human spirituality, 130

Brewer, Billy (cunning-man), 114–15, 134–5

brewers, 20, 59, 60–1 103

Bristol, 18, 52, 59, 126,

British Empire, 156–86, 218

Browne, Dr Stanley George (medical missionary), 158–60

Bryant family, 18, 25

Buchan, Peter (demonologist), 34

Buckingham Palace, 222

Buckinghamshire: 74; Burnham, 63

Buddhism, 143–5, 152, 177, 226

Burn, James (autodidact), 57

burning: burning in child witchcraft abuse, 248, 250; burning in magical rites: 23, 25, 26, 58, 60, 114, 118, 123, 128, 174, 209–10, 236; burning sensations caused by witchcraft, 30, 97; fires caused by witchcraft and magic, 20, 224; human body products burnt to prevent them falling into witches' hands, 196; language of pain, 30; milk teeth burnt for luck, 206; notion that witches were burned during the Middle Ages, 153, 216

Burns, Robert, 35

Byron, Lord (George Gordon), 35, 50

Caithness: 70–1, 114–15; Latheron, 87

Cambridge University, 47–8, 149

Cambridgeshire: 56, 85, 231; Bottisham, 197; Great Paxton, 26, 30, Horseheath, 196, 216, 257

Cameroon, 246–7

Canada, 84, 157, 223

Cannon, Walter B. (physiologist), 96

Caravan Sites and Control of Development Act (1960), 214

Cardiff, 24, 88, 128, 134, 233

cards, and magic, 26, 118, 119, 128, 135, 147, 121–2, 151

Caribbean, 168–72, 238–9

Cary, Dr Nat (pathologist), 245

Castlereagh, Lord (Robert Stewart), 9, 50

cats, and magic, 12, 26–7, 41, 63, 198–9, 230

cattle, and magic, 13, 16, 23, 57–9, 86–7, 116, 181–2, 203–4

cauldrons (witches' props), 88, 198–9

census (decennial), 23, 100, 116, 123, 173

ceremonial magic, 5, 145–7, 152, 193, 234

chapbooks, 27, 34, 57–8

Charles, Prince of Wales, 172

Chartism, 40, 52

Chester, 31, 44

children: accused of witchcraft, 244–51, 255; bully witches, 21, 88, 196; folklore of children, 207; follow parents into witchcraft, 30, 228–9; mortality, 77; no longer taught about witchcraft, 207–8; taught about magic through stories, 57, 184; victims of *muti*-murder, 243–4; victims of spiritual abuse, 244–51, 264–5; victims of witchcraft and cursing, 11–12, 20–1, 48, 76, 119, 195–6, 204–5, 232

Chirological Society of London, 118

cholera, 42, 166, 174

chovihani (Romany word for 'witch'), 127, 232–3

Christian Science, 147–50, 189–90

Church Army, 222

Churchill, Winston, 207

cinema: 205–6; *The Exorcist*, 221–2

cities and towns: Caribbean migration, 238; Christian Science, 149–50; church building and missions, 75; conditions conducive to witchcraft, 18–19, 236; the cunning-craft's urban profile, 20, 22, 24, 59–60, 63–6, 113–15, 132, 202–3; fortune-tellers based in towns and cities, 118–20, 122–3; ghost sightings and stories, 41, 230; growth, 18; Irish immigration, 44; late twentieth-century re-emergence of urban magic, 236–51; middle class fears, 52; pro-Empire speaking tours, 179; quackery in towns, 201; Roma fortune-tellers, 125–6, 214;

cities and towns *(continued)*
sanitation and domestic plumbing, 76; seen as progressive, 23; urban occultism, 5, 146, 164; urban policing, 66, 203; urban witchcraft underestimated, 71, 73, 77; witchcraft suspicions and assaults, 18–21, 29–31, 59–60, 63, 68, 70, 71, 78, 87–9, 94–7, 99, 102, 195–6, 205, 209, 210, 262

Clare, John (poet), 37, 57

Clark, James, 66

clergy: accused of being witches, 94, 166; believers in witches and demons, 10–14, 70–1, 123, 153–4, 158–60, 185–6, 197, 221–2, 228, 251–8; decline of demonology, 33; international Pentecostal churches and child witchcraft, 245–9, 255; leaders of the drive against belief in witchcraft and 'superstition', 17, 39, 49, 51, 116, 154; magistrates and authority figures, 14, 16, 17, 123; observers of popular manners, 10, 110, 125, 128, 173, 178, 197; proponents of witchcraft belief, 32–3, 35, 36–7; revival of demonology and the deliverance ministry, 153–4, 251–8; throwers of curses, 45, 47–8; unable to persuade people to disbelieve in magic, 53–4

climate change, disbelief in, 38

Clodd, Edward (folklorist), 75

clothes: cunning-folks' conspicuous dress, 24, 64; damaged by witchcraft, 135; magical items worn beneath clothes, 136, 197; stolen by fraudulent magicians, 129

Cock Lane Ghost, 141

cognitive behavioural therapies (CBT), 130

cold-reading (esoteric technique), 133, 135

Columbia University, 130

concealed ritual objects, 22, 27, 61, 164

concealed thoughts, about witchcraft and magic, 7, 73–4, 78, 164, 170, 175–6, 183

Congo, 158–61, 247

Consult the Oracle (1899), 120

corp creagh (Scotch-Gaelic effigy magic), 63, 111

Cornwall: 65, 88, 116, 133, 227; Boscastle, 225, 234–5; Camborne, 50; Helston, 227; Newlyn, 60; Penryn, 133; Pool, 115; St Austell, 234–5; St Ives, 53; Tintagel, 235

council houses, 212

counselling, 38, 134–5, 240–1, 253–4

County Durham: Hartlepool, 126

County Police Act (1856), 65–6

Courtney, 'Sir William', 52

courts of law: African colonial witchcraft ordinances, 182–3; appeals to prosecute witches, 59, 88; curses thrown in court, 45; difficult to prosecute cunning-folk and other magicians, 23–4, 63–7, 91, 108, 115–17, 126–7, 143, 175; difficult to prosecute witch abusers, 21, 68; increasing prosecution of witchcraft vigilantes, 67–8, 78, 97–9; increasing regulation of 'quacks', 201–4; legality of witchcraft slander, 80–3; limited prosecution of curse-throwing beggars, 62; permissive towards the metaphysical economy, 241–2; sympathetic to witchcraft vigilantes, 31–2; witch prosecutions of the early modern era, 9, 27, 89; witchcraft recriminalised in postcolonial Africa, 246

Covell, Benjamin (cunning-man), 134–5

covens, 218–19, 235, 253

cow doctors, 107

Crehan, Fr Joseph, 221–2

'crisis of faith' (Victorian agnosticism), 139–140, 155, 263

Crowley, Aleister, 147, 152, 188–9, 234

Cruikshank, George, 50, 52

crystal balls, 66, 113, 118, 119, 121, 135

crystals, magical, 107, 215, 222

Culpeper, Nicholas, 33, 57

'cultural competence', 240–1

Cumbria: 23; Carlisle, 18; Garsdale, 103; Kendal, 236

cunning-craft, cunning-folk: 23–5, 63–7, 106–17, 198–201, 202–4; accused of being witches, 94, 115–16; ancient and European versions of the cunning-craft, 23, 62; Christianity, 107, 113, 203; clients travel long distances, 134; costs and business methods, 16, 24–5, 58, 62–3, 66, 108–10, 112–17, 199–200; decline of the cunning-craft, 202–4, 213; demand clients wholeheartedly believe in magic, 8, 24–5, 53–4, 132–3; dress, 24, 64, 108, 113, 115; magical artifacts and scientific instruments, 24, 64, 107, 113–15; magical services and methods, 16, 23–5, 53, 58–9, 62–3, 86, 93–4, 96, 103, 113, 117, 199–200, 203, 234–6; names and terminology, 23, 107, 116, 202; not the only providers of unwitching services, 106–7, 118–29; psychologically soothing functions of magic, 129–38; recent revival of the cunning-craft, 234–6; reputations, 25, 64, 107–8, 115, 199; taught clients about witchcraft, 93–4, 97, 128, 213, 220, 263; threatened by the legal system, 23–4, 63–7, 200–3; urban profile, 20, 22, 24, 59–60, 63–6, 113–15, 132, 202–3

curses: British cursing, 47–8; 'cursed' becomes main word for being afflicted by evil magic, 223–4; cursing wells, 46–7, 51, 91–2, 206; generational curses, 257; Irish cursing, 42–6; Roma curses, 233, 254–5

Darwin, Charles, 75, 140, 150
Davenport Brothers (showmen), 141
Davies, Owen (historian), 36, 71, 81, 135, 211, 266 n. 3
decline of British witchcraft, 187–8, 195–8, 202–13
Democratic Republic of Congo, 250, 265
demonology, 33–5, 50, 54, 153–4, 251–8
demons and imps, 16, 26, 29–30, 88, 97, 175, 194, 221, 222, 253, 255, 256–8
Denmark, 23, 84
depression, and 'cursed' people, 129–38, 191, 193
Derbyshire: Bakewell, 134; Chesterfield, 122, 125–6; Pilsley, 222; Pratt Hall, 197
devil, the: and Baphomet, 150–2; connected with mesmerism, 71; declining belief in, 208; deliverance ministry and the revival of devil belief, 221–2, 249, 252, 256; and demonology, 33; depicted as a hare, 84; and exotic magic, 167, 174; linked with cunning-folk, 64, 110, 113; story of the horseshoe, 61; witches' relationships with, 35, 50, 97, 153–4, 196, 249
Devon: 25, 49, 51, 56, 58, 67, 85, 88–9, 97, 116, 131, 210, 227; Ashburton, 131; Barnstaple, 95, 99, 101; Bideford, 62; Bow, 132; Bradworthy, 64; Brixham, 96, 196; Clyst St Lawrence, 196; Colaton Raleigh, 97; Cotleigh, 196; Cullompton, 123; Dawlish, 53, 113, 132; Halberton, 102–3; Horrabridge, 210; Lamerton, 224–9; Launceston, 114; Newton Abbot, 115, 131; Okehampton, 114; Ottery, 94; Paignton, 196; Peters Marland, 36; Slapton, 76; Torquay, 127, 196; Totnes, 99; Tavistock, 58, 225; West Down, 114; Whitchurch, 228; Woodbury, 67

dialect (words for witchcraft), 19, 85–7, 127
Diana, Princess of Wales, 172, 222
diet, 54, 77, 111, 239
Dinka people, 180
doctors (practitioners of orthodox medicine): believers in witchcraft and magical powers, 98, 145–6, 158–60, 184, 190–1, 211, 253; biomedicine's increasing capacity to heal disease, 201–2, 211–12; Britain's general practitioners outnumbered by spiritual healers, 237; challenges of working in a multicultural society, 238–40, 245; consulted by ill people before they resorted to magic, 1, 20, 60, 85, 131, 176, 192, 221, 240, 253, 257; 'doctor' title used by professional magicians, 20, 25, 58, 64, 107, 116–17, 133; first medically qualified women, 145–6, 190–1; growing regulation and the 'war against quackery', 143 166–7, 201–2; limited effectiveness of treatments for depression, 132; opposed by Christian Scientists, 148–9; proponents of mesmerism, 69; recent partnerships with spiritual healers, 240–1, 253; rivalry with cunning-folk, 200–2; sceptical investigators of alleged supernatural appearances, 41–2; supporters of magical societies, 145–6, 193; unavailability of orthodox medicine to European colonialists, 162, 164; vivisection, 145–6
Dogme et Rituel de la Haute Magie (1854–6), 145, 151
dolls, and magic, 26, 63, 96, 111, 209–10, 216–17
Dove, William, 66
ducking (swimming) alleged witches, 15–16
dreams, and magic, 12–13, 120–1, 145, 184, 247, 249, 257
Dorset: Blackmore Vale, 62; Bridport, 18–19; Burleston, 196; Stalbridge, 114; Turners Puddle, 11–14
'dragon's blood' (tree resin), 107, 122
dukkerin (Roma magic), 123–9, 213–15
Dumfriesshire: Locharbriggs hill, 90
Duncan, Helen (spirit medium), 204
Dupotet, 'Baron' Charles, 69
Durham, 60, 88, 95, 119, 254
Dworkin, Andrea, 99–100
dyn hysbys (Welsh conjurors), 202–4

East Anglia, 27, 49, 88, 231; *see also* Cambridgeshire; Essex; Norfolk; Suffolk

East India Company, 172–5
East Riding of Yorkshire: Beverley, 24; Seaton Ross, 205
eBay, 258
Eddy, Mary Baker, 147–50
Edinburgh, 22, 32, 59, 83, 146, 154, 232
education: claims that education eradicates superstition, 50–1, 72, 140, 211, 267 n. 16; development in Britain, 54, 75, 101, 149, 190; formal education not antithetical to magical beliefs, 10–14, 32–3, 36, 70–1, 92, 139–55, 156–60, 183, 185, 195, 257
effigies, and magic, 26, 63, 96, 209–10, 216–17
Egypt, 2, 26, 124, 151
Egyptology, 185, 216
electricity: 76, 212, 231; influence on magical notions, 70, 114–15, 148, 192, 201, 227, 230
elf-shot, 87
Ellel Ministries, 256–7
Elliotson, John, 69
Ely, 60, 88, 231
emigration (from and within the UK), 43, 111, 118, 157
enclosure, 40, 52
Enlightenment, the, 4, 10, 13
Epping Forest Gypsies, 125–6
Epsom Downs races, 125
Essex: 89, 132–3; Canewdon, 91, 206, 234; Colchester 233; East Donyland, 98; Easthorpe, 68; Hadleigh, 64; Ostend, 90; Sible Hedingham, 117; Tiptree, 196
Etsy, 258
Ettrick, William, 10–14
Euahlayi people, 162–5
European Union, 241–2
evangelicalism, 54–5, 71, 125, 171, 214, 255, 257
Evans, George Ewart, 233
Evans-Pritchard, Edward, 156–7
evil, protective power of, 62
evil eye, 29–30, 85, 87, 96, 114, 120, 174, 196, 203, 207, 209, 231–2, 239–40, 260
Exeter, 58, 64, 67, 93, 96–7, 123, 131
Exorcist, The (1974), 221–2

faith healing: 24–5, 53–4, 130, 132–3; *see also* belief
familiars, witches', 16–17, 26–2, 30, 55, 64, 85, 117, 180

family, and witchcraft, 11–13, 18, 21, 30, 94–5, 106–7, 117, 119, 195, 225–8, 247, 254–5
fantasies (about witchcraft), 7, 29, 104, 144, 150–2, 184, 252
farmers, 14–17, 23–5, 29, 37, 42, 57, 59, 65, 66, 80–3, 87, 90, 94–5, 99, 107, 110–12, 116, 131, 134, 136, 157, 168, 179, 184, 196, 197, 200, 225, 290 n. 6.
Faty, Malibu, 243–4
Favret-Saada, Jeanne, 62, 135
feminism, 99–101, 145, 148–9, 177, 190, 219
festivals of mind, body and spirit, 222
Ffynnon Elian (cursing well), 46–7, 51, 91–2
First World War, 192–3, 200, 214
Firth, Violet *see* Fortune, Dion
fishermen, sailors and fisher-folk, 59, 60, 62, 81–2, 83, 84, 86, 87, 94, 99, 114, 116, 133, 167, 208–9, 283 n. 31
folklore and folklorists: 73–80; believers in the reality of witchcraft and magic, 74–75; censorious and inhibited, 104; findings, 23, 42, 84, 91, 101–11, 114, 174, 192, 196–7, 200, 203, 206, 207–8, 209, 212, 229–30, 231, 233, 235, 238; methods and difficulties, 74, 77–8, 231, 238; notion of 'pagan survivals', 74, 75, 150–3, 185, 216–19; pseudo-scientific ideas, 70; sceptical and chauvinistic, 75; social identity, 74
folk sector, 237
food: becoming cheaper and more abundant, 75–6, 111; food allergies supposedly caused by demons, 257; rationing, 204; scarcity, 54, 77, 162; used medicinally in *unani tibb*, 239; and witchcraft, 11, 20, 29, 126, 165, 167, 238, 257
football, and evil magic, 246, 255
Forsyth, J.S., 34–5
Fortune, Dion, 188–95
fortune-tellers, 118–23
Fox sisters (Margaret, Kate and Leah), 140–1
France: alliance with Britain during the Crimean War, 42–3; conduct of unwitchers, 62, 135; conscription for war with Revolutionary France inspires magic, 25; currency of witchcraft belief, 223; example of the French Revolution inspires sympathy for magical belief,

32, 36; French demonstrators bring mesmerism to Britain, 69; French folklorists less inhibited than British folklorists, 104; idea that witches possess black books and sexual powers, 232; later nineteenth-century *occultisme* movement, 145; Éliphas Lévi develops Baphomet, 150–1; longstanding connection between toads and witchcraft 29; Anna Kingsford's French studies and magical attacks on distinguished French scientists, 145–6; magic sparked by British troops fighting on the Western Front during WWI, 200; Jules Michelet develops the concept of pagan witchcraft, 151–2; Napoleon's rule and witchcraft, 9; origin of 'swimming' witches 15; Paris branch of the Golden Dawn, 146; ready availability of grimoires, 58; Revolutionary threat to Britain nourishes apocalyptic ideas, 13; 'stiff upper lip' ethos promoted after the fall of France in 1940, 207; tarot cards, 122; temporary home of Victoria Climbié and Marie-Therese Kouao, 247–8

frauds (associated with magic), 5, 7, 40, 42, 44, 64, 112, 116, 126–9, 204, 241–2, 261, 263

Fraudulent Mediums Act (1951), 204, 241

Frazer, Sir James, 216

Friedkin, William, 221

Galen (physician), 239

Gallup poll, 223, 246

Gardner, Gerald (father of Wicca), 152, 218–19, 223, 235

Gary, Gemma (modern tradition witch), 236

gentrification (rural), 233–4

Germany: campaign against quackery, 201; concept of the witch hare, 84; biblical criticism, 140; immigrants import European magic to Australia, 164; missionaries in Africa, 160; origin of the deliverance ministry, 252; tarot cards, 122

Geschiere, Peter (anthropologist), 246

Ghana (formerly the Gold Coast), 160, 179, 181–2, 184, 244, 249

ghosts, 32–3, 40–2, 50, 56–7, 74, 110, 153, 206, 223, 230, 237, 239, 254

Gigha, Isle of 79–84

Glasgow; 44, 240; University of, 33

glassware, 28

Glastonbury: Dion Fortune and western esotericism, 189, 193; legend of St Dunstan and the Devil, 61; location of witchcraft-related accusations and violence, 196; locus of the New Age movement, 236

Gloucestershire: Moreton-in-Marsh, 197; Slad, 196

Gorer, Geoffrey, 206

gold, 22

Greece, 26

Gregor, Rev. Walter, 110

grimoires, 58, 120, 147,

Groome, Francis Hindes, 125, 128

'gypsies', etymology, 124; *see also* Roma people

Gypsy Lore Society, 124

Gujarat, Gujarati people, 173–4, 239

gunpowder, as a magical ingredient, 58

Guyana, 171

hags (witch stereotype), 81, 85, 103–4

Hailey, Lord William Malcolm, 178, 182

hair, 12, 17, 25, 58, 93, 120, 196

Haiti, 170

hakims, 239

Hall, Ann and Thomas, 40–2

Hamilton, Dr Lillias, 190–2

Hampshire: 253; Aldershot, 128

Hardy, Thomas, 73, 133

hares (and witchcraft), 26, 80–5, 112, 229, 232

Harries, John, 34

Harries, Rt Rev. Richard, 255

Harris, John (autodidact), 50

Harrison, Henry, 66

Harvey-Bloom, Rev. J. (folklorist), 197

Hawker, Rev. Robert Stephen, 276 n. 37

hawkers, 14, 126–7

Hayden, Maria (spiritualist medium), 141

health, relationship with spirituality, 129–31

Hebrew, 12, 24, 28, 50

hedge witchcraft, 223–4, 235–6

height, of people, 18, 111

Henderson, Alexander, 107–12

herbs and herbalists, 24, 25, 33, 53, 57, 61, 110, 113, 117, 142, 160, 164, 167, 169, 198–202, 214, 215, 236, 239

Herefordshire: Orcop, 90; Walford, 96

Hermes Trismegistus, 145

Hermetic Order of the Golden Dawn, 122, 145–7, 193

Herne, Mother (white witch), 198–201

Hertfordshire, 231, 233
Hester, Marianne (feminist scholar), 100
hexafoil (symbol), 152–3, 197
Highlands of Scotland, 49, 73, 78, 80–8, 231–2
Highways Act (1959), 214
Hinduism: Hindus of South Asian heritage in the Caribbean, 171; Hindus of South Asian heritage in the UK, 239; influence on British colonialists, 175–7; influence on Christian Science, 150; influence on *obeah*, 171; Kali (goddess) and cholera, 174; *vaids* and Hindu concepts of supernatural evil in the UK, 239; and witchcraft in India, 172–4
Hole, Christina (folklorist), 209
Home, D.D. (spiritualist medium), 141
homeopathy, 142
'honest doubts', 139–40
horse races, and fortune-telling, 125
horsemen, 107, 208
horseshoe, 21, 60–1, 131, 206, 236
Hull, 24, 53, 59, 64, 67, 178, 209,
Huntingdonshire: Woodhurst, 60
Hutton, Ronald (historian), 235, 266 n. 3
Huxley, Elspeth (author), 184
Huxley, Thomas (scientist), 75

Ibbortson, Elizabeth, 19
Iceland, 19
imperialism (British), 156–86
Industrial Revolution, 18
internet, the, and magic, 258–60
Inverness: 111, 134; Kiltarlity, 231–2
Ireland, Irish people, 42–8, 84, 92, 103, 111, 124–5, 140, 167, 171, 200, 215
Islam: concepts of supernatural evil and supernatural healing, 239–40, 250, 259; Islamic extremism, 38, 155; Muslims of South Asian heritage in the UK, 239; and *obeah*, 169, 171
Italy, 29, 121–2, 152
Ivory Coast, 244–50
Izzard family, 26, 30

Jack the Ripper, 113
James I of England and VI of Scotland, 27–8
Jamaica, Jamaicans, 168–72, 238–9
Jefferies, Richard (writer), 74
Jenkinson, Sago (cunning-man), 64
jinns and *jinn* removal, 239–40, 250, 259

Kaguvi, Sekuru (Shona spirit medium), 182
karma, 226
Kelly, Aidan (Pagan author), 235
Kent: 23, 35, 52, 160; Hoo, 29
Kenya, 179, 182–4, 244
Kikuyu people, 179, 184
Kingsford, Anna (occultist), 145–6, 211
Kingsley, Charles (writer), 170–1
Kingsley, Mary (explorer) 178
Kinshasa, 250
Koch, Rev. Kurt E. (demonologist), 252
Kols (people of Uttar Pradesh, India), 173
Koran, The Holy, 239–40
Knights Templar, 151
knives, 22, 36
Knott, Olive, 200, 212

Lackington, George (bookseller), 34
Lanarkshire, 23
Lancashire: 18, 63, 85, 88; Bacup, 119; Blackpool, 76, 118, 214; Bolton, 78, 88, 106; Bury, 16; Clifton, 204; Pendle Forest, 90; Rochdale, 64; Salford, 119; witch trials, 90
Lancaster, 24
Lancaster University, 236
Lang, Andrew (folklorist), 74–5
language, of witchcraft and magic: African magic words, 180; British dialect words, 19, 85–7, 116; Gaelic magic words, 87; Romany magic words, 124–127
Lark Rise to Candleford (1945), 74
Larner, Christina (historian), 99
Latham-Jones, Cassandra (modern wise-woman), 237
Latin, 24, 64, 145, 152, 197
Lecky, William (historian), 140
Led Zeppelin, 188
Lee, Rev. Frederick George (demonologist), 153
Leeds, 18, 20, 24, 29–30, 49, 59, 66, 78, 88, 114
Leeds University, 230
Leicester, 240, 242
Leicestershire: Coalville, 97
Leland, Charles (folklorist), 75, 124, 152
Letters (scam mail), 242
Lévi, Éliphas (occultist), 145, 150–1
Lewis, Isle of, 87, 95, 102
liberals, 51–2
liberalism, 6, 204

life expectancy, 18, 77, 202
lighting, 19
Lilly, William (astrologer), 57, 106
Lincolnshire: 64; Grimsby, 196; Long
    Sutton, 99; Louth, 65; Stamford, 70;
    Stickney, 51, 53; Swineshead, 70
literacy, 49, 54, 57, 59
Liverpool, 44, 59, 66, 71,
Livingstone, Dr David (explorer), 178
Llanelian yn Rhos, 46–7, 51, 91–2
Lodge, Oliver (scientist), 192–3
London, 18, 26, 29, 31, 34, 41, 44, 45, 58–9,
    64, 69, 76, 78, 88, 95, 111, 118, 120, 122,
    141, 143, 145, 146, 149–50, 152, 161, 164,
    172, 181, 189, 193, 205, 221, 238–51, 253,
    255, 262, 265
Lord, Henrietta (Christian Scientist),
    149–50
Lord's Prayer, 25, 65
Lovett, Edward (folklorist), 192
Luckenbooth brooches, 22–3
lucky heather, 233
Lundy, John (pseudonym), 224–9
Lyall, Sir Alfred, 175

madness (and magic) 20, 70, 123, 136, 197
magistrates (JPs), 14, 17, 24, 30–3, 36, 44,
    47, 48, 53, 59, 63–8, 88, 91, 95, 97, 99,
    116, 126, 127, 172, 174–5, 183, 185–6,
    196
magnetic resonance imaging (MRI), 130
magnetism (pseudo-scientific concept),
    69–70, 114–15, 142–4, 147–9, 155,
    189–90, 193–4, 262
Maka people, 246–7
makutu, 165–8
Man, Isle of, 84
Manchester, 18–19, 44, 59, 76, 78, 88, 119
Manning, Carl, 244–50
Manning, Edward ('wizard'), 116–17
Manning, Frederick (Pākehā Māori), 167
Māoris, 165–8
Maple, Eric (folklorist), 91, 206, 234
marks, witches', 16–17, 50
Marx, Karl, 161
Mathers, Samuel MacGregor (occultist),
    122, 147
Mau Mau uprising, 179–80
McGougan, Catherine (supposed witch),
    80–4
McNeile, Hugh (clergyman), 71
mechanics' institutes, 50, 69–70, 154
Medical Act (1858), 143

mental health care, function of unwitching
    129–38
Mesmer, Franz Anton, 69
mesmerism, 68–71, 98, 114–15, 142–3,
    148–9
Metropolitan Police Act (1829), 65
Metropolitan Police Service (London), 65,
    244, 251
Melland, Frank (anthropologist and
    magistrate), 185–6
Methodism, Methodists, 35, 50, 51, 54, 91
Michelet, Jules (historian), 151–2
middle classes, 10, 16–17, 23, 41–2, 49, 52,
    57–9, 139–55, 188–95, 218–19
Middlesex Hospital, 71
midnight, 'the witching hour', 24, 62, 136,
    208
Midwives Act (1902), 202
Mill, James, 172
Millington, Rev. Thomas S. (theologian),
    153
miners and colliers, 59, 95
missionaries, 51, 157, 158–60, 166, 178, 179,
    181
mobbing of witches, 16–18, 30, 59, 68, 97,
    115, 183, 262
Montrose, 62
Moon Goddess (Wicca), 219
Moore, Rev. Carter (clergyman), 47–8
Morant Bay rebellion, 170
Moray: Kellas, 134
More, Martha (beggar), 62
motorcars, 208
movies, 205–6; *The Exorcist*, 221–2
Mozambique, 244
Mull, Isle of, 154
Multiculturalism, 6, 186, 220, 221–60, 264
Murray, Margaret (writer), 185–6, 216–18
Murrell, James, 64
Museum of Witchcraft and Magic, 218, 225,
    234, 235
Muslims, 239–40, 250, 259

Nafsiyat Intercultural Therapy Centre,
    240–1
najar see nazar
Napoleon, 9, 50, 142
Napoleonic Wars, 13, 25
National Insurance Act, (1911), 188
National Health Service, 118, 212
nazar (evil eye), 239–40
Nehanda, Mbuya (Shona spirit medium),
    182

neighbours: decline of neighbourliness changes in the concept of black magic, 258; involved in witchcraft diagnoses and cures, 18, 56, 60–1; suspected of witchcraft, 12, 14–15, 16, 18, 29–31, 53, 59, 62, 68, 80–3, 86–8, 94–7, 100–3, 111, 195, 204–5, 224–9, 231–5, 247

Neil-Smith, Rev. Christopher (exorcist), 253

Netherlands, 29, 201

neuroscience, 130

New Age movement, 222–4, 226–7, 236, 252

New Poor Law, 40, 45, 52, 101–2

New South Wales, 162–5

New Zealand, 165–8

Newall, Venetia (folklorist), 238

Newcastle, 59

newspapers, 3, 21, 23, 36–7, 39, 41, 49–50, 66

Nigeria, 181, 243–4, 255

night, 24, 62, 136, 208, 247

Nongqawuse (Xhosa prophet), 181–2

Norfolk: 208; Beeston, 90; Buckenham, 154; East Dereham, 196; Flordon, 48; Great Yarmouth, 59; Hardingham, 95; King's Lynn, 215; North Lopham, 205; North Walsham, 67; Runham, 53; Salthouse, 90; Sheringham, 90; Shipdham, 135; South Lopham, 205; Weybourne, 90

North Yorkshire: 88; Goathland, 229–30; Middlesbrough, 59, 68; Scarborough, 195; Stokesley, 24–25; Swaledale, 85

Northamptonshire: 57; Chipping Warden, 40; Croughton, 116–17; Towcester, 127

Northover, Robert and Mary (vigilantes), 19, 30–1

Norway, 84, 87

Norwich, 24, 88, 95, 96,

Norwood Gypsy's Fortune Teller, 120–1

Nicholas, Mary (supposed witch), 16–17

obeah, 168–72, 238–41

occult revival: early nineteenth-century, 68–71; later nineteenth-century, 122, 139–55; twentieth-century, 188–95, 218–19, Chapter 9

Office of Fair Trading (OFT), 242

Okely, Judith (anthropologist), 232–3

old age, 14, 16–19, 21, 30, 53, 59, 85, 97, 103–4

'old witch' (stereotype) 18, 30, 53, 59, 103–4

omens, 74, 192

On the Origin of Species (1859), 140

Olcott, Henry (theosophist), 143, 177

Olukoya, Dr D.K. (Pentecostal minister), 255

opiates, 12

Opie, Iona and Peter (folklorists), 207–8

opinion polling (magical beliefs), 206, 223, 240, 246

Orkney, 32, 232

Owen, Robert Dale (socialist), 141

Oxford United, 255

Oxford University, 11, 55, 140, 217

Oxfordshire: 74; Beckley, 41; Bicester, 41; Black Bourton, 47; Deddington, 41, 197; Enstone, 42; Hook Norton, 42; Horspath, 41; Little Tew, 40–2; Otmoor, 52; Sandford St Martin, 42; Somerton, 53; Stanton St John, 104; Witney, 41

paganism: and the devil, 150–1; and folklore, 74–5; modern pagan magical practitioners, 235, 259; modern pagans move to the countryside, 234; and witchcraft, 2, 68–9, 151–3, 154, 185, 216–19

Paine, Thomas, 13, 142

Pākehā Māori, 167

Palko, Betty (clairvoyant), 222

Palmer, Kingsley (folklorist), 230

Pan (pagan god), 151–2, 219

Paris, 122, 145, 146, 152, 248

Parker, Katie, 162–5

Parkinson, Richard (wizard), 66

Parliament (Westminster), 50, 59, 76, 241, 251

Parsons, Elizabeth (supposed witch), 19, 30–1

Pasteur, Louis, 145–6

Paterson, James (clergyman), 10

Pearson, C. Arthur (publisher), 120

Pentecostal Christianity, 245–58

Perkins, William, 34

Perry, Rev. Michael, 254

Perry, Mr (cunning-man), 53

Perth, 23

Peterborough, 60

Pharmacy and Medicines Act (1941), 202

pills, 25, 66, 142

piseogs, 46

placebos, 20, 24–5, 30, 96–7, 129–38, 210

Plymouth, 59, 60, 88, 97, 113, 116, 133, 226

Plymouth Brethren, 189

pneumonia, 202

Podmore, Frank (psychical investigator), 148, 191

poison, and witchcraft, 19–20, 28, 29, 50, 53, 63, 66, 136, 160, 169–70

poison oracle, 159, 180, 182,

police, 15, 16, 30, 31–2, 40, 44, 47, 63–8, 97–8, 102, 114–15, 119, 120, 123, 126, 127, 129, 136, 164, 184, 199, 202–3, 214, 215, 216, 226, 228, 244, 251, 263

politics, and belief in magic, 51–2

Poor Law, 40, 45, 52, 101–2

Pope Paul VI, 222

'popular superstition', hostility to, 39–52

Porter, Enid (folklorist), 85, 89, 231

Porter, Roy (historian), 201

Potato Famine (Ireland), 44

poverty (and witchcraft): 14, 45, 101–2, 117

powders (magical), 25, 100, 118, 123, 169, 176, 180

Powell, Baden (theologian and mathematician), 140

Powell, William, 17

prayers and psalms, 25, 58–9

Presbyterianism, 32–3, 51, 251

Priestley, Joseph, 13

priests (Roman Catholic), 45, 221

Prince, Derek (Pentecostal pastor), 257

Project Violet, 251

psychiatry, 130–1, 192–4, 238, 240–1, 252–3

psychic attack (concept), 188–95, 220, 224

psychic powers, 160, 176–7, 188–95, 224, 232, 234–5, 242, 254, 259

psychosomatic effects, 20, 24–5, 30, 96–7, 129–38, 210

publicans, 31, 42, 59

quackery, 201–2

Quantock hills, 197

quicksilver, 22, 107

racism, 75

radio, 212, 246

Raj, the, 175–7

Raphael (astrologer), 57–8

Rastafarians, 238

Reade, William (explorer), 180

red thread, 61, 206

reflexology, 222

reform, 23, 40, 76

regulation, of magic, 10, 23–4, 63–8, 201–4, 213, 219–20, 240–2, 253–4, 258–65

Renfrewshire: Dunrod Castle, 90; Inverkip, 90

revival of magic, 221–65

revolution, fear of, 52

Reynolds, Mallaci 'Kapo', 172

Rhondda Valley, 43, 125–6

Richards, Rev. John, 253

ritual: 62, 121, 167, 183–4, 240; 'high' ritual magic, 5, 145–7, 152, 193, 234; markings, 164; *muti*- and ritual murder, 243–4; paganism and ritual witchcraft, 216, 219; Satanic ritual abuse, 7, 252; therapeutic qualities, 136–7

Rogers, Rita, 222

Roma people: 5, 6, 40, 63, 64, 120, 123–9, 193, 204, 213–15, 227, 232–3, 255, 260, 263

Rosa, Salvator, 55

Rosicrucians, 145

rowan trees, 21–2, 61, 112, 206, 291 n. 28

Rowntree, Benjamin Seebohm, 77

Roy, Olivier, 155

Rudge, Rev. James, 53–4

ruqyah, 239–40

Sanders, Alex, 223

Santal people, 173

Sarbah, John Mensah (lawyer), 181

satanic ritual abuse, 7, 252

servants, 11–14, 16, 35, 44, 56, 59, 94, 102, 103, 111–12, 116, 118, 127, 151, 162, 184

settler colonialism, 157, 162–8

scepticism about magic, 9–10, 12, 23, 32–3, 35–42, 48–52, 57, 72, 75, 110, 139–40, 154, 156, 237, 240

Scandinavia, 87

schooling, 45, 50, 51, 54, 75, 151, 156, 190, 195, 207, 218, 256

scissors, 22

Scot, Reginald, 35

Scotland, 9, 10, 19, 21–3, 32–3, 51, 61–4, 70, 78–88, 94, 99, 105, 107–12, 114, 116, 124, 134, 207, 209, 231–2, 255

Scott, Walter, 50, 54

scratching, of witches, 16–20, 29–30, 32, 53, 59, 60, 68, 78, 94, 95, 97, 105

Seaga, Edward, 171–2

Second World War, 204–5

secrecy, 7, 14 22–3

Senegal, 246

Shakespeare, William, 19, 27

shamanism, 163–5

Sheffield, 18–19, 78, 88, 119, 134, 189, 194, 226

Sherbro, island, West Africa, 161

Shetland Isles: 87, 232, 255; Unst, 99

shoes, 22, 61, 164

Shona people, 182

Shropshire: 131–2; Market Drayton, 70; Oswestry, 63; Prolley Moor, 89–90

Sikhs, 239

silver, in magic, 22, 231–2

Sinclair, George (demonologist), 33

Skye, Isle of, 231

slavery, 9, 161, 165, 168, 170–1, 178

sleep paralysis, 20

Small, Elizabeth (Rom woman), 64

Small, William (preacher), 51

Smith, George (politician), 124

Smith, James, 80–5

Smith, Kathyrn (folklorist), 229–30

Smith, Pamela Colman (tarot artist), 122

Smith, Rodney 'Gypsy', 125

Society for the Prevention of Cruelty to Animals, 23

Society for Psychical Research, 148, 164, 176, 191

Somerset: 21, 25, 56, 63, 85, 89, 196–7, 230; Bishops Lydeard, 206; Blagdon, 95; Charlton Horethorne, 95, 198–201; Chew Magna, 94; Crowcombe, 206; East Lambrook, 98; Frome, 90, 102; Kingsbury, 102; Langport, 196; Shepton Mallet, 205; South Petherton, 115; Taunton, 20, 94, 114–15, 132, 134–5, 181, 195, 196, 205; Templecombe, 113; Wadeford, 230; West Chinnock, 115; Wiveliscombe, 18; Wookey Hole, 230

'something in it' (qualified belief in witchcraft), 157–8, 183–6

South Africa, 157, 160, 178, 182, 183, 244

South Yorkshire: Barnsley, 88, 119–20; Rotherham, 119–20

Southcott, Joanna, 35

Southport, 88

spells, 58–9, 121, 209, 219, 294 n. 82

Spinoza, Baruch, 149

spiritual healers, 107, 174, 237–44, 259

spiritual warfare, 257

spiritualism: adapted by Theosophy, 143, 177; allegedly demonic 148, 154; and the Fraudulent Mediums Act, 204; and healing, 141–3, 234–5; influence on other occultists, 145, 148, 218; influence peaks during the Interwar era, 192–3; mediums appear on television, 222; mediums unduly worried about the Unfair Commercial Practices Directive, 241–2; notion of 'bad' or malicious magnetism, 142–3, 155; origins and development, 140–1; spirit communication, 141–2; witchcraft technique, 97

spirituality and relationship with mental health, 129–31

spoons, 22

St Dunstan, 61

St Lucia, 172

St Mary's Hospital London, 244–5

Staffordshire: 26; Tipton, 196

Stebbings, Isaac, 14–16

Stevenson, Gina (fraudulent spiritual healer), 242

Stobart, Eleanor, 250

stories, and magic, 25, 56–7, 64, 83–4, 89, 97, 110, 112, 115, 127, 163, 178, 186–7, 197, 200, 205–6, 227, 229–32, 238, 246, 252, 259

stress, and witchcraft, 30, 81, 96, 105, 226, 257

Studley Horticultural and Agricultural College, 190–2

Suffolk: Blaxhall, 233; Ipswich, 24, 88, 119; Lowestoft, 59, 94–5, 131; Risbridge, 117; Wickham Skeith, 14–16;

suicide, and witchcraft, 77, 131–2, 181, 195–6, 204, 210

sulphonamides, 202

Sunderland, 13

superstition, 32–9, 48–52, 160–2, 192, 207, 218, 233

Sussex: Brighton, 69–70, 120, 150; Eastbourne, 98; Hastings, 102; Henley Common, 102

Sweden, 84

Swedenborg, Emanuel, 145

swimming, of alleged witches, 15–16

Tacky (*obeah* man and revolutionary), 169, 238

Tanzania, 183, 244

tarot cards, 122, 147, 151, 242, 258, 259

Tedworth Drummer, 141

television, 205–6, 212, 222, 230, 231

Thembu people, 180

theosophy: 143–5, 176–7

Thomas, Keith (historian), 106

Thompson, Edward Palmer (historian), 210

Thompson, Flora (writer), 74

three-fold law, 226
Tilley, Christopher, 92
toads, 26, 28–9, 63, 85, 96, 114, 208
Tobago, 172
tohunga, 167–8
tolerance, of magic and radical spiritualities, 155, 186, 204, 221–4, 251, 252
Tongue, Ruth (folklorist), 209
tractors, 208
traditional witchcraft, 235–6
traditions, magical, 26–30, 42–8, 57, 84–92, 120, 145, 148, 169–71, 175–7, 189, 194, 199, 204, 206, 207, 223–4, 227, 230, 234–41, 247–8, 251, 259
Traveller people, 111, 124–5, 127, 214, 232–3
Trinidad, 171–2, 238–9
trolls, 19, 87
Truro, 21
typhoid, 18, 58, 76, 111, 166
Tuckett, 'Dr' (cunning-man), 58, 64

Uganda, 244, 246
Ullah, Samira, 250
unani tibb, 239
uncertainty, humans find acutely stressful, 81
underground railway, London, 76
Unfair Commercial Practices Directive (2008), 241–2
United States of America *see* America, United States of
University College Hospital, 69
urine scrying, 117
upper classes, 14, 23
Uttar Pradesh, 173

Vagrancy Act (1824), 24, 63, 65, 118, 120, 143, 204
Valiente, Doreen, 219
vaids, 239
Vardos, 124
Vedic healing, 239
vegetarianism, 54, 145
violence, 16–21, 31–2, 60–1, 65–8, 78, 97–101, 173, 181, 196, 248–9
vivisection, 145–6
'voodoo death' (concept), 96–7
voodoo dolls, 26, 63, 96, 209–10, 216–17

Waite, Arthur Edward (occultist), 122, 147
Wales: 34, 44, 52, 125, 197, 202–4, 212; Aberdare, 215; Ebbw Vale, 201; Lampeter,

202–3; Llandudno, 189; Llanelian yn Rhos, 47, 51, 91–2; Llanfoist, 16–17; Llangammarch Wells, 150; Llangurig, 203; Llanidloes, 116; Mathry, 196; Merthyr Tydfil, 88, 95, 100, 134; Monmouthshire: 100–1; Narberth, 21; Penydarren, 134; Presteigne, 127; Pwllheli, 203; Rhondda Valley, 43, 125–6; Swansea, 88, 233; Troedyrhiw, 43
Walker, Rt Rev. Dominic, 254
Wallace, Alfred Russel (scientist), 69, 141, 211
Walsham, Alexandra (historian), 92
Walton, Charles (murder victim), 217
warts (magical cures for) 12
Warwickshire: 196–7; Binton, 90; Long Compton, 98, 197–8, 217; Lower Quinton, 217; Stratford-upon-Avon, 103; Tysoe, 21; Welford, 90
Watkins, William (vigilante), 16–17
Wells (Somerset), 88, 114
Wesley, John, 35, 48, 54
West Country (also see under 'Dorset', 'Devon', 'Somerset' and 'Cornwall'), 4, 59, 63, 78, 85, 88–9, 105, 114, 116, 209, 227, 234–6
West Midlands: 18, 78, 88, 253; Brierley Hill, 95; Dudley, 88, 119, 126, 215; Tipton, 196; Wednesbury, 96, 119, 205
West Yorkshire: Halifax, 119; Huddersfield, 85; Ossett, 253; Otley, 117; Wakefield, 66, 78, 88
Western Isles, Scotland, 79–88, 95, 99, 102, 154, 201
Western Sahara, 243
Whyte, Betsy (author), 232
Wicca: 2; creation and practices, 218–20; development, 223–4, 235; influence on the notion of black magic, 226, 229; origins, 150–3; professional magical practitioners, 259; three-fold law, 226
widows, 45, 99–101, 123, 132, 232–3
Wilberforce, Bishop Samuel, 69
Williamson, Cecil, 218, 234
Willox family (cunning-folk), 107, 113, 134
Wiltshire: Heywood, 98: Trowbridge, 204–5
wirreenun (shaman), 163–5
Witch of Endor, 28, 37, 48, 55, 153, 208
Witchcraft Act (1736), 9–10, 23–4, 31, 63–4, 83, 204
witchcraft ordinances (Africa), 182–3
Witchcraft Today, 218–19

witches: anti-witchcraft violence tolerated by Georgian magistrates, 30–3; attack in spirit form, 144, 152, 246–7; bullied and intimidated, 14–15, 21, 96–8, 196; child witchcraft, 247–50; command familiars, 16–17, 26–8, 30, 55, 64, 85, 117, 180; did not figure in every case of black magic, 7–8, 93; dislike being talked about, 78, 175–6; hedge witches and traditional witchcraft, 235–6; hereditary propensity for witchcraft, 30, 185, 227–8; identities and characteristics, 14, 81–5, 88–91, 93–104, 167, 180, 197, 208–9, 231–3, 246–50; men accused of witchcraft, 14–16, 99, 224–9; protected by the Victorian police and magistrates, 67–8, 78, 97–8; relationship with the devil, 35, 50, 97, 153–4, 196, 249; represented as pagans, 150–3, 216–19, 223–4; said to be unconscious mesmerists, 69–70; shapeshift into animal form, 26, 80–5, 112, 180, 229, 232; stereotypically women, 81, 85, 99–104, 247; supposed magical techniques, 12, 26–30, 86, 96, 160, 232, 246–7; supposed witches' responses to witchcraft accusations, 98–9; trials and prosecutions, 9, 14, 21, 27, 89, 182–3, 246; victims of violence, 16–21, 59–61, 65, 67–8, 97–9, 101, 105, 117, 161, 166, 173–4, 180–1, 196, 246–51, 264–5; witch bottles, 8, 22, 62, 63, 93, 113, 122–3, 169, 197, 203, 236, 292 n. 40; witch-finding ordeals, 14–16, 159, 172–3, 182; witch-scratching, 16–21, 29–30, 32, 59–60, 68, 78, 94–5, 97, 101, 105, 117, 196
witchcraft *see* black magic
witching hour *see* midnight

Wolverhampton, 59, 65, 95, 106
women: and education, 145, 149, 190; empowered by spiritualism, 140–1; female witch stereotype, 80–1, 85, 91, 95, 99–104, 173–4, 247; feminists drawn to Christian Science, 147–50; overrepresented as fortune-tellers, 118–23; protest through ghosts and witchcraft, 40–2; register higher levels of magical belief, 206, 223; Rom women and *dukkerin*, 123–9, 213–15; and solitary spellcraft, 235–6; voting rights, 101, 149, 188; and wicca, 219; young women visiting fortune-tellers, 44, 127, 199
Woodford, Susan (supposed witch), 11–14
Worcester: 94
working classes, 10, 17, 23, 25, 32, 36–7, 42, 52, 59
Wrightson, John, 24–5

Xhosa people, 181–2

yantra, 176
yoga, 171, 236, 257
York, 77

Zadkiel (astrologer), 57–8
Zambia, 180, 182, 183, 185
Zande *see* Azande
zeitgeist: late nineteenth-century shift towards the occult, 139–55; late twentieth-century multiculturalism and magic, 221–4, 251–4; 'stiff upper lip' ethos of the 1940s and early 1950s, 205–8
Zimbabwe, 179, 182, 183,
Zulu people, 179, 243–4